Russian Women,
1698–1917

Russian Women, 1698–1917

Experience and Expression, An Anthology of Sources

Compiled, edited, annotated, and introduced by
Robin Bisha, Jehanne M Gheith,
Christine Holden, and William G. Wagner

INDIANA **INDIANA**
University Press
Bloomington & Indianapolis

This book is a publication of

Indiana University Press
601 North Morton Street
Bloomington, IN 47404-3797 USA

http://iupress.indiana.edu

Telephone orders 800-842-6796
Fax orders 812-855-7931
E-mail orders iuporder@indiana.edu

© 2002 by Indiana University Press

All rights reserved

The paper used in this publication meets the minimum requirements of American National Standard for Information Sciences—Permanence of Paper for Printed Library Materials, ANSI Z39.48-1984.

Manufactured in the United States of America

Library of Congress Cataloging-in-Publication Data

Russian women, 1698–1917 : experience and expression : an anthology of sources / compiled, edited, annotated, and introduced by Robin Bisha, Jehanne M Gheith, Christine Holden, and William G. Wagner.
p. cm.
Includes index.
ISBN 0-253-34084-5 (cloth : alk. paper) — ISBN 0-253-21523-4 (pbk. : alk. paper)
1. Women—Russia—History. I. Bisha, Robin.
HQ1662 .R877 2002
305.4'0947—dc21
2001007444

1 2 3 4 5 07 06 05 04 03 02

Contents

Illustrations appear on pages 151–158 and 291–298.

Acknowledgments

From the outset the preparation of this volume has been a collaborative effort, involving not only the compilers and editors but also a large number of colleagues, students, friends, and family members. Without the generous assistance and encouragement of these people, we would not have been able to complete the project, and we therefore wish sincerely to thank all those who have helped and supported us for the past several years.

At the top of our list of those to thank are the many colleagues who suggested, translated, and helped annotate individual documents; without their help this volume would not exist. The list of these colleagues is long and follows these acknowledgments (the translator of each document also is indicated at the end of the translation). As the reader will discover, the collection includes a wide variety of documents, ranging from handwritten memoirs and archival materials to printed and published sources. The style of language found in the documents, too, is quite varied, ranging from literary and academic or journalistic genres to the specialized languages of the state and ecclesiastical bureaucracies and the cryptic scribbling of personal documents. Many of the sources were written or published in Old Church Slavonic or eighteenth-century secular Russian; still others were written or published in the more standardized Russian language and orthography that developed during the nineteenth century. The technical and linguistic problems encountered in the process of translating these documents were daunting, as were the tasks of standardizing our terminology and producing translations that preserved the nuances of the original while being readily accessible to English-speaking students. We owe a tremendous debt of gratitude to our translators and to the people who checked the translations—Greg Bruess, Eve Levin, Michelle Marrese, Carolyn J. Pouncy, Nadya Peterson, and, especially, Karin Elliot—for providing us with such excellent translations and expert advice. Assistance on aspects of Russian cultural practices also came from Olga Demidova, Natalea Skvir, and Kira Stevens. Unfortunately, when completing the final version of the book we were compelled to abridge and modify several translations, and to omit a few entirely, for which we apologize to the original translators. We fully accept, of course, responsibility for the results of these editorial decisions.

Developing the structure for a book that would be useful for history and literature courses relating to the Russian Empire and more broadly to Europe proved to be a challenge. In working through this problem, we were fortunate to have the opportunity to discuss our ideas with colleagues and students at several conferences, seminars, and workshops. In this regard, we thank in particular the participants in the workshops on Women in Slavic Culture, held over the years in association with the Summer Research Laboratory at the University of Illinois at Urbana-Champaign, and those at special seminars held at Duke University and at Williams College for their helpful and encouraging comments and suggestions.

The evolution of the book benefited enormously from the feedback received on such occasions. At a later stage, we received similarly constructive criticisms and advice from the readers of the manuscript, Beth Holmgren, Ann Hibner Koblitz, and an anonymous reader, and from Gary Marker and Pat Tracy, who kindly read individual chapters. Special mention should be made here, too, of Barbara Norton, who as a member of the "editorial collective" for several years played a significant role in the planning, conceptualization, and early work on the book. Without her expertise, intelligence, and good humor, it would have been difficult to bring this book into being.

In addition to receiving suggestions from colleagues regarding documents to be included in the collection, we spent more time than we care to remember searching for and sifting through pertinent documents. In doing so, we were assisted enormously by the library staffs of our own institutions, Duke University, Kalamazoo College, the University of Southern Maine, the University of Texas at El Paso, and Williams College. Substantial help also was received from the exceptionally knowledgeable staffs at the Slavic Library at the University of Illinois at Urbana-Champaign, the Slavonic Collection of Helsinki University Library, the Russian State Library in Moscow, Ladd Library at Bates College, the Russian State Historical Archive in St. Petersburg, the State Archive of the Russian Federation in Moscow, and the Russian State Historical Archive of the City of Moscow. We are also grateful for the assistance given us by Slavic reference librarian–scholars June Pachuta Ferris of the University of Chicago and Diana Greene of New York University. Again, without the assistance and professional expertise of these people we could not have completed this collection, and it is with pleasure that we acknowledge and thank them for their help.

We also are grateful for the financial and other forms of support provided by our respective institutions over the years that we were working on this project. Such support proved invaluable. We especially thank, however, the Women's Studies Program and the Faculty Professional Development Fund of the University of Southern Maine; the Devonwood Foundation of North Carolina; the Women's Studies Program and the Department of Slavic Languages and Literatures at Duke University; and the President, Dean of the Faculty, and Francis C. Oakley Center for the Humanities and Social Sciences at Williams College. Their support enabled us to travel to research collections and conferences, to hold working weekends, and to present seminars at Duke University and Williams College.

Our work on this volume happily coincided with the great strides made in computer technology and electronic communication over the past decade. Although frustrating at times, this technology enabled us to continue working collaboratively even though we were separated spatially, sometimes by even greater distances than normal. In this regard, the computer access, hospitality, and encouragement provided by Joe Pope, head of the Department of Historical and Critical Studies, University of Central Lancashire, Preston, England, and John Klier, head, and assistants Lia Kahn-Zajtman and Juliet Summerfield, of the Department of Hebrew and Jewish Studies, University College, London, England, were much appreciated. We are grateful to the staffs of the computing labs and centers of information technology at our respective institutions for patiently helping us work through the various obstacles and glitches we encountered—and occasionally created due to our own ignorance. Christine Holden in particular would like to thank Laurie Grant, administrative assistant in the Gorham history office, and Kyle Stuart, student assistant, for their help, and the staff at the Lewiston-Auburn College Computing Lab for its assistance and guidance as she mastered the intricacies of electronic data transmission and retrieval.

Finally, we especially thank Janet Rabinowitch, editorial director at Indiana University Press, who encouraged us to undertake this project, patiently supported our efforts, and continually offered thoughtful and knowledgeable advice on the structure and contents of the volume. Truly, without her encouragement and support we could not have completed the project, and we remain indebted to her for her valuable assistance.

List of Translators

Amy Singleton Adams is associate professor in the Department of Modern Languages and Literatures, College of the Holy Cross, Worcester, Massachusetts.

Jennifer L. Anderson, Ph.D., is an adjunct instructor in the Department of History at Columbus State Community College, Columbus, Ohio.

Joe Baird is associate professor of Russian and English at Western Michigan University, Kalamazoo.

Valentina Baslyk, Ph.D., is a freelance translator in Montréal, Québec, Canada.

Justyna Beinek, Ph.D., is a graduate of the Slavic Department, Harvard University, Cambridge, Massachusetts.

Laurie Bernstein is associate professor in the Department of History, Rutgers University, Camden, New Jersey.

Gregory Bruess is associate professor in the Department of History, University of Northern Iowa, Cedar Falls, Iowa, and chair of the Russian and East European Studies Program.

Diana L. Burgin is professor in the Department of Modern Languages, the University of Massachusetts, Boston.

Pamela Chester, Ph.D., is an independent scholar and associate at the Davis Center for Russian Studies, Harvard University, Cambridge, Massachusetts.

Irina H. Corten is associate professor of Russian Language and Literature, University of Minnesota, Minneapolis.

Jane T. Costlow is professor in the Department of German, Russian, and East Asian Languages, and the Christian A. Johnson Professor of Interdisciplinary Studies, Bates College, Lewiston, Maine.

Karin V. Elliot, M.A., is a freelance interpreter, translator, and translation editor in Alexandria, Virginia.

Carol Apollonio Flath is associate professor of the Practice of Slavics, Duke University, Durham, North Carolina.

Melissa Merrill Floyd is an independent scholar in the Washington, D.C., metropolitan area.

Sibelan Forrester is associate professor in the Department of Modern Languages and Literatures, Swarthmore College, Swarthmore, Pennsylvania.

Catriona Kelly is reader in Russian and a fellow of New College, Oxford University, England.

Martha Kuchar is associate professor in the Department of English, Roanoke College, Salem, Virginia.

Sally Kux, Ph.D., is deputy director for Democratic Initiatives, Bureau of European and Eurasian Affairs, U.S. Department of State, Washington, D.C.

Eve Levin is associate professor in the Department of History, The Ohio State University, Columbus, and editor of *The Russian Review*.

Adele Lindenmeyr is professor and chair of the Department of History, Villanova University, Villanova, Pennsylvania.

Gary Marker is Professor in the Department of History, the State University of New York at Stony Brook.

Michelle Lamarre Marrese, Ph.D., is a visiting assistant professor in the Department of History, Northwestern University, Evanston, Illinois.

Rebecca Epstein Matveyev is assistant professor in the Department of Russian, Lawrence University, Appleton, Wisconsin.

Katherine Moskver is assistant professor in the Department of Russian at the United States Air Force Academy, Colorado Springs, Colorado.

Karen L. Myers, Ph.D., formerly visiting assistant professor in the Center for Russian, Eastern European, and Eurasian Studies at the University of Iowa, Iowa City, is associate director, Corporate and Foundation Relations, Brandeis University, Waltham, Massachusetts.

Willow Najjar is a graduate of the University of Minnesota, Minneapolis.

Thomas Newlin is associate professor in the Department of German and Russian, Oberlin College, Oberlin, Ohio.

Barbara T. Norton is professor in the Department of History, Widener University, Chester, Pennsylvania.

Catherine O'Neil is assistant professor of Russian in the Department of Languages and Literatures, University of Denver, Denver, Colorado.

Nadya L. Peterson is assistant professor in the Russian and Slavic Division of the Department of Classical and Oriental Languages, Hunter College of The City University of New York.

Teresa L. Polowy is associate professor of Russian, University of Arizona, Tucson.

Carolyn J. Pouncy, Ph.D., is assistant editor of *Russian Studies in History* and an independent scholar.

Denise Price is a graduate of the University of Minnesota, Minneapolis.

Melissa M. Reid is a graduate of the University of Minnesota, Minneapolis.

Karen Rosneck, M.A., M.L.S., is a library staff member at the University of Wisconsin, Madison, and an independent researcher and translator.

Laura Elyse Schlosberg, Ph.D., is a financial analyst in the Office of the Provost, Budgets, Planning, and Institutional Research, Duke University, Durham, North Carolina, and an instructor in History at Duke University.

Ruth Sobel, Ph.D., is honorary senior lecturer, the Defence School of Languages, Beaconsfield, United Kingdom.

Karla Thomas Solomon, M.A., is an independent researcher living in Moscow, Russia.

Lisa Renée Taylor, Ph.D., is a librarian at the University of Georgia, Athens.

Igor Timofeyev, a graduate of Williams College who received an M.Phil. in Russian and East European Studies from Oxford University and a J.D. from Yale Law School, is serving as a judicial clerk.

Christine Worobec is professor of history, Northern Illinois University, DeKalb.

COMPILERS AND EDITORS

Robin Bisha, Ph.D., recently received an M.A. in Journalism and Mass Communications from the University of North Carolina at Chapel Hill. She previously taught in the history departments of Kalamazoo College, Kalamazoo, Michigan, and the University of Texas at El Paso.

Jehanne M Gheith is associate professor in the Department of Slavic Languages and Literatures at Duke University, Durham, North Carolina.

Christine Holden is associate professor in the Department of History at the University of Southern Maine, Gorham. She previously taught in the Department of History at Bates College, Lewiston, Maine, and also worked for the Maine State Legislature as a nonpartisan legislative assistant.

William G. Wagner is Brown Professor of History and chair of the Department of History, Williams College, Williamstown, Massachusetts.

Note on Transliteration and Dates

How to transliterate Russian words is always a juggling act: one wants to remain true to the Russian alphabet and sounds, aim for consistency, and retain those spellings that are already familiar to the reader of English. We have used a modified Library of Congress transliteration system, keeping names for which there already exists an accepted spelling in English (e.g., Emperor Peter, Tsarevna Sophia). We have retained the soft sign, with the same exception (e.g., Olga, Tatiana). Additionally, for female names ending in "iia," we have kept the "iia" when the "i" is stressed, and generally dropped it in other cases, so that we could retain spellings that are more familiar to English-speaking readers (e.g., Maria). Yet we have also made some choices away from familiarity and for consistency (e.g., Tolstoi, rather than the more familiar Tolstoy); Tolstoi is becoming a more usual transliteration, and we want to encourage what we hope is a trend.

Dates are given as in the original document; Old Style dates therefore have not been converted to New Style dating.

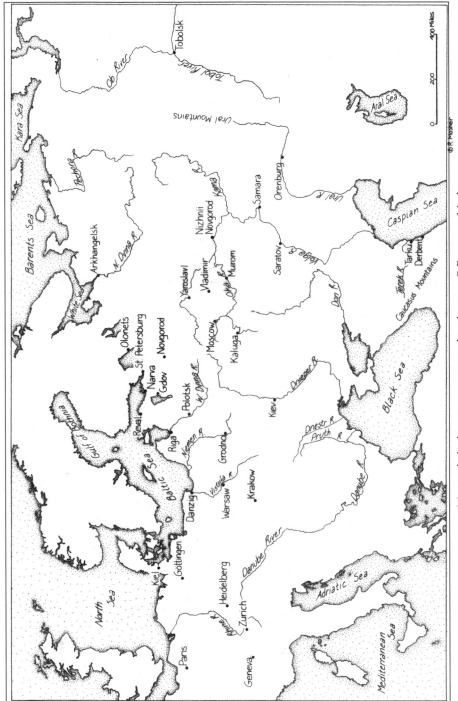

Map includes locations mentioned in the text. © Rosemary Mosher

Timeline

1682–1725	Reign of Peter I, the Great (1662–1725).
1696	Peter becomes sole ruler and begins to rule in his own right.
1697–1698	Peter makes "Great Embassy" to Europe.
1700–1721	Great Northern War against Sweden.
1701	Peter orders women to wear Western-style clothing.
1702	First Russian printed newspaper, News (Vedomosti), is published.
1703	City of St. Petersburg is founded.
1712	Peter marries Catherine, his mistress.
1714	Decree is issued on single inheritance; restricts inheritance rights of women.
1716	Natalia Alekseevna (Peter's sister) founds first charity home in St. Petersburg for the sick and elderly, as well as for abandoned children.
1718	Peter has his former wife, Eudoxia, dragged from her monastery and publicly tried for alleged adultery.
1718, 1725	Women are commanded to appear at Peter's assemblies and evening balls.
1718–1724	New census is carried out, culminating in introduction of the "soul tax."
1720	Decree is issued ending the requirement that a wife follow her husband into exile.
1721	Patriarchate (Orthodox Church) is abolished and the Holy Synod is established.
1722	Decree is issued forbidding forced marriages. Table of Ranks is introduced. Peter issues decree changing the rules of succession.
1725–1727	Reign of Empress Catherine I (1684–1727).
1726	Catherine founds the Russian Academy of Sciences.
1727–1730	Reign of Emperor Peter II (1715–1730).
1730–1740	Reign of Empress Anna Ivanovna (1693–1740).
1730	Law of single inheritance is abolished; effect is to expand the inheritance rights of noblewomen and, eventually, women of other social groups.
1731	Practice of allowing the use of land for daughters' dowries is restored.
1740–1741	Reign of Emperor Ivan VI (1740–1764).
1741	Regency of Anna Leopoldovna for son, Ivan VI. Death penalty is abolished, later rescinded.
1741–1761	Reign of Empress Elizabeth (1709–1761), daughter of Peter the Great.

1750	Professional theater is established in the city of Iaroslavl'.
1753	Senate ruling grants noblewomen full control over their property; later extended to other women.
1755	Moscow University is founded.
1756	First professional theater is created in St. Petersburg.
1757	Academy of Fine Arts is founded.
1761	Retirement home for widows of "serving people" is established.
1761–1762	Reign of Emperor Peter III (1728–1762), husband of Catherine the Great.
1762	Decree issued to free the nobility from obligation of state service.
1762–1796	Reign of Empress Catherine II, the Great (1729–1796).
1764	Catherine establishes the Imperial Foundling Home in Moscow. Church lands are secularized; many monastic institutions are dissolved.
1764–1765	First institutes (boarding schools) are founded for girls of noble rank (and of lesser rank) at the former Smolnyi Convent, St. Petersburg.
1765	Catherine abolishes marital fees.
1767–1768	Catherine's Legislative Commission meets.
1772	First Partition of Poland.
1773–1774	Pugachev rebellion.
1775	Reform of provincial administration is ordered, establishing corporate bodies for the nobility.
1779	First regular fashion magazine, *The Monthly Fashion Essay*, is published.
1783	Ekaterina Romanovna Dashkova is appointed director of the Russian Academy of Sciences.
1785	St. Petersburg Obstetrical Institute is founded. Charters to the Nobility and the Towns are issued, securing corporate privileges and establishing limited personal rights for members of the nobility and urban-based estates.
1786	Decree is issued founding public schools.
1793	Second Partition of Poland.
1795	Third Partition of Poland.
1796–1801	Reign of Emperor Paul I (1754–1801).
1797	Paul alters the law of succession, excluding women.
1798–1800	War with France.
1801–1825	Reign of Emperor Alexander I (1777–1825).
1801	Moscow Obstetrical Institute is founded. Right to own land is extended to non-nobles. Marriage of Praskovia Kovaleva (1786–1803), daughter of a serf blacksmith and leading actress and singer in the Sheremetev Theater, to Count Nikolai Petrovich Sheremetev (1731–1809). He freed her (1798), and later all her relatives (1801), from serfdom.

1803	Decree is issued on voluntary emancipation of serfs.
1805–1807	War with France.
1810	*Memoirs* of Natalia Dolgorukaia (née Sheremeteva, 1714–1771) are published, the first woman's autobiography in Russian.
1812	Napoleon invades Russia.
1812–1815	War with France.
1817–1864	War in the Caucasus.
1819	St. Petersburg University is founded.
1823–1833	*Ladies Journal (Damskii zhurnal)* is published.
1825	Decembrist Rebellion.
1825–1855	Reign of Emperor Nicholas I (1796–1855).
1828	Formation in the Imperial Chancellery of a Department for the Administration of the Institutions of Empress Maria (schools for girls, and rest homes and similar institutions for women and girls).
1830–1831	Uprising in Poland.
1834	Russian noblewoman Princess Dorothea Lieven maintains a famous salon in Paris; her correspondence appears later in *The Private Letters of Princess Lieven*.
1843	State regulation of prostitution is introduced. Orthodox Church establishes primary schools for daughters of the parish clergy.
1845	An official statute of the Russian Secondary School for Girls states that "woman, as a lower creation appointed by nature to be dependent on others, must know that she is not fated to rule but to submit herself to her husband, and that only through strict fulfillment of her responsibilities to her family can she assure happiness and gain love and respect both within the family and without."
1853–1856	Crimean War; Russian women serve as nurses.
1855–1881	Reign of Alexander II (1818–1881).
1857–1858	Secondary schools for girls are authorized and developed, through both the Ministry of Education and the Department for the Administration of the Institutions of the Empress Maria.
1858	Opening of a seven-year school (*gymnasium*) for girls of all social ranks in St. Petersburg.
1859–1862	*Daybreak (Razsvet)*, the first "thick journal" for women, is published in St. Petersburg.
1859–1863	Women are allowed to audit lectures at some universities.
1860	Maria Trubnikova (1853–1897), Anna Filosofova (1837–1912), and Nadezhda Stasova (1832–1895) establish philanthropic organizations with feminist goals: to find cheap housing, meals, and jobs for working-class women and to start sewing workshops.
1861–1874	Alexander II institutes "Great Reforms," including abolition of serfdom (1861).

1863	Women, held responsible (without evidence) for student riots, are expelled from university lectures by government order. Nikolai Chernyshevskii's novel *What Is to Be Done?* is published.
1863–1873	A women's publishing cooperative is established in St. Petersburg; active members include Anna Engelgardt, Elizaveta Beketova, and Aleksandra Markelova.
1863–1864	Polish rebellion.
1865	University of Zurich, Switzerland, opens its doors to women students. Russian medical faculties admit women as the annexation of Central Asian territories creates a demand by Muslim women for female physicians.
1866–1868	*Women's Herald* (*Zhenskii vestnik*) is published in St. Petersburg.
1867–1873	More than a hundred Russian women study at the University of Zurich, mostly in medicine.
1869	Opening of the first Russian university-level lectures to women: the Alarchinskii Courses in St. Petersburg and the Lubianskii Courses in Moscow; women are not yet allowed to matriculate.
1872	Opening of the Guerrier Higher Courses for Women in Moscow; establishment of the women's medical (midwifery) courses at St. Petersburg Medical-Surgical Academy.
1873	State decree bars women studying in Zurich from employment in Russia after January 1, 1874, because of their exposure to radical ideas.
1874	Populist movement, "to the people," arises.
1876	Opening of higher courses for women in Kazan and Kiev.
1876–1879	Populist organization "Land and Freedom" is active; in 1879, it divides into two groups, "Black Repartition" and the "People's Will," the latter of which adopts terrorism as a tactic.
1877–1878	War with Turkey; Russian women again serve as nurses.
1878	First-recorded strike by women workers takes place in two St. Petersburg tobacco factories. Vera Zasulich, 26, shoots and wounds the military governor of St. Petersburg, General Fedor Fedorovich Trepov, as a protest against his order for the flogging of a prisoner. Although she admits her guilt, a (male) jury acquits her. Establishment of the Bestuzhev Higher Women's Courses in St. Petersburg by a group of supportive faculty members.
1876–1891	*Women's Education* (*Zhenskoe obrazovanie*) published in St. Petersburg.
1881	Sofia Perovskaia is one of a group hanged for the assassination of Alexander II; Jessie Helfman is also sentenced, but dies in childbirth in prison. Vera Figner assumes leadership of the "People's Will" terrorist group.

1881–1894	Reign of Emperor Alexander III (1845–1894).
1882–1883	Admission to the women's medical courses is closed.
1883	Sofia Vasilevna Kovalevskaia (1850–1891) accepts a position in mathematics at the University of Stockholm in Sweden.
1883–1884	*Friend of Women* (*Drug zhenshchin*) published in Moscow.
1885	Night work for women factory workers prohibited. Russian musician Anna Nikolaevna Esipova (1851–1914) is appointed pianist to the Russian Imperial Court.
1886–1900	Closure of all higher courses for women except the Bestuzhev Courses in St. Petersburg, which reopen in 1889.
1889	Kovalevskaia is granted tenure and takes the chair of the mathematics department at the University of Stockholm. Maria Tsebrikova writes *Letter to Alexander III* as a political statement. N. N. Golitsyn publishes his *Bibliographical Dictionary of Russian Women Writers*.
1891	S. I. Ponomarev comments on and supplements this work with his *Our Women Writers*. "Great Famine" affects twenty provinces; reinvigorates social activism.
1894	Russian Chief of Police reports that 42 percent of the 114 Russian women studying abroad are "disloyal."
1894–1917	Reign of Emperor Nicholas II (1868–1918).
1895–1917	Women's Mutual Philanthropic Society established as an active political force for women.
1895	Nicholas II increases the quotas for the St. Petersburg course and establishes the St. Petersburg Women's Medical Institute, which leads to full medical qualifications.
1895–1898	Women tobacco and textile workers in St. Petersburg engage in major strikes.
1897	Law is enacted limiting regular factory workdays to eleven-and-a-half hours.
1898	First Congress of the Russian Social Democratic Labor Party (Marxist orientation) convenes.
1899	Society for the Protection of Women is founded.
1899–1900	*Women's Cause* (*Zhenskoe delo*) is published in St. Petersburg.
1901	Nadezhda Konstantinovna Krupskaia, 32, becomes secretary of a faction of the Russian Social Democratic Labor Party (the faction later becomes known as the Bolshevik Party), a post she holds until 1917. Formation of the Socialist Revolutionary Party.
1902–1903	Widespread peasant unrest occurs.
1904	Separate women's sections in Gapon labor assemblies are organized.

1904–1917	*Women's Herald* (*Zhenskii vestnik*) published in St. Petersburg.
1904–1905	War with Japan.
1905	Women are among the demonstrators at the Winter Palace in St. Petersburg on 22 January fired on by troops; the event ("Bloody Sunday") initiates the Revolution of 1905; unrest continues until 1907.
	General strike ensues in October.
	October Manifesto is issued, extending civil rights and promising an elected legislative assembly.
	Women's organizations are formed: the All-Russian Union for Women's Equality, the League of Equal Rights for Women, and the Women's Progressive Party.
	Constitutional Democratic (*Kadet*) Party is established.
1905–1908	Women can again attend university lectures.
1906	Fundamental Laws are issued; First Duma (elected legislative body) convenes.
	Women in Finland (an autonomous Duchy within the Russian Empire) obtain the right to vote.
	Peasants receive the right to leave the commune freely.
1907	Social Democratic activist Aleksandra Kollontai organizes public meetings, mostly of women, supposedly to hear lectures on maternal hygiene; meetings are broken up by the police when speakers refer to social exploitation and support women's right to vote.
	Police arrest Bolshevik revolutionary Inessa Armand, 32, who has dedicated herself to political reform after bearing five children. Having discussed political issues with Lenin, whom she met in 1903, she subordinates her efforts on behalf of women's rights to working for the wider cause of emancipating workers.
1907–1909	*Union of Women* (*Soiuz zhenshchin*) published in St. Petersburg.
1908	The All-Russian Congress of Women (postponed from 1902 due to war and revolution) is the last public gathering of Russian feminists before the 1917 revolutions. Kollontai, who publicly supports class solidarity and opposes feminism (as "bourgeois"), goes into exile to avoid arrest.
1909–1910	*Women's Thought* (*Zhenskaia mysl'*) published in Kiev.
1910–1917	*Women's Cause* (*Zhenskoe delo*) published in Moscow.
1910	Congress on the Struggle against the Trade in Women meets in St. Petersburg.
1910–1911	Duma enacts the Stolypin land reforms, seeking to undermine the peasant commune.
1911	Women are granted the right to matriculate in medical, pedagogical, and other specialized institutions of higher

education; graduates of the higher courses are allowed to take the state examinations to qualify for a university degree.

1912   Russian composer Ella von Schultz-Adaievski (1846–1926) publishes her opera, *The Dawn of Freedom*.

Inheritance laws are reformed, extending the rights of women.

1912–1913   First All-Russian Congress on Women's Education occurs.

1912–1914   Women tobacco and textile workers in several cities engage in major strikes.

1913   Women are admitted into the medical faculty of Tomsk University in Siberia; over the next few years, women are admitted to particular departments at other universities.

1914   Law establishes the right to marital separation.

1914–1918   First World War.

1917   Bread riots and demonstrations by women in Petrograd lead to wider demonstrations and to the mutiny of the Petrograd garrison and the February Revolution; Nicholas abdicates for himself and his son, ending the Romanov dynasty and the monarchy; Provisional Government is established.

Provisional Government expands the political and civil rights of women.

October Revolution establishes Soviet rule.

Abbreviations

GA RF — State Archive of the Russian Federation (*Gosudarstvennyi arkhiv Rossiiskoi federatsii*) [Moscow].

LOII — Leningrad Branch of the Institute of History (*Leningradskoe otdelenie instituta istorii*).

PSZ — *Polnoe Sobranie Zakonov Rossiiskoi Imperii* (Complete Collection of Laws of the Russian Empire). 1st series, enactments 1649–December 11, 1825; 2nd series, enactments December 12, 1825–February 28, 1881; 3rd series, enactments March 1, 1881–1913. St. Petersburg, 1830–1917.

RGALI — Russian State Archive of Literature and Art (*Rossiiskii gosudarstvennyi arkhiv literatury i iskusstva*) [Moscow].

RGIA — Russian State Historical Archive (*Rossiiskii gosudarstvennyi istoricheskii arkhiv*) [St. Petersburg].

RGIAgM — Russian State Historical Archive of the City of Moscow (*Rossiiskii gosudarstvennyi istoricheskii arkhiv goroda Moskvy*).

Russkii arkhiv — *Russian Archive*; journal, published 1863–1917.

Shchukin — Petr Ivanovich Shchukin. *Sbornik starinnykh bumag, khraniashchikhsia v Muzee P. I. Shchukina* (Collection of Ancient Documents, Preserved in the Museum of P. I. Shchukin). Moscow, 1896–1902. 10 vols.

Spb. — St. Petersburg.

TsGIA Spb. — Central State Historical Archive of St. Petersburg (*Tsentral'nyi gosudarstvennyi istoricheskii arkhiv Sankt-peterburga*).

Russian Women,
1698–1917

Introduction

When a woman wears a long dress at home, it
evokes the nineteenth century, when the concept
of the keeper of the hearth still existed.
—Aleksandra Marinina[1]

These lines—spoken by a fictional post-Soviet politician who has broken the
law to acquire a woman who will keep his hearth and, thus, further his career—
express the nostalgia that some Russians now feel for the Russian empire. In this
romanticized view of Russia before the revolution, women confined their activities to the domestic sphere. Marinina's politician conceives of the nineteenth-
century Russian woman as a gracious hostess who dressed for a day at home as she
would for a reception so that she would always be prepared to extend hospitality
to her husband's guests. Having rescued his "keeper of the hearth" from the life of
a prostitute and provided her with a fine apartment and sumptuous table, the
politician expects her to remain ignorant of his affairs but to take full responsibility for the functioning of the home. He recognizes that women in his time are
no longer confined chiefly to the domestic sphere, yet he senses that his effort to
recreate the vanished imperial past will serve him well in contemporary Russia. Is
this literary memory, in which the Russian empire is the site of a life of grace
and luxury for homemakers, an accurate evocation of women's lives in imperial
Russia?

Questions about women's lives, thoughts, and activities have been of major interest to scholars for only a relatively short time. Previously, historians were interested primarily in empires, states, and nations and in the rulers, warriors, and
political actors—predominantly male—who were seen as shaping them. Reflecting this tendency, scholars of Russian history focused on the expansion of Russian control across the Eurasian steppe, chronicled the affairs of the Russian state,
and examined the workings of society and the economy of serfdom. Literary critics studied the works of the great male authors, for the most part not even recognizing that women were among the most noted authors of the imperial period. In
the fields of both history and literature, women were thought to occupy a domestic realm that did not merit investigation. Until the 1970s historians rarely concerned themselves with household and domestic matters, which were thought to
be the female domain, and studies of women and their literary works were seldom
made. In that decade, however, scholars began to expand investigations of social,
intellectual, and political history to include serious study of women's past participation in politics, their work, and their position in society, among other topics.

The family as well was subjected to scholarly scrutiny. In recent years, scholars have turned to women as producers of cultural products. Authors now incorporate information on women, and the insights of scholars who have uncovered the history of Russian women, into textbooks. Students can take courses on Russian women's history and Russian women's literature in many colleges and universities. Yet, no compendium of texts presenting this history through the eyes of the women who lived it exists in any language. This book presents Russian women in their own words citing the diversity of their experiences in the Russian empire.

What were women's lives like in imperial Russia? Did they, as Marinina's politician implies, live in comfort and gentility? Does the diversity of women's experiences in imperial Russia even allow us to make such generalizations? To answer these questions, students must consider the history of women in imperial Russia and the context in which Russian women lived. Even if one agrees that all Russian women were subject to patriarchal control in the family and in society, the nature and operation of this control must be viewed against a broad historical backdrop.

HISTORICAL AND SOCIAL FRAMEWORK

Women's character and their roles in society became issues for explicit discussion in the imperial period of Russian history, which encompasses the reigns of Peter I ("the Great," r. 1682–1725) through Nicholas II (r. 1894–1917). Peter's attempts to remake Russian society in the image of Europe included a transformation of noblewomen's attire and participation in court entertainments. While this change did not bring about a proto-feminist revolution in eighteenth-century Russia, it did suggest that social and cultural life could be organized along varied lines, allowing the roles of women in Russian society to be seen as changeable, rather than as part of an immutable, natural order. Of course, by the eighteenth century Russian women did not occupy the same place in society nor perform the same tasks as they had in previous centuries. But earlier changes in women's roles had occurred in an evolutionary manner, with minimal intervention by the state. With the exception that Christianization brought the introduction of a new form of marriage and accompanying sexual mores, a process that began in the late tenth century and extended for several centuries, the historical record in Russia contains little evidence before Peter's return from his Grand Embassy to the major European capitals in 1697–1698 of direct governmental attempts to determine the role of women in society.

By contrast, under Peter I Russian women and men alike became tools to be used in the building of a modern imperial state: for Russia to become a European great power, the appearance and conduct of the Russian nobility, both women and men, had to match those of their European counterparts. Peter's reforms of women's roles in court and noble society constituted an attempt to move the Russian state clearly into European great-power status, not to correct a perceived inequity in the status of women within Russian society. The changes in women's lives were matched by a similar transformation in the lives of men. For women as well as men, moreover, both the character and pace of change in their lives resulting from Peter's policies varied widely, depending on their social position.

These changes took place on a vast canvas. By the outbreak of World War I, the Russian empire extended in all directions from the central Russian steppe to encompass lands from present-day Poland to the shores of the Pacific Ocean, from the Arctic Ocean to the deserts and mountains of Central Asia. Peter the Great was the first Russian ruler to call himself emperor, and the imperial period in Russia's history is usually dated from his reign, a time when the Russians already ruled a vast territory inhabited by numerous ethnic groups. Peter added the Baltic provinces to this territory, and his successors continued to expand the empire, in particular to include large parts of Poland, the Caucasus, and Central Asia. Historians estimate that the population of imperial Russia was about 15 or 16 million in 1719. The population had more than doubled by the end of the eighteenth century, doubled again by 1855, and reached 168 million by 1913, only four years before the revolutions of 1917. Hence during the eighteenth and nineteenth centuries the Russian empire constituted by far the largest and most populous state in Europe. Then, as now, though, many considered it also to be among the most backward.

One aspect of imperial Russia's perceived backwardness was the rigidly defined social hierarchy that came to be enshrined in Russian law during the imperial period. Legally, a person was born into a social status, or estate, and in most cases remained in that category throughout her or his life. A girl inherited her father's social rank at birth and, as a rule, took on that of her husband at marriage. For most Russians during the imperial period this meant membership in the peasant estate. And until formally emancipated in 1861, a high percentage of peasants—well over half in the eighteenth century and nearly half by the mid-nineteenth century—were serfs. The bondage of Russian peasants was codified in the seventeenth century, and during the eighteenth century the social and economic position of the serfs deteriorated until they had become virtual slaves of their landlords. While a substantial number of peasants belonged to the imperial family or to the Russian Orthodox Church (until 1764, when church lands were secularized), the largest owner was the nobility, which owned over half of all Russian peasants in the eighteenth century and somewhat less than half by the mid-nineteenth century.

Although serfs were legally bound to the land, and not to the person of the landlord, they were traded in the same manner as slaves and exchanged in the same way as other forms of property.[2] Contracts for the sale of serfs routinely placed the value of serf women considerably lower than that of serf men. Most peasants lived in rural villages and engaged in agriculture for their living and to fulfill their obligations to their landlords, although many supplemented their income through trade, craft production, carting, and other activities. The lands farmed by peasants were controlled by a council of heads of households, almost all of whom were men. Since serf owners generally worked through these village councils to maintain their control, the institution of serfdom served to reinforce patriarchal authority within the village and in individual households. In most Russian areas, particularly in central Russia, land was perceived by peasants as belonging to the village and was reallocated periodically to families based on the number of adult work units in the household. A work unit consisted of a married couple: a peasant man could not receive an allotment of land unless he had a wife to work with him. Agricultural work was divided along gender lines, but the work of both men and women was vital to family survival. Even after emancipation, village affairs remained largely under the control of peasant men. Membership in the village community was vital to survival, and both women and men were expected to marry and fulfill responsibilities to the community. Those who were expelled from or isolated from the village community struggled, whatever their gender.

Scholars face a daunting task in the construction of an account of the lives of peasants in imperial Russia. Most peasants were illiterate, and few records of their observations and thoughts are available. What historians know about peasant life in the eighteenth and early nineteenth centuries has been gleaned largely from the records of estate administrations, the army, the Russian Orthodox Church, and other non-peasant sources. Ethnographers began to record their observations of village life in the early nineteenth century. After the reforms of the 1860s educated observers regularly wrote about peasants, and peasant courts recorded snapshots of individual lives, but only a small minority of peasants had the opportunity to learn to read and write. The lives of peasant women are even more difficult to trace than are those of peasant men. Historians and ethnographers have relied on court records, reports of educated people who observed peasant life, and the embroideries and tools women left behind to reconstruct their daily lives.

If peasants occupied the bottom of the social pyramid, the top was held by the serf-owning nobility, which comprised about 2 percent of the population of the Russian empire in the eighteenth century. Being in the position of both a hereditary estate and a service caste, all noblemen, until freed from compulsory service in 1762, occupied posts in the military or the expanding civil service or at court; even after 1762, most noblemen continued to enter state service, if sometimes only for a short period. Noblewomen from elite families also served in the imperial household as ladies-in-waiting and maids-of-honor. Until the abolition of serfdom in 1861, a high (though steadily declining) percentage of nobles relied on the estates that were farmed by their serfs for their provisions and most of their income, a dependency that often continued in different forms even after 1861. Noble families gained status by their proximity to the sovereign, rank in state service, and the number of serfs they owned. Only a few nobles owned large numbers of serfs, however, and women of these families often managed vast estates while their husbands were away. Women of the elite enjoyed access to the imperial court, imported luxuries, and education. But most nobles possessed much more modest means, and many lived in conditions similar to those of peasants.

Most of the remaining Russian population could be divided into four broad and internally diverse social groups: the clergy, the *raznochintsy* (people of diverse ranks), townspeople and merchants, and workers. Sons of the clergy normally remained within the clerical estate and often took up their fathers' posts. If a priest had no sons, then his daughter generally married a cleric who followed in his father-in-law's footsteps and often took over his position. Women played important roles in Orthodox parishes; priests' wives assisted their husbands with parish activities, and other women filled important positions, for example, that of baker of the communion host. The *raznochintsy* emerged in the eighteenth century, as the imperial estate system itself was developing. Often from the clerical estate, these were men who managed to elevate or alter their status by gaining an education and entering either state service or some nontraditional occupation. Many gained personal nobility as a perquisite of state service. Level of wealth was linked to social rank only in the merchant estate, which itself could be entered through the payment of prescribed fees. Within this estate, merchants could move up and down within a guild system based on the declared value of their assets and the payment of a corresponding levy. Women of merchant families played active roles in family businesses, staffing shops located in or near their dwellings, booths at local trading rows, and displays at regional commercial fairs, and they could carry on trade in their own right. Scholars have noted that a primary goal of this group was to attain noble status. Merchants could gain noble status through a combination of amassing a certain amount of wealth and serving state interests. When achieving personal nobility proved out of reach, some merchant families married their daughters into impoverished noble families. Men of the merchant estate who married noble women, however, did not receive their status. This sort of social mobility was visible to contemporaries, but historians have discovered that the estate system in general masked both social mobility and change. Whereas the nobility, the clergy, the merchantry, and the peasantry all constituted formal legal estates, imperial law never established a category for workers, even after 1861, when large numbers of peasants began moving to the cities and engaging in industrial labor. Legally, peasants remained peasants, no matter where they worked or lived. Nor did the estate system comfortably accommodate the professional and other occupational groups that emerged and grew rapidly in the nineteenth century.

Whereas the estate system helped to determine the lives of all Russian subjects, politics and government affairs involved few men and even fewer women. The autocratic system of government placed one individual of the ruling family at the head of the entire state apparatus. Surprisingly, more often than not during the eighteenth century this turned out to be a woman. Peter the Great left neither strong male heirs nor clear rules for succession, with the result that he was succeeded by his wife, Empress Catherine I (r. 1725–1727), a commoner by birth. Catherine and the Empresses Anna (r. 1730–1740) and Elizabeth (r. 1741–1761) proved to be undistinguished rulers, and in some cases less than energetic in conducting state affairs. By contrast, Catherine II ("the Great," r. 1762–1796) took an active interest in government and imperial expansion. Believing that his mother should have abdicated the throne in his favor, however, Catherine's son Paul (r. 1796–1801) banned women from ruling Russia in their own right. Paul's action reflected the more typical situation for women. With the exception of Eka-terina Dashkova's terms as director of the Imperial Academy of Sciences and the Russian Academy in the 1780s, during the eighteenth and early nineteenth centuries it was accepted that noblewomen would serve only in positions in the courts of members of the imperial family, rather than in the regular state service. With rare exceptions, members of other social groups, whether male or female, also were excluded from state politics and government. And in the countryside, since landlords fulfilled most governmental functions for their serfs, serfs seldom encountered government officials until after the Emancipation.

If most of the population was excluded from direct involvement in politics and state affairs, the actions of the imperial state nonetheless affected the lives of everyone. In this regard, war and its consequences often constituted major turn-ing points in Russian history, from the reign of Peter the Great through the fall of the Romanov dynasty in 1917. The Great Northern War that Russia fought for all but a few years of Peter the Great's reign affected the entire population, as did Peter's extensive state-building policies, which were designed to strengthen Rus-sia's military capacity and position in European politics. Several of these policies affected women directly. One of Peter's early aims, for example, was to create a cultural milieu at the Russian court similar to that which he had seen in Western Europe. To achieve this, women were required to wear European style clothing—tight bodices and hoop skirts were very unlike the loose caftans worn by most Russians at the end of the seventeenth century—and to interact with men in so-ciety. For high society, Peter introduced the assemblies (*assamblei*), at which women conversed, drank, and danced with men. This radically new form of so-cial interaction was received well by the Russian elite, as was the new attire (al-though a little more slowly), but other elements of Peter's plan to create a European-style haut monde met considerable resistance. Peter's vision of the new Russia required educated men to run the modern state and educated women to populate the assemblies and raise future generations of state servants. For the first time, noblemen were required to demonstrate proficiency in reading, writing, and other subjects to obtain positions in the Russian civil and military service and to receive permission to marry. Recognizing that it would take a long time for Rus-sia to create adequate educational institutions, the emperor planned to send young women and men abroad to Europe for education. This initiative was some-what successful with men, but noble families refused to send their daughters abroad; however, private education with tutors and governesses for noble girls did catch on quickly.

The effects of Peter's military and state-building efforts were no less profound, albeit different, for women of other social groups. The conscription of male peas-ants and members of other unprivileged social groups into the reorganized and ex-panded standing army, and for various construction projects, not only disrupted the lives of large numbers of women but also left many women as widows or living without their husbands in villages and towns (until 1874, the term of military service was twenty-five years; thereafter, for most men it was six years). Deprived of the status and protection provided by a husband, these *soldatki* (soldiers' wives) were especially vulnerable to oppression within the extended family and village. Many women, belonging to families whose male heads were ascribed to new mining, metallurgical, or other types of enterprises, were compelled to relocate to places distant from their native villages and to adapt to drastically changed living conditions. In addition, like all members of the "taxed" population (which included everyone except the nobility, officialdom, and clergy), women felt the burdens of increased state exactions and obligations. Peter's reforms of the Orthodox Church organization seem actually to have increased the number of female as well as male dissenters from the official church. It seems likely, therefore, that the experience of Peter's reign by most non-elite women was negative, although—as we shall see—some women were able to exploit the disruptions and dislocations wrought by Peter's policies to their own advantage.

The Empresses Anna, Elizabeth, and Catherine II all presented themselves as the heirs of Peter's tradition of reform, and all three empresses in fact fostered the further development of the arts in imperial Russia and deepened Russia's involvement in European cultural life. Elizabeth and Catherine II both sponsored efforts to reform the imperial Russian legal system. In addition, Catherine II expanded the empire into formerly Turkish and Polish territories and reformed the administration of both town and countryside. Her Legislative Commission (1767–1768) brought together men of most social ranks and provided a wealth of information about the empire. Catherine also initiated a discussion of the future of an economy based on serfdom. Her efforts extended to improving education in imperial Russia and expanding its availability to women and people of non-noble rank. She founded the first state-run school for girls in Russia as well as the Russian Academy, assigning the latter the task of compiling the first comprehensive dictionary of the Russian language. Her interest in Enlightenment thought led to a flood of European publications of both factual and fictional literature becoming available in Russia, in both their original languages and Russian translation. After the peasant uprising led by Emilian Pugachev (1773–1774), however, which engulfed a large part of the empire in violence, Catherine discontinued discussion of possible alternatives to serfdom; the outbreak of the French Revolution similarly limited discussion of political reform.

In the early nineteenth century, war again deeply affected the Russian population, as imperial Russia became involved in the conflicts provoked by revolution in France and later Napoleonic ambition. In 1812 Russians were called on to resist Napoleon's invasion of Russia. The entire population had to respond to this event, through either flight from the invaders, increased taxes, or conscription and struggle to repulse Napoleon's forces. The War of 1812 was a powerful experience for a generation of Russians, and the literary journals, which began to be published in the postwar period, are filled with memoirs of the war. Among the most well known of women's accounts of this period are Nadezhda Durova's memoirs of her service in the Russian army (in male dress).[3] Most women's accounts emphasize the harsh conditions of refugee life and separation from their families during the war.

The defining experience for many noblemen of this generation resulted from their service in the army, fighting across Europe and, after Napoleon's defeat at Waterloo in 1815, during the occupation of France. Many Russian officers returned from France with new ideas about government and citizen's rights, to some degree actually encouraged by Emperor Alexander I (r. 1801–1825), which spurred a group of them to attempt to overthrow the autocracy in 1825. Their unsuccessful revolt resulted in the execution of some conspirators and the exile of many more. Several of the wives of the conspirators, known as Decembrists because their revolt took place in that month, joined them in exile in Siberia. The Decembrists' wives were elevated by Soviet historians to the status of Russia's first female revolutionaries. They were not, however, politically active in the direct ways that later women revolutionaries would be. The conspirators' societies did not include women, nor were the wives part of the planning or execution of the Decembrists' design to replace autocracy with constitutional rule. Nonetheless, the Decembrists' wives did suffer hardship in exile and, together with their husbands, were deprived of their noble titles and of contact with their children.

The defeat later suffered by imperial Russia in the Crimean War (1853–1856) provided the catalyst for a reform program that altered almost every aspect of life in Russia. Designed to transform imperial Russia into a modern state that could compete economically and militarily with the great powers of Europe, this program, known as the Great Reforms, eliminated the bondage of peasants, created an independent judiciary, and transformed the judicial process, education, the military, and local governance. While perhaps embarked on with a motivation similar to that underlying the reforms of Peter the Great in the early eighteenth century, the Great Reforms involved the public far more in their planning stages and required much more extensive social change than the earlier reforms had. Their effects, moreover, were greatly to spur both public discussion of and demands for further reform and clandestine political activity. The era of the Great Reforms therefore can be seen as marking the emergence of "society," generally understood as educated society, as an important impetus for social, legal, and political reform, although the roots of this development lie in the preceding decades.

Although the Great Reforms freed the peasants from bondage to their noble lords, the state nonetheless continued to rely on the village commune as the basis for local administration and justice. Peasant villages were collectively responsible to the imperial Russian state for the payment of taxes and debt obligations for land redemption. Similarly, the male head continued to exercise great power over the subordinate members of the household. But if the reforms did not grant peasant women extensive new rights, they did give women access to outside arbitrators for familial disputes. The reform of local government and the judiciary placed representatives of the state within the reach of women. Peasant women turned to the new courts, including the newly established peasant cantonal (*volost'*) courts, in such large numbers that educated observers took special note of the trend. For those who believed that the patriarchal family was, and should remain, the backbone of Russian society, the use of the courts by peasant women was alarming. Conversely, some members of educated society, especially women, presented sympathetic views of the struggles—legal and otherwise—of peasant women in Russia's villages. But for most members of educated society the post-reform peasant woman came to be seen as a backward, unsympathetic character.

In the late imperial period, more and more peasant men left the villages for industrial work, leaving women to carry the burden of agricultural work in the villages. Some peasant women, however, also were drawn to the cities to find work. The majority of these women took up difficult and vulnerable positions as domestic servants. Many women engaged in needlework or became laundresses or retail clerks, while others became industrial laborers, with women workers eventually coming to predominate in the tobacco-processing and textile industries. Whatever their occupation, however, women received wages that usually were not adequate to cover their living expenses. In addition, women who migrated to the cities were vulnerable to exploitation without the buffer of the extended family. Such women often found themselves recruited into prostitution, which was legal and regulated in the Russian empire, and became prisoners of debt bondage to the keepers of brothels. Many city women supplemented their meager incomes by renting corners of their crowded apartments to newcomers.

Reflecting the Great Reforms' spur to public activism, after the late 1850s members of the educated public also moved into active work (intellectual or otherwise) on specific problems of significance in women's lives. In the late nineteenth century, workers and peasants and their advocates also took up work on so-called women's issues. In this new political context, women played prominent roles in both the conservation of imperial Russian society and the efforts to transform it.

Charitable work provided a particularly important area for such female activism. Following Russian custom, which assigned the senior female in the household responsibility for giving alms to the poor, noblewomen in eighteenth- and nineteenth-century Russia fed and housed impoverished female relatives and wards and ministered to the poor and unfortunate in their communities. In the nineteenth century empresses followed the example of Maria Fedorovna (1759–1828), the wife of Paul, and focused their activities on philanthropy and education. Maria Fedorovna accepted her roles as wife and mother, carved a space for activism by building on these roles, and developed imperial education and charity into an enterprise equivalent to other departments of the government. Indeed, a department for the "Institutions of the Empress Maria Fedorovna" was added to the emperor's administration in 1828. The empress presided over the expansion of state-run education for girls to most major Russian cities and to the middling social estates. The wives of Emperors Nicholas I, Alexander II, and Alexander III continued to sponsor the development of education for girls, directing most of their activities toward the middling and lower social estates by founding primary and secondary schools for girls of all estates. Empress Elizabeth, wife of Alexander I, founded one of the first official women's organizations in Russia, the Women's Patriotic Society, which coordinated women's charitable activities during Napoleon's invasion. Its continued existence and significance were secured by the financial support of the Empress.

After the Great Reforms, more opportunities for charitable and social work opened up for women, including paid positions in fields such as medicine and teaching. Women had their first opportunities to practice nursing during the Crimean War (the same war in which Florence Nightingale served for the British). They again served as nurses with the Russian army in the Balkans in the war with the Ottoman empire in 1877–1878. Some women found employment providing medical care for rural populations. Others organized charitable societies to support impoverished women who had turned to prostitution and, later in the century, societies to aid workers. Women also played an important part in temperance societies. As was the case in Western Europe, these charitable societies both provided women with training as political activists and became a source of later feminist organizations.

In the political realm, the forces of reform, revolution, and conservatism first met in violent confrontation in the revolution of 1905–1906, an event to which Russia's loss in the Russo-Japanese War of 1904–1905 contributed significantly. Nicholas II was forced to create a legislative body, albeit one with limited powers, to break the revolutionary coalition. From 1906–1914 the Duma, the new Russian legislative assembly, regularly included the questions of suffrage for women and the improvement of the legal and civil rights of women among the issues it debated. Among the political parties that emerged from the revolution were several explicitly feminist organizations, reflecting a split among politically active women between those who advocated separate organizations to promote issues of importance to women and those who believed that real equality for women could be achieved only through a social (and socialist) revolution. When the struggle to define Russian society culminated in the revolutions of 1917 and the triumph of the Bolshevik Party in the Civil War, women had played active roles on all sides of the conflict. While the roles of women were not generally held to be the most important issue of the time, the participation of women in revolutionary, liberal, and conservative movements was a factor that forced reconsideration of their position and the scope for their activities in all sectors of Russian society in the late imperial period. Many of the women whose works are featured in this anthology were recognized for their activism on behalf of a variety of political programs.

This intense period of debate and change in the activities and roles of women culminated in the programs introduced by the young Soviet government to transform Russians into good Communist citizens; this effort included work specifically directed at women. Hence the period at issue in this book is punctuated at either end with high governmental policy on the transformation of women's lives. Officially, the triumph of Soviet power and the rule of Stalin put an end to the discussion of women's role in society, with the "woman question" being declared resolved in the 1930s. These chronological boundaries delimit a period in which the roles and status of women were perceived by some to be an open question and by others to be a vital matter of state policy, at least in part determining the position of imperial Russia as a world power.

PERIODIZATION OF RUSSIAN WOMEN'S HISTORY

As the preceding survey indicates, politics and governmental affairs did touch the Russian population at key points in the imperial period, despite the autocratic character of the regime. Certainly, Russia was very different after the reforms of Peter the Great, the Napoleonic Wars, the Great Reforms, and the Revolution of 1905 than it was before each event. What effect did these major events in Russian history have on Russian women? Does the rhythm of women's history follow the same rhythm as the general narrative that had been constructed before the experiences of women were considered significant? Thirty years of research in the field allow scholars now to identify the watersheds of the history of Russian women. Greater access to Russian archives, the new freedom of Russian scholars from the dictates of Marx and Engels in the construction of research projects, and the removal of barriers that had prevented collaboration between Soviet and foreign scholars are providing the opportunity to answer questions raised by early investigations, as well as to pose new ones.

In spite of daunting barriers to scholarly research on the past of Russian women that both Russian and foreign scholars faced, by the early 1990s a considerable body of historical scholarship and literary criticism on women and their works existed. In introductions to *Russia's Women: Accommodation, Resistance, Transformation*, Barbara Evans Clements, Barbara Alpern Engel, and Christine Worobec constructed a framework for Russian women's history that divides Russian history into two periods: a period of accommodation to patriarchy before the reforms of Peter the Great and of transformation of society after these reforms, which accelerated after the Great Reforms of the 1860s.[4] Natalia Pushkareva, a specialist on pre-Petrine Russia, and the only scholar thus far to attempt a comprehensive analysis of the history of women throughout Russian history, concurs. According to Pushkareva, "All important events in the history of Russian women in the eighteenth century and all the changes in social, political, legal, and familial status are connected directly or indirectly to the metamorphosis in the Russian state initiated by Peter the Great."[5] Clements, Engel, and Worobec and Pushkareva also agree that the patriarchal familial and political system offered women some opportunities for empowerment. The importance of marital alliances and women's honor benefited noblewomen both before and after the Petrine reforms. Elite women held and managed serfs as well as estates—and increasingly in their own right from the 1730s onward. The division of labor in the peasant household resulted in parallel male and female hierarchies that gave the senior female considerable power in her sphere. Peasant women also informally exercised power through their responsibility for perpetuating many of the rituals that ensured the cohesion and reproduction of the family and the community. Women thus had a stake in maintaining the patriarchal system. Partly for this reason, and partly as a result of the complex and often subtle ways in which the patriarchal system operated, women in traditional Russian society rarely resisted patriarchy directly and openly.

While women did not begin to challenge patriarchy openly in the early eighteenth century, the findings of scholars who are just beginning to examine the history of women in eighteenth-century Russia confirm that the status of women began inexorably to change after the Petrine reforms. Pushkareva argues that the rule of women in this century is the key factor in explaining the changes. Whatever the merits of this claim, recent research shows that women—at least among the nobility—gained a greater voice in family affairs in this period. At the same time, and probably not unrelated, the right especially of noblewomen to own and actually control their property also gained greater strength in law. Available evidence would suggest, too, that women first began to write reflectively in the eighteenth century.

The search for open resistance to patriarchy in Russia provides a good example of the way in which historical research builds on and revises earlier studies. In the 1970s those researching the past of Russian women first considered the participation of women in the revolutionary movement that developed when the government failed to follow through on the promise of the Great Reforms. Scholars noted that, with few exceptions, revolutionary women did not speak out against inequities in the treatment of women. Instead, women in these movements eschewed the benefits of privilege to devote themselves fervently to bringing about change that would end the misery of peasants and workers. Scholars first found critics of patriarchy in Russia among male socialist writers of the 1850s. Richard Stites' pathbreaking study of the women's liberation movement in Russia asserts that the debate about the position of women in society was constructed by men and only later joined by women. Recent scholarship, by contrast, suggests that women confronted "the woman question" much earlier.[6] Examination of the writings of salon hostesses of the 1820s and 1830s reveals that women thought about the question of their particular roles in society at an even earlier date. Activism by women on behalf of women began in Russia in the 1860s, somewhat later than similar activity started in the United States and England. In the late nineteenth century Russian women activists struggled for the right to education for women, for greater access to a variety of occupations, especially professional ones, and for an improvement of their legal rights. Only after men received the right to vote for representatives to the Duma that was formed after the Revolution of 1905 did women begin to argue for female suffrage.

Scholars agree, then, that the watersheds in the history of women in the imperial period are the early eighteenth-century reforms of Peter the Great and the

Great Reforms of the mid-nineteenth century. The Petrine reforms strengthened the position of women in the family and promoted the idea of education for women. The Great Reforms extended the options for women to participate in society and economic life. Disappointment with the limitations of these reforms inspired some women to join in a life-and-death struggle for the overthrow of the autocracy, which they considered the only way to bring about real change in Russia. The pace of change clearly accelerated after the Great Reforms, while the scope of change broadened under the impact of rapid industrialization and urbanization.

It is important to remember, of course, that these various developments affected different groups of women differently, and at different paces. Education, professional occupations, and involvement in political organizations remained largely the domains of women from elite and middling social groups, for example, although by the early twentieth century even peasant women were gaining access to the lower levels of education and working-class women were becoming politically active. Women from the peasantry and the lower urban strata experienced the Petrine reforms and the Great Reforms, and the industrial upsurge after the 1880s, differently than did women from elite and middling social groups. In this regard, scholarly attention thus far has focused disproportionately on certain social groups and aspects of women's lives and on the period after the Great Reforms. Hence, major gaps remain in our understanding of the history of Russian women. Nonetheless, the research accomplished to date has enabled scholars to establish the broad outlines for such an understanding.

THEMATIC ORGANIZATION AND DOCUMENT CHOICES

The present collection of documents, unique in its intent to combine history and literature, both reflects the current state of knowledge in the field and introduces new information for consideration. We chose the title *Experience and Expression* in an effort to unite two aspects of social and cultural life that often are separated from each other. While fictional and historical texts do differ in important respects, we believe that reading them together creates a fuller portrait of women's lives and their representation in imperial Russia. Hence we have attempted to combine experience and expression by including documents, philosophical and political writings, and creative works that document the activities of women in imperial Russia mainly from the point of view of women themselves.

We chose the chapter themes (female ideals, life in the family, sexuality, education, work, religious life, and political activity) carefully after intense discussions of the categories of experience that shaped the lives of Russian women. All women lived their lives in the shadow of feminine ideals that influenced both their behavior and others' treatment of them. Women in imperial Russia were intimately bound by family ties, so tightly that family is often difficult to disentangle from other categories of experience in their writing. Each woman experienced her body, chose how and whether to express her sexuality, and experienced the consequences of her choices. These choices, of course, were complicated both because women were influenced by social norms and because there was a limited range of choices open to women. While the educational opportunities and work responsibilities of women differed, based on their place in the social hierarchy, all women learned and worked in some fashion. The vast majority of Russian women subscribed to some form of Orthodox Christianity, and the Orthodox Church dominated spiritual life in the empire. These categories of experience link Russian women with larger communities. Our final category, "Opposition and Activism," reflects the experiences of women who stepped outside the traditional community to comment on its insufficiencies. Some hoped to reform Russian social, economic, and political life, while others aimed to destroy existing structures and build entirely new ones.

In addition to deliberating extensively on the framing of women's experiences, we also thought hard about the question of which women's voices to feature in our collection. To some extent, our choices were determined by the material available in archives and published sources, the recommendations of colleagues, and the desire to include aspects of women's lives that are underrepresented in existing translated sources. Insofar as we have been able to locate appropriate texts, we have included documents that open windows onto the experiences of Russian women of all social ranks through their own words.

As one might expect, the writings are not easily divided into categories of experience; some of the texts address several of the themes, and some have been excerpted in more than one chapter. In including excerpts from a document or text in more than one chapter, we have attempted to convey a sense of the life courses Russian women followed. Most of the women identified themselves as Russians and were products of, or participants in, an Orthodox religious tradition. Hence we offer a diversity of voices from within the dominant culture of the Russian empire. We made this decision to ensure that we could provide a coherent context within which the documents should be interpreted. Our areas of expertise lent themselves well to this task; we hope that scholars with different specialties will take on the task of presenting the views of women who lived as members of the groups that were subject to Russian imperial rule.

Illuminating the process of construction and reform of an idea (ideas) of female gender identity in Russia guided us in the selection of the literary and documentary works contained in this anthology. Few of these works have ever been available in English, several have never been published in any language, and with rare exceptions they are the work of women. In shaping the collection, we attempted to define the main ideas and institutions that impinged on women's self-definitions. Hence, in some cases—for example the proverbs that express commonly held notions of the definition of womanhood and the role of women in society, religious teachings about women and their roles, and some laws—the aim of a text was to form a collective understanding of women and to discourage, or even prevent, their forming an independent identity.

In spite of considerable pressure to conform, women of all social estates and political beliefs reveal in their writings a determination to act and think independently. One expects to see this attitude in the works of thinkers who challenged the status quo of opinions about women, their roles, and their status. It is also apparent, however, in the actions of less politically inclined women (documented in letters, petitions, and observations of their behavior) and in defenses by conservative women writers of the received ideas about womanhood that determined social acceptability. We specifically attempted to avoid skewing the selections toward the feminists or proto-feminists of Russia in the eighteenth and nineteenth centuries by selecting a wide variety of texts; thus the evidence of independence of thought and activity exhibited by virtually all of our authors and subjects points to an important way this documentary and literary collection allows readers to challenge paradigms of Russian history, women's history, and the development of women's literature. When they were written, these texts provided a similar opportunity to Russian women: the growing debate on women's issues in nineteenth-century Russia enabled women to pick and choose among competing viewpoints to form their own opinions and identities.

While it is probably clear that *Russian Women* can be usefully read in Russian and European history courses, it is important to point out that this volume will also be useful for students of literature. Not only does the anthology include a number of literary texts, but the selections also provide information about the questions that students frequently ask in classes about women's writing: What were the inheritance laws for women? What were women's roles in the family? How did marriage work? What kind of education did women get? The texts provide this information in a memorable way as the women themselves weave the narrative. The texts also provide a strong basis for comparison with the lives and writings of women in other cultures, making this a good companion volume for course readings about Western European, North and South American, Arab, African, and Asian cultures.

This collection allows readers to consider the history of imperial Russia without the imposition of a periodization created by scholars relying primarily on evidence produced historically by male writers and participants of the era. We chose a thematic organization to allow readers to develop their own ideas on the issue of periodization. Readers who are familiar with the accepted tropes of Russian historical writing will notice immediately that these selections call these notions into question. For example, Ekaterina Kuskova's memories of her schooling make one wonder if the policy of Orthodox religious training and Russian nationalism in education was particularly successful despite the attention historians have given it (see chapter 4).

Although we have included the works of some famous personalities of the period in the anthology, it was not our intent to highlight exceptional women. Instead, we aimed to place women in the stream of social, cultural, political, and economic life in imperial Russia. By focusing attention on women and women's analyses of Russian life, we offer the reader the opportunity to see them as a part of the fabric of Russian society, rather than as unusual entities who stood outside the flow of history. Since many of the women featured in these texts are, indeed, ordinary, we cannot always provide readers the satisfaction of learning the resolution of a dispute or the fate of a featured actor—we simply do not know. With the intent of providing English-language readers access to voices from a wide spectrum of opinions, we have also tried to avoid duplicating work that is already available in English. The works of several Russian women revolutionaries, for example, are already available. Hence, few documents presented here focus on women who deliberately sought to transform the entire social order.

We have provided short introductions to each chapter to allow the reader to place the documents in context. Chapter introductions are intended to familiarize the reader with the topic, whereas document introductions provide information necessary to understand a particular text. As readers may not be fully conversant with the institutions and personalities of Russian life, or with the language itself, we have also attempted to assist the reader in other important ways. First, each selection has been annotated to provide information essential to understanding the text. Second, we include a timeline of major events in the history of imperial Russia that provides the context for analyzing women's experience of life and culture during this period. Third, we provide a glossary of terms and a map showing locations mentioned in the documents. An extensive guide to recent scholarship in English is included for readers who would like to study Russian women in more detail. Beyond this minimum of explanatory material, we intend to allow the women of imperial Russia to speak for themselves and readers to draw their own conclusions.

Notes

1. Aleksandra Marinina, *Chuzhaia maska* [*A Stranger's Mask*] (Moscow, 1998), p. 30. An author of mysteries, Marinina is one of the most popular writers in Russia today.

2. For examples of advertisements for such sales, see Daniel H. Kaiser and Gary Marker, comps. and eds., *Reinterpreting Russian History: Readings, 860–1860s* (Oxford: Oxford University Press, 1994), p. 294.

3. Durova's work is available in English translation; see the Suggested English-Language Readings.

4. Barbara E. Clements, Barbara A. Engel, and Christine D. Worobec, eds., *Russia's Women: Accommodation, Resistance, Transformation* (Berkeley and Los Angeles: University of California Press, 1991).

5. Natalia Pushkareva, *Women in Russian History from the Tenth to the Twentieth Century*, trans. and ed. Eve Levin (Armonk, N.Y.: M. E. Sharpe, 1997), p. 121.

6. Richard Stites, *The Women's Liberation Movement in Russia: Feminism, Nihilism, and Bolshevism, 1860–1930* (Princeton, N.J.: Princeton University Press, 1978); Jehanne M Gheith, *(Not) Writing Like a Russian Girl* (forthcoming, Northwestern University Press).

1. Defining Ideals

INTRODUCTION

This chapter presents several examples of the attempts made during the imperial period to define an ideal of womanhood. By "ideal" we mean the representations and expectations of women and the prescriptive norms for women articulated within communities and social groups or by religious, state, or other bodies, or even by individuals, as a means of shaping the identities and behavior of women. Such efforts could take many forms, ranging from peasant proverbs, rituals, and folk tales to sermons, canonical rules, state laws, advice manuals, scholarly studies, and fictional literature. Several of these forms are contained in this chapter, while others—because of their subjects—are in later chapters. Indeed, to some degree, nearly all of the documents contained in this volume either explicitly or implicitly express some feminine ideal. For example, while the religious writings at the beginning of this chapter explicitly present different aspects of an Orthodox conception of women, the contrasting descriptions of peasant women given by Aleksandra Efimenko and A. S. Saburova in chapter 2 also employ implicit ideals of women as a standard of judgment. Similarly, the legislation governing women's education, presented in chapter 4, reflects changing conceptions of the roles and desirable attributes of women, just as the fictional stories and autobiographical accounts found in several chapters were meant to edify as well as to inform or entertain. As these and other documents make clear, expectations of women throughout the imperial period were conflicting, a tension particularly apparent in the case of sexuality (see chapter 3), with women expected to be both chaste and desirable.

Given the nature of ideals, one must be careful not to accept them uncritically as a reflection of reality or actual experience. With documents from any historical source it is necessary to ask whose ideal is being represented and with what purpose. It is also useful to ask what mechanisms, if any, were available to enforce particular ideals of womanhood. In some instances community pressure or community-sanctioned or -tolerated violence operated to compel women to conform to particular ideals or norms of behavior; in other instances, ideals and norms were backed up by the coercive power of a religious body or the state. In still other cases, only the amorphous pressures exerted by moral suasion, peer groups, or public opinion might be involved. Hence, how different and competing ideals acted upon and affected different groups of women in imperial Russia varied considerably. Multiple and competing ideals of womanhood coexisted in imperial Russia.

Although a multiplicity of ideals had also existed in Muscovy, among the sharpest breaks between the two periods was the expansion and transformation of the sources of ideals of womanhood and the variety of purposes for which such ideals were used. To be sure, peasant and other communities, clerics and ecclesiastical bodies, and state authorities in both periods articulated and endeavored to enforce various ideals and norms of behavior for women. These ideals and norms changed in significant ways, however, during the imperial period. Particularly after the mid-nineteenth century a host of social, professional, and political groups vied with church and state in attempting to reshape conceptions of and behavioral norms for women.

The unevenness of sources makes it difficult to determine the variety of ideals of women that existed in Muscovite Russia. We know more about the ideals propagated by or prevalent among clerical writers, princely families, and the service elites, for example, than we do about the ideals that circulated among other groups of the population. The Orthodox Church clearly was an important source of ideals of womanhood during the Muscovite period, as it continued to be during the imperial period, but the degree to which the population at large had assimilated the ideals propagated by the Church is difficult to gauge. At the risk of oversimplification, however, it would appear that most Muscovite ideals of women revolved around their familial and domestic roles. Both positive and negative images of women, as well as canonical rules and state law, reinforced the subordinate position of women in the family and society and the roles played by them in the maintenance and reproduction of the family. Hence, where the image of women as temptresses, conniving sowers of discord, and unclean persons suggested the need for male control, the image of piety, modesty, and self-denying service to the family and the unfortunate encouraged submission to senior male authority and subordination to family interests. Conceptions of female virtue helped to preserve the family's honor and thereby protected and promoted its interests. Female piety and virtue could culminate in a monastic or holy life, but usually only after a woman's marital and domestic responsibilities had been fulfilled. With rare exceptions, female saintliness lay in the strength and example of a woman's faith, often embodied in her actions as a wife or mother, not in her exercise of power or military prowess.[1]

The Petrine reforms modified and augmented, more than displaced, these Muscovite ideals of women, and initially affected primarily women of the nobility. Hence, while the familial and domestic roles of women continued to be stressed, the manner and form of their fulfillment began to change. In particular, Russian noblewomen now were expected to conform to what were presented as European standards and models with respect to dress, fashion, comportment, and involvement in public activities, pastimes, and education. The sources for these standards and models included European literature, nonfiction writing, and art, to which members of the Russian nobility were exposed in ever-increasing volume. Peter's successors in the eighteenth century not only continued and extended his efforts to refashion elite Russian women in the image of their European counterparts, but also complicated them with the reality and representation of female rule. The result of their efforts, again initially among the social elite but then percolating both outward from the capitals of Moscow and St. Petersburg and—more slowly— downward into middling social groups, was uncertainty, flux, and a blending of old and new ideals. For example, Enlightenment notions of education and a new stress on the social and public importance of motherhood were combined, in both state pronouncements and secular writings, with preexisting conceptions of the role and subordinate position of women in the family. Similarly, as the selections by Anna Labzina in chapters 3 and 5 demonstrate, Orthodox and Enlightenment ideals could be combined in complex ways to limit or defend female submission to male authority and to promote or resist new sexual mores. In the nineteenth century, new ideals of romantic love and companionate marriage similarly could either reinforce or challenge the ideal of patriarchal authority, just as the ideals of maternity and female piety were used both to justify and to resist an expanded social role for women.

Initially only a minority of the Russian nobility assisted the autocratic project of Europeanization. The nature of the autocratic system, however, both limited the possibilities for resistance to the autocratic ruler's designs and provided substantial incentives for conformity with them. As the eighteenth century progressed, the allies of the state in the process of Europeanization increased and the changes that were being promoted became more broadly and deeply assimilated, albeit within only a small part of the population. But already by the end of the eighteenth century the processes of change begun or accelerated by Peter had produced an open debate over cultural ideals and values that would expand and intensify in the nineteenth century. This debate became particularly intense and more inclusive after 1855, with the rapid expansion of education, publishing, and professional groups and the relaxation of state censorship. The debate involved a multiplicity of issues, including the character of Russian culture, Russia's relationship with Europe, the desirability of different political and social reforms, and the nature of and means to overcome social injustice.

Termed by contemporaries "the woman question," the discussion of the position, role, and rights of women came to occupy a prominent place in this public debate, especially after 1855. People argued over what types of education should be available for women, what forms their domestic, spousal, and maternal activities should assume, what their role outside the home should be, and what legal rights they should enjoy. For many participants, the preservation or improvement of the existing position of women represented not only an important issue in its

own right but also a way to defend or transform the autocratic political and social order. Hence the debate over competing ideals of womanhood in late imperial Russia formed an integral part of the political, ideological, and cultural
conflicts that marked this period, and the preservation or transformation of the
position of women often represented a means as well as an end. In constructing
their different ideals of womanhood, moreover, the participants in this debate—
which now included many women—drew on a wide variety of sources, including
an idealized Russian past, contemporary European and American examples, pu-
tative national folk traditions, historical and scientific studies, theology, ideological doctrine, and so on. Church and state, themselves divided on these issues,
thus confronted a proliferation of competitors in their efforts to define and in-
culcate feminine ideals.

The emergence of competing ideals, however, affected different groups of
women differently. Whereas elite and educated women not only were exposed to
the full range of such ideals but also could participate in their definition, and
urban women generally had the possibility of being exposed to a broad range of
alternatives, the range of exposure for peasant women was more limited. The
overwhelming majority of peasant women remained in the countryside, subjected
chiefly to the ideals and norms of village culture and the Orthodox Church. The
nature of the sources, of course, makes it difficult to trace ideals for peasant
women during the imperial period. While proverbs (such as those cited at the beginning of each chapter) offer some guidance, they are hard to date and often
contradictory. Peasant custom varied from place to place and in any case was
often unclear and, especially after the mid-nineteenth century, in flux. Nonetheless, available evidence suggests that among the peasantry the ideal woman was
one who kept her health, bore many children, worked hard, and carried out her
roles within the household and community without disrupting them. Marriage at
an early age was expected, although religion provided some cultural space for single women. Even among the peasantry, however, by the latter part of the nineteenth century alternative ideals, images, and fashions had begun to penetrate
into the village through a variety of channels.

The selections in this chapter present a variety of views on the character and
role of women expressed during the imperial period. They move from ideals
articulated by Orthodox writers in the eighteenth century to some of the competing visions formulated by secular writers—female as well as male—in the nineteenth and early twentieth centuries. Several of the selections offer a critique of
an ideal that the authors suggest was accepted by all of Russian society. In some
texts, the authors make their points indirectly, a rhetorical technique that was,
and is, an important aspect of Russian discourse. Often the reader is required to
extrapolate the author's "ideal woman" from what the author describes as negative qualities or from proposals that she or he makes for change. Although the
range of ideals represented is limited, it nonetheless provides an indication both
of the variety of ideals of womanhood that emerged in imperial Russia and of the
public debate over the nature and role of women that took place after 1855.

EIGHTEENTH-CENTURY SERMONS

Given the low levels of literacy in early eighteenth-century Russia, even among elites, for most people an understanding of their religion came from sermons. The following two documents express conflicting opinions that believers might have heard from Orthodox priests. One sermon passes on a misogynist view of women that had been part of Orthodox teachings since John Chrysostom, Patriarch of Constantinople. The sermon has been viewed as a personal attack against the Byzantine Empress, but more likely was a part of the Patriarch's general ascetic outlook. The other sermon shows the role of women in the early Christian movement. Christians were considered rebels in Rome until the fourth century, when Roman Emperor Constantine adopted Christianity. In the Roman Empire, as elsewhere, many Christians willingly went to their deaths as martyrs for their faith; eastern and western Christian churches venerate martyrs. Particularly after 1855, to support their proposals Russian writers advocating an expansion of the social role of women cited the importance of women martyrs in the construction of the Christian church (see the selections by Maria Vernadskaia in this chapter and by Ludmila Gerasimova in chapter 5). Such citations indicate that these images of women continued to be presented throughout the imperial period, and that these ideas had become a common part of Russian culture.

A. On Chastity

It is never acceptable for a monk to eat with a woman, or drink with her, or to have dealings with women or otherwise to have knowledge of them. In living with women, the temptation to adultery is great. Even if you are like a stone, you are a man, having a common nature in the Fall. You have fire in your loins; will it not ignite? What does the Word say? Place a candle on the hay; then you can say that the hay does not burn. Do not say it to me, but to Him who knows the mysteries, who is coming to gather your thoughts, for He is a judge of thoughts and intentions and uncertainty of the heart.

You eat with women, drink and tell tales with them, and laugh ceaselessly with them, and after all of this you still want to be called pure. For this reason, abstain! Continence! Restraint! Fruitful pallor of countenance!

It is fitting for you to have bad clothing. Because of your weak nature, stay away not only from conversations about women but also from thoughts of them, which are brought to us by a demon. All who look upon a woman sin with lust. For it is said, "Whosoever looketh on a woman to lust after her hath committed adultery with her already in his heart [Matt. 5:28]."

In truth, is His commandment so terrible? Is continence so great a task? For what is a woman? A decorated snare, deceiving men with love of pleasure, with a clear face and high neck and flashing eyes. Smiling with her cheeks and singing with her tongue, fouling with her voice and bewitching with her words, swishing her skirts, dancing with her feet, killing men with her deeds. For it is said, "Having wounded many, she struck them down." Likewise, "many have been seduced by the beauty of a woman, which kindles passion like fire [Eccles. 9:8]."

What is a woman like on earth? She is a source of evil, a treasure-house of uncleanliness bringing death with her conversation, a sin for the eyes, death to the spirit, a spear for the heart, a destroyer of youths, a banner of hell, a fallen desire.

What is a woman? A slanderer of saints, a serpent's resting place, the Devil's consolation, an incurable sickness, a treasure that inflames, a temptation for the saved, an incalculable evil, a whore by day, an inn where one cannot rest, the Devil's accomplice.

What is a woman? She is the love of evil, a shameless animal, an uncontained striving, an unbridled bond, an unmasking of secrets, a louse on the top of your head. She is a teacher of sin, the food of evil, an insatiable destroyer.

What is a woman? She is worldly thought for a man, slumbering sloth, a reviver of grief, a painted snake, a willful enemy, daily vanity, a storm in the home, a flood for a man, an untamable animal, a refuge for adulterers. She is the Devil's weapon, lustful mindlessness, universal death. "For," as a wise man said, "all evil is small in comparison with woman's evil."

To Christ Jesus, our Lord, glory now and forever and for all ages.

B. Holy Martyrs

Saying about the Holy Martyrs Marfa and Maria, her sister, and the Holy Martyr Monk Karion.

In the days of the wicked Caesars,[2] the saints were tortured in the name of Christ. Marfa and Maria were two sisters, virgins. They prayed to God and hoped to die as martyrs in his name. A military commander happened to walk along the street past [Marfa's] home. And Marfa bowed down before the door. She and her sister called out, saying to the commander, "We two are Christians." The commander and his servants heard this, and the sisters again cried out, "We are Christians." And the commander said to them, "Go home, and I forgive you for the sake of your youth. It is not proper to kill you." And Marfa said, "O Commander! A martyr's death is not death, but life everlasting." And the commander, having heard this, became very incensed, and placed her before him for he wanted to lay hands on her. And her sister Maria approached her and said to the commander, "That which my sister said I also say." And a young man followed after her, a monk named Karion, [and he] cried out, "As Marfa and Maria said, I also am a Christian."

And the commander gave the order to hang them on three crosses. Their mother stood and said, "My children, you will be saved, as you have taken the crown from Christ." And Maria answered, hanging on the cross, "You also will be saved, my mother, with the fruit of your womb, as you have offered the fruit of your womb to Christ."

Maria said to the executioner, "Be patient with us a little, while we sing a song, each of us, to God." He left them hanging with Karion, who was a very young man, but perfected in mind about Christ.

First Marfa said, "I lift my eyes to you, the one who lives in heaven. As the eyes of slaves turn to their masters, and as the eyes of a slave woman turn to the hands of her mistress, so are our eyes turned toward our Lord God until he bestows gifts upon us." And after the end of the singing, Marfa said, "Do any of the brethren want to come and kiss us?"

And Maria said, "Do not say this, O sister, lest there be many." And Marfa answered, "Do not be ashamed of death, which is for the sake of Christ, sister. For today we will be in the heavenly Jerusalem." And everyone remaining there came up and wanted to kiss the two of them. And when he came near, the executioner cut off their honored heads, and they gave their spirits into the hands of the Lord with joy. Their mother stood there, [and] being strong to the task of suffering, she told of eternal life. She, strong in grace for [her] children, had brought her fruit to God like a ring of gold, so that they might rejoice in eternal life, in light everlasting.

Source: Both sermons are located in Miscellany (17—[unknown year]), Uppsala University Library Slavic Manuscript Collection, no. 59, ff. 55v–56v and ff. 75v–76v.

Translated by Jennifer L. Anderson.

CHRISTIAN FAMILY DUTIES

St. Tikhon

The following passages on the duties of spouses, parents, and children are drawn from Instructions for Christians, *initially written sometime after 1771 as a pastoral letter by St. Tikhon of Zadonsk (1724–1783) and first published posthumously in 1784. The sections given here were apparently added from St. Tikhon's other writings in a synodal edition published in 1789, which by 1870 had been reprinted forty-one times by the Moscow Typography of the Synod Press and numerous times both by the St. Petersburg Typography of the Synod Press[3] and several provincial and private presses. The* Instructions *therefore were broadly disseminated in Russia for much of the imperial period and were widely used for both clerical training and pastoral teaching. Canonized in 1861, and reputedly the inspiration for the character of the saintly Father Zosima in Dostoevskii's novel* The Brothers Karamazov *(1880), St. Tikhon had taught in various ecclesiastical schools before serving as Bishop of Voronezh between 1763 and 1767. In the latter year he retired to the Zadonsk Mother of God Monastery, where he devoted himself to a spiritual life, charitable works, and writing. He produced a large corpus of writings, especially on moral theology, devotional and spiritual matters, and pastoral questions. His works reflect the influence of contemporary Western European theological writing and, in turn, had a strong impact on Russian Orthodox writing, pastoral teaching, and spiritual life in the nineteenth century. The teachings reproduced here were repeated in many of the Russian Orthodox catechisms that were published in the nineteenth century. The tension found in these teachings between the ideals of mutuality and equality of spouses and that of patriarchal authority later contributed to the debates that took place within the Church after 1855 over the positions and roles of women in the family, society, and the church.*

Article 54 On the duties of husbands and wives, or those who are married
(1) Both husbands and wives should enter into marriage of their own free will and by their own full agreement. Marriage without the agreement of both parties cannot be solid. Both those parents who forcibly convince [their children] to marry and those priests who see that one or the other of the parties does not agree, and marries them anyway, sin grievously and should be suitably punished because every evil in marriage comes from this. (2) Having righteously entered marriage you should preserve love and faithfulness to each other until the end of life. (3) The husband should not leave the wife and the wife should not leave the husband until death, but, as they promised and agreed, remain inseparable until the end. (4) If either a husband or wife sees a worthy reason for separation, then neither should separate from the other, but, rather, they should ask their pastor, their diocesan bishop, to examine the matter and then wait for a resolution from him. (5) Some husbands and wives think it is right to leave one another as a form of abstinence, but this is a very dangerous practice because instead of abstinence, a terrible sinful adultery could result in one or the other of the parties. For this reason, when a separation occurs for the sake of abstinence, then, if they are to subject themselves to this temptation, there must be agreement by both parties both about the time period [of the separation] and about whether they can bear this burden. (6) The apostle says to the married: "A wife's body does not belong to her but to her husband, and just so a husband's body does not belong to him but to his wife. Don't deprive one another except by agreement until the time of fasting and prayer", etc. [1 Cor. 7:4, 5]. . . . (8) A husband should not treat his wife like a slave but like a help-meet, yet the wife must submit to her husband because the apostle teaches: "Wives obey your husbands as the Lord." And a little further on: "The wife must fear her husband." [Eph. 5:22, 33] (9) When a husband and wife share a single morality and have good morals, then matrimony will be prosperous and excellent, for there will always be unity of thought, agreement, and peace. This makes for great prosperity. (10) When a husband has sound morals and a wife has unsound morals or when a wife has sound morals and a husband unsound ones, then there cannot be agreement and peace between them, just as there can be no meeting between straight and crooked trees. The person who has sound morals will always have to bear suffering and a cross. For this reason, it would befit him to learn patience in such a situation and by means of patience to bear any evil that occurs and to conquer it. (11) We see throughout history that many wives corrupt their husbands and lead them to their deaths. For this reason, husbands should not indulge their wives and let them do whatever they want, but rather should attempt to restrain their scandalous whims. Be on the watch for this kind of behavior. The snake came to Eve and tempted her. Eve, having been tempted,

tempted Adam and led him after her unto death. The very same thing happens today. That same ancient snake comes to the wife, tempts her and, through the woman, involves the husband in illegal matters. The husband should be cautious and not always fulfill the wife's will and counsel, do not let her possess you or lead you wherever she wants. Eve always has her morals. Love her only up to a point that will not be repulsive to God. Let her, according to the apostolic word, fear you and not you her, and let her submit to you and not you to her.

Article 55 On the duties of parents and children
Parents:
The most important thing is for the parents to train their children in the fear of God and good morals. Without this, all teaching and training are nothing. Many parents teach their children foreign languages, others teach them the arts, but neglect Christian teaching and training. Such parents raise their children to the temporal life but do not admit them to eternal life. . . . (3) God's law, consisting in the Ten Commandments, is the rule of the Christian life. Virtue consists in words, deeds, and thoughts that agree with God's law, but every deed, word, or thought that goes against God's law is a vice and a sin. For this reason, all Christians must know it and live according to the rule. Therefore, teach your children to know God's will and to keep His commandments. . . . (5) For the general memory it is useful to know where the word of natural law and God's law agree: "Do unto others as you would have them do unto you." . . . (7) Sin, if left unpunished, becomes the reason for other sins also: the habit of sin is very terrible. For this reason, Christians, love your children in a Christian way, punish them, and they will be in good order and kind. . . . (9) Small children have a rule for themselves in their parents' lives: what they see in them, they will also do. Hence, when parents live in luxury, then their children also live that way and even more so, as we see, and thus the morals of the parents are transmitted to the children. For this reason, Christians, when you want your children to be upright and good, you must also be upright and good, and use every means not to lead them into temptation; otherwise you will accomplish nothing.

On the responsibilities of children:
(1) The conscience itself tells people to respect and love their parents. Even heathens taught and made into law the first [commandment] of God to honor one's parents. The word of God also insists on respecting parents: "Honor your father and mother." [Exod. 20:12; Eph. 6:2] Therefore, Christian, give respect to those who bore you and you will be blessed. . . . (4) Do not begin any matter without your parents' advice and permission, but, rather, ask for their advice and permission in everything. Do not offend by your own impertinence or the things you try to do will not be successful. . . . (6) Be especially careful [not] to offend with rude words and deeds, but with all courtesy speak to them [your parents] and let them know and experience that you love and respect them. . . . (8) Do not leave your parents in any need or insufficiency but help them and obey them, especially in old age. Remember how much they worked for you, and give them their due

service. . . . (10) If you make a mistake and somehow offend them, then admit it in your conscience. If you notice that they are offended, do not delay but fall before them immediately and humbly ask for forgiveness; then you will not fall under God's judgment. (11) Even the heathens included in their books great punishments for those children who did not respect their parents. And in God's Holy Law there are horrible punishments for those unfortunate children: "Those who speak spitefully to their fathers or mothers will die a horrible death," etc. [Exod. 21:17; Deut. 27:16] Such children are indeed monsters of the human family and are vile before both God and humans.

Source: "Nastavlenie khristianskoe," in *Tvoreniia izhe vo sviatykh ottsa nashego Tikhona Zadonskago* ["Instructions for Christians," in *The Pious Works of Our Father Tikhon of Zadonsk*] (Pskov, 1994); reprint of the 5th ed. (Moscow, 1889), vol. V, pp. 139–77. Excerpted from pp. 159–64.

Translated by Jehanne M Gheith.

THE IDEAL FAMILY

MARIA KORSINI

The following selection is from a collection of essays and tales written by Maria Antonovna Korsini (1815–1859), a member of the nobility and a graduate of the Smolnyi Institute in St. Petersburg.[4] Korsini published several volumes of miscellaneous prose fiction and didactic essays for adults and children between the mid-1840s and the mid-1850s. Much of her writing was directed at youth, particularly girls, and sought to provide readers with guidelines for social behavior. The volume from which this excerpt is taken consists of a series of essays that define fundamental social institutions and relations, religious precepts, and behavioral norms, followed by fictional sketches that illustrate how the points made in the essays might be applied in daily life. The excerpt here is from an essay on the family and provides ideals for the roles of the mother and the father in the family. Like St. Tikhon, Korsini drew on religious sources and language to define these roles. Despite similarities, however, her views differ from those of St. Tikhon in significant ways.

FAMILY

1. MOTHER

We sometimes find it difficult to define the most ordinary things. Perhaps this is because, having them constantly in front of our eyes, we do not try attentively enough to grasp their deeper meaning. Hence, even the question I am now proposing does not seem to be a difficult one to resolve, but nonetheless would anyone be able to answer it satisfactorily? Would any of you, my readers, be able to say what a mother is?

You already know that a mother[5] loves you tenderly from the first minute of your life. This love is so strong and so constant in her heart that it gives her the patience to endure much for the sake of your tranquility. As babies you were sometimes unbearable for others, but for her you were not only always sweet but also more precious than anything in the world. She gave you her milk, which was your first food, because you could not and did not know how to accept anything else. With what delight did your mother admire you when, having satisfied your hunger, you fell asleep on her breast. How quietly did she then put you into a peaceful cradle and let down the transparent curtains, so that the wind would not blow on you or a tiresome fly would not disturb your sweet sleep.

As soon as you awakened, your mother greeted your first smile. She then played with you and amused you, and if you were crying, she comforted you and tried to guess the cause of your tears. Her love made understandable your wordless conversation. She knew how to distinguish between your movements and could guess your demands from the sound of your voice. Thus did she care for you both day and night, especially when you happened to fall ill.

And even now, when you are not well, is it not she who sits next to you for entire nights, forgetting her own sleep and comfort? Is it not she who during these times observes all your movements and listens to your breathing? And your every moan strongly wrings her heart. At such times she has only one consolation—to pray to the Savior, asking Him to fortify her strength and to preserve you, who are necessary for her happiness on earth.

Do you understand whom you call mother? It is the person who lives for you and who cares about you every minute, who began a new existence when you started your life. Remember the past, when your mother played with you as if she were a child herself. Even now she wants to participate in all your pursuits, and therefore you often study and rest together. Her care of you lasts her entire lifetime. Your kind mother, having given you your existence, not only adorns it with bodily strength and health, but also cultivates your souls in order to instill in them true virtues.

Your past is filled with sweet, unforgettable memories. You like it, and it belongs to you. During minutes of meditation and sorrow, you can delve deep into it and it will console you, because in it you will find the person who brought you up with love and to whom you should be eternally grateful.

2. FATHER

Let us now move to that being at whose name your heart throbs involuntarily. Remember your father. You often see him preoccupied, tired, and pale, but you do not know that he is fatigued by labor and that he is working for you. He is

unceasingly taking care to provide his family with that which is not only necessary but also pleasant. The family presents us with a touching picture of deep
feeling, activity, and mutual indulgence.

A man chooses a female friend for his entire life, and if this choice is made with
her agreement, then they promise to love one another. One helps the other in
everything good, and together they endure all sorrows. They must divide between
themselves their dwelling and their fortune. Religion unites their two lives into
one, and blessing their eternal union, God sends them children for their complete
earthly happiness.

To a wife are entrusted the responsibilities that are particular to her abilities
and her character. Her dominion is kindness and gentleness. She looks after the
domestic tranquility of her husband, so that when he returns home after his labors
he finds order and sees the desire of his friend to afford him pleasure in important
matters as well as in minor ones. She raises her babies and is the first to pronounce
for them the name of God and to make them pray. She also ensures that the servant performs her duties and that quietude and peace reign in her house. A
woman is given inexhaustible patience, which helps her to endure the screams of
children, lack of sleep, and many minor domestic unpleasantries.

A father has different obligations: He protects the peace of his wife and children. He ensures that they lack nothing in life and that prosperity always surrounds them. The existence of the entire family often depends solely on the
father's labors. Mental abilities act more strongly in a man; his dominion is
thought and will.

Source: M. Korsini, *Mysli i povesti, posviashchennyia iunoshestvu* [*Thoughts and Tales
Dedicated to Youth*] (St. Petersburg, 1846). Excerpted from pp. 16–23.

Translated by William G. Wagner and Igor Timofeyev.

REVIEW OF A VICTIM

VISSARION BELINSKII

*Vissarion Grigorevich Belinskii (1811–1848) was perhaps the most famous literary
critic of the nineteenth century. One of the first* raznochintsy *critics, in the 1840s he
helped to found the "Natural School" of Russian literature, a movement that focused on
the need for writers of literature to participate in the work of social reform and that valued unidealized portrayals of Russian life. The Natural School was an important transitional movement to Russian realism.*

*In the literary review included here, Belinskii sums up what were common cultural
attitudes about women in nineteenth-century Russia. Written in 1835, the review dates
from the Romantic phase of Belinskii's career. Although Belinskii himself later partly re-
pudiated the attitudes expressed here, the review both demonstrates the emergence of a*

public debate over the role of women in Russian society and provides an example of how analyses of fiction by women were used in this debate. Belinskii's style is typical of commentary on works by female authors: in what is ostensibly a review of a novel, for most of the article he focuses on the problems of women writing and then turns briefly to the novel itself.

A VICTIM. A LITERARY SKETCH.
A WORK BY MME. B. MONBORNE.[6] TRANSLATED FROM THE FRENCH

In recent years in Europe or, rather, in France (which is almost the same thing) a sort of dull rumble of protest has begun against the most sacred of civil and religious institutions—marriage; people have begun to discover some sort of doubts regarding its legality and even necessity. Now this rumble has turned into a kind of furious outcry, and the doubts have begun to be advanced for all to hear, in the form of some sort of axiom. There is no theoretical proof, nor, indeed, thanks to the absurdity of this idea, can there be. So they have resorted to another method, the practical, and chosen art as their weapon, which in France has never existed for its own sake but has always served some external, practical goals. And so, from the leading lights of French literature to the ragtag fraternity of literary hacks, they all, secretly or openly, have armed themselves against marriage; with all of them, in every work of literature, this *arrière-pensée*[7] has begun to creep through. But the women writers, at whose head appears the famous George Sand[8] and who are as numerous in France as the untalented rhymesters and novelists in Rus', the women writers, I say . . . but wait a moment . . . allow me to stray for a moment from my subject . . . I have a dreadful fondness for digression; it's my hobby-horse. . . .

What is a woman writer? Does a woman have the right to be a writer?

Everything in the world has its purpose, everything is splendid within the bounds of its purpose and bad outside of it; this is the eternal, immutable law of providence. A woman-amazon, some kind of brave Bradamante,[9] in a poem, perhaps, is no more than ludicrous, but in reality she is a creature repulsive and monstrous to the highest degree.

The whole world is a man's field of activity; the whole world is his domain; what sort of field, what sort of world is given into the domain of a woman?

No matter how close, no matter how limited the circle of activity chosen by a man, still every conscious activity is a path to the completion of a life's exploit, and the life's exploit is equally difficult and fearsome for everyone. But the just and loving providence of God, laying upon man the burden of his life and exploit, calculated and weighed the strength of his human nature, and in this intention gave him a new source of strength, located outside of himself, in that mysterious sympathy, in that elevated spiritual harmony, in that pure ethereal flame of love which unites him with woman. Woman is the guardian angel of man in all the

steps of his life: it is her vigilant, solicitous glance that he meets at his very appearance in the world and, clinging to the source of love and life, it is to her that
he addresses, with unconscious love, his first smile; it is her name that he pronounces in his first, infantile babble; her love guides him until the very moment
when life tears him from her tender, maternal embrace; afterward her gaze wakes
in him, an unbridled youth, a flame of noble passions, impulses to the highest
deeds and intentions, strengthens his soul that seethes with an excess of strength,
and tames the wild impulses of his unbridled will and unconsciously directs him,
the young, powerful lion, toward his goal with redoubled energy, drawing him
with the sweet reward of her reciprocated feelings—this last bliss that is possible
on the earth, after which there is nothing left for a person to desire for himself.
And what need, if death or life circumstances do not allow him to drink the vial
of bliss to the bottom, or if, rather than the charms of reciprocity, he should taste
the torment of rejected love? . . .

But if man is fated to the bliss of reciprocity and the bliss of unification, then
she, always she, in the years of his manhood, is the radiant guiding star of his life,
his support, his source of strength, which does not let his soul chill, grow hard,
and weaken. In old age she is the pale ray of the sun, reminding him that once for
him there was another sun, bright and fiery, that sumptuously illuminated the
road of his life and gave him to taste all the human joys!

Thus, the field of woman is to arouse the energy of man's soul, the ardor of
noble passions, to support feelings of duty and aspiration for the elevated and the
great—that is her destiny, and it is great and sacred! For her—the representative
on the earth of beauty and grace, priestess of love and self-sacrifice—it is a thousandfold more praiseworthy to inspire "Jerusalem Liberated"[10] than to write it herself, just as it is a thousandfold more praiseworthy to hand her chosen one a shield
with the device "With it or upon it!"[11] than to throw herself into the heat of battle with weapon in hand. Consolation in the miseries and woes of life, joy and
pride of man, she is the pliant vine, the green ivy that winds around the proud
oak, the fragrant rose that grows under the shelter of his powerful branches and
embellishes the solitude and severity of his life, doomed to activity and struggle.
An object of reverential passion, a tender mother, a devoted spouse—there is the
great and holy exploit of her life, there is her great and sacred destiny! Nature
gave man mighty strength and audacious daring, rebellious passions and a proud,
inquisitive intelligence, a wild will and an aspiration to creation and destruction.
To woman she gave beauty rather than strength, she replaced the excess of intelligence with an excess of tender and refined feeling and determined that she must
be a vestal of the fire of gentle and elevated passions: and what a marvelous harmony in this opposition, what a loud, full, and resounding chord these two entirely different instruments constitute! The upbringing of woman should har-
monize with her purpose, and only the beautiful sides of being should be open to
her ken, while about all else she should remain in sweet, simpleminded ignorance;
in this sense her one-sidedness is a virtue in her; to man the whole world is open,
all the sides of being.

What then is a woman writer? Does woman have the right to and can she be an authoress?

The depictions of Sappho and Corinna are splendid, as poetic reveries, as creations of fantasy; but what are they in actual fact?[12] Amazons, Bradamantes, "academics in bonnets, seminarists in yellow shawls!"[13] The mind of woman knows only a few aspects of being or, to say it better, her feeling has access only to the world of devoted love and submissive suffering; omniscience is horrible in her, repulsive, while for a poet the whole boundless world of thought and feeling, passions and deeds must be open. We know many women-poets, but not a single woman-genius; their creations are short-lived, for woman is a poet only when she loves, not when she creates. Nature sometimes spares them a spark of talent, but never gives them genius: Corinna vanquished Pindar at the Olympic Games, but Pindar vanquished Corinna in posterity, for posterity applauds the creation, not the creator, and you cannot buy it off with elegance of bearing or charm of face! And that is why, when you read a woman's work that breathes with living, unfeigned emotion, glitters with sparks of talent, then you unwittingly feel regret, thinking what such a woman could be and to what she could turn the splendid gift of nature—the flame of her feeling.

Woman should love the arts, but she should love them for pleasure, and not in order to be an artist herself. No, a woman-author can never love, nor be a wife and mother, for self-love is not in harmony with love, and only genius or elevated talent alone can be alien to petty self-love, and only in a man-artist can the egoism of self-love even have its poetry, while in woman it is repulsive. . . . In a word, a woman-writer with talent is pitiful; an untalented woman-writer is ludicrous and repulsive.

And should this, and can this, offend woman? Everything is splendid and elevated within the boundaries of its purpose, and everything should be proud and happy in its purpose, for that is the will of Providence. Who has not considered himself a poet in his youth, who has not taken an excess of feelings for the flame of inspiration, who has not written verse? This weakness is pardonable in a man; but he, too, is ludicrous and repulsive if, to spite rationality and against the will of nature, he makes the sin of his youth into the sin of his life, for in such a case he is a pretender, a rebel against the eternal statutes of providence. What should be said of a woman? . . .

But my digression is already overly long and, probably, boring also, and all because I don't like women writers! Let them be! I address myself to the interrupted thread of my reasoning. I had stopped, I seem to recall, at the fact that in France women writers had arisen against marriage with particular embitterment. Need one speak of what these women want, what they are trying to achieve? If they were merely carried away by false but poetic ideas about that good-natured little oldster, Platonism, or the no-less-false and no-less-poetic thoughts of renunciation of all human feelings and bringing them as a sacrifice to some sincere idea—let it be so! But no, this Saint-Simonism[14] is very understandable, this thirst for emancipation: the source lies in the wish to have the chance to satisfy corrupt passions.

Une femme emancipée[15]—this word might be very accurately translated with a single Russian word, but unfortunately its use is permitted only in dictionaries, and not in all of them at that, but only in the most extensive.[16] I will add only that a woman-writer is, in a certain sense, *la femme emancipée*.

But for what reason have the writers begun to rebel so against marriage? The reason is evident: they are unable to distinguish the idea of marriage from abuses of marriage. Do not fear for marriage, do not dread the emancipation of women: all that is rather endearing and amusing nonsense, but not the least bit dangerous.

Yes—perhaps, the time is not far away when people will not only cease to take up arms against marriage but will cease to make a trade of it; when women will not only cease to play author but will even cease to believe that women-writers ever existed!

And what of my novel, what of my "Victim"? Where is she? I had already forgotten about her, absorbed in the thoughts that she awoke in me. Or, rather, what can I tell you about her? How can I tell you an old, worn-out piece of news for the hundredth time? But there's nothing for it, I'm not glad but I'm ready—the desire is greater than the necessity. Thus, be so good as to observe: *A Victim. A Literary Sketch* is one of a thousand-and-one philippics against marriage. What happens is that a villainous guardian falls in love with his niece and runs after her, but the poor orphan was a girl *comme il faut*,[17] and moreover already loved another. Uncle was left with nothing and was furious with rage. To avenge himself on her, he forces her to marry a scoundrel who does not believe in anything, squanders her fortune, and makes her unhappy. But why then did she marry him? you will ask. Does France have no laws against force? Oh, it has, and very just ones, even very indulgent toward the freedom to choose and change husbands and wives. So then what is the matter? It is this: the girl had a weak character, and did not dare to oppose her hateful uncle, although she knew she had the right not to obey him, but the author had to find some way to nag at marriage, though here it's not to blame in either spirit or body. In fact, splendid logic! A girl perishes through weakness of character, and it's marriage that is to blame! But enough, the novel is so bad, so stupid, that it's not worth either criticism or attentive scrutiny. Madame Monborne does not have even a spark of talent and, probably, enjoys the same kind of authority in France that Messieurs A, B, C, and D, and the like have here in Rus'.

Source: V. G. Belinskii, "Zhertva. Literaturnyi eskiz. Sochinenie g-zhi Monbori [sic]. Perevod s frantsuzskogo," *Polnoe sobranie sochinenii* ["A Victim. A Literary Sketch. A work by Mme Monborne. Trans. from the French by Z. . . . ," in *Complete Collected Works*), vol. I (Moscow, 1953), pp. 221–28. Originally published in 1835. Excerpted.

Translated by Sibelan Forrester.

QUESTIONS OF LIFE

Nikolai Pirogov

In the mid-nineteenth century, intellectuals throughout Europe debated the extent to which women should be educated and the goals of their education. Nikolai Pirogov (1810–1881) was one of the earliest to argue that women were capable of much more than social dancing and motherhood. Encouraged by the Grand Duchess Elena Pavlovna[18] and concerned about the lack of trained medical personnel in Russia, Pirogov, a doctor, organized the first group of Russian women to work as army nurses. During the Crimean War (1853–1856), he led his Sisters of Mercy of the Exaltation of the Cross to the front lines of imperial Russia's battle against the combined forces of England, France, Turkey, and Sardinia. The women (the society had 163 members, most of them from the privileged social estates) acquitted themselves well under fire. The English also fielded their first female nurses during this war, but the English women worked in hospitals far behind the lines of battle.

The performance of the nurses impressed Pirogov so much that he took up the cause of the education of individuals according to their talents, rather than according to traditions about who should occupy what positions. In this excerpt from his essay "Questions of Life," originally published in 1856, Pirogov went a step further in his thinking to consider the effects on social life of artificially limiting women's education. He hints at the roles women will be expected to fill in the future. Yet, while striving to convince women that they must be ready for these roles, he continues to see them chiefly as companions and assistants of men.

Truly, upon entering the world a woman is less than a man and is subjected to the sad consequences of the dissonance of her basic upbringing under society's direction. She is more seldom judged able to win her daily bread for herself by her labors and to live completely independently from men. The commercial sector of society weighs less upon her.

Her upbringing ordinarily turns her into a doll. It dresses her up and puts her on stage, on show for gawkers; it makes her act like a puppet on strings, manipulated by her upbringing. The strings wear away with time, and through the rents and tears in the stage curtain she begins to perceive what had been so carefully hidden from her. No wonder that the thought then comes to her of trying to walk on her own like a human being. Emancipation is the idea.

An emancipated woman is perhaps even more than a man, although she can't, according to our laws, become a soldier, a government official, or a minister. But, on the other hand, is it possible to turn a man into a wet nurse or a mother who rears her children until they reach the age of eight? Can he become a social connection or the flower and ornament [of society]?

Only the shortsighted vanity of people building altars to heroes looks at mothers, nurses, and nannies as members of a second-degree, subservient class. Only commercial materialism and ignorant sensibilities see in a woman a creature that is subservient and beneath themselves.

Thus, let women understand their high destiny in the whirlwind of human life. Let them understand that they, in tending a child's cradle, in supervising the games of childhood, and in teaching mouths to prattle their first words and their first prayers, become the chief architects of society. The cornerstone rests in their hands.

Christianity unveiled woman's destiny to her. It put forth as a model for humanity a creature who was just taken from her breast. Both Martha and Mary[19] were made participants in the words and conversations of the Savior. It is not the position of woman in society, but her upbringing—which is central to the upbringing of all humanity—that demands reform. Let the thought of educating herself to this end, of living for the inevitable struggle and sacrifices, awaken the whole of the moral existence of woman; let inspiration bless her will—and she will know where she should seek her emancipation.

The woman, to whom inspiration has not been given, who is not fated to be Mary, who is immersed in everyday life, who hasn't learned to hear the voice of that Will—let her remain in her own circle. Let her seek pleasures, enslave herself in decency and decorum, emancipate herself, and do whatever she wants with the followers of various views, with people who live well even without solutions to life's questions. Her way doesn't converge with the way of those who believe in the ideal.

But the woman, who in moments of holy inspiration hears the summons of the Most High Will to go, and who, hearing the noble call to comfort the poor with sympathy, to live for the future within the struggle, and to make a reciprocal sacrifice, embodies the readiness to sacrifice herself: let such a woman stretch out her hand and say, "Yes, I am ready."

Source: N. I. Pirogov, "Voprosy zhizni," *Sochineniia* ["Questions of Life," in *Works*] (Spb., 1900). Excerpted from pp. 40–45.

Translated by Joe Baird.

DESTINY OF WOMEN

MARIA VERNADSKAIA

Maria Nikolaevna Vernadskaia (1831–1860) expands on Pirogov's idea that women have a variety of talents, arguing that women's potential must be developed and that women are obliged to do their share of the work in the economy. In the next selection she proposes a set of ideals different from many of the other authors in this chapter. The first Russian woman whom historians identify as a professional economist, Vernadskaia promoted English liberalism in the journal Economic Index, *which she edited with her husband. Like English liberal economic theorists, Vernadskaia saw in women a vast labor force that could be put to use in fostering capitalist, industrial economies. In her work Vernadskaia had two main aims: to convince society that women were suitable for work and to convince women to enter the labor force. Using irony, she argued strongly that women's limits are not inherent but, rather, constructed. In this excerpt, Vernadskaia asserts women's equality with men in labor and shows the advantages of the participation of women in the workforce for both society and female individuals.*

What is a man? A human being. What is a woman? A strange question—she, of course, also is a human being. If that is so, if we decide to recognize woman as a human being, then all that is human in nature must be accessible to her, and it must be accessible in reality. A woman can feel, can think, can crave education, can understand the desire to become useful in some way. Finally, a woman can work and toil for her own benefit as well as for the benefit of the public. No one would repudiate this, but then is it necessary to devise separate principles of morality and honor for women, to prescribe special duties for them, to restrict their education, and, finally, even to ascribe to them certain special virtues and vices? If woman is the same sort of being as is man, then the principles of honor and morality should be the same for both.

No vices are exclusively man's or exclusively woman's. All people, whichever gender they are, are excited by the same passions. Therefore, all people are subject to the same vices when they yield to their passions, and they have the same virtues when they gain a victory over their passions. To be concerned with arranging a woman's life, with determining her social status, and with the fulfillment of special obligations invented for her by society means not to recognize her as fully human, however strange this may sound.

So much is being said at present about women's roles and duties, about how they comprehend and carry out these duties, and so forth, that we do not consider it superfluous to cite here those opinions that people generally hold about women and to list those duties that are prescribed for them. It usually is said that women's duties are simple and uncomplicated but, at the same time, extremely important, honorable, and even sacred. Therefore, women are accused of being insane if they shun their natural calling and strive to participate, in some unattainable way, in the affairs of public life. It is alleged that they fail to see the duties that are so high, so noble, and so easy for them to perform because nature itself ordains it. Labor brings enjoyment to woman unless, of course, she becomes infected with dangerous and false ideas; whereas failure to fulfill her natural obligations brings forth terrible evil, not only for the present generation but also for the next.

Now we shall inquire into what these duties consist of, whether or not a woman can fulfill them, and, more importantly, whether or not she should. A woman . . . But first, let us digress a bit. When speaking of women, one cannot avoid saying a few words about young, unmarried women. After all, a woman is not born married, and her early life and the ideas instilled in her since childhood cannot help but play an important role in her married life. We shall not speak here of spinsters. Few people take notice of them, although they, too, are human beings like all others and, perhaps, many of them are much more estimable than married women. Nonetheless, we shall limit ourselves to young, unmarried women who eventually will marry.

What are the duties of young, unmarried women? The question seems very simple. There is no doubt that every person has certain responsibilities; however, to define accurately and clearly the duties of unmarried women is not as easy as it might seem at first glance. Of course, if this question is taken seriously, then there is much to be said; but first we shall take a look at just what kind of duties are commonly prescribed by society for young, unmarried women. Their first and foremost duty is to be well dressed—in particular, to wear a corset from morning onward. (Whether or not this is good for one's health is another question.) Then begins the performance of customary, daily duties: obligatory piano playing and singing, and then endless embroidery of completely unnecessary, decorative collars. Why embroider them? you might ask. Because a woman must always be occupied, and embroidery is the most respectable type of work for her; there is nothing more harmful than a young woman's being idle all day long.

Embroidery is fine, but labor is only good when it is productive and, therefore, useful; unproductive work is not only useless, but seriously harmful in two ways. First, it is harmful because it causes expenses, though they may be quite minor. Second, it causes harm in a moral sense, because to work in this manner is to deceive oneself or others—or both at once. If this be the case, it is better not to do anything—at least then there will be no extra expenses and no deceit. However, if a young woman is endowed with reason, and has been well raised and educated, can she really not find some sort of pastime that is suited to her abilities and is useful to others—or, at least, to herself? If not, then she must be recognized as the least useful person on earth, and she will be looked upon not as a help but as a future burden to her husband.

Some people say: "Why not occupy oneself with music? This pastime can be helpful and pleasant for oneself and for others. And why not take up needlework after all? In family life, could it not even be profitable?" Of course this is so, if one has a talent for music and studies it seriously. Needlework is useful also, if it is not confused with the completely useless type of needlework that is done a greater part of the time.

How then can a young woman occupy herself? There are a great many activities she could take on, if only she is willing to pursue them. For example, why should a young adult woman not busy herself with the task of looking after her younger brothers and sisters? And if she does not have any, why not occupy herself with the study of pedagogy—a science that would eventually prove very useful to her as a mother and teacher of her own children. And why not occupy herself with the study of medicine—particularly the study of children's and women's diseases? Both of these pursuits would not only be helpful to a young woman as a future mother, but would also be useful to many other people, because in many situations and illnesses women are more inclined to consult with another woman than with a man.

Examples have even been cited in which an illness developed as a result of a woman being too embarrassed to consult with a male doctor or to explain to him in detail all the symptoms of her illness. With a woman, though, a female patient does not need to have this false modesty: she can describe all the details of her illness. And it seems to me that a woman healer, who herself is susceptible to similar kinds of illnesses, will have more compassion for the sick woman than will a male doctor, who has no direct understanding of these illnesses.

If a young woman can hope to own land someday, why does she not busy herself with a thorough study of agronomy and agriculture? Would this not be appropriate for her and her future family? Several tasks have already been suggested here as examples, but to enumerate all the tasks that women are capable of performing would be to repeat what has already been published in "Women's Labor."[20]

Now let us look at the moral duties of young women. The first and single most important duty for her is pretense in all respects. According to general understanding, pretense is the ideal feminine virtue! Of course, this is not openly acknowledged; but, considering all the moral duties of young women, I think many people would agree that only by means of this pretending can she fulfill all the obligations that are assigned to her. A young woman must always be in the same mood—she must always be affable, polite, and cheerful; she must always be graceful in both dress and movement, as well as in her expressions. Even if she is suffering morally or physically, she may only do so in a graceful manner. For example, if she is crying, then she must not forget to cover her face with a handkerchief, because, when crying, one almost invariably makes an unpleasant grimace, and this must not happen to a young woman. Physically, she is allowed to suffer only from certain types of illnesses. She may have a headache or a slight fever, but she must never fall victim to an illness that is not elegant. Is this not pretense?

Is it ever suggested to a young woman, or does she herself have any understanding, that we must, as much as possible, with all our God-given strength, struggle against our passions, suppress our weaknesses, develop in ourselves that which is good, and finally, not be distressed over trifles, and not succumb under the burden of the first trouble we encounter? No, this is not taught to young women, and few of them realize it themselves.

Practical mothers say to their daughters: "Don't cry over nonsense. This is not the proper time. Guests could come and think that something has happened to us. And besides that, N. N.[21] may stop by to see us today, and your eyes and nose will be red . . . you would be at a disadvantage." And such words compel the young woman to hold back her tears—not because she understands that there is no reason to cry or because she has been consoled—no, she will remain just as upset as before. Instead, she does not cry because she does not want anyone to think that she has quarreled with her mother, that she is prone to tears and has a habit of crying over every trifle, or that she gets red eyes and a red nose when she cries. Is this not outright deception of outsiders in the name of family secrecy? The goal is not to have peace in the family, but to make it so that others will think there is peace. The goal is not to rise above petty everyday unpleasantness, but to let others think that we are above such unpleasantness. Is this not deception or pretense?

A calm disposition is a wonderful quality, when this quality actually exists, but not when it is nothing more than "moral rouge." A fine complexion improves one's appearance, but rouge not only fails to enhance it but [also] spoils it. Like any deception, it cannot have a pleasant effect for long, and disenchantment must follow. One cannot always sustain a single mood; in order to accomplish this, one would have to cease being human. For a short time it is possible to conquer one's real feelings, but what can we call this if not, to use the word again, pretense?

To pretend always, in all situations, is impossible. In the end, a person must give in to moral respite, and the greater the effort put forth, the stronger the reaction will be. Because of this, it often happens that young women who are very sweet, very kind, very affable, and very graceful in public quite often turn out to be completely different in their family circle. This is very natural: they are tired of the difficult role they have been playing in public, and nature demands that they rest. Since a young woman regards her duties largely as a role, it is understandable that during the intermission between one session of pretending and the next she gives in much more often to her temper than she would permit herself to do if she were generally allowed to behave in a more natural manner. In the family circle, when we can rely upon the fact that outsiders will not see or hear us, we allow ourselves to pout, frown, and harshly—sometimes even rudely—to answer our brothers, sisters, and the rest of our household's members. These are our kin—consequently, we need not stand on ceremony with them. This means that amiability, refined politeness, and evenness of temper are nothing more than ceremony, that is, nothing more than pretense.

Let us state once more that everyone must tirelessly fight against their weaknesses and passions, and should not excuse themselves by saying that they do not have enough strength for this battle, because moral strength can grow stronger, as do muscles, from constant exercise. This should be done with the conviction that one's main responsibility is to improve oneself morally, because all of humankind consists of separate individuals, and if every one of them cares about his or her own improvement, the improvement of humankind will be so much the greater. This improvement should be real and not feigned. Until now, however, people have been pursuing mainly the goal of appearing to be better and, as a consequence, deceiving others and at the same time squandering their energies on this pretense—energies that could be used for actual improvement.

We have already said enough about young unmarried women. Now let us suppose that the young woman, who until now has lived as we have described, gets married, and let us focus on her life in marriage. We will not discuss the true responsibilities of women or, better to say, of all human beings—responsibilities consisting mainly of striving, to the extent of one's strengths and abilities, to benefit oneself, one's family, and one's society, since all of that is interconnected. Every individual constitutes a part of a family; every family, a part of society; every society, a part of all humanity. Therefore, one cannot do harm to oneself without detriment to all humanity, and the common excuse—"Who cares about this? I do harm only to myself"—is completely invalid. But let us reiterate the prevailing opinions about the duties of women.

First, every woman should be attractive and healthy—a peculiar expectation, for it would seem that beauty and health are a gift from God, and we are not able to bestow it upon ourselves. Nevertheless, plain and sickly women are punished by society for their misfortune as if it were some sort of crime. Often one hears words such as: "Well, now, how can he (a certain husband) be blamed for ceasing to love her (i.e., his wife)? You see, when he married her, she was decent looking, but now she has become a real ape. Judge for yourself whether it is possible to love her—she's always ill." That is how women are judged, and, instead of compassion, they get only accusations for their misfortune, and who accuses them? If it were men, that perhaps would be understandable, but it is mainly women who blame them.

By accepted norms, then, sickly and plain women are no more worth mentioning than are spinsters, although in reality it sometimes happens that plain or sick women are loved incomparably more than beautiful or healthy ones. Let us return, however, to the question of women's responsibilities and how these responsibilities are understood.

A woman, before anything else, should worry about the preservation of her youth and beauty, and must therefore be greatly concerned with her attire; she always should be elegantly dressed and have a becoming coiffure. A woman should be an excellent hostess, and should even have some knowledge about the preparation of food, because when the dinner is plain, it is not so much the hired cook who gets blamed as the lady of the house, for one of her primary duties is to make sure that her husband is pleased with his dinner. She should strive to spend as little money as possible, while at the same time always be dressed both gracefully and appropriately for her status in society. She should not ignore the pursuit of fine arts, such as music; on the contrary, she should devote as much time to them as possible. She should cultivate social acquaintances, while at the same time staying close to home. She must offer counsel and friendship to her husband (and for this, of course, she should be well educated) and, finally, every woman should be a perfect mother, that is, a superior nanny and good governess constantly watching over her children and never letting them out of her sight.

This is all wonderful but, in truth, can any woman fulfill all these duties? No, of course it is impossible. Even if she had one hundred hands and one hundred eyes, even then it would not be possible for her to carry out even a half of such elaborate tasks. So, what is the inevitable result? Constant accusations against women to the effect that they do not understand their duties and do not carry them out. Indeed, they do not carry them out for it is physically impossible for anyone to do so. Therefore, they must choose one of the following two: either attend to all of the expected duties superficially and very badly, or focus wholly on one of the womanly tasks, for instance, the elegance of one's costume. Indeed, the latter might even be preferable in the sense that, at least, a woman would not be deceiving herself or other people. She would not be harming her young children by misguided upbringing, would not be bothering her hired cook with senseless interference in the kitchen, and would not be claiming the right to congratulate herself on the fulfillment of all her duties.

Is the situation of women indeed so wretched? Can it be that they are able only to function as dressed-up dolls capable of speaking but not reasoning, or that they find themselves in such a hopeless situation that they can only appear useful and pretend to carry out their responsibilities? This would be dreadful but, luckily, the situation of women is actually much better or, to put it more accurately, the improvement of each woman's lot depends upon herself. It must be added, however, that in order to achieve this aim she must discard many prejudices, must part with many pleasant habits of an idle and carefree life, and must exchange much of what is pleasant for that which is useful.

The responsibilities of women, properly understood, are not so very complex and difficult. First of all, there is no such thing as purely womanly responsibilities; there are only human responsibilities. Every person, regardless of gender, has a duty to be useful, but to be useful is not easy: for this purpose it is necessary for people to work on themselves. Not only must they enrich their minds with knowledge, but they must also struggle constantly with their passions and bad inclinations, which exist to some degree in every person. One must study oneself and, according to one's tastes and capabilities, choose an occupation for oneself that would be useful for both family and society. Only when a person is truly useful, only when her work brings actual benefit to society—only then can she claim social rights and hope for freedom and independence, for only then would she be worthy of them. Useless members of society, regardless of their sex, will always be more or less subordinate, and to tell the truth, this is rightfully so.

What do women need to do? They need to study, work, and cultivate their intent to be useful. They should not shy away from those endeavors that are accessible to them, since the field of work open to women is already fairly extensive now, and with time it will expand further. Most important, they must cease scorning labor, slandering themselves, and instilling false limitations in themselves.

One may ask: When do women slander themselves and which shortcomings do they instill in themselves? Naturally, they slander themselves when they say that their character is too weak, that their nerves are too weak, that they are too sensitive, that their imagination is too excitable, and so forth. This is similar to thinking that women have no abilities whatsoever, but facts prove this to be entirely untrue.

Recall how women conducted themselves during the era of early Christianity. Take the church calendar for example, and many names of women martyrs will speak for themselves. Read about the lives of women saints, and you will be convinced that women at that time were not inferior to men either in strength of will or in the power of their conviction. Think of how women conducted themselves in the frightening era of the French Revolution. Study history, and you will become convinced that women were in no way morally inferior to men.

Look at our own time, at our private lives. Almost everyone could recall several cases when in difficult circumstances—for example, during a sudden dangerous illness, death, or painful separation from loved ones—women have shown much more presence of mind and have endured their suffering with greater determination than men. Finally, think of our midwives and nurses—how much patience, how much heart, how much self-control do they manifest in critical moments! Here, it seems, is already enough evidence of the moral power of women. Regarding their intelligence, it has been amply proved through their literary compositions, as well as the skill with which some of them conduct their business affairs, manage their property, and rear children. Weak nerves, delicate sensitivity, fervent imagination are nothing more than instilled shortcomings.

Take two children, a girl and a boy, from nearly any family. What beliefs are instilled in them? The boy is constantly told that he is a man, that it is a disgrace for him to cry or be afraid, and that he must exhibit the strength of his will because he is a man. As for the girl, she always is commended for her sensitivity, until finally she begins to regard sensitivity as a virtue. Hence, she becomes maudlin, always with a gushing heart, and ultimately drives herself to some kind of nervous sentimentality. What is at fault here—nature or education? The same things can happen with the imagination. Because of some peculiar preconceived notion, educators focus on developing a girl's imagination. But if you raise the girl in the same way as the boy, teach her the necessity of having a strong will, and develop both her imagination and intellect, these instilled shortcomings will disappear on their own.

"Fine," say many, "that's all wonderful. But who will watch the household and cherish the children if women begin to occupy themselves with other pursuits?" The answer is: those women who have the ability and the inclination to do so will rear children and manage their households. What would then happen to the households and children whose mothers are unfit for those tasks? This question may be answered by posing another: are there not, at the present time, just as many households which are poorly managed and where children are brought up in a haphazard manner? Think about it, and immediately several examples will come to mind. What do these households and children stand to lose if they no longer are subjected to inept supervision? I think that they will lose nothing, on the contrary, they will gain something. In the meantime, bad housewives and bad mothers can become wonderful actresses, doctors, merchants, or scholars and, instead of being a burden, can be a real asset to society.

Nearly all of men's professions are accessible to women, and women cannot use their physical weakness as an excuse because, as civilization progresses, the advantages and even the necessity of physical strength are becoming less and less important. Even a very weak woman, if she has a revolver in her hands, can overcome the strongest of savages armed only with a tomahawk. A woman who sits in a quiet and comfortable train carriage will reach her destination faster than the strongest man on horseback.

With time, the value of brute strength will lessen even more; as for moral strength, women even now are equal to men. If society would only realize that women must be useful, that they must work, that they are created not just for pleasure but also for serious activity—then women would take an equal place to men in society and would have equal rights, for anyone who works for the benefit of others is entitled to having a place in society commensurate with his or her contribution to it.

Women must not wait for men to determine their place in society. This should not be so because until women learn to take care of themselves they will be no more than moral children. It is a well-known fact that children must obey those who are older, that is, those who are smarter and stronger than they. Is it not high time for women to come out of their infancy and, by virtue of their endeavors, take the rightful place in society that they deserve?

Source: Maria Nikolaevna Vernadskaia (Shigaeva), "Naznachenie zhenshchiny," Sobranie sochinenii pokoinoi Marii Nikolaevnoi Vernadskoi ["The Destiny of Woman," in The Collected Works of the Late Maria Nikolaevna Vernadskaia] (St. Petersburg, 1862). Excerpted from pp. 116–35.

Translated by Denise Price, with Melissa M. Reid and Willow Najjar.

"THE" RUSSIAN WOMAN

EVGENIA TUR VERSUS NATALIA GROT

In an exchange in 1869, Evgenia Tur (1815–1892) and Natalia Grot (1828–1899) debated the proper role of women in Russia through literary criticism, the same medium Belinskii used to establish his positions on women. Evgenia Tur (pseudonym of the Countess Elizaveta Vasilevna Sailhas de Tournemire) was a prominent author, critic, and journalist in the second half of the nineteenth century. She wrote prose fiction and founded and ran a periodical, Russian Speech. Tur also regularly published critical articles and semi-autobiographical essays in some of the best-known publications of the day, including Library for Reading, Time, and Notes of the Fatherland. Grot was the author of numerous articles, children's stories, and memoirs, for example From the Family Chronicle: Memoirs for My Children and Grandchildren (St. Petersburg, 1900). Wife of the well-known scholar Ia. K. Grot, she was well known as a writer in her own right. Tur and Grot argue in the following excerpts about Elena Nikolaevna Stakhova, the heroine of Ivan Turgenev's On the Eve (1860).

Although Turgenev's later novel Fathers and Children (often translated Fathers and Sons, 1862) overshadowed his earlier works, On the Eve was also the subject of much debate in the press. The novel, and its critics, used literature to discuss social and *political issues, particularly the nature of Russianness and of Russia's relationship to the West. Stakhova, rather than choosing to marry any of her Russian suitors, marries In-sarov, a Bulgarian freedom fighter, and follows him to the Balkans.*[22] *Insarov dies on the way; Elena chooses not to return to Russia but to become a nurse and carry on his rev-olutionary activity. Grot and Tur, like other Russian writers in this period, use their dis-cussions of the family as a metaphor for the social and political order more generally. The issues they explore include whether (and if so, how) women should take initiative, how women can be involved in social activism, and the meaning of female self-sacrifice. In effect, their exchange negotiates the various versions of the ideal woman seen in other selections in this chapter.*

The excerpts below appeared in the newspapers Our Times *and* Moscow News. *Grot wrote the initial article, which Tur answered; Grot then responded.*[23]

A. "ELENA NIKOLAEVNA STAKHOVA"

"Turgenev's Elena (in the novella *On the Eve*) is the best Russian woman we've met in Russian literature since the time of Pushkin's Tatiana" they tell us, adding, "God grant us more such women."[24] Before we accept Turgenev's authority un-conditionally, his view of women's role and position, let's look more closely: Does Elena Stakhova deserve the honor of being put on a pedestal? Can she satisfy all the demands of our developing, embryonic Russian life? Can our society desire that there be more such women?

We confess that even as we repeat this foolish wish, we are thinking of images very different from Elena Stakhova—as much of a contrast to her as is a mature, enlightened, Christian society, consciously moving toward a clear goal—the op-posite of a half-educated, non-rational society. But, we will be told, this image is taken straight from life, from the real world; art is closely connected with life and takes its creations from it.

Even in Russia, I'll answer, in real life there are images higher and better than this one. And this image is presented not as a second Oblomov,[25] not as a sharp criticism of one of the unhappiest sides of our Russian life, our chaotic, uncon-scious education. Elena is presented as a new image on the threshold of a new life. Therefore we have the right to demand that this heroine be complete, ideal per-fection. The title *On the Eve* indicates the breadth of the author's task. *On the Eve* of what? we ask with terror, having read his novella: on the eve of bright, new ac-tivity so that, having awakened, we can make up for lost time and shake off the apathy that always masters those who live without goals or meaning?[26] Or are we on the eve of a final, terminal scramble onto a false path after futile, weak efforts to abandon it? If the author had wanted to present the type of a woman com-pletely coinciding with our last proposition, then he couldn't have created any-thing better than Elena. But he, of course, had a different goal.

Elena perfectly embodies the element of destructiveness. A broad nature, not created to submit to anything except unrestricted fantasy and to drag along in the circle of petty duties, humble aspirations, and secret sacrifices. Exempt from the heart's foolish ability to get used to its surroundings, Elena is called not to create, but to destroy, and she fulfils her role superbly in Turgenev's novella. We are certain that she will probably turn many young, inexperienced heads and sow in them many false convictions. Maybe Elena will even find female imitators, but we comfort ourselves with the thought that in our times they will be few. Is this the kind of character who will have a beneficial influence on our society? Why does our society need the destructive principle? Why does it need destruction when it is, in essence, so little created? We need to develop ourselves and not destroy; we need to educate the younger generation.

But let's turn to Elena Nikolaevna Stakhova's biography. We'll look at her in the two most important phases of a heroine's life: when she is growing up and in the time of love, when every girl's dearest, highest dreams are realized. Elena did not receive any education in childhood; her mama gave her over to a sentimental governess who interested Elena in literature. But abstract occupations alone couldn't satisfy the girl's loving and active soul. She wanted activity, activity for good: "She thought, worried, and was tormented about the poor, the hungry, the sick; she dreamt about them and asked her acquaintances about them." But is that really all she could do for them? No, she sometimes "gave them alms."

Despite our insufficient development, despite the system of serfdom,[27] which is false and repulsive to human relations, we think that even in Russia, and even in isolated, faraway provinces, there are women who in silence and obscurity mark their existence by lofty Christian deeds, active love for their neighbors, caring about children's education, self-renunciation, and tranquil family relations, whose sanctity is surely understood even when children don't think parents deserve complete sympathy and respect. In creating his ideal, the author could have chosen to draw from these purely national sources, the most vital sources of inspiration.

We find Elena, who is presented as a model of Russian womanhood, to be completely different. Her relationship with her mother is so savage and unnatural that it can't be justified even by a bad upbringing. I won't even mention Elena's relationship with her father because she had grown especially cold to him. It surprised us very much that in this type [Stakhova] there is a lack of femininity, gentleness, [and] patience. It's clear to us what resolved the drama of Elena's life: her shallowness and vanity, her inability to create a circle of activity for herself, her inability to invest others' lives with empathic love, and, especially, her unfeminine daring and determination. This, at any rate, explains why she abandoned both her parents' home and her fatherland without any doubts or regrets.

Moving to Elena's love, we will discuss only what surprised us unpleasantly. It seems to us that in a Christian society love itself must have a particular character. True love even in a man is a hesitant feeling, tacit, humble, and shy because the one who loves places the beloved unattainably high. And this is all intensified in women because of their inborn modesty, which makes them incapable of taking the initiative in affairs of the heart.

In Elena Stakhova love manifests itself in a completely different way. The whole picture of this love grossly offends decency—beginning with Elena's daring resoluteness in seeking the first explanation with Insarov and ending with the last scene before the wedding (when Elena gives herself to her hero [who is still physically weak] with the words "so take me!"). This is all repulsive to true femininity. Is the depiction of this love as ideal worthy of the brush of an artist? And one whose word carries weight and force in society, who is an acknowledged authority in contemporary literature, should be especially careful that his types do not lead society into fatal errors.

Every day we see examples of how dangerous it is in our age of fleeting freedoms, thoughts, and openness (*glasnost'*), in our age of not acknowledging authority, to contradict contemporary authorities in any way. But truth is more valuable than anything else. So we have decided to give a candid account of our impressions on a topic so important to us, women, even though we are not sure that in our journals even the name "woman" will provide protection from those rude attacks that, for some time, have met anyone who deviates even a little not from general opinion but from the views of a well-known literary circle.[28] Our inalienable right to participate in discussions about women will, in many people's eyes, justify this protest against unconditionally worshipping the model Turgenev created for us. We consider it necessary to repeat in brief the basic ideas of our critical essay.

We not only do not feel obliged to accept the character of Elena as exemplary, but we even find that her character is not entirely faithful to women's true nature. If the awakening life of our society and its struggle against external obstacles to implement truth and goodness demand, more than ever, returning women from artificiality to life, all the same, a woman like Elena does not correspond to contemporary needs. In order to become a real friend, helpmeet, and support to men in all life's circumstances, in all life's painful trials; in order to be a worthy educator of the next generation, a woman should be able to join to self-renunciatory love more enlightenment, more practical abilities, more multi-facetedness of heart and mind, more understanding of the Christian religion than we find in Elena Nikolaevna Stakhova.

A. The Russian Woman (*Russkaia zhenshchina*).[29]

B. "A FEW WORDS REGARDING 'THE RUSSIAN WOMAN'S' ARTICLE, 'ELENA NIKOLAEVNA STAKHOVA'"

The newspaper *Our Times*, which constantly astonishes readers with its critical articles, has recently published a new work of criticism with the strange signature, "The Russian Woman." We consider it necessary to say a few words in this regard.

In seeing such a contrived signature a question arises: what is a Russian woman? Up to now we have been acquainted with two sorts of Russian women: some have been educated in a foreign way and are almost alien to our way of life; others have not received any education and vegetate in their fathers' homes. The latter are not familiar with thought and stagnate under the coarse despotism of family slavery. Up to now there has been no middle ground. Families in which parents and children, husbands and wives, apparently recognize their rights and responsibilities have begun to spring up in Russia only recently, very recently. I said apparently recognize, but I will not say "have recognized" because Russian life still has a long way to go to work this out.

Here is why the signature "The Russian Woman" surprised us: we, it is true, are acquainted with high-society people, with reflections of Frenchwomen and Englishwomen, with female landowners, with clerks' wives, with merchant women, and with simple Russian women (who, by the way, should not go last in this pitiful list), but we have to confess that up to now we have not met a Russian woman. Is the Russian woman who wrote the article that appeared in the paper Our Times an exception? Let's get acquainted with the views and ways of thinking of this newcomer whom we do not want to prematurely accuse of being a pretender.[30]

"The Russian Woman" sees in Elena Stakhova the embodiment of an ideal, an example presented by Turgenev for imitation, a pattern according to which all Russian women must be cut out: it is very easy to see that this judgment is artificial and groundless. Turgenev created his heroine with love, but it doesn't follow from this that he claimed to make her an ideal Russian woman and to present her as a pattern of perfection to be worshipped and imitated. True, he gave his heroine intelligence, beauty, passion, and a strong will, but, practically all heroines in novels are given these qualities. Where and when did Turgenev express the idea that all Russian women should be this way? We will add that a woman capable of loving warmly, strongly, spontaneously, and devotedly, a woman capable of valuing a man who would give all of himself in the service of his motherland—such a woman is, without a doubt, rare. From this point of view, of course, one could wish that there were more Elena Stakhovas in Rus'. Do many women (especially Russian!) understand that love is not the main objective of a man's life, that a man first of all belongs to his native land and only then to his wife and family? The majority of our women—and what a large majority!—want to be a man's main concern and the center of his attention at all times. In a word, they definitely want to be his first concern and only then allow civic or other activity. Can one cast stones at Elena because she is not like this and, loving the ugly, poor, and clumsy Insarov, follows him to far-off places, recognizing what labor and deprivations she will share with him, how many wounds, physical and moral, she will have to heal, how many bitter moments she will have to live through because his life, as she knows, belongs inseparably to liberating his fatherland and only then to her. This consciousness demonstrates self-renunciation and the complete absence of an egotistical feeling of love. But that is not how "The Russian Woman" of the newspaper *Our Times* thinks. "Elena perfectly embodies the element of destruction," says "The Russian Woman": "Elena is called not to create, but to destroy, and superbly fulfills this role."

But what does Elena destroy? Despite all our desire to understand the meaning of "The Russian Woman's" words, our efforts have been in vain. Was it Insarov Elena destroyed? This proposition is so crazy that we hurriedly dismiss it, knowing that "The Russian Woman" possesses common sense, even if not brilliant logic. Elena cannot be blamed for Insarov's cold, as a result of which he got pneumonia and then consumption. So is it her family Elena is trying to destroy? But what is a family? A family in the narrow and contemporary meaning of the word is a husband and wife and their young children. According to the law—divine and human—as adults, children strive to separate from their families and create their own families. True, Elena left her parents willfully and married without asking permission, but who is to blame for this? Only she herself? To marry against the will of your parents is a great misfortune, but this misfortune is often unavoidable. Can we really not allow a woman the right at least to decide her own fate and that of her heart?[31]

We do not share the opinion of many that a literary work must provide a lesson. The public has the right to demand from an author only that his novella or novel does not offend basic, immutable moral laws: lessons and exhortations are not his affair. This has long been widely known, but regarding the critical article of "The Russian Woman" one constantly has to repeat what is already well known. Turgenev's novella *On the Eve* expresses, among other things, the idea that there was no one for Elena to love until meeting Insarov—there wasn't even anyone to truly respect. It was impossible to respect her shallow, foolish, extravagant, and almost depraved father. It was equally impossible to become attached to, respect, or love her shallow, sentimental, tearful mother. If it's absolutely necessary to search for lessons in novels and novellas, then we'll yield and search for them. In life, as in novellas, daughters run away from their parents' homes, but in Turgenev's novella this phenomenon is a lesson that relates not to daughters but to mothers. Let mothers like Anna Vasilevna Stakhova remake themselves and take care of their children. Then, of course, they will inspire love and respect in their daughters, gain their trust, and, in that case, they will certainly not be abandoned.

And does the heroine of the novella *On the Eve* have to be considered culpable even for having a broad nature? We confess that until now, in our simplicity, we have considered broad natures an especially fortunate occurrence. Only broad natures are capable of full development and of noble and energetic activity. "The Russian Woman" demands from women exclusively secret sacrifices and humble aspirations—in general, a passive and suffering role. But why insist on secret sacrifices and humble aspirations when we're talking about a girl full of youth and life, a girl who is in love for the first time? A girl is a free creature who has the right to live, love, and, out of love, choose a husband for herself. Girls are indisputably freer than women. What is this asceticism that puts a monk's hair shirt on a young creature who is full of life and [that] wants to force secret sacrifices and humble aspirations on a splendid, living creature? But further on there's an even more significant—and immoral—phrase: "Elena is exempt from the heart's foolish ability to get used to its surroundings." What is this: to get used to one's surroundings? Doesn't this mean to become reconciled to them? And from complete reconciliation it is not far to complete agreement and even sympathy. And if the surroundings are coarse, dirty, depraved? Are you also supposed to get used to these? All our society's wounds have festered from this capacity to be reconciled with reality, from this passive attitude toward life and its phenomena, from this indifference to good and a still greater indifference to evil. God save us from advocates of this kind of morality!

"The Russian Woman," without adducing any proof, accuses Elena of "the inability to create activity for herself (terrific!) and the inability to invest others' lives with empathic love." We ask, what kind of activity can a girl create for herself among us? Men are freer and stronger than women, but where and when have they been able to create activity for themselves if life itself has not been able to offer it to them? Where is a girl supposed to find activity? That's easy to answer. The only activity that she has access to is helping the poor and taking care of the sick, and for that one needs a vocation. A girl can be splendid and not have this vocation.

"To invest others' lives with empathic love!" But how can you do this when there is no one to love? You can demand fulfillment of duty, but you can't demand love and respect. Love and respect come into being because of and depend on the qualities of those around us; to forcibly uproot them is just as impossible as forcing them on someone. That would mean not acknowledging freedom of the spirit, freedom of thought, freedom of feeling.

We have often heard Russian nannies say: "Little one,[32] love your brother."[33]

"Yes, but nanny, he beats me."

"Never mind—he's your brother."

"Love a Russian," says "The Russian Woman." "But there aren't any," Elena could reply, or "They don't inspire love in me."

"Never mind—they're still Russian," answers "The Russian Woman."

We have to add that we don't see the sensual side of her [Elena's] love anywhere; we don't even see it in the words "Take me," from which only those who have the unenviable advantage of possessing a depraved imagination and unclean thoughts have tried to make something dirty and base. But we must not forget that such people soil not only what they touch but even what they look at.

"The Russian Woman," having entered the slippery arena of journalism, timidly backtracks and says that it's dangerous to contradict the authorities, and that the name of woman does not protect against rude attacks. We venture to note that rudeness to men and women is equally blameworthy but the woman who takes pen in hand and exposes her article to print does not have the right to plead women's privilege. In literature there is an author and a critic, and it doesn't matter whether they are men or women. Women should not hide behind their dresses, and if you're afraid, then you'd better sit in the *terem*,[34] or, failing that, then within the four walls of your own home.

We'll say a couple of words in conclusion. Whoever is for the right of a woman who has attained majority to choose her own husband is also for the inviolability and sanctity of marriage. Free choice is the necessary condition for this. Excessive strictness is extremely harmful in everything. Let's save our censure for novellas and novels that are truly immoral. As for moralists who punish the love, passion, and enthusiasm of a free person in the name of conventional and therefore vulgar morals, one can only smile and say in the words of Talleyrand:[35] *pas trop de zèle, surtout pas trop de zèle.*[36]

Evgenia Tur

C. "A RUSSIAN WOMAN'S REPLY TO MME. TUR"

When we wrote our modest critique of one of the characters in the novella *On the Eve*, we, naturally, did not hope to be favored with the attention of the respected authoress Evgenia Tur, who has long been working in the literary field. We also didn't think that a retort of this kind could come from the pen of a woman. And, we confess, we expected even less that our authoress would so decidedly announce her claim to be not only the first, but what's even better the only Russian woman by development, nationality, "familiarity with thought," and the ability to express this thought in the Russian language. Evgenia Tur was clearly offended at another Russian woman's daring to express her thoughts in print. Otherwise why did she, from the very first line, attack not the essence of the matter but the "contrived signature of A Russian Woman?" We don't understand why this pseudonym is worse than that of "Evgenia Tur," all the more so as the one who wrote the above-mentioned critique grew up in the very heart of Russia and therefore has a perfect right to call herself "A Russian Woman." Tur harshly proclaims that up to now, in all the broad expanse of our fatherland there have not been and are not now any Russian women, that all of Russia is populated with "half-foreign women stagnating under the despotism of family slavery" and who therefore do not have the right to call themselves Russian women. Such a merciless sentence on a whole society can hardly be just. Our authoress, it appears, firmly believes that while she is working in the literary field, no other woman author, who would dare to raise her voice in the sphere of thought, can or should appear in Russia. However, this confidence is justified by Tur's sincerely admitting that among all her Russian acquaintances, she still hasn't met a Russian woman. This fact proves, at least, that she has a perfect right to consider herself the only Russian woman capable of thinking, feeling, and writing competently in her language.

Looking at our entire article from this strange point of view, Tur uses all her female curiosity to try to discover who dared to encroach on her literary monopoly—and what amusing guesses she makes. "A Russian Woman" is not only not old but is much closer to the younger generation than the respected authoress herself.

We confess that we did not expect to be met by such hostile hints on the part of a woman. These cannot be justified even by the sharpest division of opinions and views, and this is not only strange in a personage sincerely enlightened but also is not appropriate in a literary matter. All this compels us to provide an explanation of the points in our article that Tur attacked especially cruelly. [We find] especially surprising the question: "What kind of activity can a girl make for herself?" We answer: "Not political, of course." In Russia it appears that this question was decided long ago in the unanimous effort of our society to reform female education, to make girls useful members of the family and of society.

The respected authoress also asks: "How can you love when there is no one to love?" It's impossible not to point out that the nanny who naively tells her charge, "Little one, love your brother," reasons much more sensibly and progressively than Tur herself, although she is presented as ridiculous. Not to love anything because everything seems worse than we are and beneath us is pride and coldness. In Tur's opinion, love comes into being because of and depends on the qualities of those around us, but in our understanding love depends on the richness of our own heart and its capacity for generosity and tolerance.

Having repeated our words that, in Russia, even the name of woman does not protect from rude attacks, Tur again came to a mistaken conclusion, that is, that we are afraid of real criticism and want to hide from it behind women's privilege. If this were true, then, of course, we wouldn't have decided to publish even a line, since we do not presume that everything we say is, without exception, true and irrefutable.

We'll add that in her anticriticism, Tur expresses not so much a need to speak the truth as a desire to gain more popularity and curry favor from those she considers strong. However, knowing Turgenev's enlightened mind, we are certain that ecstatic and unconditional worship probably wearies him more than rare and not so unconditional contradictions and that, sated with praise, he will sooner turn to Tur herself with the words she took from Talleyrand: *"Pas trop de zèle, surtout pas trop de zèle."*

"A Russian Woman" (Russkaia zhenshchina)

Source: "Elena Nikolaevna Stakhova," *Nashe vremia* [*Our Times*], no. 13 (10–20 April 1860), 207–10; "Otvet Russkoi Zhenshchiny g-zhe Tur," *Nashe vremia* ["A Russian Woman's Reply to Mme Tur," *Our Times*], no. 18 (15–20 May 1860), 284–87; Evgenia Tur, "Neskol'ko slov po povodu stat'i Russkoi Zhenshchiny," *Moskovskie vedomosti* ["A Few Words Regarding 'The Russian Woman's' Article," *Moscow News*], no. 85 (17 April 1860), 665–67.

Translated by Jehanne M Gheith.

THE EMANCIPATION OF WOMEN

ARIADNA TYRKOVA

Like Maria Vernadskaia, Ariadna Vladimirovna Tyrkova (1869–1962) calls for women to support themselves and share the burdens of society. A member of the Kadet party,[37] Tyrkova had both served time in prison for her activism and lived abroad in the society of Russian radicals. She wrote her history of women's treatment under patriarchy while her political views briefly held sway, during the rule of the Provisional Government (February to October 1917).[38] Representing a growing segment of the population that had long struggled for both the rights for and responsibilities of women, Tyrkova articulates yet another ideal for Russian women, an ideal that is quite similar to that developed by Vernadskaia. Reflecting the changes in the political situation that had taken place with the establishment of the Duma in 1906, however, Tyrkova has added equal political participation for women to her conception of women's appropriate public role. Unlike Tur and Grot, Tyrkova argues about living women, rather than literary characters, and she unambiguously values the political activity of Russian women: these differences indicate the enormous changes that had occurred in imperial Russia over the course of the more than fifty-five years that separate these documents. Revolution in the political system and the emancipation of women are clearly linked in Tyrkova's writing; she expected women's participation in the new Russian regime to change the very character of government. They would do so, however, by introducing into the political process qualities that many of the authors in this chapter believed to be specifically feminine.

I. The Russian revolution gave political rights to Russian women citizens; it opened before them the road to equality.

This enormous change serves not only the female half of the Russian population but also Russia as a whole. It is the death sentence for one of the most ancient and tenacious forms of slavery, the subjugation of woman. Attempts were made to elevate this slavery to a law of nature, to authenticate it with rituals, with customs, and with the arbitrary interpretation of church canon. But at the heart of it all lurked echoes of the law of the jungle, by which [one's] rights and freedom were determined by the power of the fist, and the master of life was the one who was better able to defend himself and attack others. From age to age, from generation to generation, it became commonplace to look on woman as an inferior creature.

Woman was considered too irrational to take part in the formation of laws— but rational enough to obey them and independent enough to pay taxes. Even when a woman headed the government—when the country was ruled by a queen or *tsaritsa*—her subjects would not allow women to be involved in the affairs of state; the tsaritsa did not have the right to surround herself with women ministers, women openly helping her run the country. Her own subjects did not have the sense to speak out loudly about women's troubles and desires and to address their requests to a female ruler.

II. An ingenious human idea came to the assistance of the first, solitary female ad-vocate of women's freedom. It was the invention of the engine. A hundred years after the invention of the engine, in countries where factory production was es-pecially developed—in Austria, Germany, France—already about half the women were earning a living for themselves through their own individual labor.

This changed the character of woman, especially urban women. Woman emerges from the darkness and confinement of small, domestic worries. She no longer sits behind the head of the family—her father, husband, or son. She her-self pays her own expenses, or at least a portion of them, and cannot but feel her-self the master of her own fate. It is no wonder that a modern woman possesses an independence that never before existed and the desire to arrange her life as she wants to, without always being subjugated to another's will.

And step by step began a reexamination of the question: is the status of woman the right one at home and in the state? Is it not time to change and reorganize many things? Is the modern state, to whom woman—unequal to man—is obliged to submit, able to take care of her?

The answer to that is simple: No. It is unable [to do so].

III. Nature has placed upon woman the difficult and sweet obligation of mother-hood. The modern state, instead of protecting and preserving both mother and child, creates conditions in which suckling infants die like flies and young women in search of work find themselves in the market of depravity.

Like men, millions of girls and women now must earn a living for themselves and their family outside the home. This female labor is needed by the state. But the state hardly acknowledges the need to educate and train women for work. Here in Russia there were always fewer women's schools than men's. There were very few technical or professional schools where one could learn a trade. Un-trained, uneducated women unavoidably find themselves working for the worst wages.

But even where women were able to perform the same work as men, they were usually relegated to a second tier. The habit of thinking about women as inferior creatures, as if half-human, was very strongly expressed in the distribution of labor. Men would get the most profitable positions and women would get what was a bit worse. Workers' unions did not accept women.[39] Employees would voice protest against those whom they regarded as their competitors. In justifying them-selves, they would cite that women lowered workers' wages. Certainly women were guilty of being paid less than men. In instances where a worker sells only his raw, physical strength, this unequal pay is understandable. But with each year, everywhere, even in agriculture, the machine replaces the flexing of human mus-cle. Already work is performed depending not on who is stronger but [rather] ac-cording to the cleverness, quick-wittedness, and conscientiousness of employees and workers. Women have realized that they would have all of these attributes, if only they were given the opportunity to study, train, and develop themselves in general. The female mind has awakened and has begun to stir; it has ceased to reconcile itself with injustice. It has gone to battle for women's human dignity.

Women's unions began to form in order to evaluate their situation and fight for their rights together. There are many such unions abroad. Millions of women are united there in strong organizations. They organize lectures, meetings, congresses; open the eyes of women to the injustices of their plight; appeal to political parties and parliaments; and demand new laws.

Disregarding the few differences in the status of women in various states, these demands essentially turn out to be just about identical in many countries, and women's societies have united into large, international unions. Delegates chosen from among American, French, German, Italian, Swedish, English, and Australian women—that is, from all ends of the earth—are meeting at women's congresses. Only women representatives from Russia, with a female population of eighty million, did not attend these congresses because the tsarist government would not allow them to organize an all-Russia women's congress.

Spreading all the time, the women's movement created a universal, women's public opinion, at first in small circles and then in wide masses. Its voice is heard ever more loudly, and its demands are shaking loose old prejudices bit by bit.

This is what women are talking about and demanding:

A woman should be equal to a man, because, just like him, she possesses intellect and a conscience.

Like a man, a woman pays taxes and obeys laws. That means that, just like him, she should send her own delegates to where the laws are written and the taxes are allocated.

A woman should be equal to a man in both state and domestic affairs. She no less than a man is in charge of the fate, the upbringing, and property of the children.

A woman should receive the same education as a man.

A woman should receive equal pay for equal work.

The labor of women and children should fall under the special protection of the state.

The state should care for poor mothers, providing support before and after the birth of a child.

IV. There is still not one country or state where all of these demands have been entirely satisfied.

Day by day the war has changed attitudes about woman. It has become increasingly clear that the unseen effort of a woman and her labor often support the entire economy of a country.

Thanks to the Revolution, Russia is the first warring nation to give women full political rights. It may seem surprising that women first achieved equality in Russia, where the women's movement practically did not exist, and that barely literate—even illiterate—Russian women took the lead from their more educated, western sisters. But among our men there is an enormous majority of illiterates. And if, despite that, Russia overthrew the autocracy and proclaimed freedom, then it came about thanks to the determined efforts of a comparatively small circle of people who fought for that freedom for decades. There were people of all classes among those who fought. And Russian women can fearlessly take from the hands of the nation full rights because in the long years of struggle they shared with their male comrades all the difficulty, all the persecution, all the blows, and together went to their death for the happiness of the people.

Deprived of rights in public life, they were men's equal in exile, in prison, and even on the scaffold. Their devotion to the sacred fight for freedom and their selfless determination often upheld the spirits of the fighters. Many of them perished unknown, falling stars that flashed across the night sky. The people already know the names of others and are learning by their example to value a woman both as a citizen in the loftiest sense of the word and as a person.

But heroines, like heroes, are always considered rare individuals. Now the time is upon us when each man and woman must be able to fulfill his or her own obligation. And they must learn first and foremost how to think. Women must forget the old, stupid saying—that thinking is not a woman's business—they must learn how to think.

There are so many female votes that elections to a significant degree depend on women. The woman delegate and woman citizen will found the new Russia hand in hand with male *citizens*. And she must think hard about the obligation, of women's share, and ease the situation of the working mother both in the country and in the city. She must petition in the cantonal *zemstvo* for schools for [those] adults left illiterate during the old regime, for maternity homes, for day nurseries, for who should look after children in the country—and how—while their mothers are working in the fields. It is no less important to arrange for the care of children in the cities, where mothers leave for the factory or workshop while [their] children stay without supervision in dark, dirty places, playing in damp, backstreet courtyards and falling under carriage wheels; half-starving, unwashed, they live like kittens without care and upbringing. And around them swarm drunkenness, theft, hooliganism, and depravity. From a tender age children are apprenticed in the street to crime and vice, with which the dregs of large cities swarm. Little thieves, experts in burglary and murder, little girl prostitutes—see with what horror life pays off the blind indifference of the government toward the interests of the child.

And everywhere, where women become lawmakers, they first take up the fight against children's homelessness. This issue always goes side by side with their campaign against drunkenness and prostitution. It will not be easy to realize all of this in a poor and ignorant Russia.

It will also not be easy to accustom people to the new attitude toward woman and the fact that after the Revolution a Russian woman has ceased to be an inferior creature.

It is this recognition, that the new right has lifted from woman the old, degrading subordination—now she is no longer a thing, given over to the power and amusement of her master, but a person—this is one of the main outcomes of equality. As soon as a woman thinks about its meaning, she will immediately raise her head and shake off her former servitude. At work here is the spiritual and moral strength of equality. All types of enslavement and every form of subjugation cripple both master and slave. When one half of the population considers itself the master of the other half, there can be no real freedom.

Only a free mother can raise free citizens and teach them to consider this freedom as a blessing to themselves and the nation.

The revolution, having given the Russian woman rights at such a difficult, terrible hour—when, for the salvation of the country, all the efforts of the people's minds are needed and the national conscience needs to burn brightly—has set her an enormous task and an enormous obligation.

We would like to believe that in creating a new Russia women will be able to introduce into politics and into public opinion the spiritual warmth, response, and sympathy toward the suffering of one's neighbor, which is characteristic of today's women. Up to this point, there has been none of this in world politics. Until now politics have been based on the peculiar and quasi-animalistic law by which the right of the powerful sounds more loudly than the right of justice and conscience. From this men have oppressed women, the ruling classes have oppressed the workers, the stronger nations or governments have encroached upon their weaker neighbors.

Woman has been the weaker, oppressed party for so long that she must become a brave defender of freedom. The revolution has set us this great and honorable task. We should cope with this task because the fate and happiness of our children depend on it, as do the fate and happiness of Russia.

Source: A. V. Tyrkova-Viliams [Williams], *Osvobozhdenie zhenshchiny* [*The Emancipation of Woman*] (Petrograd, 1917). Excerpted from pp. 1–16.

Translated by Amy Singleton Adams.

Notes

1. For examples, see Daniel H. Kaiser and Gary Marker, comps. and eds., *Reinterpreting Russian History: Readings, 860–1860s* (New York: Oxford University Press, 1994); Serge A. Zenkovsky, ed., *Medieval Russia's Epics, Chronicles, and Tales* (rev. ed., New York: Dutton, 1974); and Carolyn J. Pouncy, ed. and trans., *The "Domostroi": Rules for Russian Households in the Time of Ivan the Terrible* (Ithaca, N.Y.: Cornell University Press, 1994).

2. The author is referring to the Roman Empire.

3. The Synod Press was the official press of the Russian Orthodox Church; publication by the press signified official sanction by the Church.

4. The school for noble girls founded by Catherine II; see chapters 2 and 4.

5. The word used here, and throughout most of the remainder of this passage, is *mamen'ka*, a diminutive form of the word for mother that expresses affection.

6. Mme. B. Monborne, author of three sentimental and historical novels published in the 1830s. *Une Victime* was published in two editions in 1834.

7. French: hidden motive.

8. George Sand (pseudonym of Amandine-Lucie-Aurore Dupin, Baronne Dudevant, 1804–1876), French writer. Sand was widely read and debated in Russia in the 1830s and 1840s. Both her works and her life were topics for controversy (Sand left her husband, lived independently in Paris, and wore men's clothing). Her works raised issues of love, sexuality, and the value of the individual.

9. A warrior maiden of Carolingian legend with several literary variants. Belinskii probably refers to Robert Garnier's 1582 play *Bradamante*.

10. The Italian poet Torquato Tasso (1544–1595) began writing "Gerusalemme liberate" ["Jerusalem Liberated"] in 1565. It was published in the early 1580s.

11. The supposed exhortation of a Spartan mother to her son as to how he should return from battle.

12. Sappho (b. 612 B.C.E.) was a famous poet of the isle of Lesbos. Her writings, which have survived only in fragments, display a lyrical intensity that few poets have matched. Corinna (5th century B.C.E.) was a Greek poet who won several poetic competitions with one of the leading (male) poets of her day, Pindar (522 or 518–432 or 438 B.C.E.). Beginning in the eighteenth century, Russian women authors frequently used these personae in their fiction.

13. The quotation is from Aleksandr Pushkin's (1799–1837) *Eugene Onegin* (1833), chapter 3, canto XXVIII, verses 2–3.

14. Claude Henri, Duc de Saint-Simon (1760–1825), writer and supporter of socialist ideals. He argued that work was a social duty, and called for an organization of industrial society on an ethical basis. Belinskii here is referring to the sexual experimentation associated with his many, and often highly visible, women followers.

15. French: *an* emancipated woman; in the next sentence, *the* emancipated woman.

16. Belinskii here refers to a vulgar word for "prostitute."

17. French: "proper, as she should be."

18. Daughter of Prince Paul of Württemberg and the wife of Grand Duke Mikhail, the younger brother of Emperor Nicholas I. A well-educated and intelligent woman, Grand Duchess Elena Pavlovna (1806–1873) devoted considerable time and resources to charitable work. During the Crimean War, she established the Community of Sisters of Mercy of the Exaltation of the Cross and outfitted the medical detachment that was headed by Pirogov. She also actively promoted the abolition of serfdom.

19. In the New Testament, Martha and Mary of Bethany, sisters of Lazarus [Luke 10:38–42]; Martha is commonly regarded as typifying the "active" Christian life as contrasted with Mary, who typifies the "contemplative" life.

20. Vernadskaia refers here to her own earlier essay, "Women's Labor."

21. Russian authors used "N.N." or "NN" to signify an unspecified person, in the way "X" is used in English.

22. In the 1860s, Bulgarian patriots were beginning to work actively for their country's liberation from Ottoman control; many looked to Russia for support.

23. Nikolai Pavlov (a minor author, editor of *Our Times*, and the husband of the author Karolina Pavlova) also responded negatively to Tur's article (see *Our Times*, no. 17 (8–20 April 1860), 262–68).

24. This quotation is from *Saint Petersburg News* [*Sankt-Peterburgskie vedomosti*], no. 48, 1860. Tatiana is the heroine of the poet Aleksandr Pushkin's *Eugene Onegin* (1833). The character of Tatiana was widely considered to be a model for Russian women.

25. Ivan Goncharov's novel *Oblomov* (1859) portrays the decline of the gentry class; the protagonist Oblomov is spectacularly incapable of taking action.

26. Grot uses the word *"deiatel'nost'*,*"* a much-used term in Russian, which has the connotations of socially or politically important action. Throughout, *"deiatel'nost'"* is translated as "activity."

27. Serfdom was abolished in 1861.

28. Grot here refers to the so-called "radical critics," who argued that literature's primary function was social reform and who were powerful arbiters of literary taste in the 1860s.

29. There are no articles in Russian, so it is unclear whether this signature should be interpreted as "A Russian Woman" or "The Russian Woman." As the dialogue between Tur and Grot develops, it becomes clear that Tur interpreted it as "The Russian Woman," while Grot, in her second article, implies that she intended it as "A Russian Woman."

30. The Russian word is *samozvanstvo* (literally "self-naming"). There is a long history of pretenders to the Russian throne, lending a rich set of associations to Tur's use of the term here.

31. This argument may be rooted in Tur's personal experience. In 1836 she nearly eloped with her tutor Nikolai Nadezhdin.

32. *Matushka* literally means "little mother"; this is a common, usually informal, way of addressing women.

33. The Russian term here is *bratets*.

34. The secluded quarters for elite women, common in Russia before the eighteenth century.

35. Charles Talleyrand (1754–1838), French statesman and diplomat.

36. French: "Not too much fervor, above all not too much fervor."

37. Term for the Constitutional Democratic Party, the main liberal political party active in the Imperial Russian State Duma after 1906. Members of the party dominated the first Provisional Government established after the collapse of the monarchy in February 1917.

38. The Provisional Government succeeded the tsarist government. A weak but liberal governing body, the Provisional Government immediately granted full freedom of speech, press, assembly, and religion; equality to all citizens; and amnesty for exiles. Tentative public support, the inability to undertake a more extensive program of reform, and the decision not to withdraw from World War I contributed to the Provisional Government's failure and the subsequent seizure of power by the Bolshevik party in October 1917.

39. On this question, see the selection by Vera Karelina in chapter 6.

2. Family Life

INTRODUCTION

In imperial Russia membership in a family provided individuals with the principal basis for their identity. Social roles were determined largely by family status and position, and family networks strongly affected social, economic, and political behavior, although among some social groups this influence was waning by the end of the imperial period. The family at this time in Russia was patriarchal, and authority within the family was distributed on the basis of sex and age. Preference, legally and usually in practice, was generally given to senior males. Reflecting this patriarchal structure, each Russian child received a name that placed her or him clearly in relationship to the father of the family—a Russian's first name was always followed by a second name, or patronymic, derived from her or his father's first name. For girls, male identity followed them into married life, where they gained the additional mark of a husband's family name. Folk wisdom among the mass of the population, "middle-class" mores among the merchants, social custom to maintain family and political influence at the highest levels of the nobility, as well as Orthodox religious teachings—all worked to define women's roles as primarily those of daughter, wife, and mother. With few exceptions, until late in the nineteenth century, women had limited opportunities to exercise political power outside the family circle or to follow an occupation, although women in poorer social groups often engaged in a trade or craft while remaining within their households. Learning her role within the family—as daughter, wife, mother, daughter-in-law, and mother-in-law—occupying herself with household tasks and children, being pious, and, for non-elite women, contributing to the household economy, were the accepted, even required, behaviors for Russian women in the imperial period. While some documents in the later chapters of this volume show that women often acted at variance with this ideal, it nevertheless remained in force for the entire period with insignificant modifications as time passed.

Women's lives in Russia, as in most pre-industrial societies, were shaped and constrained by the expectation that they would marry. As we saw in the previous chapter, Orthodox teaching held that marriages should be voluntary (see St. Tikhon's *Instructions*), a principle that Peter the Great also established in imperial law. But since the main goal in marriage at all social levels was not the individual's happiness but the family's financial health and social position, in general decisions about marriage partners were made by the senior members of the family. By the middle of the nineteenth century, however, there was greater opportunity for personal preference to be taken into account in marriage decisions, particularly among the educated and privileged strata of society. Most Russians apparently accepted this situation and acquiesced in the needs of the family, if sometimes reluctantly. Those who opposed their families' demands regarding marriage partners appear to have been the exception. Nevertheless, the exceptional cases (such as that of Natalia Dolgorukaia [1714–1771], who opposed her family's advice that she give up her politically doomed fiancé) are more widely known to historians than are those of the great majority who complied with the patriarchal social order.

During the eighteenth and nineteenth centuries, as cultural contact with Western European societies increased, Russian society at the highest social level began to acknowledge concepts such as romantic love and companionate marriage. But religious precepts and legal norms worked to reinforce patriarchal family relations, for example, by placing a wife under the authority of her husband and requiring her to live with him, making divorce or legal separation difficult, and strongly favoring males in inheritance law. As a result, most women had limited control over their own persons, even though, surprisingly, they could control their own property. In contrast to most women in Western Europe and North America, Russian women in the eighteenth century had acquired the right not only to inherit real as well as personal property, but also to dispose freely of their property, including their dowries. For some women, particularly those from privileged social groups, this ability to control their own property did allow greater personal independence. By the later nineteenth century the roles within the family began to alter as more women sought out opportunities for education and jobs (some forced by economic circumstances, drawn by new opportunities, or inspired by new ideas; others encouraged by their mothers and, occasionally, male family members). But for most women in imperial Russia, members of the peasantry, there was little change from the cycle of caring for younger children in the family (in preparation for their own children), courtship rituals and the companionship of other young girls in the village, and marriage (probably an arranged one), followed by entering a husband's household and assuming the role of daughter-in-law and, eventually, mistress of the household.

Nonetheless, after the late 1850s both the ideal of the patriarchal family and the position of women within it were subjected to increased pressures for change. Although the extent of change varied widely by social group and geographic location, the general trend was toward an increased respect for women within the family and an expansion of the sphere of authority and independent action, especially among married women. For women in the privileged[1] and educated strata of society, at least, the intensified influence of the ideals of romantic love and companionate marriage, the widespread critique of arbitrary patriarchal authority (within as well as outside the family), and demands for a better social and legal position for women appear to have generally resulted in greater independence in choosing whom, when, and even whether to marry. These pressures for change likewise resulted in improved family life. The rapid expansion of education and employment opportunities among women of the elite and middling social groups (see chapter 4) had a similar impact. Women from the unprivileged and poorer groups of society, especially in rapidly expanding cities but also in rural areas, also increasingly worked for wages outside the home (see chapter 4). However meager, the income from such work appears for at least some women to have enhanced their status and authority within the family and to have enabled them to escape their abusive or negligent husbands, by both legal and illegal means. After the abolition of serfdom in 1861, peasant households were divided at an increased rate into smaller units, which, in some instances, apparently mitigated the harsh conditions of family life among peasant women. At the same time, there was a rapid growth of migratory labor for extended periods among peasant men. In some districts, in fact, the extent of such male migratory labor was so great that women effectively headed the majority of households in a village. Yet despite such pressures for change, the patriarchal structure of the family remained pervasive in some form at all levels of society.

Discussions in the press, in the *zemstva*, and in the Duma after 1906, as well as at various conferences of women and of professional organizations throughout the late imperial period, had only a belated and modest effect on the legal arrangements of families at this time. Such public discussions nonetheless helped prepare the ground for major changes in women's family lives that would come about with the new family laws passed first by the Provisional Government after the February Revolution in 1917 and then by the Bolshevik government after the October Revolution.

PRINCESS DASHKOVA'S DOWRY

Before the 1917 Revolution (as indeed after), the overwhelming majority of Russian women expected to become wives and mothers; for most women, material support for their adult lives began with marriage portions provided by their fathers or occasionally by mothers or other relatives. Generous dowries given to young noblewomen not only cemented unions with young noblemen, solidifying families' positions in the social order, but also provided support for noblewomen both during marriage and, if necessary, in widowhood. Women of other social groups likewise were expected to bring some property into their new families. In the course of the eighteenth century noblewomen acquired the right to manage their own property, including their dowries, even during marriage, and this right eventually became generalized in imperial Russian law.

Dowries not only marked the occasion of betrothal and marriage, but also provided a young woman with valuable and useful goods to begin her wedded life. The following document recorded the portion the rich and generous Roman Larionovich Vorontsov settled on his daughter Ekaterina when she married Prince Mikhail Ivanovich Dashkov, thus taking on the name by which she is better known in history, Ekaterina Romanovna Dashkova (1743–1810). The large number of signatories to the document is an indication of the public significance of marriage, especially among the nobility. Dashkova's dowry, worth 22,917 rubles in 1759, marks her as a member of the aristocratic elite. An early favorite of Catherine II, and a participant in the events that brought Catherine to power, Dashkova was the director of the St. Petersburg Academy of Sciences and the only woman ever appointed president of the Russian Academy of Sciences.

"AGREEMENT BY COUNT ROMAN VORONTSOV IN GIVING HIS DAUGHTER EKATERINA ROMANOVNA IN MARRIAGE TO PRINCE DASHKOV. 12 FEBRUARY 1759"

On the twelfth day of February of the year one thousand seven hundred and fifty nine, I, lieutenant general and gentleman-in-waiting cavalier Roman Vorontsov, son of Larion, have agreed to give my daughter, the maiden Ekaterina Romanovna, in marriage to second lieutenant Prince Mikhail Dashkov, son of Ivan, of the Palace Guard of the Preobrazhenskii Regiment, and to my daughter I have given as a dowry the following things of value: diamond earrings valued at five hundred rubles; a diamond ring valued at one thousand rubles; a string of large pearls valued at nine hundred rubles; a green emerald ring valued at one hundred rubles; two rings with a portrait and cluster of diamonds valued at two hundred rubles; a diamond pendant valued at one thousand rubles; a wedding robe valued at three hundred rubles; a bright brocaded *samara*[2] dress valued at four hundred rubles; a brocaded, white and gold robe valued at one hundred and seventy rubles; hoopskirts: one of light-blue brocade[3] valued at two hundred and fifty rubles, one of white brocade valued at two hundred [rubles], one white and gold valued at two hundred [rubles], one of white damask with appliqués and flowers valued at one hundred and fifty rubles, one of purple moiré with appliqués valued at one hundred and fifty [rubles], one of brocaded chamois with light-blue flowers valued at one hundred and thirty-five rubles, one of scarlet lustrine with silk lacework valued at ninety rubles, one of light-blue lustrine valued at seventy-five rubles, one of scarlet satin with appliqués valued at eighty-five rubles, one of white satin with appliqués valued at eighty-five rubles, one of wavy taffeta with appliqués valued at sixty rubles, one of striped taffeta with appliqués valued at fifty rubles, one of scarlet taffeta with appliqués valued at forty rubles, one of scarlet satin with quilting valued at fifty rubles; women's jackets: one of scarlet lustrine valued at sixty rubles, one of scarlet satin valued at twenty-five rubles; a woman's jacket with a white satin skirt valued at forty rubles; underskirts: one white embroidered with gold and flowers valued at forty rubles, one of white *gros de Tour* satin embroidered with silk valued at thirty rubles, one of scarlet satin smocked with silver netting valued at thirty rubles, one of satin with silver netting valued at twenty-five rubles; a brocaded cape with fox fur lining trimmed with ermine valued at two hundred and seventy rubles; a silver brocade cloak with ermine valued at one hundred and twenty rubles; a white patterned wool skirt valued at thirty rubles; two dozen shoes valued at thirty rubles; linens: three dozen Holland chemises valued at four hundred rubles, two dozen men's Holland undershirts valued at two hundred rubles, two tablecloths of patterned Chinese silk and four dozen napkins valued at two hundred and fifty rubles, eight dozen ordinary tablecloths and eight dozen napkins valued at two hundred and fifty rubles, five changes of bed linen valued at five hundred rubles, twelve Holland kerchiefs valued at twenty rubles, six Holland scarves and a dozen silk stockings valued at forty-eight rubles, a dozen cotton stockings valued at thirty rubles, two cotton hoopskirts with underskirts valued at sixty rubles; four cotton women's jackets valued at twenty rubles; four muslin undergarments valued at forty rubles; three dozen muslin kerchiefs valued at one hundred and forty rubles; nine pairs of embroidered muslin cuffs valued at one hundred and fifty rubles; six evening bonnets valued at one hundred and sixty rubles; four dozen pocket handkerchiefs valued at one hundred and seventy rubles; one dozen silk kerchiefs valued at twenty-four rubles; four dozen washcloths valued at fifteen rubles; a fine *samara* outfit valued at three hundred rubles; seven lace bonnets valued at one hundred and forty rubles; a lace bonnet for bed valued at sixty rubles; a nightcap trimmed with lace valued at forty rubles; six pairs of men's lace cuffs valued at two hundred rubles; four pairs of women's cuffs valued at three hundred and fifty rubles; neckerchiefs with lace valued at twenty rubles; one-and-a-half dozen men's embroidered cuffs, valued at one hundred and ten rubles; a bed upholstered with raspberry red moiré and with gold galloons valued at one thousand rubles; bedding with lace detailing valued at five hundred rubles; a white satin blanket valued at fifty rubles; a light-blue satin blanket valued at fifty rubles; a mirror with silver fittings valued at one hundred and seventy rubles; various ribbons valued at fifty rubles; two whalebone skirts valued at forty rubles; a man's bathrobe valued at seventy rubles; twelve fans valued at two hundred rubles; a gold snuffbox valued at two hundred rubles. The total value of the dowry comes to twelve thousand, nine hundred and seventeen rubles along with money to the amount of ten thousand rubles toward the purchase of villages, with the whole of the dowry and money amounting to twenty-two thousand, nine hundred and seventeen rubles.

With this marriage contract Lieutenant-General and Gentleman-in-Waiting and Cavalier Roman Vorontsov, son of Larion, has given his above-named daughter in marriage to Second Lieutenant Prince Mikhail Dashkov, son of Ivan, of the Palace Guard of the Preobrazhenskii Regiment, and with her has given a dowry of a total value of twenty-two thousand, nine hundred and seventeen rubles and has affixed his hand. To this agreement Captain Fedor Bibikov, son of Ivan, was a witness and has affixed his hand. [There follows the names and ranks of fifteen other men, all belonging to the elite Palace Guard of the Semenovskii Regiment and some belonging to prominent and powerful noble families.] The agreement was written by the scribe Petr Ivanov of the St. Petersburg Registry of Deeds. Concluded by order of Secretary Ivan Iazykov on the 12th day of February of the year 1759. This agreement has been recorded in the St. Petersburg Registry of Deeds. For the [cost of] registration, twenty-two rubles, ninety-two kopecks. For notarization, twenty [kopecks?] per page; twenty for transfer; eleven and three-fourths kopecks were received by the supervisor Mikhail Avramov. I, Prince Mikhail Dashkov, ascertained that all is correct in this agreement.

Source: "Sgovornaia grafa Romana Larionovicha Vorontsova, o sgovore docheri svoei Ekateriny Romanovny za kniazia Dashkova, 12 fevralia 1759 goda" ["Agreement by Count Roman Vorontsov in giving his daughter Ekaterina Romanovna in marriage to Prince Dashkov, 12 February 1759"], in Shchukin, vol. IX. Excerpted from pp. 53–55.

Translated by Thomas Newlin.

SYNOD DECREE ON UNDERAGE MARRIAGES

The minimum ages of marriage prescribed by the Russian Orthodox Church in the eighteenth century were twelve for girls and fourteen for boys. The Synod decree of December that follows was based on a Senate[4] decree of the same month. The two decrees demonstrate the concern of both the government and the Church that peasants and priests were violating even these limits to serve their own ends. Specifically, the Synod decree indicates that some male heads of peasant households, who enjoyed great control over all areas of their families' lives, were choosing to marry their sons in childhood to young adult women. The primary object of such marriages was to recruit, as early as possible, additional adult workers for the peasant household; these young women, however, also became subject to sexual abuse by their fathers-in-law, leading predictably to conflict-laden domestic situations. This practice, known as snokhachestvo, was quite common.

"SYNOD DECREE ON UNDERAGE MARRIAGES, DECEMBER 1756."

The decree of Her Imperial Highness, the autocrat of all Russia, from the Holy Governing Synod to the Synod member the Most Holy Dmitrii, Bishop of Riazan and Murom, concerning the text [here] revealed, conveyed to the Holy Governing Synod from the Governing Senate:

Among the state peasants[5] an undesirable custom is in widespread use, in that they marry their underage sons at eight, ten, and twelve years old. And they choose as their brides maidens aged twenty and older, with whom, in many cases, the fathers-in-law fall into incest.[6] This behavior, which is as much in opposition to the law as it is a cause of the disintegration of the peasants' families, happens because of nothing more than the priests' avarice. At the extreme, some of these blood-minglers are sentenced to death, and their houses broken up, as a result of which the remaining peasants are wrongfully required to assume an extra burden in taxes,[7] as well as for the support of their archpriests and priests. By grabbing money and other things greatly in excess of their authorized fees,[8] they [the priests] act to oppress the peasants.

According to Her Imperial Highness's decree, the Holy Governing Synod has ordered all members of the Synod, all dioceses and most holy hierarchs—and where there is no such person, the spiritual consistory—to send a decree in which they will write what the Holy Governing Synod wants and without a doubt expects, just as in all the dioceses the most holy hierarchs must affirm it to the spiritual leaders. Without fail they should observe those entering matrimony, that they be of age for such a ceremony as authorized in the holy regulations, and the rest of the pairing be in order for this sacrament, in terms of the laws and the spiritual regulations of the leaders. The pastors especially should go forth to speak most strongly about that which is required, although it will be best of all in those circumstances for those who are most holy hierarchs and spiritual leaders to exercise caution and themselves deliver most strongly the affirmation and instructions, so that before the performance of the marriage ceremony, all those [to be married], as specified and legislated by the holy regulations, will without fail have been observed and warned of that which applies to the meaning of the Governing Senate's text given above.

As regards archpriests and priests taking money from the state peasants before the marriage ceremony as a form of oppression, however, no such requests from anyone have been investigated in the Holy Synod and there is no news of such. On this topic, nonetheless, the most holy hierarchs should also affirm most strongly to whomever it concerns that any fees taken in excess of those authorized for the performing of the marriage ceremony [in whatever form these are tendered][9] may absolutely be confiscated.

The Synod member the Most Holy Dmitrii, Bishop of Riazan and Murom, is ordered to implement that which is written above, according to Her Imperial Highness's decree, and the same in other places where the decrees of the Holy Synod are sent.

Signatures: Issued under the seal of Secretary Andrei Sorokin and Mikhail Ostolopov. Corrected by Chancellor Ilarion Nedlikov, 14 January 1757, and later recorded in the register sent by the Executorial Registering Offices.

Source: RGIA, f. 796, op. 37, d. 533, ll. 4–5 ob.

Translated by Carolyn J. Pouncy.

FROM 1797, A JOURNAL

Varvara Tatishcheva

Varvara Aleksandrovna Tatishcheva's journal of her marriage to Fedor Vasilevich Tatishchev captures the rhythm of a noble family's life, particularly its peregrinations between the capital and the country home. Covering the years 1803–1823 (from her marriage to her death), Tatishcheva's daybook also provides documentation of one family's experience during the years of the Napoleonic Wars (1807, 1812–1815). This small daybook, bearing the title, "From 1797," was found between two much larger documents in a large folder in the Tatishchev family archives. Early entries in the book list expenses, but in 1803 Tatishcheva began to note the major events of family life: births, deaths, and visits. While relatives make up the majority of the visitors, Fedor Vasilevich often seems no less a visitor in his own home. Upon Tatishcheva's death in 1823, her son continued the chronicle of family events. The frequent and long absences of Tatishcheva's husband were common among noblemen in state service; during such absences their wives often managed their estate.

DAYBOOK OF VARVARA A. TATISHCHEVA

1803, on the 6th of [month illegible] was our wedding. We married in the afternoon.

1804, the 4th of April. At 2:20 in the morning daughter Agrafena was born at Peleshko.[10]

[1805], the 7th of July. A daughter was stillborn.

1806. At 1 o'clock in the morning on the 23rd of February daughter Agrafena passed away. Fedor Vasilevich [was not here?].

1805. Brother Spiridon Vasilevich passed away on February [1] at five o'clock in Petersburg. He was 30 years old.

1803, May 6. [*sic*] Brother Ivan Vasilevich passed away at twenty-six in Petersburg.

1807, 29 June. I miscarried a girl of four and a half months.

1807, May 10. Uncle Ivan Vasilevich was killed in the navy.

1808, May 30. On Saturday at 7:30 daughter Varvara was born in Petersburg on Mokhovaia [street] at the Zamiatins'.

1809, August 12. Son Nikolai was born at Peleshko on Thursday at ten o'clock in the morning.

He died in 1810 on August 30, a Wednesday, in the afternoon. He was sick for only ten days.

1811. Daughter Agrafena was born on March 7, on Tuesday, at twelve o'clock at Peleshko. Martianova was her godmother.

1812. On August 20 Fedor Vasilevich was selected for service in the civilian militia. He spent five weeks in Petersburg, then on September 20 participated in a campaign near Polotsk[11] on Sept. 10.

28 September I delivered son Spiridon on Saturday at eight o'clock in Fedor Vasilevich's absence. Iurii Vasilevich and Paraskovia Ivanovna were his godparents.

6–7 October there was an attack and they took the fortress. He [We assume Fedor Vasilevich is meant here.—eds.] was in Peleshko on leave from 23 November until he left again for the regiment on 7 December.

1814. December 28 Fedor Vasilevich left Danzig for Kiev [Kiel may be meant here.—eds.], on campaign with the prisoners of war.

1813. 28 [May] there was a battle near Danzig. It continued for ten hours.

21 August he was in a battle at the taking of Lanfori.[12]

21 September. [Mentions another city, illegible, taken in battle] For the battle of 28 May he received an award.

1814. Fedor Vasilevich returned from campaign 5 May and arrived from Taraskovich with brother Petr Aleksandrovich. 9 June he left for Petersburg for good with his unit.

For the Polotsk battle Fedor Vasilevich received the Cross of [St.] Vladimir, of the fourth class with the bunting and the medal on the light-blue ribbon.[13] On the 26th Fedor Vasilevich came back from the service to Peleshko for good. He spent two years in the civilian militia.

1815. May 2nd at four o'clock in the afternoon son Fedor was born at Peleshko. Iurii Vasilevich and our eldest daughter Varvara were his godparents. He died the same year on August 30 at twelve o'clock in the afternoon. He was sick with a severe cough.

1816, January 2. The children and I were in Petersburg. We returned safely on 5 March of the same year. We bought a forte-piano for Varinka [familiar form for Varvara]. We paid 600. We hired a Frenchwoman to be with our son beginning on the 20th of March at a cost of 1200 rubles per year. Madame de Jarbé, the Frenchwoman, set off May 15.

1816, November 5. A daughter was stillborn at four o'clock in the morning, and I was seriously ill with fever and with [the afterbirth] the day after my labor and [I bled so].

1817. From the first days of June the weather was absolutely awful and cold.

1818, 4 January. The children and I arrived in Petersburg. We hired a Mamzel [Mademoiselle] on 3 March. We returned safely from Petersburg on 6 March. On 10 March we [tuned the forte-piano].

April 15. We heard thunder and there was lightning and snow was still falling and it was cold. The lengthy spring storm was severe and continued for three hours.

1818, 24 June. My brother Petr Aleksandrovich passed away. He was thirty-two years old.

26 August of the same year. I delivered a stillborn girl.

1819. To the 2nd of January winter still hadn't come. There was warm weather, without snow or rain. Everyone went about on wheels.[14]

January 7. Fedor Vasilevich and I went alone to Petersburg. I passed two weeks and returned on the 23rd to Peleshko and he stayed to live in the city a while longer.

23 March. He returned safely from Petersburg. On the 26th we both went to [Riga] and returned home on the 27th.

April 16. My portrait and that of Fedor Vasilevich and the three children was painted by the artist Ivan Aleksandrovich Aleksandrov. 1819. Varinka's portrait was drawn at 11, Grushinka's [familiar form for Agrafena] at 9, and Spiridon's at 7.

June 5, in Veshno, three *versts* from us, a threshing [barn] burned from a strong storm.

June 31[sic]. Because of an injury, I miscarried a child of three months.

True winter set in on 22 October. It brought cruel frosts, down to 33 degrees [below zero Celsius, or 22 degrees below zero Fahrenheit]. I went to Nikandrovo on 15 December.

1820, 1 January. Fedor Vasilevich went to Petersburg. He arrived home in February, on the 20th.

Madame Koval entered our household. She arrived from Petersburg on 29 February.

The children started to study the forte-piano. On 20 March we left for Petersburg.

1820, December 2. We returned safely.

1821, March 12. Mr. [Sbegard] taught the children to dance. He brought Madame LeBon, a Frenchwoman, with him. Spiridon's teacher, Mr. Shtemberkh, is a German who plays three instruments. They started classes in Petersburg on the 1st of March.

They elected Fedor Vasilevich to the Gdov[15] Assembly of the Nobility for this year. He arrived from Petersburg on 15 January and in a few days he was in Gdov. Varinka began to study on 20 March.

30 August of the same year, Madame LeBon went to Petersburg because of an illness. The new mamzel, DeCalame, came to us. In addition to French, she knows history, geography, and arithmetic. She teaches lessons in drawing, music, singing, carving, and all sorts of handiwork for 1500 rubles. They started classes 2 September.

November 20. Winter still hasn't started. Fedor Vasilevich traveled on the slippery, foul road. Then he left for Gdov for the assembly, then to Petersburg for extremely important [business].

4 December. He still hasn't returned and winter hasn't arrived yet. It's raining like October.

[25] December. Before Christmas, Fedor Vasilevich arrived from Petersburg for a little while. Winter started only on Christmas itself and continued to be the real thing. The frosts are cruel.

1822

7 January. The day after Epiphany. Fedor Vasilevich left again for Petersburg. On Saturday, the 10th of the same month, I wrote via Egorka Nikolskii. I wrote more letters on the 14th via Penteshka Ozerskii and again on the 18th I wrote via Vaska Otekin. On the 18th I received two letters from Fedor Vasilevich from Petersburg. I wrote again on the 19th via Obka Bobrovskii.

20 April. The children went to the *bania*, but I bathed in the tub.

22. I received a letter from Fedor Vasilevich from Gdov. On the 24th I wrote him in Petersburg.

24. Brothers S. V., D. V., and N. V. and all their children and governesses were here and on the 26th we went together to brother Iu. V. and then to Akerina's. We returned on the 28th.

30. Fedor Vasilevich returned from Petersburg through the cities of Narva[16] and Gdov.

From 1 May began the raise in the salary for our mamzel[s?] to 2000 per year.

20 May. Varinka fell ill, was lightheaded and nauseous.

27. The whole family went for a ride. On the way home, Grushinka fell ill with a fever and a cold and she lay in bed for an entire day.

30. Fedor Vasilevich set off for Petersburg on post horses. Having returned, they saw the procession of the tsar and all his entourage.

10 June. He returned from Petersburg, having been very ill there and upon arrival he lay with fever and sharp pain for an entire day.

17 June. Having gone for a ride, I took fright and fell from the coach, from the wagonette. I am two months pregnant and I hurt the back of my head.

20 June. We were all in the *bania*.

21. The doctor in Shemanovo in Gdov district let Vaniushka's blood without any problems. The next day his arm healed.

22 June. [We had a crowd] at two o'clock in the afternoon and Grushinka received gifts for her name day.[17]

1 July. [Another crowd and lilacs were given as gifts.] The great heat continues.

5 [July] Uncle Sergei Aleksandrovich arrived and stayed in the [barn]. He left on the 9th.

26th of the same month, my Friend, Fedor Vasilevich, left for Petersburg. I received a letter from Varvara Andreevna and her husband, Konkov, delivered by their man Ignatii.

2 August. In the night I fell desperately ill and lost a horrible amount of blood and, at six o'clock, miscarried a son of three months. I was sick for a long time and Kriger was here from afar twice. All this assistance took place in the absence of Fedor Vasilevich.

8 August. Fedor Vasilevich found me ill upon his return from Petersburg.

29th of the same month. He went to the city of Gdov for the Assembly of the Nobility. On 3 September he returned home.

20 September. Selivanov and his wife arrived and stayed for three days.

26. Sent a messenger to Zkliuka with a letter for sister Olga Vasilevna.

11 September. Brother Nikolai Semenovich passed away in Petersburg.

8 October. Sister A. V. arrived with A. Al. They stayed until the 14th.

28 October. It's snowing but the weather is still somewhat warm. We all went to the *bania*. I rode in a four-horse coach lit with lanterns, behind the wives in [another] coach.

[By a different hand, most likely that of Tatishcheva's son Spiridon]

1823. 15 February at three o'clock in the afternoon, Maminka [familiar term for Mama] passed away from fever and a stroke. She will be buried on Thursday in Petersburg. Maminka was thirty-seven.

Source: LOII, f. 131. 10a, No. XCVII, packet III.

Translated by Robin Bisha.

MEMOIRS

GLAFIRA RZHEVSKAIA

The following four selections illustrate relationships between mothers and daughters. Although they demonstrate some of the types of relationships and feelings that could develop between mothers and daughters, they obviously do not represent the rich range of relationships and feelings—positive as well as negative—that could and did exist in different families. All four selections, moreover, concern women of the nobility. They therefore reflect the experiences of only a small part of the Russian population. The selections by Aleksandra Efimenko and A. S. Saburova later in this chapter provide some insight into mother-daughter relations among the peasantry, at least as viewed by outsiders.

While the selections are not meant to suggest that negative relationships predominated between mothers and daughters, they do reveal some of the difficulties that could arise in a relationship where mothers were expected to exercise authority over their daughters, to oversee their preparation for adult life, and, often, to play a prominent role in arranging their marriages. Indeed, much of the enmity between mother and daughter seen in the selection we include by Ekaterina Dashkova stemmed from the unsuccessful marriage that Dashkova arranged for her daughter.

The writings of Glafira Ivanovna Rzhevskaia (née Alymova) (1759?–1826) illustrate some of these difficulties. Rzhevskaia, born in the eighteenth century and a graduate of the first class of the Society for the Education of Young Ladies of the Nobility (or Smolnyi Institute, founded in 1764), reveals in her autobiography the strain women might feel from numerous pregnancies. This excerpt from the autobiography focuses on her mother's extreme reaction to Rzhevskaia's birth. It also reveals the distance in relationships with family that many students of the Smolnyi and other women's institutes experienced. Girls entered these boarding schools at a very young age and remained until age eighteen. During this time, as a rule, they could see their parents and other family members only during brief vacations and Sunday parental visits.

_____

My entry into this world was not met with joy. A child born at her father's death, I began life with sinister omens of the wretched fate that awaited me. My distraught mother could not bear the presence of her poor nineteenth child and removed my cradle from her sight, and a father's tenderness could not answer my first cries. It was forbidden to divulge the fact of my birth, a sorrowful occasion. A kind nun took me under her protection and was my godmother. I was baptized as if by stealth. After a year had passed they persuaded my mother, though with difficulty, to have a look at me. She hugged me in the presence of relatives and friends who had gathered for this important occasion. The day when that event had taken place was one of sorrow and tears. My father had already blessed me before my birth and bequeathed me my name. This circumstance often consoled me in my sad orphaned state. I was constantly reminded of my mother's dislike of me. While I lived near her I had not noticed it at all and had not suffered from it; on the contrary, though I was a child I could see that the strictness with which she treated my brothers and sisters did not include me; I did not understand the reasons for it. I was not afraid of my mother, but I tried to please her in every way. She caressed me no more than the other children but smiled at me more often, always with tears in her eyes. When, at the age of seven, I was separated from her and was placed in the Smolnyi convent, I started to be aggrieved by everything I had had occasion to hear up until then. My sensibility developed, seeing the caresses with which my friends' parents showered them. Out of fifty girls I was almost the only one who had not experienced parental tenderness. A kind of adoration that my person aroused in all those around me could not re-place the feeling that was lacking for my happiness. I had reason to doubt my mother's love for me. Finally, after seven years, the long awaited meeting with her took place. In one moment her kindness effaced all the past impressions and her trust opened before me a touching image of virtue struggling with adversity. My mother's grief strengthened even more my attachment to her; I trembled at the sight of sufferings that distorted her noble features. Her grave demeanor evoked a feeling of respect and gave weight to her speeches, from which I learnt, with weightiness, about the sacred obligations of spouses, parents, and children. Her whole life was an example of the most perfect adherence to the principles of the Gospels. Her counsels struck a deep root in my heart. Looking at her, listen-ing to her, I did not cease to weep for my wretched fate that for so long had kept us apart and was soon to separate us forever. It was my misfortune to lose her soon afterward.

My feelings toward my mother, feeble at the beginning and almost phantom-like toward the end, had been artificially nurtured by me. Without encourage-ment, they vanished within three months.

Source: Glafira Ivanovna Rzhevskaia, "Pamiatnyia zapiski Glafiry Ivanovny Rzhevskoi," *Russkii arkhiv* ["Memorial Notes of Glafira Ivanovna Rzhevskaia," in *Russian Archive*], vol. IX (1871), pp. 2–3.

Translated by Ruth Sobel.

LETTER TO HER MOTHER

Maria Ivankova

We have already seen that fathers were often distant from their families, in particular from their young daughters; mothers, however, often remained important sources of emotional support or upheaval during women's married lives. While some mothers were idealized in memoirs, documentary sources reveal that the mother-daughter relationship was often problematic. In a letter dated 23 September 1749, Maria Ivankova expresses distress about her unhappy marriage in terms that reveal her dependence on her mother for emotional support and her fear that she will not receive it.

Social conventions discouraged women from seeking support from anyone outside their family circle. Whereas many women corresponded with and maintained visiting relationships with relatives and friends, only in the late nineteenth century would married women begin to escape customs that made it difficult for them to discuss their marital problems with others. After the Great Reforms (1861–1874), as women began to organize into study groups and philanthropic circles, they found camaraderie with other women like themselves. Faster forms of transportation and communication were developed, and communication with family members helped to ease the isolation of the married woman on distant rural estates who, as we saw with Tatishcheva, often spent months without other adult company.

My dear madam mother Daria Ivanovna I wish you with all my heart dear madam many years of health and all manner of prosperity.

As for me and the children if you kindly do not mind recalling as of this letter I by the Lord's will for all of my unstintingly grievous and execrable sorrows and intermittent blindness am still alive. I received your letter for which I humbly thank you and with regard to which I most humbly beseech you not to deprive me of your parental correspondence that I always sincerely hope to receive. But most of all I most humbly and servilely beg you my dear madam light of my eyes not to withhold from me your parental blessing and not to forget me in your prayers. As to why I am not writing to you in my own hand truly I am not able to see well enough not only to write but to read either, and for my needs the girls have to lead me out blindfolded.[18]

Because of my various eye ailments I've been sitting inside with the windows shut for almost three months and not only for these three months but for more than three years I've barely been able to see and during the whole thirteen years since I got married I have constantly suffered from intermittent blindness and now am almost completely blind and all this because of my tears of unceasing grief because of your disapproval and my husband's cruelty. What's more he's a scoundrel he knocked my eyes out and cut them out [too] and smashed my whole head to which not only God himself but many others are my witness. Some ten doctors and physicians have treated me over the years mentioned above but it didn't help at all and they say that nothing will help in the future either. I cry every day now that's what I use my eyes for. Because of the unbearability and cruelty of my husband and his letters to me and your disapproval toward me my eyes get worse and worse and certainly no one can cure them.

As for writing that you wish me a long life and pray to God for it I truly do not wish for life or for health either and most humbly and servilely beseech you my dear madam mother not to ask God's mercy about this but rather to pray for me as a mother that I not go blind and that my bitter and unhappy life soon end. My life is so miserable that it would be better were God to grant me death rather than to have such a detestable foul and loathsome existence. Please my dear mother light of my eyes beseech the Lord most zealously and as a mother to bring my life to a Christian end as soon as possible.

As for my children the Lord will not deny them his gracious mercy. At this point of course I don't desire villages or anything else in the world [for them] and as I wrote to you before if you see fit to allow a divorce out of love for my children that's fine if you don't see fit then so be it.

I behaved badly toward you before because of my husband's unbearable cruelty toward me but now I'm not that way at all and don't want to be in the future and am truly filled with contrition and have lost my eyesight. As to why I didn't write to you before and didn't tell you about my husband's cruel behavior toward me I didn't want to cause a big quarrel between you or expose him rather I wanted to make things better and make him love me but instead I just made things worse for myself. It's impossible to recount everything about him if the Lord allows me to see you face to face [lit., "to see your eyes"] I will tell you everything about myself and the letters written in his hand will bear witness for me. At the moment it's impossible for me to come see you in Moscow because of my eyes. As soon as the Lord makes me a little better and it's possible I'll come see you.

The whole [crop from the] orchard has been sold only not all the money has been received as soon as I get it I'll bring it to you myself. There truly isn't any hay or straw at Vasilevo we'll have to buy it all ourselves I wouldn't begrudge you such a trifle. There isn't any of the old flax left either and the new flax still isn't ready to harvest only the flax at Vasilevo is very poor please don't be angry about it or attribute it to niggardliness. I'm sending you one hundred skeins of their flax they really are spinning it here and I'm sending a small crock of salted fish as well. We had twenty nets out in both ponds for two whole days and all we caught is what's in the crock and we even topped that off with loaches from the bottom [of the pond]. You don't have to believe me your peasants will all be my witness they all know that I sent men out to fish. Maybe since I'm blind they are deceiving me. As for ordering your elders to sow the rye on time and not to leave any ground fallow if in earlier times I was ready to be of service now truly I can't see anything or run things even in the house. The children sit all day and night without anything to eat I swear by God. All my children dear madam most humbly and servilely bow down to you and beg for your continued charity.

Please my dear madam mother light of my eyes show your most exalted divine and maternal mercy toward me forgive me and pardon me for all my bad behavior and rudeness toward you. God takes back sinners and forgives them when they repent whereas you are my own parent and it is in your power to grant me maternal forgiveness as one borne by you and pardon me and bestow on me your maternal blessing not just in spoken form but in all your letters you haven't sent me any parental blessing as the Lord himself knows I cried my eyes out over this more than anything please my dear madam mother light of my eyes show me mercy as Christ did with sinners please in all your letters grant me your gracious parental blessing so that in reading your letters I have the tender joy of hearing your gracious parental blessing. Because of my husband I was deprived of your parental blessing may God grant that his soul in the future likewise be denied God's mercy and heavenly kingdom whereas truly inasmuch as I can and until my dying day I will make every effort to secure your freedom if I don't go blind or if it doesn't happen by itself.

Unstintingly trusting in your generosity I remain dear madam mother your most humble daughter and servant Maria Ivankova and in requesting your parental blessing servilely bow down to you.

23rd day of September
of the year 1749
from the village of Kotlovo

Source: "Pis'mo M. Ivankovoi k materi, 23 sentiabria 1749 goda" ["Letter from M. Ivankova to her mother, September 23, 1749"], in Shchukin, vol. X. Excerpted from pp. 319–21.

Translated by Thomas Newlin.

LETTER TO HER DAUGHTER

EKATERINA DASHKOVA

In the eighteenth and nineteenth centuries many Russian women eagerly awaited motherhood. Ekaterina Dashkova, according to available sources, was no exception: like other elite women of the late eighteenth century, she saw motherhood as a duty to God and society that should also bring joy to both mother and child. However, her relationships with both her son and daughter proved difficult. In this letter to her daughter Anastasiia

*Mikhailovna (1760 or 1761–1830 or 1831, m. Shcherbina), she discusses arrangements
for her deceased son's illegitimate children. As often occurred in Dashkova's relations with
her daughter, she was disapproving of the younger woman's intentions and behavior. This
short letter gives the reader a taste of the bitter flavor of Dashkova's pen.*

*Dashkova's letter, written sometime in 1807 or 1808, also highlights several impor-
tant aspects of imperial Russian law. Until the late nineteenth century, imperial law denied any legal rights to illegitimate children and did not allow their adoption except by
special consent of the emperor. Since Dashkova's son had no legitimate children, his estate eventually passed to a male cousin (males excluded females in collateral lines), after
deduction of the share due his widow. While the inheritance was being sorted out, however, Dashkova was seeking to have trustees appointed who could manage and protect
her late son's estate and arrange for the payment of his very substantial debts.*

In light of all the business entrusted to him, I will be very glad if Nikolai
Nikolaevich Novosiltsev[19] were to oversee the trusteeship of the estate of my unfortunate late son; he is fair-minded, and that way the creditors will be satisfied
despite your dissolute extravagance. If Fedor Ivanovich Kiselev refuses to be the
trustee, then Pavel Aleksandrovich Rakhmanov[20] alone will do. For the state is
always duty-bound to oversee trusteeships; such a guarantee of peace of mind is
all the more essential since you, by virtue of your depraved behavior, warrant no
trust whatsoever. I solemnly repeat that my son did not want the impossible: i.e.,
to adopt illegitimate children begotten during the lifetime of his still-living wife.
Rather he wanted them to become upstanding tradespersons of middling means,
which was all he could provide them with given his sizeable debts. He himself
saw fit to inform me of this. I likewise solemnly aver that he never intended to
entrust them to you, and during his final illness requested that his friend take
them. You boast that you'll petition the Emperor to bend the law and subvert
the sacrament of wedlock sanctified by the Holy Writ,[21] and that to satisfy your
whim and conceit he will permit you to adopt these illegitimate children while
the wife is still alive. This is a fantasy truly worthy of your deluded state of mind.
You promise that you will pass on your estate to them, even while your estate
and your ill-starred inheritance are laden with debts; you want to tend to their
upbringing, yet you ruin them, tearing them away from their mother, who alone
has a natural and legal right to them. Then in the first fit of rage that comes over
you you'll throw them out the window. I opened the way to you for a reconciliation of sorts, but you forsook everything that the dictates of my heart—common sense, humanity, and Christianity—offered up to you. Later on I found out
that after you joined the imperial family in mourning, you took it into your head
that you were the Empress, and in the church where the body of your unfortunate brother (which should have awoken only feelings of sorrow on your part)
lay before you, summoned the chief of police and gave him most unseemly orders and shouted and swore that my niece Norova and my friend Martha Ro-

manovna [Wilmot][22] hadn't rendered the last Christian rites. Your hysterical voice shook the whole church, and everyone was aghast at this ungodly frenzy of inhumanity and viciousness and at your intent to abuse your mother within everyone's hearing; all of Moscow now speaks your name with revulsion. I have forgiven you seven times—for things only an angel of mercy could forgive. Recall how you came to me in the village at night, not wanting to see me, gathered together my peasants, and after a prayer service (which most assuredly was not to God's liking) passed out money to them and said bad things about me and about my friend, who alone consoles an abandoned mother in her sorrow and grief. This rebellion that you tried to instigate; the orders you gave my peasants; and the various slanders against me that you tried in vain to encourage in Moscow, prove that the time has come for me to take measures to protect myself from you. In hopes of vexing me and strengthening your own hand, you favor and surround yourself with all those members of the family whose conduct I do not approve, and abuse and despise all those who love me. This whole ungodly campaign against me vindicates me before God and society. If you do not leave Moscow within a fixed period of time, I will resort to my last legal option, incarceration,[23] in order to save you from carrying out any further criminal or evil designs and to protect myself and my home. I will remind you once more as a mother who has lived in sorrow into old age and who has been loath to mete out punishment, that following the dictates of my conscience I find it necessary and just to put you in prison, lest you cause another disgraceful scene such as you caused in the church, lest you subvert my peasants, and lest your malice fell innocent victims.

Source: "Kopiia s pis'ma kn. E. R. Dashkovoi k docheri" ["Copy of a letter from E. R. Dashkova to her daughter"], in Shchukin, vol. IX. Excerpted from pp. 66–67.

Translated by Thomas Newlin.

DIARY OF A YOUNG NOBLEWOMAN, ON HER MOTHER

If parents among the nobility initially had resisted the pressures exerted by Peter I to send their daughters abroad to be educated, by the mid-nineteenth century this practice was not uncommon among the noble elite. This entry from an unidentified young noblewoman's diary of her life in Geneva, Switzerland, in the 1860s reveals both her deep emotional attachment to her mother and the sentimental mode of expression of the time. By the 1870s a number of Russian women circumvented tsarist restrictions on higher education for women by studying at the University of Zurich. Many of these women were drawn into radical politics while in Zurich and engaged in revolutionary activities upon their return to Russia.

20 January 1865 Geneva. Countryside from Berthet to Florissant[24]

I am sixteen years old today. I feel very emotional: my tears flow without my knowing why. Each [of my friends] gave me a little souvenir and as a group some books, with English ones predominating. A beautiful gray silk dress from Mama; if only she were here, I should be happy. I often think: was it a good idea for Mama to have me brought up here so far from Russia? I don't like Russia that much, and I realize that leaving Switzerland would make me unhappy far from all those here. I still have five long months ahead of me, to get used to the separation. I will spend them being happy, happy as much as possible, come what may.

1 May [18]65.

We are returning from Coppet, the château of Madame de Staël.[25] My heart is boiling. What emotions I have had today. Madame de Staël!!! I have finally seen her portrait. What a grand manner! That is what I would like to be. Genius is inscribed in her eyes and what a mouth for sublime words! Happy, happy the Duchess de Broglie to have been the daughter of such a mother!

What have I just said? Shame on me! I, the daughter of my sweet, adorable, gracious mother, should envy a daughter her mother! And why? Because that mother was a woman of genius, celebrated throughout the whole world . . . I am ashamed, I blush and . . . I wish I had lived when this woman did.

3 June 65.

Mama! Mama!! Dear Mama!!! tomorrow, tomorrow, at this time, Mama will be here! I will finally see her; oh, Mama!

3 July 65. Paris, Hôtel de la Paix

I haven't opened my diary for a month. Don't I have anything to say? No, my heart was full, very full, but I couldn't sort out my thoughts. To see Mama and to leave the *pension* were two occurrences too enormous for me to grasp. For a month, I have laughed and wept, wept and laughed.

I'm now in a new phase of my life. Switzerland, Mlle. Pelet, my classmates, my professors, all that is in the past. Past, gone, past forever. I weep often, and Mama, when she sees me weeping, weeps too. The other day, in the evening, we kept embracing each other, weeping and not speaking. Mama wept softly and copiously; why was she weeping? I wanted to ask her that, but I didn't dare, I thought it was insensitive.

5 July 65

And now Mama is also sad; I sense that my little suffering as a young schoolgirl is mingled with a larger and more serious suffering. I would like to be consoled by

Mama, and I sense that it's almost she who needs to be consoled, supported. What is going on? But there is something, certainly, there is something in the air that we are breathing. Is some misfortune waiting for me? Mama, dear and poor Mama! My heart is wrung every time I look at her.

Dear God, preserve my mother for me.

9 JULY 65

Mama got a letter from Russia this evening. After reading it, she remained like a statue, cold and motionless. Then she took my head in her hands and strongly, with a type of detachment, she said to me: "Listen, pack up everything, quickly, quickly, we are leaving Paris tomorrow." I embraced Mama and quickly set to work. Mama is sleeping, but her rest is fitful. Poor Mama! I love her so ardently and deeply, and there is mixed up with that an indefinable sentiment that grips my heart, which disturbs me. I'm afraid when I think about her, and the more I think about her with devotion and ardent affection, the more this feeling of fear and even of *terror* completely overcomes me. The heart has unfathomable mysteries, Mlle. Pelet told me one day. I see that she was correct. There is something mysterious in my heart having to do with Mama. . . .

Source: "Vypiski iz dnevnika neizvestno, 1865 goda" ["Extracts from the diary of an unidentified (person), 1865"], in Shchukin, vol. X. Excerpted from pp. 396–401.

Translated by Christine Holden.

ALEKSANDRA LEVSHINA MOURNS HER SISTER

Throughout the imperial period most families included several children. With the rate of infant and child mortality approaching 50 percent, mothers gave birth frequently but saw only a few of their children live to adulthood. Perhaps the precariousness of childhood explains the strong sibling bonds found in Russian families of the eighteenth and nineteenth centuries. Aleksandra Petrovna Levshina, a favorite of Catherine II and a graduate of the Smolnyi Institute, mourns her sister in this letter to the empress, who had encouraged the schoolgirl to write to her of her feelings.[26] The letter, originally in French, was written sometime after Levshina left the Smolnyi Institute in 1776.

#XVIII (14) [n.d.]

Your Majesty!

Forgive me if, out of an excess of painful grief, I humbly present the sounds of my sorrow to Your Majesty. My poor sister has died. Nothing could save her—neither Your interventions, nor any amount of care, nor her Youth. If almighty God had heard my prayers, which I have long expressed, then it should've been I and not she who had died. Alas! What am I doing on this earth? From the time I lost Your precious friendship, I have daily reproached myself for my life. All that was needed to poison it even further was this new misfortune. Oh, most gracious Sovereign, I am very, very unhappy. But what am I doing, bringing this sad picture to a heart that is so good, so compassionate toward the forlorn? Yet, because this is so, I have a right to the solicitude that You are so kind as to express. Your Majesty, deign to remember Your good deeds and take pity on a heart that has always been devoted to You.

I remain, with the deepest respect and the most complete humility, Your Majesty's humblest and most obedient servant

A. Levshina

Source: Appollon Maikov, ed., "Perepiska imperatritsy Ekateriny II s A. P. Levshinoi," Russkii vestnik ["Correspondence of Empress Catherine II and A. P. Levshina," in Russian Messenger], vol. 247 (Nov. 1896): 344–45.

Translated by Martha Kuchar.

RECOLLECTIONS OF CHILDHOOD

Anna Volkova

The merchant district of nineteenth-century Moscow was an environment branded by the Russian intelligentsia as socially backward and culturally stultifying. It was not known for producing writers or intellectuals, especially of the female sex. In 1847 Anna Ivanovna Volkova, née Vishniakova, was born in this district to one of Moscow's most conservative merchant families. Seemingly destined for social invisibility as the daughter of a merchant, she instead overcame a scanty formal education and an early, intellectually stifling marriage to edit a pioneering feminist periodical called Women's Friend (1882–1884) and to write hundreds of articles for numerous periodicals on issues concerning women, children, education, charity, and social reform. Although Volkova was not the only merchant daughter to surmount the conservative traditions of her class and create an independent life for herself, her long career in journalism represented an unusual achievement.

Volkova wrote a memoir of growing up in her grandparents' dark, old-fashioned mansion in Moscow's merchant district, and left instructions that it be published at her expense after her death, which occurred in 1910. The memoir recounts not only her unhappy childhood but also many of the customs generally associated with traditional Russian households of the merchantry and nobility. This excerpt describes young Anna's relationships with her parents and servants. It is particularly interesting for its insights into how one girl dealt with what she, at least as an adult, regarded as an emotionally and culturally repressive family environment. Although Volkova does not say how old *she was when the events she describes in this excerpt took place, she must have been quite young, for her mother died when she was only nine years old.*

According to the stories of my elders I was very willful, mischievous in early childhood, and stubborn. At a sharp cry from elders or servants, when I was very little, I would begin to cry, to yell. In general, even later rude treatment always aroused in me an unconscious desire to express a protest by means of obstinacy and tenacity, for which I was punished—made to stand in the corner and whipped. I do not remember affectionate words or tenderness from Mother or Father.

I remember an incident when I was lying on the bed in Mother's bedroom, and she, leaning over me, placed a piece of black bread soaked in vinegar on my head and gave me spirits to sniff from a little vial. Father stood next to her and held plates with frozen cranberries, which were intended for my ears. At that time these procedures were considered completely effective for curing carbon monoxide poisoning. I remember that Nanny,[27] too, was present during these treatments.

Nanny's image remained in my memory in the most attractive form; she used to caress me, and this caress is unforgettably memorable to me. In the evenings my brother was with Mother, when she was home, but I sat with Nanny in the nursery and listened to fairy tales about Ivan Tsarevich,[28] imagining myself the Tsarevna. The fairy tale was told every day, and for the most part in one and the same manner: after the story was finished, Nanny kissed me and put me to bed. Later this beloved Nanny of mine fell ill and she was taken to Golitsyn Hospital,[29] where we, my brother and I, went to visit her. The doctor at the hospital was Tikhomirov, who treated the entire Vishniakov household, starting with members of the family and ending with the servants. Nanny fell ill during Easter Week and died in the summer, which they kept from us children, telling us that relatives had taken Nanny away to her village.

I remember the night when Nanny was in the hospital. They had a maid to sleep with us children; she lay down on the floor, so there wasn't the usual fuss with the ironing board and chairs for Nanny. I could not fall asleep for a long time—I felt very sorry for Nanny; that evening no one told me a fairy tale and no one kissed me. I buried my head in the pillow and began to weep bitterly, trying to keep my mouth pressed against the pillow more firmly, so that the maid would not hear, but she slept. Convinced that she was asleep, I raised myself on the bed, kneeled and began to pray to God for Nanny, so that she would get well soon and come to me. In the course of time I consoled myself, and stopped crying and missing Nanny, especially because I saw her in the hospital very often. New impressions replaced old ones, but the presence of our Nanny and her caresses could not disappear without a trace in my life.

At about the same time I also loved my wet nurse.[30] She often came to us from the village and brought village treats in the form of eggs, cookies made from rye flour, nuts, etc. What especially attracted me to my wet nurse was her kind face; it seemed to me that she resembled an angel. The best days for me were those when I saw my wet nurse. I threw myself on her neck and kissed her soundly, soundly. I never embraced and kissed anybody at that time except my wet nurse and Nanny. I felt something especially pleasant whenever I heard that my wet nurse had arrived from the country. I immediately ran to the maids' room and settled down on a maid's bed together with my wet nurse: there were no chairs in the room; there were two beds and a table. Over one bed was a cupboard built into the wall; the edible belongings of the servants or leftovers from the master's table, placed at their disposal, were put into this cupboard. Having jumped onto the bed, I would open the cupboard and take from there everything that seemed the best to me, to feed to my wet nurse. Understandably, later I caught it for disposing of the maids' food without permission, but every time I forgot about these punishments and, upon the next arrival of my wet nurse, again headed for the cupboard for edibles. What explains this attachment to my wet nurse—the treats that she brought from the village or the unconscious need to love somebody and experience affection— it is difficult to say. Perhaps it was both together.

[Volkova here describes a time when she and her brother set fire to a bed and almost the whole room by lighting a candle under the bed.]

Many other pranks of mine and my brother were less dangerous, and some were even completely harmless. But I held the advantage in all childhood tricks, both in initiating and implementing them, so I also bore the brunt of the punishment. Fantasies popped into my head one after another and were immediately put into effect.

Once during Easter Week I was dressed in a green-and-white checked, silk dress, and my hair was curled, but, in all probability, it was poorly combed out, so my hair got disheveled. Mother, seeing me with disheveled hair, sent me to Nanny to put pomade on my hair. Nanny was not to be found in the nursery, and I dealt with it myself. Thinking to please Mother, I took pomade with practically all my fingers and put all of it on my head; then I smoothed my hair a little and appeared before Mother. Mother was horrified at the sight of the large quantity of grease on my head, and sent me again to Nanny to wipe it off my head, but I found that it was impossible to wipe so much grease off with a towel, and it was necessary to wash my hair. Having looked for water in the nursery, I thought it convenient to head for Grandmother's room and from there upstairs, to where Uncle Nikolai lived. Upstairs was the very thing; no one was there, and on the washbasin there was lots of water standing in a white bowl. Without thinking long I stood on a chair, poured water into the basin, and washed my head with soap, but I could not wash all of it off. The grease of the pomade mixed with the soap and created something unimaginable on my head. Seeing such lack of success in my undertaking, I added more water to the basin and, kneeling on the chair, set about lowering my entire head into the basin. Streams of dirty and greasy water poured from my head and began to flow onto my dress. I seized a towel and began to wipe my dress, smearing dirt over the entire outfit. The critical moment of my escapade had arrived, and at that moment someone entered the room and caught me at the scene of the crime. Looking like this I was taken to Mother, who, infuriated, ordered Nanny to wash my head properly and to put on a new dress, and then to bring me to her. Nanny carried out all of this, and Mother made me stand in the corner and told me that the next day I would be given neither *kulich* nor *paskha*, which brought me great sorrow, because I loved both.

Source: Anna Ivanovna Volkova (née Vishniakova), "Vospominaniia detstva," *Vospominaniia, dnevnik i stati* ["Recollections of Childhood," in *Recollections, Diary, and Articles*], ed. Ch. Vetrinskii [V. E. Cheshikhin] (Nizhnii Novgorod, 1913). Excerpted from pp. 7–12.

Translated by Adele Lindenmeyr.

ON PEASANT WOMEN'S LIVES

ALEKSANDRA EFIMENKO

The following selection, by the noted ethnologist and historian Aleksandra Iakovlevna Efimenko (1848–1918), paints a grim portrait of life within the peasant patriarchal family. Efimenko spent much of the 1870s and 1880s studying the records of peasant courts and observing peasant life firsthand, initially in the northern Russian province of Arkhangel'sk and then in Ukraine. Her essays during this period, published in the collection Studies on the Life of the Folk *(Moscow, 1884), helped to shape contemporary images of the peasantry, albeit from a populist perspective. Like other populists, Efimenko believed that the moral and other values of the peasantry could serve as a basis for the renewal of Russian society generally. Her essays focused especially on peasant legal customs, which she considered to provide a model for general legal and social reform. For example, note the differences between Efimenko's discussion of peasant women's dowries and the elaboration of Dashkova's earlier in this chapter. Both Efimenko's emphasis on peasant women and her portrayal of them, however, were unusual among pre-revolutionary observers of the peasantry.*

Efimenko's essay, like the selections by Lidiia Avilova and A. S. Saburova that follow it, poses the problem of how peasant family life can be studied and understood in its own terms when much of the evidence derives from outside observers. In this regard, the three selections taken together reveal as much about the different values and attitudes of the authors as they do about family life among the Russian peasantry.

With respect to women, the Great Russian[31] extended family has incorporated almost entirely the patriarchal ideas of the *zadruga*,[32] and the nuclear family has borrowed much from the extended one. Hence, among the peasants, the position of a woman even in the nuclear family is defined to a significant degree by ideas drawn from the way of life of the extended family.[33]

What position does a woman occupy in the extended family?

If she is a young maiden, her destiny, the whole meaning of her existence, is to leave her family for another one through marriage. If she is married, that is, has been brought into one family from another, she is linked to her present family only through her husband. If he dies, she can return to her own extended family, but, of course, she can also remain in her husband's extended family, in either case to work as hard as she is able in return for support. Hence the position of a woman above all lacks stability—there are no organic ties linking her with the family—and this is one of the reasons why a woman occupies the lowest place in the extended family. Her entire meaning in such a family is to contribute as much work as possible to the household economy and to provide the extended family with new members, chiefly sons, who are its real representatives. Young girls are only tolerated as a necessary evil.

The role of women in such a family is by necessity extremely unenviable. True, a woman is a member of the extended family, in the same way that any of *her* newborn children is considered a member, just as a manservant or a maid. But a woman cannot be a full member [of the extended family], as a man is, and cannot have a voice in managing the affairs of the family. She must only work, work, and work. Any man in the family is senior to her. She cannot even eat at the common table together with the men, but must serve them. It follows naturally from this, in the highest degree subordinate, dependent, and almost slavish position of a woman, that she must be burdened with work. Will someone in a superior position work if the work can be passed on to an inferior? And in reality, a woman works perhaps even more than a man and as much as her physical strength will bear. She nurses the children and clothes herself, her husband, and her children, and sometimes even other members of the extended family, from head to foot; she also must grow and process the hemp for the clothing herself. She prepares the food and carries it on her shoulders, sometimes for long distances, to those working in the fields. It is her job to look after the cattle, to feed and water them, to milk them, to make butter and cheese, to carry water and firewood, and to do whatever other domestic chores there are. Women often help men with work that is considered to be chiefly men's work, for example, fieldwork, and sometimes they even replace men completely in this work. But a man will never replace a woman, even in the slightest way and even if she is ill, considering women's work to be beneath him.

In Great Russia, a woman's manner of life does not change even when she is pregnant. Frequently a woman will feel the labor pains anywhere, for example in the forest where she goes to cut firewood, and will give birth right there, without any help, and then carry the child home. How many stories did we hear in Arkhangel'sk province of women giving birth in a field or in the stubble, because there was no time to lie down during an intensely busy period, or in the forest where they go to collect berries and mushrooms, trying to lay in a reserve of provisions for the winter.

Among the positions occupied by a woman there is one that, apparently, gives her greater privileges: the position of the senior woman, the *bolshukha*.[34] But in what does her power consist? She manages the other women, divides the work among them, holds the keys to the larders and the storerooms, and in general oversees the domestic economy. Despite all her apparent power and significance, however, with respect to the family she is not distinguished in any way from the other women. She cannot take part in the management of general matters, whereas any male reaching adulthood has the right to do so, so she nonetheless is considered lower than any adult male.

Apart from this, the position of the remaining women differs very little. There is almost no difference in the burden of obligations imposed on each of them and in the equality or, more truthfully, the absence of any rights except the right to be fed and clothed. The position of a young woman in her own extended family is not much better than that of an outsider who has married into the same family. True, out of a natural feeling of parental love the parents of a young woman, especially the mother, try to do what they can for a daughter. But the extended family comes first, and in relation to it a young woman is not a daughter, but the same as the other members of the family. Hence a young maiden bears the same burden of common family work as a married woman does.

A young maiden knows that if not today, then tomorrow, her turn will come to be sold out to another family (young girls in the Great Russian family are given in marriage in turn), and it is impossible to go into another household with empty hands. A young woman must spin and weave a dowry for herself, so that her future relatives see that she is able to fulfill her obligations as she should and that she will clothe her husband and children. Moreover, she must prepare even more clothes for herself, since in the new household there will be no time to think about herself; even without this there will be much to do. At the wedding, gifts will have to be given to the future relatives so that they look more affectionately on her when she arrives as a bride, and it is necessary to earn the means for such gifts. Life as a young maiden is short and there is much to do. A young maiden by herself cannot cope, and, of course, her mother helps as much as she can and both secretly and openly takes her side. Sometimes young women at their own expense cultivate silkworms, or have their own garden; they also spin, knit, and sew on the side. The earnings of a young woman, of course, are used for her dowry. When a young woman marries, her family will supplement her dowry if it is insufficient in some way and will pay the wedding expenses. But then the young woman marries, and all her reckonings with her [original] extended family are at an end. She is already an outsider, a member of another extended family, and no longer can rely on her own extended family for anything.

The position of a married woman is determined, in the first place, by her relations with the extended family and, in the second place, by her relations with her own family and husband.

With respect to the extended family, in the Great Russian family a married woman above all is a daughter-in-law,[35] especially of her husband's father.

The whole burden of the domestic work described above falls chiefly on the married women, that is, on the daughters-in-law. They must work both for the extended family and for their own family. With respect to their obligations to the extended family, there is a strict division of labor among them based on clear rules sanctified by time and having acquired the force of law. In the Great Russian family, generally the daughter-in-law who has the greatest physical strength and is not suited for other work is assigned to look after the livestock. In those families where the father/father-in-law[36] is senior, he can assign the daughter-in-law toward whom he is least well disposed to look after the livestock or to do the most arduous and unpleasant work. The remaining women in turn must take care of all the kitchen chores and manage the domestic chores, that is knead the bread and cook the food and carry it to those working in the fields. Each woman manages these chores weekly, from Monday morning to the following Sunday evening. Only those daughters-in-law in their first year of marriage are excused from these chores, and even then not in all families but only in those where concord and love rule among family members.

In addition to working for the common household economy, each married woman also must work for her own family. And there is a lot of work for her own family: she must clothe her husband and children from head to foot, and moreover help to clothe her father-in-law, unmarried brothers-in-law, or other unmarried members of the family.

In addition to work within the household, women also have to undertake a significant amount of work in common with the men, for example, fieldwork. Among the Little Russians[37] who resettled onto the steppes of the southeastern provinces and, under the influence of the Great Russians, adopted the large extended family, even though Little Russians generally are not inclined toward this form of family, women bear an unbearable burden of work. "In the summer they never live at home, but constantly wander in the steppe, pasturing the livestock. At lambing time they must sit entire nights in the cold, protecting the lambs from dogs. In addition, they mow the hay and reap the grain and collect firewood. The women also must go out to protect the grain, and for this they travel as far as five *versts* to the farmstead,[38] often ragged and hungry, with children in hand and bearing a cradle. There, under the scorching sun, they sit for whole days. Frequently in such cases one or another woman is carried from the steppe ill or even dead."[39] Although these facts relate only to one locality, they are not without significance for a characterization of the burden to which the position of women within the extended family leads.

Such is the position in which a woman finds herself. And no protest on her part and no easing of her lot are possible as long as the extended family structure is preserved. A husband oppresses his wife, but the extended family and the family oppress them both. If by some means a woman managed to make her husband aware of the need to alleviate her position, her lot nonetheless still would not become easier. The family would compel the husband to demand from his wife the fulfillment of what it considered to be her obligations. If he did not begin to direct his wife toward the path of truth and virtue with sufficient firmness, the family would begin to direct him. The barbaric principle of the responsibility of one person for another is applied in full strength in the family adhering to kinship principles.

The guiding principles of spousal relations worked out by folk wisdom are not applied everywhere and are not followed with equal consistency. The more a given stratum of the population or a given locality enjoys the level of welfare which among the masses is generally associated with a correspondingly greater degree of development, the more practice deviates from a consistent observance of the principles that are recognized strongly in theory. Conversely, the poorer and more ignorant the masses, the more consistently the coarse practices of spousal relations are carried on, to such a severe degree that, in the end, a wife is reduced to the level of an animal, which works as hard as possible and in return receives only constant cruel blows from its master. A change for the better in the material conditions of life for our peasantry [therefore] probably also would soon change the relationship of a husband to his wife for the better.

Does the peasant woman gain anything from the exchange of forms entailed by the replacement of the extended family by the nuclear one? Perhaps this change also means as little for her as the replacement of the purely patriarchal *zadruga* by the Great Russian extended family having an economic character?

Women have struggled much, and to this day continue to struggle, to destroy the extended family. As long as this form is strongly adhered to, a woman passively submits to her bitter lot. But as soon as she senses the possibility of a life based on other principles, a consciousness of the harshness of her present position and a passionate striving to change it immediately awaken in her. Kinship principles, already weakened, find in her an adversary embittered by an age-old oppressiveness that has lain on her like an unbearable weight. She turns all of her weapons to the struggle against these principles. Her weapons, artfully deployed, are cunning, slander, constant disputes over trifling matters, and such like. The effects of these weapons in each separate instance are completely insignificant, but taken together they constitute a decisive force.

By using various means to make common family life unbearable, by constantly acting on her husband, who quite apart from this already is wavering in his instinctive adherence to kinship principles, [a woman] thus achieves her goal of dividing the family.[40]

In believing that women are the enemy of the old order, the people are right. But, of course, it is necessary to look for the fundamental cause of this not in women: they only relate more receptively to the influences of new principles that promise at least somewhat to alleviate their position. The unanimity with which peasants heap all the blame for the new order on women is remarkable: the *baby*, so they say, are always committing excesses and are unable to get on together. If one objects that there was a time, and not so long ago, that tens of *baby* got on together, the peasants usually will make some profound remark about other times. "Times now are completely different, and nothing now happens as it did before." Despite their simplicity, these words nevertheless express sufficiently clearly a consciousness that some fatal forces are beginning to intrude into life through the actions of people despite their personal views, tastes, and wishes.

The destruction of the extended family is the first step toward the liberation of women. If folk wisdom has transferred entirely to the nuclear family its theories of dependence and the absence of rights that have been worked out by the principles of the social conditions of the extended family, and the application of these principles to the spousal relations of the nuclear family also is demanded, nonetheless the circumstance that the nuclear family does not provide as propitious a field for the practice of these principles as does the extended family remains in full force. The person of the husband alone simply does not have the physical possibility of concentrating in itself the pressure exerted by the extended family and, in the name of its old ideals, required by folk wisdom. A woman, standing face to face with only her husband, can always employ her physical, moral, or mental superiority, if she has them, in order to win for herself some share of freedom, the acquisition of which is unthinkable under the pressure of the extended family, and women frequently exploit this advantage of their new position.

In addition, in the nuclear family we encounter an influence that paralyzes somewhat the strength of the savage traditional views of women. This paralyzing influence is the structure of the nuclear family in economic respects, which necessitates some share of independence for women. For the successful conduct of the family's household economy, in which at first there are only two workers, a husband and a wife, a strict division of labor is necessary. True, there is a division of labor even in the extended family. But there women are deprived of any independence. They are simply machines for the fulfillment of certain tasks previously allocated and prescribed by the family. By contrast, in the nuclear family a woman enjoys almost complete independence in her sphere, since by necessity the husband must entrust this sphere to her—the sphere of the domestic economy—as he has no physical possibility of interfering in it. A wife in the nuclear family therefore usually manages almost entirely her sphere and the products of her economy. She can, for example, sell butter, milk, eggs, baked bread, and such like, and with the money received she can buy what she likes and engage in various trades. A husband does not interfere in the affairs of a wife's economy because there is not enough time remaining to him from his own troubles and cares. This actual practice becomes a custom, according to which a husband considers himself *not to have the right* to manage the appurtenances of his wife's economy.

There is another custom, widespread everywhere among our peasantry, a custom flowing directly from the extended family order but in its new application in the nuclear family exerting a favorable influence on the position of women. This is the relationship of a husband to the dowry of his wife. Giving a dowry to a young woman about to be married, the extended family has an interest in guarding the dowry against encroachments by the family that the woman is entering.

In some localities an inventory of all the things given to the woman is openly made, so that she can bring them back in entirety if she happens to return to her own extended family. From this arises the custom according to which a dowry began to be considered the inviolable property of a wife, that is inviolable for the family that a woman had entered and where in the vast majority of cases she remained forever. This custom has become rooted so firmly that it has been transferred in entirety to the nuclear family. It appears in the latter with a new significance that it did not have in the extended family: it has begun to serve as a point of support for women in their attempt to improve their position. The causes of this lie, on the one hand, in the more independent position of a wife, as mistress and complete manageress of the domestic sphere of the nuclear family, and, on the other hand, in the freshness of the memories of that order under which a wife's property was defended by her extended family, which was not averse to asserting its claims to this property.

In the nuclear family a woman works no less, and sometimes perhaps even more, as the peasants themselves recognize, especially if there are young children and it is impossible to take on anyone as help. But on the other hand she is manageress of her own labor: she now applies not only the strength of her muscles but also her quick-wittedness and her mind and knowledge—her spiritual strengths. She now sees clearly that her welfare and that of her children depend on her mind and industry. By necessity a woman in the nuclear family must cast aside torpor and apathy, the products of her previous slavish position, since her new position calls into action strengths that were paralyzed by the absence of their use in the extended family. Here is another of the reasons why a woman strives so much for the nuclear family: she instinctively senses that it will provide at least some scope for her suppressed spiritual strengths.

The important meaning the economic principle has in the peasant spousal union is apparent especially when the person of the husband, with his petty tyrannical and despotic ways, is eliminated and a woman remains as a widow. Precisely here can be seen clearly the tremendous difference between the position of a woman in the extended and the nuclear families. Nothing can be more degrading than the role played by a widow in the extended family. She has lost that small source of support that she had found in the significance of her husband and in his natural protection and defense: there is no one to whom she can complain about insults and oppression or from whom she can request defense. And precisely the most difficult work is imposed on her. She becomes the object on which each member of the family can vent his anger.

There is no more difficult lot for a peasant woman than to be a widow and a father's daughter-in-law. There are two fates for a widowed woman: to return to her parental family, if she is childless, or to marry. But she has lost her natural place in her parental family and usually it is no better for her there than in the family of her late husband. And far from all widows manage to remarry, since peasant men prefer young women to widows, who are valued significantly less.

How is the position of a widow defined in the nuclear family? It is defined quite originally, with the economic principle emerging in sharp relief from this definition. The *statutory* share[41] inherited by one spouse from the property of the other is completely unknown to the people. These artificial quarter and seventh parts, having no foundation, are unnecessary to the people, who decide the matter much more simply and reasonably. If a widow has children, then she inherits all her husband's property, that is, more accurately, she does not inherit his property but receives it in use. Moreover, she is obligated to use the property in the interests of the children. If she does not concern herself with these interests, squanders the property, or remarries, a trusteeship composed usually of the parents or relatives of the husband is appointed over the property. If she remains forever a widow, then she can manage the property until the children are grown and desire a division. She then receives for maintenance a share equal to that of the sons, or lives with and is maintained by one of them, or, finally, all the sons are obligated to take part in supporting their mother.

The position of a childless widow, however, is defined particularly originally. If she had not lived long with her husband, then she is not recognized as having a right to the husband's property, since she did not in any way merit or *earn* this right. In this instance she receives her dowry, something from the husband's property, for example his wedding clothes, which by custom are given to her as if in memory of her husband, and then she remarries, returns to her parents, or leaves and finds paid work. But the husband's property goes to his parents or relatives. If she wishes to remain with the person who received her husband's property, however, usually the father-in-law or the brother-in-law, that person does not have the right to deny her shelter. But if she lived for a long time with her husband, then by her labor she has earned the right to all the husband's property, and no one can dispute this right with her, for the recognition of which no will is necessary. The sense of justice in a peasant would be extremely upset if someone began to contest an inheritance with such a wife by relying on the law. The highly humane manifestations that this sense [of justice] sometimes can reach are apparent from a custom that is widespread across all of Arkhangel'sk province. If a young woman or an older woman lived for a lengthy period with a man without a formal celebration of marriage, then after his death she is recognized as his heir, despite any relatives and regardless of whether or not she had children by him. When we asked the peasants to explain this custom, they told us that a woman who lived a long time with a man, worked with him and for him, and cared for him, had a greater right than anyone else to his property.

Source: A. I. Efimenko, "Krest'ianskaia zhenshchina," *Izsledovaniia narodnoi zhizni* (*vypusk I, Obychnoe pravo*) ["Peasant Women," in *Studies on the Life of the Folk* (*part I, Customary Law*)] (Moscow, 1884). Excerpted from pp. 68–69, 74–75, 76–77, 78, 79–80, 83, 87–88, 89–90, 90–94, 95–96, 96–98.

Translated by William G. Wagner.

FEMALE POVERTY

As we saw both in the Synodal decree concerning the fate of peasant daughters-in-law in the eighteenth century and in Efimenko's account of peasant family life in the nineteenth century, poverty could have devastating effects on family relations. Poverty among the peasantry remained pervasive throughout the imperial period, despite the rapid commercial and industrial growth that took place at the end of the nineteenth century. The Imperial Foundling Homes (established in St. Petersburg and Moscow in the 1760s) accepted a veritable flood of infants from peasant women too poor to raise their children. Lidiia Avilova (1864?–1943) presents a literary view of such a poverty-stricken mother who has embarked on a journey to the city to give up her youngest child and search for work as a wet nurse. Avilova's "On the Road" was published in 1892, a year of severe famine and a cholera epidemic.

A. S. Saburova took up a similar subject fourteen years later in the form of an analysis of village life, published in 1916 as an article in the journal The Protection of Motherhood. It is likely that Saburova was a member of the landowning nobility of Moscow province. Her arguments reveal more about her own self-perception, ideals, attitudes, and aspirations than they do about the conditions of peasant life. The juxtaposition of Avilova's compassion and Saburova's harshly critical "rational" approach to peasant women reveals splits that divided Russian society and prevented a unified approach to the problems of female poverty, unemployment, and infant mortality in the late imperial period. Given the date of Saburova's article, it is unlikely that any of her proposals were implemented, if indeed they were ever considered seriously. Within a year of the article's appearance, however, the Russian countryside was beset by a massive agrarian revolution. The selections we include indicate how literary and historical texts worked, in different ways, to accomplish social change.

A. On the Road

LIDIIA AVILOVA

It was the middle of the night. In the large third-class hall, dimly lit with gas burners, there were lots of people: they slept on benches, they slept sprawled out on the floor, with a tightly bound canvas bag stuffed under their head. From time to time the doors opened and slammed shut, letting in clouds of cold air. You could hear movement all around, the whistles of steam engines carried in from outside, along with the even tapping of wheels approaching and then again growing distant; voices rang out. The door slammed again, and now the bell trembled and flew out in the hall itself.

"Good Lord, is that for us?" asked a woman, bustling about in confusion, straightening her kerchief and groping around her for everything she could find. She was sleeping on the floor, and beside her, wrapped in rags, lay a small child.

"Hold on lady, don't hurry," a young man spoke to her from a bench; he was somewhat foppish in the way salesmen are, with an ugly self-assured face. "Goodness, how quick you are! I told you, we have to sit here till almost daybreak."

"Akh, brother, I'm worried we'll miss it. Shouldn't we ask?"

"What's the point of asking? I'm telling you. We're going to the same place, why butt in ahead of time?"

"Are you sure you know?" asked the woman.

"Sure I'm sure. I'm going there, too; what's the deal?"

He pulled a crumpled cigarette from his pocket, straightened it out, felt around for a match, and started to strike it against the wall.

"What a lot of room you've got there," he began again, taking a drag on the cigarette and stretching out on the bench, "and I can't turn around up here." The woman was sitting on the floor, and her face, frightened at first, grew calm now and took on a concentrated, dull expression.

"It's not bad, there's space," she answered, "but there's a draft on the floor. I'm frozen."

"Never mind, you'll warm up on the train. Most likely you'll be crawling under the benches again. Like a stowaway. Clever! You gave folks some entertainment when your kid there started squealing. We were splitting our sides! He's crying, and over there, 'Tickets please!' How that one didn't guess, it's surprising!"

"Maybe he guessed but he's a good soul. After all, conductors have souls too, brothers," commented an old man, a neighbor on the bench. "Where are you going, Auntie?"

"To Moscow," the woman answered thoughtfully.

"From the famine country, is that it? To get a job?"

"I want to work as a wet nurse. That's my child; I'll put him in a state home, and I'll be a wet nurse."[42] She sighed deeply, put her chin in her hand, and set to thinking. The young man spit and laughed gaily.

"Oh, you hungry ones; you may be hungry, but you're taking illegitimate kids to the state homes," he observed in a mocking tone, and narrowed his eyes. "Well, you're not bad looking . . . I noticed you this evening. Just awfully crudded up."

The woman was upset. Her lips trembled, and her eyes looked out in fear.

"Never mind! You'll get washed up properly in town. Wet nurses make a good living; invite me to come see you." He started laughing, but she didn't say a word back and kept looking straight in front of her.

"You're a widow, are you?" the old man spoke to her.

"A widow."

"It's bad in your parts this year?"

"Oh how bad! There's nothing there," the woman answered and again sighed.

"God is angered!" the old man concluded; and moaning, turned over on the rough bench.

"There are still two more of them, older," the woman started quietly. "Good Lord, how to give them food and drink without their father? We've a big family, we've not split up: everyone takes joy in their own, but who needs orphans?"

"And the old folks, are they alive?"

"The old folks. My father-in-law's all right, but my mother-in-law. . . . 'I'll run you out, with your children.' And how are the little ones guilty? And tell me, Granddad, why do people have such cruel hearts? They're ready to drive you from the earth, they've no pity."

"Hey, Auntie, ask me, I'll take pity on you," again the young man laughed. "I'm kind. You don't believe me?"

The woman looked askance at him and fell silent.

"It's bad, bad!" she started again, as though to herself. "It's all because of our poverty. In earlier years we didn't live like rich folks, but we didn't know such need. If my dead husband could see it. . . . There's nothing left of our livestock. If we hadn't sold them—they'd have died before spring anyway."

"It's a familiar story!" said the old man. "Where's it better now?"

"It's bad everywhere, everywhere!" sighed the woman. "And who are you?"

"Me? I'm a driver. Also not a happy business. . . . What did you sell your horses for?"

"For next to nothing; we gave it away for next to nothing. And what a horse it was!"

The young man again started striking a match against the wall.

"Auntie, hey, Auntie, so are you going to invite me to come see you?"

"We sold everything, we ate everything. Maybe it's sorrow that makes my mother-in-law like an animal. Not long ago Mashutka—that's my daughter—comes up to me, 'Mama,' she says, 'cut me off a piece of crust, Grandma won't give it to me, and I'm so hungry.' I'm sorry for the girl; I looked around, there was no one in the hut, only me and Mashutka. I went up to the table, cut off a tiny piece of bread, I give it to Mashutka and say, 'Hide it, don't let Grandma see, she'll start scolding again.' Mashutka held onto the bread, even her little eyes were shining, she holds it, shaking. . . . "

The woman stopped. Whether she saw in her mind her daughter, happy, with a crust of bread in her hand—whether she rested with that vision—or if it was difficult for her to say what happened to Mashutka next, in any case she bowed her head, and tears ran down her face.

"She saw, she took it away," she went on. "Semka was on the stove, he saw it all. My mother-in-law's in the door, and he yells to her, 'Grandma! Aunt Maria is stealing bread, she's giving Mashutka bread. See, there's a piece tight in Mashutka's hand.' Mashutka started crying and screaming. My mother-in-law grabbed her by the shoulders, ready to shake her: 'Give it back,' she yells, 'give back the piece!' She started beating her, Mashutka's face was pale, she's holding the bread in her hand, and won't let go. And I fell on my knees in front of my mother-in-law: beat me, I say, leave my child alone. What did the child do to you?"

"And then? Did she take it?" asked the old man.

"She took it," the woman answered quietly, and grew thoughtful. "My little boy is exhausted with hunger, too, what holds his soul together! Such a wee one, he didn't understand. 'Mama,' he'd say, 'I want some soft bread.' And where was I to come by it? Those with fathers still have everything to eat, but it's easy to hurt my orphans. Good Lord! Where's people's pity? 'I'll run you out,' she says, 'with the children. You're eating me out of house and home.' And what's to eat up? I don't eat it up myself, nor do I drink anything, I give it to the children. The one that's nursing's in a bad way, bad. . . . At first he always cried, but now he's stopped even crying."

"How can you have abandoned your children? They'll be treated worse without you."

"Akh, I've abandoned them," the woman shook her head. "At least my eyes won't have to see it. . . . Perhaps their gran will take pity on them when they've no mother, pity will speak in her. When I started to say goodbye, Mashutka collapsed, they couldn't tear her hands from me. . . . She wound around my neck and held tight. . . . "

She sobbed and wiped her face with her hand.

"Will we see each other?" The woman was silent for a long time and suddenly began to speak in a different, peaceful, and even voice: "I'll become a wet nurse; they say the pay's not bad, I'll send some money to the village right away, and in the letter I'll tell them to give my children soft bread to their heart's content. I'll buy some clothes, I'll send Mashutka a scarf. . . . When I can, I'll send food, a little sugar and some tea. . . . All to my own ones!" The woman became thoughtful. A slight shadow moved across her face, her lips set into a smile.

"If you find work!" observed the old man. "You think there aren't a whole lot like you in the city? You'll really have to make the rounds! They pick over your sisters quite carefully indeed. They'll see a sick child—and head the other way. It's not an easy business."

The woman winced; at once her smile disappeared and fear again showed in her eyes. She turned quickly toward the benches. On one slept the young man, his legs crossed, and whistling through his nose; next to him sat the old man, counting something on his fingers with great concentration.

The woman cast him a glance that mingled entreaty and desperation, but when she met his serious, cold face, she turned away, hugged her small knees with her hands, and grew still. If these people had beaten her or threatened her with death, she would not have been as horrified or have suffered as she did now. Again she saw Mashutka, but not a joyful Mashutka, with bread in her hands. She saw her hungry, offended, among people without pity or heart. And she no longer had a mother; her mother had gone away, because she could not help; she had gone away so her eyes wouldn't see. . . . These eyes looked wide as though they were mad; her hands grew numb and deadened from cold. . . .

An engine heaved heavily, doors started banging insistently.

The young man jumped up and rubbed his eyes, looked through the window, and stretched.

"Look, now you can get a ticket," he said, yawning. "And you, my beauty, you're not sleeping? You'd better worry about a ticket, too. What, are you traveling first class?" He looked about, straightened his hair with his hand and pulled his cap down. "The old man's already gone. Looks like he's rolled off. Soon it'll be our turn."

He stretched once more and headed for the door.

A pulley started to creak and whine. Bundled figures started rising from the floor with moans and groans. An early, gray morning glimmered weakly in the large windows.

Source: L. A. Avilova, "V doroge," *Pisateli chekhovskoi pory* ["On the Road," in *Writers of the Chekhovian Period*], ed. S. V. Bukchina (Moscow, 1982), vol. II, pp. 218–22.

Translated by Jane T. Costlow.

B. Why Infants Die in [Peasant] Villages

A. S. SABUROVA

They die due to the backwardness and carelessness of parents, to bad care, filth, infection and accidents, and to the indifference and ignorance of mothers. In our area (Moscow province, Podolsk district), with few exceptions, *baby* present a picture of the most unrelieved unawareness, coarseness, and indolence—an extremely backward element, with all the inadequacies of this condition. They constitute a brake on the family, women who are lazy and cynical, knowing how to do nothing and trained for no craft, thieves, idle, crude, believing in nothing except personal gain. Peasant men are much better, more tractable and responsive, and the children, as everywhere, are the same, good until spoiled by the example of adults. To struggle with peasant women using only words is tremendously difficult. Many thirst for the death of their children, and not always because of poverty, but frequently because they are unwilling to care for them; children up to five or six years old hold no interest for peasant women since they will not be able to work for some time, and when they fall ill, peasant women rejoice that perhaps "God will take them to Himself." They therefore are indifferent to caring for them, to accidents, and to infections and epidemics, so that admonitions to look after children remain mere words. Herein lies the source of the children's misfortunes and that of the entire village—the backwardness of these women, which makes them inert, indifferent to any sort of enlightenment (if this is accompanied by any extra trouble) and even cruel, like unconsciously cruel wild beasts that know no culture. For women, and for young and adolescent girls—few attempts are made to enlighten them. One also can speak endlessly about our young and adolescent girls, but it's all the same—most depressing and distressing. All view children as boring and an unavoidable evil. Even more, one could say that all the adults in our area greatly exploit the labor of children, and older sisters especially exploit young orphan girls. We have had instances of crimes (the poisoning of infants) caused by the fatigue of young dry nurses and of craziness accompanied by arson, due to the desperate position of girls aged fifteen to sixteen and younger who were enslaved by sisters. It seems to me that lectures and advice alone will not suffice here; it is necessary to institute some form of control over how parents, and especially peasant women, treat children and young girls, hinder their education, beat and torment them, compelling them to work beyond their strength, and this begins from a very early age, with children being considered something like beasts of burden. But there is control over animals, there is a society for the protection of animals, and in other countries control even exists over adults and over universal literacy. Among us, girls aged eight, ten, twelve are beaten cruelly so that they do not go learn a trade (for example to the women's handicrafts school that I am trying to establish), and the backwardness of the domestic circumstances of these girls (and future women and mothers) remains unrelievedly in full force; to struggle with the logic of peasant women is impossible. So from generation to generation the most horrible backwardness and coarseness of relations continue, examples of thievery, exploitation, indolence, and stepping out in the women's world of the village, since young girls tend the children, maidens dress up and walk about, and mothers sit in taverns, beg, are unable to manage a household, and count on others, complaining more than working. And meanwhile there needn't be real poverty among them.

The blame for all this lies in [the peasant women's] savage backwardness, their horrifying conceptions of life, and a complete absence of moral foundations, which shocks everyone who comes into our area and who has dealings with them and sees their world view. It is understandable that among such women children die like flies, die from everything, die without any help, and to save them one frequently must use force.

Disinfection, after or during an epidemic, does not occur here at all. There also are no bathhouses in our entire district, and no one ever washes (except the workers on our estate), but they only climb onto stoves where they cook and sweat and then crawl back down. Because of all this, no household is without a rash or skin diseases of all kinds, and masses of households are infected with the "French disease."[43] There are masses of cases of scrofula, rickets, and tuberculosis, not to mention those crippled due to carelessness. No one takes any medicine, and if you take something to the children and beg the mothers to give it to them, they laugh and very rarely pay any attention to such entreaties. "Take the children away as long as you like," is all you hear, "we don't have the time to deal with them." At night sick or neglected children are beaten from age two to three months, and when they cry or hinder sleep, they are beaten instead of being bathed and settled or fed, or they are stuffed with muck, filth, and, previously, vodka but now methylated spirits or whatever comes to hand, "so that they sleep."[44] Obviously many young children cannot survive such a regime, and they perish in great numbers. I know families where only one of eleven children has survived. It seems to me necessary to dispatch a special detachment for the salvation of young children up to two years old and to undertake a campaign against mothers, a campaign that includes conferring some rights, because words and lectures will not help here. It is necessary to show how one should look after and care for young children, and perhaps to give incentives to those who wish to do well, since those who do and do not wish to do well are in the same position—they understand and know nothing and don't know how to help themselves even if they want to do so. Crèches are good, but only in the summer months. Perhaps, there could be cafeterias for the backward and the convalescent or the infirm and the hungry, and constant oversight by a directress who would stop by peasant huts, leave medicine, soap, linen, *kasha,* and so on and compel each household to contribute some share to a monitoring agency, since the people are corrupted by charity alone. It seems to me that these directresses should wear uniforms and have certain rights, i.e., a right of oversight, to levy fines and award prizes, or something of this sort—visible and tangible, since our directress, modest and without rights, came to nothing, heard only ridicule and questions—such as who is she? and why is she interfering?—and was horrified that among these peasant women there is neither compassion, nor the fear of God, nor faith, nor law, but only ignorant and blind hostility against all fate, authorities, the priest, school, landowners, the police, and life. . . . With them all conversations end hence: that life is hard for them, that they don't need anything that increases their work. Such is their logic. It seems to me that for the protection of infancy it would be good to bring in something akin to those "small families of Madame Monod" that exist in France,[45] where numerous family centers constitute a hub of culture, with their "directing mothers" occupied especially with the children of soldiers killed in war. Perhaps it would be possible to become acquainted with Madame Monod and write an appeal to single Russian women, female Russian landowners, especially those who are childless and well-to-do, to take five or six orphans and bring them up, working with a "directing mother" to care for their physical and moral upbringing, using measures proposed by Madame Monod based on the French model?

It seems to me that for our own backward region something clear and visible is necessary—an office, a sign, a uniform, and clinics, first aid, incentives, a modest disbursement of goods, and also prizes for a healthy infant, just as at livestock exhibitions incentives are given "for well-formed steers," and so on—since it is impossible to imagine the depths of village backwardness and its accompanying gloomy and dreadful logic and indifference to kith and kin, so horrifying to the soul. In their drab life there really is much pain, work, and weariness. But children are to be pitied more. . . . Perhaps it would be possible to specially train young girl-nurses (preparing them for their future mission—to be mothers) with readings and practical instructions, without, however, overloading them with work—but lightening it and offering incentives where possible, illuminating this question differently (that a clean and healthy, satisfied infant causes less trouble to adults than a sick, hungry, unclean, etc., one); perhaps entertainments and gifts could be offered to the young nurses, in that way helping them to advance by treating them well. Perhaps the directress, together with the crèches, could establish a kindergarten in this facility, a small courtyard where it would be possible to play or to work or study, or a small garden where it would be possible to plant and cultivate, at the same time telling stories, reading, and developing both the children, their nurses, and the mothers who come visit, gradually, at odd moments, even during the preschool years, fostering through play an understanding of studies, cleanliness, joy, mutual assistance to one another, i.e., the education and religion so clearly absent from our village life.

In general I think it is sufficiently clear what can be done, but the question is, how does the Guardianship Board[46] regard the matter? Does it have the means? In an amount sufficient for each minimal salvation center, since even though relying on charity alone is unnecessary and harmful, basic centers of protection are impracticable without incurring expenses, and to expect sympathy immediately from a backward population that desires nothing seems to me utopian. We have not accomplished anything serious with a single traveling directress who has no office or real life.

Nevertheless, I am full of hope for a better future and think that, having devoted effort to the development of women at these centers for protecting infants, we can expect, and certainly there will be, the most gratifying results; I also think that the difficulty will consist only in getting things moving at the beginning and in finding directresses, but we can always count on the young generation because it is impressionable and receptive; what is more, I think that all these cruelties are due more to ignorance and lethargy than to real malice, and no one has ever enlightened peasant women in this sense. It seems to me that such directresses of salvation from child mortality will need not only a knowledge of physical nursing, like that of paramedics,[47] but [also] special courses on the physical and moral sides of life and a knowledge of the village, the ability to approach peasant women and inspire their trust and respect, understanding their conditions and views on everything, but standing higher than they in education and culture, knowing how to impart one's knowledge and demands firmly and convincingly but without imposing them and without despairing at the backwardness and rebuffs of peasant women or without being offended by mockery and distrust or cynicism, while not making concessions. These centers for the protection of infants and aid to mothers must be educative centers of village hygiene and philanthropy, of nurture, and of education, not merely a help to women but also an awakening of their human feelings for children.

Source: A. S. Saburova, "Otchego umiraiut v derevniakh malenkie deti," *Okhrana materinstva i mladenchestva* ["Why Infants Die in (Peasant) Villages," in *The Protection of Motherhood and Infancy*], vol. 1 (1916), pp. 127–32.

Translated by William G. Wagner.

THE FORCED MARRIAGE

Evdokiia Rostopchina

Evdokiia Petrovna Rostopchina (née Sushkova, 1811–1858) was an author of poetry and prose and a salon hostess. She traveled in the highest circles of society and was acquainted with the most famous literati of her day, including the poets Pushkin and Lermontov.[48] *Rostopchina's first poem, "Talisman," was published without her permission by Petr Andreevich Viazemskii*[49] *in 1831. When they discovered this fact, her family became upset and made her promise not to release any of her works for publication until after she married; Rostopchina, in fact, did not publish again until after her marriage in 1833. She then frequently used the pseudonym "Clairvoyant" ("Iasnovidiashchaia").*

Most of Rostopchina's poems are written from a female perspective. Several, such as "Advice to Women" (1838) and "How Women Should Write" (1840), explore gender as a theme. Her prose works include the society tale "Rank and Money" (1839) and the novel A Fortunate Woman *(1851). She occasionally wrote politically oriented poetry, most famously, this poem, "The Forced Marriage" (1846), an allegory of the relationship between Russia and Poland. Because of this poem, she was not permitted to live in the capital, St. Petersburg, and she lived in Moscow from 1847 until her death.*

In addition to its political meaning, Rostopchina's poem also presents the difficulties that could arise for wives who refused to comply with the patriarchal controls placed on them, insisting on maintaining a sense of a separate self in marriage. In this poem Rostopchina comments on the colonial relations between Russia and Poland that existed from the 1770s, when a large part of the latter was absorbed into the Russian empire, until the Russian Revolution.

"THE FORCED MARRIAGE"
DEDICATED [IN THOUGHT?] TO MICKIEWICZ[50]

The Old Baron

Come gather here, my men and vassals,
Upon your master's gentle call!
Judge, without fear of my disfavor—
The truth, I wish to hear it all.
Judge a dispute you all know well:
Though I am mighty and renowned,
Though I am thought all-powerful—
I am not master in my home:
One's disobedient all her life

To me—my own rebellious wife!
I gave her charity as an orphan
And took her in her poverty,
I raised the strong hand of a sovereign
To give my patronage to her;
I clad her in brocade and gold,
Surrounded her with countless guards,
And, so that enemies won't approach,
I stand above her with a sword;
But gloomy and dissatisfied
Is my ungrateful, thankless wife.

I know—with lies, with calumny
She libels me to everyone;
I know—for all the world to see
She curses my roof, shield, and home,
And looks askance beneath her brows,
She scowls, repeating slanderous vows,
She weaves intrigues, sharpens a knife,
Blows up the flame of civil strife;
She whispers with a monk besides,
My crafty, my perfidious wife.

And in exultant satisfaction,
My enemies observe us both,
They flatter her vain pridefulness
And tantalize her trait'rous wrath.
My tongue's not crafty, though it's strict!
Give me advice that will be wholesome,
Judge, which of us two is correct?
Now hear the unsubmissive woman:
Let her try to defend herself,
My criminal, felonious wife!

The Wife

Am I a friend, am I a slave—
God only knows! Was I the one
Who chose a cruel spouse for myself?
Was I the one that took that oath?
I lived in freedom and good fortune,
I loved my precious liberty;
But I was vanquished and imprisoned
When evil neighbors preyed on me.

I've been betrayed and sold—no wife,
No, I'm a captive in this life!

In vain the sovereign potentate
Attempts to gild the fatal yoke;
In vain he wants to change to love
The vengeance that to me is holy.
I don't need his munificence,
I do not want his constant guard—
I'll teach the obstinate myself
To pay the debt of peaceful honor.
By him alone am I oppressed—
I am his enemy, not his wife.

He forbids me now to speak
The language of my native land,
He will not let me bear the mark
Of my inherited coat of arms;
Standing before him I dare not
Take just pride in my ancient name
And, like my glorious forebears,
Go pray within my age-old temples:
The miserable wife is forced
To bow down to another's laws.

He's sent to exile, into prison
All my best and faithful servants;
He's left me to the persecution
Of slaves—his spies and vile informers.
He brings me as a wedding gift
Disgrace, oppressed captivity—
And now my murmurs he'll forbid?
Since I am suffering such a fate,
Taken by force, can it be
A wife must hide it silently?

September, 1845
On the road, between Krakow and Vienna

Source: E. P. Rostopchina, "Nasil'nyi brak: ballada i allegoriia," *Talisman. Izbran-naia lirika. Neliudimka (Drama). Dokumenty, pis'ma, vospominaniia* ["The Forced Marriage: Ballad and Allegory," in *Talisman. Selected Lyrics. The Unsociable Woman (A Drama). Documents, Letters, Memoirs*] (1845; reprint, Moscow, 1987), pp. 109–111.

Translated by Sibelan Forrester.

DIVORCE

Defining marriage as a religious institution, imperial Russian law largely ceded control over the definition and administration of divorce law to the ecclesiastical authority of each officially recognized faith with respect to its own adherents. Most of the population consequently came under the jurisdiction of the Russian Orthodox Church, which narrowly restricted the grounds for divorce (in the eighteenth and nineteenth centuries, to adultery, prolonged disappearance, penal exile to Siberia, and sexual incapacity due to physical causes arising prior to marriage; see St. Tikhon's Instructions in chapter 1). As a result, the incidence of divorce among the Orthodox population remained extremely low throughout the imperial period, despite rapid increases after the mid-1860s and again after the 1890s. Until 1914 imperial law also formally prohibited marital separation, although exceptions were made via special administrative processes and, particularly after the early 1880s, the civil courts recognized the legitimacy of separation in certain instances. The only marriages that were easily dissolved were those that were non-canonical, that is, concluded between two people of too-close a blood relationship (or spiritual relationship— Russians had well-defined rules for including godparents and children in marital prohibitions) or between people who were already legally married to someone else. Such non-canonical unions were regularly annulled, regardless of the circumstances, when discovered or reported to ecclesiastical authorities. Otherwise, formal marital dissolution was difficult to obtain in imperial Russia, and attempts to relax the law from the 1860s onward proved to be a source of conflict within and among the state bureaucracy, the Orthodox Church, newly emergent professional groups, and different ideological movements.

The next four documents illustrate the difficulties created by the intersection of imperial law, Orthodox doctrine, and ecclesiastical policies, as well as the central role of the Church in dissolving marriages. The first case resulted in the forced return of the bigamous wife to her first husband, in spite of the fact that all three parties wished to leave the second marriage intact. In the second case, the Moscow Spiritual Consistory instructed the district police authorities to collect the required tax for submission of petitions from the complainant before informing her that she did not have valid grounds for divorce. The ultimate disposition of the third case is unknown. The fourth document relates the testimony of peasant women in civil cases heard before the peasant cantonal courts and magistrate's courts.[51] In the first two and the last selection, we have tried to reproduce the grammar and spelling of the original documents.

A. Zhenka Anna

September 29, 1750. By the authority of the above-mentioned decisions of the Spiritual Consistory decisions sent by the communication from the office of her Imperial Highness, *Zhenka* [wench] Anna, daughter of Lukian, and Sergei Khristoforov were interrogated and in the interrogation they said,

This is the thirty-fourth year from her birth in Reval. Her father was Luk Shorin, son of Afanasii, a soldier of the Reval Garrison Regiment. Her mother was Paraskeva Ionia, daughter of Nikifor. In bygone years, and she cannot remember when, both her mother and her father died. And in a past year, and she cannot remember which, only that it was about sixteen years ago, she was given in marriage by her father to the soldier of the Dorpat Garrison Regiment, who is now of the Reval Garrison in the Estland Regiment, Sergeant Mikhail Kalugin, son of Mikhail. She was married in the Church of St. Nikolai the Miracleworker in Reval by a priest whose name she does not remember. She lived with him [Kalugin] for about twelve years. They had four children who died in infancy.

In 1744 she, Anna, because of intolerable beatings from her husband, ran away from Reval to St. Petersburg and lived in the Moscow Coachmen's District at a coachman's for about a week, but she does not remember how he was called. Then she went to Kronstadt, to the aforesaid Estland Regiment, to the soldier Stefan Tarasov's widow Avdotia, daughter of Andrei, who was then married to [a sailor] whose name she does not remember. She does not know where Avdotia now resides. She had known Avdotia in Reval. Marfa, daughter of Denis, the mother of Anna's first husband, Sergeant Kalugin, was the godmother of Avdotia's child. Upon arrival at Avdotia's, Anna informed her that she had run away from her husband because of the intolerable beatings he inflicted on her. Avdotia told her that she had a letter permitting her free habitation from the Estland Regiment. And with this letter, calling herself Avdotia, daughter of Andrei, Anna lived in Kronstadt at a naval doctor's, whose name she does not remember, for twelve weeks.

Then she came to St. Petersburg and served in the home of Count *Gosudar*[52] Iaguzinskii with the above-mentioned's [the count's] chef, Ivan Fedorov, for two years. Then, having left him, she lived at some foreign tailor's, Andrei, son of Petr, for about seven months, and after leaving him she lived at a silversmith's, at the snuff-box maker's, the foreigner Matfei Bok, son of Matfei, in a rented apartment for about three months.

The late General Fieldmarshal Prince Repnin's servitor Sergei Khristoforov, son of Matfei, would come to Bok's, why she does not know. At that time Sergei asked Anna if she had a husband. To that question she answered that she was a widow. With those words, he proposed to her. She was married to him in 1747 in October, but she does not remember the exact day, in the Church of the Resurrection in the Admiralty suburb by the priest Ioan Fedorov. And in addition, the marriage license was signed by the snuff-box maker Matfei Bok, who did not know that Anna had run away from her husband and was marrying Khristoforov while she was already married to a living man, since Anna had showed him and her second husband Khristoforov [the letter?] and had not told them and had called herself Avdotia, the soldier's widow from the Estland Regiment, Stefan Tarasov's widow, Avdotia, daughter of Andrei. And at her marriage to Khristoforov Anna tore up that letter.

In March of this year, 1750, while in St. Petersburg, Anna's first husband, having identified Anna, now married to Khristoforov, wanted to bring suit against

Khristoforov but did not because Khristoforov and Kalugin came to terms about
the situation. Kalugin was to receive a given sum and there would not be any suit.
Khristoforov gave Kalugin sixty rubles. In return, Kalugin gave Khristoforov a
handwritten letter, which is now at the institution of the *Kamennii Kalininskii Dom*
Commission[53] with three examination reports. The first, Sergeant Kalugin, now
lives at the regiment in Reval. Anna has told the absolute truth without any lies
and if this testimony turns out to be false, then she will be fined a sum to be determined by decree. By the request of the St. Petersburg Spiritual Consistory Naumov affixed his hand.

Source: TsGIA SPb, f. 19, op. 1, t. 2, d. 352, 5–6 ob.

Translated by Robin Bisha.

B. Varvara Kondratevna

To [the Moscow Spiritual Consistory]
        Peasant of Moscow province, Volkolamsk [*sic*] district, Annenskii
canton, village of Danilovo, Varvara Kuzminina Kondratevna, currently living in
house no. A17, Ilinskii Street, [Moscow]

Petition

With the present petition I have the honor humbly to request the Spiritual
Consistory for the following:

Being legally married for seven years to Vasilii Kondratevich Kondratev, a peasant of Volkolamsk district, I am no longer able to live with him for the following
reasons:

During the whole time I lived with him I have not seen a peaceful day. He has
not worked his whole life from the day of our marriage, and even if he worked, [he
did so] very rarely, since no one would keep him due to his drunkenness. And [I
had to undertake] factory work in order to support him, that is to maintain, feed,
and clothe him. But all this was nothing. Recently he not only has got drunk, but
has treated me outrageously all the time, beaten me, smashed glass, and swiped all
sorts of things from our apartment. As soon as I come back from the factory where
I work, the last that was in the apartment was carried off by him and squandered
on drink. All this has driven me to bed and I have become ill.

On the basis of what has been related, I humbly request that you summon me
and my husband in order to give me a full divorce. Varvara Kondratevna, and due
to her illiteracy, signed by Mikhail Shelepaev. 1911.

Source: "Divorce petition of Varvara Kondratevna to the Moscow Diocesan Consistory, 1911." RGIAgM, f. 203, op. 759, d. 111, l. 1.

Translated by William G. Wagner.

C. Aleksandra Dvorskova

To the Moscow Spiritual Consistory.

Report of the Priest Nikolai Benevolenskii, Church of St. Nikolai in the New Settlement.

I have the honor of reporting to the Moscow Spiritual Consistory that in execution of the Edict of the Consistory dated 31 July 1912 No. 10247 I summoned for admonition[54] the peasant woman Aleksandra Vasilevna Dvorskova, who, having abandoned her husband, declared to me that she had left her husband Timofei Markov Dvorskov as a result of his ill treatment of her; she does not wish to become reconciled with him and to remain living with him in a marital union, and [she] gave a written attestation of this, which is attached to this report.

Church of St. Nicholas in the New Settlement, Priest Nikolai Benevolenskii.

9 August 1912.

[Added to the report:] Dvorskova's written testimonial was forwarded to the Transbaikal Consistory on 18 August.[55]

Source: "Clerical admonition to a wife in a divorce action," RGIAgM, f. 203, op. 483, d. 123, l. 2.

Translated by William G. Wagner.

D. Abused Peasant Women

IA. LUDMER

[Petition from one Stepanova:][56]

My husband led me a dance he were always tormennting me with beatings so as I couldnt hardly stand it Yesserday he beat me so crooly half to death so that blood ran out of my nose and mouth and he made great blue and purple marks on me and Im ill now from them beatings and aside from them beatings he gave me he took off of me propperty worth 100 rubles and is keeping it for himself contrary to what he should.

[Vlasova the *soldatka*'s story:]

My husband whose drunk day and night treats me cruelly, he tore my hair out and hes making merry hell with me. My life is quite unbearable. Ive all the work on the farm to do and in the house and a little son and my mother in law to look after. My husband beats the child unmercifully. Yesterday he grabbed my head and squashed it between his knees and thrashed me pitilessly with his soldiers belt so that even his own mother bowed down before him and begged him not to kill me.

[Shirokova's story:]

I married my husband four year ago we had a proper church weding since then ive had no life from that shirokov but beatings he gave me and alsorts bulying that kind. Lastyear we both of our own goodwill agreed a seperation and shirokov he let me go "go where you will" he says. And i Domna i have my own home now but my husband he still has a grudge agin me and he comes round to me twice and invites me round he says weel talk but i knows his grudge agin me an i never went withim nowhere. But not long since i had to pay a visit somewhere and i was cummin back alone when i sees my husband cummin he says whereve you been i says been payn a visit an he takes a swing at me an hits me in the eye so i fall down he grabs my hair an beats me half to death and shoves my face in the mud so i cant scream but i dont know how i did scream in a bad voice. My dorter in law come out she heard a voice she knew she stopt when she saw me starts screamin too. And then he screams at her shut your mouth if you doan want the same yousel. So i got back home somehow an when i feel i cant take what he done to me i tells the elder. So i has to go to the cantonal court when they sees the marks on my face they says go to the magistrate we cant deal with beatings an so your honor may i dare to fall before you i most humbly beg you dont leave me without your honors mercy i want the laws protecshon agin his beatings.

[Another *soldatka's* story:]

My husband a conscript discharged from duty came to spend the night with me because he was hangin roun with nowhere to go and he started to treat me real bad then he chucked me out the house with our little girl.

Source: Ia. Ludmer. "Bab'i stony," *Iuridicheskii vestnik* ["*Babas'* Groans," *Juridical Herald*], no. 11 (1884), pp. 450, 459, 462, 465.

Translated by Catriona Kelly.

Notes

1. By "privileged" social groups are meant those—chiefly the nobility, higher guild merchants, and clergy—that enjoyed such privileges as exemption from the soul (capitation) tax or corporal punishment; conversely, "unprivileged" social groups, essentially all other social groups, were those not enjoying such privileges.

2. The adjective *samara* apparently referred to a type of woman's two-piece dress.

3. This document refers to a number of different luxurious fabrics, including brocade, damask, moiré, chamois, lustrine, *gros de Tour* satin, and holland cloth. Muslin, a much more common fabric, is also mentioned.

4. Created by Peter I in 1711, the "Governing Senate" in the eighteenth century was the highest administrative and judicial body of the state.

5. Peasants were classified into several different categories in the eighteenth century: these included state peasants (who were subordinated directly to and administered by the state administration), crown peasants (who were owned by the imperial family), serfs (who were owned by private landlords), and *odnodvortsy* (owners of a single homestead).

6. In Russian *krovosmeshenie*, literally, "the mingling of blood."

7. Even though taxes on the peasantry were assessed according to the number of adult males, the entire community was responsible for them, so that the death of some members of the village and the disintegration of peasant households meant a heavier burden for those who remained.

8. A chief source of income for parish clergy, and of friction between them and their parishioners, were the emoluments received for the performance of prayers, rituals, and various other services.

9. Brackets in original.

10. Peleshko is the name of their estate; its exact location is unknown.

11. An ancient city on the Dvina River, south of St. Petersburg and west of Moscow; located in present-day Belarus.

12. We have not been able to find a reference to this battle, but it appears to have been one of the many minor engagements fought between the Russian and French armies as the latter withdrew through Germany in 1813.

13. The Order of St. Vladimir was founded by Catherine II in 1782 and awarded for acts of military bravery, as well as for a lengthy period of civil service. The ribbon is usually red moiré, with black edges.

14. In winter, Russians replaced wheeled carriages with sledges for easier travel on frozen roads and rivers.

15. Gdov was founded as a fortress town in 1431 and became a city in 1780. It was the capital of the district of the same name.

16. A city on the Gulf of Finland, west of St. Petersburg, located in present-day Estonia.

17. Russians of the Orthodox faith celebrate the feast day of the saint for whom they are named.

18. Ivankova wrote in a style typical of correspondence in her time—with very little punctuation and almost no paragraphing. To reflect the rambling style of the original while assisting our readers in understanding Ivankova, we have added paragraphing to the text but left it relatively free of punctuation.

19. A close confidante of Emperor Alexander I at the beginning of his reign, Nikolai Nikolaevich Novosiltsev (1768–1838) continued to play a prominent role in state affairs until his death.

20. We have not been able to identify either Fedor Ivanovich Kiselev or Pavel Aleksandrovich Rakhmanov, although both were members of prominent and influential noble families.

21. With his autocratic status, the emperor had the power to grant exceptions to the law in particular cases. In the nineteenth century a special bureaucratic department was established to receive and process petitions requesting such action.

22. Martha Wilmot, who was a kind of surrogate daughter for Dashkova, and her sister Catherine were long-time residents of Russia; their accounts of their experiences are in The Marchioness of Londonderry and H. M. Hyde, eds., *The Russian Journals of Martha and Catherine Wilmot* (London: Macmillan and Co., Ltd, 1935).

23. Imperial Russian law granted parents the right to have their children incarcerated for disobedience and disrespect.

24. The punctuation and ellipses are as given in the original. In the Shchukin text the diary is presented in French, which would have been the language at the school. Many young Russian women used French as their first language.

25. Geneviève, Madame de Staël (1766–1817), daughter of the royalist finance minister Jacques Necker and his wife Suzanne, a *salonnière*. A noted author and social critic, she was exiled from France to Switzerland by Napoleon.

26. On this correspondence, see chapter 4.

27. The Russian nanny (*niania*) is a common figure in both fiction and real life. Many children were as close to their nannies as they were to their parents.

28. Prince Ivan is a character who appears in many Russian folktales. In some portrayals he is a heroic and fearless knight; in others, a too-proud elder son who is bested by a more lowly brother. Often, as appears to be the case here, he is the suitor of a beautiful princess and must perform some heroic or mighty deed in order to win her hand.

29. Located on Grand Kaluga Street, now Lenin Prospect, the Golitsyn Hospital was built in 1796–1801 by the architect M. F. Kazakov. It now forms a part of the largest municipal hospital in Moscow.

30. During the eighteenth century it became a common practice among the European aristocracy and sometimes the middle classes to employ women from the countryside to nurse infants. Many memoirs testify to the strong attachment between children and their wet nurses.

31. As an ethnographic and geographic term, "Great Russia/n" referred to ethnic Russians and the territories populated chiefly by them, particularly in European Russia. It acquired this meaning in the seventeenth century, with the incorporation of the left-bank Ukraine into the Russian Empire.

32. The *zadruga* is the extended family community existing among Serbian peasants, which nineteenth-century Russian ethnographers commonly believed represented the original form of family structure among all Slavic groups.

33. In Russian, *rodovoi byt*. The root of the adjective, *rod*, refers to the patrilineal kin-group.

34. The term *bolshukha* is untranslatable, but means the senior woman in and mistress of the household.

35. In Russian, *snokha*.

36. In this passage Efimenko refers to both the father (*otets*) and the father-in-law (*svekor*) in relation to the *nevestki*, which can mean either daughters-in-law or sisters-in-law. In relation to each other, of course, the wives of the father's sons would be sisters-in-law, and they and the father's unmarried daughters also would be sisters-in-law.

37. The terms "Little Russia" and "Little Russians" were used commonly at this time to refer to Ukraine and Ukrainians, in part reflecting the belief (among Russians) that Ukraine was an integral part of Russia as a whole.

38. Efimenko here seems to mean a smaller, outlying farmstead separated from the main village settlement.

39. The source of this quote is not given.

40. Peasant families generally followed a "life cycle" by which they would grow larger as adult children married and had their own children, and then at some point they would divide into two or more smaller households.

41. Under imperial law, a surviving spouse had the right to inherit in unrestricted ownership one-seventh of the immovable property and one quarter of the unbequeathed movable property of the deceased spouse. Husbands and wives were treated equally in this instance.

42. That is, the Moscow Imperial Foundling Home, established in 1764 on the initiative of Catherine II. On the practice of peasant women becoming wet nurses, see note 30 above.

43. That is, syphilis.

44. During World War I the sale of alcohol was banned, leaving drinkers to resort to other intoxicating liquids such as methylated spirits.

45. Saburova appears to be referring to Marie Valette Monod, a French publicist and author in the latter part of the nineteenth century who wrote extensively on morals, education, and philanthropic activities by women. Among her works is *The Mission of Women in Time of War* (Paris, 1870).

46. In Russian, *"Popechitel'stvo,"* presumably the parish guardianship boards established in 1864 to provide elementary education and to undertake charitable work within the parish.

47. Saburova uses the feminine form, *fel'dsheritsy,* i.e., women who had received a lower level of medical training and often were utilized by the *zemstva* to provide medical services to the rural population.

48. Mikhail Iurevich Lermontov (1814–1841), romantic poet and novelist, best known for his novel *The Hero of Our Time* (1840).

49. Prince Petr Andreevich Viazemskii (1792–1878), a poet, literary critic, and (from 1841) member of the Academy of Sciences.

50. The Polish poet and patriot, Adam Mickiewicz (1799–1855).

51. In these cases, the women were seeking the right to live separately from their husbands, a request that the civil courts granted with increasing frequency, particularly in cases involving abusive behavior by the husband. The cantonal courts were established by the judicial reform of 1864 and were composed of peasant judges; they dealt with minor civil and criminal cases involving the local rural population. Also created by the judicial reform of 1864, the magistrate's courts—or justice of the peace courts—similarly had jurisdiction over minor civil and criminal matters for the general population.

52. A title equivalent to lord, or governor; Anna emphasizes Iaguzinskii's high rank by using both titles.

53. We have not been able to determine the function of this particular institution. In the second half of the eighteenth century, however, a number of commissions bearing similar names were established to oversee the construction of stone buildings in major cities (*"kamennyi dom"* signifies a building made of stone).

54. Under the divorce procedure established by the Russian Orthodox Church, a priest was required to admonish each spouse to reconcile before a divorce action could proceed.

55. This addendum suggests that Dvorskova's husband currently was living in the Transbaikal Diocese, in eastern Siberia.

56. The language throughout this selection has been rendered into the equivalent in colloquial and uneducated English.

3. Sexuality

INTRODUCTION

"We have no sex here!" asserted a Russian who participated in a simultaneous television broadcast between the Soviet Union and the United States in 1990. She clearly implied that sex is a Western "import," a Western corruption of Russian mores. While this now famous—and oft-repeated—statement may have been made jokingly, it also indicates that how sexuality is discussed and conceptualized varies by culture. There is a range of possibilities: sexuality can be celebrated, feared, repressed, boasted of, taken for granted, or some combination of these. The Russian Orthodox Church, for example, which had far-reaching influence in Russian culture, held sexuality to be both a source and sign of human sinfulness and an essential aspect of a Christian marriage. It therefore tolerated human sexuality while seeking to confine it within marriage and to curb what it defined as deviant sexual behavior. Within its own ranks, the Church required the parish (white) clergy to marry while it limited episcopal appointments to members of the monastic (black) clergy who had taken a vow of sexual abstinence. The teachings of the Church contributed to a strong tradition in Russia of considering sexuality improper and to a corresponding silence around the topic. Censorship by the state and Church also played a role here: many of the bawdier works—even of such well-known authors as Pushkin and Lermontov—could not be published. Yet side-by-side with this tradition of silence existed a folk literature of resistance and erotic tales and a tradition of carnival that reveled in the earthier sides of sexuality. During the Russian Silver Age (1890s–1910) there was a shift in the public sexual ethos. In this period sexuality became the subject of major philosophical debate; it also was a time of acknowledged sexual experimentation. In the Silver Age sexuality was frequently discussed in spiritual terms, and it was regarded as an important source of artistic creativity as well as human self-fulfillment.

Sexuality does not exist in isolation: how people think about sexuality and the body, and, for our purposes, in particular the female body, affects such societal issues as the organization of family life, the existence and character of prostitution, abortion, and birth control. It also has an impact on power relations, for example, within the peasant household or between (female) serf and (male) landowner. Conversely, other societal, political, and religious issues and goals affect the conceptualization and regulation of sexuality. For example, the desire to reinforce patriarchal authority and to protect the interests of the kin group, to assert the moral and institutional authority of the Orthodox Church, and to preserve social order all shaped attitudes toward and the legal rules regulating human sexuality in imperial Russia. Hence, how sexuality is conceptualized and codified reveals much about what a society values.

In this regard, state law and Orthodox teaching and sanctions worked throughout the imperial period to limit sexual activity both to marriage and to acts deemed "natural" and consistent with the procreative purpose of a Christian marriage. Severe legal disabilities were suffered by illegitimate children and stringent restrictions were placed on divorce, particularly for the Orthodox population; for the latter, among the few grounds for divorce were adultery and sexual incapacity. Sexual behavior considered to be deviant—which included adultery, fornication, homosexuality, bestiality, certain forms of intercourse, rape, and sex involving children—could incur both criminal and ecclesiastical penalties. While pandering, too, was criminally punishable, in the nineteenth century the state indirectly recognized sex outside of marriage through the introduction of a system of state registration and inspection of female prostitution. For its part, in its catechistic and other instructional literature the Orthodox Church stressed the sinfulness of sex outside of marriage, emphasized the procreative purpose of sexual relations, and taught that, for the few able to achieve such self-discipline, celibacy represented a higher state. The faithful, moreover, were enjoined not to enter a church to take the sacraments for a period after having engaged in sexual intercourse. And as the first sermon in chapter 1 demonstrates, a misogynistic tradition existed within the Church that associated female sexuality with impurity, temptation, and sin.

In imperial Russia, then, as in many cultures, the female body was feared as well as desired, sought after and yet seen as something that must be regulated and controlled. The documents in this chapter demonstrate the many ways that female sexuality—among all social groups—in Russia was regulated through marriage mores and social opinion, through laws, and through Church teaching and edicts. The chapter also shows how women sometimes internalized these controls and imposed them on (other) women. Conversely, it provides examples of ways that women protested or refused such controls, sometimes by using the system to make their protests (as in the case of Irina Globina) and sometimes by moving outside the system or attempting to transform it (as in the case of Marina Tsvetaeva and Sofia Parnok).

Many of the documents in this chapter overlap with those in other chapters, especially those in chapter 2, on family life. We have included them here to raise the issue of where these topics intersect and to ask readers to interpret some of these overlapping dynamics in terms of sexuality, rather than, primarily, in terms of choices about family roles or education.

Although sexuality is often thought of as private (or non-existent, as in the opening quotation), many of the selections in this chapter suggest that there also has long been an indirect public discourse on sexuality in Russia; this is seen in legal and church documents, in the advice given by older women to younger ones, and in autobiographical statements. The chapter begins with a letter and three personal narratives by women who lived in the eighteenth century. Their writings reflect a range of attitudes about sexuality, showing the ways that this topic was talked about or, more accurately, talked around. As with many of the other selections in this chapter, much is revealed about attitudes toward sexuality and the female body and little is made explicit.

SEX AND THE EIGHTEENTH-CENTURY NOBLEWOMAN

The following four selections describe different aspects of sexual mores for eighteenth-century Russian noblewomen. These include how women understood and discussed pregnancy (Tsaritsa Praskovia), issues of modesty (Aleksandra Levshina), unwelcome pursuit by an older and powerful man (Glafira Rzhevskaia), and how deeply both the silence around sexuality and the conflict between old and new sexual mores could affect women (Anna Labzina). Tsaritsa Praskovia Fedorovna (1664–1723) was a descendant of a powerful Russian noble family, the Saltykovs. From the high position of a noble-woman, Praskovia ascended even higher when Tsarevna Sophia, then regent of Russia, selected the young woman to marry her brother Ivan. Ivan and Peter I, half-brothers who reigned jointly, were grandsons of families—the Naryshins and the Miloslavskiis—who were competing for control of late seventeenth-century Russian politics. Praskovia and Ivan's marriage was intended to produce heirs who would strengthen the Miloslavskiis' claim to power. Although Praskovia gave birth to several girls, she never produced a son who could have inherited his father's claim to the throne. After Ivan's death, Praskovia actively supported Peter's program of reforms. Her letter, the earliest of these entries, shows that women did speak frankly with one another about matters of the body. In reading this letter from dowager Tsaritsa Praskovia to her daughter Ekaterina Ivanovna, we gain an understanding of how people of the Petrine period employed religious beliefs and practice to help them cope with difficult aspects of their lives. We also glimpse, in the advice Tsaritsa Praskovia offers her daughter about understanding developments in her body, the camaraderie of women in dealing with childbearing and health.

A. On Pregnancy and Female Health

Tsaritsa Praskovia

May 1722

Tsarevna Ekaterina Ivanovna! May God's grace and the mercy of the Holy Mother of God and your father's and my blessing be upon you. Write to me more often about your health and about your husband's and about your daughter's. And I write to you, my light, Katiushka,[1] and I support you with God in your sorrows and illnesses; place all your hopes on the Lord God and on the Holy Mother of God. May He, the All-Merciful Lord and the Holy Mother of God complete the uncompleted [tasks] now and in the future. And don't kill yourself with sorrow,[2] don't destroy your soul, also keep your creed like the apple of your eye so that in the future you will stand with Christ in common belief although what you will suffer is unknown. Don't bring down upon yourself our curse or that of the Church. The sovereign really sympathizes with you and wants to help somehow, only since he hasn't seen you, he can't do it; in the end, it is necessary for you to be in Riga. And keep Okunev,[3] who has been sent to you, as long as you need him. Convey my greetings to your husband and my granddaughter. And about myself, I write that I lie in complete illness and weakness. Since Christmas I have not been able to use my legs, only my arms, and Sister[4] can also do little continuously. I have sent more words with Okunev.

And I sent my granddaughter toys; give her the little barrel and the little basin.

And forgive me, Tsarevna Katerina, if the Lord creates something, remember. I am already in my great griefs and unbearable sorrows; I don't know if I will live long, and if I live, I would only kill myself with my great sorrows. And you write about your stomach and from your letter I don't know if you really are pregnant; there are such cases in which it doesn't show. While your father was here, I was that way. I knew for a year that I was pregnant, and that's how it turned out. Write more about your disease; can the doctors help you? And we haven't heard about the departure from Moscow, but I know that it will soon be time to go, and I will go straight from Moscow to the waters.[5] Write before that, please, really: will you go to Riga or not? And if you aren't pregnant after all, it is necessary for you to visit Olonets, the mineral waters, for such a disease, and you write that there is a swelling, and for such diseases and damage from female weakness water is really useful and it cures. My sister Princess Nastasia was cured of such diseases at the waters, and she doesn't swell up and her side doesn't hurt and her monthly weakness has become regular. If the doctor's medicine doesn't serve, then you need to go to the waters at Olonets. The writer, your mother, I send my blessings.

About that which is written, my light Katiushka, fulfill my command. Ts[aritsa] Praskovia

Granddaughter, my light, comfort your father and mother, don't rile them up. With this, the writer your old grandmother greets you. Ts[aritsa] Praskovia.

Source: M. Semevskii, *Tsaritsa Praskov'ia, 1664–1723. Ocherk iz russkoi istorii XVIII veka* [*Tsaritsa Praskovia, 1664–1723. A Study in 18th-Century Russian History*] (reprint; Moscow, 1989). Excerpted from pp. 194–95.

Translated by Robin Bisha.

B. A Letter on Modesty

ALEKSANDRA LEVSHINA

Aleksandra Petrovna Levshina, one of Catherine II's favorites, has been introduced in chapter 2, in an excerpt in which she mourns the loss of her sister; in the selection in chapter 4, she describes life at the Smolnyi Institute, a school for young noblewomen founded by Catherine II. Here, in a letter of 14 May 1773, she notes the seemingly prurient interest in her of Count Ivan Ivanovich Betskoi (1703–1795). Betskoi held important posts during the reign of Catherine II, including being president of the Imperial Academy of Fine Arts, chief trustee of the Imperial Foundling Home, and a trustee and member of the Board of the Society for the Education of Young Ladies of the Nobility (the Smolnyi Institute). In the following selection Levshina asks for the advice and protection of the empress; she expects Catherine II to understand her sense of modesty about the female body. It is unlikely that Levshina would have asked a male ruler for this kind of protection. It also should be noted that nude swimming with people of the same sex was common in Russia.

14 MAY 1773

Mr. Betskoi[6] has this minute informed me that he wants to teach us how to swim and that he has chosen me to be his subject. Doesn't Your Majesty find that his kindness goes a little too far? The worst of it is that he says You agree with his project. I beg You, have mercy, dissuade him, especially since we have among us some highly skilled swimmers; for that matter, I swim quite well myself. Therefore, either Mr. Betskoi will not be teaching us to swim or we will not be using the pond.

Source: Appollon Maikov, ed., "Perepiska imperatritsy Ekateriny II s A. P. Levshinoi," *Russkii vestnik* ["Correspondence of Empress Catherine II and A. P. Levshina," *Russian Messenger*], vol. 247 (Nov. 1896), pp. 310–49. Excerpted from p. 325.

Translated by Martha Kuchar.

C. Courtship Intrigues

GLAFIRA RZHEVSKAIA

Like Levshina, Glafira Ivanovna Rzhevskaia (née Alymova) has been introduced ear-
lier; in chapter 2 her relationship with her mother was the primary focus. Rzhevskaia,
too, attended the prestigious Smolnyi Institute. Also like Levshina, but in more detail,
Rzhevskaia discusses Ivan Ivanovich Betskoi, in particular she refers to the powerful at-
traction the seventy-five-year-old man felt for the eighteen-year-old Rzhevskaia. In the
eighteenth century, marriages between older men and younger women were common in
Russia, as throughout Western Europe. By the end of the century, however, this age gap
was shrinking, and it declined even further in the nineteenth century. Rzhevskaia notes
the intense confusion between the roles of daughter and wife, father and husband, which
the relationship with Betskoi entailed. She also describes the ways that her attachment to
her future husband became the subject of court intrigue; in this way, she shows that
among the social elite sexuality was inseparable from and implicated in political life. The
selection from Rzhevskaia's memoir not only details the dynamics of attraction and
power relations between Betskoi and Rzhevskaia, but also hints at Rzhevskaia's school-
girl crush on the headmistress Mme. Lafond.

Mme. Lafond directed this establishment for thirty years with rare wisdom and placed on a firm footing the system of upbringing accepted there. She threw herself wholeheartedly into work. She maintained a firm and vigilant watch over those persons who had to assist her in the success of her enterprise so that they would carry out their obligations conscientiously; it was as if she was educating them before she put trust in them. She exhibited the same care in choosing servants, which is so important in an institution where purity of mores is considered to be the cornerstone of all virtue.

Before I tell you how dear she was to me personally, I have to say how valued she was in general. She was the subject of my first attachment. No one who came after her could replace her for me. She was my mother, my guide, my friend, she was my patroness and my benefactress. I fully understood that when I reached such an age when I could comprehend my different feelings toward her. To love, honor, and revere her was a necessity for me. At that time my feeling resembled a strong passion. I would give up nourishment for her caresses.

It only remains for me to tell about Iv. Iv. Betskoi, who played such an important role in my life from my childhood until my marriage. I have difficulties in defining his character. The more I think about him, the more indistinct he becomes. But there was a time when his influence on me resembled a spell. Having the possibility to mold me in any way he liked, he lost this right due to his own mistake. I say it with regret, but I do not wish to deviate from the truth. Facts will prove that we, despite free will, cannot run away from our fate.

We were taught to respect this remarkable and revered old man as our father and protector. He was like that to all the pupils until the last moment of our stay in Smolnyi; to the most deserving he attempted to provide the greatest advantages and in such cases was fair without a trace of partiality. His relations with me were of a different kind. From the first moment he had seen me, I became his favorite child, his treasure. His feelings reached such a degree that I became the object of his most tender sentiments, of all his thoughts. This predilection in no way was a disadvantage to the others, because I used it for their good. I asked nothing for myself, I tried to get everything for my friends who were grateful to me for my impartiality and because of it loved me even more. I did not cease to ask him on behalf of all those who needed his protection, and my requests were not in vain. He always fulfilled my requests. Wishing to give some pleasure to the pupils he would inform me about it in advance and executed his intention at my most insistent requests, and so the joy that he brought was ascribed to me.

I have already mentioned my attachment to Betskoi. My infinite feeling had no special price. All the sacrifice was made by him, while I only submitted to the entrancing feeling that constituted my happiness. But he did not inspire such trust in me as Mme. Lafond. I poured out my feelings to her; when I was with him I was happy without saying a word. I used to ask Mme. Lafond whether my actions were good or bad. She knew how to direct my thoughts in such a manner that my behavior always conformed to her advice. Soon Mr. Betskoi stopped hiding his feelings toward me and announced publicly that I was his favorite child, that he was taking me under his tutelage, and made a solemn oath about it to my mother by lighting a lamp in front of an icon of the Savior. Before the world he adopted me. Three years passed as a day among constant amiabilities, attentions, caresses, and tender care that completely enchanted me. At that time I would gladly devote my life to him.

Mr. B. started being more attentive than ever; neither cold nor bad weather would keep him. He would come to me daily, toward the end even twice a day. He would be occupied only with me, he would talk about my future. Noticing that I understood nothing and that I became fed up with this sort of conversation, he decided to act as if in accordance with my character and inclinations, but in reality he was managing me in his own way. Trying to distance me from all those who enjoyed my trust, he arranged it so cleverly that no one dared reveal to me his intentions, while they were so obvious that when I remember his behavior, I wonder at my stupidity. At first he tried to blind me with expensive gifts, but I used to refuse them saying I did not need them. Then, jokingly, he would ask me in front of everyone what I would prefer to be: his wife or his daughter. "Your daughter," I would answer, "because I could live with you and no one would think that I loved you out of interest and not for yourself; they say that you are very rich." "But you have nothing." "Do I lack for anything?" He would laugh until tears would run down his face and change the conversation, but I paid no attention to all this, as if it did not concern me.

Seeing that I did not know the world and that even the suspicion of evil would make me indignant, he tried in every way to convince me that everybody was out there to deceive me and in this way to distance me from the world. He would not leave my room even when I was out of the house and would wait for my return. When I woke up I would see him beside me. In the meantime he would offer no explanations. Trying to instill in me an aversion toward marriage with anyone else, he wished I would decide to marry him as if out of my own free will, without any coercion on his part. His passion reached such extremes that it was no secret for anyone though he used to hide it under the guise of fatherly tenderness. I did not even suspect this. At the age of seventy-five he would blush, would admit that he could not live without me. It seemed to him a most natural thing that a girl of eighteen, who knew nothing about love, would give herself to a man whom she liked. His reasoning was correct but he was mistaken as to the means of achieving his aim. I repeat, had he been somewhat more frank, I would willingly have become his wife. Meanwhile other men were trying to find favor in my eyes.

Mr. Rzhevskii proposed to me. I promised him nothing, saying that I depended on Iv. Iv. B.,[7] whom he should approach in this matter. He wanted to know whether I was inclined toward him and whether I would accept his proposal. I answered that I would do it only with the consent of the person who replaced my father and that without his approval I would not give anyone my hand or my heart.

I hastened to tell Iv. Iv. about all that happened. To my great amazement this man, usually so mild and tractable, became angry and fell into despair. I was at a loss what to do, I imagined that I had committed a very great *faux pas*, but still I wanted to know what it was exactly. Having calmed down, he explained his outbreak, saying that I had grieved him by thoughtlessly tying myself down, by giving my word to a man whom I did not know. At the same time he painted a gloomy picture of how I was cheated, how the name of the Empress was used in a wicked way, and finally said that he would die of grief if I were to be unhappy. All this was enough to instill in me a revulsion against any marriage. I assured him that I did not at all insist on that match, that I renounced it completely and submitted my will to his in all that concerned my fate.

I thought no more about Rzhevskii's proposal. Iv. Iv. received him very well and made an excellent show of playing the tender father. He made a plan of how to behave and undoubtedly would have achieved his purpose if it were not for an event that wrecked his intentions. Firstly, in his conversation with Mr. R. he assured him that the obstacles were created by me, that I was resisting his desire to find me a husband; he asked him to be patient and promised to act to his advantage. Unfortunately, he found a man who was more cunning than himself. While he was teaching me, Count Orlov[8] tried to explain the matter to me. But I had become so accustomed to being mistrustful that the influence of Iv. Iv. could not be undermined. Orlov did not spare him when talking to me about him, but I was angry that the purity of his intentions was being put into doubt. On his part Iv. Iv. communicated to me adverse opinions about my fiancé.

With the help of Count Orlov's cousin who lived at court, I became more closely acquainted with Rzhevskii and slowly became attached to him. This was unexpected. I became firm and consistent in my actions. Then Betskoi became ever more active and decided to organize my fall from grace at the court of the Grand Duchess,[9] presenting me to the Empress as an ungrateful person and as a duplicitous one to my fiancé, while presenting them all to me as unjust and contemptible. I could never stand court life. I wished to take my leave of it and marry Rzhevskii. All this was taking place in spring, prior to the departure to Tsarskoe Selo,[10] where Rzhevskii, with my consent, found lodgings for himself in order to see me every day. The Empress was openly favoring my marriage, though, using persecution, Betskoi was compelling me to hide my intentions and even put off my marriage for two years. As he was unable to put to naught the whole affair, he was hoping that time and the power of intrigues would help. And indeed, on the day when I was packing to leave, while Betskoi was pacing up and down the room, the Grand Duchess sent for me. She was in tears and told me that the Empress commanded me to stay in the city. I asked the Grand Duke to try and reverse this order. He went twice to the Empress and told us that there was some mystery involved. The Empress did not want to say anything and only mentioned to him that she did not wish to hinder me and, in accordance with my wishes, allowed me to breathe at liberty and to have a rest from his wife's jealousy. He added that my insistence would be futile, that he did not believe any of it knowing my truthfulness and my inability to invent an unforgivable lie. The Grand Duchess flared up, I became angry and suddenly left. Betskoi was waiting for me, he arranged everything his own way. He assured me that he had just returned from the Empress who told him that at the insistent request of the Grand Duchess, she had decided to leave me in the city without the knowledge of the Grand Duchess's husband in order to remove me from him. The story seemed plausible to me. The Empress, wishing to ensure harmony in her family, could indulge the caprices of her daughter-in-law. But I could not forgive the latter her behavior in relation to me in an instance where she alone was to blame. I could not contain my indignation. Instead of calming me down, Betskoi became irate, saying that this disfavor could finally destroy my reputation, about which in any case unflattering rumors were abounding. I swore that I no longer wished to stay at court, where I had become the apple of discord. This was what he was waiting for. Immediately he conjured before my eyes the most alluring pictures of life among friends, under a father's roof. He immediately wanted to transfer his house to me, to surround me with all the people I was attached to in Smolnyi, to bring an orchestra from Germany, instruments from England, to give me means to improve my music and painting, to give balls, play comedies, etc. My grief turned to joy; I surrendered to the wisdom and benevolence of my protector. He should have maintained this mood of mine, to hasten to fulfill his intentions. Everything would have been lost if anyone had opened my eyes to the truth. He left me no time to say good-bye to their Imperial Highnesses and took me back to Mme. Lafond.

I wanted to see my fiancé; they dispatched someone to invite him to come the next day, but he declined under the pretext of illness. Then they started to abuse him, saying that he was a vile and base courtier who was attracted to me only because of the advantages and who abandoned me when I fell into seeming disfavor. I tried to defend him; such unfounded accusations did not agree with the purity of my heart and my exalted feelings.

To amuse me Betskoi took me for a drive and, as luck would have it, we met Rzhevskii, who earlier had said that he was unwell. I became sad, but my pride revived my shaken soul. Passing next to Rzhevskii I noticed signs of joy that promised the explanation of all that happened. After my return to the palace in the company of my sister, I received through the maid a note from Rzhevskii, who asked me to meet him in secret from the old man as he had something important to communicate to me. And indeed in the presence of my sister he disclosed to me the secrets by which I was surrounded in order to place insurmountable obstacles between us. He confessed that he himself was deceived, suspecting that I was unfaithful to him, and tried in every way to find out the truth; he told me that the Empress said to Count Orlov that Betskoi pestered her the whole day and in my name asked her to leave me in town to prepare my trousseau. On my part I told him how all this had come about. Everything became clear and this explanation brought about the desired denouement.

Being certain of Rzhevskii's feelings, I forgave Iv. Iv. Betskoi everything, and in order not to embarrass him completely I hid from him that I was aware of all his trickery. He, on the other hand, continued his intrigues to the very end, but lost completely; because his stratagem was discovered he had willingly to agree to our marriage. Out of respect for him I submitted to his authority. As a father he was necessary for my happiness, while his only desire was to become my husband. I began by making my peace with the Grand Duchess, who considered herself offended by my treatment of her in circumstances that were in no way her fault. I wrote to her without my guardian's knowledge. We explained everything, and the past was forgotten. I returned to the court where everybody took a keen interest in my forthcoming marriage.

Then he (Betskoi) brought to the fore a long-forgotten condition, namely the promise to go and live in his house, which had earlier frightened Rzhevskii and which Betskoi believed would break the engagement. He humiliated himself so far as to beg me, representing this as necessary for the protection of our reputation, that we would, at least for several months, go and live in the house he had arranged for us. At long last I managed to persuade Rzhevskii to agree to this plan. Then the intrigues ceased, but Iv. Iv. still hoped to shatter my decisiveness and to woo me by insistent constancy. Before the altar, as the sponsor at the wedding, he told me of marriages that fell apart during the actual ceremony and incited me to do the same. My marriage put an end to all the disputes. With daughterly tenderness I tried to console Iv. Iv., but my efforts were in vain. My friendship could not satisfy his passion. Caught between my husband's love and Betskoi's friendship, my situation became intolerable. Both felt offended by me and tormented me.

There was no possibility of satisfying their claims; I had to choose one or the other.

In the behavior of Iv. Iv. I clearly saw the intention of causing a quarrel between me and my husband, pushing him away from me by insults, and trying to woo me by tenderness and promises of wealth. He was looking for an opportunity to have me under his control without trying to win my consent. I managed to stop him in time. Having proved to him the enormity of his guilt and having offered to make peace in any way, I explained to him that neither myself nor my husband would stay any longer in his house, I told him that his own peace of mind depended on it, and promised to show him my attachment all my life. He would not even hear about it and, seeing that all his insistence was in vain, swore revenge.

Source: "Pamiatnye zapiski Glafiry Ivanovny Rzhevskoi," *Russkii arkhiv* ["Memorial Notes of Glafira Ivanovna Rzhevskaia," *Russian Archive*], vol. 9 (1871), pp. 10–31. Excerpted.

Translated by Ruth Sobel.

D. Sexual Mores in Marriage

ANNA LABZINA

The following selection is from the autobiography of Anna Evdokimovna Labzina (1758–1828), who was chiefly raised by her deeply religious and pious mother. Her father, a middling nobleman and official in the mining service in Siberia, died in her early childhood. Nearing death, Labzina's mother married off her daughter Anna at age thirteen to Aleksandr Matveevich Karamyshev (1744–1791), fourteen years her senior and a former ward of her parents. Karamyshev had been educated at Moscow University, then studied at Uppsala University in Sweden, and was in the early stages of a successful career in the state's mining service. The author of several works on mining and economics and a corresponding member of both the Russian and the Swedish Academy of Sciences, Karamyshev appeared to embody the liberating ideals of the Enlightenment. He used these ideals, however, to justify his gambling, carousing, and loose sexual morality. At first glance, then, the unhappiness and misery Labzina experienced in her marriage to Karamyshev seems to have derived from the conflict between the values, ideals, and behavioral expectations of traditional Russian culture and those of the Russian Enlightenment. On closer inspection, however, Labzina's conflict with her husband reveals a more complex process of cultural interaction and personal self-definition, as her subsequent activities attest. (In this regard, refer to the selection from Labzina's autobiography in chapter 5.) After Karamyshev's death, Labzina married Aleksandr Labzin (1766–1825) and together with him played a prominent role in the Masonic movement in St. Petersburg and in the religious revival that took place in early nineteenth-century imperial Russia.

Labzina wrote her autobiography in 1810, during her far happier marriage to Labzin, and apparently never intended that it be published. It first appeared in 1903. The excerpt here demonstrates how little education about sex the young Russian noblewoman received before her marriage, a phenomenon that was common throughout Europe in the eighteenth century. According to her own account, Labzina entered marriage with no knowledge of sex at all. In this regard, her experience was similar to that of Levshina and Rzhevskaia.

We arrived in the city. All sorts of merrymaking started at our house in which I could not participate. My husband took his niece Vera Alekseevna to live with him. During the day all were together, but when we went our separate ways to sleep at night, his niece came to our room and lay down to sleep with us. And if it seemed crowded to her, or for another reason that I did not understand then, they sent me to sleep on the couch. Since I still could not collect myself after the loss of my mother, I was glad to be alone so I could think in freedom and get up early as was my habit, but which my husband did not allow, ordering me to arise no earlier than ten o'clock. For me, this was torture and terrible anguish: not to see the sunrise and to lie there, although I was not asleep. That life reduced me to such a weak state that I could not sleep a wink, and I grew thin and sallow; I was in this state for about four weeks.

My mother-in-law became distressed about my health and also lost sleep. One night she wanted to see if I was sleeping. Having entered the room very quietly, she found me lying on the couch and my husband with his niece. Seeing this, she began to tremble and went away. The next day she came to me, because I could no longer get up due to the ache in my head. Once we were alone, she asked me why I was sleeping on the couch. I answered, "I was told that Vera Alekseevna was crowded and uncomfortable. Not thinking of myself, I wanted her to be comfortable."

She began to cry and reproached me for my insincerity because I had not told her earlier. I answered that I considered this unnecessary. "And I would ask you, as my mother and benefactress, to leave me here when you go to Petersburg.[11] I am in no way necessary to you and I can be useful to others. I assure you that I will indeed not complain about your son; I will reproach myself for my inability to love or please my husband. What kind of joy could it bring you to see in torment the one you love and who has done you no wrong and who could have loved your son if he wanted it? Be so kind, take me to the village so that I can die there surrounded by my friends! And you, of course, will not refuse to do me one last kindness and stay with me now. It is pleasant to me to see you, and I love you no less than my own mother. Remember, that I was entrusted to you at my mother's death and except for you I have no one in the world. My relations and friends are all far away and separated from me!" She cried bitterly and said, "What is the matter with you, my friend, that you are killing yourself? God is kind, all will come right! We will pray and hope. It seems to me that your husband loves you. Otherwise, why would he have married you? No one forced him."

"This is strange love! Not everyone loves in this fashion. And isn't this the upbringing they call the best and enlightened? Why did you take me out of my blissful condition and make me feel such deep sorrows so early? You knew me intimately and knew I was living among friends and that their love elevated me and made me happy. What will become of me now? Oh, how I want to be united with my honored mother!

"There is only one thing that still makes my heart beat; that is love for my brother who sees everything in me. Look after him, dear mother, and do not let him feel the loss of everything."

She embraced me and said, "Compose yourself, my invaluable daughter and friend! You will find everything in me: I will share everything with you." That day she never left my side.

Toward evening I became feverish and delirious, and they say I raved, calling my mother and all of my friends to take me with them. My mother-in-law sat near me the entire night in fear and even despair. My husband left for the mines. In the morning they called the head physician who said that I had a severe and dangerous fever and he doubted that I would live through it. My mother-in-law threw herself on her knees before him saying, "Save her, for God's sake, and use every means for her recovery! You are a friend of her mother's and you have to know the reason for her disease: the powerful shock of everything created by the loss of her mother and her excommunication from her friends have made this disease."

For twenty-one days I was without hope! My mother-in-law sent to the village to have Nanny brought to me and for Uncle and Aunt to come. I was surrounded by my friends, yet did not feel how much sorrow I had created for them. They had me confessed, and the priest administered the Last Rites. On the twenty-first day I came to my senses and the first thing that appeared before me was my nanny, and I thought it was a dream. I sighed and closed my eyes. On the next day I began to hear and understand what they were saying. The physician said that now there was hope for life. To tell the truth, it was very unpleasant for me to hear this: I would have left this earth with joy then. I saw my husband kneeling, crying bitterly. This so touched me that I made an effort to lift my hand and give it to him. He noticed my movement and approached me. I looked at him, took his hand, and pressed it to my heart. He fell on his knees and began to sob. My mother-in-law and relatives convinced him that he would reactivate my illness with his grief. Even so, I had already noticed that all who were dear to my heart were with me. I asked about my brother and they brought him to me immediately. He embraced me and asked, "Now you are not going to die and your Sasha[12] is not going to be an orphan?"

Even so, my recovery was very slow. For two months I couldn't walk by myself, I was terribly thin, bile had spread all over my body, and I had a heavy cough. The physician was afraid of consumption, however, from time to time it got better and in December [1772] I was completely healthy already. My husband had spent very little time away from me during this time, and his ministrations over me greatly reassured me. And I, as much as I could, tried to show him my feelings: with what joy I accepted his services and how grateful I was to him. My mother-in-law and all of my relatives rejoiced at my tranquility and complete recovery. Uncle and Aunt left for the country, but my mother-in-law would not allow Nanny to leave; she gladly stayed with me.

One day I asked my mother-in-law, "Where is Vera Alekseevna?"

She said to me, "Do not speak of her to me. I do not want to see her!"

My calm did not last long. In the evening, I was sitting in my room reading. My husband came to me, caressed me, and asked, "Why are you angry at poor Vera Alekseevna?"

I told him he was mistaken in thinking that I was angry with her. "I even asked your mother about her. She ordered me to be silent and not remind her of Vera Alekseevna, saying that she did not want to see her. So, ask her how Vera Alekseevna made her angry. I don't even know if it's been a long time since she's been here or why."

My husband said, "From the beginning of your illness she was hung out to dry and driven away for no reason by my mother."

This surprised me a great deal. "Knowing the gentleness and kind disposition of my mother-in-law, what you have said really surprises me. Your mother would not treat her so harshly without reason, and especially since she is her favorite granddaughter. You should have tried to find out the reason and make her beg your mother's forgiveness."

He told me to do this and also to ask her to let Vera Alekseevna live with us until our departure. I said that I was forbidden to speak of her, so I could not do this. He looked at me with a very angry countenance and said, "I demand that this request be fulfilled. Otherwise, you will receive neither love nor caresses from me and everything will be taken away from you again. I am going to her now and will spend a much nicer night there than here. Do you think that I don't know that this is your undertaking?"

Crying, I answered that what he had said to me had not been in my thoughts, "And you yourself tell me that during my illness she was chased away. How could I take part in it?" He left, not saying a word.

My mother-in-law waited for us for a long time but finally gave up. She came into my room, and seeing me alone and tearful, she started to ask me questions. I told her everything. She grew absolutely furious, but I said, "What are you going to do with me? You are taking away my composure again. He will be going to her, you know. He wanted to spend the night there tonight. I just don't know, can you make this better? People may trumpet about his behavior, and that would be unpleasant for you. Oh, dear mother, why did you rush to make me unhappy, not finding out his character before our marriage?[13] To my misfortune, I see that he has nothing saintly about him. I fear that he will even lose his respect for you, then what will you do? Find the means, if you can, now to save me."

I no longer remember how it took place, but in a few days Vera Alekseevna turned up to live with us until our departure, and my life was nothing but suffering. Thinking that I would complain about his actions, my husband appointed his niece my supervisor to keep me from going anywhere or speaking with anyone. But I had no such intention. My mother-in-law ordered that Vera Alekseevna be with us only during the day; after supper she would go immediately to her room. But during the day, when we were sitting alone, there was such vileness that it was impossible to watch. I was compelled to bear it all because they would not let me go. Looking at all of that, I closed my eyes in shame and cried. Finally, I stopped crying. I decided not to live with my husband, and to remain in Siberia, but I kept quiet until we had packed.[14]

Source: Anna Evdokimovna Labzina, Vospominaniia Anny Evdokimovny Labzinoi, 1758–1828 [The Recollections of Anna Evdokimovna Labzina, 1758–1828] (St. Petersburg, 1914). Excerpted from pp. 36–40.

Translated by Robin Bisha.

REGULATING SEXUALITY

A. Exile for Indecent Behavior

The events described in the following selection took place in the 1760s, very close in time to those described by Levshina, Rzhevskaia, and Labzina. This is a legal document, however, rather than a personal narrative; unlike Levshina, Rzhevskaia, and Labzina, most of the women described in the text are from either the merchant or other non-noble estates, and not all are Russians. As was typical at the time, sexual behavior is not named directly in the document. Rather, the acts for which the women are to be punished are described as "idle pleasures" and "indecent behavior." The punishment for these "pleasures" was exile and marriage: the first priority was to remove these women from the scene of the crime, after which they were to be married off. Marriage, then, was considered a means by which female sexuality could be controlled or made less dangerous. In the nineteenth century the sexual character of offenses was indicated more explicitly and, especially prior to the 1850s, penitential confinement in a convent was frequently used to control and "correct" sexual behavior.

By the royal order of Her Imperial Highness those widows and wenches who engage in idle pleasures and in indecent behavior are to be exiled to Siberia and Orenburg. These women have been brought to the Main Police Office and their names are shown on the enclosed register. The appropriate amount of money from the Treasury is to be allotted for the cost of this banishment; and there [in Siberia and Orenburg], based on consideration and circumstances, these women are to be married off to local residents or exiles.

THE REGISTER OF THOSE WOMEN AND WENCHES WHO ARE ORDERED INTO EXILE:

For indecent behavior:
Moscow merchant Pavel Baleter's daughter, an unmarried girl Anna Pavlova.
Moscow woolen-cloth merchant Fedor Medviedev's daughter, an unmarried girl Avdotia Fedorova.
Navy assistant skipper Grigorii Sobolev's wife, Praskovia Andreeva.
Soldier of the Preobrazhenskii Regiment of the Imperial Guards Afanasii Romanov's wife, the widow Praskovia Sergeeva.
Soldier of the Chancellery of Constructions Prokofii Maslov's wife, the widow Natalia Fedorova.
Worker of the Navy Hospital Akim Vorotnikov's wife, the widow Anna Ivanova.
Soldier Andrei Kopytov's wife, Varvara Ivanova.
French midwife's servant, Anna Anofrieva.
Recruit Ivan Volkov's wife, Anna Ivanova.
Sailor Nikifor Svatov's wife, the widow Matrena Ekimova.
Soldier Timofei Makarov's wife, the widow Praskovia Grigoreva.
Carpenter's daughter, an unmarried girl Anna Petrova.
Soldier's daughter, an unmarried girl Anna Ivanova.
Of Turkish origin, having taken on the Greek Orthodox faith, Maria Vasileva.
Locksmith Osip Viman's wife, Anna Ivanova.

SENATE RULING, 20 DECEMBER OF 1765.

It has been ordered that the aforementioned widows and wenches be taken to the Main Police Chancellery in order to be sent away according to their destination.

REPORT TO THE SENATE FROM THE MAIN POLICE CHANCELLERY, 3 FEBRUARY 1766.

With this report the Chancellery informs that one of those women sent here for deportation, Ekaterina Fedorova, wife of the trumpeter Fedor Sivov, has been overcome with a fever. After the physician's examination [it was the physician's opinion that] she will not only be unable to travel to her assigned destination, but she is incapable of any movement whatsoever; for the reason of her illness this Fedorova has been placed under the care of Andrei Mikhailov, the archpriest of the

Church of Transfiguration of the Lord; and another soldier's wife, Irina Vlaseva, died. The other women have been sent to the St. Petersburg Provincial Chancellery.

REPORT TO THE SENATE FROM ST. PETERSBURG PROVINCIAL CHANCELLERY, 7 APRIL 1766.

Which informs that among those women sent from the Main Police Chancellery for deportation to exile, were a woman of the Catholic order, Anna Ivanova, and her underage daughters, Anna and Elizaveta, who have expressed their desire to espouse the Greek Orthodox faith; therefore, the [St. Petersburg] Provincial Chancellery inquires of the Senate what is to be done with them in the light of the edict of the Empress Elizaveta Petrovna of 28 September 1743, which exempts foreigners from punishment for minor offences when they espouse the Greek Orthodox faith.

THE RULING OF THE SENATE, 18 MAY 1766.

It has been ordered: that woman of the Catholic order, Anna Ivanova and her two daughters, be sent away from the Chancellery where it is deemed right by the law, in order to be accepted into the Greek Orthodox faith; and later Anna is to be freed and not be exiled because of the aforementioned edict of Empress Elizaveta Petrovna of 28 September 1743. A signed pledge [from Anna Ivanova] is required, stating that she would abstain from indecent behavior, and would not dare to attempt those indecent acts under threat of actions against her according to the law.

Next, all the other women and wenches have been deported into exile to their assigned places.

Source: "Kopiia s dela ob otpravlenii v Sibir' i Orenburg na poselenie zhenok i devok durnogo povedeniia, 1765–1766 gg." ["A Copy of the Case of Exiling Women and Wenches of Indecent Behavior to Siberia and Orenburg, 1765–1766"], in Shchukin, vol. VIII. Excerpted from pp. 354–56.

Translated by Robin Bisha.

B. Regulation of Peasants' Sexuality

Moving into the nineteenth century, we begin with two official documents, one an Edict of the Holy Synod and the other a petition of a peasant woman to the Holy Synod. These documents show both the extensive role played by the Orthodox Church in the regulation of sexuality in general and different aspects of the ways in which sexuality was thought about and regulated with regard to female peasants. The edict demonstrates the complicated relations of power between the landowner Chesnovskii and the priest Silet-skii, a battle that takes place over the rights and bodies of female peasants as well as over competing sexual mores. Among the many duties of parish priests was the performance of rituals like marriage and funeral rites for both serfs and landowners, so that the priest served as a link between the two groups. It is important to note that the decision of the Synod, while supportive of the female peasants, would be difficult to enforce. The second document, the petition of Irina Globina, was submitted forty-five years later. It reveals the kind of punishment that women were given for such sexual violations as fornication and indicates that peasant women could and did use the legal system to redress their wrongs.

---

1. Edict, Sexually Abusive Landowner

Regarding the petition of provincial secretary[15] Iosif Chesnovskii for the removal from his property of the Priest Andrei Siletskii, for refusing to conclude marriages. Submitted to the Holy Synod, 1827.

On the 25th of January of the year 1828, in accordance with the decree of His Imperial Majesty, the Holy Governing Synod heard the report of the Right Reverend Parfenii, Bishop of Vladimir,[16] in response to the decree of the Holy Synod of the 22nd of April of the past year 1827, regarding the furnishing of information with respect to the petition of Provincial Secretary Iosif Chesnovskii, which complained about the inaction of the Vladimir Diocesan Authorities[17] in connection with his requests concerning the refusal by Andrei Siletskii, parish priest of the Kuzemsk cemetery church in Murom[18] district, to conclude marriages between his serfs and his encouragement of their insubordination to him, Chesnovskii, and which requested the removal of Siletskii from the superintendence of his peasants in the performance of the religious rites that take place among them.

In his report, the Right Reverend Bishop of Vladimir relates: firstly, the noble landowner Chesnovskii brought two complaints against the Priest Siletskii to the Vladimir Consistory: the first, of the 1st of June, 1826, concerns the legal reckoning with Father Siletskii for the incitement in his peasants of a spirit of insubordination and enmity toward him that reached such an extent that they denounced him, Chesnovskii, to the civil government for debauchery with their wives and the seduction of their underage daughters; and they denounced his wife for oppressing them with excessive manorial work. To expose Father Siletskii in the above-mentioned actions, Chesnovskii presented a letter written by Siletskii to the clerk of the Melenkov lower land court,[19] Aleksei Popov, asking that beneficence be shown to the peasants upon the submission by them of the declaration against Chesnovskii.

The Consistory denied Chesnovskii's request, first because by the decision of the Vladimir Criminal Chamber[20] in the case regarding his debauchery with his peasants' wives and the forcible corruption of their underage daughters, on the basis of the unanimous testimony of the peasants themselves and of their wives and girls, and also on the basis of the testimony of the clergy of the Kuzemsk cemetery church, among whom Father Siletskii explained that a serf woman and a serf girl belonging to Chesnovskii had confessed to him, Chesnovskii was left under suspicion,[21] as a consequence of which he was deprived of the management of his peasants, with this function being transferred to his wife.

Second, [the Consistory denied Chesnovskii's request because] Father Siletskii already had borne an appropriate punishment for encouraging the peasants in their disobedience to Chesnovskii, and the Diocesan Authorities cannot undertake a new examination of the letter, since it was already considered by the Criminal Chamber when it decided the case against Chesnovskii. And in the last request, submitted on the 1st of November of 1826, regarding the refusal of Father Siletskii to marry peasants who had become widowed but were still underage, and even some who had reached the legal age for marriage; also regarding the infrequent reading by the Priest in the church of the imperial manifesto of the 12th of May, 1826, concerning the submission of peasants to their owners[22] and regarding the prescriptions to those who perform marriages, the Vladimir Diocesan Authorities likewise denied his [Chesnovskii's] request for the removal of Father Siletskii from his superintendence of the peasants, because first of all the petitioner Chesnovskii does not explain how exactly the Priest does not perform marriages, whereas the Priest testifies that he refused to marry Chesnovskii's widowed peasants Emelian Isaev with the widow Agripina Leontieva because of the disparity in their ages and the failure of Leontieva to agree to this, and Fedor Petrov with the young maiden Avdotia Gerasimova because of her denunciation of Chesnovskii for the corruption of her virginity, and this case had not at all been settled at that time; there were no other weddings for three years.

As concerns the imperial manifesto of the 12th of May, 1826, it was always read by Siletskii in the church on Sundays and on holidays, and Chesnovskii has not presented any proof or evidence in refutation of this. Second, because Chesnovskii has been deprived of the administration of his peasants, he does not have the right and must not introduce any order with respect to his estate and use petitions for the marriage of his peasants. Third, the contents of the letter written by Father Siletskii to the clerk Popov by no means show an encouragement of the peasants' insubordination to their landlord, but the obligation of a pastor to keep his flock away from debauchers, and Father Siletskii was not found by the government to be guilty. Consequently, the removal from his place and position which follows with respect to the civil authorities for the encouragement of peasants to insubordination should, since no such encouragement was revealed in this case, not be regarded as an acknowledgment of his guilt and as a punishment, but solely as a legal measure of precaution on the part of the spiritual authorities.

On the basis of the information submitted the following is decreed: to deny the request of Provincial Secretary Iosif Chesnovskii for the removal of the parish priest of the Kuzemsk cemetery church, Andrei Siletskii, from the performance of religious rites for his peasants, as well as to deny all his other requests, for the same circumstances and reasons that the Diocesan Authorities justly and legally left his requests without satisfaction. The Right Reverend Bishop of Vladimir should be sent this decree to declare to the petitioner Chesnovskii, but with the addition that a stern reprimand be given to the Priest Andrei Siletskii for his illegally testifying that the peasants confessed to him about the fornication of Chesnovskii with their wives and his seduction of their daughters.[23] It is also clear from the report of the Right Reverend Bishop of Vladimir that the landowner Chesnovskii was unanimously denounced by his peasants for committing forcible fornication with their wives and for corrupting the virginity of their young daughters of ten years of age and younger, and that he was tried in the Criminal Chamber, by whose decision he was left under suspicion and deprived of the administration of his estate, with the latter being transferred to his wife. All this notwithstanding, he continues to issue orders on the administration of his peasants and enters into their houses under various pretexts, and in this way without hindrance can continue his seductive and, for his peasants, harmful actions. The Ober-Procurator of the Synod therefore is called upon to discuss with the Chief Administrator of the Ministry of Internal Affairs whether it would not be beneficial to remove the said Chesnovskii from further participation in the management of the peasants on his estate, with a reliable barrier erected to this end, and to subject his behavior to vigilant supervision. For this purpose a copy of this ruling will be given to the office of the Ober-Procurator.

[The ruling of the Holy Synod was signed by the members of the Synod on 13 March 1828.]

Source: RGIA, f. 796, op. 108, d. 345, ll. 15–19 ob.

Translated by William G. Wagner and Igor Timofeyev.

2. Penance for Fornication

IRINA GLOBINA

Your Most Exalted Highness and Majesty
Great Sovereign Emperor
Alexander Nikolaevich,
Autocrat of All Russia, Gracious Sovereign!

Petitions the peasant woman Irina Fedorova Globina of Tobolsk[24] Diocese, Berezovsk District, Village of Kondinsk, and my petition concerns the following points regarding a reduction of the period of penance imposed upon her [sic] by the Diocesan Authorities for fornication.

By a decision of the Tobolsk Spiritual Consistory I was sentenced for fornication to a seven-year penance[25] in the Village of Shorkalsk, Trinity [word unclear].

2. I have a house in the Village of Kondinsk, whereas for no fault of the petitioner the penance is directed to be performed in the Village of Shorkalsk, which is 45 versts from the Village of Kondinsk.

3. Submitting to the will of the Spiritual Government, I am ready to fulfill it, but I consider the punishment imposed on me to be very severe, all the more so since I would be absent for such a long distance as to be ruined completely; the very Period of Penance is so long that to endure this punishment is beyond my Physical Strength. Therefore, I humbly and loyally request that it be ordered to accept my petition and ordered that the Period of my Penance be reduced, and if it is impossible to do this, then assign my Penance in the same Village of Kondinsk in which I live, or otherwise I will bear large losses, for which in due course I will bring a [law-]Suit. November 29th, 1871, subject to submission to the Holy Governing Synod. Signed by Kazak [word unclear] Grigoriev Yakov.

This petition was written down from the words of the petitioner by Berezovsk Constable Peasant Ioakim Ivanov Bukanin.

The place of this petition is the Village of Kondinsk.

[Written in the top margin of the petition] Report—it is not necessary to travel beyond the place of residence to perform a penance.

[Outcome: The Holy Synod reduced the period of Globina's penance to four years and transferred its place of performance to her local church.]

Source: "Case of the petition of the peasant woman of Tobolsk province, Berezovsk district, village of Kondinsk, Irina Fedorova Globina, regarding the reduction of the period of penance imposed on her by the Diocesan Authorities for fornication. Submitted to the Holy Synod, 1872." RGIA, f. 796, op. 153, d. 456, 11. 1–1 ob.

Translated by William G. Wagner and Igor Timofeyev.

C. Arranging of Marriages

1. Peasant Practices

The next two documents describe the process of arranging marriages among the peasantry and nobility. Both the similarities and the contrasts between the practices of these two social groups should be noted. The first selection is taken from Ethnographic Collection, a series published by the Imperial Geographic Society that consisted of material submitted by provincial correspondents or members of the Society on local peasant life. The excerpt here is from the 1853 issue and describes the practices among peasants in a village in Tver district of Tver province, which is located north of Moscow in the central industrial region of Russia. Two cautions are in order. First, the description was provided by a parish priest who, despite his involvement with the village community, most likely would have been an outsider. Second, peasant practices and rituals varied substantially within as well as between various regions, making generalization based on individual examples difficult. Despite these limitations, however, the following selection still offers valuable insights into peasant attitudes toward both marriage and female sexuality.

Peasant weddings, like all others, begin with matchmaking. The young man tells his parents whom he would like to have as a wife. Then the parents go with him to visit one of the girl's neighbors and make a proposal; she dresses up in her finest clothes and receives the matchmakers; the bride and bridegroom look each other over. Then the parents of the young man ask the girl's parents whether they would like to observe his way of life. They go to his village, question his neighbors on everything that they need to know about the young man, and look over his house, barn, and livestock. Afterward they go home and tell the girl what they saw and heard, and when they learn her decision, they inform the suitor. If the girl agrees to marry him, their parents agree on a day for the "handshaking" (*ruko-bit'e*). Until that day, both the groom and the bride have the opportunity to change their mind and refuse.

On the day of the "handshaking" the father of the bridegroom brings a bottle of wine and a pie to the bride's house and gives them to her father; both of them sit down and talk; then a candle is lit before the icons and they say a prayer; finally they offer their hands to each other, making sure to wrap them first in the hem of their fur coat or *armiak*.[26] At this point the girl begins to sob loudly, or, as the peasants say, to *wail*. She repeats these words: "My dear father NN and mother NN, don't light the bright-white wax candle, don't bring your coat-hems together, don't beat your hands together, don't destroy my virginal beauty, don't give away my hand-made linen to be soiled by strangers' hands." Then she turns to each of her friends, crying and asking them to weep for her grief, and her friends weep and wail along with her. Meanwhile the fathers, having slapped their hands together and exchanged a kiss, sit down at the table and serve each other the wine that the groom's father brought. Then they set the day for the wedding. When the groom's father is about to leave, the bride gives him a towel to take to the groom: once she has done this she can no longer refuse the marriage. From this time on until the wedding day, the bride weeps loudly every morning and evening in her father's house, and everyone everywhere calls her the *princess*, and the groom the *prince*. And it is at this time that both sides begin preparations for the wedding.

On the eve of the wedding the princess goes to the bathhouse, accompanied by her girlfriends; there they bathe and drink beer. The princess comes out of the bathhouse wearing a white veil and starts off for home, with her friends following behind her. When they reach the crossroads near the village, the princess begins to wail at the top of her voice: "Oh, I will be left a miserable orphan at the great crossroads, at the end of the big wide street, at the edge of the open field; I will turn in all four directions and pray to my Lord God." She prays and then goes home. She walks up to her house, stands at the gate and wails until her father or mother comes out to meet her. She repeats these words: "My dear Father NN and Mother NN, look out your front window, onto the big wide street, see me out here, oh, woe is me. Here I am, woe is me, walking with my flock of swans—with my dear friends. They all have scarlet dresses, but me, poor orphan, mine is white. Rise up, you stormy winds, rock the oaken gate-posts, open the big wide gate."

She goes inside, prays, sits on the bench and starts wailing again, thanking her father and mother: "Thank you, my dears from the bathhouse, for the soap, the silky
birch twigs, the crimson steam." Then she turns to her best friend, lamenting,
"Comb my unruly hair, make me a brown braid so tight it won't come undone tomorrow." Her friend fulfills her request. When she's done wailing and lamenting,
the princess bows all the way down to the floor to all her friends and, saying her
farewells, parts from them.

On that same evening the father of the bridegroom comes to see the bride
again, bringing presents from him; he brings her a *grivna*-[worth][27] of honey, shoes,
stockings, a mirror, some gingerbread, soap, whitewash, and rouge. The bride accepts all these things, and they seat the bridegroom's father at the table and serve
him some food and drink, and when he leaves, the bride sends the bridegroom a
wedding towel or triangular kerchief, and the mother of the bride sends her future
son-in-law ten eggs.[28]

Source: "Byt krest'ian tver'skogo uezda, tver'skoi gubernii, sviashchennikom N.
Le-bedevim," *Etnograficheskii sbornik, izdavaemyi Imperatorskim geograficheskim
obshchestvom* ["Daily life of the Peasants of Tver district, Tver province, reported
by priest N. Lebedev," in *Ethnographic Collection, Published by the Imperial Russian
Geographical Society*], no. 1 (St. Petersburg, 1853). Excerpted from pp. 184–92.

Translated by Carol Apollonio Flath.

2. Advice of an Elderly Woman

*The second selection in this section, published in 1858 in a journal concerned with
the upbringing and education of children, presents some strong opinions about the best
way to arrange marriages so that they will be successful. It also describes the enormous
role that parents had, not only in arranging marriages but also in the couple's fate after
a marriage had taken place. Although sexuality is not discussed directly, it is assumed
that marriage is the place in which sensuality will be expressed. Scholars debate whether
the practice of not being direct about sexuality minimizes or exaggerates its importance.
Certainly emotional attachment is in the foreground of remarks the "Elderly Woman"
offers, but her advice, on one level, is about negotiating a safe outlet for the expression
of sexuality.*

*An "Elderly Woman," who speaks with great authority, focuses throughout on im-
proving the conditions of marriage for women. Furthermore, in a discussion of old maids,
she claims that an unhappy marriage is at least as bad as not marrying; this was a very
progressive opinion for the period. Nevertheless, other ideas she presents about aristocratic women and marriage were powerful societal norms: she considers that women are
born to love and that they are happiest in being helpmeets for men in marriage. She also
focuses on male desire, foregrounding what it is that men want in women—rather than
explicitly considering what it is that women want in men. We see variations on this theme
in subsequent documents in this chapter.*

VI. YOUNG LADY—BRIDE-TO-BE. COMING-OUT PARTIES. CIRCLE OF FRIENDS.
FORMS OF ADDRESS. FRIENDLINESS.

I was discussing the upbringing of a young lady: the development of her mind
and heart and the atmosphere her parents should create for her. I move on to that
time when she becomes a mature young lady, a bride-to-be, when her parents start
thinking, as is usually said, "about arranging their daughter's fate." There are those
who speak ill of mothers concerned about marrying off their daughters; but such
ridicule isn't worthy of attention. A woman's goal is to be a wife, a man's lifelong
partner, and what's strange about a mother who is concerned that her daughter
achieve her goal? After all, nobody laughs at fathers who are concerned that their
sons become respectable citizens. No, in this respect, a mother's concerns are
strange only if they destroy the dignity that must surround every young lady, only
if these concerns are inappropriate to that important undertaking at which they're
directed.

Marriages are arranged in our society either indirectly through matchmakers or
directly by introducing the bridegroom and the bride-to-be. It's hardly necessary
to discuss the first method because anyone who thinks about it seriously will recognize its unsoundness. One may buy things through brokers; but joining the lives
of two people who don't know each other through a third party, unknown to the
pair, is decidedly absurd. People say that parties who are introduced to each other
even without matchmakers, whose acquaintance is not limited to two-three meetings, as usually happens in the presence of first-rate matchmakers, get to know
each other as little as those who see each other only once, because bridegrooms
and brides-to-be usually conceal their characters extremely well. It's easy to raise
the objection that, in any case, it's easier to get to know each other's proclivities
in the course of a year than in one evening; moreover, one must admit there is
something humiliating about matchmaking through matchmakers, about "view-
ings,"[29] etc., especially for the bride-to-be who is inspected like a piece of mer-
chandise. This is why the best method is direct introductions at social gatherings.
The latter method is frequently employed in more educated circles. One mustn't
forget, however, that parties, balls, receptions, etc., fulfill only the needs of matchmakers, that is, they introduce young people to each other but don't bring them
closer together. Even if parties who see each other only at balls, concerts, and
large gatherings, frequently fall in love, that kind of love is dangerous because it
rarely lasts. You still have to come back to earth; you can dance all night at a ball,
but you can't dance forever . . .

This is why, if parents want to secure their daughter's happiness, they must
know the bridegroom well; he must be on intimate terms with the family and his
bride-to-be. The bridegroom and the bride must see each other not only in strait-
laced salons or in the noisy brilliance of ballrooms, but also in a peaceful family
setting, in an atmosphere, amid those activities that will be central to their lives.
Let parents, as long as it's within their means, take their daughters into society, to
balls and shows (on condition, of course, that these pleasures not become, under

any circumstances, their children's specialty); but most importantly they should be concerned about creating a close, intimate family group. If there's a place love can develop, strengthen, and purify itself, then it's surely not balls, but the family hearth. It's the hearth parents must devote all their attention to, and it's the hearth that, with their daughters' help, they must make inviting.

The first condition for any kind of intimacy is, of course, honesty. Don't invite people you don't want in to see your house; but at all costs don't invite those who haven't expressed a desire to accept your invitation: then your home will be more appreciated, and will, consequently, be more attractive. Many want to impart, at all costs, as much brilliance to their circle as possible, and because of this try to attract to it a social class higher than the one they themselves belong to. It's excusable of course for parents to think that such honored guests will succumb to their lovely daughters' charm and marry them, but, first, such occurrences are rare, and, second, even if they occur, then one mustn't forget that happiness lies not in a good match but in compatibility, as I've already said. Some families try especially hard to become intimate with men from a higher social class not because they have designs on them as bridegrooms, but only because they would like to enhance the value of their circle and the importance of their daughters. But for what purpose? To attract others? Frankly, one can call men who succumb to such a ploy shallow and insignificant. This would be the same as falling in love with a young lady's attire instead of [with] the young lady herself. . . . No, there's no point in expecting our daughters to be happy with bridegrooms enticed by such things. . . . This is not the way to attract young men to your circle, this is not the way to advance your home's value and significance; it's with your personal qualities: with the good mind and heart of your children, and with that order, that harmony, which reigns in every good family.

Discussing upbringing, I expressed an opinion about those qualities men like to see in women. Discussing family life, the family hearth, I must remind parents who are raising daughters that they must make an effort to teach them to be friendly and courteous in society. Friendliness and courtesy make everyone compelling. Unfortunately, we pay little attention to this. Our women are either completely unfriendly or too amorous; that is, in society, they either sit strait-laced, frowning, flirt too blatantly, or they fall in love with every man who's paid them a compliment. There's almost no golden mean.

VII. TENDER ATTACHMENTS. GENUINE AND FALSE ATTACHMENTS. CHOOSING A GROOM. PARENTS' ROLE IN CHOOSING.

If everybody needs to love and be loved, then such a need is especially strong in a woman. Thirteen-, fourteen-year-old boys sometimes pay court to girls and women, fourteen-year-old girls often fall in love. I could give several examples of highly touching, poetic scenes; but this would take me beyond the topic at hand. And most importantly it wouldn't be necessary because who hasn't witnessed such scenes? . . . The need for love increases with age. Sensuality and a natural yearning for a family and family life intertwine with an intimate need for compassion, a simple desire to marry, etc. At this time, many elusive and indiscernible threads gently move the heart. Beginning with a crush on a teacher, continuing with a heartfelt fondness for a cousin, attachments in a young heart appear quickly, disappear, one giving way to the other. . . . I anticipate being reproached for expressing such an opinion on fickle attachments, but I don't think this would be fair. Let each of my readers look back dispassionately on her past. . . . Who hasn't fantasized about cousins, who hasn't stayed up all night after a ball deep in thought, who hasn't listened in trepidation for the ringing of the bell, anticipating his arrival, who hasn't been racked by jealousy when he's invited another to dance the mazurka, etc.? Different men were the objects of our tender feelings, but, at the time, it seemed that we were harboring eternal love. If at the very moment when we were looking at a fading bouquet and remembering the ball and the man we spent most of it with, the man who was so kind and attentive, if at that moment someone told us that our love would be over in a heartbeat, that we would fall in love the very same way a second and third time, we wouldn't have believed it, we would have been offended by such a comment. Meanwhile . . . time would move on, love would move on, and a new one would appear. . . . Such fickle feelings of course exist only until we reach a certain age; if a forty-year old woman sometimes falls in love with every man who is kind to her, or who isn't kind to her, one must look upon such types as exceptions, but we're not concerned with exceptions. . . . If feelings are so easily aroused in a young lady, then clearly one must be careful if they're meant to become the basis for an indissoluble bond, for marriage. What if one were to take seriously feelings aroused by an attachment formed at a ball, and upon seeing one's daughter become fond of this or that man, one were to marry her off without thinking, without reflecting, and this ephemeral feeling then suddenly died, then what? Eternal regret, eternal remorse, grief and unhappiness. . . . No, in order for marriage to be based on love, one must find out what that love consists of, one must take a closer look at it.

Of course this is difficult for a young lady to do herself, but this is why her parents must do it. First of all, in my opinion, a young lady can experience true, sensible love no earlier than at twenty years of age, when her outlook on life and her character have been established; then the young lady, if she's sufficiently intelligent, can better judge people, better understand what to expect and what to look for in a prospective husband. Of course, there are types who remain childlike even at twenty, and there are others who develop earlier . . . but here I'm talking in general, believing that parents themselves must take a closer look at their children's upbringing.

In vain do parents start discussing marriage, prospective bridegrooms, etc. when their daughters are barely sixteen. First, it's too early; at that age, young ladies can't make an informed decision, can't completely understand and assess their responsibilities. Second, discussions on this topic at any time, but especially at this age may be harmful. They will instill in her the need to marry at any cost. A young lady's main goal, of course, is to be a man's lifelong partner and a mother, but we can only perform these noble duties conscientiously and honestly if we marry men we're able to love and respect. Those unable to marry under these conditions would be better off if they didn't marry at all because nobody should assume responsibilities they're unable to carry out conscientiously. I knew many old maids who were household irritants, but I knew others who were good angels to their families. The latter dealt with their loneliness by forging emotional attachments with their younger sisters and brothers and elderly mothers and aunts. I knew an old maid, a landowner, who was a genuine benefactor for her district. I don't deny that an old maid's situation is sad and sorrowful; however, it's not so desperate that fearing it, one marries the first man who comes along, deceiving oneself into believing one is emotionally attached, and sometimes even admitting one is not. An unhappy marriage, a consequence of which is an unhappy family, is harder to bear for an old maid than loneliness.

And so, to address what I had started out with, I repeat that the most genuine and sound age for love is twenty. But age of course can't serve as the only guarantee of its endurance. In order to be convinced of the soundness of love, it's necessary to examine its beginnings, its basis. Sometimes a young lady, who has become close to someone in childhood and finds herself in intimate relations with him, will grow accustomed to him as a family member—this closeness, this acquaintance they regard as love. If, because of this closeness, young people are compatible in the areas of their education, upbringing, train of thought, age; in one word, if they're right for each other, suited to each other, then such an attachment may last; but if there is no compatibility, they must renounce their attachment. The young lady can test it herself: better yet, her parents can do it, and try to point out to their daughter the lack of compatibility, to say nothing of the recipient of the tender feelings. If he's honest, good, and not blinded by love and vanity, he'll be anxious to remove himself from an inclination rooted in unsound beginnings. For an attachment to be considered durable, compatibility is necessary in the areas of character, age, education, understanding.

It's difficult to generalize what kind of people are compatible because a vivacious spouse may be compatible with a gloomy one, and the shortcomings of one may be offset by another; two easygoing people often get along swimmingly, but often they don't get along at all, etc. In this respect, parents should be guided by experience and observation, etc. As far as the compatibility of ages, I think it's best when a husband is five to ten years older than his wife; a large age difference, in my opinion, makes happiness between husband and wife doubtful, although here, too, there are many exceptions for psychological and physiological reasons. Similar educational backgrounds are obviously essential. Only when she can understand his interests and appreciate his good qualities, can a wife be a true friend to her husband. Everyone has a circle of friends he's grown accustomed to, and is comfortable with. And the wife, joining her husband's circle and occupying a place of honor in it should, of course, come from a similar educational background, and the reverse is true: a husband's education should not be inferior to his wife's circle, otherwise both risk losing their affection for each other. Here we're

talking about a general education, not a specialized one, otherwise our requirement would be absurd: the wife of a mathematics professor must know all the sub-
tleties of his field, etc. If parents recognize that their daughter can find pleasure in
family life and be a good wife outside a brilliant setting; that she and her prospective husband have compatible characters and educational backgrounds; that they
have clearly established a reciprocal emotional attachment; and finally, that her
prospective husband is energetic and active, then one can count on this couple's
happiness.

N.V.-V-va

Source: "Sovet starushki materiam, imeiushchim docherei," *Zhurnal dlia vospitaniia*
["An Elderly Woman's Advice for Mothers Who Have Daughters," *Journal for
Child Rearing*], vol. IV (1858): 331–42. Excerpted.

Translated by Valentina Baslyk.

D. Should Men Be Chaste?

MARIA POKROVSKAIA

*The genteel marriage that the Elderly Woman advocates in the preceding selection
seems far removed from the world of prostitution, but Maria Ivanovna Pokrovskaia
connects them in the following essay. Pokrovskaia (1852–1921?) was a doctor, journalist, and activist, a not uncommon combination in late imperial Russia that reflects
the expansion after 1860 of both educational and occupational opportunities for women
and civic activism by women. From 1904 to 1917 she edited* The Women's Herald,
*the longest-running feminist journal in Russia's history, and frequently published arti-
cles dealing with the social consequences of prostitution. In writing "On Cultivating
Chastity," she used the work of the French philosopher and author Jean-Jacques Rousseau (1712–1778) to argue for early education and control of male sexuality, as a way
both to lessen prostitution and to improve marriage. Furthermore, Pokrovskaia claimed
that parents, especially mothers, have a crucial role in training their sons to respect
women.*

SECTION II.

The question of the chastity of men has been urgently entering the scene. We
find ourselves hearing the opinion more and more often that men, just as women,
must be equally pure before marriage. If men and women touch on this question
in society, then often a heated debate arises between them. The main theme of
the latter is usually the possibility or impossibility of male chastity before marriage.

There is no contradiction as far as women are concerned in this instance. Long
experience and daily observation prove completely that they can [be chaste prior

to marriage]. But regarding men opinions strongly diverge. An insignificant percentage assert that for them chastity before marriage is entirely possible. But the overwhelming majority maintain the absolute opposite opinion. The frailty of men in this situation is acknowledged equally by these men themselves and by women. "We cannot," insist the men. "They cannot," the women, like an echo, repeat.

In support of this opinion the advice of doctors usually is brought in. Until now the latter have insistently assured young men that their nature necessarily demands sexual relations as soon as they reach sexual maturity. Otherwise they are threatened by various nervous illnesses. And since it is not possible to marry at the age of 15 to 18 years, then inevitably one must resort to prostitutes. In this way a habit is formed which later is very difficult to struggle against. It takes hold of a man at a time when there cannot be any talk of firm will. Later, when the youth matures and arrives at the conclusion that it is shameful for a decent person to enjoy purchased love, he attempts to struggle with himself. But he rarely succeeds in this. He lacks strength of will, and his companions act toward the opposite effect both by their example and their ridicule. Here the advice of doctors joins forces. All this influences the unformed youth in such a way that he himself is convinced of the impossibility of being chaste.

"We are not built like you. We cannot. It is in our nature," assure the men.

If they all without exception spoke and acted this way, then nothing would remain for women but to believe it. After all, who knows? Perhaps male nature really is such that dissipation constitutes its insurmountable inclination. But there are facts that give us the right to regard this supposed impossibility with skepticism. It is well known that in England, America, Sweden, Norway, and other states a society called the "White Cross" has been created, the members of which, young men, take a vow to preserve their chastity until marriage. This serves as proof that men themselves admit the possibility of abstinence. On the basis of this women should insist on the latter, and not agree with the opposite position.

On this question it is interesting to become acquainted with the views of J. J. Rousseau. In earlier times his theory of upbringing enjoyed great fame. And even now in many regards it has not lost its value. Rousseau arrives at the conclusion that male chastity depends on existing viewpoints. A youth begins to lead a corrupt life not because his temperament demands it, but as a result of social opinion. It is not nature that inspires this in him, but example.

Undoubtedly anyone who has looked closely at the youth of our capitals has become convinced as to how right Rousseau is in asserting that young men from the provinces in the beginning of their stay in the capitals are much more modest and moral than they later become. The evil of big cities depends to a significant degree on the corruption of good morals. This corruption, like poison, infects even those innocent young men who arrive in the cities. Their corrupt comrades, the indifference of their elders to the morality of youth, the loneliness of the new arrivals—all this facilitates the development of a flippant attitude toward serious things.

Rousseau says that until the age of twenty a youth develops and grows, and this is why he needs for this goal all the strength of his organism. Until this age chastity is completely natural and lies in nature itself. It is later that abstinence becomes a requirement of morality.

He thinks that since upbringing plays a large role in the development of sexual needs, then it is up to the youth's educators either to restrain or hasten this development. The body wins or loses depending on whether we slow down or hasten sexual maturity. It is desirable therefore that a youth be acquainted with sexual relations not earlier than when he matures into a real man, when he possesses the proper strength and fortitude.

We consider it essential to add to this, that a youth's organism attains complete maturity around twenty-five years old. Therefore one should not marry earlier than this age. And we know that at this time young men almost always have already completed even their higher education and family life has become accessible to them. Therefore the use of prostitutes cannot be justified by the impossibility of marriage.

Rousseau acknowledges that the attraction of one sex for the other is perfectly natural. However, in his opinion one's choice and preference here depend on the familiar views, habits, prejudices, and customs. Therefore, in order to know how to make the appropriate choice of the object of one's love it is essential to acquire the habit of judgment. True love always enjoys respect. However the beloved object appears in the eyes of others, the man who is truly in love will unfailingly respect her. Although they call love blind, still it sees in the given subject such qualities that escape the attention of indifferent people. Therefore it is first of all necessary to teach the child respect for other people. A person should not despise another person, no matter in what position the latter finds himself. The child must speak of people with love, with pity, but never with contempt.

Love and respect toward all men, pity, but not contempt—this is what Rousseau demands as the basis for cultivating chastity in children. And he is right. Debauchery without doubt develops on the soil where these qualities are absent. Is it possible to say of those youths who use the services of prostitutes, that they love and respect other human beings? Of course not. Undoubtedly these feelings are completely absent in them. He who loves and respects his fellow man will not debase another and do violence to his human dignity.

The cultivation in a child of love and respect for his fellow man, no matter in what position the latter finds himself, is the foundation stone of chastity. All the efforts of parents and educators should be directed toward this if we wish to destroy the dreadful evil that is consuming modern society. The family [and] the mother serve as the first educators of a child. On them first of all lies the obligation to plant a spark of love and respect for humanity in the soul of the child and to nurture it there.

It should be particularly valuable to mothers to develop in their sons a respect for people, for women. For this reason she should direct all her energies so that her children do not become witnesses of ugly scenes. If such scenes are unavoidable, then it is better to remove the child as soon as possible. Send him for a walk, let him go outside to play. The mother should value respect for women. Then why does she slander them in the eyes of her grown or adolescent sons so often? A conversation begins about the young girls who came to visit their house and who could be the brides of their sons. Yet the mother for some reason or another finds this marriage to be inappropriate. Then she begins to use all her strength to lower and discredit the young women in the eyes of her sons.

These mothers analyze in detail not only their physical qualities but their spiritual ones as well. She is heartless, she is a coquette, she will probably be a bad wife and mother. She is extravagant, she spends a large amount on finery, she is not entirely modest, she runs after young men—these and all sorts of other faults are discovered in her by the mother.

Fear for her son so blinds the mother that she destroys with her own hands the possibility of his finding any happiness in family life. Hearing from his mother that this girl, that girl, and the third are creatures that are good for absolutely nothing, unworthy of love and respect, the son arrives at the conclusion that all women are like that. Then he marries without feeling any respect for the woman he has chosen, governed by sexual attraction alone. If the wife does not obtain her husband's respect in the very beginning of the marriage, then their family life has barely a chance of being happy. Passion passes, and there is no respect. What then remains between them? Habit? But habit cannot make conjugal relations so good that the couple's mutual shortcomings are forgiven and forgotten. Habit does not prevent mutual misunderstandings and bitter scenes from arising. It cannot ease one's life and smooth over life's storms. In this way even the best woman cannot constitute the happiness of the son, thanks to the extreme concern of his mother.

If only mothers would undertake as a rule to act in the opposite fashion, if they would teach their sons to respect women, no matter what position they were in, no matter what flaws they possessed, then the most ordinary woman could constitute the happiness of her son, because respect would force him to reconcile himself to the imperfections of his wife.

M. I. Pokrovskaia, a woman-doctor.

Source: Maria Pokrovskaia, "O vospitanii tselomudriia u mal'chikov," *Na pomoshch' materiam* ["On the Cultivation of Chastity in Boys," *For the Assistance of Mothers*], no. 3 (1901), pp. 103–112. Excerpted.

Translated by William G. Wagner.

E. Prostitutes' Petition

Although the Russian Society for the Protection of Women (RSPW) saw itself as inviting a broad cross-section of Russian society to the 1910 Congress on the Struggle against the Trade in Women, invitations went only to other salvationists, medical-society representatives, government bureaucrats, university professors, feminists, temperance orga-

nizations, and delegates from district and municipal councils. Several worker-activists attended, but they numbered five in an audience of nearly 290 representatives from the professional and upper classes. The congress was an important and multi-faceted event, and two speeches made at the congress by women activists are included in later chapters (chapters 4 and 6). But prostitutes, curiously, had no place at the congress purporting to illuminate all aspects of prostitution.

When a congress organizer read aloud the following "petition" addressed to the congress and signed by sixty-three prostitutes, this marked the only hearing given to prostitutes themselves. Congress priorities focused on abolishing the government system of issuing licenses to brothels and streetwalkers, discussing the circumstances that gave rise to prostitution, and developing philanthropic solutions. Yet the signers of this petition ignored all three of these questions. Their priority was much more immediate: ending the injustice of a system that examined and incarcerated them for venereal disease, but let syphilitic male clients go about their business "unimpeded and with impunity." Most congress participants hoped to use the meeting as a springboard for promoting the abolition of government regulation of prostitution. Significantly, the prostitutes who wrote the petition did not judge abolition per se. Instead, they simply complained of its most unfair and paradoxical aspect, examinations and incarceration for women but not for men. This petition is particularly remarkable because prostitutes in imperial Russia did not leave written records of their lives, and even sympathetic reformers tended to lack a full awareness of their situations.

Having learned from the newspaper that on April 21 of this year the All-Russian Congress for the Struggle against the Trade in Women will be convened, at which many issues concerning our unhappy life will be discussed, we the undersigned request that the esteemed members of the congress grasp our situation and do not refuse our humble request.

Many of us for various reasons became prostitutes at a very early age, when we were in tolerable health and we were not suffering from any kind of venereal diseases, of which the most horrible for us, as for everyone, is syphilis. Meanwhile, as time goes on, every one of us unfortunates becomes infected. This is due to no fault of our own, but because syphilitic men, whom it occurs to no one to examine, are indiscriminately permitted as guests. [The medical police] require us to be healthy, they make us go to examinations, they put us in the hospital for the tiniest of scratches, but nobody requires the same of our guests. They are allowed to infect us unimpeded and with impunity, and transform us in the future into miserable cripples from whom anyone would turn away in horror. Indeed, our guests are not little children, and they should understand that it is wrong to spread illness and that they do not have the right to pass on syphilis, even to loose women. We, you know, are also human beings, our health is valuable to us, and our old age will not be sweet without it.

Not daring to trouble the attention of the honored congress for long, we humbly ask you to discuss this issue and try to arrange things so that sick guests are not allowed to come to those of us who are healthy, and that health is required of them, as it is of us. They who participate in this business are no better than we.

We humbly request that you give our paper a turn and read it at the congress. Maybe it will find kind people who will understand that it is cruel and insulting to have one's health ruined when one is young, and that everything is only demanded from one side, that is, from us. We earnestly request that you look after us.

Source: "Proshenie ot zhenshchin, zanimaiushchikhsia prostitutsiei," *Trudy pervogo vserossiiskogo s"ezda po bor'be s torgom zhenshchinami i ego prichinami proiskhodivsh-chogo v S.-Peterburge s 21 do 25 aprelia 1910 goda* ["Petition from Women Who En-gage in Prostitution," in *Works of the First All-Russian Congress on the Battle against the Trade in Women and Its Reasons. Held in St. Petersburg, 21–25 April 1910*], vol. 2 (St. Petersburg, 1911–1912). Excerpted from pp. 511–12.

Translated by Laurie Bernstein.

MUSIC HALL SONGS

A. Cruel Romance

In spite of all the difficulties that married life could present (see especially chapter 2), many young women eagerly awaited marriage. As we have seen, until well into the nineteenth century (and, for many women, beyond that), their parents sought partners for them, and arranged marriages remained common. Partly under the influence of ideas of romantic love, however, in the nineteenth century at least non-peasant women in-creasingly searched for grooms themselves. The following document provides a look at romance from the point of view of popular music of the late nineteenth century.

Traditional Russian folk song had begun to be influenced by printed songbooks (pe-senniki) by at least the last quarter of the eighteenth century. The late nineteenth and early twentieth centuries, however, witnessed an explosion of new kinds of popular song, transmitted not only through printed songbooks (one of the most widely disseminated forms of mass-market publication) but also by word of mouth and, in the early twenti-eth century, increasingly by phonograph recordings. Apart from the chastushka (comic poem), two of the most popular genres were the "cruel romance" (an evocation of tragic love) and the shansonetka (a comic song, from the French chansonette), performed in the café-chantants, popular cabarets, of Russian cities by raucous soubrettes. Cre-ated by professional songwriters rather than gifted amateurs, these genres, however, cir-culated anonymously, advertised by the name of their singers rather than their composers or lyric-writers in songbooks and in collections of libretti sold to accompany phonograph records. Among the most popular women performers of the cruel romance was Varia Panina, while Maria Vasileva made large numbers of shansonetka recordings. Both ro-mances and shansonetki had their own genre conventions. In the cruel romance singers, both male and female, lamented the infidelity of their sweethearts or shed tears by the

*lilac-shaded grave of the dear departed. The following romance illustrates this conven-
tion; the popularity of romances suggests the importance of romantic love in the thinking
of Russians in the late nineteenth and early twentieth centuries.*

O how I loved your eyes so dear[30]
When in them glowed a light of gladness;
O how I loved them when a tear
Showed in them of unhidden sadness.
　　O how I loved, I loved, I swear!

O how I loved your glance to see,
That told what thought was in your mind:
In silence you would talk to me,
My heart and your eyes intertwined.
　　O how I loved, I loved, I swear!

Your voice gave me delight,
O how its sound did me enrapture,
And how I longed to sleep at night,
Hoping my dreams its notes would capture.
　　O how I loved, I loved, I swear!

I loved your spirit's smoldering fires,
And o, how pleasant was your mind!
O unforgotten, still desired,
Each day such joy with you I'd find!
　　O how I loved, I loved, I swear!

Source: Polnyi russkii pesennik: 1000 pesen [Complete Russian Songbook: 1,000 Songs]
(Moscow, 1893).

Translated by Catriona Kelly.

B. *Shansonetki*

　　The shansonetka *(from the French* chansonette) *or music-hall song was popular in
the late nineteenth and early twentieth centuries. Unlike the "cruel romance," the point
of the* shansonetka *was outrageous sexual innuendo, the more improbable the better. In
one popular* shansonetka, *the singer presented herself as the owner of a typewriter-hire
business whose machine had been "damaged" by an elderly male client; in another, a
soubrette complained that her "little pussy" had been frightened at first by her lodger's
"fierce bad tomcat," but was beginning to get less timid as she got used to him. Often,
too, the* shansonetka *performers provocatively boasted of their power to manipulate men
and strip them of their savings, and of their success in transforming themselves from low-
paid female employees (servants and seamstresses) into glitzy music-hall stars. Although*

the spectators at café-chantants[31] were overwhelmingly men, and some "women of ill repute," phonograph recordings took the new sexual stridency to less exclusive audiences. The motif of social self-betterment through sexual manipulativeness was also present in cinema dramas of the 1910s, such as Evgenii Bauer's A Child of the Big City *(1915), many of whose spectators were "respectable," working-class women.*

The two songs that follow show how sexual innuendo could be expressed indirectly ("I Was Sitting") and directly ("Here and There"). In these two songs, women are both the (assumed) singers, that is, the agents, and the objects of male desire.

---

1. *I Was Sitting in My Kitchen*

> I was sitting in my kitchen
> When the chimney sweep came in.
> I was startled and admiring,
> As I watched the man begin.
> He surveyed my narrow chimney,
> And at once began to clean,
> At the double, woof, I say!
> > How he swept and swept and swept it,
> > How he swept it long and wide,
> > Left and right and in the middle,
> > Up and down, from side to side.

> But only a few days later,
> The thing again began to smoke,
> And burn: the soot had caught afire,
> O, I said, that's not a joke.
> And I sent my maid to fetch him:
> He came at once and set to work:
> At the double, woof, I say!
> > How he swept and swept and swept it,
> > How he swept it long and wide,
> > Left and right and in the middle,
> > Up and down, from side to side.

2. *Here and There*

> I was born in St. Petersburg,
> This town is my birthplace, my home,
> When you live somewhere that's so superb,
> You feel no temptation to roam.
> You walk along Nevsky at night,
> And the street's always packed—
> Oh, you'll not find such pearls

As the Petersburg girls,
Never mind where you look, that's a fact!
    Girlies here, girlies there,
    Girlies, girlies, everywhere! [repeat]

My sister's new husband, you know,
Is a slobbery, doddery old trout:
They got married five days ago,
But old Baldy's beginning to pout:
She gives him the runaround
With whole strings of young beaus:
He's got horns to wear
Where he should have his hair,
And things are far worse than he knows!
    Cousins here, cousins there,
    Cousins, cousins, everywhere! [repeat]

When I've finished singing this song,
I'll go back to my room and get dressed,
The line of young men will be very long,
Everyone wants a tête-à-tête.
They nag me to come and dine,
But how can I fit them all in?
If I make rendez-vous,
With you, and you, and you,
I get hassles from him, him, and him!
    They want me here, they want me there,
    They want me, want me, everywhere! [repeat]

Source: Both from: *Polnyi sbornik libretto dlia gramofona [Complete Collection of Librettos for the Gramophone]*, pt. 3 (Moscow, c. 1910).

Translated by Catriona Kelly.

GIRLFRIENDS: TSVETAEVA TO PARNOK

While the shansonetki *focus on heterosexual desire in a playful way, other approaches to sexual desire were also openly expressed at the turn of the century. The poet Marina Tsvetaeva (1892–1941) embodies the complicated range of Silver Age sexuality. She was married and a mother, and she was also romantically involved with women, most famously with the poet Sofia Parnok (1885–1933). The poems that follow are from Tsvetaeva's "Podruga" ("Girlfriend") cycle of 1914–1915; they are addressed to Parnok. These poems, together with Parnok's poetry addressed to Tsvetaeva, chronicle a passionate love. They also take sexuality out of the realm of family life that is so central to the "Elderly Woman's" vision of sexuality. The relationship between Parnok and Tsvetaeva lasted from 1914 to 1916. These poems are an example of direct and intense expression of female sexual desire (as in poem 9); many also detail the delights of androgyny. Poems 1 and 10 describe the first meetings of Parnok and Tsvetaeva in haunting, elusive, and sensual images.*

1.

You're happy then? You won't admit it!—Hardly!
Well, let it be!
You've simply kissed, methinks, too many people.
And hence—your grief.

I see in you the heroines of Shakespeare's
Tragic plays.
You are the tragic youthful lady
Whom no one saves.

You are so tired of mouthing love's recurrent
Recitative.
The iron bruise there on your bloodless hand speaks
Expressively.

—I love you!—Like a cloud of thunder over
You hangs—a pall!
Because you are sarcastic, searing hot, and
The best of all.

Because to you, my steep-browed demon, surely
I'll say goodbye,
Because—despite all efforts mad to save you!—
You still shall die!

Because this thrill I feel, because of—surely
It's not a dream?
Because of the ironic charm in knowing
You're not—a he.

16 October 1914

6.

How tiny snowflakes sparkled merrily
On your gray, my sable fur.
How long we combed the Christmas market for
The brightest ribbons that there were.

How on those pink unsweetened waffles I
Just gorged myself—I ate all six!

How in your honor I felt tenderness
For every chestnut mare we met.
How reddish-coated hawkers—blaspheming
With vigor, tried to sell us rags,
How simple peasant women marveled at
Us strange and fancy Moscow gals.

How when the crowd was finally scattering,
We neared the church and slipped inside.
How on an ancient *Bogoroditsa*[32]
You simply riveted your eyes.

How noble, good, and wan her visage was,
With sad and melancholy gaze,
Encircled by the pudgy Cupids on
The eighteenth-century icon-case.

How after sighing: 'Oh, I want her so!'
You suddenly let go my hand.
With such solicitude you lit and placed
A yellow candle on the stand . . .

—Oh cultivated, ringed-in-opal
Hand! My whole unlucky plight!—
How recklessly I promised you
To steal the icon that same night.

How stomping like a soldiers' regiment,
—The sunset and sound of bells,—
In blissful spirits, just like name-day girls,
We hit the nunnery-hotel.

How swearing to you I'd get prettier
Until old age, I crossed my heart,
How three times straight—oh you were furious!—
The king of hearts showed in my cards.[33]

How you then took my head between your hands,
Caressing each and every wisp,
How on that small enamel brooch of yours
The flower cooled my lips.

How I across your tapered fingertips
Traced patterns with my sleepy cheek,
"How like a boy!" you told me teasingly,
How much you liked a girl like me. . . .

December 1914

9.

There you go about your business,
And I can't touch you passing by,
But I long for you—too eternally,
For you to be for me—some passerby!

"Darling!" said my heart, immediately:
I forgave you all—and utterly,
Knowing nothing,—and unknowingly!
Love me, please, o love just me!

Your lips convey to me—through their curvature,
Through their exacerbated arrogance,—
As do your forehead's stern protuberances:
Seize this heart by storm, not chance!

Your voice—its hint of gypsy throatiness,
Your dress—a black silk coat-of-mail,
Everything about you pleases painfully,—
Even that you are not beautiful!

Beauty, you'll not wither with the summertime!
Not a flower,—you're a stalk of steel,
Wickeder than wicked, spicier than spicy,
From what island—transported here!

As you snap a fan, or twirl a walking-stick,—
In your each and every move I sense,
And in every wicked fingerlet,—
Woman's tenderness, boy's impertinence.

With my verse all laughter parrying,
I reveal to you and the world-at-large,
Stranger with the brow of Beethoven,
All in you that lies in store for us!

14 January 1915

10.

How can I not remember
That scent of tea and White Rose,[34]
And Sèvres porcelain figures
Above the blazing fire. . . .

You wore: a black knit jacket
With a wing-shaped collar,
I—a splendid dress of
An almost golden faille.

I can recall your face as
You entered—no trace of makeup,
And stood, biting a finger,
Your head held to the side.

Your power-loving forehead
Beneath its heavy red helmet.
—Not a boy and not a woman,
But something that's stronger than I!

I rose in an unforced motion
As people gathered around us.
And somebody jocularly
Said: "Get acquainted, gentlemen!"

And in a protracted motion
You put your hand in mine and
Upon my palm that sliver
Of ice affectionately leant.

With somebody glancing sideways,
Already sensing a skirmish,
I half lay in my armchair
And twisted my ring to the side.

You took a cigarette out,
And I immediately lit it,
Not knowing what I'd do if
You looked me in the eye.

And I recall our glasses—
Above a blue vase—clinking.
"Oh, be for me Orestes!"[35]
And I gave you a flower.

You laughed—at what I was saying?—
And from your black chamois handbag
You drew in a lengthy gesture
A hankie and—let it drop.

28 January 1915

15.

In your first woman you
Loved beauty found in few,
Ringlets of henna hue,
Lure of the *zurna's* blues,[36]

Flint's—beneath her horse's—sound,
Smooth rhythmical dismount,

And, sown with semiprecious
Seed pearls, two Turkish slippers.
And in your next, you loved
Arch of a subtle brow,
Carpets of *peau de soie*
From rosy Bukhara,[37]
Hand all beringed and sleek,
Beauty mark on her cheek,
Always tanned under blonde,
And sights of midnight London.

For something else, it's clear
You found your third girl dear . . .

—What will your heart retain of me,
Wanderess, in its memory?

14 July 1915

Source: Marina Tsvetaeva, "Podruga" ["Girlfriend"]. Written in 1914–1915. Originally published in Paris in 1976. For the full cycle, see Marina Tsvetaeva, *Sobranie sochinenii v semi tomakh* [*Collected Works in Seven Volumes*], vol. 1, pp. 216–28 (Moscow, 1994). Excerpted.

Translated by Diana L. Burgin.

Notes

1. Katiushka and Katerina are both nicknames formed from her given name, Ekaterina.
2. Ekaterina's husband, the Duke of Mecklenburg, was considered cruel even by Peter I. It is likely that this is the cause of the sorrow to which Praskovia refers.
3. Okunev was a trusted servitor in Tsaritsa Praskovia's household. She used him to keep an eye on her daughter.
4. Probably refers to Praskovia Ivanovna, the youngest of the dowager tsaritsa's five daughters.
5. Here and in the following sentence, Tsaritsa Praskovia refers to mineral springs that were valued for their medicinal effects. The Russian refers specifically to "chalybeate waters," which indicates heavy concentrations of iron.
6. Throughout the correspondence, Levshina refers to Betskoi as Betskii.
7. That is, Betskoi.
8. Most likely Count Grigorii Grigorevich Orlov (1734–1783), a favorite and lover of Empress Catherine II. A nobleman and military officer, Orlov helped to overthrow Peter III and elevate Catherine to the throne, for which he was richly rewarded. Orlov also was president of the Imperial Free Economic Society, which he helped to found, and a patron of writers and scholars.

9. Each member of the imperial family maintained a court; the Emperor or Empress presided over the most important one. Catherine's son Grand Duke Paul and his wife, Grand Duchess Maria Fedorovna, had their own courtiers and, given the animosity between mother and son, considerable political rivalry developed between the adherents of the two courts.

10. Tsarskoe Selo is a suburb of St. Petersburg, the site of one of the imperial family's favorite palaces.

11. The family was preparing to move to St. Petersburg as a result of Karamyshev's appointment to a position there.

12. Sasha (a diminutive for Aleksandr) was younger than Labzina.

13. Karamyshev had been away for a long period of study and state service before the wedding.

14. Labzina accompanied her husband to St. Petersburg, remaining with him until his death.

15. A provincial secretary ranked twelfth, or near the bottom, in the Table of Ranks established by Peter the Great in 1722. Held by low officials in provincial service, it conferred only modest status.

16. Part of the central Russian heartland and the central industrial region, Vladimir province borders Moscow province on the east.

17. That is, the Vladimir Spiritual Consistory.

18. Bordered by the Oka River, Murom district is in the eastern part of Vladimir province.

19. Between 1775 and 1864 this was a magistrate's court established at the district level and staffed by the local constable.

20. Prior to 1864 this was the high court for criminal cases within a province, staffed by personnel appointed by the government.

21. Prior to the judicial reform of 1864, tsarist courts had the option in criminal cases of leaving the defendant "under suspicion," which indicated that the evidence suggested guilt but was insufficient to establish it satisfactorily. Since prereform judicial procedure generally weighted evidence on the basis of social status, it seems likely that in this case the testimony of serfs against their master was accepted but discounted.

22. The manifesto of 12 May 1826 was issued as a response to reports from the governors of several provinces that serfs and state peasants were refusing to fulfill their obligations to their masters or the state due to the spread of false rumors. The manifesto declared all rumors to be false, reminded serfs and state peasants of their duty to fulfill their obligations, and threatened punishment for the failure to perform these obligations, the dissemination of false rumors, or the composition of petitions based on them.

23. The issue here appears to be Siletskii's revelation of what had been confessed to him.

24. Tobolsk province was located in southwestern Siberia, just east of the Ural Mountains.

25. A punishment imposed by the church for certain sins or violations of ecclesiastical rules. Penance generally included both the public performance of prescribed religious acts and the temporary denial of certain comforts or pleasures. The Orthodox Church used penance particularly to enforce its norms of sexual and marital behavior.

26. A peasant's coat made of heavy cloth.

27. Ten kopecks (colloq.).

28. In Russia, eggs usually come in tens rather than dozens.

29. The Russian original refers to *smotriny*. The word *smotrina* comes from the Russian root *smotr*, which literally means "to look."

30. The narrator of the lyric can be identified as a woman by the feminine past tense ending in the original Russian.

31. These were cafés and bars with musical entertainment.

32. *"Bogoroditsa"* literally means "The Mother of God"; in Russian Orthodoxy this is the common way of referring to Mary. There are many different icons of Mary as the Mother of God, and they are among the most revered images of Russian Orthodox believers.

33. The king of hearts indicates romance, particularly the love of a man. This is one of the many images of fortune-telling in this cycle; see also Parnok's poem of 1915, "Fortune-Telling" (*"Gadanie"*), in which she mentions a "red king."

34. "White Rose," in English in the original, was a fashionable perfume at the time. This scent is a heavy, sweet fragrance that originally came from England.

35. In Greek mythology, the son of Agamemnon and Clytemnestra, who, with his sister Electra, avenged his father by slaying his mother and Aegisthus.

36. A *zurna* is a musical instrument that resembles an oboe.

37. Located in present-day Uzbekistan, Bukhara (Bokhara) was a major trading and cultural center on the Silk Road from China to the Ottoman Empire; it was ceded to the Russian empire in 1868.

Tsaritsa Natalia, mother of
Peter the Great, by an unknown
artist, early eighteenth century.

Empress Aleksandra Fedorovna
(Princess Charlotte of Prussia),
wife of Emperor Nicholas I,
with two of her children.
Engraving by Thomas Wright.
Artist, George Dawe.

From N. Shil'der, *Imperator Nikolai
Pervyi* (Spb., 1903), vol. 1.

Wet Nurse with a Child,
by Aleksei Venetsianov
(1780–1847), early 1830s.
The State Tretiakov Gallery,
Moscow.

Peasant women bathing
infants along the
Volga River, 1897.
Keystone-Mast Collection,
UCR/California Museum of
Photography, University of
California, Riverside.

(*Top*) A peasant wedding (*lubok* print). From *Velikaia reforma* (Moscow, 1911), vol. 4.

Peasants haying in the village of Volkhovo, Volga region.
Library of Congress, Prints & Photographs Division, Prokudin-Gorskii Collection.

Woman weaver, Torzhok, Tver
province, late nineteenth century.
Courtesy of Timothy Mixter.

Weaver, by Natalia Goncharova
(1881–1962), 1912–1913.
National Museums and Galleries of
Wales, Cardiff.

Women workers assembling shells at the Sormovo metal-working plant,
Nizhnii Novgorod province.

From *Illiustrirovannaia istoriia SSSR* (Moscow, 1977).

Shansonetki at the annual Nizhnii Novgorod Fair: the Gustov sisters.
Dmitriev collection, State Archive of Nizhegorod Region.

Brothel prostitute and client. He: "Tell me, please, how'd you wind up here?"
She: "Real easy. My lover went to Novgorod for a while. I got bored . . . and
now I'm in debt."

From Lebedev, *Pogibshiia, no milyia sozdan'ia*, Slavic and Baltic Reserve,
New York Public Library.

(Top) Pilgrims at the Serafim-Diveevo Trinity Convent, Nizhnii Novgorod province.
Dmitriev collection, State Archive of Nizhegorod Region.

Nuns and novices at the Serafim-Ponetaevka All-Sorrows Convent, Nizhnii Novgorod province.
Dmitriev collection, State Archive of Nizhegorod Region.

4. Work and Schooling

INTRODUCTION

Work and schooling are broad and elusive categories. For women in imperial Russia, schooling, or education, could be formal or informal, and it could take place in the home, in specialized institutions, or in other venues. In this chapter we have focused on the growth of formal education for women, a process that came to exert a strong influence on the lives of many women. Work of some sort was nearly universal among women in imperial Russia; it was performed both inside the home and outside it, was paid and unpaid, and was sometimes predominantly of a physical character, and sometimes more intellectual in nature. Since many of the documents in chapter 2 describe women's domestic work, here we have concentrated on other forms of work by women, chiefly but not exclusively those performed outside of the home. We have linked the categories of schooling and work in part because our historical subjects often did so, seeing in formal education a means either to better prepare women to perform their familial and domestic roles or to enable them to earn a supplementary income or independent livelihood. But we have also included both categories in this chapter because the growth of formal education for women, particularly after the late 1850s, did in fact substantially expand their occupational opportunities, in ways that helped in turn to provoke public debate over what constituted "women's work."

Still, it should be emphasized that throughout the imperial period for most women work remained centered on the family and the household. The work that women learned to do, through the observation of older siblings and mothers and often through formal schooling, was to fit them for the various roles they were expected to play in their families and households at different stages in their lives. As the documents in chapter 2 demonstrate, how these roles were performed varied, depending on social position and wealth. Even similar types of work within the household could take on different forms and significance. Whereas noblewomen were expected to supervise the kitchen and the estate, for example, direct involvement in the production, preservation, and preparation of food was central to the peasant woman's life; while for noblewomen, who often produced goods for churches, monasteries, and the poor, needlework was a mark of refinement and charity, for peasant women weaving and sewing garments were essential functions in the household economy. Broadly speaking, the responsibilities of noble and merchant women within the household tended to be more administrative, and those of women from the peasantry and poorer urban strata generally involved more physical labor, with women from the clerical estate and "middling" social groups falling in between. In whatever form, however, nearly all women performed gendered roles within the household.

Virtually all women, too, endured the physical rigors and dangers of childbearing. Since reproduction was as important as production in terms of its contribution to the household economy, and for the nobility, to the preservation of a family's status, the bearing and raising of children was a necessary occupation for nearly all women. But how the latter responsibility was performed varied, based on social standing and wealth. Whereas a wealthy noblewoman would oversee the servants, mostly peasants, charged with caring for her children, a peasant woman would have to take on much of this responsibility herself, depending on the composition of her household. Even most noblewomen, however, played some direct role in their children's upbringing, an involvement that sometimes extended into the children's adulthood. Support of one's family members thus constituted a major occupation for women in imperial Russia, and for many women, particularly from the nobility, merchantry, and other privileged social estates, marriage represented a form of career.

In addition to their domestic and familial occupations, women engaged in other types of work, either within or outside the household. Throughout the imperial period, large numbers of peasant women were involved in petty trade and the production of a wide variety of craft goods, activities that almost certainly expanded over time (in addition to the documents in this chapter, see the description of peasant life by Aleksandra Efimenko in chapter 2). Women of the unprivileged urban estates similarly engaged in trade and craft production and in providing various services. The rights of married women from the nobility and merchantry to own and manage their own property, rights consolidated and expanded during the eighteenth century, enabled many such women to administer their estates independently and to become involved in commercial and manufacturing ventures. Spurred on in part by imperial example, women from more wealthy noble and aristocratic families undertook charitable work in a more organized and systematic fashion, an activity that gradually percolated down the social pyramid. At the very apex of this pyramid, not only was the empire ruled by a handful of women during most of the eighteenth century, but, beginning with Catherine II, empresses and other women of the imperial family also founded and actively supported educational institutions, foundling homes, hospitals, nursing orders, and other types of charitable organizations.

Invoking the abolition of serfdom in 1861 as a crucial dividing point in Russian history, though a valid argument in many cases, can be misleading when applied to the experience of women. The domestic role and ideal of women transcended this divide, for example, and the processes of economic development, expansion of formal education, and cultural change that powerfully affected the lives of most women at an accelerating pace after 1861 had begun long before this date. Nonetheless, Emancipation and the "Great Reform" period of the 1860s and 1870s in general mark an important watershed for Russian women with respect to both work and schooling. For peasant women, the abolition of serfdom resulted in an increased rate of household division and facilitated male seasonal out-migration, trends that made more women the mistresses of their households and that generally strengthened their position in the household, even though they often also intensified the burden of physical labor for women. Peasant women also gained an expanded opportunity to engage in wage labor and, apparently, more secure control over those forms of personal property considered their own. Wage labor for peasant women involved either work on a neighboring agricultural estate or in a nearby rural manufacturing enterprise or migration to a town or city. This last phenomenon increased considerably after the early 1880s as a result of the rapid growth of industry. Most peasant women who migrated to the cities engaged in domestic service, although large numbers of women also worked in craft shops, laundries, and similar trades. They also showed up increasingly as workers in industrial enterprises. By the early twentieth century, certain industries—for example, textiles and tobacco processing—had become heavily feminized, a process accelerated and extended to other branches of industry by the First World War. Many female peasant migrants to the city also turned eventually to prostitution, on an occasional or full-time basis, until able or compelled to abandon the trade (in addition to the speech by Dementeva in this chapter, see the relevant documents in chapters 3 and 6).

While the rapid industrial growth of the late nineteenth and early twentieth centuries reduced the demand for certain craft goods produced by both peasant and urban women, it increased the demand for others, with the result that dislocation was balanced by new opportunities. Particularly in expanding cities, the development of retail and service industries similarly offered opportunities for women as shop workers, shopkeepers, managers of taverns and restaurants, independent seamstresses, telephonists, and so on. Emancipation and the processes of industrialization, commercialization, and urbanization thus often altered the location, forms, and conditions of non-domestic work by women from the peasantry and poorer urban strata, but not its necessity or pervasiveness.

For many noblewomen, the economic dislocation resulting from the abolition of serfdom and the idealism of the Alexandrine reform era intersected with the expansion of formal education for women and with cultural changes to create the incentive and desire, and in some cases the necessity, to undertake new forms of employment. These changes in employment in turn both compelled a redefinition of what constituted "women's work" and helped to undermine the system of social estates. As women from different estates pursued similar forms of employment and came to identify themselves in a variety of new ways, the social estates, according to which the Russian population was officially categorized, weakened.

Although there had been some church-based antecedents, systems of formal education began to develop in imperial Russia only in the eighteenth century, chiefly as a result of the state-building efforts of successive rulers and the imperial government. Demanding more systematic and specialized training for military and civil servitors, Peter I brought numerous foreign specialists to Russia, sent noblemen abroad to Europe for education, and established a number of lower and specialized schools to provide the type of personnel needed to staff the expanding army, the new navy, and the growing civil administration. His successors pursued similar policies. As part of their efforts, the Imperial Academy of Sciences was opened in 1725 and Russia's first university, Moscow University, was established in 1755; each of these institutions included an affiliated secondary school. In the latter part of her reign, Catherine II endeavored to introduce a regularized system of public schooling in all provincial and district towns. Although her efforts met with limited success, they provided a foundation for the educational reforms of Alexander I, under whom gymnasiums providing secondary schooling were established in all provincial towns and four new universities, the elite Alexandrov Lycée, and several specialized institutes were opened. Paralleling these efforts by the state, the Orthodox Church created a system of clerical education during the eighteenth century that helped to transform the clergy into a closed estate. In addition, over the course of that century numerous private *pensions* and similar schools were established by individuals, often foreigners, and home tutoring for the children of the noble elite became common. In the nineteenth century the number of state, ecclesiastical, and private educational institutions expanded dramatically, although it was not until after the late 1850s that systems of primary schooling began to be developed to any significant extent.

Formal education for women developed within this general context and was marked by several broad trends. With the notable exception of Catherine II's provincial and district schools, which were coeducational, access to and the curriculum of educational institutions initially were based on sex and social status. The goal was to train men and women, but overwhelmingly men, for the particular roles they were expected to play in their family, society, and state service. Over time, however, and particularly after the late 1850s, the student body in schools and higher educational institutions became socially more mixed, and the curriculums of women's schools and higher educational institutions became academically more rigorous, moved closer to that for males at parallel levels, and grew more oriented toward preparing women for occupations outside the home. As was the case with respect to formal education for males, moreover, formal education for females was skewed disproportionately toward secondary and higher education, with primary education becoming more widespread only after the 1860s.

Although Peter I had demanded that women, as well as men, of the noble elite be properly educated, and in 1724 had decreed that convents teach basic literacy to children of both sexes, education for girls occurred mainly in the home until well into the nineteenth century. It was, moreover, chiefly the noble elite that could afford to hire governesses and tutors to educate their daughters. The provision of formal education for women began only in 1764 and 1765, when Catherine II established first the Smolnyi Institute for girls of the nobility in St. Petersburg and then the Novodevichii Institute for the daughters of commoners. Girls at both schools followed a twelve-year course of study, with instruction at Smolnyi including religion, Russian and foreign languages, arithmetic, history, geography, drawing, dancing, music, sewing, and social manners, and instruction at Novodevichii emphasizing more practical subjects and domestic economy (in addition to the documents in this chapter, see the letters by Aleksandra Levshina and Glafira Rzhevskaia in chapters 2 and 3). Similar training in "women's crafts" was provided for girls at the Imperial Foundling Homes, the first of which was founded in Moscow in 1764. As noted above, girls also were admitted to the two- and four-class public schools opened in provincial and district towns beginning in the early 1780s. Although the number of female pupils in these schools remained small both absolutely and in comparison with the number of male pupils, female enrollment rose steadily, so that by 1802 girls numbered approximately 2,000 of the total student body of just over 24,000. Under the patronage of the Dowager Empress Maria Fedorovna (d. 1828), widow of the assassinated Emperor Paul, and other royal women, the number of institutes and schools for women increased steadily during the first half of the nineteenth century and by 1845 totaled thirty-six. As in the case of the Smolnyi and Novodevichii Institutes, the curriculum of these schools was designed to suit the social standing and the expected social and familial roles of the students. Beginning in 1843 the Orthodox Church also established a number of schools for daughters of the parish clergy. Again, these efforts of the Church and the state (or local society acting under royal patronage and prodding) were supplemented by private efforts (see the petition by Anna Virt in this chapter).

However limited and modest, these early measures contributed to the expansion of literacy especially among women of the social elite and added to the number of women able to participate in literary and journalistic activities. In so doing, they helped fuel the demand made, beginning in the late 1850s, by male and female members of the nobility and of middling social groups for both greater access to and higher quality education for women (for example, see the documents by Nikolai Pirogov and Maria Vernadskaia in chapter 1). This demand, a central strand of the "woman question," often was linked to the desire to enable women to play a broader role in society through non-domestic employment. Secondary and higher education were seen not merely as means to self-improvement but also as essential prerequisites for a self-fulfilling occupation that would also benefit society. Partly in response to the resulting pressure for educational reform, the opportunities for women to pursue formal education at all levels expanded substantially after the late 1850s. At the outset of Alexander II's reign, for example, the approximately five thousand parish schools operated by the Orthodox Church provided the most extensive system of formal primary education available in the empire. But of nearly 100,000 students in these schools, only about 10 percent were girls. By 1911 this system had expanded to include 38,239 schools with 2.6 million pupils, of which about 600,000 (23 percent) were girls. In addition, by 1913 there were 77,839 primary schools operating under the jurisdiction of the Ministry of Education, mostly in rural areas, with a total enrollment of nearly 5.8 million pupils, of which 1.86 million (32 percent) were girls. To these schools must be added a number of trade and craft schools operated by the Ministry of Education, several other state agencies, and monastic institutions.

At the secondary level, gymnasiums for women were established beginning in 1857, both by the Ministry of Education and under the auspices of the Department for Institutions of Empress Maria; by 1915 there were nearly 950 women's gymnasiums and eighty-eight progymnasiums (see the statute on women's gymnasiums in this chapter). Between the late 1860s and 1913 the Orthodox Church also established seventy-four Diocesan Women's Schools, which provided a comparable education, primarily but not exclusively for women of the clerical estate. As a result of such developments, women constituted approximately half of all students enrolled in schools at the secondary level in 1913 and over half of those in secondary schools under the jurisdiction of the Ministry of Education (323,577 of 567,430, or 57 percent).

Similar advances occurred, albeit in a more uneven way, in women's higher education. Beginning in 1859, but only until the government prohibited this practice in 1863, individual universities allowed women to audit lectures. The lack of opportunity in imperial Russia led a number of women in the late 1860s and the 1870s to pursue higher education abroad, chiefly in Zurich and Geneva. Partly out of concern for the "morals" and the political loyalties of such women, and partly as a result of the strenuous efforts by the advocates (which included several prominent women) of higher education for women, the government permitted series of special lectures for women. These were established in St. Petersburg and Moscow in 1869 and continued into the 1870s, evolving into programs of Higher Women's Courses in these and several other cities. Although these courses provided university-level education for women, they received no material support from the state, which also refused to grant formal recognition to the women who completed their course of study. As part of the conservative reaction following the assassination of Alexander II in 1881, the government closed all of these courses in the mid-1880s, although it soon relented in part and permitted those in St. Petersburg to reopen in 1889 (see the petition by Elena Likhacheva in chapter 6). Higher Women's Courses were allowed to reopen in other cities beginning in 1900, and by 1914 there were such courses in eighteen cities, enrolling 23,534 women. In 1911 the graduates of these courses were permitted to take state examinations at universities and to receive university degrees. In addition to these courses, the Women's Medical Institute was established in St. Petersburg in 1895 (see the statute in this chapter), and by 1914 four such institutes existed in the empire. After 1900 several other specialized institutes for women also were established in various fields, especially pedagogy, and in 1911 women were permitted to enter several higher institutes in pedagogy, medicine, and some other fields. In 1913 women were admitted to the medical faculty at Tomsk University, and over the next several years the government permitted other universities to admit women to particular departments (see the decree of 1915 in this chapter's section, "Admissions to Universities"). As a result of these developments in imperial Russia, by 1915 women constituted roughly a third of all students in higher educational institutions.

This expansion of formal education for women, especially at the secondary and higher levels, helped open new occupations and careers to women. The large increase in the numbers of schools, hospitals, charitable and social organizations, and similar institutions, as well as the expansion of publishing and the periodical press, that followed in the wake of the reforms of the 1860s and 1870s provided educated women with opportunities for work outside the home. Women found non-domestic employment as teachers, medical assistants, midwives, nurses, doctors, journalists, editors, publishers, ethnographers, geographers, court stenographers, administrators, and so on (examples are included throughout this volume). They also became increasingly active as writers, actors (on stage and on the screen), dancers (in cabarets, music halls, and, more venerated, ballet productions), musicians and singers, and artists (see several examples in this volume). One effect of this expansion of the fields of non-domestic work women engaged in was to blur the boundary between "women's work" and work performed by men. This blurring gave rise to conflicts over the areas of appropriate work for females, and women fought out these issues in a multiplicity of venues, from professional and artistic-intelligentsia arenas to schools, craft shops, factories, trade unions, and peasant huts. The expansion also undermined the social categories into which Russian subjects were formally divided, as women from diverse social backgrounds were drawn into similar educational and occupational experiences and public discourses. A third effect was to contribute to the rise in female literacy; although by 1897 literacy rates had reached only 13.7 percent among rural women and 38.3 percent among urban women, these percentages almost certainly were higher by 1917. The figures conceal, however, substantial differences between women of different social backgrounds and generations. Nonetheless, they indicate the differential impact of educational expansion on different groups of women and the wide cultural as well as social and economic disparities that existed among them at the end of the imperial period. If the world of work and schooling had changed dramatically for Russian women during the imperial period, it had changed more dramatically for some individuals than for others.

THE EMPRESS AND THE PHILOSOPHER: CATHERINE II–VOLTAIRE CORRESPONDENCE

Empress Catherine and the French philosophe Voltaire (the pen name of François Marie Arouet, 1694–1778) corresponded, in French, for many years. Catherine looked to Voltaire to support and recognize her as a follower of Enlightenment ideals, that is, of tolerance and liberal social reforms. The French author, jailed and exiled on several occasions, flattered Catherine, perhaps hoping to count on a place of exile if needed. In these letters they exchange ideas about the curriculum and purpose of the Smolnyi Institute, which Catherine is at pains to distinguish from St. Cyr, the apparent model for it. Located near the palace of Versailles, St. Cyr was a French school founded in 1685 by Louis XIV, the "Sun King," and his mistress Madame de Maintenon for the daughters of impoverished nobility. Catherine contrasts its curriculum, based on religious piety but within the artificial constraints of court life, with her emphasis for the Smolnyi Institute on education, preparation for marriage, and freedom of spirit. She also coyly refers to her own writing of plays, while asking Voltaire, a playwright and man of letters, to edit some French classics which the Smolnyi pupils might perform.

---

86. CATHERINE TO VOLTAIRE
30TH JANUARY/10TH FEBRUARY 1772 [BESTERMAN 16546][1]

. . . You are aware—for nothing escapes you—that five hundred young ladies are being educated here in a convent formerly intended for three hundred brides of our Lord. The young ladies, I must confess, surpass our expectations: they are making astonishing progress, and everyone agrees that they are growing up as delightful as they are full of social accomplishments. Their morals withal are irreproachable, without, however, having the rigid austerity of recluses. For two winters, now, we have started to make them act comedies and tragedies, and they acquit themselves better than the professionals here. I admit, however, that there are only a very few plays that are suitable for them; their superiors would rather avoid their performing any which might arouse the passions too soon. They say there is too much love in most French plays, and even the classic writers have often suffered from this national taste or trait. To have plays commissioned would be impossible; good ones are not written to order at so much a page; they are the fruit of genius. Bad or insipid plays would spoil our taste. What should we do? I really do not know, and I turn to you for advice. Should we select isolated scenes? That is far less interesting, I think, than whole plays. No one could judge the matter better than you. Please help me with your advice. . . .

89. VOLTAIRE TO CATHERINE
FERNEY, 12TH MARCH 1772 [BESTERMAN 16587]

. . . I am extremely interested in your account of your five hundred young ladies. Our St. Cyr has less than two hundred and fifty. I do not know whether you make your girls perform tragedies; but I think that dramatic recitation, of tragedy or comedy, is an excellent form of education. It lends grace to mind and body, and trains the voice, deportment, and taste. One remembers a hundred passages that one can later quote as occasion demands. This adds to the pleasures of society and does all the good in the world. It is true that all our plays are concerned with love;

it is a passion for which I have the deepest respect, but I agree with your Majesty that it should not be developed too soon. One could, I think, take several selected comedies, and cut out the parts most dangerous to young minds, while retaining the interest of the play. There would be perhaps not twenty lines to alter in *Le Misanthrope*, and less than forty in *L'Avare*.[2] If the young ladies perform tragedy, a young man of my acquaintance wrote one only a short while ago, in which love can certainly not be said to play a role.[3] . . . I shall send it to your Imperial Majesty as soon as it is in print. If you consider that our classic authors can provide dramatic material suitable for the curriculum of your St. Cyr, I shall order tragedies and comedies from Paris in loose-leaf form; I shall have blank sheets of paper sewn between the pages, and on these I shall dictate the changes necessary to preserve the virtue of your fair young ladies. This little task will be a pleasure for me, and will not harm my health, feeble as it is. Moreover, I shall be sustained by the pleasure of doing something to please you.

I suppose that your battalion of five hundred girls is a battalion of amazons; but I do not suppose that they banish men. Certainly in performing plays, at least half of these young heroines must play the parts of heroes; but how will they play the role of old men in the comedies? I await your Majesty's instructions and orders on all these points . . .

What I admire about you, Madam, is that you do everything to perfection: you make your court the most delightful in Europe, while your troops are the most formidable. This mixture of grandeur and grace, of victories and fêtes, strikes me as charming. . . .

91. CATHERINE TO VOLTAIRE
2ND/14TH APRIL 1772 [BESTERMAN 16644]

Sir, your letter of 12th March gave me very great pleasure. Nothing could be more fortunate for our community than your proposal. Our young ladies perform both tragedy and comedy. Last year, they put on *Zaïre*,[4] and for the New Year they performed *Semira*, a Russian tragedy, indeed the best tragedy, of Monsieur Sumarokov, of whom you have heard.[5] Oh Sir, you will oblige me immensely, if for the sake of these dear children you will undertake the task which you call a pleasure and which would be so difficult for anyone else. You will thereby give me a most feeling token of that friendship of which I am so distinguished an object. Moreover, these young ladies are all charming, as all who see them agree. Some of them are already fourteen and fifteen years of age. I am sure they would win your approval if you saw them. I have been tempted more than once to send you some letters I have received from them and which were certainly not devised by their teachers; they are too childish for that: for the moment, every line brims with innocence, charm, and high spirits. I do not know whether this "battalion of girls," as you call them, will turn out to be amazons, but we are very far from wishing to turn them into nuns, or wear them out by constant caterwauling in church, as the practice is at St. Cyr. On the contrary, we educate them with a view to making them the delight of their future families; we want them to be neither prudes nor coquettes, but agreeable young ladies, capable of raising their own children and running their own homes.

This is how we set about casting the plays. We tell them that such and such a play will be put on, and ask them who wants to play such and such a part. Often, a whole class learns the same part, and then we pick the girl who acquits herself best. In the comedies, those who play the male roles wear a sort of long coat that we call the fashion of the particular country. In the tragedies, it is easy to dress our male leads in a way suited both to the play and to the performers. The old men's parts are the most difficult and the least successful. A big wig and a stick do not make a young girl look old and wrinkled: these parts have been rather lifeless so far. . . .

100. CATHERINE TO VOLTAIRE
17TH/28TH OCTOBER 1772 [BESTERMAN 16920]

. . . As soon as the translation is ready of our favorite Russian comedy, it will be on its way to Ferney. Perhaps after reading it you will say that it is easier to make me laugh than other monarchs, and you will be right. Basically, I am an extraordinarily light-hearted person. Opinion here is that the anonymous author of these new Russian comedies,[6] though he shows talent, has grave faults; he knows nothing about the theater, and his plots are weak. However this is not the case with his characters, which are well sustained and drawn from everyday life. There are flashes of wit, he makes you laugh, his morality is pure, and he knows his nation very well. I do not know whether all this will come over in translation. Talking of comedies, Sir, may I remind you of the promise you were kind enough to make me nearly a year ago, to adapt some good plays for the use of my educational institutes? . . . [7]

Source: Voltaire and Catherine the Great: Selected Correspondence, trans. and ed. A. Lentin (Cambridge, 1974). Excerpted from pp. 129–30, 131–32, 134–35, 143–44.

THE *INSTITUTKA* AND THE EMPRESS: LEVSHINA–CATHERINE II CORRESPONDENCE

The letters which follow represent part of an exchange (other letters are found in chapters 2 and 3) between Aleksandra Petrovna Levshina, an institutka, or a student at the Smolnyi Institute,[8] and Empress Catherine II. Levshina was one of the first pupils at the school, referred to in the letters as the Society for the Education of Young Ladies of the Nobility. She entered the Institute in 1770 and graduated in 1776. From among a select group of her favorites, Catherine handpicked Levshina for a special honor; they became pen pals, their correspondence spanning nine years, roughly spring 1771 until spring 1780. All but one of Levshina's letters (#V [3]) and part of another (#XI [7]) were originally written in French.[9]

The letters offer good evidence that the Smolnyi Institute, at its inception at least and unlike the closed institutes of the nineteenth century, afforded its young women many opportunities to venture outside the school premises and, to a certain extent, interact with the public. In contrast to the memoirs of students who attended the Institutes in the nineteenth century, Levshina's letters describe a life of varied amusements, both on the Institute's grounds and elsewhere, from strolling in the gardens of the Summer Palace to visiting young cadets at their military school. Her writing reflects her spirited, independent, and for the most part self-confident disposition and perhaps the atmosphere of the Institute as a whole.

#I (16) LEVSHINA TO CATHERINE II[10]

Your Majesty will of course recall the kind permission You gave me to write to You from time to time. I make bold to write You these few lines, in order to tell You that the Society presents its deepest respects to You, especially the Gray Order.[11] As for me, I am just as I was when You graced us with a visit—I skip and jump, I run, and in the evenings I play "wolf." But what a difference from that evening when, while playing the game, we were honored to hold Your Majesty's wonderful hands. Because they really are very beautiful. I so much wanted to kiss them, but I didn't dare. Now Your Majesty knows all our amusements. From time to time I also read, but that doesn't last long because I always have fun and games on my mind. Your Majesty will please remember her promise to visit us more often. I will close now because I've heard that long letters can be tiresome, and I would not want my letter to bore You, Your Majesty, on the contrary. Therefore I have the honor to remain Your Majesty's most humble and most obedient servant.

Pitch-dark Levushka[12]

#II (1) LEVSHINA TO CATHERINE II

Your Majesty!

A new opportunity has presented me the honor of writing to You, for I bring You thanks for Your kindness in allowing us to visit the wonderful palace where so charming a Person as You resides. How many charming things we saw there! I will describe them in detail for You, for Your Majesty is probably not aware of all that You possess. When we entered the grounds, we truly did find ourselves in heaven. Beautiful birds, trees, and so on—everything was so magnificent that I imagined I'd been transported to an enchanted palace by some sorceress. I don't understand how Your Majesty could have left all this and gone off to Peterhof to look at woods and mountains when here You have such wonderful things. I would remain here and admire them a month long. The exhibit of natural history with its shells and other objects is very nice. As for all Your precious jewels, Your scepter, Your crowns and orbs—they are very beautiful; their brilliance blinds the eye. But since I don't know the value of these items, I don't like them as much as the portrait gallery, and therefore please explain to me, what do You use them for? You can't wear all of them at the same time—why have things that serve no purpose? As for the portrait gallery, that's an entirely different matter; true, You cannot wear all the portraits on Your person, but they afford You great pleasure—I approve of the money You've spent on them. I've heard they are expensive, but then again they are good things. When Your Majesty comes to visit us at our school, we don't talk about the diamonds You were wearing; we talk about how beautiful You are. That is my opinion. I know very well that people will say I am a little fool; but I love things that give me pleasure and amuse me. We also visited Your library; there was a pulpit there and my friends told me to give a sermon, but I am least of all a sermonizer and I broke out laughing, as is my custom. All the girls have instructed me to express to You their deepest gratitude for the kindness You showed us. Levushka remains, with deferential respect,

Your Majesty's humblest and most obedient servant

Pitch-dark Levushka

27 June 1771

#VIII (5) LEVSHINA TO CATHERINE II

Your Majesty!

Pardon me, Your Majesty, for bothering You with my nonsense; but this time it's in order to thank You for kindly allowing us to go out for a stroll.[13] How many wonderful things we saw! Two magnificent palaces, an enchanting park, a brand-new portrait gallery, but what gave me the greatest pleasure was a certain character placed in Your room. As soon as I saw her I jumped for joy and bliss; in short, I can't describe the pleasure I felt at that moment. I imagined how happy I would be if I were a sorcerer and could bring her to life and make her talk freely about the things I always think about. But tell me please, Your Majesty, what sudden whim makes You want to keep a Turkish divan in Your room? This disturbed me a great deal. You can't tell me that some Turkish man or woman visits You? Or that You've put that divan there for comfort? As far as I know, the Turks have a rather unattractive way of sitting down; of course, it is a matter of Your taste, which is surely very good. Let us change subjects, therefore, to the Summer Garden. Had Your Majesty been hiding behind a corner and watching us, You would have seen how ecstatic we became. Believe me, it sounded as if fifty apes were taking a stroll; on top of everything, people were crowding us from all sides—from the back and the sides; in a word, it seemed that all of Petersburg was in the garden that day—I don't know why since, except for the fact that we went for a stroll that day, our appearance hadn't changed at all. But that's what it means to belong to You; everyone looks at us with pleasure, and we enjoy seeing the people because they shower us with kindness.

Monsieur Count or Prince—I don't know his title—did us the courtesy of treating us to a darling serenade that he prepared for us beforehand. As You can see, Your Majesty, I've managed to include in this letter of thanks talk about portraits, divans, and musicians. I assure You that all this is very interesting. Thus I always come across as a flighty creature. Indeed this is one of Madame de Lafond's[14] nicknames for me; it suits me. I will take the liberty of reminding Your Majesty not to remain in Tsarskoe Selo too long without being so kind as to visit us. The whole Society assures You of their deep respect, especially the white capes, and I have the honor to remain, with the deepest esteem, Your Imperial Highness's most humble and most obedient servant

Pitch-dark Levushka

25 May 1773

#IX (1) [CATHERINE II TO LEVSHINA]

Here is my reply to your two letters, madam, apropos of which let me mention in passing that the first was written in so cramped a hand that if you continue to write in this manner you will give me the added expense in six months of having to purchase eyeglasses with which to read your letters. Nevertheless, I will always find them pleasant, whether I have to read them with glasses or without. Please tell Madame de Lafond for me that the big girl in white with the dark complexion and a nose like a parrot's who in times past cried out at every arrival and departure of mine from the convent, that this girl writes just as naturally as she is and that her letters are filled with joy. I always like it when the beauty of nature is left on its own without any compulsion or added refinements; I find pitch-dark Levushka, with her frivolity and unexpected pranks, entirely to my taste. Keep going, madam, keep going. In three years I will come and kidnap you from the convent, and no matter how much you'll see fit to scream and curse, you will see Tsarskoe Selo, about which you've formed such a negative opinion. Despite your negative attitude and since you love the truth, you will be forced to admit that it is a delightful place and incomparably more beautiful than the garden of the Summer Palace, which you girls in white adorned on the very day when some guinea-fowl were on the loose there and when you turned the heads of everyone in town. Similarly it's him you need to ask about the Turkish divan in my room in the Summer Palace; he usually puts whatever he wants into my room. I myself placed in it only your portrait, the one madam Molchanova drew. This is my favorite thing; it will never leave the place I've assigned it or, more accurately, which you assigned it. If you don't understand this, ask your schoolmistresses for an explanation—they certainly know about it. I find that the serenade the prince sang for you was a very good idea. He likes to please you; he has seen how you came into the world and desires the best for you because he loves to see his country prosper, and your education contributes to it. In particular he likes you, and do you know why? Because you are sweet. My letter is quite long enough, isn't it? The last thing I want to say is give my regards to the brownies, caress the little blues for me, give the gray sisters a kiss, and hug the white capes, my oldest friends. Also extend my sincere regards to Madame de Lafond and at the same time convey to her all those feelings which she has successfully instilled in you; this can only give her great pleasure.

#XI (7) LEVSHINA TO CATHERINE II

Your Majesty!

You love me forever. "Oh! How happy I am! I'm the happiest of all people!" My happiness will be complete if You promise to visit us again in one year and if You keep Your word; that is the main thing. Take care, take care if You deceive me. Did You know that I am very dangerous when I get angry and so I strongly advise You to fear me a little; I will give You a little example of how I get when I'm angry. You can't imagine the kind of audacity that lurks in me—yes, audacity, that is it precisely. So here it is! Your Majesty treats us as if we were people unable to read or write in Russian. Allow me to tell You—*et ne vous deplaise*,[15] we know as much Russian as You do, *à la bonheur*,[16] our conversation skills may not be too strong but our reading and writing ability warrant a higher opinion from You than at present. We put on a decent show for the English; they were so pleased with it that they talked about it endlessly.

I have the honor to be, with the most profound devotion to You,

Your Majesty's
Most humble and most obedient servant
Pitch-dark Levushka

19 March 1875 [*sic*]

#XII (8) LEVSHINA TO CATHERINE II

Your Majesty!

First of all, we visited the Summer Garden in most festive form.

Our second trip was to Peterhof, or, better, to Your magical kingdom. After we looked the palace over, we went down to the enchanted garden; it struck me as the dwelling place of the gods, and from one moment to the next I kept expecting a certain deity to appear, but in vain. The deity of that enchanted place was unfortunately in Moscow. Having feasted our eyes on all the beautiful things and objects of art collected in that place, we turned to feasting on all the objects of nature collected upon the wonderful dining table. Philosophy is all the more fascinating and useful when, for example, lengthy discussions about a chicken, and all philosophical viewpoints about its characteristics, come to an end once the chicken is carved and meets the mouth. To tell the truth, this resolution is a bit savage for us ladies, but people with a hearty appetite ignore such trivia. After dinner we rode carriages to Monplaisir. What a fitting name! So there, in broad outline, is a description of our trip to Peterhof. The trip to the Cadet Corps was also quite interesting and deserves a detailed description of its own. Our delight was partly mixed with fear because for the first time we heard gunfire and every shot made us shudder and shrink back at least a half foot. God knows what would have happened to me if the gunfire and cannon blasts had continued any longer; I didn't know where to hide my ears and I kept thinking that my poor head would become the target of the cannons and grenades. I'll be less timid next time and therefore I ask Your Majesty not to laugh at me. After this lesson in the camps, we went horseback riding, which was wonderful. One of the horses, known by the name "Big Prancer," was making frightening jumps and prancing on its front legs while cutting some sort of capers with its back legs. After this ritual ended, some dwarfs appeared; they invited us to visit their nice little park. We saw one of the dwarfs on the road home; he was trying to get a bear to dance. The day ended with a magnificent festival in the garden: there was a comedy, an opera, and a ballet. We left feeling more than satisfied with such a wonderful day; however, we still have one small wish. It would seem, after You went to so much trouble for us, that we should do something in turn. Monsieur Betskoi[17] won't take it upon himself to give us permission to put on a little festivity for the cadets; we beg permission from You, dear Sovereign, to let us repay our considerable debt to them; were it to remain unpaid, we would be thought of as dishonorable.

I remain, with the deepest respect, Your Majesty's most humble and most obedient servant

Pitch-dark Levushka

18 June 1775

Source: Appollon Maikov, ed., "Perepiska imperatritsy Ekateriny II s A. P. Levshinoi," *Russkii vestnik* ["Correspondence of Empress Catherine II and A. P. Levshina," *Russian Messenger*], vol. 247 (Nov. 1896), pp. 310–49. Excerpted.

Translated by Martha Kuchar.

FATHERS AND DAUGHTERS

A. A Caring Father's Note to His Young Daughter

VASILII TATISHCHEV

Father-daughter relationships often were limited to obligations, financial and otherwise, as was Dashkova's with her father, who provided a generous dowry while leaving her upbringing to his brother (see chapter 2). Yet some fathers took a much more active interest in their daughters, thinking about their upbringing and education even while away on civil service assignments. Vasilii Tatishchev and Mikhail Speranskii were two such fathers, and their letters to their daughters are included here for this reason.

The concern of historian Vasilii Nikitich Tatishchev for his daughter's education, and his involvement with the group that brought Empress Anna Ivanovna to the throne in 1730, ensured that Evpraksiia Vasilevna Tatishcheva (1715–1769 or 1770) would make a successful marriage. Shortly after ascending the throne, Empress Anna proposed a marriage for the young Tatishcheva to Mikhail Andreevich Rimskii-Korsakov, who had just returned from a long period of study abroad and was related to one of Empress Anna's ladies-in-waiting. To facilitate the match and the success of the marriage, the Empress contributed, in addition to her august blessings, gifts and money amounting to several thousand rubles. This marriage produced two children and was happy, though short, ending with Rimskii-Korsakov's death.[18] Evpraksiia's second marriage, to S. A. Shepelev, was more like that of her father and mother. Tatishchev had petitioned for separation from his wife in 1728, accusing her of dissipation, unfaithfulness, and attempting to poison him. Instead of torturing each other, the Shepelevs agreed to live separately and not make any claims against the property of the other. This sort of arrangement was fairly common, but not strictly legal in most cases (refer to the discussion of divorce in chapter 2 for more on this issue). Evpraksiia was seven years old when she received this letter from her father.

My Dear Evpraksiia Vasilevna, Hello.

I am sending you a length of azure damask for a dress, but it is necessary to keep the brown one for the future; my portrait doesn't look much like me, which is not my fault, but you can recognize me and you will have it to remind you of me. Don't lose it, and don't ruin it! I don't have any news about you yet. Where are you? What are you doing? Are you studying diligently? If only I knew that you had the desire, I would give you more. Together with this, be in God's grace, as I wish.

V. Tatishchev
Uktus,[19] 18 Dec. 1722.

Instead of damask, since it had stains, and I couldn't look for another, I am sending you two ends [from bolts of fabric] and a [length][20] of nankeen.

Source: "Chetyre pis'ma V. N. Tatishcheva k docheri," *Arkheograficheskii ezhegodnik za 1986 god* ["Four Letters of V. N. Tatishcheva to His Daughter," in *Text Study Annual for 1986*] (Moscow, 1987), Letter no. 1, p. 299. Excerpted.

Translated by Robin Bisha.

B. A Diplomat Writes to His Daughter on Self-Reliance

MIKHAIL SPERANSKII

Perhaps because his wife, Elizabeth Stephens, died in childbirth (1798), Mikhail Mikhailovich Speranskii (1772–1839) also took an active interest in his daughter's development. Speranskii, a noted diplomat and imperial advisor in the first quarter of the nineteenth century, corresponded with his daughter while he was away on business, keeping her apprised of his activities and offering her advice on her intellectual development. In this instance, he was writing from Irkutsk, in eastern Siberia, where he was serving as provincial governor-general. While Tatishchev included study among material concerns,

Speranskii focuses his attention on his daughter's education. This change reflects the growing importance of education and its more comprehensive character in the nineteenth century.

Irkutsk. 4 February 1820

I begin my letter where you ended yours. It is certainly unfortunate, my dear Elisaveta, that fate keeps separating us. Of course, no one can understand you the way I can, for the delicate sentiments of the soul are best understood in the heart, not in the mind. By the way, to the extent that we can perceive the inscrutable ways of Providence, it seems to me that this separation, which Providence has given us, has some beneficent purpose. It teaches both of us patience; in particular, it teaches you to be self-reliant, to examine your own feelings, to discuss them with others, and to act. To what extent this study and this practice will be necessary in your practical life you will find out in due course. Why are women for the most part weak, indecisive? Because they have long leaned on someone else, have relied on someone else even in trivial matters. This is convenient for men but most inconvenient for women. One can always summon a certain amount of that weakness or, more accurately, that duplicity which a woman sometimes needs; all that is required for it is modesty, or even just an accurate account of mutual relations. But strength of soul and emotion will not always be found when it is sought. One must have it in ready supply.

Goodbye, my dear. May the Lord be with you.

Source: "Pis'ma M. M. Speranskago k ego docheri iz Sibiri," *Russkii arkhiv* ["Letters of M. M. Speranskii to His Daughter from Siberia," *Russian Archive*], vol. 6 (1868), pp. 1681–1811. Excerpted from p. 1736.

Translated by Martha Kuchar.

PRIVATE SCHOOLING

During the greater part of the eighteenth century, Russian girls even of the middling and upper classes had few options, apart from private tutoring at home, for receiving an education. Even after formal schooling had become available, most families continued to prefer tutoring at home for their daughters. Study in private schools, many of them run by women of foreign origin, became a popular alternative in the early nineteenth century to home tutoring or study in the Institutes. The following documents present curriculum and evaluations from a private school in imperial Russia in the early nineteenth century and the experiences of a young woman studying in a foreign finishing school in the 1860s.

A. Petition to Establish a School

ANNA VIRT

Anna Virt, a Russian German, had to gain the approval of the Director of Schools for Moscow province (the recipient of this petition) and of the Schools Committee of Moscow University for permission to open a school. Almost six months passed between the initial petition and the opening of the school in February 1818. Virt established her own curriculum and hired teachers for all the subjects; she taught reading and writing in Russian, French, and German as well as handwork, hiring five additional teachers, all men, to complete the curriculum. Although Virt chose the curriculum, the school was subject to inspection by the Director of Schools of Moscow province; one of his reports is translated here.

Your Honor.
To the Director of the Schools of Moscow Province Collegiate Councilor
and Cavalier[21] Petr Mikhailovich Druzhinin.

From the foreigner, Moscow native Anna Virt

Petition

As the bearer of a certificate for the teaching of French, German, and Russian languages, I wish to open a school for reading and writing in the above-named languages for young children of the feminine sex. As a consequence of this [desire], I most humbly beg to obtain the appropriate permission to do so. I propose a two-hundred-ruble per girl annual charge, and I have the honor to present a schedule of the hours they will be studying. 21 August 1817 Anna Virt

Schedule of Academic Subjects by Hour

Monday	8–10 o'clock:	Reading in German
	10–12 o'clock:	Embroidery
	2–4 o'clock:	Embroidery
Tuesday	8–10 o'clock:	Reading in French
	10–12 o'clock:	Reading in Russian
	2–4 o'clock:	Writing in German and Russian
Wednesday		Dancing
		Sacred history and Catechism
Thursday	8–10 o'clock:	German conversation
	10–12 o'clock:	German and Russian grammar
	2–4 o'clock:	Writing

Register of the Pupils Studying in Anna Virt's School

Name	Age	Status of parents	Time of entry	Abilities	Diligence	Behavior
Aleksandra Ketcher	13	Titular Councilor[22]	8 Feb. 1818	Good	Diligent	[All pupils
Anna Golovina	13	Fencing Master	8 Feb. 1818	Fair	Fair	exhibit
Maria Anderson	12	Foreigner	8 Feb. 1818	Not bad	Diligent	GOOD
Nastasia Savchenkova	14	Collegiate Assessor[23]	8 Feb. 1818	Good	Diligent	BEHAVIOR]
Maria Savchenkova	12	" "	" "	Good	Diligent	
Elena Bostelman	14	Foreigner	8 Feb. 1818	Weak	Fair	
Elisaveta Manners	12	Foreigner	8 Feb. 1818	Good	Diligent	
Sofia Otmar	9	Foreigner	8 Feb. 1818	Good	Painstaking	
Elisaveta Shchekoldina	12	Townsman	10 Mar. 1818	Fair	Fair	
Avdotia Dranitsyna	13	Priest	1 May 1818	Good	Diligent	
Iiulia Velikoselskaia	9	Titular Councilor	25 May 1818	Good	Diligent	
Elisaveta Odintsova	13	Provincial Secretary[24]	20 Aug. 1818	Fair	Diligent	
Sofia Bostelman	9	Foreigner	20 Aug. 1818	Fair	Fair	
Donna Ushakova	14	Townsman	25 Sept. 1818	Fair	Lazy	
Nadezhda Zaikovskaia	10	Physician	11 Jan. 1819	Fair	Fair	
Maria Shtal	9	Foreigner	4 Feb. 1819	Not bad	Painstaking	
Varvara Vasileva	13	Captain[25]	10 Mar. 1819	Fair	Fair	
Amaliia Shram	11	Foreigner	16 Apr. 1819	Good	Diligent	
Vilgemina Shram	9	" "	" "	Weak	Fair	
Maria Karlyzeeva	9	Collegiate Assessor	13 May 1819	Good	Fair	
Maria Fisher	14	Foreigner	20 May 1819	Not bad	Diligent	
Elisaveta Fisher	11	" "	" "	Fair	Fair	
Anna Knopp	13	Foreigner	2 July 1819	Weak	Fair	
Aleksandra Pristlei	11	Foreigner	11 Aug. 1819	Not bad	Fair	
Elisaveta Pristlei	9	" "	" "	Stupid	Lazy	
Ekaterina Rasinskaia	11	Collegiate Councilor	19 Aug. 1819	Weak	Lazy	

Register of the Pupils Studying in Anna Virt's School (continued)

Name	Age	Status of parents	Time of entry	Abilities	Diligence	Behavior
Natalia Vasileva	9	Commissar[26]	11 Sept. 1819	Not bad	Fair	
Anna Peluz	8	Foreigner	21 Sept. 1819	Good	Painstaking	
Elisaveta Rule	7	Foreigner	11 Jan. 1820	Weak	Decent	
Anna Sokolova	12	Titular Councilor	22 Jan. 1820	Pretty good	Fair	
Sofia Frovein	11	Foreigner	24 Feb. 1820	Stupid	Decent	
Ekaterina Maslovicheva	10	Court Councilor[27]	6 Apr. 1820	Good	Painstaking	
Anna Stabrovskaia	12	Court Councilor	21 Apr. 1820	Good	Diligent	
Elisaveta Markova	11	Titular Councilor	2 May 1820	Not bad	Decent	

Subjects taken:

1. Several have finished the Catechism and others have reached the 12th Article.

2. In Russian, some have finished grammar and others have reached the verbs. They are beginning to study reading and writing.

3. In French grammar, some have passed syntax, others are taking etymology.

4. In German grammar, some have passed syntax, others are taking etymology and have passed easy translations from German into Russian.

5. Calligraphy in all three languages.

6. In arithmetic, they are continuing fractions and beginning the rules of simple numbers.

7. They do embroidery on a hoop; they sew and knit.

Friday	8–10 o'clock:	French conversation
	10–12 o'clock:	French grammar and reading
	2–4 o'clock:	Writing in French
Saturday		Rehearsal

Anna Virt

Remarks:
His Honor the Director of the Schools of Moscow Province Provincial Collegiate Councilor and Cavalier Petr Mikhailovich Druzhinin visited this school 3 July 1820 and inspected the entire institution.

Source: "Delo o zhenskoi shkole Anny Virt v Moskve, 1817–1820 gg." ["The Matter of Anna Virt's Girls' School in Moscow"], in Shchukin, vol. VII, pp. 271–79.

Translated by Robin Bisha.

B. Diary of a Young Noblewoman: Curriculum and Teachers

The second document offers a glimpse into the life of a young Russian noblewoman attending school in Geneva in the mid-nineteenth century (for another excerpt from her diary, see chapter 2). Since her diary entries were published anonymously, we cannot establish why she was living abroad during her school years or who her parents were. It is clear, however, that she felt at home in the company of girls of the European ruling class. Her comfort in this milieu demonstrates that Russian nobles were part of a general European elite and that this group shared similar values about education for women across national boundaries. Her concerns and style are reminiscent of those of Levshina and differ from those of Kuskova (later in this chapter).

EXTRACTS FROM MY DIARY. . . .

28 JANUARY 1865

On the evening of the 26th I enjoyed myself very much; I ordered little cakes, and a large spiced punch, and eclairs and sandwiches: Mlle. Pellet allowed us to dance. We jumped around till 10 o'clock, and laughed like crazy people. It was always the tall American man, with his red cravat, who made us make these endless "poussades";[28] he had come to speak to Mlle. Pellet about gymnastic lessons; Mlle. Pellet was busy and had told Mlle. Léonie to receive him. She had laughed so much that the American had said to her, "I shall come back in an hour, when you will be calmer." It was very impertinent, but Léonie forgave him because of his red tie, quite disheveled and not very new. Each time we met this chimpanzee, we laughed till we cried; there was no way not to laugh, and why wear red ties when one came into a *pension* of young women? Mlle. Pellet scolds us, but that means nothing, she understands us. I love Mlle. Pellet so much! If only she were not under the thumb of that awful Mlle. Borck! No one except Catherine A. likes Mlle. Borck. She flatters Catherine and gives her presents, that's the secret of this great friendship. It is quite different with Mlle. Léonie, Lina D., and myself: we quarrel frequently, we make up quickly, and then we laugh a lot! We three make more noise than all the others together. It was great yesterday, during the geometry lesson. Just at the moment when M. Bort had asked me a problem, I looked at Lina, to find the answer in her shining eyes and her pretty crooked nose, when suddenly she pulled a small red handkerchief out of her pocket and put it under her chin. Pouf! I let out a monstrous burst of laughter, and so did all the other young women. M. Bort was disconcerted, and looked at Mlle. Pellet. Mlle. Pellet didn't move; she knew it would be useless, and that the crazy laughter was controlling things; M. Bort just folded his arms and waited. Luckily the lesson was almost over; the bell rang, and M. Bort left the class calmly, without saying anything to us. Tomorrow Lina D. and I will go to see him to make our apologies and to explain our laughter. Mlle. Pellet is displeased, but hasn't said anything, and for us, that's as bad as if she had borrowed all Mlle. Borck's awful German vocabulary.

. . .

1 MAY 65.

On our return Mlle. Pellet took me in her carriage with Mlle. Léonie and Lina D.; we talked the whole time about Madame de Staël and her works, of which I only knew *Corinne*;[29] Mlle. Pellet told us about the topics [in her book on] Germany and also told us several anecdotes about Napoleon. I don't like Napoleon: he seems to me someone who is too large in his faults, and too small in his soul.

Source: Shchukin, vol. X. Excerpted from pp. 396–401.

Translated by Christine Holden.

STATE SCHOOLING: REGULATIONS AND EXPERIENCE

The expansion of state-run schooling in the latter part of the nineteenth century marked a transition in the curriculum at the secondary level from an emphasis on religious instruction, foreign languages, social manners, and basic homemaking skills to an academically more rigorous education that included subjects in the social and natural sciences. Since women were not yet admitted as degree candidates at universities, completion of eight years of secondary school was for many women the highest qualification they achieved; it qualified them to work as governesses or as teachers in public and parish schools. Some women continued their studies abroad; others took courses and examinations in Russia to qualify as doctors, pharmacists, and other medical professionals.

The following two documents illustrate this transition. The first is an excerpt from the statute of a school for girls established in 1827 by the Women's Patriotic Society, a charitable organization founded in 1812 by the Empress Elizabeth and other ladies of the aristocracy, initially to provide relief to victims of the wars against Napoleon. The second document, which was promulgated in 1870 and revised an earlier statute of 1857, consists of excerpts from the statute on women's gymnasiums and progymnasiums under the supervision of the Ministry of Education.

A. Women's Patriotic Society, School for Girls

STATUTE OF THE SCHOOL ESTABLISHED BY THE WOMEN'S PATRIOTIC SOCIETY, APPROVED 7 APRIL 1827.

5. The purpose of the program of moral education is to teach the students to be good wives, solicitous mothers, and exemplary mentors for their children, and to teach them the skills they need to be able to provide for themselves and their families by means of their own hard work.

6. To this end, the subjects taught are: (a) morality, based on Divine Law; (b) the essential sciences; (c) useful needlework skills; and (d) fundamentals of home management and housekeeping.

Source: 2PSZ, ii. (1827), no. 48,406: 701–705. Excerpted.

Translated by Carol Apollonio Flath.

B. State Women's Gymnasiums and Progymnasiums

STATUTE ON WOMEN'S GYMNASIUMS AND PROGYMNASIUMS OF THE MINISTRY OF EDUCATION, APPROVED 24 MAY 1870.

REGULATION

General Provisions

1. Girls' Gymnasiums and Progymnasiums under the authority of the Ministry of Education have the good fortune to enjoy the Supreme patronage of Her Imperial Highness the Sovereign Empress.

2. Girls' Gymnasiums and Progymnasiums are establishments intended for non-resident students of all social estates and religious creeds.

4. Girls' Gymnasiums consist of seven grades, each one with its own year-long course of study, but for students preparing for teaching careers, an eighth, supplemental grade may be established as well, with its own year-long, and, where possible, two-year course of study (Articles 27 and 28).

5. Girls' Progymnasiums have three grades, with a year-long course of study for each grade, but, where possible, they may include a greater number of grades.

[Administration and Staffing of Gymnasiums and Progymnasiums]

8. Direct administration of a Gymnasium or Progymnasium is entrusted to the Headmistress, who is selected by the Administrative Council. The Headmistress of a Gymnasium is approved for her position by the Minister of Education, and the Headmistress of a Progymnasium—by the Superintendent of the school district. Where funds permit, a Gymnasium or Progymnasium employs supervisors, selected by the Headmistress and confirmed in their positions by the Administrator of the school district, who serve as aides to the Headmistress.

9. Headmistresses or supervisors certified as governesses or teachers may teach in a Progymnasium and in the lower three grades of a Gymnasium one academic subject of their own choosing, for which they receive special compensation.

10. The Administrative Council consists of persons of both sexes, selected by those associations and societies representing the social estate that sponsors and maintains the Gymnasium or Progymnasium. The Administrative Council is chaired by one of its members, selected by the Council for a three-year term; the person occupying this post may be reelected for new terms as well. The Director of a Boys' Gymnasium, or, where there is no Gymnasium—the Permanent Inspector of Schools, and the Headmistress of the Girls' Gymnasium or Progymnasium are, by virtue of their positions, standing members of the Administrative Council.

11. Additionally, the Administrative Council includes a female Administrator selected by the Administrative Council from among the most distinguished citizens of the town, who can use their influence to enhance the well being of the Gymnasium or Progymnasium. During Council meetings, this Administrator occupies the place of honor.

17. The Pedagogical Council of a Gymnasium or Progymnasium, chaired by the Director of the Boys' Gymnasium, or, where there is no Gymnasium, the Permanent Inspector of Schools, consists of the Headmistress of the Girls' Gymnasium and the Progymnasium and all the people who work in the academic program and the program of moral education of these institutions. One of the instructors is selected by the Pedagogical Council to serve as Secretary.

22. Male instructors of a Girls' Gymnasium and Progymnasium are selected by the Chairman of the Pedagogical Council from among the teachers of Boys' Gymnasiums, Progymnasiums, and provincial schools, as well as from among persons certified as domestic tutors and teachers; female instructors are selected from among certified governesses and teachers. They are all approved in their positions by the Superintendent of the school district.

Note: In Progymnasiums having three grades and in the lower three grades of Gymnasiums, teaching positions are given primarily, where possible, to persons of the female sex.

Academics

24. Required subjects include, in Progymnasiums with three grades: (1) Scripture; (2) Russian language (explanatory reading and introduction to basic grammar); (3) Russian history and geography, abbreviated, with a supplemental survey of all the parts of the world; (4) Arithmetic (the first four operations on whole numbers, concrete numbers, and the concept of fractions, with practical application in keeping accounts, where possible); (5) penmanship; and (6) needlework essential for practical application in the home.

Note: In Progymnasiums having more than three grades, the course of study is expanded to match the academic program of the corresponding grades in Gymnasiums.

25. The following are required subjects in Girls' Gymnasiums: (1) Scripture; (2) Russian language (grammar and introduction to the most important works of literature); (3) Arithmetic, as applied in accounting, and fundamentals of geometry; (4) Russian and World Geography; (5) Russian and World History; (6) fundamental concepts of Natural History and Physics, with supplemental instruction relating to home management and hygiene; (7) penmanship; (8) needlework; and (9) gymnastics, if the school has the necessary facilities.

26. Elective subjects in Gymnasiums and Progymnasiums include: French and German language, drawing, music, singing, and dancing.

27. In addition to the general seven-year course of study, Girls' Gymnasiums may offer a special course for those wishing to acquire the right to work as governesses and teachers.

28. Students in the special course are provided instruction in the primary provisions concerning moral education, as well as the methods of teaching the subjects in the academic course of study in Girls' Gymnasiums. In addition, they perform practice teaching under the direction of teachers and instructors of the Girls' Gymnasium, following specific rules approved by the National Minister of Education.

43. Students awarded gold or silver medals upon graduation from the general course of study in a Girls' Gymnasium, and who have also taken the supplemental year-long course, are qualified as governesses.

44. Students not awarded medals, but who have earned a degree attesting to their successful completion of the general Gymnasium course and who have taken the supplemental year-long course, are granted the right to serve as governesses.

45. Students not awarded medals, but who have completed the general course of study in a Gymnasium, are granted the right to serve as primary teachers and teachers in the public school system. The same right is granted to students who receive a certificate attesting to their completion of the course of study in a Progymnasium or the lower three grades of a Gymnasium if, having reached the age

of sixteen, they perform the duties of a teacher's aide for half a year in a primary school.

Source: 2PSZ, xiv, pt. 1 (1870), no. 48,406: 701–705. Excerpted.

Translated by Carol Apollonio Flath.

C. Memoirs

EKATERINA KUSKOVA

Ekaterina Dmitrievna Kuskova (1869–1958) was a noted political activist in the late imperial period and during the Russian Revolution and Civil War. Exposed to revolutionary ideas during her youth in Saratov, a city on the Volga River to which a number of political activists had been exiled, she was an early proponent of Marxist ideas. Although she renounced her social democratic beliefs in 1899, she remained active in radical politics and after the 1905 Revolution helped to found the Constitutional Democratic (Kadet) Party.[30] She grew disillusioned with the party almost immediately, however, and resigned from its Central Committee. While avoiding party membership thereafter, between 1906 and 1917 Kuskova contributed regularly to the opposition press and published or edited several short-lived journals. An opponent of the Bolshevik seizure of power in October, she became a leading figure among the democratic opposition and was expelled from the Soviet Union in 1921. She lived the rest of her life in Berlin and Geneva. The memoirs excerpted here, which reflect Kuskova's democratic orientation, were written and published in emigration.

In this excerpt, Kuskova recounts key aspects of her education in provincial cities. She began her formal education in 1877, following the classical curriculum for girls in gymnasiums in Samara and Saratov.[31] Although the classical curriculum for both boys and girls emphasized Greek and Latin, the girls' curriculum also devoted much effort to preparing young women for their roles as wives and mothers, for example by including instruction in needlework. While study in the gymnasium prepared boys for university study and eventual civil service, the main non-domestic occupation envisaged for girls was teaching, particularly at the primary level. Rather than accept this limitation on her prospects, however, Kuskova developed into a politically active journalist.

I never recall my mother, even in later times, with a book or a newspaper. It seems to me that she never read. But on the other hand my father was always bringing home whole briefcases of books, and he would often read them over tea and dinner. He himself taught my sister and me to read and write very early on: at the age of six I was already reading children's fairy tales and I really liked to retell them to my father. But my mother did not like to listen:

"Don't bother me with such foolishness, Katenka. Nothing of the sort ever happened. . . . It's all foolishness. Why don't you help me rinse the berries instead? . . ."

In Samara

My father sent off for the educational program at the Saratov gymnasium for girls: he had been trying for a long time to get us transferred to Saratov—and he started to prepare us for it himself. I clearly remember those lessons with my father: you could ask him any questions at all, and he explained everything so well and so clearly. Sometimes my mother would come to our lessons with some mending or embroidering in her hands. But I always thought that she didn't hear anything that was going on around her; my father so often lowered his voice and threatened us with his finger: quiet! My mother was sleeping. . . . Her health kept getting worse and worse. The doctor often came to see her, and he would make her stay in bed for whole weeks at a time. Then I became the mistress of the house. At the age of nine or ten I already had a firm handle on all the details of housekeeping, I was great at making *pel'meni*,[32] I put mustard plasters on my mother's back, and my father often called me "a little mama."

In Saratov

We arrived in Saratov in the fall of 1879. My sister had no problem getting into first (that is, seventh) grade[33] at the Mariinskii gymnasium for girls. But in my case, things were difficult for a while: because of my age they would not let me into the grade level where I should have been, based on my knowledge. My father nonetheless insisted that they let me into the fifth (third) grade, promising to leave me for a second year in the next, more difficult set of classes. So we became schoolgirls in Saratov. School was easy there: the preparation our father had given us became evident. We both quickly moved up into the ranks of the best students, almost without studying at home. The only problem was posed by the language classes: our mother did not know a single foreign language, and our father was very weak in them.

The Saratov Mariinskii Gymnasium

It would probably be worthwhile to comment on the absolute indifference of the teachers of those times to our physical development. What a difference there was when I observed Moscow and Petersburg gymnasiums, much later! In Saratov we not only had no notion of excursions or physical exercise, but even during the long recess we were let out into the spacious yard not so that we could get some exercise after being in the stuffy classrooms. On the contrary, they were keeping an eye on the decorum of the young girls' behavior.

I also do not recall that there was any kind of spiritual upbringing. Education— yes. We learned a lot in school, at any rate, and in the upper grades—thanks to a chance selection of teachers—even serious religious interests were awakened in us. But at that time, nobody at all even thought about any kind of upbringing, whether patriotic, religious, or aesthetic, and nobody inspired any ideas in us. Later on, when I heard that school firmly hammers into the souls of the students three concepts—autocracy, Orthodoxy, and national pride—I was surprised: nobody hammered such concepts into us. In order to hammer in any elements at all of an ideology, the teachers themselves need to have that ideology, and for the teachers to inspire that ideology in the souls of the students, they have to have self-sacrificing zeal or simply a sincere desire to inform, to infect the students with a feeling or an idea. As far as I remember, nobody performed those kinds of ideological operations on us. Later on, when I became personally acquainted with several teachers, I became convinced that they did not have even the slightest recollection of that devotion to autocracy or Orthodoxy. And whenever any kind of harmful "ideology" suddenly turned up from outside, the school was completely powerless to do battle with it or to counteract it with anything of its own.

People usually say that the old schools of prerevolutionary Russia did not provide any knowledge at all, that everything that was told to the students by the teachers lay like a dead weight in their young minds, that it did not contribute to their intellectual development, did not inspire spiritual inquiries, and was in no way connected with life. I do not think that this should be expressed so absolutely. Even the old schools provided some amount of knowledge in a systematic sequence. If one takes into account the level of knowledge and development in the society of that time, then one must pay a considerable debt of gratitude to the old schools, as well. They did not bring up children, but they nonetheless provided knowledge. And in any case, the schools were on a higher level, as far as spiritual concerns go, than the environment from which its charges came.

Besides that, the personality of the teacher and his attitude toward his work meant a lot. A conscientious and enlightened teacher in the old school could have a considerable influence on his students, in terms of their development. Dull-witted people could do nothing even as far as simply conveying information. We spent seven years in school studying foreign languages. And we learned absolutely nothing. If somebody spoke another language at home, or if they had had governesses as a child, they managed to get something out of the lessons taught by the Frenchwoman, Mlle. Terrä, or by the incredibly dull-witted German master, Neiburg. The rest never even got a handle on declining nouns and conjugating verbs. Even now it is difficult to remember what took place during those lessons. In any case, they did not give us any of the joy of learning foreign languages, and they gave us a lot of grief: during exams, nobody could correctly translate even a short paragraph or write a dictation passage. Not wanting to get stuck in the same grade for another year or to take a make-up exam because of those subjects, students would simply drop the foreign language halfway through, or even a year or two before graduating: it was not worth it to waste time, and besides, those subjects were not required.

The same could be said of the lessons on Divine Law. We had a very handsome and incredibly lazy priest. And we never knew what he wanted. Of course, there could be no question of any kind of "religious inspiration." He listlessly told the story of the Old and New Testaments, listlessly said prayers and the texts of the catechism, and he really liked to joke around. His jokes were rude and not in the least bit clever. What could you get from a person like that, as far as religion goes? For that matter, there was never any talk of religion. The priest himself, it seems, was sure that religion was not something to be touched upon. He very often said:

"At home, I figure, you don't even cross yourselves. That's just how it is. Why bother. . . . But you should learn your prayers: the bishop will be at your exam. . . . "

Every morning at school we went to a general prayer gathering; those who were late were strictly reprimanded and their names were recorded in the conduct-book, while those who came to the prayer gathering saw it as a formality that, if you failed to observe, resulted in "punishment." Hardly anyone actually prayed. The intelligent teachers understood quite well all the discomfort involved in this kind of religious formality.

Three subjects—by a happy coincidence—roused our delight, and we devoted all our efforts to them: history, physics, and literature. Literature, by the way, was only for a short time—only in second (sixth) grade. Now, when I recall those lessons, I do not even remember exactly what delighted us so: the subjects themselves, or the way they were taught, or, finally, the teachers. . . . At least in the last year of school there was some kind of school infatuation: half the students were "in love" with S. I. Kedrov, the history teacher, and the other half were "in love" with I. P. Iuvenaliev, the physics teacher. This love was expressed by students "chasing" after them into the halls, by "encounters" somewhere outside, and finally, by contemplating them—with an adoring expression on one's face—during class.

S. I. Kedrov taught history wonderfully. He was a good public speaker, and we scribbled down entire sets of notes during his lectures. Sometimes, while portraying some historical event in vivid colors, he would say:

"This won't be on the exam, of course. You don't need to know it in this much detail . . . I'm just talking about this in passing. For yourselves, read such and such."

How we loved his "incidental" stories! After I graduated from school, when I met with him quite often, he would complain:

"It's really torture teaching history in this accursed pit! I don't dare depict for my students even a true picture of the liberation of the serfs or the reforms of the 1860s. I can't say a word about the social attitudes of that time. . . . You can go on as much as you want about appanage princes or Vladimir Monomakh. But it's strictly forbidden to talk about how Russian society lived, what kinds of battles they had with the government, what finally caused our defeats, and what victories we gained. The school principal quakes, the head of the school quakes, all you hear at meetings is: 'Sergei Ivanovich! For heaven's sake, be more concise. Sergei Ivanovich, it seems that you're leading them far off the path.' . . . Is that really teaching? I once offered to arrange something like a history seminar, where the students could learn how to do independent work on historical materials. And I'm not glad that I proposed it: the head of the school literally became hysterical. . . . Stupid people. They don't understand that on the side, these same students are being dragged over to such extreme opinions, which we could paralyze by developing their abilities to think in the least bit critically. Real dimwits from antediluvian bureaucracies!"

But during his classes we took delight in his lively explanations, which were rare in our school, his talent for eloquence, and his unflagging desire to provide the true meaning of historical events in a manageable form. And we were always so sad when the bell proclaimed that class was over. Sergei Ivanovich would immediately be surrounded, showered with questions and requests to recommend some book to read—to the dissatisfaction of our class mistress.

"Children, is this really possible!" she would say with her lips pursed. "Maybe he urgently needs to leave, and you're blocking his path. . . . How awful!"

But we really liked spending even just one extra minute with this lively and intelligent person. Yes, the personality of a teacher and his interest in his subject is a huge factor in teaching at a school. Many of us found our way to independent intellectual work—work not simply for the sake of an exam—precisely through Sergei Ivanovich. After his classes the world began to appear so immensely wide, and one's own self seemed so uncouth and ignorant. . . . And in the upper grades, when we were instructed to organize independent study groups, the students responded with such joy: after all, in those groups you could go much further in studying unclear information about the world than you could go in your school lessons with your favorite teachers.

Another person who evoked an active love for knowledge was the physics teacher, I. P. Iuvenaliev. Living with his family, he spent all his income on the acquisition of various types of equipment and instruments for our physics laboratory. At that time, school provided such miserly allocations for any undertakings "irrelevant" to the textbook that I. P. Iuvenaliev's contribution was far from superfluous. He also completely changed the method of teaching. Before he was there, the students simply memorized passages that were intended for the exam. He extensively set up a method of teaching with experiments. He was able to put into effect only one of his dreams, which was accomplished much later by all the new, progressive schools: that the experiments not simply be demonstrated to us, but that we ourselves would use the equipment and the means of analysis. There was not enough room for this in the laboratory, and there was not enough equipment, either. All he could do was designate, by turns, assistants to be "on duty" and sternly demand that they work capably with the equipment in his modest laboratory.

Physics and chemistry were the only subjects that provided some notion of natural history. Botany, biology, and chemistry were given in only tiny doses, and only from the textbook. In our times (the 1880s), the "classical system" of education, established by the Minister of Education, D. A. Tolstoi,[34] was fully in place. This system consisted not only in the study of ancient languages. Its significance was much larger, and its goal was determined by Tolstoi himself. In 1871 he introduced into the State Council[35] a bill to change the charter of gymnasiums and progymnasiums, which had been sanctioned by imperial order of the tsar during the time of the Reforms (November 19, 1864). The Minister declared all the progressive measures of the last twenty-five years to be erroneous. As is known, those progressive undertakings consisted in "bringing the schools closer to the demands of life"—an age-old dream of forward-thinking teachers. Tolstoi, though, proposed that the classical system of education and instruction be completely restored, for "the adaptation of the secondary school program to practical goals has become, if not the only cause, then at least one of the major causes of the materialism that has such a strong hold on our young people."

So we studied "without any practical goals," without experiments and science, so as "not to fall into materialism." The poor Minister did not understand that if the schools refused to allow in life and its demands, then that life would burst into the souls of the young generation by some other means. That's how it was. At no other time did "extracurricular," mostly secret education and instruction have such success as during the time that Tolstoi's reactionary system was in effect. Thousands of groups of young people covered all of Russia, and through these groups, completely without the interference of the schools and their teachers, the young people got access both to "materialism" and to the unique idealism of that time.

The old system of education was especially obvious in literary classes. One would think that nothing could be livelier than literature. It provides free range for the teacher's talent, to acquaint students with the spirit of their national literature and to study the art of other nations. But if in our old schools, natural science, which imparted "materialism," was dangerous, then literature was so many more times dangerous—even Russian literature, the internal flame of which could not be extinguished even by the Cerberus-like vigilance of censorship.[36] Well, for example, how could you give young people access to the Gogolian literary period when the seditious critic Belinskii was always declaring that it was with Gogol that the period of naturalism [Natural School] began in Russian literature. It would be better to restrict the young people to old Russian literature. . . . Therefore, we spent an infinite amount of time analyzing "The Lay of Igor's Campaign."[37] And we covered Gogol and Pushkin "briefly";[38] we never got to Turgenev, Dostoevskii, and Tolstoi.[39] Of course, there was no point in even talking about the journalist-critics: Belinskii, Pisarev, and Dobroliubov—forbidden fruit![40] You could only get all of this in some other place, on the side. . . . At the same time that everyone outside of school was absorbed in reading L. N. Tolstoi's famous novel *War and Peace*—discussing his characters, his philosophy—in school we did not even dare make a sound about it. *The Silver Prince* was still permitted—after all, it was about the time of Ivan the Terrible![41] But Lev Tolstoi, whose "underground" works were already being passed around from person to person, was not accessible to schoolgirls.

So this "brief" program, which excluded the authors and works that were having the greatest effect on society of that time, fell to the lot of the young literature teacher, Orlov. I don't know where he turned up from in Saratov. But at the beginning of the school year, in the next-to-the-last class period, an unusual-looking person came in. He was not in a dress-uniform, and the first thing that amazed us was his coiffure: long, curly hair—"like a poet," we decided—framed a very pale, nervous, and irregular face with beautiful brown eyes. He immediately enchanted us, won us over. I no longer remember whether he stuck to the course of instruction, but I clearly remember how he immediately led us into the heart of Russian literature in a completely different way. He paid a particular amount of attention to Pushkin. Along the way, in order to clarify the difficulties confronting all Russian writers of that time, he also traced out the era of Nicholas I, and Pushkin's friendship with the Decembrists—in general, he strayed quite far from the "school reader" [on the Decembrists, see chapter 6]. Orlov's lessons positively captivated us. Walking out of class and answering many of our questions on the way, he would recommend that we read books—as our class mistress later said—"which were hardly written for an Institution of the Empress Maria." Soon the literature teacher's discrepancies went quite far. He assigned us a composition on "The Poet and the Mob"—to do a close reading of Pushkin's famous poem. Orlov used no less than three class periods to draw us into the circle of ideas of a poet who was casting off the "ignorant mob," the "uninitiated people" for the sake of acquiring enough space "for inspiration, for sweet sounds and prayers" . . . Our class mistress always sat in on Orlov's classes, without budging. And during those three class sessions she made no attempt to hide her deep indignation at "this unworthy sermon within the walls of this kind of institution!" Shaking all over, with red spots covering her face, several times she made gestures as if she wanted to stop him, to defend us from the harmful ideas of the young literature teacher. And he probably forgot where he was. . . . This time he spoke about Pushkin without any rapturous, worshipful admiration. . . . He reproached him for "his scornful treatment of the suffering people" and he ascribed this to the pernicious influence of the imperial-feudal society on the poet.

When he walked out after the last of these "explanatory lessons," our poor "kinswoman" of Gusev, the gendarme colonel,[42] addressed us with what was, I must say, a really stupid speech:

"Children, children! There's been some sort of misunderstanding here. Teachers shouldn't say such things in an institution of the empress. . . . In the first place, you should know that Pushkin himself was a member of the court and that he always wrote for his ruler, and not at all for the mob. The entire story of the life of our poet, who was true to his ruler, speaks to that fact. And in the second place, girls should pay attention to the poetic aspect of verse, and not to the content at all. . . . "

Our poor Maria Vasilevna was not good at oral presentations and she immediately became confused. . . . And Elena Shiriaeva's beautiful eyes were mockingly staring at her, from the third bench. Always silent, somehow cold, she would become remarkably alive during Orlov's classes. She could not stand Gromova's speech:

"After all, many of the Decembrists were also courtiers," she spoke out sharply.

"I would ask you, Miss Shiriaeva, not to speak about criminals in class. . . . If a teacher . . . If people. . . . " And suddenly, her tears were flowing! Whether the class mistress had burst out crying because of her own helplessness or out of furious passion over our being corrupted—she was crying bitterly.

Young people have no pity. Especially when they contemplate weakness. We not only did not sympathize with poor Maria Vasilevna, but several of us even chuckled at her: what a joke, she's upset because of the Decembrists! I should also say that in second grade several of us were already in illegal organizations and Orlov's sermon fell on fertile soil. The essay on "The Poet and the Mob" interested us and even gave rise to a lively discussion in the organization that I belonged to. And Gromova's worrying and useless diatribes only added fuel to the fire. We started working excitedly on our topic; we argued, we read each other passages from what we had written, and finally, we handed in our notebooks to Orlov. . . . I wrote seventy whole pages, Shiriaeva and M[uromskaia] also handed in full notebooks. After that we had two or three more literature classes. Then— a finale which seems to have been unheard of in the history of the school. The director of the school, extraordinarily pale and agitated, came to Orlov's class. He walked straight up to the lectern and said something to Orlov. Orlov also turned pale, jumped up quickly, and turning to us, said:

"Goodbye!"

Then they both walked out. The class period was not yet over, and our class mistress suggested that we "work on something independently." It was only a few days later that we found out what had happened: Orlov had been arrested right there in the school. And several days later we found out that all the notebooks with our compositions on "The Poet and the Mob" had been sent to the governor of Saratov, who was the trustee of our school. The story spread . . . This was in the spring of 1884, before exams. I had a habit of skipping a lot of classes—after all, this was half a year before the death of my mother.

When the incident of the tendentious compositions on "The Poet and the Mob" was discussed, the school board resolved: to severely reprimand the students who had incorrectly worked on this topic and to let them stay in the school. And secondly: to expel the students who had missed a large number of classes without bringing notes from their parents explaining the reason for their absences, but granting them the right to take exams without attending lectures. I turned out to be the only one in that situation of not attending school. My sister Mania cried bitterly when she found out about that decision. But for that matter, I was almost glad: it was quite unbearable to keep up with my responsibilities at home, take care of my mother, and "pass for" a student at school.

Source: E. K. Kuskova, "Davno minuvshee," *Novyi zhurnal* ["The Distant Past," *New Journal*], vol. XLIII (1955): 98–106, 111–12; vol. XLV (1956): 149–66. Excerpted.

Translated by Rebecca Epstein Matveyev

ADMISSION TO UNIVERSITIES

As noted in the introduction to this chapter, the imperial government long resisted the demand that women be admitted to Russian universities. Hence women were twice permitted to audit university lectures, between 1859–1863 and between 1905–1908, before being barred again by the government. In 1911 graduates of Higher Women's Courses were allowed to take the state examinations at universities and thereby qualify for a university degree. But women were first admitted as regular university students, to the medical faculty at Tomsk University, only in 1913. Thereafter, the government granted women permission to enroll as students in selected faculties at other universities, a process that accelerated when the outbreak of World War I increased the need for trained medical personnel.

STATUTE ON THE ACCEPTANCE OF PERSONS OF THE FEMALE SEX INTO PARTICULAR DEPARTMENTS OF CERTAIN RUSSIAN IMPERIAL UNIVERSITIES, APPROVED 17 AUGUST 1915.

On the seventeenth day of August, 1915, His Majesty the Emperor, as recommended by the Council of Ministers, has deigned to command:

I. To allow the acceptance into the medical and the physics and mathematics departments[43] of the Imperial University of Kazan', into the medical department of the Nikolaev Imperial University in Saratov, and into the law department of the Imperial University of Tomsk, to fill vacancies left open after the acceptance of regular students, within quantitative limits established by the Minister of Education, of persons of the female sex who have the documentation specified in Paragraph 1 of Article 2 of the Rules for the testing of persons of the female sex on their knowledge of the course of study in institutions of higher learning and on the procedure for their acquisition of academic degrees and the title of Secondary School Teacher.

III. To grant the Minister of Education the right to allow, upon recommendation by university councils, the acceptance of persons of the female sex to particular departments of all Russian imperial universities on the grounds specified above.

Source: Sobranie uzakonenii i rasporiazhenii pravitel'stva, izdavaemoe pri Pravitel'stvuiushchem Senate [Collection of Government Statutes and Directives, Published by the Governing Senate], 1915 (26 November), no. 334, pt. 1, pp. 3259–60. Excerpted.

Translated by Carol Apollonio Flath.

MEDICAL SCHOOLING AND PRACTICE

As women in the Russian empire were both admitted to formal educational institutions and gained access to new occupations, the boundary between "women's work" and the types of work performed by men sometimes blurred. One response, as we have seen, was to base school curricula on the domestic and social roles that women were expected to play and that were considered suitable for women. As women began to be employed increasingly in new occupations outside the home, the imperial government—as well as the Orthodox Church—attempted to direct them, through the educational system, into areas deemed consistent with their nurturing qualities and "natural" propensities. The principal occupations so regarded were teaching and medical practice. A pattern can be observed in both areas: women were first permitted to work in what were considered the least skilled and lowest status positions and often they could work only with female students or patients. Over time, however, changing circumstances and their own efforts enabled women to gain access to higher levels of training and more prestigious positions.

The following documents illustrate this process with respect to medical practice. The first is the statute of the Belostok Obstetrical Institute, founded in 1817, following the establishment of similar institutes in St. Petersburg in 1785 and Moscow in 1801. These were the successors of midwifery courses for women first introduced in the 1750s. The second document is the statute of the Medical Practitioners' School for Women established in Moscow in 1879; such schools were intended in part to enable women to practice medicine in a limited way—but without allowing them to earn a university-level degree. The third document is the statute of the St. Petersburg Women's Medical Institute, which was founded in 1895 and which provided university-level medical training. As noted above, women finally were admitted to regular university medical departments beginning in 1913.

A. Belostok Obstetrical Institute

STATUTE OF THE IMPERIAL BELOSTOK OBSTETRICAL INSTITUTE, APPROVED 30 JUNE 1811.

INTRODUCTION

1. The Belostok Obstetrical Institute is an educational institution charged with training a certain number of lay midwives every year, primarily for the Belostok and Grodno Provinces.

4. The direct internal supervision of this educational institution is entrusted to a Senior Teacher, who is also its Director. All the personnel there are subordinate to him.

5. A Junior Teacher and two midwives are delegated to assist the Director. In addition, the service staff should include a laundress, a cook, and a workman.

Chapter I: *General Academics*

7. The course of study should be designed in such a way as to ensure that before students are released for practical study in the maternity clinic they will have been given Theoretical instruction in everything that a midwife has to know; for this reason it is divided into two sections or grades: Theoretical and Practical.

9. The Theoretical and Practical courses of study last one year each.

[Chapter II. *Theoretical Study*]

11. The subjects taught are the following:

1) The structure, connections, function and use of the soft and hard reproductive organs not so much in Anatomical detail as in their relevance to obstetrics. This course includes an elaboration of the differences between a woman who has reached puberty and one who has not; between a virgin and a married woman, between one who has given birth and one who has not;

2) Pregnancy, its variations and duration, the changes that take place during this time in the body as a whole, as well as in the soft reproductive organs, the abdomen and breasts; pregnancy-induced fits, and the indications and determination of the stage or periods of pregnancy;

3) The time of implantation of the embryo in the uterus, its gradual development, and [its] position;

4) The fetal membrane and other parts relating to it, such as the placenta, umbilical cord, and amniotic fluid;

5) Childbirth, its stages and their indications, explanation of the labor contractions and their differentiation from so-called false contractions; other phenomena or changes taking place during this time, both in the body as a whole and in the reproductive organs in particular; the determination on their basis of the stages of labor, or its periods; the various possible positions of the baby as it passes out of the uterus through the pelvis, such as head, face, feet, knees, or buttocks down, and the recognition of these positions; birth itself and the delivery of the placenta; the postpartum cleansing;

6) Obstetrical examinations, both as a whole, i.e., the body as a whole, and the reproductive organs in particular in the abdomen and the breasts, both external and internal;

7) The care of a pregnant woman: recommendations for food and drink, the surrounding air, behavior, physical activity, and so on;

8) Assisting at natural childbirth;

9) The proper care of the newly confined mother and newborn infant;

10) Instruction on abnormal childbirth requiring artificial assistance, and elaboration of the various causes that can give rise to it;

11) Demonstration of cases and methods when and how a midwife can assist at abnormal childbirth. These include primarily the proper positioning of the

woman in labor, the use of enemas and lubricants, artificial breaking of the waters, separation and removal of the placenta, methods for changing the baby's position, and so on;

12) Instruction on apparent infant death and ways of reviving the baby;

13) Determination of the ability or inability of the mother to nurse her baby, the selection and qualities of a good wet nurse.

15) Instruction on abnormal childbirth should not cover those methods of assistance that involve advanced obstetrical science or skills, such as the use of medicines and instruments; it should only enable them to identify those cases where they should seek the advice and assistance of a doctor or obstetrician.

Chapter III. *Practical Training*

16. Upon completion of the theoretical course of study, and when testing ensures that first-year students have acquired sufficient knowledge and skill in turning infants using mannequins and performing other skilled manual operations, they are promoted into the second, practical course; i.e., they begin practical training in the Clinic.

17. The clinical exercises consist of:

1) Practice in obstetrical examinations, developing the ability to confirm pregnancy, to estimate the stage or period of pregnancy, etc.; for this purpose, twice a week, in the presence of a senior or junior teacher, they practice examining pregnant women who are being treated in the Institute;

2) Proper ways of behaving around pregnant women; preventing and overcoming obstacles, either those that might complicate childbirth itself or those that might cause trouble or discomfort afterward for the mother or the baby—or both of them together;

3) Assistance during childbirth itself, for example: the preparation of a suitable bed for the mother, instruction on when and how to work with the labor contractions and how to ease the process of labor and delivery for the mother; prevention of injury to the external reproductive organs, especially the perineum; handling the infant and helping it emerge from the mother; binding and severing the umbilical cord and assisting in the expulsion of the placenta;

4) Care for women after birth, for example: bathing them and maintaining hygiene, the administration of enemas, binding of the abdomen, preparation and application of poultices, etc.;

5) Handling of newborn infants, for example, bathing, diapering, etc.

19. All these exercises must be performed by the students under the direct supervision of teachers and a skilled midwife.

[3] *The Midwife*

55. The particular duties of the midwife include the direct supervision of: housekeeping; the preparation and distribution of food and the laundering, care,

and changing of linens, the behavior of students, cleanliness in the rooms, the bathing of new mothers and the bathing and diapering of infants, etc.

Source: 1PSZ, xxxi. (1810–1811), no. 24,695: 760–67. Excerpted.

Translated by Carol Apollonio Flath.

B. Moscow Medical Practitioners' School for Women

STATUTE OF THE MEDICAL PRACTITIONERS' SCHOOL FOR WOMEN
AT THE MOSCOW MARIINSKAIA HOSPITAL FOR THE POOR,
APPROVED 2 MAY 1879.

REGULATION

The Mission of the School, Its Staffing, and Administration

1. The mission of the Medical Practitioners' School for Women at the Moscow Mariinskaia Hospital for the Poor is to train women to perform the duties of medical practitioners.

3. The instructors in the school are the doctors and pharmacist of the Mariinskaia Hospital; they are selected by the Chief Doctor.

Conditions and Rules for Accepting Students

7. Women (unmarried girls, widows, and married women) of all estates, eighteen to thirty years of age, are eligible for acceptance as students.

8. Students are selected annually at the beginning of August; a woman wishing to be considered for acceptance applies to the Chief Doctor, providing the following documents: (a) birth certificate; (b) certificate of estate; and (c) diploma from an educational institution, if relevant. Both married and unmarried women who are minors (under twenty-one years of age) are also required to provide evidence that their husbands, if they are married, or guardians or parents, if they are not, do not object to their matriculation.

Course of Study, Subjects Taught, and Examinations

11. The academic course of study lasts for two years.

12. The following courses are taught:

1) Human Illness and Health (basic information about anatomy, physiology, hygiene, pathology, therapy and first aid).

2) Hospital practice (rules for caring for patients, minor surgery and bandaging).

3) Basic pharmaceutical knowledge and practice (including an introduction to the natural sciences). All these subjects are taught according to programs

compiled by instructors and approved by the Chief Doctor with the consent of the Medical Inspector.

13. Every day during their time outside of the classroom, students work in the wards, caring for patients under the supervision of doctors; during the second year they alternate service as medical practitioners in the hospital and the outpatient clinic and as apprentice pharmacists in the pharmacy.

[Duties, Rights, and Benefits of Students]

18. After completing the course and becoming certified, graduates have the right to begin working in medical facilities and to enjoy the rights and benefits granted female medical practitioners according to the existing regulations of those facilities.

Source: 2PSZ, liv., pt. 1 (1879–1880), no. 59,577: 335–36. Excerpted.

Translated by Carol Apollonio Flath.

C. St. Petersburg Women's Medical Institute

STATUTE OF THE ST. PETERSBURG WOMEN'S MEDICAL INSTITUTE, APPROVED 1 JUNE 1895.

REGULATION

1. The mission of the St. Petersburg Women's Medical Institute is to provide persons of the female sex with a medical education, with a primary focus on treating women's and children's illnesses and on midwifery.

14. Direct supervision of the students and management of the Institute's residential facility is the responsibility of the Inspectress, who is selected by the Director and approved for her position by the Minister of Education, upon the recommendation of the Superintendent of the school district. The Inspectress's staff includes Assistants, selected by her and approved for their positions by the Superintendent of the school district upon the recommendation of the Director of the Institute.

18. The Institute accepts as students Christian persons[44] of the female sex between the ages of twenty and thirty-five. In exceptional cases the Institute may accept, with the permission of the Administrator of the school district, persons over thirty-five years of age.

19. Those wishing to study at the Institute apply to the Director, providing: (a) certificates of age, estate, and religious creed; (b) a diploma from the educational institutions specified in Article 20; (c) a document from the police attesting to their good character; written permission from their parents or, if their parents are deceased and the student is under twenty-one years of age, guardians;

and (d) other documents, which the administration of the Institute may consider necessary.

20. Persons who have graduated from a Gymnasium or equivalent educational institution must take a test in Latin that follows the standards established for acceptance into Universities. Tests are given in the Boys' Gymnasiums located closest to the residence of the applicant; if a town has several Gymnasiums, the test is given in the one designated by the Superintendent of the school district. Graduates of the Higher Women's Courses in St. Petersburg who have passed the standard test in Latin and graduates of Girls' Gymnasiums who are entitled to take such a test are accepted into the Institute without testing.

22. The following courses are taught in the Institute: (a) anatomy; (b) normal histology and embryology; (c) physiology; (d) general pathology; (e) specific pathology, therapy, practical diagnostics, and medical chemistry; (f) organic and inorganic chemistry; (g) physics; (h) mineralogy, botany, and zoology (with comparative anatomy); (i) pharmacognosy and pharmacy; (j) pharmacology, including principles of prescription writing, toxicology, and instruction on mineral waters and water cures; (k) anatomical pathology, with histological pathology; (l) obstetrics (with clinical practice); (m) gynecological diseases (with clinical practice), pediatric diseases (with clinical practice); (n) hygiene; (o) surgery (including bandaging); (p) operational obstetrics (in obstetrical and gynecological clinics); (q) syphilology and dermatology (with clinical practice); (r) ophthalmology (with clinical practice); and (s) nervous and psychological diseases (with clinical practice).

24. The Institute offers a five-year course of study, divided into ten semesters. Four of the five years are devoted to medical training in the Institute; during the fifth year students perform clinical practice under the supervision of experienced doctors or work in special women's and children's hospitals or clinics, as well as in maternity clinics.

27. Those who successfully complete the Institute's course of study receive a diploma granting them the title of "female doctor," which gives them: (a) the right to practice without restriction anywhere, subject to the regulations concerning independent doctors; the name of the person granted the diploma, in accordance with Article 95 of the Medical Code, is entered into the list of doctors entitled to practice medicine in the Empire; (b) the right to prescribe strong medicines from pharmacies; (c) the right to serve as doctors specializing in women's and children's diseases, without the rights of civil servants, in Women's Institutes, Gymnasiums, pensions, schools, and other women's educational and charitable institutions, as well as in women's and children's hospitals and maternity clinics, and also in communities of Sisters of Mercy and medical establishments associated with police departments anywhere; (d) the right to be entrusted by Provincial Medical Boards with the management of zemstvo medical districts and the rural hospitals and casualty wards located in these districts, as well as certain rural treatment facilities, and also the management of special urban women's and children's hospitals and treatment facilities and women's and children's departments of gen-

eral hospitals and treatment facilities, and duty in all departments of these hospitals and facilities; and (e) the right to be invited to serve as assistants to the Medical Examiner during medical forensic investigations involving women and children.

28. Female doctors are not permitted to manage urban general hospitals or other such treatment facilities and men's departments of those hospitals and medical facilities, or to perform the duties of doctors in qualifying examinations for military service or to conduct independent medical forensic analysis upon demand by judicial institutions.

Source: 3PSZ xv. (1895), no. 11,760: 364–67. Excerpted.

Translated by Carol Apollonio Flath.

PROSTITUTION AS A PROFESSION: SPEECH OF ALEKSANDRA DEMENTEVA

Aleksandra Dementeva was a schoolteacher and member of the philanthropic Society for the Care of Young Girls in St. Petersburg. Her speech to the 1910 Congress on the Struggle against the Trade in Women is noteworthy because she was the only participant to solicit responses from prostitutes directly. Although prostitution in fact presented women from the working class and peasantry with income and freedom otherwise hard to achieve in the world of urban Russian female labor, Dementeva could only conceive of prostitution as sheer misery. Nonetheless, she revealed aspects of the trade that most observers either ignored or overlooked without slighting the high incidence of venereal disease among prostitutes and the abuses they suffered in the state regulation system. (On prostitution, see also chapters 3 and 6.)

In the fall of 1903 I began to visit Kalinkin Hospital,[45] where once and sometimes twice a week in the evening I read to and conversed with sick prostitutes. My work in the Society for the Care of Young Girls in St. Petersburg prompted these visits. It is known that this Society organizes dormitories for young women and Sunday meetings; the residents and female visitors frequently disappear over the horizon, and their further fate remains unknown to the Society. Of course, the majority of cases are explained by the fact that they got married, or left Petersburg, or moved to another region of the city, but all the same, one's heart is occasionally seized by the notion that they left to lead a wanton life. Naturally, in such an event they will not go where they are known by honest working women, but in my opinion, the Society for the Care of Young Girls should also extend aid to these young women.

The only place where it is possible to approach so-called "fallen women" freely turns out to be Kalinkin Hospital, where the medical-police committee[46] sends sick prostitutes who have been picked up on the street or were at their obligatory examinations.

I visited this hospital for five years (excluding the summers) and, with a sense of astonishment, I must point out that in all that time I met only two girls who had attended Sunday meetings, and not one from the dormitories.

During these visits I became closely acquainted with the hitherto unknown to me world of "the fallen," and I learned in my soul the chilling details of their lives. The best means for drawing close were readings, after which I would converse with separate individuals. At first they avoided me, and several even regarded me defiantly and hostilely, asking why I come to a hospital that everyone is so afraid of and runs past. But little by little they not only got used to me but they [also] began to treat me with trust; they would tell me the stories of their fall and subsequent misadventures.

I was more than once witness to the terrible desperation that came from consciousness of the total impossibility of changing their painful situation and returning to the path of honest labor. Time does not permit me to retell everything I heard, but I cannot fail to tell the sad story of one of them who died from consumption in September 1909, in the twenty-fourth year of her life. Vera A., the daughter of a corporal in the gendarmes, having received a primary education and some training in a simple, patriarchal family, worked at one of the St. Petersburg train stations. When she was fourteen, a dressmaker acquaintance deceived her parents and secretly sold her to a monk, bringing her to him several times and receiving money, part of which she also gave to the girl. Having noticed that the girl had money, her older brother and sister told their father; forcing her to admit everything, he brutally beat her and threatened to kill her for the shame she had brought down on his head. During the night, the beaten, embittered girl ran away from home to the woman responsible for her fall. She, fearing the father's wrath, hid the girl with her "aunt," who was none other than the brothel keeper of a den. The latter persuaded the girl to apply for a license (*blank*) in order to escape the authority of her father.[47] From that time on, she broke with her family and was given up as lost. She turned into the most desperate prostitute, very quickly contracting both syphilis and consumption. Not long before her death she made peace with her family, but, consumed by horrible illness, she was not able to become an honest worker, and death appeared to be her best escape.[48]

In Kalinkin Hospital, I first became aware of the horror surrounding these young women, almost children, who are forced to seek wages in the capital. Only she who is nearly a complete physical freak is left alone. Danger awaits her everywhere and anywhere; everyone tries to push her down the road of vice. Neither the intelligentsia, nor her brother-worker, nor middlemen in the trade in women, leave her in peace. It is necessary to hear from them themselves the sad details of their misadventures for it to become clear how it is almost impossible for a girl, sometimes almost a child, who is deprived of an education and the support of a family, to withstand temptation in this maelstrom of life in the capital. Don't judge her but, rather, the society that indifferently permits this. And, really, once a girl falls and goes along the evil path, there is no going back, especially because they almost all without exception very quickly contract a terrible disease and become alcoholics. It is also impossible to judge them for this because, in addition to the fact that they must drink at their "guests'" demand, they, particularly at the start of their wanton lives, not yet having lost their feminine modesty and in order to forget, drown their shame in wine. I shall never forget how an eighteen-year-old girl during one of the conversations sadly said, "Ah, only here with you is it possible to speak like a human being, but when I'm free I'm never sober." Involuntarily, I remarked to her, "Nastia, aren't you ashamed to drink at your age." To this she answered reproachfully, "Well, would you approach our life sober?" And I was ashamed of my remark. Aware of how gloomy their life is in the hospital, with its compulsory character, I tried to brighten up somehow the time of their treatment. Thanks to the sympathetic attitude of the hospital administration, I succeeded in organizing several literary-musical evenings, which lifted the spirits of the patients. Attending a May 8, 1909 meeting at which the organizational plan of the First All-Russian Congress for the Struggle against the Trade in Women and Its Causes was discussed, and having heard paragraph two, where it says who can be participants at the congress, I could not forget that there would be no representative from among those for whose sake it was convening. Though I myself was aware of how difficult this would be to implement, it nonetheless seemed to me that it would be extremely valuable for the congress to find out directly from them themselves about their needs and sufferings, because there are few, even among those who sympathize with them, who are closely acquainted with this world of outcast women. Then I decided to gather their opinion directly on this issue and convey it to the congress.

In the beginning of March [1910] I gathered the patients from the third ward (about two hundred people) in the big auditorium of the Suvorov Military School,[49] in the building of the so-called "committee" of the main building of Kalinkin Hospital, and I acquainted my listeners with the goals of this congress. I suggested that they speak out on the issues that I would propose, and I promised to tell the congress everything they told me, and, at its close, acquaint them with its work.

There were six such meetings in all. I would propose issues, and those who wished to speak would raise their hands and speak out in turn. Incidentally, I must point out that they all spoke very sensibly and they observed surprising order, which would have been difficult to expect from such an undisciplined group. This is really a very painful issue, and they all regarded it so seriously that I had no trouble leading our conversation and maintaining order.

Above all I asked them to relate the conditions of their life. It turned out that from all 128 people present at this meeting, only two lived in their own apartments, several lived in brothels, and the overwhelming majority lived with "landladies." They paid such a landlady from 75 to 100 rubles and more for bed, board, and laundry. The landlady supplies them with all the necessities (clothing, etc.) for a debt, which they pay off gradually. The consequence of this is eternal indebtedness, because the prices for everything are excessively high, and, as a result, after two or three years of such living at the "landlady's," they leave with nothing, because she holds her residents' things for security on the debt.

To the question of why they prefer to live at a "landlady's," rather than independently, they gave the following reasons:

1. Prostitutes are rarely accepted at free apartments, and the police bother them so much that life is made unendurable.

2. The majority began the life of a prostitute when they were already living at the "landlady's," who also serves as a procuress who entices a girl onto the path of vice, and in such a way makes her into a hopeless debtor from which there is no escape.

3. Several openly said that they are so weak and characterless that they would not settle independently and that they get something from their landlady, although they also understand that everything is much more expensive.

To the question of why there are so few residents of state-licensed brothels in the hospital, they answered that both the brothel keepers and their private doctors do not like to send [brothel prostitutes] to the hospital and that they compel them to be treated at home. When asked about the conditions in these homes, the following incident occurred. One girl, not particularly young, started to praise the living conditions in a so-called "first-class house" so effusively that, according to her, it sounded like paradise on earth: they are free to go when and where they please; they have the right to refuse a "guest"; most important, they have all accumulated a huge amount of money on the books. She, for example, saved 600 rubles in six months, and several already had 1,000 rubles and more. But the others very passionately protested, saying that there is no such place, and that, on the contrary, life in a "house" is worse than in prison and that, aside from the necessities, they are thrown out of there with nothing because everything written in the books goes for the personal living expenses of the residents. At that one of the girls told the very sad tale of her life in one such house in the city of Narva. I understood quite well that the first girl was none other than a recruiter of less experienced girls for state-licensed brothels. This is a fairly common phenomenon in the hospital: these agents get in as patients or relatives on visiting days, and above all they lie in wait for those who are discharged from the hospital, taking with them those unfortunates who often do not know where they will lay their head.

On the question of their attitude toward the medical-police examination, everyone unanimously characterized it as very burdensome, especially before they are accustomed to it: it is carried out so rudely and heedlessly of feminine modesty that it prompts many of them to come to the examination drunk. While discussing this issue many spoke out very heatedly about the injustice of examining women only, justifiably saying that they all contracted their infections from men. One of the girls insisted with great vehemence that she herself could point out to someone a hundred syphilitic men whom no one had required to seek treatment.

On the question of what compelled them to take the path of vice and depravity, many pointed out that they were drawn into it by pimps who took advantage
of their dire straits and sometimes also their moral situation. Several, due to their
inexperience and youth, did not even comprehend at first what they were getting
into, fancying that they had been offered honest labor. Many said frankly that
they did it consciously, attracted by the idea of having the chance to live without
working and in luxury.

On the question of whether they had found satisfaction in this relatively inse-
cure, idle life, and whether they were satisfied with their fate, in one voice they
passionately insisted that their life is disgusting, and they vied with each other to
relate the horrible details of their life. I cannot find one positive word and expression to convey in all I heard. One seventeen-year-old girl, Olga L., described
how one evening, when she was drunk, they grabbed her and brought her to the
police station, where an inspector made her vile propositions. When she angrily
refused him, he beat her, tore her clothes, and pushed her, humiliated and dressed
only in her slip, into the men's wing. There they took pity on her and left her in
peace. In the morning they released her with a black eye, a split lip, and in her
tattered clothes. But she did not dare lodge a complaint, because the prostitute is
always considered guilty.

Another showed me dark spots on her breasts—the remains of burns from a
guest who extinguished cigarettes on her body.

It is impossible to convey all the humiliations, indignities, and insults that prostitutes endure from everyone with whom they have some kind of relations. Everyone tries to humiliate, to insult these unfortunate women, aware that their deeds
will go unpunished because no one stands up for them.

Then I asked, "Who, not wishing to remain in such terrible circumstances,
tried to get released from the license, but then returned again to her former way
of life?"

Several people raised their hands and wanted to say why they were recidivists.
All of their stories, with only small differences, were very similar to one another.
It turns out that it seems easy to get rid of a license; one has only to request this
from the committee. But it is almost impossible to return to a working life—the
rules interfere with this. In the first place, they write "lives by her own means" on
a passport,[50] which really interferes when a girl seeks a job. In the second place, for
the first two or three months after a license has been returned, agents pursue a former prostitute, forcing her, sometimes with the aid of doormen, to undergo a medical-police examination from time to time. Of course, under such conditions it is
difficult to find a place or a job. Because in the majority of cases, she has nothing
when she leaves the landlady, in order to find food and shelter she has no alternative but to return to her former life. To be released from the license and engage in
her trade secretly is also not easy, because then she must hook up with a so-called
tomcat-pimp, who, it is true, protects a woman from the persecution of medical-
police committee agents and exams, but who himself generally terrorizes and
fleeces the unfortunate so much that it is not clear which of the two evils is worse.

In the majority of cases, the complete lack of work and the terrible scourge of an infectious disease that almost all prostitutes contract enslave the unfortunate woman forever, depriving her of the possibility to break loose from these conditions, [making it seem] as though they were not repulsive to her—in spite of the most sincere desire to construct her life in another fashion.

In conclusion I proposed to them that they point out what they themselves would propose to ease their lot. On the basis of the answers, my interlocutors were divided into two categories: those who proposed measures to ease the conditions of a prostitute's life, and those who came up with the means providing an opportunity to leave such a life.

The first asked whether it was possible to restrain the police, who persecute them completely arbitrarily.

Individuals in the second category, those who are requesting help in leaving the dissolute life, yet again repeated their complaints about agents who persecute them even after they have ceased to engage in prostitution.

Several expressed a wish to construct apartments or houses of industriousness, where those who wished could leave their vile trade and find shelter for a while. Resting somewhat, getting a little medical attention, getting somewhat used to work, they would leave there physically and morally reformed. Of course, in these houses the syphilitics must be separated from the healthy.

I heard many other depressing tales and unbearable dramas, but it would take too much time to relate them. I think that what was said sufficiently depicts all the horror of the prostitute's position. Society does not have the right to permit such enslavement of a woman, even if she practices the infamous trade. I will not delude myself that prostitution will disappear from the face of the earth, at least in the near future, but I find it unjust that all the weight of this evil falls exclusively on the woman. For this not to be so, it is necessary above all to abolish regulation. Women will always be found who, for one or another reason, will sell themselves, but it is their personal matter from which no one else has the right to derive profit.

Right now, thanks to regulation, this vile and burdensome trade is considered state business. The government retains special agents for the apprehension of prostitutes, it invites doctors to supervise them, and not only does it tolerate but it [also] encourages houses of depravity. All this is done to protect the health of men. But aside from the fact that many doctors have proven that protection of the kind that now exists is fairly problematic, who has the right to subject a woman to such shameful humiliation for the sake of protecting men who wish to indulge in debauchery?

Regulation pins a shameful label on a woman for her entire life. It makes it almost impossible to return to an honest life, and it leaves her in slavish dependency to her landlady or pimp.

The number of prostitutes will certainly fall considerably when regulation is abolished because, in the first place, it is directly advantageous to all those involved with this business for there to be more prostitutes and for the supply to be constantly replenished by fresh, young bodies. In the second, there will be more of an opportunity for those who feel the burden of their situation to break away from the whirlpool, for in the majority of cases they have not fallen because of their own guilt. Our society devotes too little care to providing women with sufficient preparation for a working life and protecting the hard-earned wages of young girls from the temptations of life in the capital. It is also too lenient toward those who push them onto the path of depravity, branding the deeply unfortunate, humiliated, and insulted woman with shame.

Source: Aleksandra N. Dement'eva, "Otritsatel'nyia storony vrachebno-politseiskago nadzora po pokazaniiam prostitutok," *Trudy pervago vserossiiskago s"ezda po bor'be s torgom zhenshchinami i ego prichinami proiskhodivshchago v S.-Peterburge s 21 do 25 aprelia 1910 goda* ["The Negative Aspects of Medical-Police Surveillance, According to the Testimony of Prostitutes," in *Works of the First All-Russian Congress on the Struggle against the Trade in Women and Its Causes, Which Took Place in St. Petersburg 21–25 April 1910*] (St. Petersburg, 1911–1912), vol. 2. Excerpted from pp. 504–11.

Translated and partially annotated by Laurie Bernstein.

PEASANT WOMEN'S WORK

In all regions of Russia there were seasonal patterns to work, depending on the climatic conditions and types of crops. During the winter months (obviously, a longer period in the north), women spun and wove, sewed and embroidered, making items for personal use (such as the dowry items described by Efimenko in chapter 2) or for sale. They also sometimes participated in woodworking. These activities provided opportunities for informal teaching, as well as for social gatherings, usually gender-segregated (e.g., the "spinning bees" referred to in chapter 5 under "Peasant Rituals"). Since peasants generally were illiterate, or at best had limited education, the information about their activities comes primarily from such literate observers as ethnographers, teachers, and government officials, whose remarks were regularly published in general, as well as specialized, journals.

The local women, in addition to taking care of the household management, slow-burn the gardens and fields, mow the grain and bind it into sheaves, and harvest flax and hemp during the summer. During the fall and winter they spin linen, hemp, and sheep's wool and weave various cloths from the yarn for their domestic needs, and, in addition, they often thresh grain together with the men. Occasionally women from prosperous peasant households invite the girls and women to their homes in the evening for so-called *popriadukhi*:[51] the guests bring their *dontsy*[52] and combs and spin a large quantity of wool all at once. These "spinning bees" (*pomochi*) are held primarily on Friday evenings, when the peasants avoid doing any heavy work at home and do not spin hemp or flax, believing it to be sinful. As a reward, the hosts serve them a hearty meal. The linen cloth is bleached during the spring and summer, and the coarse cloth is fulled during the fall and winter at home or in water mills that have fulleries. Some of the women are able to dye the woolen articles that they make for domestic use, and to weave waistbands.

Source: Member-Assistant [of the Society] Mashkin, "Byt krest'ian Kurskoi gubernii, Oboianskago uezda," *Etnograficheskii sbornik, izdavaemyi Imperatorskim russkim geograficheskim obshchestvom* ["Daily Life of the Peasants of Oboianskii District, Kursk Province," in *Ethnographic Collection, Published by the Imperial Russian Geographic Society*] (St. Petersburg, 1862), vol. V, pp. 100–101.

Translated by Carol Apollonio Flath.

PROPERTY MANAGEMENT

A principal occupation of Russian noblewomen was the administration of their properties, both those they owned themselves and those that belonged to their husbands. The following two selections reveal key aspects of property management (related documents also appear in chapters 2, 5, and 6). Many Russian women acquired and bequeathed significant holdings through inheritance, even though imperial inheritance law reflected the interests of the state and the patriarchal family, particularly the noble family. Inheritance law divided property into two types: movable and immovable. Immovable property, generally the more valuable category and the more heavily regulated, consisted chiefly of land, including that inhabited by serfs. Prior to the abolition of serfdom in 1861, Russians thought about wealth more in terms of the number of serfs owned than the quantity of land. Throughout the imperial period, apart from a brief interlude between 1714 and 1731, imperial law prescribed a system of partible inheritance for both immovable and movable property that favored males but granted widows and female relatives some rights. After 1731 the rights of women expanded, most importantly to include receipt of their share of an inheritance in outright ownership. Restrictions on the testamentary disposition of patrimonial property, that is, immovable property that already had passed by inheritance within a kin-group, meant that widows and female heirs generally received some immovable property, as well as movable property, in inheritance. By the middle to latter part of the eighteenth century, Russian women—initially noblewomen, but then also women of other social groups—had acquired the right to manage and dispose freely of this property, as well as of property acquired by other means, even if they were married. (Peasant inheritance practices were governed by different principles, which are described by Efimenko in chapter 2.)

A. Correspondence of Tsaritsas Ekaterina and Praskovia

Tsaritsa Praskovia's correspondence with Tsaritsa Ekaterina and Prince Aleksandr Menshikov[53] centers on the property left by Tsarevna Natalia Alekseevna (Peter I's favorite sister) at her death in 1716. Of this property, the tsar had granted Dowager Tsaritsa Praskovia Fedorovna (1664–1723) an island near St. Petersburg. The grant was announced in a letter from Ekaterina Alekseevna to Praskovia Fedorovna, and she also negotiated the settlement between Menshikov, who had already occupied the property, and the dowager tsaritsa. In the end, Menshikov was allowed to keep the island, while Praskovia Fedorovna received other property instead. Although the dowager tsaritsa did not triumph in this instance, she was a powerful member of the royal family and Peter's court. She maintained estates in several provinces; her holdings consisted of no fewer than 2,477 households of craftsmen and peasants.

Your Majesty, my dear sister-in-law, Tsaritsa Praskovia Fedorovna![54] May you and your gentle Majesties the Tsarevnas thrive for many years.

I report to you, my Sovereign, that His Tsarist Highness is, glory be to God, in good health, and we hope that we will be on our way from here soon, since the landing at Shona has been put off because it is late. I beg you, my Sovereign, don't refrain from writing to me, which I really desire.

With this, I inform you that Krestovskii Island which used to belong to Sovereign Tsarevna Natalia Alekseevna,[55] of blessed memory, His Tsarist Highness deigns to give to you, and you will deign to possess it. From now on may your health be committed to God's protection. I remain

Ekaterina[56]

From Copenhagen on 10 October 1716.

My Little Father, His Most Serene Highness Prince Aleksandr Danilovich! May you and Her Highness Princess Daria Mikhailovna and your dearest children and your newborn daughter and your sister-in-law Varvara Mikhailovna thrive for many years.

If you like, my light, by your leave, command that we be informed of the health of you all. Hey, hey, hey! I wish with all of my good heart to hear about your health. I report, your Highness, Prince Aleksandr Danilovich, that his Royal Highness and the Sovereign Bride[57] have granted me Krestovskii Island [which formerly belonged to] Sovereign Tsarevna Natalia Alekseevna, of blessed memory, and I command you to give us that island by the order of Their Royal Highnesses. With this, I remain

Ts[aritsa] Praskovia

From the town of Nikolskii, 19 November 1716.

Source: No. 9: 1716 oktiabria 10. "Pis'mo Gosudaryni Ekateriny Alekseevny k Tsaritse Praskov'e Fedorovne, o pozhalovanii eiu Krestovskago ostrova" [10 October

1716, "Letter of Her Majesty Ekaterina Alekseevna to Tsaritsa Praskovia Fedor-ovna on the bequest to her of Krestovskii Island"]; and no. 10: 1716 noiabria 19. "Pis'mo Tsaritsy Praskov'i Fedorovny k kniaziu Menshikovu, s pros'boiu chtoby on prikazal otdat' pozhalovannyi ei Krestovskii ostrov" [19 November 1716, "Letter of Tsaritsa Praskovia Fedorovna to Prince Menshikov, with a request that he order that Krestovskii Island, which has been bequeathed to her, be given up"], *Pis'ma russkikh gosudarei i drugikh osob tsarskago semeistva* [*Letters of Russian Sovereigns and Members of the Royal Family*] (Moscow, 1861). Excerpted from pp. 7–9.

Translated by Robin Bisha.

B. Request of Baroness Stroganova

The Stroganov family first became associated with the Perm region, a district in the Ural Mountains, in the sixteenth century, establishing business enterprises in the met-allurgical industry and the salt trade. The family almost exclusively dominated the met-allurgical industry until the end of the century. Because of the size and complexity of Stroganov family property holdings, legal disputes, many over inheritance, occurred fre-quently. The Baroness Stroganova's request to Catherine II reveals some of the under-lying ambiguity for women inherent in Russian inheritance law in the eighteenth century. The Baroness wishes to transfer patrimonial property to her daughter Anna. However, Anna Chernysheva was the offspring of her mother's first marriage to Aleksandr Islenov. The fact that Anna was not a member of the Stroganov patrimonial line makes this re-quest particularly problematical. Repeatedly stressing her old age and widowhood, the Baroness attempts to elicit Catherine's sympathy as another woman. The Baroness con-cludes her request by emphasizing that her other daughter, Varvara Aleksandrovna, is already financially secure and has no need for additional property. The Empress's deci-sion is unknown.

Most-Kind Empress!

The great motherly care of Your Imperial Majesty toward all the public as well as the private needs of Your loyal subjects, as well as Your most gracious and right-eous attention to these requests, gives me occasion to be so bold as to approach the august kindliness of Your Majesty with this, my most humble request.

Many former ill-fated adventures in the building of my house have necessitated my contracting large debts, amounting to the sum of 230,000 rubles. Among these are debts to my son-in-law, Count Ivan Grigorevich Chernyshev,[58] amounting to 85,386 rubles. By obligation, I certainly should, and want to, repay these debts. However, widowhood, disease, and old age no longer permit me to undertake these necessary, though at my age extremely overwhelming and unbearable, re-sponsibilities and cares. Therefore, to put these problems behind me and to facil-itate the speediest payment of these debts, it occurred to me, Most-Kind Empress, with the consent of my aforementioned son-in-law (who has held a mortgage on all my immovable estates since 1775), that I will have to sell the businesses and foundries on the patrimonial estate in the Perm viceroyalty. Since funds generated through the sale of a single estate will not satisfy payment of my debts to Count Chernyshev, I therefore will place all the patrimonial estates located in other regions, remaining after the sale, into the eternal hereditary and perfectly free possession of my daughter, Anna Aleksandrovna, wife of Count Chernyshev. She will return, upon receipt of the money, according to the law, the above-mentioned mortgage on all of the immovable estates given to her husband by me; and, with his guarantee, he will bind himself and his successors to provide the support required by me every year until my death, according to the conditions stipulated between us.

As for my other daughter, Varvara Aleksandrovna Shakhovskaia, she not only doesn't find anything offensive in the ratification of patrimonial estates to my daughter and her sister, the Countess Chernysheva, but, rather, from the warmest love for her sister and having no need to add the property, [considers] this is perfectly to her satisfaction.

I dare, Most-Kind Empress, to approach Your most maternal Imperial Majesty to humbly ask for the mercy of monarchal benevolence in sanctioning this proposed distribution of my remaining immovable estates for the use of my daughter the Countess Chernysheva and her successors, in eternal heredity and perfectly free possession. This, my humble request, I submit at the hallowed feet of Your Majesty.

Most-Kind Empress, I am the humble slave of Your Imperial Majesty

Maria, Baroness Stroganova

Source: "Spisok s prosheniia baronessy M. Stroganovoi imper. Ekaterine II" ["Transcript of the Request of the Baroness M. Stroganova to the Empress Catherine II"], in Shchukin, vol. X, pp. 182–83.

Translated by Karen Rosneck.

THE WOMAN WRITER

A. Society's Judgment

ELENA GAN

Writing was one of the few respectable ways women could earn money in the nineteenth century. Elena Gan, the author of the following story, was the pseudonym of Elena Andreevna Fadeeva (m. Rzhishcheva, 1814–1842). Gan was widely considered the finest woman writer of her time by her contemporaries, including Vissarion Belinskii, the leading critic of the day (whose work is featured in chapter 1), and the writer Ivan Turgenev (also see chapter 1). She spent much of her life in the provinces. In 1830 she

married Petr Gan, an artillery captain, and, due to his profession, began a series of
moves, mainly to provincial towns. Gan had three children, a son who died young and
two daughters who both became writers (Elena Blavatskaia, famous as the popularizer
of Theosophy, and Vera Zhelikhovskaia). In 1836 Petr Gan was posted to St. Petersburg, where Elena began her literary career. At first, she worked closely with Osip
Senkovskii, the editor of Library for Reading, where she frequently published her prose
until 1840, when she and Senkovskii parted ways. In her short life Gan wrote eleven
works. Her fiction includes Ideal (1837), Utballa (1838), and A Useless Talent,
which was left unfinished when she died in 1842. Throughout her fiction, Gan focuses
on the need for the emotional emancipation of women. Many of her heroines do not fit
into society and provide a kind of judgment on it, quite explicitly in Society's Judgment
(1839), a semi-autobiographical work about a woman writer whose husband is in the
military. The following excerpt from the novella, like many of Gan's works, describes
marital discord; it also focuses specifically on the difficulties of being a woman and a
writer, especially in Russian provincial towns.

The change of apartments is an epoch in military life; on the other hand, the
transfer itself takes a good while—but for the moment they're still not thinking
about that. Officers generally worry about whether there will be lots of wealthy
landowners near the future station—[and] will they be hospitable, will they like
soldiers? The commander, armed with receipts, mulls over the good and bad
points of housing in such-and-such a province, while the commander's wife is
mentally packing into carts her little caps and turbans, if she's possessed by the
mania for fashion—and books and music, if she has pretensions to enlightenment;
before the fact she distributes into a huge traveling carriage her children, her nannies, her servant girls and Pomeranians.

For two months there are preparations and bustle, and then the awaited moment arrives—trumpeters shaking on gray horses give the signal, ranks of horses
set out, a lively song strikes up, and, by God, they're off on the broad journey!

Stopping places, dinners, nights' lodgings, days of rest follow each other in
lengthy order, unchanging even at holidays; the surroundings change slowly, like
settings in a provincial theater. . . . The son of Apollo, artificially seeking poetic
metaphors from everything, might compare our procession to some kind of idyl-
lic moment in human life, but those of us who know campaigns not from the pic-
turesque descriptions of retired writers but from experience can find no more apt
comparison than with boring, apathetic prose: they're both varied by commas and
periods!

The last day's march has come; the promised land is near!—we've arrived and
unpacked, and you look around you: new faces, habits, new relationships. [E]very
step in society is like stepping on thin ice: you grope and test where it's best to
place your foot. In any case, young people don't take long to settle in: two or three
quadrilles and they're acquainted, friends, in love; all the difficulties remain for
the ladies, the wives of the officers and commanders.

Societies so love dancers with shining epaulettes that they're not subject to strict selection; the women gentry and town ladies receive them with favor, the landowners and town gentlemen invite them to dinners and evenings to appease their feminine commanders. But soldiers' wives—oh, that's a different matter! Judges of the feminine sex view their newly arrived rivals with a less than indulgent eye, dissecting severely their costumes, their facial features, their characters. These are two nations alien to each other, two divergent elements—they unite into one friendly whole neither easily nor quickly.

What if, unhappily, one of these arriving ladies is distinguished from the others in some way—by beauty, talent or wealth! If the [local] villainess-gossip outstrips her and brings news of her to new apartments, and even before her arrival arouses curiosity, incites rivalry, wounds pride, gives out the bitter taste of jealousy—what if this gaunt, yellow-faced figure sharpens her teeth ahead of time on an unknown, but already hated, victim?

"But what could so strongly upset women's passions? What kind of superiority, what sort of difference?" my dear readers will say.[59] Oh my God! I repeat: a small digression or stepping out of the general circle of what's considered normal, a relief on the smooth wall of society. Imagine a marvelous lieutenant's wife, of striking beauty; a captain's wife born in North America, thrown by chance from the shores of the Mississippi to the shores of the Oka together with her million-dollar dowry or just with some additional rank; a writer[60] who at some point in her leisure time has written two or three stories, which later showed up on the typesetter's bench.

"What? The wife of a captain or a lieutenant who's a writer? . . . That's ridiculous! That can't be!—many will object. It's true, [de] Genlis wrote, but she was a member of court, a countess!—Staël wrote, but her father was a government minister.—They both received a higher education, but the wife of a capt [sic]. . . . "[61] However, let's suppose, just for a joke, that in the crowd of newly arrived officers there appears, on the arm of one of them, a woman-writer. Everyone knows beforehand that she's coming, they collect rumors about her, they tell stories both true and untrue—at last she's arrived, she's here. . . .

Ah! How to see her! No doubt she bears the mark of genius on her brow; no doubt she talks only of poetry and literature; she pronounces her opinions like improvisations, uses technical terms, carries a pencil and paper with her to write down her happily occurring ideas! . . .

With similar preconceptions people gather to look over the newly arrived writer.

A week goes by, two. . . .

"*Ma chère*, come to dinner at my house on Thursday."

"What's the occasion, a name day?"[62]

"No, Madame *** is dining with me—you know, the writer."

"Ah, I'm delighted, we'll see what a woman-writer looks like."

"And you, Avdotia Trifonovna, do you want to make her acquaintance?"

"Not exactly to make her acquaintance, but I'll come to take a peek."

"Have you read her work?"

"Oh no! I don't have time to read such nonsense."

"What exactly has she written?"

"Not much—trifles, probably stolen from the *Revue étrangère*."[63]

"Oh, no, my little dear, it's pure imitation of Marlinsky."[64]

"Ha, ha, ha! * * *"

"Allow me as well to enjoy your dinner on Thursday!" exclaims the herald of all grand occasions in . . . county. "For the sake of your beauty! I've long wanted to meet with her, to speak with her about wit and talents, to pose several questions, to pronounce sincerely my opinion of her creations, hmm . . . I think she'll take my advice with gratitude!"—he adds with blessed self-confidence, smoothing the rose-colored lapels of his blue velvet waistcoat.

"Ah! my dear! I've heard that if she's inspired, then regardless of where she is, at a ball, in a carriage, or on the riverbank, right there she immediately begins to declaim."

"Ah, if only she'd be inspired on Thursday!" explains the naive country miss.

"And do you know, they say that in her novels she copies all of the heroines from herself."

"How is that?"

"It's very simple: whoever takes a pen in hand, winds up describing himself."

"But how is that possible, if you please? Not all of her heroines are baked in one mold! One is a country girl, another's a society lady, another's exalted, still another's colder than ice; the first is Russian, the second's a German, the third is absolutely wild—a Bashkir, isn't it?"

"Oh, but you've forgotten," exclaims the quick-witted poet, "that she's not simply a woman, but a woman-writer, that is, she's a special being, a deformed whim of nature, or better: a monster of the female sex. There are people born with a bird's head or chicken's legs. Then why not allow that her soul, created in the form and likeness of a chameleon, pretends to be thus-and-so, draws its own portrait, and then takes on a different form."

"Ah, you see . . . "

"Well, if that's how it is, . . . " two or three ladies utter in a sing-song voice, believing blindly in all the pronouncements of the great poet.

"Well, then, tell me please," says an honored old lady who has grown gray in blessed ignorance of the things of this world, "tell me, she writes the way they print it in books? That is, the way she writes, that's how they print the word?"

And on an affirmative response she expresses the desire to see the woman who knows how to write the way they print in books.

The fateful Thursday arrives, the poor writer goes in the innocence of her soul to dine, not suspecting that they've invited her for show, like a dancing monkey, like a snake in a flannel blanket; that the women's glances, always sharp in analysis of their sisters' qualities, have armed themselves for the meeting with a hundred mental lorgnettes, in order to take her apart hair by hair, from her cap to her slippers; that they expect from her inspiration and bookish speeches, stunning thoughts, a magisterial voice, something special in her step, her bow, and even Latin phrases mixed with Hebrew—because a woman-writer, according to general opinion, can't help but be a scholar and a pedant, and why is that? I can't say!

Good Lord, when you think how many people write all their lives and spread their imaginings freely through the world—and no one thinks of patenting them as scholars simply because they compose with words! Then why, as soon as a poor woman-writer puts one of her aforementioned imaginings on paper, does everyone unanimously transfer her into the ranks of the scholars and pedants? . . . Tell me, whence and to what end comes such unsolicited reverence of talent?

And then she can't get on with anyone. Some imagine that she'll immediately seize their form and transmit them alive into a journal. Others eternally imagine a satanic smile on her lips, a satiric attentiveness in her eyes, a betraying espionage—even when, truly, any espionage would be a jug taking water from the air[65]—it's as though everything in her isn't quite as it is with other women. . . . I don't know what, but something isn't right!

Judge then by this pale story one thousandth of the lot that awaits the poor woman-writer, how she wanders the earth, everywhere an uninvited guest, eternally becoming acquainted. Barely do they get to know her in one place, barely grow accustomed to seeing in her a *woman* without the terrible modifier "writer," barely have kind people embraced her—when suddenly the campaign, a change of apartments—again you begin with the alphabet.

Source: Elena Gan, "Sud' sveta," *Dacha na Petergofskoi doroge: Proza russkikh pisatel'nits pervoi poloviny XIX veka* ["Society's Judgment," in *The Cottage on the Peterhof Road: Prose of Russian Women Writers of the First Half of the 19th Century*], ed. V. V. Uchenova (Moscow, 1986), pp. 148–244. Excerpted from pp. 148–53. Originally published in *Biblioteka dlia chteniia* [*Library for Reading*] in 1840.

Translated and partially annotated by Jane T. Costlow.

B. To My Critics

Evdokiia Rostopchina

This poem was written in 1856, toward the end of Evdokiia Rostopchina's life (for more on Rostopchina see chapter 2). In it, she describes her sense that with the ascendance of the "radical critics" in the 1860s her writing has become devalued: many women writers (for example, Evgenia Tur) expressed similar sentiments. In this poem, Rostopchina celebrates her distance from a socially oriented realism, already apparent in the preceding story by Elena Gan and which was quickly becoming the dominant aesthetic of the day.

I do not wonder, really, I'm not angry
That they rise up at me so spitefully:
I'm sooner proud of that abuse from journals,
My heart will not be stung by calumny.
I've parted ways with this new generation,
My path leads from it to another goal;
In concepts, in my soul and in conviction
I belong to quite a different world.
I respect and call to other gods,
And I speak another, different language;
I'm alien to them, absurd—I know it,
But I am not abashed before their judgment.
I do not seek with craft and with incitement
To set one class against another class;
I do not wish to boast before society
Of mystic love and sanctimoniousness;
I do not rush toward robbers to embrace them,
I do not bring my praise to the depraved;
I do not stir my father's dust with a curse
And do not write lampoons about the dead!
Without complaint, nor bitterness, nor anger
I look at life, at people and the world . . .
But then from left and right, in compensation,
Anathemas above my head are heard!
The throng of friends and brethren is far distant—
They've passed on to their rest, their song is done.
No wonder that, a solitary priestess,
It's at an empty altar that I stand!

November 1856

Source: E. P. Rostopchina, "Moim kritikam," *Talisman. Izbrannaia lirika. Neliudimka (Drama). Dokumenty, pis'ma, vospominaniia* ["To My Critics," in *Talisman. Selected Lyrics. The Unsociable Woman (A Drama). Documents, Letters, Memoirs*] (1845; reprint, Moscow, 1987), pp. 156–57.

Translated by Sibelan Forrester.

WOMEN AND THE MILITARY

A. Letter to Peter I

ANNA MENSHIKOVA

While accounts of Peter I's activities rarely mention women except as the object of his reforming zeal, several women played active roles in supporting the military campaigns that occupied most of Peter's reign. He corresponded regularly with these women, and they often accompanied him on campaign. These women were some of the main supporters of his Westernizing efforts. Ekaterina Alekseevna (Marfa Skavronskaia, more commonly known as Catherine I) later married the tsar and became Russia's first empress. Daria Mikhailovna Menshikova sent supplies to her husband's army and accompanied him on many of his missions during the Great Northern War against Sweden (1700–1721). When she and Catherine were not on campaign with their lovers (later husbands), they often lived together with other female relatives and friends. The first letter included here, probably written in 1704 or 1705, is typical of the correspondence of the period in that questions about health make up the majority of its contents. Yet, as in this letter, most of the correspondence concerns the fate of Russia's war effort.

Our joy, Merciful sovereign, dear captain, the right hand of God preserves your health. We thank you, my [sic] Little Father, for your kindness, that you granted to remember us and gladdened us by writing of your health, about which and henceforward, we beg grace, that we will not be deprived of this joy. We congratulate your worship that by your efforts the Mitau castle[66] has been taken. Also through your efforts we here have received some amusement, and we thank you very much for this kindness, and we along with this newborn henceforward wish to congratulate you. We petition, my [sic] Little Father, for your grace, that you will deign to wish to see us, by your grace, of which we are unworthy and by which we tearfully beg your kindness to see your worship. Following this, we entrust your health to God's preservation. Anna Menshikova. Varvara. . . . Katerina Herself Third. Auntie Not-So-Clever. Stupid Daria. After them, Petr and Paul, begging your blessing, they petition.[67] 3 date of October.

Source: Pis'ma i bumagi Petra velikogo [The Letters and Papers of Peter the Great], vol. III (1704–1705). This letter can be found in the notes to document no. 917 on pp. 788–89.

Translated by Robin Bisha.

B. Memoirs of a Campaign

VARVARA BAKUNINA

While most women followed Russia's wars from their homes (like Varvara Tatishcheva, in chapter 2), throughout the eighteenth century other women accompanied their husbands on campaign. In 1796, at the age of twenty-three, Varvara Ivanovna Bakunina (née Golenishcheva-Kutuzova, 1773–1840) was one of only two women who were permitted to accompany their officer husbands to the Caucasus during the Persian campaign of that year. Bakunina performed the important function of chronicler of the campaign, which was part of Catherine II's policy of territorial expansion in the Caucasus as well as her response to Persia's invasion of Transcaucasia and the capture of Tbilisi in the fall of 1795. The Russian troops, under General V. A. Zubov, began their march south in the spring of 1796. They took Derbent on May 10 and accepted the surrender of Baku and Kuba in mid-June. In November they reached the Kura and Araks rivers but were ordered to withdraw the following month, after Paul succeeded to the Russian throne and began to alter the course of Russia's foreign policy.

Bakunina's memoirs of the campaign, originally written in French, cover the first three and a half months, up to the point at which the troops are about to enter Kuba. The main events of the narrative are the siege of Derbent and the capture—and subsequent escape—of Sheikh-Ali, Derbent's young ruler. Bakunina's telling of these events is interspersed with incisive commentary on the army's leadership as well as detailed accounts of daily life on the road and the surrounding environment. Her remarks frequently show a sharp ethnographic eye and penchant for debunking stereotypes about the Orient and its inhabitants.

It is the lyrical digressions, however, in which Bakunina departs from the reportage genre and speaks about her own fears, thoughts, and emotions, that turn her text into a fascinating autobiography of an eighteenth-century Russian woman aristocrat. The military expedition becomes a canvas onto which the writer projects a record of her changing sense of self in a form "suitable" for a woman. The narrative frame she chooses— ostensibly, she writes a letter to her "dear sister"—reveals the ways in which she experiments with the genre of an epistolary journey-diary, made fashionable in the 1790s when Nikolai Karamzin published his Letters of a Russian Traveler.[68] *Although Bakunina's work was produced in the same period, it was not published until 1887 in Russian translation.*

I.

I want to describe the events of the ill-fated Persian campaign, while its most minute details are still fresh in my memory. I dedicate this story to you, dear sister; you will read it with sympathy on account of our friendship, and you will forgive me the shortcomings of my writing style and exposition, as you have usually been kind and lenient toward me. You are no greater expert at politics than I am, so you will not start criticizing me when I begin to talk about it or about the war and military affairs.

On March 1, 1796, our regiment received an order to leave our quarters and move to Kizliar. To my great joy, it was decided in Kargalinka that I would follow my husband during this expedition; my husband and another colonel were allowed to take wives with them, for which I was very grateful to the count.

On April 13, the crossing of the Terek River began and two days later, the whole army had already marched thirteen versts on the other side of the river. Count Zubov arrived on the following day; all the soldiers were under arms, and they welcomed him with rapture. We ate together at Colonel R.'s. The count was quite friendly, but his friendliness seemed insincere, and it seemed that he constantly tried to control himself, as if afraid that people might forget themselves in front of him. In short, he looked like a man in fear of losing his superiority—superiority that he had not earned but which was established artificially because of his status. When I got to know him better, I became certain that my first impression was not mistaken.

On April 18, Good Friday, the whole army was fully assembled, and when all preparations were finished, we started to advance. We marched sixty versts, which took us twelve hours. The heat was unbelievable; the soldiers were exhausted, but they were determined to court fame. Having arrived at the camp, everyone got some rest [and] became more cheerful, and the following day we continued our march in good spirits. After we had gone for fifteen versts on a relatively good and pretty route, which often took us through a forest, we set up our camp near the village of Kazi-Iurt, located on the bank of the Sulan—quite a wide and deep river, with a very rapid current. I went for a walk on the riverbank and stopped at the village where I was very well received by a certain prince and his family who lived in this village, which they owned. It turned out that they knew our grandfather B. M., and when they heard our last name, they tried to show us kindness in every way possible and they treated us to dried fruit and nuts.

The wife of the prince was an elderly woman, and, it seemed, very wise, as far as I could tell after talking to her with the help of an interpreter. Her two daughters were very pretty and dressed quite well. I was only surprised by a rather strange local custom: women receive strangers without wearing a veil, while the husband does not enter his wife's room during the length of the visit; he takes the guests to the door of his wife's room and leaves. Isn't it strange and completely contrary to the customs of the East?

The first day of Easter we spent at our camp. The soldiers were busy that day placing pontoons for our crossing of the Sulan. We went to the morning service and mass, even though we were in a non-Christian land. The weather was foul; we sat all day locked up in our little house. Generals, colonels, and others all came with greetings. According to our Easter custom, we exchanged triple kisses but instead of *paskha*, we ate very salty and bad Lezgin cheese.[69]

III.

[On May 1, Bakunina was ordered to stay behind the army, which was getting ready for the siege of Derbent.[70] Bakunina and M. K.—the other woman who accompanied her husband during the campaign—lived in what she calls a "wagon-burg," a storage place for the army engaged in siege and combat, guarded by a handful of soldiers.]

IV.

Since there was nothing to do during the siege [of Derbent], my husband came to visit me on May 4 and allowed me to return his visit. On May 5 I arrived at the camp, and, thanks to my eloquence, managed to elicit permission not to return to the accursed "wagon-burg." This is how I stayed in the camp, without any fear or uneasiness. Regardless of the siege, everything was following its course; every day I took a walk on the beach, collecting shells and stones and climbing the mountain, where there were many springs of fine water flowing down into pools of cut stone. Everywhere you looked, soldiers were assembling batteries for bombing the city, all the while being within range of a Persian rifle shot; many soldiers were wounded.

During one of my many walks, I met a wounded soldier from our Vladimir regiment, and he made a strong impression on me. But, after a few days, I became accustomed to such sights. How is it that what initially startles us does not impress us nearly as much when encountered again? Doubtless, I did not become insensitive to the suffering of others, but, subsequently, stories about the wounded and the killed did not leave such a depressing impression on me as they did in the beginning. How miserable we would have been, if time and habit did not weaken our impressionability.

I must confess that my first night in the camp was not very quiet; constant shooting and the whistle of flying bullets did not make for particularly pleasant music to my ears. My sleep was also interrupted by the incessant cry "Khabarda" which echoed in the city; it is a customary Persian cry that tells city dwellers to be on guard, to which they were responding in a chorus. If you add to this the bellowing of the bulls and the braying of the donkeys, of which there were plenty in the city, you will have a good idea of the horrible noise in the city every night. However, the force of habit can do a lot: it was only during my first night that the noise kept me awake, and the following night I slept wonderfully.

On May 8 we started firing from the batteries that were located opposite the ill-starred tower where the Russians had suffered a setback. The shots were well aimed and made a breach in a short time. Then the army went in for the assault, and chasseurs and grenadiers of the Voronezh regiment took the tower despite the unyielding and desperate resistance on the side of its defenders. They were a select Persian army who had volunteered to defend the tower. They all fell in battle; not even one was taken prisoner. Our soldiers also worked miracles.

Derbent was taken on May 10. Some are sure that the Persians offered to surrender under the same conditions the day before, but they were refused; our superiors wanted to bombard the city at any cost and to make as much noise as possible. Indeed, I think that if our first attack at the tower had not taken us down a peg, we would have wanted to take Derbent by storm, ignoring the fact that the Persians were ready to surrender without a fight.

V.

Perhaps you have read the report about the taking of Derbent in newspapers, and you will be very surprised that my story does not agree with it in the least. Believe me: I did not miss a detail, and as for the forest of shining bayonets, the old man who fell on his knees, etc., all that is nothing but a figment of M.'s imagination; it is an elegant fiction that exists only in his mind. Sheik-Ali was brought to the Count disarmed, with a saber on his neck, and so was his entourage; it meant that they offered their heads in order to atone for their sins and they were fully dependent on the Russians' mercy. Kadyr-Bek—the richest and most influential of Derbent's inhabitants and chief among the khan's advisors—addressed the Count with a speech in which he said that if the Count intended to punish anyone, let him turn his wrath upon Kadyr-Bek and the other advisors, but spare Sheik-Ali because of his tender age. What devotion, and what magnanimity!

The Count calmed them, saying that the Empress's mercy knew no boundaries, and that he could promise them pardon in advance. Nonetheless, he added, Sheik-Ali must atone for the fault committed against the Russians, to whom he had closed the gates of the city after previously turning to them for help; because of this, he would be detained in our camp until the Empress thought fit to return his freedom and all rights to him, which he should earn with his obedience and devotion.

And so, Sheik-Ali stayed in our camp and a part of his entourage was sent back. His older sister—Parezhi-Khanum—had always been on the side of the Russians and did all she could to persuade her brother to receive Sav. and open the city gates when our army came; during the siege, she often sent her messengers to the Count to express her devotion and gave him some very important pieces of advice. Therefore she was entrusted with the government of Derbent and given the title of ruler. Weapons were taken away from the inhabitants, but some refused to give them up and kept them. One strong garrison stayed in the city and Sav. was appointed commandant of Derbent.

Parezhi immediately asserted herself, as did her colleague—S.—who was obliged to share with her the reins of government in Derbent. At that time, it was also decided that Sheik-Ali would follow the army. There were competing opinions on this subject: some people, including myself, thought that this was not altogether safe and that it would be better to send him to Astrakhan.[71] Not being particularly foresighted, I thought, nevertheless, that he could easily escape; perhaps it was a premonition of the troubles that his escape caused us. Of course, I expressed my views on this matter; they laughed at me, and those for whom the Count's decision was sacred tried to prove that I myself did not know what I was saying. I fell silent; but when Sheik-Ali took advantage of the carelessness of his guards and the silly trust shown him and escaped, it was my turn to laugh at those who had said that I reasoned like a child.

VI.

The whole week that we spent on the bank of the Rubas was very lively. No later than the eve of our departure, we traveled a verst away from our camp to drink tea. I felt like returning home on foot, and, because it was already late, it had become completely dark by the time we arrived home. Suddenly, I learned that Ben.'s and Bul.'s brigades were ordered to take the field, under the latter's command, on the following day at three in the morning. I was extremely tired and quickly had to pack, see to everything, and get up at two in the morning. It seemed to me very rude on the Count's part: we had spent the whole afternoon with him, and I asked him a few times when we would depart, to which he answered each time that nothing had yet been decided. Later on, I became used to such peculiarities and the perpetual mystery that shrouded the most irrelevant events, probably to add a little importance to them.

I am also indebted to my journey into Persia for my becoming more courageous and getting rid of all the fears inculcated in me through my upbringing and my sedentary life. No mountain, no stream can scare me now; there is no such thing as a dangerous route for me; I can easily endure cold weather, dampness, [and] intense heat, and I can manage without many things which seemed absolutely essential to me before.

Source: Varvara Ivanovna Bakunina, "Persidskii pokhod v 1796 godu. Vospominaniia Varvary Ivanovny Bakuninoi," *Russkaia starina* ["The Persian Campaign of 1796. The Memoirs of Varvara Ivanovna Bakunina," *Russian Antiquary*], vol. 53 (1887), pp. 343–74. Excerpted.

Translated by Justyna Beinek

C. Deposition about the Women's Death Battalion

MARIA BOCHKAREVA

From the eighteenth to the early twentieth century, a number of Russian women served as soldiers and officers in the imperial army. The best known of this handful of women is Nadezhda Durova, who disguised herself as a man in order to join the army and who fought in the Napoleonic wars. Beginning with the Crimean War (1853–1856) women served as nurses, but the first woman to serve openly as a woman-soldier was Maria Leontevna Bochkareva (née Frolkova, 1889–1920). Bochkareva, a semiliterate peasant woman from the central Siberian provincial capital of Tomsk, had a diverse and very public military career between 1914 and 1919. Following her arrest by the Bolsheviks in December 1919 as an alleged counterrevolutionary, she provided police interrogators with four depositions, between January and April 1920, describing her military activities during World War I and the Civil War. She was executed in May 1920.

Bochkareva's most extensive deposition, taken on April 5 and from which the following excerpt is drawn, offers both direct and indirect evidence about the experiences of this female soldier in the period of the war and the 1917 revolutions. The deposition raises a number of important issues about gender identity, the fluidity of political affiliation, the possibilities of and limitations on social and sexual mobility, and the impact of war and revolution on women.

In 1914, I went to war out of a feeling of patriotism, and wished to die for my country. From Tomsk in 1914, in October, I sent Nicholas II a telegram about my wish to enter military service. I received an answer from Nicholas II—I was accepted into military service as a volunteer. They enlisted me in a lower rank in the 25th Tomsk reserve battalion. In this battalion I was trained in military science and shooting, and after two and a half months was sent with a marching company to the front—near Molodechno.

Upon arrival at the front, the marching company was attached to the 5th Army Corps, 7th Division, 28th Polotskii Regiment. During my entire stay at the front in this regiment, I was wounded in battle four times; for participation in these battles I received all four grades of the St. George Cross.[72] On the 1st of May 1917 I met Rodzianko[73] at the front. During a conversation with him the commander of the Polotskii regiment informed Rodzianko that there was a woman-volunteer in the regiment who had been at the front from the beginning of the war and whose courage and bravery set an example for the men. Rodzianko wanted to see me personally; I went to him, and he kissed me[74] and ordered a new uniform sewn [for me] and sent me to Petrograd.

Upon arrival in Petrograd, I gave a report in the Tauride Palace[75] to the members of the Provisional Government. In the report, I said that the soldiers were not listening to their commanders and were fraternizing with the Germans. Rodzianko asked me what would help lift the spirit of the soldiers. I suggested he could assist this by forming a volunteer women's battalion. They told me that my idea was splendid, but it was necessary to report to Supreme Commander-in-Chief Brusilov[76] and consult with him. I went with Rodzianko to Brusilov's Headquarters. In his study Brusilov asked me, "Do you have confidence in women?" and told me that the formation of a women's battalion was the first in the world. "Won't women disgrace Russia?" I told Brusilov I was uncertain about women but [added], "If you give me full power, then I guarantee that my battalion will not disgrace Russia—but only if there are no committees."[77] Brusilov told me he believed me and would try in every way to help in forming a women's volunteer battalion. I was glad to hear it. Then I returned to Petrograd.

On the day after my arrival, I was introduced to Kerenskii[78] at the Winter Palace.[79] I was invited to dinner. After dinner Kerenskii greeted me and told me he would permit me to form a women's battalion of death in my name, i.e., Bochkareva's Volunteer Women's Battalion of Death. On 22 May 1917 I appeared at the Malii Mariinskii Theater in Petrograd. I made an agitational speech appealing to women to join my battalion. In my appeal, I told the women that the soldiers in this great war were getting tired, that it was necessary to help them and give them moral support. With this, I enrolled 2,000 women volunteers.

They provided me with barracks in Torgovaia Street in Petrograd; they issued uniforms and equipment, and provided instructors. I proceeded with the training of my battalion. In this period I sent away 1,500 women because of their loose behavior. And with [the remaining] 500 women, I began to form the battalion. On 27 June 1917 I was present for the blessing of the standard[80] of my battalion at St. Isaac's Cathedral. General Kornilov,[81] in the presence of Kerenskii and other members of the Provisional Government, handed the standard over to me and promoted me to ensign. On 1 July 1917, after a Te Deum[82] in Kazan Cathedral, I set off with my battalion for the front near Molodechno, where they assigned my battalion and me to the 1st Siberian Corps. On 8 July my battalion and I took part in a battle near Krevo. Two lines of German trenches were captured. When we found ourselves in Spasskii Forest, the [Russian] soldiers abandoned us to the mercy of fate, and I remained behind, alone with the battalion. On the morning of 9 July, the Germans crossed over to the offensive, and the battalion and I retreated. During this [action], I received a serious concussion and was taken unconscious from the battle zone. They sent me to Petrograd to the hospital, where I lay for one and a half months. For this battle, I was recommended for a gold weapon,[83] but did not receive the weapon and was promoted to second lieutenant.

When I recovered, I received an order from General Kornilov to inspect the women's battalions[84] and to attach those suitable to my battalion. I traveled to Moscow, inspected the Moscow women's battalion, and found it unfit for military action. I went to the front to my old battalion and decided not to take women any more because I was disappointed in women. At the front I took over a military district, which I guarded until the overthrow of Kerenskii.

I received a telegram from Soviet authorities that I should disband my battalion; this I did at once. This was the autumn of 1917. After disbanding the battalion I left for Petrograd. In Petrograd they arrested me at the station. Afterward I was called to Smolnyi where a gentleman I didn't know spoke with me and suggested I enter the service of Soviet power: "You are a peasant and must defend your people." But I told him I was exhausted from the war and didn't want to take part in a civil war. This gentleman gave me money, and I left for home in Tomsk.

I considered the Bolsheviks my enemies and the country's enemies. Upon arrival in Tomsk I lived with my father and mother, and occupied myself with housekeeping: I washed clothes and sewed for myself. In this period, before the New Year of 1918, I had an old wound in my right leg open up, and I went to Moscow to be treated. When I arrived in Moscow, they again arrested me at the station. I did time in the guardhouse; they transported me to Butyrskaia prison, made an inquiry about me in Tomsk, and held me for two months. I lay in the prison hospital with a wounded leg. Then they freed me. I returned to Tomsk. My leg worsened. It was too hard to live in Tomsk, and my 15-year-old sister and I left for Vladivostok,[85] where I appealed to the American Consul for assistance, to give me the means and opportunity to go with my sister to America to be treated. The Consul helped me, and I was sent by steamship to America.

In San Francisco, in America, the women made me welcome: they greeted me and arranged a dinner. From San Francisco I went to New York, where I arranged for my sister to study free of charge. I went to Washington where I spent a month and a half in the hospital. In Washington, I visited the Russian Ambassador, Boris Aleksandrovich Bakhmetev, who asked me about Russia.[86] On the holiday of the Revolution, I was invited to dinner by President [Woodrow] Wilson. Wilson received me as the first woman officer, and said he considered it an honor to see me. I told Wilson that I considered myself a very lucky woman, that I came from the common folk and was seeing the representative of a free country. Wilson asked me: "Who is right and who is to be blamed in Russia?" Then I told him, "I understand this problem too little and am afraid of finding myself in an erroneous position." With this my conversation with the President of America, Wilson, ended. After two weeks I went to New York and from there by steamship to England.

I arrived by train in the English capital, the city of London, where I stayed at the Savoy Hotel, where I lived at the expense of the well-known wealthy suffragette, Miss [sic] Pankhurst.[87] This suffragette arranged a meeting for me with the English War Minister. I asked the War Minister to present me to the King of England.[88] My wish was fulfilled. In the middle of August 1918 the King's secretary arrived by automobile and handed me a slip of paper saying that the King of England would receive me for five minutes. I put on my military officer's uniform and my Russian decorations, and with my interpreter, Robenson [sic], I went to the King's palace.

I went into a hall, and after a few minutes the door was flung open and the King of England entered. He had a strong resemblance to Tsar Nicholas II. I went toward the King. He told me he was very glad to see the second Joan of Arc and as a friend of Russia [said,] "I salute you as a woman who has done much for Russia." In reply I told him I considered it great good fortune to see the King of England. The King asked what party I belonged to and whom I trusted; I told him, "I don't belong to any party, and I trust only General Kornilov." The King told me the news that Kornilov had been killed. I told the King, "I don't know whom to trust now, and I don't think I'll fight in the Civil War." The King said to me: "You are a Russian officer. It is your direct duty in four days to go to Russia, to Arkhangel'sk;[89] I rely on you to take an active part." I said to the King of England: "Yes, Sir!"

[When] I arrived in Arkhangel'sk, I went to General Murashevskii [sic],[90] to whom I said, "I have arrived from England to receive an official assignment." The General asked me to sit and said, "I'm glad you have arrived. A new army is just being formed here; therefore, I request that you form a small military volunteer unit—but not a women's, a men's [unit]." I told him I didn't want to take part in military action in time of civil war. The General screamed at me, "You are a Russian officer, and you refuse the order you are given!" I said to him, "Don't shout at me; in my life I have seen people more important than you, and I do not permit you to shout at me!" Then the General ordered me arrested. They wanted to arrest me, but my adjutant, Colonel [L. G.] Filippov, then and there talked it over with the English General Poole.[91] He [the adjutant] said they should not arrest me. They took the interpreter and the adjutant away from me, and I spent seven days under house arrest. This was in the first days of September 1918.[92]

On New Year's Eve, an order was published in the paper declaring that I had done much for Russia in the German war and that central Russia would value this work in the future, but now they had no need of my work; they are managing without women and asking me to discard my military uniform and epaulettes. I was terribly insulted at this, went to the Governor General of Arkhangel'sk, Miller,[93] and told him that no one had the right to take the uniform and epaulettes away from me; I hadn't committed any treason and refused to do what General Murashevskii ordered because I considered myself an invalid and didn't have the energy to form a military detachment. I argued with Miller. I went to General Poole's assistant. I told him I had given everything for Russia, that now I was a sick woman and I didn't accept the order because I could not fulfill it—and they had treated me so dreadfully for this. He told me he would clear all this up; and in three days there appeared in the newspaper an order stating that Lieutenant Bochkareva had the right to wear a military uniform and epaulettes and to be on the list in the reserve ranks with a salary of 750 rubles a month. This was 3 January 1919.

Until July, I lived on the salary I received, on the list of the reserve ranks, doing nothing. In July, I learned from the newspaper that an expedition was assembling to set off for Siberia. It was a military expedition, which had to deliver machine guns, shells, and uniforms to Kolchak's army.[94] The captain of this expedition was a naval officer, Savitskii.[95] I went to Governor General Miller and asked his permission to go with this expedition to Siberia, to my native land. This permission was given to me.

On 10 August 1919 I left Arkhangel'sk with Captain Savitskii's expedition.

I arrived in Tomsk. I found my parents in distress. Then and there my brother-in-law began saying I'd made a mistake: "Look, three barges of frozen Red Army men stand in the Ob [River], and you sympathize with our enemy." I told my brother-in-law and my husband, Bochkarev,[96] with whom I'd not lived for twelve years, that I had sympathized with the Whites. But now I understood I was completely mistaken, and therefore I would go to Omsk to Kolchak and ask him to let me retire entirely from military service and [give me my] pension. I spent a week in Tomsk and left for Omsk.

On arrival in Omsk, I presented myself at Headquarters to the general on duty, and reported to him that I had no strength to do anything and asked that they give me retirement with pension as a battalion commander, with the uniform of a staff-captain.[97] He told me that Kolchak wanted to see me and set an appointment for me on Sunday, 10 November. I arrived on Sunday at 12 o'clock at Kolchak's house. I went into Kolchak's study. When I entered, Kolchak and Golitsyn[98] both stood up and greeted me. They said they both had heard much about me and asked me to sit down. Kolchak began to talk to me: "You request retirement, but such people as you are vitally necessary now. I commission you to form a volunteer women's sanitary detachment (the First Women's Volunteer Medical Squadron of Lieutenant Bochkareva)." He said, "There are many typhoid cases and wounded, but there are no hands to nurse the sick. I hope you'll do this."

I accepted Kolchak's suggestion. Kolchak turned to General Golitsyn and said, "Give her an apartment and instructors immediately, so she can give a lecture tomorrow to call women volunteers to her medical detachment." And he gave orders that they should give me an advance of 200,000 [rubles] for the formation of the detachment. Already on 11 November there were distributed around the whole of Omsk posters with appeals [announcing] that the well-known organizer of volunteer detachments, Lieutenant Bochkareva, had arrived from Arkhangel'sk and that she would be in the Gigant Theater today to deliver an appeal to women to form a women's volunteer medical detachment. On 12 November I gave the same speech at the Kristall Theater. From both meetings I immediately recruited 170 women volunteers—and thirty men. Four officers were assigned to me: a chief of staff—a colonel, and a paymaster—a lieutenant, and an adjutant with the rank of lieutenant.[99]

On 13 November I went to get the money from General Golitsyn, 200,000 [rubles], and wagons so I could prepare my people for the retreat from the approaching Red Army. But Kolchak and Golitsyn and the commander of the garrison had already left. I was then terrified—I did not know what to do with my people. Not for the world did they want to remain in Omsk, but there was no money and no means of transport. It was then that I became completely disappointed in Kolchak and in everything, and swore that I would do nothing more for their benefit. I telephoned the doctor at the cadet corps and suggested he take my two hundred medical attendants. He took them, and on the morning of 14 November, on horses supplied locally, I left for Novonikolaevsk. I presented myself at Headquarters to the general on duty, to whom I handed over the four officers of my medical detachment staff and six clerks. I told the General, "If you treat me so basely, abandon me in Omsk without money and without means of transport, I cannot serve you—I'm leaving for home in Tomsk." The General told me to hand in a report to Commander Sakharov;[100] "There is an order for you to go to Irkutsk, and there you will be given means and everything [necessary] for the formation of a women's volunteer medical detachment." I went to General Sakharov and said I couldn't serve any more.

I went to Taiga Station, where I tried again to see Kolchak and clarify my position. But I didn't see Kolchak, although I met Sakharov at the station. He told me he was busy now and said I should go where I was ordered; but I left for Tomsk.

I lived in Tomsk five days under the Whites; then the Soviet authorities came. I presented myself to the commandant of the city of Tomsk, gave him my revolver, told him who I was and what I did for the Whites, and offered my services to the Soviet authorities. The commandant said he had no need of my services, but when he needed me, he'd send for me. The commandant took my pledge not to leave town, and they let me go. They said they wouldn't arrest me.

I lived at home, threw off my military uniform, and put on a woman's dress; I decided to do nothing more and began, with my sister, to sew overcoats for soldiers. On Christmas, at 2 o'clock in the morning, near the Old Cathedral, I was arrested. Later I was put in the Tomsk prison, from where they transferred me to Krasnoiarsk.[101] I acknowledge myself guilty before the Soviet Republic, in that I sympathized with Kolchak and the Whites and formed a women's volunteer medical detachment and that I personally agitated for and didn't prevent my name's being used as propaganda for volunteer formations. I declare my evidence to be correct, in attestation of which I give my signature, Bochkareva.

Military examining magistrate of the Special Section of the VChK[102] with the 5th Army, Pobolotin.

Source: "Protokoly doprosov organizatora Petrogradskogo zhenskogo batal'ona smerti," *Otechestvennye arkhivy* ["Protocols of the Interrogations of the Organizer of the Petrograd Women's Battalion of Death," *Archives of the Fatherland*], no. 1 (1994), pp. 50–66. Excerpted from pp. 59–64.

Translated and partially annotated by Barbara T. Norton.

Notes

1. This refers to the 107-volume edition of Voltaire's correspondence edited by Theodore Besterman and published in Geneva between 1953 and 1965.

2. Molière's *The Misanthrope* (1666) and *The Miser* (1668).

3. Voltaire's *Les Lois de Minos.*

4. Tragedy by Voltaire (1732).

5. Russia's best-known pseudo-classical dramatist; his *Semira* was first performed in 1751. Voltaire had corresponded briefly with Sumarokov in 1769.

6. Catherine refers to her own works, *O Tempora!* [*O Vremya*] and *Mme. Vorchalkina's Nameday,* 1772.

7. The rest of the letter discusses the truce negotiations and Catherine's hopes for a speedy peace treaty ending the Russo-Turkish War.

8. *Institutka* referred to a young woman studying at any of the institutes that were modeled on Smolnyi.

9. The documents translated in the following letters are based on the Russian translation of the French made by Apollon Maikov (1821–1897). Many of the present notes are based on Maikov's extensive annotations to the letters.

10. Except for letter #XV below, Catherine's letters to Levshina had already been published in the mid-nineteenth century (Maikov, "Introduction," pp. 310–12), though Levshina's letters had not. Catherine's letters found in the archive appear to be drafts and differ from the published versions in mostly minor details (except for the previously unpublished letter #XV below). None of Catherine's letters are dated or signed, but all are written in what is evidently Catherine's handwriting.

11. Each class in the Institute wore a uniform of a particular color. The eldest group wore white and the next group, Levshina's, wore gray.

12. Levshina signs most of her letters with the peculiar nickname, *Chernomazaia Levushka*. "Levushka" is an affectionate diminutive of Levshina's surname; *Chernomazaia*, translated as "pitch-dark" to correspond to the etymology of the Russian word, refers to her dark complexion (letter #IX [1]). Starting with letter #XVII (13), however, the last five letters are signed "A. Levshina." This reversion to the formal style coincides with two events: Levshina's departure from Smolnyi once her term there had ended (1776) and an apparent rift between Catherine and Levshina for reasons that have not yet been determined.

13. Maikov's note (revised): The students' first promenade took place May 20, 1773, in the Summer Garden. The serenade was performed on a bugle horn by Count Grigorii Grigorevich Orlov (on Orlov, see chapter 3, note 8).

14. On Mme. de Lafond, see the selection by Rzhevskaia in chapter 3.

15. French: don't be upset. Particularly prior to the patriotic reaction provoked by Napoleon's invasion of imperial Russia in 1812, the Russian aristocracy commonly spoke French among themselves.

16. French: luckily.

17. Ivan Ivanovich Betskoi (see the selections by Levshina and Rzhevskaia in chapter 3).

18. Evpraksiia's grandson, born on her estate of Bobrovo, wrote extensively about her life in *Grandmother's Stories: Memories of Five Generations* [*Rasskazy babushki: Iz vospominanii piati pokolenii*] (1878; reprint, Leningrad, 1989).

19. A city in Siberia.

20. The Russian reads *brata*.

21. Collegiate Councilor was the sixth highest of the fourteen civil service ranks in the Table of Ranks established by Peter I in 1722; until 1856, attainment of this rank by a non-noble conferred hereditary noble status. The title of Cavalier signified appointment to the emperor's honor bodyguard for ceremonial occasions.

22. The ninth highest rank in the Table of Ranks (see previous note 21); it did not confer hereditary noble status on a non-noble.

23. The eighth highest rank in the Table of Ranks (see note 21); until 1856, attainment of this rank conferred hereditary noble status.

24. The twelfth highest rank in the Table of Ranks (see note 21); it did not confer hereditary noble status.

25. The eighth or ninth highest military rank in the Table of Ranks (see note 21); until 1856, it conferred hereditary noble status.

26. A local administrator not included in the Table of Ranks (see note 21).

27. The seventh highest rank in the Table of Ranks (see note 21); until 1856, attainment of this rank conferred hereditary noble status.

28. A type of dance.

29. On Mme. de Staël, see chapter 2, note 25, and on *Corinne*, below, note 61.

30. On the Constitutional Democratic Party, see chapter 1, note 37.

31. Both ports on the middle reach of the Volga River and the administrative centers of Samara and Saratov provinces, respectively.

32. *Pel'meni* are small meat dumplings.

33. It is likely that in noting two forms of grades, Kuskova is providing equivalents familiar to her readers outside of Russia, as the piece was published in an émigré journal.

34. Dmitrii Andreevich Tolstoi (1823–1889), a conservative statist official who strongly influenced educational policies while serving simultaneously as Chief Procurator of the Holy Synod (1865–1880) and Minister of Education (1866–1880). He tried, largely unsuccessfully, to devise a system of education that would limit a person's education to the level and type deemed appropriate to his or her social position and that would provide the requisite expertise without fostering subversive ideas.

35. Established in 1810 to review legislative proposals on a consultative basis and composed of high dignitaries appointed by the emperor, the State Council was one of the chief legislative bodies in the empire; after the establishment of the State Duma in 1906 it was composed of elected as well as appointed members and constituted a conservative upper chamber.

36. Cerberus is a dog of classical mythology, usually depicted with three heads. He guarded the entrance to the underworld.

37. *The Lay of Igor's Campaign* [*Slovo o polku Igoria*], the most famous work of—reputedly—Old Russian literature. The historical event it describes was a battle in 1185; the date of the composition of the document is disputed.

38. A poet, author of prose, and playwright, A. S. Pushkin (1799–1837) is considered by many the creator of the modern Russian literary language. Nikolai V. Gogol (1809–1852) was a novelist, playwright, and short-story writer; he had a keen sense of humor, and his works are important in the development of nineteenth-century Russian literature.

39. Two of Russia's greatest writers, Fedor Dostoevskii (1821–1881) and Count Lev (Leo) Tolstoi (1828–1910).

40. D. I. Pisarev (1840–1868) and N. A. Dobroliubov (1836–1861) were radical journalists and critics. For Belinskii, see chapter 1.

41. A novel by the poet, playwright, novelist, and satirist Alexei N. Tolstoi (1817–1875).

42. We have not been able to identify this apparent literary allusion.

43. Russian universities included the following departments: historical-philological, physical-mathematical, juridical, and medical.

44. Not included in the 1879 statute of the Moscow Medical Practitioners' School, this restriction affected especially Jewish women, who in the 1870s and 1880s had formed a significant percentage of the students in the Women's Higher Courses in several cities and in those medical courses that had been open to women.

45. St. Petersburg's Kalinkin Hospital, originally a home for confining "women of debauched behavior," had become the most prestigious venereal and dermatological hospital in Russia by the middle of the nineteenth century. Among its facilities was a locked ward for prostitutes whom local medical-police physicians had diagnosed as suffering from infectious venereal diseases.

46. In the mid-nineteenth century, the tsarist government ordered all cities in the Russian empire to organize "medical-police committees" to enforce the regulation of prostitution.

47. The term "license" (*blank*) referred to the so-called "yellow ticket" that allowed women to practice prostitution without prosecution, so long as they submitted to regular medical-police surveillance.

48. This story parallels a similar, and romanticized, situation in the novel *What Is to Be Done?* (1863) by the radical writer and critic Nikolai Chernyshevskii (on both, see chapter 6, note 38).

49. Apparently, one of the cadet schools in St. Petersburg that prepared boys for service as military officers.

50. The tsar's subjects were required to carry a domestic passport at all times for identification and control. When women applied for a yellow ticket, the latter was substituted for their passport.

51. A spinning bee.

52. A tool used in spinning and also by joiners.

53. The son of a palace cook, Prince Aleksandr Danilovich Menshikov (1673–1729) rose to great prominence, influence, and wealth after becoming a confidante and confederate of Peter I.

54. The text reads "Paraskevia," an alternate spelling of Praskovia.

55. Natalia Alekseevna (1673–1716) was Peter's younger sister, his favorite, and a partisan of his reforms. Peter left his heirs in her care after the forcible tonsure of their mother, Tsaritsa Evdokiia. Natalia Alekseevna was one of the first members of the royal family to move to St. Petersburg.

56. As Empress Catherine I (Ekaterina Alekseevna) was barely literate, all her letters were dictated to a secretary. She signed with her own hand.

57. Peter I and Ekaterina Alekseevna were married publicly in 1712. Crowned empress in 1724, she ruled Russia from 1725 to 1727 as Empress Catherine I.

58. Ivan Grigorevich Chernyshev (1726–1797) was one of Catherine's closest advisors throughout her reign.

59. The word in Russian is *chitatel'nitsy*, which distinguishes the readers as female.

60. The word in Russian, *pisatel'nitsa*, clearly shows that the writer is a woman.

61. Mme. de Genlis and Mme. de Staël were both important and well-known writers of the late eighteenth century. On Mme. De Staël, see chapter 2, note 25. De Staël's novel *Corinne, ou l'Italie* helped to create the image of a woman creator as improviser—an image Gan seems to allude to in her own story.

62. Each Russian celebrates both a birthday and a name day; the latter is the day in the liturgical calendar devoted to the person's patron saint. The celebration usually included a festive dinner and presents.

63. A journal published in St. Petersburg (1832–1863) that reprinted articles, stories, and other material from European periodicals.

64. Marlinsky was the pseudonym of Aleksandr Aleksandrovich Bestuzhev (1797–1837), an enormously popular writer of highly elaborate, romanticized fiction. He wrote in the 1820s and 1830s, primarily on the life of soldiers set in Russia's "exotic" Caucasus Mountains. The later generation of writers viewed his work as the epitome of saccharine, exaggerated romanticism.

65. That is, completely without aim or function.

66. A city in Latvia, now known as Jelgava, founded as a fortress by the crusading order of Livonian Knights and the residence of the Dukes of Courland. It became part of the Russian empire in 1795.

67. Anna Menshikova was Aleksandr Menshikov's younger sister (on Menshikov, see note 53 above). Varvara and Daria Mikhailovna were the Arsenev sisters, daughters of a Moscow nobleman who served at one time as the military governor of a Siberian territory. Menshikov's younger siblings and the Arsenev sisters lived together in his home in Moscow during the Northern War. Daria married Menshikov in 1706. Auntie Not-So-Clever was Peter's pet name for Anisia Tolstaia. Katerina Herself Third was the signature of Peter's future wife and empress Catherine I. Peter and Paul were the infant sons of Peter I and Catherine (who were not yet married). Both children died in infancy.

68. Nikolai Karamzin (1766–1826), prose stylist and historian.

69. Lezgins (Lezguians, Lezgians, Lesghis): this term was used by Russians to designate inhabitants, regardless of the diversity of ethnicities in the region, of the basin of the Samur River from the Caucasus Mountains to the Caspian Sea south of Derbent.

70. Derbent is a port on the western shore of the Caspian Sea in the Dagestan region in present-day Russia. The city has changed hands several times since its founding in the fifth century. Through the Treaty of Gulistan in 1813, Derbent, together with the whole Dagestan province and northern Azerbaijan, was ceded to Russia by Persia.

71. A major port city at the mouth of the Volga River, near where it empties into the Caspian Sea.

72. An award given for military valor. All imperial Russian awards and honors had four grades.

73. Mikhail Vladimirovich Rodzianko (1859–1924), member of the moderate Octobrist party, President of the Fourth Duma, and Chair of the Temporary Committee of the Duma which helped constitute the Provisional Government. On the latter, see chapter 1, note 38.

74. A traditional Russian form of greeting for men and women.

75. The eighteenth-century palace that served after 1906 as the home of the Duma, Russia's parliament.

76. General Aleksei Alekseevich Brusilov (1853–1926), Supreme Commander-in-Chief of the army in 1917.

77. Political committees set up in the army by the soviets (councils of workers, peasants and soldiers) at the time of the February Revolution to serve as supervisory mechanisms on behalf of the soldiers. They often undermined military authority and discipline.

78. Aleksandr Fedorovich Kerenskii (1881–1970), served in the Provisional Government as Minister of Justice (March 3–May 5), Minister of War and Navy (May 5–July 2), and Prime Minister (July 25–October 25).

79. The former Imperial residence; after the February Revolution, the Winter Palace became the headquarters for the Provisional Government.

80. That is, the battalion's flag.

81. Lavr Georgievich Kornilov (1870–1918), Commander-in-Chief in Petrograd, later to replace Brusilov as Supreme Commander-in-Chief.

82. A service of thanksgiving.

83. An honor bestowed on members of the military for valor in battle or meritorious service.

84. Additional women's battalions had been formed elsewhere on the model of Bochkareva's.

85. An important port city in the far east of Siberia.

86. Although the Provisional Government had been overthrown, some of its embassies remained in place abroad, awaiting the outcome of the Civil War.

87. Emmeline Pankhurst (1858–1928), usually referred to as "Mrs.," was a leading figure in the British suffrage movement. On a visit to Russia in 1917 she had declared Bochkareva "the greatest woman of the century."

88. George V (r. 1910–1936), who was a cousin of both Nicholas II and Empress Alexandra.

89. A major port city in northwestern Russia and entry point for Western Allied military support for the Whites.

90. Marushevskii was commander of the Arkhangel'sk front.

91. Major General Frederick C. Poole, Commander of the British Expeditionary Forces in Russia.

92. From this point on, presumably the dates are New Style.

93. Evgenii K. Miller, interim head of the Arkhangel'sk government.

94. Anti-Bolshevik forces in Eastern Russia commanded by Admiral Aleksandr Vasilevich Kolchak (1871–1920), nominal head of the White movement.

95. Bochkareva misremembered the name. In fact, she is referring to Captain B. A. Vilkitskii (1885–1961).

96. Bochkareva had married Afanasii Sergeevich Bochkarev in 1905.

97. *Shtabs-kapitan*, one rank above her present rank of lieutenant (*poruchik*).

98. General N. N. Golitsyn, main commander of Russia's volunteer detachments.

99. Bochkareva does not identify the fourth officer.

100. General K. V. Sakharov, Commander of the Northern Army and Commander-in-Chief of the Western Siberian front.

101. A regional capital just to the east of Tomsk.

102. The military branch of the Cheka (the Soviet political police).

5. Religion, Piety, and Spiritual Life

INTRODUCTION

Religion remains among the least studied aspects of the history of Russian women during the imperial period. Until recently, relying chiefly on the writings of prerevolutionary lay critics of the Orthodox Church, historians generally have emphasized the ways in which religious institutions and beliefs served to reinforce patriarchal social and political structures and, thereby, limited and oppressed women. Social and cultural historians similarly have noted how the efforts by the Orthodox Church to impose its moral and social ideals challenged and restricted the social and ritualistic roles played by women in medieval and early modern Russia. More recent scholarship, by contrast, has shown the importance of religion as a source of identity, self-expression, spiritual fulfillment, and even authority for women during the imperial period, as well as the ways in which religion provided both women and men with a means to resist political, ecclesiastical, and other forms of authority. Hence, while religion clearly exerted a strong influence on the social and cultural lives and experiences of Russian women prior to the revolutions of 1917, it did so in diverse and often contradictory ways.

Nonetheless, three broad trends with respect to women and religion are discernable throughout the imperial period. First, while the overwhelming majority of Russian women continued to profess religious beliefs to a greater or lesser extent, processes of cultural change and educational development initiated or accelerated by the Petrine reforms contributed to the growth of religious indifference and militant secularism, especially among elite and educated women. Second, the schism in the Russian Orthodox Church and the appearance of mystical Christological groups in the late seventeenth century, as well as the exposure to forms of evangelical and dissenting Christianity later in the nineteenth century, resulted in greater religious fragmentation and diversification among women, thereby making religion a more personalized source of identity for many women. Different religious groups, moreover, often assigned different roles to women, thereby adding a religious dimension to the dialogue over the nature of women and their appropriate social roles. Finally, the nineteenth century witnessed a remarkable growth in the expression of religiosity by women, both in their actions and through writing and art. The religious experience of women in imperial Russia thus paralleled that of European women generally at this time in its diversity, complexity, and apparently conflicting developments.

Indeed, the breadth of religious diversity among Russian women should be emphasized. The overwhelming majority of Russian women, of course, adhered to the Orthodox faith and thus accepted the legitimacy and authority of the state church. Although its position as state church was a mixed blessing, the Russian Orthodox Church nonetheless enjoyed considerable privileges with respect to access to state authority, state subventions and reinforcement of doctrinal positions, and the ability to evangelize and conduct missionary activities. Despite these advantages, however, and the severe restrictions imposed on the activities of other organized religions and religious groups by the state, particularly prior to 1905, a significant number of Russian women could be found among the Catholic, Protestant, and Jewish populations of the empire. Women also figured prominently in the schismatic and sectarian groups that began to emerge in the late seventeenth century, to the point that contemporary Orthodox observers often attributed the strength and growth of Old Believer communities chiefly to their female members. It is clear that the number of Russian women belonging to such groups, as well as to evangelical Christian movements, was increasing rapidly in the late imperial period. Hence, the range of religious experience and expression among Russian women under the empire was extremely broad. The impossibility of doing justice to such a wide range of religious groups has led us to concentrate in this chapter on Orthodox women, who composed by far the largest group.

Even among Orthodox women, however, the range of religious experience and expression was broad, differing by social position, educational level, cultural ambiance, and geographic location. An illiterate peasant woman living in a remote village, for example, generally experienced and understood Orthodoxy, and expressed her religiosity, in different ways than did a well-educated and well-traveled noblewoman or a cultured *intelligentka*. Indeed, it has been argued that the "popular religion" of the peasantry did not constitute a form of Orthodoxy at all, but rather consisted of a syncretic amalgam of paganism, folk beliefs and traditions, and popularized Orthodox rituals and practices. This argument, too, has been challenged by recent scholarship, which emphasizes the legitimately Orthodox components of peasant religious beliefs and practices and locates the distinctiveness of popular Orthodoxy in the differences between "premodern" and "modern," or "popular" and "cognitive," forms of Christianity in general. In any case, while the differences in the religious experiences and understandings of Russian Orthodox women must not be disregarded, they should not be overemphasized either. Despite local variations, Russian Orthodox women shared common liturgical, iconographic, and sacramental worlds, recognized common saints and a common deity, and turned to the latter for comfort and intercession in times of need. For most Russian women, the major milestones in their lives and many of their daily activities were accompanied by Orthodox rituals and invested with religious meaning.

These rituals served to reinforce Orthodox ideals and teachings that sought to define norms of behavior, moral values, and appropriate social and religious roles for women. Women were enjoined to defer to the authority of their parents and husbands, for example, to deny themselves in working for the material and moral welfare of their families, to concentrate their activities on the fulfillment of their domestic responsibilities, and to confine their sexuality to marriage and the purpose of procreation. A variety of rituals and proscriptions emphasized female uncleanness, and women were barred from clerical functions. Exceptionally strict observance of religious ideals, conversely, enabled some women to gain unusual authority or autonomy as Holy Fools, spiritual eldresses, or *chernichki*, i.e., single women who lived pious, ascetic, and celibate lives alone in a peasant village and who supported themselves through craft work, reading the Psalter for the dead, and the performance of other religious functions. At least among the peasantry, women also appear to have played a disproportionate role within the local community in the preservation and transmission of religious culture.

Within this general context the imperial period witnessed a significant transformation in the relationship of women to the Russian Orthodox Church, although the sources and precise contours of this change remain largely unstudied. During the latter part of the eighteenth century and into the early nineteenth century, a domestic ideal of women that stressed their maternal and educative roles and their nurturing qualities came to predominate in official Orthodox writing. Religious activism and religiously based charitable work and social activism by women grew substantially during the nineteenth century, as did both the number of convents and the number of women entering them, to the point that by the early twentieth century Russian Orthodox monasticism had become predominantly female. Informal religious communities of Orthodox women also proliferated after 1764, when the state secularized monastic land holdings and closed a large number of convents and monasteries, and in the nineteenth century religiously connected nursing orders of women began to emerge. Such developments, in combination with the example of the roles now played by women in secular society and in religious groups such as the Old Believers (see the selections on E. V. Iguminshcheva and Anastasia Kerova in this chapter and that on the resistance of peasant women to marriage at the beginning of chapter 6), contributed to the growing pressure on the eve of the First World War for an expansion of the role of women within the Orthodox Church. The Council of the Russian Orthodox Church that met in 1917–1918 responded to this pressure by modestly expanding the voice of women in parish and diocesan governance and their role in other areas of church life.

THE RELIGIOUS RITUALS OF DAILY LIFE

The first two documents illustrate the pervasiveness and significance of religious rituals and symbolism in the lives of women at all levels of Russian society during the imperial period. For the overwhelming majority of Russian women, the main milestones in their personal life cycles and in those of their families were marked by deeply symbolic religious rituals that stressed the interconnections within the family and the community and among the human, divine, natural, and, often, supernatural worlds. Religious fasts and festivals also played prominent roles in structuring the yearly life cycle of Russian women, providing them with opportunities not only for spiritual expression but also for celebration, amusement, and sociability. Even on a daily basis, many of the household tasks performed by women were influenced by religious beliefs, accompanied by religious rituals, and given religious meaning. Religious rituals, practices, and symbols, too, provided women with a medium through which they could both express their spirituality and attempt to influence their world and their personal lives. The popular religion of the peasantry in particular has often been described as a mixture of beliefs that expressed an animistic and supernaturalistic view of a world inhabited by willful and arbitrary demons, spirits, and similar forces, which, nonetheless could be manipulated or invoked to deal with or prevent disasters or otherwise affect the circumstances of one's life. Regardless of whether one accepts this view of peasant religion, women from all social groups clearly called on Christian saints and especially the Mother of God to intercede on their behalf when they encountered difficulties or distress in their daily lives. Observing and participating in religious rituals and practices also constituted powerful mechanisms of social and cultural integration and differentiation, both within and between local communities and within and between social, ethnic, and religious groups. Since some religious rituals were performed exclusively either by women or men, observance and participation also helped define gender roles. In short, religious rituals heavily influenced and gave meaning to the daily lives of Russian women, regardless of the social group to which they belonged.

A. Peasant Rituals

As the following selections demonstrate, religious symbolism, ritual, and practice infused nearly every aspect of peasant life, helping structure and reinforce its fundamental institutions and relationships. The religious rites and customs that accompanied birth, death, and marriage, for example, emphasized the importance of the family and supported its internal structure (for marriage customs, see also the selection on peasant practices in chapter 3). Religious fasts and festivals also helped delineate the annual rhythm of village life and provided occasions for important social activities, such as courtship and marriage. As the selections also make clear, Orthodox Christian beliefs and symbols, earlier pagan practices and beliefs, folk traditions, and a belief in the malevolent actions of witches and sorcerers (see the documents on witchcraft in this chapter) coexisted and intermingled in peasant religious culture, providing a rich medium through which peasants both understood and attempted to influence their environment and their individual and collective fates. Within this religious culture, different roles frequently were assigned to women and men, so that the expression of female and male religiosity varied in significant ways. Moreover, it appears that women bore the primary responsibility for preserving and transmitting village religious culture, which may help explain their prominence in efforts to protect religion and religious institutions from the challenges that arose in the late imperial and early Soviet periods.

Like the selection in chapter 3, these excerpts are taken from the 1853 issue of Ethnographic Collection. *They relate to districts in Nizhnii Novgorod and Tver provinces, both of which are located in the central industrial region of Russia, east and north, respectively, of Moscow. Both accounts were provided by local parish priests and therefore reflect the perspective of an outsider to the peasant community, one who was educated in an Orthodox seminary and who most likely was originally from the clerical estate. As the variety of such documents demonstrates, the sources and character of peasant religion made for significant variation in content and expression from place to place. Peasants belonged to a wide array of religious groups, with religious boundaries often running through, as well as between, villages (as examples, see the documents relating to Kerova and Iguminshcheva in this chapter). Such diversity suggests that care must be taken in drawing general conclusions about peasant religious culture and its impact on women.*

When a village is threatened with an epidemic (for example, the recent cholera), several old maids—elderly, unmarried women known for their Christian way of life—will meet at night and walk together in a circle around the village, carrying an icon and lighted candles in their hands and singing religious songs. Some of them walk behind with a plow, plowing the earth in the absolute certainty that no plague can cross the line they make. At the stroke of midnight, one of the girls will steal up to the bell tower and begin to ring the bell, sounding the alarm. The frightened villagers come running out of their houses, looking around in all directions to see if there's a fire somewhere; seeing nothing, they run to the church, and, meanwhile, the girl slips away unnoticed. They say this is directed at the witch who inflicts people with the deadly plague, to scare her so that she won't dare come near the village.

During a cattle plague it is customary to hold a public prayer service out in a field. All the livestock are herded through a deep, specially dug ditch, with a wood fire burning at its entrance.

During Holy Week,[1] the women, girls, and young men put on their best clothes and go outside; the streets fill with young people—happy, healthy, and handsome: they are all overjoyed at the coming of a fine spring and the warm sunshine; they dance and scatter across the soft green grass like a flock of butterflies. Beginning with the first Sunday after Easter, everyone runs outside the church after mass, and all kinds of games begin; several groups form for round dances and the air fills with the sounds of happy singing. Then, every evening up to the Fast of Peter[2]—or as the country people call it, the *rusalkas'* feast day—especially on holidays, all the young people gather on the open square in front of the manor house to amuse themselves; several large circles form, singers gather into choirs, and musicians appear with horns, maple-wood flutes and reed pipes, concertinas, balalaikas, and fiddles. The singers sing happy songs, and the musicians play their instruments; two by two, young couples come out into the center of one of the circles, and a dance begins; in another circle, a game of tug-of-war starts up; in a third, they play tag. In one place children play; in another, old people watch the young ones enjoying themselves, recalling the times of their youth, wondering how their own hot, playful blood could have cooled so without their noticing it. On Trinity Sunday[3] everyone gathers on the square after dinner, and a single, long line forms for the round dance. Playing music and singing happy songs, they head for a small, nearby grove; there, after various games, the young people weave themselves wreaths out of green twigs and spring flowers, which they put on their heads. Thus adorned, they walk to the big lake, where they throw their wreaths into the water, and in the evening they return to the square and enjoy themselves until dawn. The young people also gather on the square during the *rusalkas'* feast. They dress someone up as a horse, with a bell suspended under his neck and a boy mounted on his back, and two men lead him by the bridle out into the open field, with the whole line of dancers following behind, singing loud songs of farewell. When they reach the field, they play various games, removing the horse's costume, "unfrocking" him. This is called "saying farewell to spring."

The local people are so blinded by superstition that they attribute even divine punishments to magic spells cast by *witches* and *sorcerers*. For example, the cattle plague in 1847 was attributed to the evil spells cast by dogs and pigs that were believed to be *werewolves*, and so during the plague several dogs and a pig were destroyed. And there were so many tales during the cholera of witches, werewolves, and sorcerers who the people believed were causing people to die! In fact, to this very day some of the local villagers still deny that the cholera was sent down by God as a punishment for the people's sins; the majority continues stubbornly to believe that it was a spell cast by evil witches and sorcerers.

CUSTOMS ASSOCIATED WITH CHRISTENING

The parents of a newborn baby choose the godparents from among their relatives and friends. They choose people who don't have children themselves or who have many, or, leaving the choice to God's will, go outside on the day of the christening and approach the first person they see, begging him to be the godparent, persisting in the certainty that this person was sent by God and that the baby's life may very well depend on him. The christening follows church ritual. After the Holy Sacraments the godfather drops a piece of wax with some hair from the baby into the font and watches to see whether it will sink; if the wax sinks, it means that the baby will die; if it doesn't, then it will live. Experience shows that the wax never sinks, but babies die very often; nevertheless the superstition persists to this very day. Afterward a dinner, or so-called *kashi*, is held. At the beginning everyone drinks toasts to the health of the newborn baby—the "newly birthed," as the peasants say—and of all christened folk as well, saying, "God grant the newborn baby and all christened folk bread, salt, and good health."

I feel it necessary to note that the peasants don't wash the new baby for six whole weeks after the christening, until the time comes for the mother to undergo the forty-day or purification prayer,[4]—so as not to cause the baby's mouth to "bloom," i.e., to develop milk-blisters. It's hard to imagine the terrible state of un-cleanliness in which the baby is kept during this time, and the bad smell that re-sults.

WEDDING RITUALS

On the day of the wedding ceremony the princess[5] gets up early, sits on the bench at the door of her house, and starts wailing again: "Dear father NN and dear mother NN, did you have a deep, peaceful sleep? Me, poor orphan that I am, I didn't sleep all night long: I spent the whole dark night thinking bitter thoughts." If the ceremony is taking place on a Sunday or holiday, the prince and princess arrive at the church for matins; the prince wears a white sheepskin coat and a blue *armiak*,[6] open in the front; the wedding kerchief he has tied around his arm distinguishes him from all the other men; it remains hanging on his arm throughout the wedding ceremony. The princess wears a fur coat, white or covered with nankeen or woolen cloth. In addition to the usual scarf worn over her hair, her head is covered by a long, broad white veil made of thin homespun linen or other fine cloth; the bride hides her face behind it from shame throughout the service. In church, the prince and princess listen to the prayer to the Savior and the Mother of God. It is worth noting that throughout the entire prayer service and wedding ceremony the princess keeps her right hand wrapped in the long sleeve of her blouse, so that she will not have to do without and will live in prosperity. The prince goes straight home from the church, while the princess, wailing loudly, visits her family graves. She stays at the cemetery for a long time, wailing and lamenting all her deceased relatives; she invites them to her banquet and asks them all for their blessing for her new life, saying, "Dear NN, I don't want gold or silver from you; I ask for your blessing as I go under the golden crown, under the silver to live with strangers." She wails the same refrain for the second relative, the third, etc., until she's addressed all her deceased relatives. A large crowd of women always stands and listens. Then she goes home, where she is met by her friends; the princess, wailing, tells them they will no longer see her virginal beauty. Finally the bride goes inside to await the arrival of the prince and the wedding party.

The prince comes for the bride in a *kibitka* drawn by a troika, fitted with numerous bells of different sizes, accompanied by the whole wedding party and bringing a barrel of beer. The guests sit down for a long dinner; those who drink alcohol get drunk; everyone partakes except the prince and princess, who do not eat or drink anything. After dinner the parents bless the princess: the father takes her icon and puts it on top of a loaf of bread sprinkled with salt; the princess bows three times before the icon and keeps her head bowed, and her father, holding the icon with the bread and salt, makes three circles with it over her head; then the princess kisses the icon, bows down to the floor, and in tears kisses her father, who is also weeping, three times. Then her mother takes her turn, blessing the bride with the icon in the same manner. Then she is blessed by her godfather and godmother, each using their own icons. All these icons will enter the household of the groom. During the blessing of the bride, the best man serves the beer brought by the groom to all the people standing outside, called the *pozoriane*.[7] After she has received everyone's blessing, the princess, weeping and wailing and covered by her veil, leaves her parents' home; the prince seats her in the *kibitka,* and all her closest friends gather around, wailing over her at the top of their voices. The groom drives the horses himself. Before they start off, the prince strikes the gateposts several times with his whip to make sure that his future wife will not miss her old home. The whole way home the best men ride along ahead of the prince, and those riding in the wedding party in front and behind sing loudly to let people know how well they were treated at the dinner. On their way out of the village, the wedding party stops, the best man goes back to the bride's house, gives a low bow from the prince and invites all the guests to come to his house, "the whole household except for the four walls." At that time the bride's friends say their good-byes to her. The party stops often along the way, and anyone who wants to drinks the spirits and beer brought along for the trip. Finally the procession arrives at the church, except for those who are too drunk, who go straight to the groom's house.

When they arrive, the prince and princess enter the church. The wedding follows the usual procedure. When the time comes to stand on the carpet,[8] the bride and groom try to step on it at the same time, for superstition has it that the one who steps first on the carpet will run things in their life. After the ceremony, the members of the wedding party ask the newlyweds: who is subordinate to whom? Instead of an answer, the princess bows down at the prince's feet and then kisses him, holding his head with her hands behind the ears: among the peasants this is considered the most sincere and, as they say, the warmest kiss: not everyone is kissed this way by the princess—only her closest relatives. Then the newlyweds are led to the refectory or onto the church porch, and the princess is "encircled," that is, her hair is fixed into the style for married women, two braids with a handful of flax woven in and a *volosnik*[9] and *soroka*[10] attached. After that the newlyweds are given a mirror, which they look into together, admiring each other. Finally, the bride is covered again with the same veil, and they leave the church; the prince seats the princess in the carriage, and they all set off for the groom's house, singing loudly.

When the newlyweds arrive home from the church, the father and mother of the bridegroom greet them with an icon and bread and salt. They bless them again, in the same way as when they were being sent off to the altar. Wise parents at this time admonish their children to love God, to obey the authorities, to honor their elders and to take care of them, their old parents. After the blessings, the best man seats the newlyweds down on a fur coat, helps them up, seats them down, and raises them up again, and seats them again a third time. He has them sit on a fur coat, rather than on the bare bench, so that they will not have to do without, and will live in prosperity. As soon as the guests have made their bows and congratulated the "good master" of the house and the newlyweds upon their legal marriage, the best man leads them into a spare room, where they have dinner alone together. On the day after the wedding the princess gives out gifts to the prince's relatives: the closer the relative, the better the gifts. They consist of linen towels of varying lengths. She begins with the prince's parents, and gives the gifts in the following manner: in the spare room the princess and the matchmaker determine who is to be given which gifts; the bride's best man carries them around to the recipients on a plate, one at a time. Holding the plate with the gifts in his hands, he stands in front of the bridegroom's father and begins to shout loudly: "Is there someone here present, a good man by the name of NN?" and, when no one answers, he continues: "Greetings to you and a hand-embroidered towel from the newlywed prince NN and the newlywed princess NN. Take this little thing, it will last you a long time; if it won't serve for your hands, maybe it will be of use for a foot cloth." At the same time the father is served a glass of beer or spirits, and the newlyweds bow down at his feet and lie there on the floor until he drinks it all and asks them to stand up. When he's finished, he takes the towel from the plate, wipes his lips with it, and tries to kiss the prince and princess; but the prince will not kiss him until he has used his own kerchief to wipe his father's lips, even if they are completely clean and dry. The peasants themselves do not know the meaning of this ritual. Gifts are given in the same way to the mother, addressed as "good mother NN," and all the guests, from first to last, great to small. The same thing is shouted to each of the guests: "Is there present here a certain NN? Greetings to you from good man NN, good mother NN, the newlywed prince NN, princess NN, this will last you a long time," etc. Each guest, after taking the gift from the plate, gives money in return to the princess, different amounts from each guest, according to their desires. When the distribution of gifts is complete, dinner is served. After dinner the guests from the bride's side of the family leave the bridegroom's home, with the bride wailing as she sees them off. In her lament she makes a deep bow to her dearly missed father, mother, brothers and sisters, etc., hitting her head on the floor.

On the third day after the wedding the princess removes her veil once and for all. In the morning, water is poured over the newlyweds, at the river or pond during the summer, by the well in winter. The guests spend a long time amusing and teasing each other and the newlyweds, until everyone is thoroughly drenched; then they go home, change clothes, and have dinner, and after dinner the new-lyweds and all the guests go out for a ride in two or three troikas with bells, singing songs. Others ride ahead, dressed in their finest clothes. In the evening the guests go home.

FUNERAL CUSTOMS

All the close relatives of the deceased come to the funeral. Women and girls wear white kerchiefs as a sign of their grief. When the deceased is carried out of the house, the women walk behind, wailing and keening loudly.[11] In the church they encircle the coffin, laying their heads on the sides of the coffin, and continue wailing. They are silent during the burial service, but when it's over, they again begin to wail, which they continue until the grave is filled in; then they go home and again wail loudly there. There are two funeral banquets for every deceased person: one on the day of the funeral and one six weeks afterward.[12] A special meal is served, which concludes with oat *kisel'* with honey. If the deceased drank alcohol, the memorial dinner includes spirits and beer; but if he didn't, it is not served. After dinner the relatives spend a long time wailing over the deceased.

Source: "Selo Ulianovka, lukianovskii uezd, nizhegorodskoi gubernii, sviashchen-nikom M. Dobrozrakovym" and "Byt krest'ian tver'skogo uezda, tver'skoi gubernii, sviashchennikom N. Lebedevim," *Etnograficheskii sbornik, izdavaemyi Imperatorskim geograficheskim obshchestvom* ["Village of Ulianovka, Lukianov District, Nizhnii Novgorod Province, Reported by Priest M. Dobrozrakov" and "Daily Life of the Peasants of Tver District, Tver Province, Reported by Priest N. Lebedev," in *Ethnographic Collection, Published by the Imperial Russian Geographical Society*], no. 1 (St. Petersburg, 1853). Excerpted from pp. 52, 54–56, 59–60, 184–92.

Translated by Carol Apollonio Flath.

B. Easter Period in the Merchant District

ANNA VOLKOVA

Anna Ivanovna Volkova (on Volkova, see chapter 2) here describes her memories of the rituals and customs associated with the Lenten fast and Easter celebrations. While her account depicts the purification of the individual and the home for the celebration of Easter in a merchant family, similar preparations would have been carried out by fam-ilies at all social levels. Women were particularly charged with carrying out, or super-vising, these household duties.

On Forgiveness Sunday[13] the entire family had to go to evening services. Afterward everyone assembled for tea, at the end of which all the servants gathered before Grandmother, bowed to her in turn, and asked forgiveness for all their transgressions, voluntary and involuntary. All the workers from the factory and clerks from the factory and office came together to Father and also bowed to him and remained in the room; after they finished paying their respects, Father rose and made a general bow with his head, with a request to forgive him, too. The factory workers and clerks answered in a chorus: "God will forgive you!"

Finally, toward eight o'clock in the evening, not long before supper, all the stepsons, daughters-in-law, sons, and stepdaughters with their children, the latter having come especially for this, assembled in the drawing room where Grandmother sat, and asked her [for forgiveness] in turn. She kissed each one and said: "God will forgive you, forgive me, too!" The same procedure was also arranged among the members of the family: younger brothers bowed to the oldest, the wife to the husband—that is, my mother to my father—children to their father and mother, to Grandmother, to their uncles and aunts. When the ritual of pardon was over, Grandmother invited everyone to the dining room for supper, and then everyone went to sleep in their own rooms, and the daughters returned to their respective homes. The ritual prescribed that married daughters were required to appear on that day to ask for their parents' forgiveness. A daughter came without fail with her husband and children of all ages, with the exception of nursing infants.

On Purification Monday[14] the servants began from early morning to clean the floors, windows, etc. Wooden tables were scraped with knives to get rid of all the evil spirits from Shrovetide. The entire family rose early and headed for morning services; then they came to have tea, not with sugar but with honey: the former was considered forbidden to be eaten during fasts; instead of white bread, which was also, in the opinion of the elders, forbidden during fasts, *kalachi, saiki, bubliki,* and *baranki*[15] were served. Dinner and supper all during Lent consisted of mushrooms in combination with vegetables; during the first, fourth, and final weeks of Lent, oil was not supposed to be served, that is, all food was prepared without oil. Softened dried mushrooms of all varieties and kinds were among the foods used; dozens of pounds of them were bought at the mushroom market during the first week of Lent. Then they served potatoes, grated, baked, or boiled; ground peas, radishes in slices, grated radishes; *kisels* made from peas and from cranberries; the ubiquitous cabbage, in big heads and as sauerkraut. Mushroom cabbage soup made from dried mushrooms, potato broth, pea soup, and similar victuals took the place of a main course; in the majority of cases they were cooked once a year in huge quantities and preserved in well-built root cellars and basements.

Easter was dealt with in our house with great solemnity. At night on the first day of Easter Week, after morning and evening services, all members of the family, including the children, who were awakened if they had not gone to church, gathered to break the fast in Father's rooms, as he was the eldest in the clan. Tables were laid in the hall; various kinds of food in diverse whimsical forms were prepared. Preparations for the Easter holiday began on the first days of Holy Week. For example, they made the form of a lamb out of butter, lying on a plate. Its horns were represented by a wax candle, cut in half and bent in the shape of horns; its eyes were made out of cinnamon; and in the lamb's mouth they put some greens, which hung down, depicting grass. The women made the *paskha* and *kulich* at home, which was an event and a special topic of conversation for the whole family, both the women and the men. Each tried to take part in preparations for the holiday. At nine o'clock in the evening on Holy Saturday[16] various appetizers were put on the table; in the middle of the table, between two large candelabras, on a huge platter was a big ham, decorated with greens and wrapped in white paper. After evening services they brought in the *paskha, kulich,* and eggs dyed red with sandalwood, and everyone sat down at the table, having exchanged kisses with each other and all the servants beforehand. Children were given a little bit of everything, and each time it seemed to us that they did not give us enough, so requests were made for additional helpings of favorite dishes, but these requests received no attention. In these cases our primary defenders before Mother were Uncle Vladimir and Mikhail Petrovich, who loved our mother very much, seeing in her the ideal of beauty and elegance.

Source: Anna Ivanovna Volkova (née Vishniakova), "Vospominaniia detstva," *Vospominaniia, dnevnik i stat'i* ["Recollections of Childhood," in *Recollections, Diary, and Articles*], ed. Ch. Vetrinskii [V. E. Cheshikhin] (Nizhnii Novgorod, 1913). Excerpted from pp. 7–12.

Translated by Adele Lindenmeyr.

MEMOIRS

Anna Labzina

The following excerpts from the autobiography of Anna Evdokimovna Labzina (1758–1828) reflect the complex ways in which Orthodox teaching and ideals regarding charity, marriage, and sexual relations helped shape the public and private lives and the self-identity of Russian women. For Labzina's background and the complex and conflictual relationship between her and her first husband, Aleksandr Matveevich Karamyshev, see chapter 3. As noted there, Labzina's conflict with her husband reveals a complicated pattern of interaction between traditional, Orthodox, and Enlightenment values.

I was already seven years old and had studied literacy, but my mother herself taught me to write, and she began to educate my heart, greatly with words and doubly so by example. In the countryside when someone happened to fall ill, my mother, eschewing medical assistance, ministered to all the illnesses herself—and God assisted her. She ministered to the desperately ill for entire days, and I was there with her serving the sick upon her orders as much as I could, given my age. At night she dispatched my nanny who willingly did everything that she was ordered to do. When she was among the dying I was always at her side, and throughout the suffering of the dying she prayed with sobs while kneeling before the cross. If a dying one was losing consciousness, she reassured him and comforted him with the hope of our Savior.

In this way the sick were put at ease so that they could await their death without so much fear. Often in such circumstances she prevailed upon me to read about the sufferings of Christ the Savior, which gave extraordinary comfort to the sick. Wherever she went she brought the peace and blessing of God with her. As the neighbors came to understand that my mother would minister to their needs, they began to bring sick people to her, and she never refused and with gladness accepted all of them, and only very rarely did they die. Moreover, she taught me various handicrafts and she fortified my body with a strict diet and she kept me outdoors regardless of the weather. I had no fur coat for the winter, and I wore nothing on my legs other than knitted stockings and boots. During the harshest frosts she sent me out on foot, donning everything of mine that was warm and dressed in a flannel housecoat. If my legs got wet from the snow, she did not order me to undress and change my stockings, but just to dry my legs. In the summer she woke me up when the sun had barely risen and she led me to bathe in the river. When we got home, she fed me a breakfast consisting of hot milk and black bread. Tea was unknown to us. After this I had to read the Holy Scripture and then get to work.

After bathing we immediately began our prayers, turning to the east and kneeling. Nanny and I read morning prayers, and how sweet it was then to pray with such an innocent heart! And at those times I loved my Maker all the more. Although I knew little of enlightenment, I was steadfast in the knowledge that God is present everywhere and that He sees, knows, and hears, and nothing remains secret from him so that it not be revealed. At that time I was very afraid that I would do something foolish, but the tender care of my benevolent and good nanny saved me from my pranks.

We sometimes arranged festive days for the peasants in the village. We would place tables in the middle of the courtyard. My mother would serve the peasants herself, and she would have us bring them beer and wine. When they returned home, I would lead them to the gates and wish them good night, and they would bless me. Very often mother herself went with me to the bathing area, and she would look out with reverence at the sunrise and relate to me the majesty of God, as much as I could comprehend at that time. She even taught me to swim in the deep section of the river. She did not want me to be afraid of anything, and at the age of eleven I could swim in a long and deep river without any help. I went boating in lakes and I steered them myself, and I worked in the garden and planted the beds by myself. My mother and I shared the work, thus lightening those bur-

dens that were beyond what I could get done alone. She never made me do anything that she didn't do herself.

In wintertime we would travel to town where we had another course of study.
Each week I went with her to the prison, and mother and I handed out money,
shirts, stockings, boots, robes, all this with our own hands and from our own earnings. If I came upon sick people I ministered to them, prepared tea and fed them,
and she did more than I. Early in the morning we washed together and bound ourselves with plasters. As soon as we showed our faces in the prison, everyone
shouted out and reached out their arms toward us, especially the infirm. Every day
we provided fare for the prison, including an especially light one for those who
were ill. Every week we fed the destitute at home, and she served them right next
to us at the table. As they departed she would distribute money, shirts, stockings,
and boots to everyone, or, to be more precise, to everyone who needed them, and
not a single poor person was left without her assistance.

There was one man at our house who had the responsibility to seek out the
poor and suffering, and he truly fulfilled this responsibility. My mother was often
ill herself, and at those times I visited the poor and the prison along with my
nanny, and we carried out her responsibilities and cared for the sick as she prescribed. Whenever someone died in prison, our servants were sent to cleanse the
body, which was then buried near our house. For the grievously ill she went to the
prison with a priest who offered salvation. Together they would carry out their
Christian obligation. She often sat with the priest in the prison deep into the
night, and they read and talked with those who were ill. Frequently the unfortunate confessed their sins in the presence of all of them, and this eased their con-
sciences. At these moments a joy radiated from her face, and she would embrace
me and say, "If you ever are in a position to do good deeds for the poor and unfortunate, you shall be executing God's law, and peace will reign in your heart.
God will anoint his blessing upon your head, and your wealth will multiply, and
you shall be happy. If you are poor and something is given to you, refuse it with
love so that your refusal will not anger the unfortunate. For your refusal you shall
be blessed, but even in your poverty you can do good: visit the sick, console the
suffering and angry. Always remember that they are as close to you as brothers,
and for them you shall be rewarded by the heavenly King. Remember and do not
forget, my friend, the instructions of your mother."

At last the day that had been fixed for our wedding arrived. Early in the morning my mother sat me down and began to speak, "Now, my friend, this is the day
on which you begin a completely new life, one you know nothing about. You
shall no longer be dependent upon me, but upon your husband and your mother-
in-law, to whom you should show unbounded obedience and true love. You shall
no longer take orders from me, but from them. My authority over you has come
to an end, and what remains is love alone and friendly advice. Love your husband with a pure and fervent love, obey him in everything; you shall not be submitting to him but to God, for God has given him to you and made him your

master. If he is cruel to you, then you shall bear it all patiently and oblige him. Don't complain to anyone. People will not come to your assistance, and all you will do is expose his weaknesses, and through this you shall bring him and yourself to shame."

I threw myself at her knees and wept, "I shall do exactly as you say, even if they become my enemies and tormentors."

I went to my ill mother and sat down. My mother-in-law had not left her. Throughout the night she said very little, and she seemed to be more or less sleeping; only from time to time she read her prayers. Morning arrived and at six o'clock the priest came, confessed her, administered the sacraments, and administered the last rites. After this my mother was at peace, but she requested that he come to her a little earlier. When he did come, she requested that he read her something relaxing, and she willed herself to sit up and to place the crucifix in front of her, and she asked my mother-in-law to take me away and to put me somewhere where she could not see me. When she had finished all of this, she summoned my brother and me to her. She kissed us and blessed us. She kissed my mother-in-law and nanny, and she summoned all the rest. She blessed all of them for their faithfulness and their attentiveness. After all of this, she lay down and began to pray, and she could no longer look at anything except the crucifix.

It was 10 o'clock in the morning on the 21st of July [1772]. She crossed herself three times and said something indecipherable, took a breath, and that breath was her last. There was no regret on her face.

They all remained as still as trees, but my mother-in-law sat and remained silent and just wept. My uncle started to say that he disapproved of my actions, that I should recall the word given to my mother at the end of her life "that you will endure and bear everything." "My friend, whom are you going against? Against God! Can you tear asunder those sacred bonds by which you are joined for all time? Who gave you this right to choose your own fate? You have always been taught to deliver yourself to the will of our Savior, and in Him alone to seek your solace and the fortress of your strength. How can you know, once you have left your husband, whether you will be content and happy, and that your conscience will not begin to trouble you? You will be exposing your youth to shame and censure, and your family will hear this and suffer. You will be disturbing the ground where your parents lie. Do you think that they will not suffer seeing you throw off all of the responsibilities of marriage? That alone should be horrible for you, and God's judgment will befall you. Do you really think that you are the only one in this world who suffers so much? Believe me, my dearest, there are marriages far worse and more unfortunate than yours, and there are wives who are left entirely alone, without friends, without support, but our Maker is still merciful to you. He gave you a sincere friend in your mother-in-law, and yet you still complain!" My mother[-in-law] suddenly threw herself on her knees before me: "I implore you on the grave of your mother and my grief: do not send me to my grave in torment! I assure you that Vera Alekseevna will not go with you. If he gains strength and I am not strong enough, then I promise that you need not accompany him, and I will stay here with you."

Then he [Karamyshev] became unwell. I sat alone with him in the evenings. He seemed very bitter to me, and I asked him, "What is troubling you? Is it your illness or something else?"

"I am growing weak. We have no children. My relatives will take back the little village that I own. What will you be left with? This pains me terribly!"

"My friend, you have begun to think about this rather late. Help is nowhere to be found. Don't worry, I shall be rich and in no way poor. My conscience is clear before God, and He shall not reproach me for anything. I am also innocent before you. I am beloved by everyone, not because of my merits, but all of this on account of the kindness of the Maker of all that is good. I have this treasure, so what more could I wish for? He has protected me and defended me up to this very minute, so why should He not forgive me in the future? Only if I were to abandon Him, but He would never abandon those who race to Him, and I have no other helper except Him!"

He looked at me with a grin and asked, "Would you consider it a sin to have another man besides me who would take my place and from whom you could have children? They would be dear to me because they would be yours, and that would comfort me very much. I have in mind such a person, in whom I could be confident that he would protect this secret and your honor. I know that the one of whom I am speaking loves you. Would you really refuse me in this?"

I stayed silent for a long time, because I had turned to stone when I heard that the one he wished to involve in this was the very one who should be my guide and mentor![17] Finally, I asked whether he was joking, in which case I would be infuriated. "No, my friend," he responded. "This is my true wish, upon which my peace of mind depends, and you should not refuse me, but rather you should obey!"

"In everything except this! This is the limit of my obedience and honor for you! Everything that you have done against me I forgave, but it impossible to forgive this! How and with whom would you want me to do this? I know that you are not well, for which you cannot reproach me in any way. Rest assured that I have learned to be virtuous before you, and none of your threats can divert me to dishonorable and abominable deeds! You can order me to do everything for you except for this shameful suggestion! I am surprised that you could speak to me about such a matter when you must surely know that I shall not heed you!" The flowing tears and sobs choked off my voice. . . .

He said, "You are so stupid! I thought that you'd finally wised up. You are now twenty-two years old, and it's about time that you stopped calling a sin and vice that which serves a person's pleasure, and I am sure that were you to think about this clearly and come to know this person, who loves you passionately, then finally you would agree with pleasure!"

"There is nothing for me to think about; you have my answer, and I have no wish to know such a person of whom you speak! It surprises me that you would know about his passionate love for me. If he told you himself, then how could he be so bold as to speak to you of such a dishonorable thing, in which you yourself would be a party? But if you brought the subject up on your own, then isn't the dishonor yours? Toward what end are you handing me over? Don't you think that this could efface me? From now on I shall conduct myself more cautiously with any man I meet so that I can be certain in advance that by my behavior I am keeping a very insolent man at the limits of propriety. You have forced me to speak the truth to you, that, in you, I never have and never had hopes of having a guide or mentor. Clearly, the Lord has deemed it useful that people completely unrelated to me would come and instruct me to be virtuous, but from you I have witnessed nothing at all except depravity! You are responsible for this yourself! The Lord has not left me an orphan here, and he has given me a father and benefactor[18] to whom my whole heart is open, and if you say another word about this to me, then I shall resolve to tell him everything about you, and to request instructions from my benefactor about what I can do in such grievous circumstances!"

Source: Vospominaniia Anny Evdokimovny Labzinoi, 1758–1828 [*The Memoirs of Anna Evdokimovna Labzina, 1758–1828*] (St. Petersburg, 1914; reprint, Cambridge, Mass.: Oriental Research Partners, 1974). Excerpted from pp. 5–6, 6–8, 21–22, 30, 42, 94–96. A full translation appears in *Days of a Russian Noblewoman: The Memories of Anna Labzina, 1758–1821*, translated and edited by Gary Marker and Rachel May (DeKalb: Northern Illinois University Press, 2001).

Translated by Gary Marker.

THOUGHTS AND TALES DEDICATED TO YOUTH

Maria Korsini

The following selection is from the same collection of essays and tales by Maria Antonovna Korsini from which her idealized depiction of the family was drawn (see chapter 1). As noted earlier, this volume was intended for young readers and consists of a series of edifying essays and fictional sketches. The excerpts here are from the introductory essay and demonstrate how nineteenth-century Russian Orthodox teaching influenced Korsini's conception of social relations, moral norms, authority, and appropriate spheres of personal and social action for men and women.

Foreword.

We receive our first impressions in our family, and the self-consciousness of the soul begins under the influence of our mother, father, brothers, and sisters; then educators help develop our abilities, and finally our encounter with outsiders—or with society—acts upon us.

But we see not only people. The boundless sky with innumerable heavenly bodies and the resplendent earth in its fascinating beauty also appear to us, and seeing them our heart throbs and our reason asks: "Universe, who has created you so wondrously?" The answer to this question is heard everywhere. It is repeated by voices flying from the sky, erupting from the ocean waves, and resounding in all earthly creations. All these voices name the highest force: the Infinite God.

With confidence in the existence of the All-Powerful Creator, we enter into completely new relationships, no longer with beings similar to us but with our Creator. Acknowledging before Him our weakness and insignificance, we feel fear; but experiencing every minute the blessings of the Divine force, we become inflamed with gratitude and love toward Him.

Observing nature, we are struck by the order, harmony, and beauty of the universe, which, as we see, is correctly fulfilling its purpose, and its unity is preserved by the fact that each of its parts executes the laws given to it. We also compose a part of this whole, and consequently we also must act in accordance with laws. But where are they? Nature cannot resolve this question. It is answered for us by inner voices, which originate from the depth of our soul and are called reason and conscience. They tell us that we, who are preserved by God, will insult him by doing ourselves harm. We therefore are obliged to preserve ourselves both body and soul, and while preserving ourselves we must also preserve those similar to us, who in relation to God have the same importance as ourselves. Thus we approach the principal rule of our life, or the foundation of all laws, which prescribes to us: love God as your Creator and Benefactor, with all your heart and all your soul; and love your neighbors as yourself. This law imposes obligations on us.

INTRODUCTION: LIFE.

Life is precious for everyone because it is the supreme gift of God. It depends on us whether we spend it in error, sorrow, and weakness or whether we sanctify and adorn each day with good. It depends on us whether we achieve true happiness in love toward God and our neighbor and in the fulfillment of our obligations. It depends on us whether this temporary life will be united, through faith and hope, with eternal life, so that already in this life a presentiment of eternal bliss will be enjoyed.

THE WORD.

Have you ever paid attention to the astonishing gradations that rule in all of God's creation? You know that a stone is the most insensible and, it might be said, the coarsest body; then follow crystals and metals. Another step, and you find more life and more sensibility in plants; ascend even higher, and there you meet animals. Finally, at the summit of the universe stands the most perfect and beautiful being: man.

In man is reflected the wondrous idea of the Deity, by which he is sanctified and separated from the rest of creation over which he rules. This incomprehensible stamp of God's omnipotence and blessing is expressed in man through the word.

In the word is invested the immortal spirit and unbounded thought. Without it we would not know what abilities we have been given nor what use to make of them. It is through the word that great undertakings are accomplished, destinies of people are decided, virtue is rewarded, and vice is punished.

Without the word we could not clearly understand either ourselves or others; without it we could not even think definably. Through the word we come closer to those who are similar to ourselves and share with them our feelings, so that it is as if we double our own life.

We feel an irresistible inclination to live among people and to tell others everything that happens to us—we feel the need of the presence of others.

FELLOW MAN[19] AND SOCIETY.

Our fellow man can be any man—a relative, an acquaintance, a friend, and an enemy. All people on earth compose one family, the protector and Father of which is God himself, which is why all people are brothers to each other. All of them are given an immortal soul and a transitory body; all are equally able to think, to feel, to desire, and to act. The joining of many people is called society.

The striving to live in society was instilled into the human heart by God Himself. In it, amongst those who love us, we reform our initial shortcomings and learn to enter into a crowd of unfamiliar people, who will demand from us the knowledge of established proprieties and will not forgive our shortcomings as generously as do our relatives.

From the encounter with worthy people we improve ourselves. Without society, work is useless and there are no true pleasures. Indeed, what would the purpose of living be then? Without our fellow man we would not have a clear understanding of God or of our own purpose.

NATURE.

One who understands and loves nature cannot be a depraved human being. As does everything beautiful, nature elevates the soul and directs it toward the good; its sympathy and caresses are accessible only to a pure heart. One should not, however, use its pleasures for evil ends. Always remember that you were created for good deeds, to help your fellow man, and not for incessant contemplation.

In our very insignificance we have the merit of having been created by God, who loves us with a tender and perfect love. He loves us because He summoned us from nothingness and made us alive with a ray of His Divinity—that ray is our soul. He loves us and, as our guardian Father, arranged everything in the world so that we could delight in everything. For a temporary habitation He gave us the flourishing earth, which is entrancing in its beauty and inexhaustible in its products. For us He kindled the sun and He adorned the moon with a diamond-like cool light. For us He illuminated the sky with the sunrise and stars and ordered the clouds to fly freely from one corner to another and to serve the earth: where with rain, and where with thunder and lightning. For us He gave the bird its voice and the flower its sweet smell, and He ordered the forest to provide shade and the ocean to roll with countless waves.

God loves us. He instilled in our hearts a strong striving to draw nearer to Him. In this striving is contained all the merits and all the virtues of man. In order to draw nearer to the highest spiritual blessing and perfection, it is necessary to elevate one's soul, to cleanse it of all earthly vanities, and to sanctify it with good.

LOVE.

In order to define man and his qualities, it is necessary to remember that he is a complex being composed of two different parts, body and soul, and that these diverse natures are inseparably united by God. Man cannot separately exist with only one or the other part, and his whole perfection consists in the fact that all the abilities given to him from above exist in permanent harmony: the lower ones, by submitting to the higher ones, would achieve their purpose.

You will easily understand that the body, which is created from the earth and which reminds us of the limited existence of animals, is much lower than the soul, which dwells reasonably and broadly within us. Our entire merit consists in the fact that our spiritual force always has precedence over and governs our physical force.

Look even at love, in its various forms, from two sides.

A child grows up; his spiritual abilities gradually awaken. How happy he is if from his early years he is given a clear understanding of God and of good! Then the first feeling of egoism is held within limits; then he will love himself for the sole purpose of preserving the most beautiful of God's gifts, his life, which he will try to adorn with true virtues. A secret voice will say to him: "Love your neighbor as yourself, he is a man just as you are—he is your brother!" A feeling of justice compels us to love those who are similar to ourselves, and the love of one's neighbor leads to the love of God.

If we express our attachment to God through unceasing prayer, outward service to Him, and fasting, and, in the meantime, we cannot withstand without grumbling the trials that He has sent us and we do not want to help our brother, then we love Him not with our soul but only outwardly, and He will not accept such love.

The soul will feel its Creator in the fulfillment of His will and in the constant activity of labor and service to one's neighbor. While the flame of Sacred love burns in it, the soul does not search for calm nor want rest, but on the contrary it wants to make sacrifices and calls for trials, and in them, as in a radiant crown, God appears to it. During the instant of such a close presence of God, the soul is ready to endure all earthly misfortunes.

We call love for our fellow man all feelings that in general are favorable to him; these have many shades. There is a general love, which we are obligated to have toward all people without exception. Perhaps it is the highest feeling on earth, but it is difficult to attain fully because then we have to sacrifice ourselves for everyone, and our fellow man receives no exceptional concern from anyone. Nature itself, as well as religion, invites us to love some people more than others, such as, for example, our family and those who have done something good for us. But there is much diversity even in these feelings. A mother loves her child differently than he loves her; we do not love those who are equal to us in the same way as we love those who are either superior or inferior in relation to us. That is why feelings are given different names: respect, esteem, benevolence, gratitude, indulgence, patronage, friendship, and many others, but all of these are only manifestations of love. From love, as from the center of the sun, flow countless rays, which spread out and beneficially fill our hearts to the extent that each can accept.

From everything that I have told you, my young readers, you have seen the relationships in which you find yourself with respect to everything that surrounds you. By examining nature, and by coming closer to people who are like us, we invariably approach an understanding of God.

With the thought of a higher Being we acquire a consciousness of good and evil, that is to say, a conscience awakens in us. This mysterious Lawgiver—and our Judge—prescribes for us the obligations that will lead us to virtue and to true happiness.

Source: M. Korsini, *Mysli i povesti, posviashchennyia iunoshestvu* [*Thoughts and Tales Dedicated to Youth*] (St. Petersburg, 1846). Excerpted from pp. 6–59.

Translated by William G. Wagner and Igor Timofeyev.

DIARY OF A YOUNG NOBLEWOMAN, DOUBTS ABOUT RELIGION

The young woman studying in Geneva (see chapters 2 and 4) here shows evidence of a more serious and independent nature, reflecting on her view of God and those who profess to be Christians but do not seem to follow Christ's teaching. In this selection, as in the earlier ones, the diary form reveals the emotions surrounding these issues.

—————————

5 MARCH [18]65

There was a large religious gathering yesterday at the country estate of M. Merle d'Aubigné.[20] We also were invited. Lise Erucolloff said that she found these gatherings ridiculous; Lina D., the A-za sisters, and I, on the other hand, enjoy them very much. Lise said that churches are for prayers, and that gardens and parks are for enjoying oneself; I replied that since God was everywhere, one could and should pray everywhere; she said that it was not the fashion in Russia; we told her that when we return to Russia we will introduce the fashion there; she said that they would put us in prison, and we told her she was silly. At that moment, we heard the voice of M. Merle d'Aubigné from the balcony: "Christianity without charity is not Christianity." Lina D. poked me with her elbow, saying, "It will be impossible for me to be a Christian, since I detest fat Lise more every day." I didn't say anything, but I became sad, troubled. As much as I can understand, the world only judges by [the profession of] Christianity, but I don't see where there is any charity. Certainly, there are great missionary and philanthropic works, but people's relations with each other are grumpy and dubious. M. Merle d'Aubigné said "Charity isn't done by words, but by one's heart and one's life." I would like to know M. Merle more closely; I would ask him how to behave.

15 MARCH 65

I have written to Mummy that I have not made my devotions and that I don't want to do them. The truth is that I don't like these long church ceremonies; I pray much better alone, in my room. But for some time, I haven't prayed at all.... I'm afraid of God. I'm afraid of returning to Russia. Why do I have to go there? Because God wishes it, Mlle. Pellet tells me. In that case, God is not a good God, if he wants something that is so hateful to me, and so I weep, I feel abandoned and . . . I do not love God.

Source: Shchukin, vol. X. Excerpted from pp. 396–401.

Translated by Christine Holden.

POPULAR PIETY AND RELIGIOUS DISSENT

A. Isidora (Daria)

The next five selections illustrate various forms of popular piety and religious dissent. The first relates in idealized form the life and religious exploits of a peasant woman named Daria from Novgorod province.[21] *Despite the didactic character of the account—it appeared in a collection of lives of spiritual ascetics meant to serve as examples for emulation—it conveys the deep piety of its subject. It also demonstrates the ways in which such piety could provide peasant women with a degree of autonomy, status, and even authority. In this instance, once Daria's familial obligations had been fulfilled, her extreme piety enabled her to gain considerable control over her movement and activities. Despite the precariousness of her existence, she was able to travel widely throughout the empire as a pilgrim, receiving both spiritual and material support on her many journeys. As a single woman who had adopted a religious form of life Daria enjoyed a greater ability than most women to undertake religious pilgrimages. Nevertheless, the phenomenon was widespread in imperial Russia, with women from all social backgrounds and even empresses regularly making such journeys. Similarly, despite Daria's humble origins, her ascetic practices and reputation for piety eventually gained for her a measure of spiritual standing and authority even among the upper strata of society, although she does not appear to have attained the status of an "eldress," that is, a spiritual guide and teacher. As Daria's experiences suggest, then, Russian Orthodoxy presented Russian women with a complex mixture of boundaries, limitations, and opportunities.*

Dariushka[22] was born into a peasant family at the beginning of the second half of the eighteenth century. Her parents died when she was only fifteen years old, and at this young age she had to care for a younger brother and sister. They were all taken in by their grandfather, a peasant of Novgorod province who was well known in the district and respected by all for his piety and brotherly love. Here is how Dariushka herself subsequently described her life in her grandfather's home in her reminiscences:

"We lived with grandfather and loved him, in place of father and mother. Grandfather was literate and lived by the word of God. As soon as the daily work was finished, he would take a book and begin to read aloud. He owned many books: the Gospels, the Bible, and a *Chetii-Minei,*[23] as well as many others. He had a calm disposition, disliked empty speeches, and was extremely sympathetic to people of God, that is the poor and the destitute. The whole family obeyed him without complaint, even though he never raised his voice but taught us everything so calmly and with even-temperedness. None of us ever began anything without a prayer, and everyone hurried to finish the most distant work by the time that grandfather would take up a book. Not only his family but also neighbors would gather in our hut with their domestic work—some spun, some wove, and some sewed or knit. It was so quiet that a fly flying past could be heard; no one uttered a word, and all that could be heard was the unhurried reading of the seventy-year-old man. And he read, and as he read he would stop and begin to explain how one should observe the law of our most gracious Savior and listen to His holy saints. We observed all the fasts and went to church on Sundays, never excusing ourselves due to work or lack of time. 'For this the Lord gave us six days,' grandfather taught us. He did not like young people's gatherings or round dances,[24] and it never entered our head to go outside: it was peaceful, calm, and good in our little hut. Our spiritual father often came to visit grandfather and we would all chat together and it was good."

So passed Dariushka's maidenly years. She had her comforts and consolations, but these were not at all the sort that girls of her age usually seek. About twelve versts from their village stood the Goritskii convent,[25] the nuns of which were beloved by the peasants in the surrounding area for their piety and good works. Dariushka's only real joy and outing was a journey to the Goritskii convent in her free time, which was quite rare. On major holidays she always went there on a pilgrimage. There she was moved by the sweetness of the harmonious church singing, she took pleasure in the duration and grandeur of the liturgy, and she loved to converse with the nuns, who themselves quickly became accustomed to her and attached to her good, meek, humble, and mild spirit. Dariushka received help from them in word and deed, and comfort during the difficult moments in her life.

As Dariushka's brother and sister grew older, the concerns for them and the thoughts for their future multiplied. Moreover, as their grandfather grew older, their material welfare and the household economy became disordered, too, and fell with all their weight on Dariushka. But her meek and humble obedience to the will of God gave her the strength to bear even these unbearable worldly burdens. Soon after, her grandfather died. Dariushka was able to manage the household economy by herself and to maintain her brother and sister until, finally, the former married and the latter found a husband.

Being left completely alone as a result, Dariushka finally felt the weight of her joyless life. A single, solitary, complete orphan! . . . And from this moment began her ascetic life of pilgrimage, in which she again found serenity and happiness. Dariushka wandered in this way for three or four months and then returned to her peaceful hut and again became an indefatigable worker, thoughtfully looking out for any opportunity where she could help someone at the cost of her own peace and labor. In her every word, in her whole life, there was so much love for each of God's creatures that her heart overflowed with a deep feeling of compassion, love, and *sympathy*, if it can be so expressed, not only for the "people of God" (which is what she called everyone, men, women, and children) but also for animals, plants, the sea, and insects; everywhere and in everything she loved God's creation, which was so dear to her. It was comforting to talk with her, and in their grief everyone who knew her turned to her, seeking from her sympathy and consolation. She especially loved her "relatives," as she called the poor and the destitute, orphans and widows. But for Dariushka this was little. Her loving heart did not allow her to be alone for long, and, indeed, after her brother and sister had died, she took in the latter's daughter, her favorite niece, Nastiusha,[26] caring for her with truly maternal love and instilling in her her own good spiritual qualities of meekness, piety, and humility. She frequently took Nastia on pilgrimages, and when Nastia subsequently reached the age of sixteen, she entered the Goritskii convent.

Thus for a long time life passed modestly for the humble Dariushka, who, in her humility, liked to call herself a "bad person," a "fool," a "madwoman," and so on. During this time, as she said, "the Lord carried her to all the holy places of mother earth." Whether she was leaving on or returning from a pilgrimage, her first thought was for the holy Goritskii cloister. Among the sisters of the convent, mothers Feofania and Varsonofia exerted a special influence on Dariushka.

During Dariushka's absence on a pilgrimage to Kiev in 1845, the ecclesiastical leadership summoned the nun Feofania and several selected sisters, including Varsonofia, to St. Petersburg to organize a new convent there (the Convent of the Resurrection). News of this struck Dariushka like thunder. After briefly thinking the matter over, she herself set off for Petersburg to her "monastic-comforters," and in such haste that she forgot to take any warm clothing with her. This was the winter of 1846. Dariushka was already over seventy, but was fresh and hale; having come to her benefactresses, she never returned to the countryside.

Hence, Dariushka arrived and settled in Petersburg. But even here her wandering on local pilgrimages did not cease, nor did her feats for the sake of God and other people. Her soul ached and pined especially for her favorite comforter-nuns, chiefly mother Feofania, whom the Sovereign Emperor Nikolai Pavlovich[27] had charged with the difficult and responsible task of organizing a new convent. Despite all her simple-heartedness and worldly naiveté, the simple Dariushka understood with her loving heart the hard position of the new cloister and gave her entire soul to comfort her favorite mother, Feofania, and to help her in her sorrow and difficulties.

The position of the new convent really was unenviable. It had been granted a large area beyond the Moscow Gate, but there was no material assistance for the construction of the convent.

But with God's blessing and help from people of God, a wooden church and tower[28] first were built by the cemetery. At the behest and with the blessing of the abbess, Dariushka settled in this tower in order to collect voluntary donations from passing pilgrims for the improvement of the newly created cloister. Sometimes she was spelled by other eldresses, four in number, who lived in small cells at the cemetery and who sometimes brought her food. (The remaining [sisters] lived temporarily in a completely different place on Vasilevskii Island.[29]) The unpretentious and modest Dariushka prayed and labored and collected donations, never complaining of her solitude, even though it was difficult for her to bear. "In the summer there was nothing," she recalls of this period of her life, "and in the winter it became terrifying: not a bird chirped, not a dog barked, and even during the day there were few people! Only recruits (soldiers) sometimes passed by or peasants with carts—and the Lord sometimes brought a pilgrim."

The donations collected generally were modest and few, but sometimes Dariushka encountered wealthy donors. Once the Chief Procurator of the Holy Synod[30] visited her, and Dariushka related to him the sorrows of the new cloister. After this conversation with the elderly Dariushka, he visited Abbess Feofania and told her of his talk with Dariushka. Soon after this the tsar ordered that 25,000 rubles be allotted each year until the cells, church, and hospital had been constructed, and then other generous donors also appeared. And so Abbess Feofania and her associates, among whom not the least of which was the humble Dariushka, built the Convent of the Resurrection, "all with labor and tears, and with prayer and love for each human soul," as Dariushka put it.

Dariushka lived in Petersburg not alone for her comforters, the nuns, nor alone for the holy cloister. Here, as before, each free minute was spent on a pilgrimage. Having reached a very elderly age, Dariushka commanded unusual quickness afoot and loved to walk, overcoming frost, intense heat, and weariness. It was not easy for a young person to keep up with her. She never spoke of herself as "walking" anywhere, but always as "running." Usually in Petersburg she liked to rush from the Church of the Annunciation on Vasilevskii Island to mass at the Church of All Sorrows (on the corner of Hedge Street and Resurrection Prospect) or at Kazan Cathedral.[31] In order to afford her this pleasure, the abbess sometimes sent her on errands, to drop off a letter to someone among good acquaintances who greatly valued the visits of this simple, loving old woman. It is notable that wherever Dariushka was sent, she first went directly to Kazan Cathedral, where she attended mass and conversed with the poor, and from there she rushed off to All Sorrows, where she again prayed during the whole service, and then she carried out her errand or went wherever was necessary. Very frequently wealthy and prominent people would come to the mother abbess with a request that Dariushka be sent to visit them, especially if someone was ill or suffering from grief. Everyone loved this kind, simple, and modest old woman, with whom it was more comforting to pray and grieve. Passersby would frequently stop and look with surprise as an important gentleman in a magnificent fur coat would be sitting in an opulent sleigh and solicitously supporting a bent old woman in a shabby black jacket who was seated next to him, or some richly dressed gentleman carefully seated this old woman in his expensive carriage before seating himself. Indeed, this was a simple, poor old woman, but she brought comfort everywhere.

In general, Dariushka especially loved her "relatives," as she called the destitute and the poverty-stricken, widows and orphans. She rendered them many kindnesses, and for this these "people of God" strongly loved her.

The strength and simplicity of Dariushka's faith were so great that in any difficulty, whatever it was and whatever it concerned, she would seek heavenly help with a faith full of modest audacity, and through her faith she would receive what had been sought. She always explained every escape from difficulty as the result of divine help, never taking any credit for herself. We already have seen examples of this above in her guileless conversations. Once during the winter, when taking loaves of bread to a respected hermit, she lost her way in a forest and nearly died. At that point she audaciously asked "father Nikola the saint"[32] to lead her to the path, and, in her words, the bushes immediately parted. There then arose instantly in her a gratitude amazing for its sincere simplicity and ingenuousness: "Thank you, Nikola, God's saint." Her limitless faith did not permit her to doubt for a moment in divine help. In her conception, God's saints are always beside us, always ready to give us help, protection, and service.

Dariushka's humility was no less striking. Once that same "good mother" took her to mass and to see the much beloved Right Reverend Bishop at the episcopal residence. Sitting in the carriage during the journey, Dariushka was glad that she would see "a good service." But when, after the mass, they went into the bishop's rooms, she grew so timid that she would not yield to any persuasion and did not want to enter the drawing room, to the point of becoming angry nearly to tears when they tried to compel her. The others had to go in without her. Accepting the blessing of the beloved bishop, they told him about Dariushka and her refusal. The bishop, with his characteristic composure, hurried to leave his guests and go out into the hall to the poor Dariushka.

"Why do you not wish to come into my room, old woman?[33] Come here."

"And when, father, does a bad person go where the bigwigs sit? Supposing they throw me out."

"Well, you'll see what happens. Come in with me." The bishop led her into the drawing room and seated her beside himself in an armchair.

Dariushka sat and did not budge, hanging her head.

"And so, old woman," the bishop asked her, "have you been to God's church?"

"Of course I have, father."

"And the Lord accepted you and did not order you thrown out?"

"Why would He throw me out? No one is kinder than He. You have only to come to Him, and He is glad to accept everyone."

"Well, so do you see, old woman of God," the bishop then remarked, "if God is glad to see you in His church, then how can I throw you out of my manse? Indeed, I'm a human being, just like you, and I receive grace from the same God."

Dariushka's face brightened. She raised her head and said merrily, "Goodness, how clever you are, father, even though you're a bigwig!"

When the Convent of the Resurrection was completely built, each nun was given a cell, or as Dariushka expressed it, "a bright and pleasant little corner." Only Dariushka did not have her own special little corner, but she went from one sister to another, and they all welcomed the kind old woman with gladness. But she herself began to feel burdened by her wandering life and the absence of her own peaceful little corner. Her advanced years and the ascetic feats of her long life of many labors had begun to tell. Noting Dariushka's desire to have her own little corner, Abbess Feofania used this to persuade the old woman to take the veil.[34]

"And they were such kind mothers to me," Dariushka related, "that they prepared everything: a white curtain on the little window and a bleached bed with a pillow in the corner, and a little table, on which was a samovar, and a cup, teapot, and sugar pot were not forgotten, and in the right corner was an icon case with an icon, before which a lamp was burning, everything had been prepared as if for a monk. Save them, Lord, do not forget them, as they have not forgotten me, a poor orphan! And so he[35] began to live in his cell, to thank God and to prepare for that journey when it would be pleasing to the Lord to send for his soul."

Hence Dariushka's wandering life came to an end, and with the name of the eldress Isidora, she occupied the peaceful little corner assigned to her—something she had never before had in her life—in her favorite Resurrection cloister, beside her kind mothers.

About four months after Dariushka had taken the veil, when she was nearly eighty years old, at twelve o'clock on 1 July 1854, immediately after having received the holy Christian Sacraments and having been ill for only a day, Dariushka died from cholera. On that day, many of the destitute, whom Dariushka had loved so compassionately during her life, were treated to a memorial meal in the refectory and given money in memory of the late eldress Isidora.

Source: *Zhizneopisaniia otechestvennykh podvizhnikov blagochestiia 18 i 19 vekov (s portretami)* [*Biographies of Native Ascetics of Piety of the 18th and 19th Centuries (with Portraits)*], July (Moscow, 1908). Excerpted from pp. 16–32.

Translated by William G. Wagner.

B. Anastasia Kerova

The fate of the peasant widow Anastasia Kuzmina Kerova was very different from that of Daria. In the late nineteenth century, peasants from several villages in Samara district of Samara province[36] gathered regularly at Kerova's hut to hear her read and discuss the Scriptures and other holy writings. While continuing to participate in Orthodox services and sacraments, Kerova and her "followers" preached the necessity of temperance, moderation, aid to the needy, and adherence to a strict moral code of behavior. An informal religious community of women also formed around Kerova and eventually was transformed into an official convent, a phenomenon that occurred frequently in the late imperial period. Despite Kerova's evident piety, however, the local parish priest and several peasants from neighboring villages felt threatened by her activities and accused her of establishing an heretical sect. Investigating these accusations, Bishop Gurii of Samara charged Kerova with heresy and prohibited her from taking part in the services and sacraments of the Church until she acknowledged her false teachings, repented, and identified her followers. While reflecting the Church's growing concern over the spread of sectarianism, Bishop Gurii's pronouncements on the case also reveal a strong desire to maintain clerical control over the definition and preaching of Church doctrine and teachings. The following document is Kerova's repentance, made to archpriest Georgii Tretiakov and submitted by him to Bishop Gurii on 22 December 1893. Gurii accepted Kerova's repentance and granted her request to enter a convent, although he secretly instructed the abbess to confine Kerova to the convent and keep her isolated from its members as well as from her relatives and supporters. But Kerova apparently managed to maintain contacts with the latter, as Gurii ordered her to be exiled in 1897 and confined in a more distant convent. While again illustrating the authority that women could acquire through piety and asceticism, Kerova's case also raises an important question about the roles women were permitted to play in the Orthodox Church, an issue addressed directly in the selection by Liudmila Gerasimova at the end of this chapter.

In the Name of the Father and of the Son and of the Holy Spirit.

I, Anastasia Kuzminishna Kerova, who have signed below and am a peasant widow of the village of Rakovka, Samara district, having been born to Orthodox parents and baptized in the Orthodox Christian Church, all my long life have confessed the Holy Orthodox faith, as set forth briefly in the Orthodox Creed. I have always believed in the Holy Conciliar and Apostolic Church, in the Sacred leadership of this Holy Church established by God, and in the Holy salvific

Sacraments of the Christian Church, and with all my heart and all my soul I wish
to quit this earthly life in unity with the Orthodox Church and in communion with
Christ our Savior and Lord, having partaken in His Purifying and Life-giving
Sacraments. If during the course of my life I have sinned in some way against
Christian truth and against the Orthodox doctrine of the Church of God, then
this was done not in opposition to or rejection of Its salvific doctrine, but due to
my ignorance and foolishness. I myself am unable to understand or make sense of
how I have become known as the heretic-teacher of a sect, the so-called Mon-
tanists[37] or Khlysty,[38] who as all know deny the necessity of belonging to the Holy
Christian Church, believe in salvation without priests or spiritual Fathers, and,
among other errors and false doctrines, propagate the soul-destroying teaching of
irresponsibility for the crimes and the depraved vices of extramarital life, even ele-
vating—so I have heard—such a shameful and in truth impure life to the level of,
it is terrible to utter, a virtue and a salvific feat.

Having been left a widow at a young age, neither by my teaching nor by my life
have I given any cause for the violation of the sanctity of marital life and the per-
missiveness of life outside it. . . . Thinking over how and why I have become
known as a heretic-leader of the Khlysty sect, I have come to, for me, the sad conclusion that this good turn may have been done me by my admirers, who in popular rumor are known as followers of my teaching . . . and by my teaching have I
not given cause for my admirers to use the basic thoughts of my teaching to construct from them a clearly false doctrine, by its very essence contrary to Christian
truth and all Orthodox Christian dogma. . . . I am deeply guilty of anticipating
the right to teach which belongs only to priests and teachers of the Church and
which the Holy Apostle Paul explicitly denied to women, and I sincerely and
frankly repent of this, my sin and error. But I fell into even this sin and error for
no other reason than ignorance and thoughtlessness. It was only after the speech
addressed to me by Your Reverence and after the conversation with the spiritual
guide appointed by Your order to look after me that I became fully convinced that
I had appropriated a right not belonging to me, and I tearfully beg Your Reverence to forgive me this sin and error. The very fact that I, a woman, allowed myself to teach without any permission of the Diocesan authorities to do so perhaps
gave my admirers, especially among the men, a reason to audaciously and bravely
take up teaching—not their affair—and, despite my will and desire, develop their
teaching to the point where it became false doctrine, and, perhaps referring to me
as a famous personage, to develop and disseminate their false doctrines as if they
had been heard from me.

I am also deeply guilty of allowing meetings to take place in my home without
any permission of the Diocesan authorities and even without permission of the
local priest, and sometimes during the day, but more often during the evening and
at night, men and women and young lads and lasses came to me and gathered at
my house. At these meetings we read acathists,[39] prayed to God, read divine and
edifying books, sang psalms and spiritual panegyrics, and interpreted, as it came
into one's head, something from the Scriptures or the Apostolic epistles and in

general from the Holy Writ of the old testament. I myself now recognize and spiritually regret that, perhaps, someone among those present at the meetings by his incorrect interpretation was able to lead and led some into error. It is even possible that young people, leaving our meetings at night, on account of human sinfulness, engaged in impermissible relations and allowed themselves to do that of which it is shameful even to speak. Then out of remorse they used my merit as a teacher, or the reputation of someone among the incorrect interpreters of the Scriptures who had been at the meetings, to cover themselves and justify themselves. Hence, although not advocating debauchery, indirectly and seemingly unconsciously I was able, despite my wish, to further it, and for this I tearfully and ardently repent and ask for merciful forgiveness and resolution. But even here I can say with audacity that I permitted myself to hold even these meetings not out of opposition to Ecclesiastical authority, but due to ignorance of their unlawfulness. . . . When the directive was issued, I don't recall in which year, that these meetings could be held with the priest's blessing and even were possible in his presence, then I began beforehand to ask for this blessing, and the priest sometimes came to our meetings and sometimes gathered us in the school and there taught us and held discussions with us. But due to old age, I have not for already nearly three years, if not longer, had anyone come to gather at my house and have myself gone nowhere. I confess that I accepted offerings of bread and money and other things, and I distributed these offerings either according to the directions of the donors or at my discretion, and concealing no sin, I used [these offerings] myself and helped my relatives.

Although I myself cannot give an account of why and for what reason I enjoyed special honor both among my fellow villagers and among the surrounding population, they really rendered me this honor without my wish for it and expressed it by bowing down to me and by even kissing my hand. I also have nowhere ever been greeted with Holy Icons and lighted candles. I have always considered and consider myself to be the greatest sinner, I honor and worship the Sole Source of our salvation, the Most Blessed Mother of the Savior, our Lord Jesus Christ, and the most saintly Cherubim and the incomparably Most Glorious Seraphim. And so here are all my errors, which I tearfully, ardently, and sincerely repent. I would wish that the naked truth about me were known by those of my admirers who for reasons and convictions known to me not only think but also proclaim about me more than I am in fact. But submitting this, my wish, to the discretion of Your Reverence, I tearfully and prostrating myself beseech You, Most Merciful Bishop and Father, to pity me an old and cursed sinner, to remove from me the damnation by which You have bound me, to my great sorrow and despair, to forgive and resolve all willful and involuntary errors committed consciously and unconsciously, and to permit the spiritual guide appointed for me by You to accept my confession and to consider me, an unworthy and great sinner, worthy of partaking in the Holy Sacraments and the Blood of Christ, so that I can quit my earthly life in peace and union with the church and with Christ our Savior and thereby inherit eternal life. I find myself in such declining years that each minute is dear to me and I could even die without having confessed and having partaken in the Holy Sacraments.

This epistle was signed in her own hand by "the sinful Anastasia Kerova." Present were:

The Archpriest of the Samara Iverskii Convent Georgii Tretiakov

The priest of this convent Gavriil Formakovskii

Abbess Feofania

Treasurer and nun Sofia, in retirement Abbess Dorofeia

The young woman Marina Nikitishna Abramova, attendant of Kerova

Source: I. G. Aivazov, *Materialy dlia issledovaniia russkikh misticheskikh sekt.* Vyp. 1, *Khristovshchina*, t. 1 [*Materials for the Investigation of Russian Mystical Sects.* Issue no. 1, *Christism*, vol. 1] (Petrograd, 1915). Excerpted from pp. 349–53.

Translated by William G. Wagner.

C. Witchcraft

As earlier selections in this chapter demonstrate, Russian peasants believed in witchcraft and the ability of an individual to harm or injure people and animals by supernatural means, words, spells, and potions. Suspected witches might be either women or men, but between the emancipation in 1861 and the revolutions of 1917 women accounted for close to three-quarters of the individuals charged with witchcraft and sorcery. This predominance of women contrasted with the pattern in Muscovy, where the ratio of male to female witches had been almost seven to three. The feminization of witchcraft in the nineteenth century reflected a growing identification of women and their sexuality, if left unrestrained, as potentially dangerous to the patriarchal society in which peasants lived. While peasant violence against suspected witches ran contrary to the provisions of Russia's Criminal Code, courts often found it difficult to identify the perpetrators since peasants protected each other, claiming that the entire community had participated in the crime. The sources below illustrate two different examples of peasants taking extra-legal action against suspected witches, resulting in the death of the victims and court actions.

---

1. Agrafena Ignateva

On 4 February 1879 in the village Vrochevo, Derevskaia canton, Tikhvinskii district,[40] the fifty-year-old soldier's widow Agrafena Ignateva, who since she was a young woman had been considered to be a sorceress[41] who had the ability to hex people, was burned alive in her hut. For her part, Ignateva, not believing the premise that she was a sorceress, however did not even try to dissuade the peasants of this, using the fear that she invoked to live at someone else's expense. The conviction that Ignateva was a sorceress found support in several cases of nervous illnesses that struck peasant women in the same place where Ignateva lived.

Around Epiphany 1879 Ignateva came to the peasant Kuzmin's home and asked for cottage cheese, but they refused to give her any, and quickly thereafter his daughter, who during her fits shouted that she had been bewitched by Ignateva, fell ill. The peasant woman Maria Ivanova of the village Perednikovo also suffered from the same illness. Finally, at the end of January 1879 in the village Vrachevo the daughter of the peasant woman Ekaterina Ivanova Zaitseva, whose blood sister had earlier died of the same illness and cried out before she died that she had been bewitched by Ignateva, became ill. Since Ivanova shouted that she had been bewitched by Ignateva, her husband, retired private Zaitsev, filed a complaint with a constable who, several days before the burning of Ignateva, traveled to Vrachevo to undertake an investigation. The peasant Nikiforov asked the peasants to save his wife from Ignateva, who was allegedly about to bewitch her, just as the ill Ekaterina Ivanova had shouted.

They locked Ignateva up in her hut, boarded up the windows, and set it [the hut] on fire. Three of the participants were sentenced to a church penance, while the others were acquitted.

2. Maria Markova

On 15 December 1895 the Kashinskii circuit court and participating jurors[42] heard a case concerning a mistaken sorceress:[43]

The wife of the peasant Petr Briukhanov developed a typical case of "grand hysteria,"[44] the cause of which, according to popular superstition, involved spoiling.[45] The mother-in-law was suspected of being the source of the spell. Once, on the first day of Easter in the presence of his mother and neighbors, Petr Briukhanov gave his wife "holy water"[46] and asked her who bewitched her. "Your mother," answered Briukhanov's wife, and at the sight of her mother-in-law standing before her, her face suddenly became transformed, she jumped as though lifted up by her hair, sang something, and with convulsive movements lunged at the seventy-year-old woman, threw her to the ground, [and] began to drag her by the hair and to strike her all over her body, demanding that she "break the spell." Her husband joined her, and the two of them began to kick the old woman everywhere. All those present looked on without saying a word; when the old man-father tried to defend his wife, one of the peasants sat on his knees and would not let him get up, while another held the door. In the end, the peasant Vinogradov suggested that they throw the old woman into a cellar so that she could exhume the spell, and with that goal in mind he brought a rope, tied it around her neck, and dragged her to the cellar, into which he, together with others, threw her, after which they gave her a tool so that she could dig up the spell. Finally, when the old woman Maria lost all her strength, they left her in peace. Meanwhile, a crowd from neighboring villages, that by now had learned a sorceress was being beaten in Sinitsy, had gathered. One of the newcomers advised Petr Briukhanov to heat up an iron bar so that he could brand the witch, for which purpose he had already set up a bonfire in the yard, but by that time Maria had fallen from the mound of earth on which she had been sitting and died.

Briukhanov's wife, who had been having strong hysterical fits the whole time, danced, grabbed incense, and yelled, "Now they are dispersing, dispersing"[47] (i.e., they are breaking the spell). All of those persons enlisted as defendants, not negating the fact that a crime had been committed, maintained that they themselves, with the exception of the young Briukhanova, had not beaten the old woman and had not intended for her to lose her life, but had simply wanted her to reverse the spell, which, in their opinion, she had actually cast. All of them, in their own words, had been "as if bewitched," as a result of which they had lost all reason.

During the juridical investigation it was established that rumors that the mother-in-law had bewitched Briukhanov's wife had circulated in the village all winter; in the neighboring village of Gorokhovo a hexed woman also appeared. Rumor ascribed this spell to the same Maria Markova (the mother-in-law). According to popular belief, the person whose name the ill person calls out, is the one who "spoiled" her. It is important to note that Olga Briukhanova was subjected to a juridical-medical examination in a *Iaroslavl' zemstvo* hospital and was pronounced to have committed the crime in a state of delirium. The expert, the district doctor Kovalev, gave his opinion that a strong fit of grand hysteria is infectious for those present, so that the accused, being normal and healthy people, in all probability must have found themselves in a situation of unconsciousness and hardly knew what they were doing.

The assistant prosecutor, evidently a surgeon by profession, incidentally said the following: the ignorance of the accused does not excuse them, [and] the jurors should "do a surgical operation" and cut off the unhealthy organisms.

The counsel for the defense, having set forth the circumstances of the case in detail, pointed out how slowly and reluctantly Petr Briukhanov came to be convinced that his mother was a sorceress and [that he] had to resort to all the methods available to him of verifying this. When he was convinced that Maria Markova was no longer his mother, but instead a sorceress, a pernicious person, an evil being, it was necessary to struggle with her in order to save his suffering wife. "On a joyous holiday, on a Sunday of goodness and love, a dark source, 'a devil,' appears particularly subversive, and in the name of goodness it is necessary to destroy evil. Thus, there was nothing evil in the mood of the accused. They found themselves in an essentially defensive position and saved the life of their neighbor with those means that appeared to them to be the most rational. Therefore, they did not have ill intent, which should be the one thing punished. One-hundred-million [-strong] Russia poses the following question to the judges: What should be done with these people who committed a crime out of ignorance? Is a 'surgical operation' really necessary? Perhaps begin with education in such a way that they can dissect the brain and put a book there? No, they place it [the book] in the hands and act not with a knife but with words. Now, when the Russian people's disease of darkness and ignorance is pointed out from the heights of the throne, then the ways of healing that disease are pointed out: school and education. It is impossible to resort to shackles together with this. To punish them—that means hitting a person when he is down, for darkness has tangled up these unfortunate people's arms and legs."

The defendants were sentenced to hard labor. Thus, new perspectives have been added to the experience of suffering. From the heart we hope that this distinctive case, weighed down by the darkness of the Middle Ages, is understood as the obscurantism of the apostles and publicly fought with the diffusion of popular education.

Source: V. N. Krainskii, *Porcha, klikushi i besnovatye, kak iavleniia russkoi narodnoi zhizni [Bewitchment, Shriekers, and Possessed as Phenomena of Russian Popular Life]* (Novgorod, 1900), pp. 77–78. Krainskii relied on the following source: *Pravitel'-stvennyi Vestnik [The Governmental Herald]*, no. 230 (1879), pp. 87–89.

Translated and partially annotated by Christine Worobec.

D. Old Believers: Iguminshcheva

The next selection in this section concerns the practices among Old Believers as well as official attitudes toward this religious group. Old Belief emerged from the schism in the Russian Orthodox Church that occurred during the latter part of the seventeenth century as a result both of liturgical reforms imposed by Patriarch Nikon (patriarch, 1652–1667) and of efforts to strengthen the central administration of the Church. Those who refused to accept the liturgical reforms and instead continued to use the pre-Nikonian liturgical practices became known as Old Believers. By separating themselves from the official Church, Old Believers relinquished access to the priesthood and thereby also to participation in the sacraments of the Church, such as baptism, marriage, and the Eucharist, which only priests could perform. To preserve access to the sacraments, some Old Believer groups accepted either fugitive priests from the official Church or the priests ordained by a separate Old Believer hierarchy that was established by a Bosnian Orthodox bishop in 1846. Hence, Old Believer groups, called concords, could be either "priestly" or "priestless."

The institution of marriage posed a particularly thorny problem for priestless Old Believers. The largest of the priestless concords, the Pomortsy, eventually resolved this problem by developing a quasi-canonical form of marriage. The rejection of this solution by more radical concords, however, further divided Old Believers. One of these concords, the Fedoseevtsy, initially had in fact followed a comparatively lenient policy with respect to marriage, for example, permitting to remain together couples who had married in the official church but later converted to Old Belief. But by the mid-nineteenth century the Fedoseevtsy had adopted the extreme requirement of strict chastity for all adherents, insisting that celibacy was the only form of life consonant with Christian belief.

Considering Old Believers to be both heretical and a serious threat, the official Church sought not only to suppress them, using the power of the imperial state, but also to discredit Old Believer groups and to reconvert their members to official Orthodoxy. As part of this latter effort, Orthodox writers frequently charged that Old Believer doctrines on

marriage led to widespread sexual promiscuity, abortion, infanticide, and child aban-
donment, accusations that—as Kerova's repentance indicates—also were made against
sectarians. The following selection reflects this tactic. When reading it, the reader should
therefore keep in mind the polemical purpose of the author, who was an Orthodox priest
to whom Iguminshcheva, herself illiterate, had related her story.

Valuable insights into the role of women in Old Believer communities, and into the
meaning of religion for peasant women, nonetheless still can be drawn from Igumin-
shcheva's account of her conversion to and then abandonment of Old Belief. Igumin-
shcheva was living in a settlement near one of the numerous metallurgical enterprises
that dotted the Ural Mountains region, a remote and sparsely settled area to which many
Old Believers had fled especially during the eighteenth century to escape persecution.
There they established cohesive and mutually supportive communities that often were
more prosperous than those of their neighbors.

My parents lived in Ufa province,[48] then moved here to the village of Urlia-
dinsk;[49] I was born here. At age twenty I was married to a cossack named Artemii
Iguminshchev. After living with him for nine years, I was widowed. My life after
this was unenviable since I had to learn to take complete charge of the household
myself, as well as raise two small children. My parents were of the Orthodox faith;
I also eagerly went to church; I even used to go on foot to the Karagaisk church
when there weren't any other churches nearby—eleven versts from our village.
That's how I lived for fifty years and more.

Across from us lived two rich brothers, Nazar and Efim Polovnikov, Old Believers of the Fedoseev concord; neither was married; their three sisters, Marfa,
Anisia, and Uliana, also unmarried, lived with them. The Polovnikovs had excellent means; they farmed and sold livestock (they had herds of cattle and
sheep); two or three kitchen servants managed this business. Among the kitchen
servants was a peasant from Tirlianskii Foundry[50]—Agafia Vasileva Dudushkina—
she's still alive even now. Fifteen years ago, about 1875, because she happened to
be in the neighborhood, this Dudushkina started to visit me, probably having noticed that I often went to church. She began trying to tempt me into converting
to their faith. "Why do you go to church?" she asked. "The followers of Nikon are
heretics! And what heretics too! We believe all of that belongs to antichrist, and
the antichrist himself sits behind the altar at the front of that very church! Think,
is salvation possible for you? Just death!" Then she began to gasp and lament "Oh
you're lost! You're lost! The antichrist has caught you in his trap! Convert to our
faith: only we can save you! We'll never abandon you; we'll always help you;
you'll never have any needs."

Being completely illiterate, I was really terrified by her words. I thought, "What
if all this is really true?" I kept thinking about this and felt so unhappy; I didn't
know what to do; should I go with them or not? But my temptress kept badgering
me with her terrible slander of the Orthodox Church; finally she convinced me
to convert to the Fedoseevtsy. Dudushkina was very happy.

The Fedoseevtsy's preceptor was a cossack in our village by the name of Andrei Emelianov Ovchinnikov. He put me on a six-week fast with a thousand daily obeisances. I did everything exactly and wanted to be baptized; but their chief preceptor, a cossack living near the city of Troitsk in the village of Samarskii—I don't recall his name—found something insufficient and again made me perform a six-week fast with the same number of obeisances. I did everything again. On the fifth or sixth week of the Great Fast[51]—it was still winter—they cut a hole in the ice over the Urliad stream, near the village; all of them, as many Fedoseevtsy as were in the village, met that evening with the aforementioned preceptor, Ovchinnikov, in the house of the Polovnikov brothers. They waited; when everyone had quieted down, they performed the usual seven obeisances before beginning the service, and we started off to the baptismal place. I was wrapped in a fur coat up to my ears, leaving only my eyes, out of caution, so I wouldn't be recognized if we happened to come across someone on the street. When we arrived at the spot, they took the coat off, undressed me, then lowered me through the hole in the ice. Dudushkina, who was to be my godmother, supported me with the help of the others; then, placing his right hand on my head, Ovchinnikov immersed me three times, pronouncing the words, "In the name of the Father and the Son and the Holy Ghost." When I was lifted out of the hole in the ice, he, Ovchinnikov, dressed me in a shift, cross, and belt. I was again wrapped in the fur coat and led back to the Polovnikovs' house where the fellow Fedoseevtsy were waiting for us. Ovchinnikov arrived at the house; he also performed the required obeisances and read something, too, that I couldn't understand at all. After that, there were congratulations on my acceptance of Christianity. On Ovchinnikov's order I was told to come back the next day. I came. Ovchinnikov was waiting for me. I joined the Fedoseevtsy in performing the usual obeisances; the preceptor ordered me to fast for a week with 1,000 obeisances a day. After this, I was allowed to go with them to pray.

Some time after that, Khionia, the wife of a cossack, Matvei Ivanov Demin, was baptized in my presence; I was the godmother. Khionia was on her deathbed when our unified concord decided to baptize her. Forgive me, God, for taking part in such profanity! Scarcely alive, she begged and pleaded with us not to baptize her; but no one heeded the voice of the dying woman. A tub of water was prepared, and the same Ovchinnikov baptized her. They immersed her in the water, holding her arms; after two or three hours she died.

When his wife died, Demin, a Fedoseev, married for a second time; the ceremony was held in the Orthodox Church. This second wife was Orthodox too; Demin drove her to the settlement at Beloretsk Foundry to be rebaptized, already pregnant. After Demin's wife gave birth to a daughter, it was necessary to christen her, but there was no one to do it since our preceptor, Ovchinnikov, had died. The Polovnikovs' kitchen servant, the aforementioned Dudushkina, assumed this responsibility then, since she was somewhat literate. The christening had to be performed at Demin's house; everything had already been prepared; the candles on the little tub had even been lit; the door had been locked and bolted; the shutters closed out of caution. Suddenly there was a knock at the door. Probably the priest had noticed the preparations for the christening and wanted to catch the Old Believers in the midst of the crime, but we immediately put everything away; the intruders found nothing. When everything was quiet, with some assurance that there was nothing to fear, Dudushkina proceeded with the christening.

Converting to the Fedoseev concord, I began to visit the Polovnikovs, but also the settlement at Beloretsk Foundry, and soon perceived the really bad deeds of our Fedoseevtsy; I found out that there wasn't a Christian among them; they were allowed to live with anyone they wanted, and didn't think there was any sin in it. . . .There was a peasant of our concord at Beloretsk Foundry named Ivan Kuzmin Neudachin. He had three adult daughters; they openly lived in a really bad manner and even gave birth to children. But something else really astonished and troubled me. It was never known what became of the newborns; I became suspicious that they might have been killed. At this time Neudachin himself left for the woods and built a hut near the foundry nearby, as if to escape. I saw that even my temptress herself, Agafia Dudushkina, had depraved relationships with the Polovnikovs. She also gave birth to a daughter, in just the same way, which she took to Beloretsk Foundry and gave to someone. I saw, as a matter of fact, that all the kitchen servants living at the Polovnikovs—I know there were no less than ten—were involved in criminal liaisons with them; each one, after becoming pregnant, left to visit the settlement near the foundry, which was some sixty versts from us. After a little while each one would return, but the child never came back. You may ask, "Where did they go?" No one knows. And the Polovnikovs' sisters lived exactly the same way. Seeing all this, I unwillingly came to this conclusion: what kind of faith is this, what kind of Christianity is this when such acts too terrible even to consider are permitted! "Did people really live this way before Nikon's time," I thought? But they're so sure they've found the only true faith, preserved since the time of Patriarch Iosif, unspoiled by Nikon! "No," I thought, "they chose a new faith so they could do whatever occurred to them." How does God stand such blasphemy and impiety! Something else struck me as well: all of our Fedoseevtsy somehow die through some misfortune—either suddenly or hurting themselves in some accident—then, ailing for a short time, they die. Nazar Polovnikov was out walking and suddenly fell down right in the middle of the yard; he was taken inside and died. But Matvei Demin's grandfather fell from the attic and died on the spot.

Seeing such impiety among the Fedoseevtsy, I stopped going to their place of worship; I started to pray at home. They noticed this and began to scold me. I responded, "I'm not going to your place anymore because you have nothing good to offer!" They opposed me, and my heart wouldn't return to you.

After this, I intended on going to church a number of times; but I was always afraid of something, as if something forbade me to go there. This lasted for more than ten years. All this time, when the bell was rung for matins on holidays or for church service, my heart would ache and ache so much that I couldn't rest. I thought, "Well now, I'll go to church!" But no, something held me back, or one thing or another would come up. Finally in 1889, during Shrove week, I promised myself that I'd go to church without fail during the first week of the [Easter] fast. The first week came; for three whole days I thought about it; I didn't sleep most of the night; I kept thinking about how I would go to church; the thought that "everyone will laugh" was always on my mind. You see how difficult it is, once you've been torn away from the church, to return. Finally, I decided and went! I fasted, attended church, confessed, and on Saturday was honored to take part in the holy mysteries of Christ. Now I go to church without fail; I thank God for taking pity on me and not allowing me to die separated from the Church.

Having related what I have seen as an Old Believer, but also how difficult it was for me to return to the Church, I ask everyone who is an Orthodox to resist the temptations offered by the Old Believers, who on the outside appear to be devout people—fasters, but inside are full of impiety so I, an illiterate woman, when I saw their strange way of life, fled from them. Believe me, a sixty-year-old woman who has finished her time on this earth. Prize the holy Church and be faithful to its children so you will receive salvation.

Source: "Rasskaz byvshei raskol'nitsy E. V. Iguminshchevoi, zapisannoi sviash-chennikom A. Zhezlovym," *Bratskoe slovo* ["The Account of E. V. Iguminshcheva, a Former Old Believer, Recorded by the Priest A. Zhezlov," *Brotherly Word*], no. 7 (1 April 1893), pp. 526–32.

Translated by Karen Rosneck

MONASTICISM

Despite the secularization of monastic lands and the dissolution of many monastic communities by Catherine II in 1764, the number of such communities and of those living in them rose sharply during the nineteenth and early twentieth centuries. The number of women entering convents increased particularly rapidly, especially after the middle of the nineteenth century. Whereas there had been fewer than 2,000 nuns and female novices at the end of the eighteenth century, by 1914 there were 73,299, compared with just 21,330 monks and male novices. To the expansion of convents and their memberships, moreover, must be added a growing number of unofficial women's religious communities and formally sanctioned service communities. While increasing in numbers and size, Orthodox convents and other women's religious communities also became almost exclusively communal in structure and more heavily engaged in various forms of educational and social welfare work. Fragmentary evidence also suggests that the social background of the women undertaking a religious life shifted during the nineteenth century, away from a predominance of widows from privileged and urban social groups toward young and unmarried women from unprivileged urban groups, the clerical estate, and, especially, the peasantry.

The reasons for, and significance of, these trends in Orthodox female monasticism are still little understood. The current state of research, for example, allows one only to guess at the motives of the vast majority of the women who entered convents and unofficial religious communities. Certainly the desire for greater spiritual fulfillment should not be discounted, but life in a convent or other religious community also offered women much more: considerable material security, support during illness and old age, one of the few socially acceptable alternatives to marriage, expanded opportunities for female sociability and self-development, a socially as well as personally meaningful vocation, and the possibility of managing sometimes substantial resources. Hence, a religious life could hold many attractions for women of diverse social backgrounds, particularly during a period of intense social, economic, and cultural change and disruption. Conversely, donations by and the patronage of women from privileged and middling social groups constituted an important source of financial support for women's religious communities. These communities drew membership and support from a broad social spectrum, suggesting that they served the religious and other needs of a wide range of women. The following four selections illuminate these and other aspects of the growth of female monasticism in nineteenth- and early twentieth-century imperial Russia, a phenomenon that paralleled the simultaneous expansion of women's religious orders in Western Europe.

A. Mavrikiia, in Schema Maria[52]

The first selection provides an account of the life of Maria Matveevna Khodneva (1778–1867), a member of the provincial nobility who eventually became abbess of the Goritskii Convent of the Resurrection.[53] The excerpt is taken from the same collection of lives of spiritual ascetics that told the life of Isidora/Daria (see the section, "Popular Piety and Religious Dissent") and should be read with its didactic purposes in mind. Nonetheless, in addition to conveying the ideal qualities of a spiritual life and female piety as exemplified by Maria, this account of her life sheds light on several of the trends in Orthodox female monasticism noted earlier. In particular, it describes both the motives for and the effects of reorganizing an idiorhythmic convent on a communal basis, including the conflict within the monastic community that often attended this conversion.[54] The selection also reveals the diverse sources of income on which women's religious communities relied, the importance both of female donors and patrons and of the sisters' own labor in supporting such communities, and the seemingly constant search for funds that occupied much of an abbess's time and energy. Important aspects of the internal structure of the convent, the nature of its relations with superior ecclesiastical authority, and the social and other activities of its members also are apparent.

On Easter day, 8 April 1778, with the pealing of bells proclaiming the joy of the Resurrection of Christ the Savior, a daughter Maria was born to Matvei Ivanovich Khodnev, a pious and good-natured noble landowner of modest means of Belozersk[55] district. When the young girl began to come of age, her parents were comforted by her good qualities: her meekness, humility, and unanswering obedience. By her eighth year she had taught herself Church Slavonic, she loved to read the *Chetii-Minei*[56] of Bishop Dmitrii and the Psalter,[57] and she knew many of the psalms by heart. But her attempts at secular education encountered insuperable obstacles. The young Maria not only was not given to French, but she also could scarcely learn the grammar of the so-called Russian secular script.[58] The young girl willingly went to church, prayed zealously, and, following the example of her parents, strictly observed the fasts without distraction (something very rare in children of young age). She loved to help the needy, and even shared any delicacies that were given to her with the poor children in the village. No one ever heard an idle word from her, and she never engaged in children's games, except for the amusement of her sister who was two years older than she.

Thus passed the first years of Maria's life, in the solitary village of her parents, far from the noise and temptations of the world!

At age eighteen, this pure soul, preparing for service to God, was sent her first test. Maria lost her father, whom she ardently loved, and after a year her mother entered into a second marriage. The former order of life was disturbed. The successor was a hot-tempered, severe, and despotic man. Unaccustomed to restraint, he demanded that the whole family eat prohibited food during all the fasts. Maria could not bear such a violation of the rules of the holy Church and so asked her mother for permission to live alone. A new, independent life began for the pious young girl. Living in a peasant hut, Maria rejoiced in her soul. All her time was devoted to prayer, contemplation of God, and labors. Noting that when peasant women went out to work in the summer they left their children without supervision, this lady-toiler began to gather the children around her and look after them while their mothers were absent. She herself prepared warm water, washed the children, combed out their hair, fed them, and changed their underclothing, washing it herself. She did this with simplicity of soul, out of compassion and love for her neighbors. She was affectionate to all, was ready to help anyone by word and deed, was prepared to serve everyone, and if someone did something for her, she would return the favor two times over. Feeling drawn to a monastic life, Maria thus prepared herself in a timely way for future ascetic exploits. She wanted to enter the Nizhegorod Convent of the Exaltation of the Cross, which at that time had been reorganized on a communal basis.[59] She hoped to work there not according to her own will and for herself, but in accordance with the duty of obedience and for the general good. But her mother did not agree to let her travel so far away, and the daughter, always obedient to her parents' will, entered the neighboring Goritskii convent in 1801.[60]

One of the oldest convents in the Belozersk region, the Goritskii Convent of the Resurrection was supported and regulated by the state, like the majority of our women's cloisters.[61] Each sister lived in her own cell, fed herself with her own labors, and supplied her own food and clothing.

Maria's first obedience in monastic life was the post of candle-tender, which meant that she had to clean and sweep the church, a responsibility that imposed on her the duty to attend every service. But having earlier accustomed herself to unceasing labor, she found the time to work for herself as well, and to serve others.

Living in a cell that had been constructed for her by order of her mother, after matins (which began at 2:00 A.M.) and early mass Maria occupied herself with preparing food from the provisions that her mother sent her. At night she secretly distributed the greater part of the food she had prepared around the cells for the poor sisters, putting it in the windows or by the doors. For a long time these sisters could not guess who was bringing them donations, until a chance event revealed the identity of the benefactress. Maria tried to expend as little as possible on herself; she herself looked after her own cow and did not disdain the most menial and difficult work. The mother superior of the convent, the aged Abbess Margarita, loved the young novice for her meekness, obedience, and concern for her salvation. She proposed that Maria become a *riasofor*[62] nun, and in 1806 Maria took the veil with the name Mavrikiia. She then performed various obediences, and finally became treasurer.

Life at the Goritskii convent was pleasing to Mavrikiia. Only one thing was not to her liking—the absence of a communal order. Each time during the reading of the Psalter [that] she heard the words "It is good, it is beautiful, that brothers live together," her eyes filled with tears. "Just so, we should live together in complete agreement, like true sisters of God (she would say to those near her). But what do we have now? Here one sister lives in complete abundance, with slaves and servants, in large cells; another works indefatigably in a shack in order to provide herself with a crust of bread, and another in old age and infirmity lives off donations, either from her relatives or from others. How can there not be envy, backbiting, enmity, and every temptation from the Devil?"

At that time the Goritskii convent was under the guidance of Archimandrite Feofan.[63]

In the winter of 1809 Abbess Margarita died. Having committed the body of the eldress to the earth, Father Feofan gathered together all the sisters of the cloister and began to question them over whom they wished to select as mother superior. All unanimously declared that they desired the nun Mavrikiia Khodneva. This selection struck the humble nun like thunder. She did not believe her ears, burst into tears, and fell on her knees before Father Feofan, saying: "I beseech you, father, spare me! They themselves do not know whom they are selecting! I am ignorant and moreover very young in monastic life. Such an obedience is beyond my understanding." Also kneeling before the sisters, she tearfully beseeched them not to lay on her the responsibility of mother superior. "You are mistaken about me, I am unworthy," she repeated, "it is my role to obey, I am not able to lead. Where is it for me to order others, [when] I myself am worse and more unworthy than all the others!" But the unanimous selection of the mother superior was an obvious manifestation of God's will, and the diocesan authorities confirmed it. Mavrikiia was ordained in the rank of abbess in Novgorod by the Most Reverend Ioasaf, Bishop of Staraia Rus, on 11 July 1810, at the age of 33.

Having taken over the administration of the cloister, Mavrikiia hurried to the Novoezersk monastery,[64] to bow before the imperishable remains of the Most Blessed Kirill[65] and to obtain the blessing of her mentor, with his deep under-

standing of God's mysteries. With complete sincerity, she confessed to Father Feofan that she did not even know how to sign her name. The elder took a piece of
paper and wrote "Abbess Mavrikiia." "So that's how you sign," he told her. And so
it happened. From that day on Mavrikiia, who had never held a pen in her hands,
began to write her name precisely and correctly, as the elder had showed her. It was
a striking experience of the strength of obedience! At the same meeting Mavrikiia
revealed to the elder her cherished desire to institute a communal rule at the
Goritskii convent. He warmly sympathized with her good intention, the more so
because he himself had introduced a strict rule and complete disinterestedness at
the Novoezersk monastery. Nonetheless, he considered it necessary to pose a question: "The cloister has no income. How would a communal rule be supported,
what are you hoping for?" "All my hope rests on the Lord God," the abbess answered, "[and] with your prayers God will provide for us." "If you have hope in God,
then He will bless you and help you. He is an inexhaustible source of charity."

There were many obstacles and temptations at the start of this good work. The
thought of instituting a communal rule was not pleasing to many nuns and
novices, who were accustomed to living, if not in prosperity, then according to
their own taste and habits. Several grumbled loudly, and others decided to leave
the convent, so that no more than forty sisters remained, including not a few who
were poor, aged, or feeble. With the instituting of common meals, the abbess set
the first example, donating her cow and whatever provisions she had.

The remaining sisters offered whatever they could find to the community. On
the joyous feast of holy Easter on 21 April 1812 the common refectory was
opened for the first time. "What gladness we felt at the time," Abbess Mavrikiia
later recalled, "I simply cannot express. None of us could restrain our tears of joy.
The sisters thanked me and assured me that they had never eaten so sweetly, even
though it was the simplest fare. And to be sure, at that point we all were not on
earth, but in heaven. After that joyful feast we began to live in complete unanimity, communally, by the mercy and grace of God for us sinners." When crusts
of bread were left from the refectory meal, the abbess herself dried them and from
time to time put them on the common table, having boiled them in hot milk.
Any food was eaten in sweetness and with thanks.

As the spiritual life of the Goritskii convent grew, the external well-being of the
cloister also grew commensurately. The ancient Cathedral of the Resurrection was
repaired and covered with an iron roof, and a broad porch with a vestry was added
to it. Behind its altar, above the grave of the two drowned princess-nuns,[66] a magnificent cathedral to the glory of the Holy Trinity was built. On the place of the
previous warm church[67] a wonderful church in honor of the miracle-working icon
of the Smolensk Mother of God was erected. Both these churches were decorated
with superb frescoes by gifted artists, Goritskii nuns. Many other buildings arose
gradually, one after the other: a strong stone fence, long buildings with cells for
the sisters, an extensive refectory hall, several craft workshops where the sisters
painted icons and engaged in various handicrafts, a bakery, a kitchen with pure
water piped from the well, and a hostel for pilgrims that admitted everyone,

without exception, who visited the convent and where everyone was offered clean quarters, a bed, food, and drink. Finally, the tenderhearted Abbess Mavrikiia, compassionate to all, found it possible to build a hospital, with a church inside, for the rest and treatment of sick women without charge.

Where were the means for all these establishments found? The Lord alone knows! The Lord, in whom Mavrikiia firmly trusted, did not betray her trust. Widows and unmarried women from wealthy noble and merchant families, visiting the Goritskii convent, donated their property to their favorite commune. There were unexpected contributions even from strangers. The tireless labor of the sisters, carried out in strict order, brought in not a little income. Moreover, Emperor Alexander I granted the cloister land along the shore of the Sheksna River, a mill, and fishing rights.

Mavrikiia administered the Goritskii cloister for fifty years. The constant labors exhausted her strength and, feeling the ailments of old age, she finally decided to lay down the responsibilities of abbess. The Most Reverend Metropolitan Nikanor wished to retain Mavrikiia in the position of mother superior until the end of her life and therefore offered to give her an assistant of her choice. But at last he had to yield to the persistent tearful entreaties of the eldress who was prostrated at his feet. Agreeing to Mavrikiia's request, the bishop asked her to indicate a worthy successor to her.

In 1858 the aged ascetic, her bodily strengths exhausted, accepted the great schema and took the name of Maria, the same name that she had received at baptism.

As the sun extinguishes itself on the western horizon, sending its last rays into the interior of the magnificent church erected by Abbess Mavrikiia, so the richly fruitful life of the worthy nun in schema peacefully passed away. In the summer of 1867 she lay down and did not arise again. During the whole period of her illness, despite her feverish state, she retained complete consciousness and peacefully gave her spirit to the Lord, Whom she had served more than sixty years through feats of monastic asceticism, as mother superior and as a nun in schema, on 18 July 1867, in her eighty-fourth year.

Source: Zhizneopisaniia otechestvennykh podvizhnikov blagochestiia 18 i 19 vekov (s portretami) [Biographies of Native Ascetics of Piety of the 18th and 19th Centuries (with Portraits)], July (Moscow, 1908). Excerpted from pp. 264–74.

Translated by William G. Wagner.

B. Autobiography

SERAFIMA

The next selection is an autobiographical account of the early life of Varvara Mikhailovna Sokovnina (1779–18??), who was appointed abbess of the Vvedenskii con-

vent in the city of Orel[68] in 1821. A member of an ancient and wealthy Muscovite noble family, Sokovnina's father was a high state official during the reign of Catherine II. Enjoying the benefits of such a privileged background, Sokovnina appeared to be well educated for her time and spoke French, German, English, and Italian. Deeply affected by the early death of her father, Sokovnina's relations with her mother grew strained. Apparently seeking escape as well as solace in a religious life, she fled from her family in 1799 but for a short time was dissuaded from entering a convent. Later in the same year, however, she entered the Trinity Convent in Sevsk, Orel province,[69] where she quickly formed a close bond with her mentor, the nun Ksanfia. Like Sokovnina, Ksanfia was a member of a wealthy noble landowning family who had been orphaned at a young age. She had entered the Trinity Convent after allegedly using the property she had inherited to help the needy. Much of Sokovnina's autobiography, only part of which is reproduced here, is devoted to her obviously very tender, intense, and complex relationship with Ksanfia. After the latter's death in 1816, Sokovnina—who had taken the name of Serafima in monasticism—remained at the Sevskii Trinity Convent until asked by Bishop Ion of Orel to become abbess of the Vvedenskii convent, which at the time was in poor repair and riven by internal discord. At Ion's request, Serafima wrote her autobiography in 1821, on the eve of taking up her duties as abbess. She remained abbess of the convent until 1844. Her autobiography was published posthumously in 1891.

The autobiography focuses first on Sokovnina's family life and the motives that led her to undertake a religious life. After entering the Sevskii Trinity Convent and taking the veil, Sokovnina reconciled with her mother and maintained close relations with her family, particularly a younger sister who had settled with her husband on a nearby estate in Orel province. The second part of the autobiography discusses life at the convent, Sokovnina's relationship with Ksanfia, and relations among the sisters generally. In this regard, Serafima's autobiography is typical of many such works in stressing the importance of strong central authority for ensuring an orderly life within, and the material welfare of, the monastic community.

An account of the insignificant history of my life must, it seems, commence with the initiator of my existence. Without any spiritual partiality I can say of him that he was a person of rare merits: he could be called not only an exemplary father of the family but also a complete friend of humanity. My mother was an intelligent woman and had many natural gifts, but she could not compare with him in spiritual qualities. I had four brothers and two sisters. Our father tried to raise us in the best manner possible. He spared nothing either for our instruction or for our education, or even for our comfort. Our house was one of joy and peaceful amusements. But our earthly joy did not last long.

Our father died at age fifty, after an illness of only three days, and his death put an end to all our earthly pleasures. Our house became a place of weeping and perpetual lament. Being young, loving my father immeasurably, and finding in him the sole source of my comfort, I nearly descended with him into the grave.

After the death of our worthy father, our mother no longer wished to take any teachers or supervisors into the household, saying that she could not occupy herself with such matters on account of her grief. I was compelled to take on the upbringing of my two younger sisters and my younger brother, despite the fact that at the time I myself was only seventeen years old. I taught them everything that I had been taught. My morning hours were devoted almost entirely to this occupation. Moreover, I had to take on myself the management of the household and all domestic matters, which took so much of my time that I was left with hardly any free hours. My health began to be ruined, and my strengths perceptibly diminished.

My mother at first showed me some sympathy, but then, as with time and due to various diversionary occupations her grief for her never-to-be-forgotten spouse began to pass, she became cool and tried to show me her maternal tenderness only when others were present. But in the absence of other people she paid almost no attention not only to me but also to her family. My social life ended together with the life of our worthy father, and from age sixteen I no longer lived for society. I no longer occupied myself with any sort of amusements or worldly distractions, I went out with my mother only when necessary to visit our closest relatives, and I found my sole consolation in the fulfillment of my responsibilities and in the reading of edifying compositions. I prayed for death, but it did not come. My sufferings multiplied, and I often sank into the abyss of despair. To add to all this, our mother suddenly took it into her head to divide the paternal estate prematurely among my brothers and to distribute it to them entirely according to her instructions, which caused them to become extremely irritated with her. I was completely consumed by an exceedingly difficult attempt to mediate between them. I thought at that moment that it would be better to cast everything aside and flee to the edge of the earth than to be a witness to the sad picture of our unhappy family.

While in this unbearable state an intelligent and learned person suggested that I read Fénelon.[70] I delved deeply into his essays with all possible concentration, and his sermon on leaving the world and on the advantages of monastic life inflamed my imagination so strongly that I was prepared hourly to follow Fénelon's instructions and escape into the solitude of the most remote hermitage.

At that time one of our good acquaintances (Princess Kasatkina) took it into her head to travel to Kiev and on the way to visit the Sevskii convent. Here are the words with which she described the convent to me: "The Sevskii convent is a heavenly dwelling place, inhabited by peaceful and meek souls and administered by three angels, who in their unanimity resemble the Holy Trinity." Her words sent me into rapture. How lovely, I thought, to live with peaceful souls, to be administered to by angels, and to enjoy a heavenly dwelling place!

The explanation of my desire regarding monastic life caused my mother to become extremely irritated with me. However much I tried to reassure her with my entreaties and persuasions, it was all in vain. She affirmed wide-eyed that Fénelon had turned my head and that I wanted to embark on an irrational undertaking.

"What a chimera," she stated, "to leave one's mother and family at such a young age and confine oneself in a convent, which is intended only for the blind, the lame, and the crippled!"

I then conceived the firm intention to leave my parental home, letting no one know of it, and to hide myself from this world, where I had suffered so many griefs.

[Sokovnina fled her mother's house in Moscow late one night and, after various difficulties, found her way to the hut of a peasant whom she had met earlier and who she hoped would help her with her plan to prepare herself for monastic life. Recognizing the danger in this plan for himself and his family, the peasant refused to allow Sokovnina to stay with him, but he offered to take a letter from her to her mother. He returned to the village the next day, bringing letters for Sokovnina from her mother and her sisters. While Sokovnina's mother entreated her to return home, her sisters warned her of their mother's anger toward her. Two of Sokovnina's brothers also soon appeared in the village and eventually persuaded her to live alone on a family estate near Moscow. Within a year, however, Sokovnina had decided to enter the Sevskii convent. Since neither her mother nor any of her brothers would help her do so, Sokovnina turned to an uncle, who with the assistance of Princess Kasatkina managed the affair. Sokovnina arrived at the convent accompanied by her niece and nephew.]

On our arrival here, we went first of all to the abbess's cell, where mistress Margarita met us. Mistress mother Ksanfia (who at that time was the chief administrator of the Sevskii convent, so that even the mistress abbess did nothing without her advice) appeared only after my relatives had gone to their apartment, while at the invitation of the mistress abbess I had remained with her in her cells. The splendid appearance of the wise mother Ksanfia, her gentle conversation, and her common sense all from the first moment compelled me to turn all my attention to her. I sat with her until midnight and could not get my fill of her delightful conversation. My heart, always prepared for true love for others, became so attached to her during this first communication with her that from that moment I could perceive from her eyes what she wished, and since my heart is very gentle, in her hands I was no more than melted wax, from which she produced whatever she wished. The Sevskii convent blossomed, like a lily, under her administration. The church, which due to its beautiful appearance attracted the gaze even of outside visitors, had no other architect than the wise Ksanfia, whom God had endowed with such a fine understanding of everything that she could do absolutely anything. She had a knowledge of style in architecture, painting, and carving, and the workers who at that time had been hired to do all the construction and decorations feared her much more than their boss, who almost never turned up here and came only for the financial reckoning when the work was finished. They responded to her slightest wish, and if anything was not done just so, she immediately compelled them to put it right or do it over. They carried out everything unquestioningly because she had the astonishing gift of combining exacting strictness with tender persuasion. The embroidered cloth on the altar and on the credence table, as well as the shroud and all the embroidered icons found in our upper church, were finished by her own hands. Her labors were tireless, and there was not the slightest thing to which she would not turn her attention. The order, cleanliness, and external good order [of the convent], which even to this day has not lost its appearance, were instituted by her alone. Everyone was satisfied under her guidance, because she showed herself to be in everything an example of true perfection. She had the special gift of recognizing the morals and abilities of her subordinates and accordingly assigned to each an obedience within her power, which each tried to fulfill with exceptional zeal.

On my entry into the cloister here, mother Ksanfia imposed three obediences on me: first, to light the icon-lamps, of which more than twenty burned daily here during her administration; second, to read the lesson during matins; and third, to keep necessary accounts and to write letters to whomever was necessary for the needs of the cloister. During her administration everything seemed pleasant to me. And although the second obedience somewhat intimidated me, given my natural bashfulness, to please her I did not refuse even it. On weekdays (when almost no one was in the convent church) I read the appropriate lessons freely, but on feast days, when there was a whole crowd of people in the church during matins, it seemed to me so wild that I scarcely had the strength to fulfill the obligation imposed on me. The only comfort was the fact that my kind mother was as indulgent as she was strong. Seeing my insurmountable bashfulness, she helped me by never leaving the lectern while I was reading, and looking at her, I forgot my surroundings and thought only about executing her will.

She herself proposed to me my refection, and I only asked her whether such food was necessary for the salvation of the soul. She told me that any mortification of the flesh was useful to the soul, and so I unquestioningly agreed to everything. At first I ate in my cell, but I soon grew bored taking such plain fare alone. I proposed to mistress mother that we take our refection together. She admitted me among her associates with great pleasure, and I went daily to eat in her cell. While her strength was sufficient, she herself prepared the refection for me. But when she began to grow weak, she entrusted this to my cell attendants, whom she herself taught to cook the food for the fasts.

Soon after I had taken the veil, my spiritual mother declared to me that she wished to leave the administration of the convent and live in even greater seclusion, and therefore she was preparing to take the holy schema.[71] This troubled me a great deal, due to my faintheartedness. Knowing all the disloyalties that her spiritual associates had shown her, however, and all the reasons that had led her to this intention, I did not dare to contradict her. She had managed the cloister for somewhat more than a year during my stay here, and now she rejected completely any monastic administration; she stepped down from the choir, even though her voice was as precise as a spiritual reed with which she led others to tenderness; and she dedicated herself to the deepest seclusion. She assigned herself a crypt for standing in the church but left me in my previous place and with my previous obediences. But this continued only for several days. Without her everything became dull for me. I transferred all the responsibilities imposed on me to others and myself withdrew into the crypt with my spiritual mother. At first the darkness was intolerable for me, and from tedium I slept until the mass itself. But then I became acclimatized, ceased to sleep, and began to feel peaceful in the crypt.

I consider it superfluous to describe to you all the sorrows and bitterness that my kind mother suffered, having set aside the administration of the convent here, perhaps because this served to redouble her humility as well as my own. But I cannot conceal from you that this always made me extremely despondent, and I was never able to conquer the excessive sensitivity of my heart. The cloister here, renowned for its astonishing order and the strict rules of its administration, began to fall into complete decay. Disorder established itself in all areas, and obediences became for all a yoke, because for one nun they were imposed incommensurably, for another not in accordance with her abilities, and for a third none were imposed at all, all of which led to such chaos that only grumbling was heard—which continues to this day. All the directions of the wise mistress Ksanfia were consigned to oblivion. People for whom she had at one time sacrificed even her own life became her clear enemies, and irrational malice against her arose to such a degree that it is impossible to describe it. Five years later she took for herself the great angelic model.[72] Since this matter had to be arranged by the convent's leaders, for some reason it somewhat calmed them with respect to her. They asked her permission to come again to her cell to seek her directions. Although she did not desire this, being always moved by true love for others, she agreed to their requests and admitted them to her cell for spiritual discussions until the very time of her death. It was a pity only that her instructions always produced so little of use for them, and these gray-haired infants were occupied solely with the fact that they argued with one another almost daily and came to her only for a judgment. She generally would reconcile them before dinner, and until evening they would be peaceful and appear before the others in complete harmony among themselves. But by nightfall they again had quarreled and had come to our spiritual mentor for a judgment. Her patience was unlimited, and she bore all of this with astonishing firmness.

Source: G. Piasetskii, "Avtobiografiia Igumenii Serafimy," *Orlovskie eparkhial'nie vedomosti* ["The Autobiography of Abbess Serafima," *Orel Diocesan Gazette*], nos. 12 and 13 (1891). Excerpted from no. 12, pp. 822–52, and no. 13, pp. 879–86.

Translated by William G. Wagner.

C. Donation to Found a Women's Religious Community

COUNTESS ORLOVA-DAVYDOVA

Not only did the number of official convents and their membership grow rapidly during the nineteenth and early twentieth centuries, but so too did the number of unofficial women's religious communities. The two trends in fact were directly related, as most of the newly established convents had been formed originally as unofficial women's religious communities. Located primarily in rural areas, these communities served as a model and an important impetus both for the reorganization of Orthodox female monasticism on a communal basis and for its reorientation toward the provision of welfare services to needy women. Although apparently composed predominantly of peasant women, especially after the mid-nineteenth century, unofficial women's religious communities commonly were founded and supported by wealthy women from more privileged social groups, as the following letters from Countess Maria Vladimirovna Orlova-Davydova to the metropolitan of Moscow indicate.

Countess Orlova-Davydova was a member of a very old and distinguished noble family. She initially proposed donating eighty desiatin of land and 100,000 rubles to secure the material well-being of the community. Apparently considering this amount inadequate, however, Church authorities pressed Orlova-Davydova to increase her donation. She subsequently did so on several occasions, ultimately providing 1,300 desiatin of land and 200,000 rubles for the foundation of the community. In 1898 the Holy Synod finally accepted Orlova-Davydova's donation and approved the founding of a women's religious community "in the name of the Mother of God 'Comfort and Consolation'." The community was to consist of twenty-five members, five of them nuns.

Your Grace, the Right Reverend Metropolitan,

I turn to You with a most humble petition to establish on my estate in Serpukhov district,[73] in the village of Shchegliatev, a Women's [Religious] Community, the essential goal of which, in addition to the performance of regular prayers, would be to serve the needs of the local population, to tend the ill, to instruct and educate young girls, and so on.

Entrusting this Community to the Spiritual Administration,[74] I would wish that Trusteeship over it be granted to me for my lifetime.

Reports and matters regarding the Community preferably would be submitted personally to Your Grace.

To secure the Community, I will donate eighty *desiatin* of land with substantial woods and with existing dwelling and outbuildings, the latter consisting of: (1) a large, two-storied stone house with a chapel; (2) a cattle yard with accommodation for herdswomen; (3) two ice-houses; (4) a barn; (5) a stone building with a laundry and bathhouse; (6) a woodshed; (7) a stable; and (8) a wooden building for workers.

In addition, I will donate capital in the amount of 100,000 rubles. With this petition I am enclosing a plan of the area to be donated. In expectation of a most gracious resolution from Your Grace, I beg Your Pastoral blessing and remain Your Grace's most obedient servant.

Countess Maria Orlova-Davydova

17 March 1894

I wish the Community in Dobrynin[75] to be in the monastic spirit of prayer, obedience, and unconcern with worldly goods, but without the external signs of monasticism; namely, the sisters should continue to wear clothes in the peasant style in order to preserve simplicity and the freedom to serve their neighbor.

An example of such an arrangement for a Community of sisters administered by a Nun is the Diocesan Community of the Intercession in Moscow.

It is desirable that the number of nuns proper not exceed three, or at most five, and that the remaining sisters in turn perform required prayers under the supervision of the nuns and be prepared at any time of the day or night to serve the many and diverse needs of the infirm, the poor, and the orphaned among the surrounding peasant population.

Countess Maria Orlova-Davydova

16 June 1894

Source: RGIAgM, f. 203, op. 400, d. 1, ll. 1–1 ob., 7–7 ob.

Translated by William G. Wagner.

D. Donations to the Alekseevskii Convent

As several of the previous selections demonstrate, leaders of convents and women's religious communities devoted much of their time and energy to finding the necessary resources to support the particular community and its activities and to maintain, improve, and expand its facilities. Fragmentary evidence suggests that female donors provided a significant share of these resources, a phenomenon that reflected in part the right of women under imperial Russian law to dispose freely of their own property. The following two documents, directing donations of various types to the Alekseevskii Convent in Moscow,[76] illustrate this phenomenon.

1.

In the name of the Father and of the Son and of the Holy Spirit, Amen.

I, the undersigned, Tatiana Fedorova Raevskaia, an Unmarried Woman from the Nobility, being of perfect mind and memory but feeling the weakness of my health and imagining that death can follow unexpectedly, therefore considered it fitting to make this will regarding my movable property, so that after my death there will be no displeasure and, averting this, the following will be executed:

1. When it pleases the Most High that my life come to an end, then for my stay at the Moscow Alekseevskii Convent I ask the Lord that the Abbess commit my body to the earth at whichever of the Moscow convents she deems appropriate; for this purpose, for my burial I have deposited two thousand rubles from an unknown person in the savings repository of the Moscow Imperial Foundling Home,[77] and from these funds the Mistress Abbess should receive three hundred rubles; all the

remaining funds should be used for my burial, prayers of remembrance, and alms, as indicated in the special instructions that I have left for her, the abbess.

2. The holy icons remaining in my cell: the Passion of Christ the Savior and two Silver Crosses with relics [in?] a pair of carved flanged cups should be given, for my stay at the Alekseevskii Convent, to the church of the convent.

3. The icon of the Savior Not Made By Hands with silver riza[78] and a starry halo with a ring of uncut diamonds, and the icon of the Most Holy Kazan Mother of God with silver riza and a crown, should be given to the hospital church at the Sanaksarskaia hermitage.[79]

4. The icon of the Most Holy Tikhvin Mother of God should be given to the church located where my surviving sister Anna Fedorovna Lavrova lives.

5. The silver found in the milk cupboard, consisting of a coffee pot, a sugar bowl, a dozen and a half tablespoons and two other spoons—one different and the other a gravy spoon, should be exchanged for vessels [presumably for church use] and given to the village of Eroppino, where the body of my late parent[80] lies.

6. My books, clothing, and other remaining property I give into the unlimited disposition of the firm ability of the unmarried Secretary's[81] daughter Katerina Grigorevna Karchashna, with the condition that she rework my silk dress into items for use in church and distribute these items to churches; and I give to my cell attendant a part of my supply of linens.

7. Upon my death I request the Guardianship Council of the Moscow Imperial Foundling Home to give to my spiritual father for prayers of remembrance three hundred rubles from my money, deposited by me with the Council on 1 June 1825; and also, in accordance with my declared instructions, to distribute to monasteries, charitable bodies, and various people the monies deposited by me with the Council at various times, for which the Council issued certificates that will be presented upon my death. To ensure the fulfillment of my will regarding my movable property, I request that upon my death this testament be given to the Mistress Abbess, with a copy being left with the council.—This will has actual and full force from the moment of my death; but during my life it may be amended, supplemented, and completely abrogated.

1 August 1827. This testament was written in accordance with the will, and at the request, of the testatrix by the Nobleman, Titular Councillor,[82] and [word unclear] Semen Lavrentev Anokhit.

[The will was signed by Raevskaia and witnessed by Anokhit and two other men. It was confirmed for execution by the Second Department of the Moscow Civil Chambers on 17 August 1832.]

2.

We the undersigned, the children and heirs of the late Moscow merchant Fedor Mikhailovich Zolotarev, present to the Moscow Alekseevskii Convent, located on Krasnoselskaia Street, the here-appended sum of ten thousand silver rubles, in the form of a deposit from our family for the eternal remembrance of our late father, on condition that this sum be used for the rebuilding and expansion of the main cathedral of the convent and that two local icons must be placed in its main iconostasis: one of the Holy Apostle Matthew, whose memory is celebrated on 9 August, and the other of the Russian Saints and Martyrs Prince Mikhail of Chernigov and his Boiar Fedor,[83] the memory of the latter of which, the Angel of our late father, is celebrated on 20 September. To this document is appended a note, by which we request the daily performance of the *proskomide*[84] and each Saturday the saying of prayers of remembrance for the deceased slaves of God indicated in the note, with the further condition that on both days of remembrance, 9 August and 20 September, and on the day that our late father died, 21 November, and also on the days when those of our relatives who are buried in the convent died, each year a special service of remembrance with a *pannychis*[85] will be performed. 21 November 1854. Moscow.

[Signed by:]
State Councillor Ivan Fedorovich Zolotarev
Moscow Merchant Ilariia Fedorova Zolotareva
Hereditary Honored Citizen Elizaveta Fedorova [surname unclear], née Zolotareva
Colonel's Wife Maria Fedorovna Semenova, née Zolotareva

Source: RGIAgM, f. 1175, op. 1, d. 63, ll. 33–34 ob., 7–7 ob.

Translated by Laura Elyse Schlosberg.

THE OFFICE OF DEACONESS:
LETTER TO THE RUSSIAN ORTHODOX CHURCH COUNCIL OF 1917–1918

LIUDMILA GERASIMOVA

While revolutionary women sought to serve the "people" by overturning the existing order, as we shall see in chapter 6, other women sought to do so through an expanded role in the Church. One means of achieving this end was through the restoration of the office of deaconess, a proposal that was first made in the 1830s but that was pressed insistently by church reformers and by several prominent monastic women in the early twentieth century. In the early Christian Church, deaconesses had performed a number of functions, relating chiefly to the care and religious instruction of women. The office had been revived by a number of Protestant churches in Western Europe during the nineteenth century, and the supporters of restoration in the Russian Orthodox Church hoped similarly to use the office as a means for enabling women to devote themselves to religiously based educational and social welfare work. Advocates of restoration disagreed over the precise role and status to be assigned to deaconesses, however, and conservatives opposed

the proposal as an inappropriate foreign innovation that violated canonical prohibitions
against the inclusion of women in the clergy. Although a proposal to establish the office
of deaconess was nearly approved by the Holy Synod in 1911, the issue was deferred for
consideration by a future Church Council, which finally met in late 1917 and 1918. The
Church Council drafted appropriate legislation but dissolved before being able to act on
it. The following selection is a petition for the restoration of the office of deaconess sent
to the Church Council by one Liudmila Semenova Gerasimova. It is worth noting that
Gerasimova composed and submitted her petition after the October Revolution, in the
midst of imperial Russia's collapse due to war and revolution and of intensifying Bolshe-
vik attacks on the Orthodox Church.

TO THE ALL-RUSSIAN LOCAL COUNCIL
OF THE RUSSIAN ORTHODOX CHURCH

Petition

With this petition I have the honor of most humbly requesting the Local
Council *to permit me to assume the office of deaconess of the Russian Church* [em-
phasis here and throughout in original], and for this purpose I ask the Council to
resolve the question now before it regarding *the restoration of the institution of dea-*
coness on the basis of the ancient ecclesiastical order existing during the time of
John (Chrysostom).[86] This action is demanded by the cultural-historical mission
of Russia, the good of the state and the people, and the good of all humanity.

Basis of the Petition

I. Woman is cast by human fate as the Holy Virgin severing the head of the serpent, the intermediary between God and people, and as a moral force. She is the
bearer of Christian love and mercy, assuming a spirit for others, a fact confirmed
by the actuality of the moral order in life. Equality of rights within a democratic
political order demands equality of rights for women within the church, and not
a division whereby men are preachers of the Word of God both inside and outside
the church, and women, only outside the church. With Christ, there are no outcasts and female slaves with lords, and there are not people of the male and female
sex, but God is in everyone. The slavery of women is a perversion of Christianity.
As a mother and an educator, a woman lays the foundation of a child's moral and
religious principles, but a slave will produce neither heroes of the spirit nor heroic
citizens. Moral decay, the desertion of soldiers, and anarchy represent the moral
failure of the Church, resulting from the evasion of its duty to provide a moral
Christian education to its flock and from the slavery of women. It is necessary to
raise women up to the heights of moral authority appropriate to them in order to
yield the widest possible Christian education. Christ Himself revealed to women

[word unclear] the deepest essence of His teaching and gave to Mary His blessing of the knowledge of God. The whole Gospel is an annunciation to the Virgin of her liberation from the chains of Old Testament law. St. Phoebe[87] and the Apostle Thecla[88] were equally the collaborators of the Apostle Paul.[89] Our national genius, a gift to us from the Holy Spirit, has decreed a moral ideal in the person of the Russian woman. Due to the physical sensitivity and nervousness and the psychological subtlety of her constitution, a woman possesses the most perfect capacity for instinctive understanding and is the bearer of mystical religious feeling. I have factual evidence of Christ's having called me to the above-mentioned mission. Can one dare to resist the Spirit of God? If a German princess has received the right to organize a society of deaconesses,[90] then can a Russian woman be denied this request?

II. What will women do in their spiritual mission for the people, the Church, *the state*, and *humanity*? Given the darkness and ignorance of the people, women will engage in culturally enlightening activity in a religious spirit that corresponds to the mystical feeling in the spirit of the Russian people, in particular in such areas as agriculture, medicine, crafts, and useful trades for the countryside. To overcome blind ritual and the abyss beyond it of the collapse of morality in life and the ignorance of the Gospels and of Christ, women will proclaim the Christian truths of the knowledge of God and undertake the moral and spiritual enlightenment of the people. Women also will engage in economic-managerial activity *in the Church*, the organization of the parish, charitable activity, [and] the declaration of the joyful news of the Gospels to adults, youth, and children and its proclamation to female Christian lay students. Women also will participate in the liturgy and the management of the church economy. Monastic institutions have lost their significance, and settlements of female intelligentsia will find their best use in the cultural-educational religious mission of the village deaconess. The people thirst for faith and for Christ. Due to the vast spaces of our motherland, a priest cannot serve the mass of parishioners. The deaconess is his collaborator; she is present to administer the last rites to someone who is dying and is caught on the road, and she gives timely help of one kind or another. Taken together, all these activities of the deaconess have tremendous state significance because they represent the organization of Russia on the basis of the principles of an internal moral order, that is, the construction of a building on a stone foundation, on a Christian stone foundation, which alone can support all of humanity. The historical mission of Russia, a spiritual-Christian one, is to show Christ to the world. Without it, Russia will lose its right to exist and the people will be excluded from the midst of the living. The responsibility for the fate of Russia and of humanity rests on you. Now, in these dreadful, fateful moments, women stand guard over the fates of Russia and the world. Woe unto you if you turn them aside.

Believing in God the Father, the Lord Jesus Christ, the Son of God, and the Divine Holy Spirit,

With the mercy of God
Slave of the Lord, a Christian person of the Body of Christ,
Deaconess of the heavenly church, daughter of a deceased priest,
Writer-journalist
Specialist in agriculture. Sister of Mercy

Liudmila Gerasimova

Petrograd
Transfiguration Street, house 3, apartment 13

Source: Letter of Liudmila Semenova Gerasimova to the All-Russian Local Council of the Russian Orthodox Church, September ?[91] 1918. GA *RF*, f. 3431, op. 1, d. 327, ll. 8–9 ob.

Translated by William G. Wagner.

Notes

1. The week preceding the feast of Easter.

2. A fast that follows Easter by anywhere from eight days to six weeks, depending on the date on which Easter falls.

3. Pentecost, which in Russian villages also constituted a harvest festival.

4. Immediately after childbirth, the mother and—if present—the midwife would wash their hands using the same soap and towel in order to purify themselves. To complete the process of purification, the mother went to church on the fortieth day after childbirth and said a purification prayer.

5. The princess was the bride, and the prince was the groom. See the selection on peasant marriage customs in chapter 3.

6. A peasant coat made of heavy cloth.

7. Essentially, these are witnesses.

8. The bride would take a small carpet to the wedding ceremony for herself and her bridegroom to stand on.

9. A thin quilted cloth cap.

10. The headdress for married women.

11. One of the cultural roles played by women in the peasant village, dating back to the pre-Christian period, was to lament the dead. Because of its associations with paganism, this role was a source of friction between women and the official Church.

12. In the Russian Orthodox Church prayers are to be said for the deceased on the third, ninth, and fortieth days after death; the prayers on the fortieth day are particularly important, because on that day the fate of the deceased prior to Judgment Day is determined.

13. The Sunday before the beginning of Lent, which in the Russian Orthodox tradition begins on a Monday and continues for six weeks.

14. The first day of Lent. Purification is an essential part of the physical, emotional, and spiritual preparation for Easter. Russian Orthodox believers observe a strict fast during Lent, severely restricting their consumption of such rich foods as meat and dairy products.

15. *Kalachi, saiki, bubliki,* and *baranki* are all forms of cakes or buns, usually sweet.

16. The day before Easter Sunday. The Orthodox Easter service begins at midnight and lasts for several hours.

17. This apparently refers to one of Karamyshev's nephews.

18. Mikhail Kheraskov, who was Karamyshev's superior in St. Petersburg.

19. The Russian word here is *blizhnii,* which has been translated as either "fellow man" or "neighbor," depending on the context.

20. Jean Henri Merle d'Aubigné (1794–1872) was a Swiss ecclesiastical writer and evangelical Protestant. His *History of the Reformation,* which he produced between 1835 and 1853, was widely read and translated into many languages.

21. Located in northwest Russia.

22. An affectionate diminutive form of Daria.

23. A book of monthly readings, usually including saints' lives, sermons, interpretations of the Scriptures, and excerpts from the works of the Eastern church fathers.

24. *Khorovody,* which are traditional Slavonic folk dances.

25. The Goritskii Convent of the Resurrection, founded in the first half of the sixteenth century and located on the left bank of the Sheksna River in Kirilov district of Novgorod province.

26. Like Nastia, an affectionate diminutive form of the name Anastasia.

27. Emperor Nicholas I.

28. Probably a guard tower by the cemetery.

29. One of the major islands in the Neva River on which a part of the city of St. Petersburg was built.

30. A high state official who was the chief secular administrator of the Russian Orthodox Church throughout most of the imperial period.

31. One of the main Orthodox cathedrals in St. Petersburg, located on the city's principal and most fashionable thoroughfare, Nevsky Prospect.

32. Probably St. Nicholas, Bishop of Myra and the patron saint of Russia as well as of sailors and children.

33. The Russian word here is *starushka,* which in this context has connotations of affection, respect, and condescension.

34. That is, become a nun.

35. When speaking about herself, Daria generally used the masculine pronoun.

36. A predominantly agricultural region in eastern European Russia whose western boundary is formed by the middle course of the Volga River.

37. An early Christian heresy that embraced a severe asceticism, marked by fasting, forbidding of second marriages, and an enthusiastic attitude to martyrdom.

38. In English sometimes called "flagellants," the Khlysty were the first Russian group of "Spiritual Christians." The name *Khlystovshchina* probably derived from a corruption of *Khristovshchina,* the original and more accurate term applied to a sect that emerged chiefly among the peasantry in the region between Moscow and Nizhnii Novgorod during the mid-seventeenth century. A central tenet of the group was the belief that Christ was not the Son of God, but the most intense example of the incarnation of the spirit of God that could occur in any true believer.

39. Collections of hymns to God, Mary, or the Saints.

40. Located in Novgorod province, a region in northwest Russia that was highly commercialized, with a mixed economy of agriculture, crafts, and industry.

41. The Russian terms for witch (*ved'ma*) and sorceress (*koldunia*) were used interchangeably.

42. Under the judicial reform of 1864, circuit courts became the court of first instance except for minor civil and criminal matters, which lay within the jurisdiction of district justices of the peace. Trial by jury for criminal cases was established at the same time.

43. The alleged witch lived in a village in Iaroslavl' province, in the central industrial region.

44. This is a medical, not popular, classification for a severe form of hysteria in which the victim experiences severe fits and loss of consciousness.

45. "Spoiling" (in Russian, *porcha*), or perhaps more accurately, bewitchment, referred to the illness, or harmful possession by demons, suffered by someone as a result of a spell or hex cast by a sorcerer/sorceress or a witch.

46. Peasants believed that a hexed or bewitched person was possessed by demons and that contact with holy objects would activate the demons, who would identify the individual who planted them inside the victim and cause her to experience convulsions. They called possessed women *klikushi*, or shriekers, because of the high-pitched sounds they made during their fits.

47. A reference to the fact that the demons were leaving her body.

48. Located in western Siberia, between the Volga River and the Ural Mountains.

49. In the Upper Ural district of Orenburg province.

50. In this region, settlements often were named after the local metallurgical factory.

51. This refers to the Lenten fast, the strictest of the four fasts observed by the Orthodox.

52. The strictest monastic rule in the Orthodox Church.

53. On the Goritskii Convent of the Resurrection, see the selection relating to the Nun Isidora above.

54. Russian monastic institutions were either idiorhythmic or communal. In the former, members owned their own cells and provided for themselves, whereas in the latter, cells and work were assigned by the superior and meals were taken in common.

55. A district in Novgorod province.

56. See note 23 above.

57. A book containing the Book of Psalms or some version of or selections from it.

58. That is, the new secular script introduced under Peter the Great in the early eighteenth century, in contrast to the earlier Slavonic, church script. The two scripts differed substantially, and although both were used during the eighteenth century, most of the literate population apparently was taught the latter.

59. A convent located in the city of Nizhnii Novgorod, which lies east of Moscow at the confluence of the Volga and Oka rivers. After being reorganized on a communal basis in 1807, the convent grew rapidly, eventually becoming by far the largest monastic and, indeed, religious institution in the city.

60. Either the dating here or this aspect of the account of Mavrikiia's life is inaccurate, as the Nizhegorod Convent of the Exaltation of the Cross was not reorganized on a communal basis until 1807.

61. The Russian term here is *shtatnyi*. After Catherine the Great secularized Russian monastic property and closed the majority of monastic institutions in 1764, the remaining monastic institutions received an annual subsidy from the state, which henceforward also regulated their size, acquisition of immovable property, and certain other matters.

62. Imperial law formally prevented women from taking full monastic vows before age forty. Women younger than that, however, could take an intermediate vow, thereby becoming a *riasofor* nun, technically still a novice.

63. All Russian convents were placed under the spiritual as well as administrative supervision of various superior, exclusively male, ecclesiastical bodies.

64. The Kirillo-Novoezerskii Monastery of the Resurrection, located in Novgorod province and founded in 1517 by the Most Blessed Kirill the White, whose remains were buried in one of the churches of the monastery.

65. See the previous note.

66. That is, Princesses Evfrosinia Andreevna Staritskaia and Iuliania Dmitrievna. Princess Evfrosinia was the aunt of Tsar Ivan the Terrible and the widow of Prince Andrei Staritskii, who was Ivan's uncle. Fearing that she was plotting to have her son put on the throne in place of himself or his own son, Ivan had her confined to the Goritskii convent. Princess Iuliania was the widow of Prince Iurii, the first cousin of Tsar Ivan the Terrible. Ivan allegedly ordered the two princesses to be drowned in the Sheksna River, which flowed past the convent.

67. A smaller church generally used in the winter.

68. The principal city and the administrative center of Orel province, a predominantly agricultural area south of Moscow in the central black earth region. Founded in 1686 by the inhabitants of Orel, the Vvedenskii convent was largely destroyed by a fire in 1843, while Serafima was abbess; it was then relocated to another part of the city and rebuilt.

69. The Sevskii Trinity Convent was founded in the mid-seventeenth century.

70. Archbishop François de Salignac de la Mothe Fénelon (1651–1715), an influential French writer, mystical Catholic theologian, and pedagogue, some of whose writings were translated into Russian as early as the mid-eighteenth century. He is best known for his innovative, though still conservative and moralistic, ideas on the education of women.

71. See note 52 above.

72. That is, the schema.

73. Located in Moscow province, south of the city of Moscow.

74. The Spiritual Administration refers to the administrative structure of the Russian Orthodox Church, in contrast to the state administration.

75. Most likely the name of the estate or village where the center of the community was to be located. The substantial increase in the amount of land to be donated for the establishment of the community may explain the apparent discrepancy between the two letters in the name of the location for the community.

76. The Moscow Alekseevskii Convent was founded in the second half of the fourteenth century by Metropolitan Aleksei of Moscow for two of his sisters, who allegedly wished to quit the world and live a religious life. Over the course of its existence the convent moved several times, finally coming to be located in the latter part of the nineteenth century on Krasnoselskaia Street on what was, at the time, the outskirts of the city.

77. On the Moscow Imperial Foundling Home, see the story by Avilova in chapter 2.

78. The metal mounting or shield of an icon, usually made of gold, silver, or brass and decorated with jewels or delicate enamel work.

79. A monastery, founded in the seventeenth century, in Temnikovskii district of Tambov province.

80. The word is partially obscured, but seems to refer to either Raevskaia's mother or her father.

81. A relatively low rank in the state bureaucracy.

82. The ninth rank (of fourteen) in the imperial civil service.

83. Prince Mikhail Vsevolodovich of Chernigov and one of his boiars, Fedor, were killed in 1246 by the Mongols for refusing to perform pagan rites.

84. In the Orthodox Church, the elaborate preparation of the bread and wine for the Eucharist during the first part of the liturgy.

85. A special office for the dead.

86. St. John Chrysostom (c. 347–407; see chapter 1) was a particularly eloquent and influential preacher in the early Christian Church who is considered among the greatest Christian expositors. His writings carry great authority in the Russian Orthodox Church.

87. According to Romans 16:1, St. Phoebe was a deacon of the assembly of Christians at Cenchreae, near Corinth. She was also a patron of Paul and was entrusted by him to deliver his Epistle to the Romans to the church in Rome.

88. According to the Apocryphal Acts of Paul, Thecla was a noblewoman and follower of Paul who preached and administered baptism. Influenced by Paul's teaching on chastity, she renounced her engagement to Thamyris, for which she was condemned to death but was miraculously saved.

89. Conservatives generally cited Paul's epistles to support their efforts to limit the role of women in the Church and to defend the subordination of wives to husbands in marriage.

90. Gerasimova appears to be referring here to Grand Princess Elizaveta Fedorovna, née Princess Ella of Hesse-Darmstadt (1864–1918). Like her sister Empress Alexandra, Elizaveta was born a Lutheran; she converted to Russian Orthodoxy several years after her marriage in 1884 to Grand Prince Sergei Aleksandrovich, a brother of Emperor Alexander III. After the assassination of her husband in 1905, Elizaveta established the Martha-Mary Cloister of Mercy in Moscow, a religiously based community of unmarried and widowed women dedicated to providing care for the sick, infirm, and needy. Elizaveta served as mother superior of the community and became a strong advocate of the restoration of the office of deaconess. A member of the royal family, she was murdered by the Bolsheviks in July 1918.

91. The precise date is not indicated.

Princess Ekaterina Romanovna
Dashkova (1743–1810),
Director of the Russian
Academy of Sciences.

Luncheon at the Belenkoe estate of the Miklashevskii family, Ekaterinoslav
province, c. 1900.
From M. Lyons, *Russia in Original Photographs 1860–1920* (London: Routledge & Kegan Paul,
1977).

(Top) A merchant family, Nizhnii Novgorod province, prior to 1900.
Musée de l'Homme, Paris.

A merchant family at their dacha, with a male servant (far left) and a wet nurse
(in traditional dress), 1910.
Courtesy of Jay West and Mikhail Zolotarev.

Portrait of the Dancer Ekaterina Aleksandrovna Telesheva, by Orest Kiprenskii (1782–1836), 1828.
The State Tretiakov Gallery, Moscow.

The ballerina Anna Pavlova (1881–1931), in costume for "The Dying Swan."
The State Museum of Theater and Music, St. Petersburg.

(Top) Students dressed for dancing at the Smolnyi Institute in St. Petersburg.
The State Archive of Film and Photographic Documents, St. Petersburg.

Lesson at the factory school of the Maliutin and Sons Company, 1890s.
Courtesy of Jay West and Mikhail Zolotarev.

(*Top*) The author Anna Ivanovna Volkova (*née* Vishniakova) (1847–1910),
late nineteenth century.
Courtesy of Jay West and Mikhail Zolotarev.

Nurses in a military hospital, Nizhnii Novgorod, caring for victims of the
Russo-Japanese War.
Dmitriev collection, State Archive of Nizhegorod Region.

Self-Portrait at the Dressing Table, by Zinaida Serebriakova (1884–1967), 1909.

The State Tretiakov Gallery, Moscow.

Almshouse for elderly women, run by the Serpukhov Guardianship for the Poor, Second District, Moscow, late nineteenth or early twentieth century.

Courtesy of Adele Lindenmeyr.

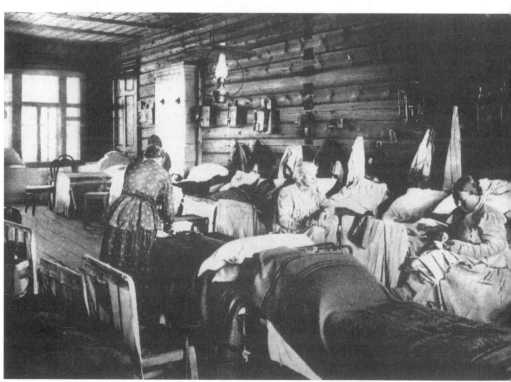

The socialist revolutionary and terrorist
Ekaterina Breshko-Breshkovskaia (1844–1934).
From *Little Grandmother of the Revolution* (Boston:
Little Brown, 1918).

The editorial board of the Social Democratic
journal *Rabotnitsa* (*Woman Worker*), 1917.
Clockwise from left: Klavdiia Nikolaeva,
Praskovia Kudelli, Konkordia Samoilova, Vera
Bonch-Bruevich, Liudmila Stal', Aleksandra
Kollontai, and Anna Elizarova.
Hoover Institution Archives.

Advertisement for Singer sewing machines, early twentieth century.
Courtesy of Jay West and Mikhail Zolotarev.

6. Opposition and Activism

INTRODUCTION

After pondering long and hard, we finally—and not entirely satisfactorily—settled on a title for this chapter. By the phrase *opposition and activism* we mean to signify not only conventional types of political action but also the wide variety of ways through which women publicly protested repressive forms of authority and sought to shape their world. The "world," of course, had different meanings for different women, ranging from the local village and region to the Russian empire as a whole or, more broadly still, to the entire "civilized" world. Although broad, our definition of opposition and activism still concerns public actions—and does not include the numerous forms of resistance to superordinate authority that could be employed in daily life. Understood in this way, many instances of opposition and activism in fact already have been encountered in this collection, for example the political activism of Ariadna Tyrkova (in chapter 1), the journalistic and professional activities of Maria Vernadskaia and Maria Pokrovskaia (in chapters 1 and 3), and the literary works of Lidiia Avilova and Evdokiia Rostopchina (in chapters 2 and 4). In this chapter, we concentrate on illustrating the evolution and variety of public opposition and activism by Russian women during the nineteenth and early twentieth centuries.

This evolution was an integral part of the growth both of political opposition to the autocratic order and of civic activism in general that occurred particularly after the first quarter of the nineteenth century. Although certainly the eighteenth century had contained its share of protests, uprisings, rebellions, palace coups, and critics of the autocratic regime or its policies, systematic and—increasingly—organized opposition to the autocratic order emerged only in the second quarter of the nineteenth century. The conventional starting point is the Decembrist Rebellion of 14 December 1825, an attempt by several groups of chiefly noble military officers to seize political power and establish, respectively, a conservative constitutional monarchy or a more radical centralized republic along Jacobin lines. While the rebellion failed miserably, it marked the first attempt to replace the autocracy with a different type of political system. The next thirty years witnessed the emergence of a discontented and radical intelligentsia, numerically quite small

and drawn principally from privileged social groups, which in a variety of fo-
rums—salons, "circles," journals, literary works and nonfictional writing, and literary criticism—developed and expressed extended critiques, from a variety of
ideological perspectives, of the fundamental institutions of the autocratic order.
The Great Reform era of the 1860s and 1870s intensified and expanded this critical and oppositional political activity, and broadened both the social composition of the radical intelligentsia and the spectrum of ideological positions that it
espoused. Liberals, radical democrats, populists, socialists, and anarchists clashed
not only over ideals and ends, moreover, but also over means, with some groups
confining themselves to the very limited modes of public and political activity permitted by the autocracy and others turning to illegal activity, underground organization, and terror. The spectrum of opposition widened still further in the late
nineteenth and the early twentieth centuries, in particular with the emergence
both of a mass labor movement and of non-Russian nationalist groups and the
resurgence of peasant unrest. Catalyzed in part by the conditions produced by the
Russo-Japanese War (1904–1905), these diverse oppositional and protest movements culminated in the Revolution of 1905, the outcome of which included an
expansion of civil rights, the legalization of political parties, and the establishment
of an elected legislative assembly (the State Duma) and a limited constitutional
order. While this new constitutional order greatly broadened the scope of allow-
able political activity, its limitations nonetheless ensured that oppositional activity continued until the autocratic order finally collapsed in February 1917.

Particularly after the late 1850s, civic activism and organization also grew
apace. Given the jealousy with which the autocracy guarded its power and the
consequent restrictions it imposed on public organization, however, the boundary between civic activism and political opposition often remained unclear, and
insensitive tsarist actions not infrequently converted the former into the latter.
Prior to 1905, moreover, the pursuit of incremental change through civic activity provided one of the few legal means for attempting to transform the autocratic
order. But during the late imperial period members especially of the growing educated and professional strata of society, whatever their motives, engaged increasingly in civic activities through a variety of groups, including philanthropic
organizations and professional associations, the new local administrative bodies
established by the Alexandrine reforms, parish councils and religious associations,
permanent societies and temporary congresses, and other forms of voluntary organization.

Women played an integral role in all of these developments. While not involved in the political conspiracies of their husbands, for example, many of the
wives of the Decembrists sacrificed their social status and families to accompany
their husbands into exile, an act later transformed by revolutionary mythology
into an ideal of women's self-sacrificial opposition to autocratic injustice. In the
1830s and 1840s women not only engaged in critical social commentary through
their literary activity but also facilitated the discussion and dissemination of critical ideas by organizing and hosting salons. After the late 1850s women as well as

men participated in the public debates, including those over the nature, status, and role of women, and in the upsurge of political and civic activism that marked the Great Reform era. Not surprisingly, women, too, expressed a diversity of ideological perspectives and disagreed over means as well as ends. In this regard, an important fissure emerged between those women who concentrated on improving the position of women through legal means and those who rejected this approach as too narrow, instead advocating a radical transformation of the entire social order. The former included women from privileged social backgrounds who used their organizational skills and social connections to gain wider access to education for women and to establish philanthropic bodies that rendered assistance to women in need. These bodies provided valuable experience for many of the leaders and activists of the feminist organizations, and eventually political parties, that emerged after the 1890s. Many of the women who advocated a more radical social transformation, by contrast, were drawn into various forms of revolutionary activity, including efforts in the 1870s to educate the peasantry or rouse them to revolution. Some, such as Sofia Perovskaia, executed in 1881 for her part in the assassination of Alexander II, turned ultimately to terror.[1] Whether liberal, feminist, nihilist, populist, or socialist, however, the women who engaged in political and civic activism overwhelmingly were educated and came from privileged or middling social groups. This remained largely the case until the end of the autocracy, although—as Vera Karelina's memoirs in this chapter demonstrate—women also participated actively in the labor movement that emerged in the 1890s. Indeed, the massive strikes that broke out in St. Petersburg in 1896 began among female textile workers.

Civic activism by women also increased and grew more diverse after the late 1850s. Here again, though, the boundary between civic and oppositional activity was uncertain, not least because the involvement of women in new forms of public activity by itself often proved controversial. Perhaps least controversial was the prominent role women played in the expansion of public charitable organizations, as patrons, administrators, and activists. Work for such organizations provided women with a way to serve others outside the home without appearing to violate prevailing ideas regarding their feminine nature and appropriate social role. Stirring more controversy, however, women with specialized training or with secondary and higher education used their expertise to pursue social reform and reform in such areas as education and public health, and, especially after the 1890s, women participated actively in the public campaigns to curb alcoholism, deregulate prostitution, and decriminalize abortion. In this regard, the growth of literacy, publishing, and a commercial press provided women with important media—journalism, nonfiction, and creative literature—through which to express critical views and calls for change. The emergence of the Realist school in art offered female artists similar opportunities. Indeed, there was a strong belief among the Russian intelligentsia that social action and literary and artistic activity were closely intertwined, with literature and art providing direct models for life and consequently a means for accomplishing social change. The fictional works included in this chapter (as well as the works by Lidiia Avilova and Evdokiia Rostopchina in chapter 2 and by Rostopchina and Elena Gan in chapter 4) should be read in this light: by depicting social life in imperial Russia critically, the authors acted publicly to promote its transformation.

Although women were engaged in all the "great issues of the day" in late imperial Russia, activists identified several as being of particular concern to women. Subsumed under the rubric of the "woman question," these issues involved first and foremost the interrelated questions of the status and role of women in the family and society. Associating the patriarchal family order with arbitrary authority, inequality, and repression, and often considering it as a surrogate for the autocratic regime, activists advocated reforms especially of family, inheritance, contract, and criminal law intended to secure the personal autonomy and equality of women in the family and to expand their opportunities for activity outside the home. Similarly, believing that employment outside the home would provide women not only with economic independence but also with personal fulfillment and a means to serve society, activists sought increased access to education and non-domestic employment for women. With the establishment of the Duma in 1906, women's suffrage became an important issue, especially for liberal and feminist women. These suffrage concerns generally were dismissed by socialist women as reflecting the "bourgeois" character of their liberal and feminist rivals. Liberal, feminist, and socialist activists alike, however, supported efforts by women workers to improve their situation through both the provision of maternity leaves, daycare facilities, and nursing breaks at work and the ceasing of such personally demeaning practices as body searches at the end of the work day. Despite such programmatic solidarity, the social distance between the predominantly educated women from elite and middling social backgrounds, who formed the core of liberal and feminist activists, and women workers—let alone peasant women—proved difficult to bridge. Indeed, as the selection by A. S. Saburova indicates (see chapter 2), women activists—like their male counterparts—often regarded peasant women as ignorant and backward and in need of their enlightened tutelage. The same social and ideological differences that in general weakened the political opposition to the autocracy in late imperial Russia thus also affected activism by women.

SERF WOMEN'S RESISTANCE: THE COUNTESS'S ORDER

Irina Vorontsova

Serf owners had long adhered to the principle of universal marriage in their peasant villages, and to increase the number of working households they often also pressed for early marriage once daughters had reached a marriageable age. The following order of Countess Irina Vorontsova reflects these concerns. Because women's work was essential for the successful operation of both the household and the village economies, and hence for peasant survival strategies, peasant elders similarly promoted universal and early marriage among village women. Indeed, sometimes orders that young women should marry were precipitated by repeated complaints by village elders or men who could not engage wives to run their households for them. At the same time, resistance to a particular marriage might come not only from a young woman but also from parents who wished to arrange a better match for their daughter. Widows could exercise greater choice in deciding whom and even whether to remarry, although the unenviable position of an older single woman in the village provided an incentive for remarriage. In some cases, too, village authorities abetted the resistance of women to marriage; in these cases, the reason usually was religious. As is evident in the case of Iguminshcheva in chapter 5, some sects of Old Believers rejected the institution of marriage altogether.

To Stepan Medvedev, bailiff of my Murom² village Vysokovo

Order

You submit that on my estates there are single and widowed youths and girls who are of age whom I command you to marry off so that they sort things out themselves voluntarily. If any of the fathers resist, then their daughters will be taken to my village in Mozhaisk,³ and a monetary fine will be laid on them for their disobedience, and, without fail, after the next fast,⁴ they will be married and you will delight me with a report about it.

Countess Irina Vorontsova

27 July 1796
St. Petersburg

Source: "Povelenie, podpisannoe grafinei Irinoi Vorontsovoi, 27 iiulia 1796 goda" ["Injunction, Signed by Countess Irina Vorontsova, 27 July 1796"], in Shchukin, vol. VII, excerpted from pp. 53–55.

Translated by Robin Bisha.

SASHA

Marko Vovchok

Marko Vovchok was the masculine pseudonym of Maria Aleksandrovna Vilinskaia (first m. Markovich, second m. Lobach-Zhuchenko, 1833–1907). An author of prose and a translator who wrote in French, Russian, and Ukrainian, she is best known for her works on peasants and for her satires of provincial life. Vovchok was educated at home and at the Kharkov Institute for Girls,⁵ an experience that is reflected in a later work of fiction, The Institute Girl *(1860). Vovchok's first published works were ethnographic sketches, based on her fieldwork with her first husband. Entitled* Folk Tales, *they were published in Ukrainian in 1857; a partial translation by Vovchok came out in*

*Russian in 1858, 1859, and 1862. Vovchok moved to St. Petersburg with her husband
in 1859, the same year that her* Ukrainian Folk Tales *appeared in two volumes, translated by novelist Ivan Turgenev. Vovchok's fictional works (which include* The Plaything *[1859],* The Merchant's Daughter *[1859], and* A Living Soul *[1868]) and, in
particular, her peasant tales were seen by her contemporaries as having a social purpose.
Many of her works foreground the lives of women and the need for emotional and domestic liberation for women. Like many of Vovchok's peasant tales,* Sasha *(1858), published prior to the abolition of serfdom, features a first-person female narrator and details
the difficulties of life under this institution. Vovchok portrays these difficulties as stem-
ming from an imbalance of power and demonstrates their effects on gentry and peasants
alike. In this story, she sets up an implicit parallel between the friendship of female characters and romantic relationships. A different type of sexual relationship, between a serf
owner and peasant women, can be found in chapter 3.*

I.

I've known her for a really long time: we're from the same village, we played
dolls together. What a sincere little girl she was, how loving, I'll tell you! If she
got to be friends with anyone, got to love them—she would be happy to give her
soul for them. She'd look into my eyes; if I wanted anything, she'd guess it and
she'd make me happy. She and I came to love each other deeply. Often it happened that she would give me all her things—and I didn't ask, she gave it away
herself: dolls, and earrings, everything, everything—and she would just smile,
looking at me.

Other little girls would begin teasing her, laughing at her: "She's given everything away, now she has nothing at all herself!"

And when we were a bit older, those same girls called her "homeless."

"Look," they would say, "You are going to be a fine housewife! You're preparing
a fine house."

And her mother often tried to talk her out of it and threatened her, but she still
just laughed.

"Well, aren't you sorry that you gave all your things away?"

"Sorry for what? I love her—what's to be sorry for? I'm not sorry.. . . . . "

II.

We were fourteen—she and I are the same age—when our mistress got married.
And she, our mistress, was no longer in her first bloom of youth. She read a great
many books, and by nature she was obstinate: she looked askance at the neighbors, got angry at people. She had no admirers, no friends. She grew thin and yellow over her books.

She was already over thirty when her brother arrived from the provincial capital for a visit, and with him a tall gentleman, so round-faced and handsome, calm, self-satisfied; he was always smoothing his chin with his hand, and paced around with measured tread, smoking a pipe.

The first few days the mistress dressed up a bit more than usual but didn't enter into conversation with her guest; and he would greet her in the morning, inquire about her health, but didn't bother himself with her either.

The master just looked at them frequently (how penetrating his eyes were, narrow and black; he had a very evil look, very cunning). He'd look, and one evening, after hugging his sister, he walked up and down the rooms with her for a long time, and all the time he was talking and talking about something, as if he were giving advice, making her see sense.

The mistress went to her room very thoughtful and thought for a long time, thought and sighed.

From that time on she was nicer to the guest, and she and he would always go for walks together and sit next to each other at dinner. And when he was getting ready to leave, our mistress started weeping. Her brother scowled. The guest saw all this; he himself felt sorry, or perhaps bored; he gave up and asked for her hand.

They got married without delay, and the young people went to live in the provincial capital.

III.

The young wife decided to take a servant girl from her own village. "Why should I take a stranger when I have my own? I'd have to pay wages to a stranger, and what kind of a servant would she turn out to be? You can't teach a hired girl."

She chose Sasha: she seemed to her to be the cleverest and quickest. They took Sasha and took her away with them. Her father, mother, sisters—all stayed, only Sasha went off to a strange place.

I cried so much, seeing her off. And she would hug me to herself: "I won't forget you, I won't forget you!"

She went away, and we had very little news of her. A year went by. Suddenly bad rumors about Sasha began to fly. Her mother, although she cried and grieved, did not want to believe them. Her father was blacker than a thundercloud and didn't say a word about his beloved Sasha. When her sisters heard about her, they would blush. People judged and analyzed, but just the same no one could say anything for certain. That was when I was summoned to the young mistress. They sent me off to her in the provincial capital.

I came to say farewell to Sasha's father and asked, "What would you like me to say to Sasha?"

"I don't know myself what to say to her," he replied, "whether I should be blessing her or cursing my dear daughter!"

He stood, folded his arms, and looked out the window.

But her mother came outside with me, all in tears, to see me to the gate.

"I send her my blessing! You tell Sasha that her mother blesses her. . . . Tell her to pray to God.. . . . "

Her sisters ran out after me. "Say hello to our sister! Say hello to our Sasha!"

IV.

It's hard, after all, to be torn away from your family, from your native region—everyone knows that! I was traveling to the mistress and all the time I was thinking about Sasha, and only one thing comforted me: I would see my faithful friend, I would talk with her, grieve a little—I'd feel better. . . . But how would Sasha receive me? And what had happened to her! Was it true what people were saying? The whole entire trip I was pondering on Sasha.

V.

We arrived in the evening. Our mistress lived in the middle of the city, on a broad street. All the houses were stone, tall, with iron roofs and big windows, and light from the windows shone out onto the street.

Sasha wasn't there; I was afraid to ask about her. Prokhor [the driver] was looking around and sighing all the time. We were all sitting in silence; and through a broken window the wind was blowing the candle.

VII.

I gathered my courage and asked the cook about Sasha. The coachman heard and interrupted, "You bow to me and ask me! Here, look. (He opened the door.) You see the little room across from us? Your Sasha is sitting in there, and here I have the key from the padlock." (He showed me a key from his pocket.)

He spoke, and I looked—what a heavy lock hung on the door. My Sasha, you poor dear!

"What," I said, "doesn't she ever come out of there?"

"How could that be? She can go where she pleases, only not out the gate of the courtyard—don't get angry!"

"What have they locked her up for?"

"Oh, there's a reason!"

"Let me in to see her," I asked him.

"With pleasure—go!"

He opened the door and I went in—it was dark as pitch in there.

"Sasha! Sasha!" I called.

Silence.

"Could she have gone somewhere?" I thought, "Broken out somehow?"

I stood there for a while and then went back into the hut.

"Did you see?" asked the coachman.

"I saw," I said.

"Not very cheery, I think, hmm?"

VIII.

Here a tiny quick little old woman came in; her little face was sharp, malicious, her manner furtive; she was always coming on from different sides, as if she was seeking where to pinch most painfully. She circled around, circled around, and she said to me, "They won't take you to see the mistress today. Go to bed." And she went out.

We sat down to supper. They called Sasha—she didn't come.

After supper everyone lay down to sleep in the kitchen, but I went on sitting in the servants' hall—I wasn't sleepy. I was sitting and thinking and waiting: "Why doesn't Sasha come running to me? And where is she? Had she gone away, or didn't she want to answer me?"

Something rustled. I raised my head—before me, it seemed to me, stood a tall boy. I looked again—it was Sasha! But her hair was cropped in a circle; she had gotten so tall and thin; her clear, lively eyes were sunken, and the color had fled from her face.

I rose, but she just stood.

"Sasha," I said, "Sasha!"

I felt so sorry for her at that moment!

She came closer to me.

"Hug me," she said. "Hug me, and give me a kiss!"

We hugged each other tight, and we kissed each other. And we began to cry harder.

"Your mother sends you her blessing, and your sisters send you greetings," I said.

She flared up, but she didn't ask me a single thing; I didn't feel like talking either. We sat hugging each other and occasionally exchanging a few words, remembering our long-ago childhood days.

IX.

The next day I was summoned to the mistress.

She had become so stout and majestic. She looked me over from head to foot, asked my name, and said to me, "See that you don't get spoiled! If you get spoiled, they'll cut off your braid[6] as they did to that nasty Sasha, and you'll be punished severely!"

She told me what to do, gave her orders, threatened me, and sent me away.

And Sasha and I began to live together. My life was no beauty, but how bitter was Sasha's! Anyone could scold her, anyone could punish her and laugh at her.

The housekeeper tormented her worst of all. At times she was quite venomous, as if she had fangs.

The old cook . . . he too wasn't above reproaching her with things: he was touchy when he was sober, would sneer at everyone, God knows for what. Sometimes it would seem to him that you looked at him the wrong way, that you were laughing at him—and he would sneer at you for something or other. But when he was drunk, he could not have been nicer. At those times he would praise everyone; and if they cussed him, he would try to talk them out of it, tell them that it wasn't good. "People, live in peace!" he said. "Don't be sad, don't quarrel, share everything with one another; if anyone wants to drink, I will let them; I would buy it for him myself, but I've already drunk everything up. Be patient. But the main thing is, live in friendship!" He loved Sasha most of all and was kind to her when he was drunk.

Only the drunken cook alone did not abuse her. Sometimes a stranger would come, a trader we knew or the neighbor girl, guests of one of the servants or the housekeeper—everyone would look, ask in a whisper, shake their head, spread their hands. . . . And she, as if she had gotten completely used to this, did not complain, did not grieve.

X.

I didn't say a word to her. Don't upset her, I thought; but then once I went into the servants' hall (it was a holiday, the masters had gone out, and the servants had scattered), I went in—the stove was lighted, and Sasha was sitting on the bench, looking into the fire, and the tears were flowing and flowing.

I sat next to her and put my arm around her. And she without looking at me began to tell me a story:

"They brought me here as a young, inexperienced girl, and I wept a great deal at the time. Every evening I would cry. Everything was strange to me, everything was unfamiliar, uncomfortable. I was so sad, so sorrowful! Once I was standing on the porch toward evening, and I was looking around and grieving; and it was already spring, the snow had shrunk and turned black, beneath the fence the tender new grass was coming up; there was still a bit of a frost, the streams and puddles were covered with a thin skin of ice. The sun was going down, crimson and red. I stood there and I remembered my dear native country so vividly! 'Lord!' I thought. 'If I could only catch a glimpse of it.' I hear, 'Sasha, why are you so sad? Don't be sad, dear!' I was amazed and frightened; I looked around—it was the master's young nephew. He approached, took my hand, squeezed it, looked at me some more, and went away. I was frightened, but it was annoying, too: What, had he been pitying me? Was he making a joke of me, laughing? After all, all of them were without pity, without mercy. Would this one be any more sympathetic? His eyes had seemed very kind to me, in fact.

"I began to ponder and thought for a long time; my sadness even dispersed, but my soul was uneasy. Then I remembered our arrival, how *he* stood timidly before the mistress, how he got flustered and tripped himself up in the conversation at dinner. I remembered that he often seemed to be looking at me from behind the door. That if I was working near a window, he would walk past and look. That night I even dreamed about him. I got up at dawn and remembered him again. And the whole day I couldn't get him out of my head. But in the evening I once again ran out onto the porch: would I see him today? Would he speak to me? I ran out, and he was already standing there, as if he were waiting for me. 'Hello, Sasha!' but I was silent. We stood there—he was looking at me, I could feel it— he was looking, but I didn't raise my eyes, I didn't say a word. Someone knocked, and we got frightened and separated immediately."

XI.

"From that time on I saw him every day, every single day! How many times I declared, 'I won't go! I don't want to!' and the next thing I know, I'm going out. And he would be so glad to see me, he would look into my eyes and always ask, 'Do you love me, Sasha?' And I, I'll tell you, I fell very much in love with him. Very much. When people began to notice and to laugh, at first I was ashamed and upset, but then—I thought, people are laughing, so what, let them! I love him, I am *his*! Why should I think of myself? Let him think. It's fine with him, it pleases him when they laugh—so laugh; if it seems offensive to him, he knows what to do. But I will obey his word, his command. Here I just live and don't worry. At home we hardly saw each other: they were watching us, but when I was being sent somewhere, I would whisper to him, and we would meet somewhere in a back street, sit under other people's gates."

XII.

"Only one day he arrived so upset.

"'Sasha!' he whispered to me. 'Aunt and Uncle have learned everything!' My heart sank.

"'Do they want to separate us?' I asked.

"'Don't be afraid, don't be sad!' he urged. But he himself was no better.

"Then we sat down next to each other and cried our fill.

"'What are we to do, Sasha?' he asked.

"'You should know,' I said. 'It's for you to decide.'

"'Oh, Sasha, Sasha! What can I decide? I'm so sad, I'm so full of craven doubt! I don't know what to do! You tell me . . . '

"'What?' I said. 'Can't you think of anything, how can you not know . . . '

"'Sasha, don't you look at me, and don't condemn me: I'm not happy with my-self either, by God! I'm always afraid . . . '

"'What are you afraid of?'

"'I've been this way since childhood. My father was stern and strict. He beat me and terrorized me. Even now I'm always hearing his voice, "Don't be bold in anything, you'll get into trouble! Go along the path quietly and cunningly—it will be all right!" I was even planning to deceive you, Sasha; I wanted to deceive you and then abandon you—forgive me! I didn't abandon you: I didn't have the strength, because I was so in love with you . . . Tell me, Sasha, tell me what to do? I'm in torment, and my head is whirling . . . Oh, Sasha, if only I could marry you!'

"'Marry me,' I said.

"'But what will people say? Think, Sasha, how people will attack us,—uncle, his wife is even more evil—everyone! All the relatives! They would peck at us, Sasha! I would gladly die now.'

"And he himself started to cry.

"'Well, let's die, if you want,' I said.

"He kept crying. And he cried a long time. Then he stood up and said to me confidently, 'No, Sasha, it's a sin to die by your own hand. Come what may—I'll marry you! I'll marry . . . God be with them all. What are they to me? Why am I afraid of them? I'll marry you and we'll start our life!'

"He gave me a kiss and went off happy."

XIII.

"I returned home—the housekeeper summoned me to the mistress. She herself was laughing maliciously: it was she who had told the mistress everything. I went. I heard a great many of all sorts of words that time, but those words didn't get to my heart—because I knew them already, expected them . . . I stood before the mistress, listened to her shouting, and her threats, and her curses, just as if it were the tolling of a far-off bell. He was flying before my eyes, and everything around was growing bright for me.

"That whole night I did not shut my eyes—I thought and thought . . . what didn't I think over during that time!

"In the morning the masters were having tea—he came in. I had not expected that he would come to them so soon. I got frightened. I saw that he hadn't slept either: he was so pale and exhausted. He looked at me, and then his eyes flashed, and he seemed so courageous to me.

"The masters were amazed. The mistress asked him roughly, sternly, 'What does this mean? Where is this coming from? What do you want?'

"The master rose and began to pace around the room, then sat down again.

"But he answered them courageously, 'I have come to you with a request . . . Sasha . . . '

"But the master interrupted him, 'Well, well, God will forgive you. Only watch out before you do something stupid.'

"'I don't know where your nephew's conscience is,' the mistress cried. 'To start talking about this again.'

"'But that's from meekness, darling; he wants you to forgive him,' said the master.

"And they started to argue among themselves. They quarreled and didn't let him say a word.

"I was listening and watching everything from behind the door. I saw that he was losing his composure; he ran up to him, seized him by the hands and fell on his knees.

"'Give me Sasha, give her to me!'

"'How? What? What?'

"And they couldn't understand what he was saying; they jumped up, they turned red. . . .

"'Give me Sasha! I want to marry her!'

"'Marry!' cried the mistress. 'Have you lost your mind? You've gone crazy. You'll be ruined! You'll perish! No decent person will allow you over their doorstep! . . . How are you going to live with a simple peasant girl, coarse, stupid?'

"And the master smoked and smoked—you could hardly see his head through the smoke, and all the time he was crying, 'He's crazy! Ah, the Lord is punishing me!'

"But *he* said:

"'Give me Sasha! (He himself was kissing the hem of the mistress's dress and catching her by the hands.) What, can't a simple girl's heart love? We are all equal before God, auntie! Give me Sasha, I'll die without her. Without her I don't want to live in this world!'

"I listened and I felt so sorry for him!

"'Let go!' interrupted the mistress. 'Get away from me. How dare you speak to me like that! I won't give you the girl. Do what you like—I won't give her up. Get out of here! Out!'

"And he fell, sobbing. And the master was pacing, and smoking, and tut-tutting.

"'Sashka!' the mistress cried suddenly.

"I went in. She snatched her scissors from the table and nodded to me that I was to come up to her—I went. She ripped at my braid, and sheared me. She cut off one braid; on the other she broke her scissors. Her hands were shaking—she was enraged.

"The master watched, he stood with his pipe. And *he* looked at her, at me, and just wept tearfully . . . But it was as if I went cold for some reason—as if some cold wind blew on me and carried everything far away from me. The mistress ordered me to gather up the hair that was scattered and thrown about, and sent me out.

"I gathered up my braids and went out. So what? I was *his* property; he was free to give me to them. Only why did he give me up?"

XIV.

"From that time on the mistress ordered that I wasn't to be let out of sight. What troubles for the housekeeper! She couldn't get enough sleep—she was always keeping watch on me. If I moved so much as a step—there would be a cry after me, 'Where are you going? Where are you going?' And for a long time I didn't see him. I didn't see him, and I was glad of it. It was as if I had stopped loving him completely. It wasn't that I was angry, it wasn't that I was offended, but I just stopped loving him—I had no need of him.

"For a long time the mistress harassed me; for a long time she persecuted me. Then he stopped coming—she began to forget and stopped her attacks on him. And the master was glad of that. He was rather slow in the uptake: it was hard for him either to be cruel or to be kind. When he did get angry, a few days later he would repent: 'Why bother me? Just do what you want—don't bother me, please. You might as well prevent a man eating his dinner.' The mistress wasn't like that; she was quick-tempered and quick at everything. 'I don't want to. I don't want to permit your nephew into my presence.' The master agreed at once. 'Give orders not to let him in, darling; although it's a bit unfortunate, one's own peace is the most important thing.'"

XV.

"I gave birth to a little boy—what a cry-baby he was, restless! I had a lot of trouble with him; after all, I was inexperienced, young, I didn't have this, I didn't have that, I had to ask people for things, to get advice from people. I had so many thoughts, so many worries! Everyone around looked at me sarcastically. Whoever dropped in on us, whoever looked in—they didn't even want to reproach me— they despised me. And the housekeeper couldn't bear it, she would yell. Only the cook was kind to us, when he was drunk. Yes, yes, there were cares and worries! But somehow my soul became quiet then, quiet. . . . "

XVI.

"One evening—I was living alone here in this very chamber where they lock me up now, so the baby wouldn't bother people with his crying—in the evening I was sitting and listening—someone was sneaking up, cautiously opening the door . . . *he* was sneaking up. I took a look and I was not happy and I didn't grieve, I only felt rather bored. He had grown thin and looked tormented. He talked a lot then, he wept a lot and caressed me; he was delighted with the baby . . . 'I,' he said, 'have been hiding in your barn all day today, I was tormented, I wanted to see you so much . . . ' I heard it all, I knew it all, I felt sorry for him, only he was completely unnecessary to me.

"But from that evening on he started coming around again. How he loved the baby! Often I would look at the two of them, often. The little boy looked a lot like him: the same gentle eyes, his whole look just like *him*.

"I felt sorrier and sorrier for *him*, I pitied him with my whole heart. I would think and think—I racked my brains. And what was going on between us? Was he at fault? Was I the cause? He would start telling about his late father, he would start to grieve and complain—and his late father would take revenge on me: stern and heavy, he had icy eyes and a stony breast, and a commanding voice. He had snow-white hair, and he was terrifying; and he pursued [us] and bent the child's helpless head lower and lower. And all the time I was imagining that *he* was a child, it was as if *he* were my child and that they were chopping off the child's right hand. Such sadness came over me all the time, but I still loved to hear about his late father: the dead man was forever spreading his shadow before me, and *he* became more pitiful to me, dearer. . . . "

XVII.

"My little boy got sick and died . . . What a life this is, Lord! Is it proper to grieve for the dead as I grieved? What kind of human life is that? Everything so disordered, everything so unclear! . . .

"*He* fell ill from grief, from sorrow. I went to him. He was glad to [see] me, how glad he was! 'I would have perished alone,' he said, 'I didn't know how to exist, what to do!'

"But when someone knocked on the door, how he trembled all over: 'Who is it? Where from? What are we to do!'

"And then they came for me: the mistress had sent them. They came and took me from him, they led me away, and he saw me off and cried."

XVIII.

"They brought me in and again they cut off my braid. Now everyone was ordered to keep watch over me; and if there wasn't time, they were to lock me up. So here I haven't gone out of the yard for three weeks. Since that time I haven't seen *him*. The cook has met him a few times; he sends greetings, he says, and is very sorrowful. He sends me gifts and money through him.

"My soul is languishing, and nowhere can I find peace for my soul, nowhere can I seek out protection. You arrived—you lightened my heart without words, you calmed me without caresses. Thank you, my long-desired one!"

And how Sasha grabbed me, how tightly she squeezed me in her arms! And suddenly she lost her strength and fell beside me as if she had been broken. Sorrow crushed my soul as well. I hugged her: "Go to sleep," I said, "go to sleep here on my lap!"

"Oh, how could I sleep," she said. "A bitter spring is rising in my heart, and boiling, and flooding my whole soul!"

XIX.

I thought and thought: how could I ease her, how could I help her? And once I said to her, "Sasha! I will go see him and find out everything: we'll be happier!"

"What is there to know? Go if you want," she replied, "but it's clear that it won't be any happier!"

"Don't upset yourself, Sasha," I urged her. "After all, he loves you, you said so yourself, and you love him. Don't grieve. Only tell me, how do I get there and how will I recognize him?"

"Go out to the corner in the evening. He will probably be standing there waiting for me. And you will know him by his good looks, by his honorable appearance. He's very blond, curly haired; he wears a black overcoat, and his walk is quiet."

I waited for a good moment and ran out to the corner, and *he* came straight to meet me; I knew him at once.

"Sasha sends greetings," I whispered.

He trembled and exclaimed, "Whose [serf] are you? Where are you from?"

"I am a village girl," I replied.

"Oh, so it was you who arrived not long ago? I know, I know everything that is going on with you there, although I am not there myself. What did Sasha tell [you to say] to me?"

"Nothing, she just sent greetings."

"Doesn't she love me any more, that she couldn't find a more heartfelt word? Tell her from me that I have neither rest nor peace, that this separation is destroying me."

"And what is she to do?" I said to him. "It's not [by] her will."

"Oh, what am I to do?" he cried. "I would be glad to steal her, but how?"

"How could you steal her? It's hard," I said. "It's hard to soothe her grief now. If only you had made up your mind to [do] something earlier. . . . "

"Yes, if I had known, had foreseen, all the torments and all the grief, I would have made up my mind. But I couldn't even think straight. They yelled at me, they stormed and threatened and reproached; they put me off the point, they befogged me! What does Sasha say?"

"She didn't say anything about that."

"Nothing! . . . A loving girl—glory be! She's probably living merrily even without me—sadness hasn't overcome her?"

"Akh," I said, "It's not you who should be offended at her! On whose behalf is she now locked up in four walls?"

"What am I to do?" he cried. "Well, I'm going to go to my uncle, I'll run [to him]! I'll throw myself at his feet, I'll ask and plead!. . . . "

"They are hardly going to listen to you."

"And I want to see Sasha! Let them take off my head, but I'll see Sasha. I'll go!"

XX.

I got frightened: what was going to happen? If only he didn't make everything worse!

He walked hurriedly toward the masters' house, and I went running after him. He [went] to the masters, and I rushed to Sasha. I was dashing around in all directions, telling her what had happened and casting around in my own mind: what would happen? But she sat motionless.

"Sasha! What are you doing?" I said to her. "My heart is stopping, stranger that I am, and you don't even stir, you don't budge!"

"Oh, my dear!" she answered laughing. "Sit down and calm yourself: you don't get thunder from a cloud! You ask me, I know better—I'll tell you."

"But he's gone to the masters!"

"I know he's gone to the masters. And he's bold while he's on his way; but when he stands face to face with them, his arms will go limp—he'll grow timid. I know him; believe me!"

Just the same I couldn't calm myself, I was constantly expecting that there would be shouts, noise, running around. But everything was quiet; the hours passed. I couldn't stand it, I stole into the masters' room; but it was already dark there—they were asleep.

Abashed, I returned to Sasha: what was this?

But Sasha just looked at me and laughed.

XXI.

The next day they sent Sasha out to get bread for tea, they sent Sasha to the seamstress. The housekeeper was raging; the coachman opened the gates wide for Sasha, joked with her; the cook (he was sober that day) shouted at everyone, heaved firewood around the hut. The young men laughed. I no longer knew what to think.

"Sasha!" I said. "What do you think? Why is this happening? Did they yield to him, or what? Why are they letting you out?"

"Yes, probably he gratified them," she said. "Don't you get upset for no reason. People are not enemies: they've thought it over and worked it all out peacefully."

"Better start crying, Sasha," I said.

"You obviously have nothing better to do with your tears! Mine aren't so abundant," she replied.

XXII.

He and Sasha saw each other, but it brought her no joy.

"What, Sasha, is he happy, I suppose, as he was before?"

"He's happy," she replied.

"And how did he work everything out?"

"He swore to them, he vowed that he wouldn't marry me. He took a vow to them—now they've calmed down: let him amuse himself!"

"Although it's insulting, at least there won't be such constant anxiety. And maybe later. . . . "

"Don't get your hopes up," she interrupted me, "he's very easily frightened. There are loves that you don't feel like showing in front of people, my dear! If she's not brightly costumed, not beautifully dressed, then they bury you up at home under the bench: 'Sit, love, comfort me, but don't go out in front of people—people will condemn you and shame your master.'"

"Oh, Sasha," I said. "He loves you!"

"Oh, he loves himself more, I'll tell you."

"No, don't sin, Sasha. It's simply that they've gotten around him, befuddled him; he's confused, but he truly loves you. How he's wasted away with grief for you!"

"Here's how. A little boy gets an apple from someone else's garden, and they beat him for it—he'll cry, after all, but he doesn't feel like giving up the apple. But you ask—he's ashamed to admit it."

"You, Sasha, are constantly looking for grief for yourself, as if that's what you live on."

"What grief! By God, it's not grief. It's just my thoughts."

XXIII.

She was always [buried] in thoughts and reflections like that, and in meditation; she spoke little, and hardly looked at anything.

And he got upset, kept asking her, then he began to suspect: "You love another man!" And how he moaned and complained! How he pleaded with her passionately, and offended her bitterly!

"Sasha, Sasha!" I said to her. "Think, and straighten out your affairs! You're just torturing yourself senselessly. How humble he is to you, how he loves you! Well, you say directly what you don't like, simply teach him."

"You won't teach him if it takes forever, dear! This literacy can't be learned. No, I have had my fill of seeking after yesterday."

"But you would live well together, in love, in harmony then!'

"Such tenderness when we're so poor!" she laughed, but she herself was thinking about something all the time. "You know," she said again, "I would just ask for death, but the grave is dark."

"God be with you, Sasha!"

"Wait, wait," she interrupted. "And he thinks that I've fallen in love with someone else, but who? There's no one for me to fall in love with. I don't want to, I couldn't . . . Why squander myself for nothing? He who is miserly is not stupid. . . . "

And sometimes when she began, then she would almost convince you.

XXIV.

Lord! What madness there was then in the whole house! The mistress and master were quarrelling about the fact that he had paid too much for a carriage; the master frowned and groaned; *our* young man was feeling jealous; the housekeeper was doing battle with the servants. When the mood would come on her, on the housekeeper—she would do nothing but sting for weeks on end. The cook, thank God, was constantly drunk at the time, so he walked around happy and just kept urging us to live amicably.

XXV.

Sasha became still more thoughtful and avoided *him*. You couldn't get her to go out either to walk or to dance. She only went to the monastery on Sundays. Then a nun—so thin, so frail—began to come visit her; she walked, leaning on a cane, and her face was so calm—probably because she was praying constantly. Once this nun came, and Sasha took her to the mistress. The nun sat there a long time, and they called for Sasha, and the mistress served tea to the nun, and ordered that she be taken back to the monastery in the carriage. I asked Sasha, "What is this?"

"Wait a bit," she said, "you'll find out everything."

XXVI.

In the evening I saw that Sasha was tying up a bundle. I was wondering what she was doing that for . . . I saw that she packed her shirts and her bit of money.

"Sasha, tell me, what is going to happen? Where are you preparing to go?"

"Farewell, dear!" she replied. "Live, don't grieve, weep a little, rejoice a little, don't chase after what belongs to someone else, but your own . . . God forbid,— don't squander your own! Remember that wealth is no help to the stupid son."

I got frightened: what was wrong with her?

"Don't be afraid, don't get frightened: I'm in my right mind. But I am going to the convent. The mistress has given her permission. She is afraid to answer to God for my soul—and she allowed it. I'm going tomorrow at first light. You tell *him* about it yourself and calm him down."

"You're so young!" I say.

"Not old, but I've been around. And you tell him too—ask him for me: let him not be anxious. I feel like getting a good rest. I'll get a good rest there."

XXVII.

Lord, what became of him when he found out! It was pathetic to watch him.

I went to see Sasha, though not often. She worked there at the convent. It was wonderful there! That convent stands outside the city, on a hill, in the forest. The green trees hung down over the wall into the convent courtyard, and the wall it-self had grown green and mossy. The cells were dark, small, but if you looked out the little window—how many flowers were blooming! What soft feather grass! At the foot of the hill you could hear a river burbling; and if you listened carefully—you could hear the wheels knocking on the pavement in the city.

"Is it nice for you here, Sasha?" I asked.

"Very nice," she replied.

"Peaceful?"

"It's peaceful."

She had become still less talkative. Occasionally she would ask about *him*, how he was and what he was doing. Once I said to her, "Sasha, you still remember him . . . Isn't that a sin?"

She smiled.

"Yes," she said, "what should I do with him, even if it is a sin? If I'm silent—will it really be forgiven?"

"And aren't you sorry for him? Tell the truth!"

"No, I regret nothing."

I asked her how it came into her head to enter a convent.

"I came here often, you know—and I began to love it. It's so quiet here, so serene. I finish up my work and sit down somewhere. I sit—the leaves rustle, the river burbles, the birds sing and twitter, there's not a human voice to be heard."

XXVIII.

As far as I could observe, she lived happily there. Everyone praised her so in the convent. And the old nun, the one who had asked the mistress for her, came to love her very much; if she walked past—she would always bless her. I was glad that she had gotten settled, and had calmed down. "Let her live in the convent! She likes it there," I thought. And then, completely unexpectedly, she died. And no one in the convent knew: she didn't call for anyone, but perhaps she couldn't call out. She died in her own cell, crowded and dark . . .

I was there at her burial. It was bright outside, clear. Candles burned around the coffin; the flame trembled, and the sun played on her face. And her face was so thoughtful, so martyr-like!

To this day *he* goes to her grave and prays there all the time. He has never wanted to marry. I have met him at the grave several times. He's so sorrowful!

"No one can cheer me any longer the way my late Sasha did. Let God be the judge of my uncle and aunt!"

Source: Marko Vovchok [Maria Aleksandrovna Vilinskaia], "Sasha," vol. I of *Tvori v dvokh tomakh* ["Sasha," in *Works in Two Volumes*] (Kyiv, 1983), pp. 145–66. Excerpted.

Translated by Pamela Chester.

LETTER TO THE TSAR

ELENA LIKHACHEVA

A journalist and historian of women's education in Russia who wrote extensively on women's topics, Elena Osipovna Likhacheva (1836–1904) also worked actively from the 1860s onward to expand the educational and career opportunities for women in the Russian empire. She served as chair of the Society for Assistance to the St. Petersburg Higher Women's Courses, which were established in 1878 by a number of faculty members of St. Petersburg University to offer higher education to women. Women such as Likhacheva had worked energetically throughout the 1860s and 1870s, often exploiting their contacts in higher state officialdom and prominent social circles, to gain greater access to education for Russian women. Their efforts bore fruit in the expansion of secondary education for women and in the establishment of higher courses for women in several cities during the 1870s. Much of this work was undone, however, by conservative state officials in the 1880s. In writing to Alexander III, Likhacheva employed some of the tactics and arguments commonly used by her contemporary Russian feminists in trying to prevent the closure of the St. Petersburg Higher Women's Courses. Her efforts were successful, and the St. Petersburg higher courses remained the only such courses available for women until the reopening of those in Moscow in 1900.

Your Imperial Highness,
Most Gracious Sovereign!

In 1878, with the permission of the former Minister of Education Count Tolstoi,[7] Professor Bestuzhev-Riumin[8] established the Higher Women's Courses in St. Petersburg with the goal of providing female students who had completed the course of study at a women's secondary school with the possibility of supplementing their general education with the study of historical and philological or physical and mathematical sciences.[9] The need for such an educational institution has already long been vitally felt by many Russian families, who have been convinced that a truly educated woman is the surest conservator of religiosity, morality, and order in the family and society. For the material support of the courses, with the permission of the Minister of Internal Affairs, there was formed at that time a special private Society, composed of people sympathetic to women's education in the spirit indicated. Soliciting in 1878 an annual allowance from the government for the St. Petersburg Higher Women's Courses, which was Most Graciously granted, the former Minister of Education Count Tolstoi testified before the State Council[10] that "these courses respond directly to the views of the government, both because they in general enable the development of women's activity in the field of education and because they can serve to prevent the regrettable phenomenon of Russian women going abroad in order to receive higher education, from which they cannot otherwise return but with ideals and an orientation that are incommensurate with our way of life."

The grand total of the sums expended for the St. Petersburg Higher Courses, without taking into account the masses of unpaid labor provided by many people, now amounts to 740,000 rubles, of which 32,500 rubles has been allotted by the State Treasury. The property of the Society for Assistance to the Courses consists of a large, well-constructed building, land, and educational equipment, all of which together are worth 300,000 rubles.

At the directive of the Ministry of Education, the admission of students into the courses had been halted since 1886 due to the review of the general question of women's education that was undertaken by the Commission established under the chairmanship of the Assistant Minister of Education Prince Volkonskii.[11] This Commission completed its work at the beginning of the past year, 1888, but the directive halting the admission of students remains in force. Meanwhile, in the spring of the current year the final graduation of students will occur and the activity of this educational institution will cease. In accordance with its obligations, the Society for Assistance to the courses consequently will be compelled to sell all its property. In its full composition, this property, which has been collected with extended effort and many sacrifices, constitutes an extremely valuable support for an institution of women's higher education. By being broken up and sold off into various hands, and thereby losing all its significance, the property will be irretrievably and fruitlessly lost to the cause of education. The creation in the future of women's higher educational institutions will again require the labor of many years and huge expenses, and the significant sacrifices already made by the government and by private people will not assist this important cause.

The Society for Assistance to the Higher Women's Courses therefore has taken the liberty of submitting to the Most Gracious review of Your Imperial Highness a most humble request for permission to accept students into the aforementioned courses from September of the current year, 1889, even though in the form of a temporary measure, until the government has confirmed a new statute on women's education.

With deepest veneration and boundless devotion,

I have the honor of being
Your Imperial Majesty's

loyal subject Elena Likhacheva
Wife of a Privy Councillor,[12] and Chair of the
Committee of the Society for Assistance to the
Higher Women's Courses

January 21, 1889
Residence:
St. Petersburg,
Furshtadtskaia Street, own house

Source: RGIA, f. 733, op. 191, d. 813, ll. 151–53 ob.

Translated by William G. Wagner.

THE WOMEN'S MOVEMENT AND ITS MISSION: SPEECH TO THE WOMEN'S CONGRESS, 1908

Anna Kalmanovich

*The next selection reflects a shift in the character of the activism engaged in by femi-
nists after the late 1890s, one that was intensified by the Revolution of 1905. Activists
for women's rights had struggled for years to obtain permission to hold a national congress. The general suspicion of the tsarist government that national congresses of any sort
could be camouflage for national political organizations interfered, but the Women's Mutual Philanthropic Society—a moderate women's organization founded in 1895 and intended to promote both the "intellectual and moral improvement" of women and the
improvement of their rights and opportunities—finally received approval for such a congress in 1902 from the Minister of Internal Affairs. A series of delays, including the
events of 1905–1906, postponed the meeting until 1908. This All-Russian Women's
Congress brought together women activists of numerous political persuasions; even a del-
egation of working women affiliated with the Bolshevik party attended briefly. The majority of delegates, however, were women of the privileged and middling estates who had
been active in the women's movement in the late nineteenth and early twentieth centuries. One such delegate was Anna A. Kalmanovich.*

*In this excerpt from a speech delivered at the 1908 Women's Congress, Kalmanovich
places the Russian women's movement in an international context. In so doing, she demonstrates how women activists in Russia, by the turn of the twentieth century, followed the
activities of their counterparts in other countries and had themselves become active inter-
nationally. For example, they maintained contacts with groups abroad and with international women's organizations and attended national meetings and international congresses.
Kalmanovich, as a liberal journalist, one of the founders of the All-Russian Union for
Women's Equality,[13] and an ardent opponent of socialist revolutionary movements, also is
typical of the younger generation of activists for whom—with the granting of an elected legislative body in 1905—women's suffrage became a central issue. One of the few Russian
activists for women's rights who proudly called herself a feminist, Kalmanovich argued that*

women could retain their political and ideological differences while still cooperating on is-
sues of importance to women. Likewise, she was atypical in her support of the
Pankhursts'[14] terrorist methods in the English struggle for female suffrage.

INSTEAD OF A FOREWORD

In the fall of 1905 I gave a speech in Saratov,[15] where I was living at the time.
My talk was on the need for exclusively women's organizations within the present-
day emancipation movement here in Russia.

This speech came about due to the following circumstances. At the time, political banquets and rallies were just beginning to be organized throughout Russia.[16] Rallies were organized even in Saratov, and the organizers naturally wanted
to make these events as ceremonial and lavish as possible. To this end, they invited representatives from various institutions and societies to give speeches. They
knew that there was a group of so-called feminists in Saratov whom they always
made fun of. But now, for the sake of decorum, they needed to invite a representative from this group, too—*Es passte ihnen so in den Kram*[17]—as the Germans say.
The honor fell to me.

And so I came to learn more about the people who organize these political
events. And this is how I realized that women are useful at these events only as
decoration, and that no one gives a thought to their interests. Women respond
innately to such situations, and of course they scurried to the rallies, thinking, in
the simplicity of their hearts, that the meetings were being held for all citizens,
regardless of gender. Quite the contrary! The organizers candidly told me that a
limited number of places were reserved for women in order to invite more needed
participants, because women would only take up space like useless, extraneous
ballast. From their point of view they were completely justified. They needed the
opinion and backing of doctors, lawyers, judges, civil servants, merchants, and
even the workers and peasants, who are usually seen as having no more advantages than women. And did they take the endorsement of women into consideration? Who needs it? Well, this may be so, but women were no longer to be
treated like minors: life itself had outgrown the narrow confines in which women
had been living until then. Like it or not, women needed to become involved in
the whole of life.

Yes, it was an intense moment. The Manchurian slaughterhouse[18] had left a
deep wound in women's souls. And so, we, the very same laughable feminists,
began to organize our own rallies using the same old tactic—we didn't exclude the
men, but we gave entrance tickets mainly to women. The hall of the Commercial
Club where we met was enormous, but it still couldn't contain the multitude of
women who came to listen. But, as always, we were accused of being isolationists,
and, what is even more amazing, these attacks came predominantly from other
women. This is why I thought it necessary to speak publicly about why we need
exclusively women's organizations.

Much time has passed since then, and many events have taken place. Fate brought me to Europe, where I thought this topic was already outdated. But after a conversation with a group of young women in Geneva, I became convinced that this was hardly the case. Even there they told me: "Young people won't join your union. It's feminist!" This is exactly what's being said right now, right here in Russia. And so the purpose of this address is to prove that these statements are unfounded; that they are fabrications created by unenlightened opponents of the women's movement who speak in a voice that is alien to women.

There are two objections to having a women's movement in Russia. Some say: "We don't need a women's movement. Unadvanced Western women may need it, but we have long since vindicated ourselves as the most progressive of our gender. Also, our men are less egocentric and more enlightened than Western men, and so we have no need to be differentiated from them. We have no need to resort to feminism. Women and men have a single mission: ours is a common struggle, and, consequently, the fruits of this struggle will belong to all of us." Alas! Vain, though sweet, illusions for which we will pay just as dearly as Western women have paid. For just as here, the West also has many, maybe even more, men who are enlightened; men lacking in prejudice and dark thoughts. In the West [the movement for] equal rights for women has had, and still has, ardent champions like D[aniel] Defoe, J[ohn] St[uart] Mill, [Gabriel-Jean-Baptiste-Ernst-Wilfrid] Legouvé, [Jean-Antoine-Nicolas de Caritat, Marquis de] Condorcet, [André-Paul] Gide, [August] Bebel, [James] Keir Hardie, and many others. As regards women, our most progressive women are undoubtedly on a par with the most advanced women in the West. And because of our country's unique conditions, Russian women have recently produced heroines that the entire civilized world admires. But these are individual personalities. I say that our masses, both male and female, have fallen far behind.

We need to have the courage to look truth in the face. We have fallen behind, and exceedingly so. But this is hardly surprising. Thank God that Russian women, with their twofold lack of rights, have still preserved a vibrant soul. Against a background of darkness and ignorance they continue to strive toward Light and Knowledge. Women's fate is the same wherever you go, just like the fate of all peoples. This is clear once you enter into contact with other nations. People are starting to do this right now by forming international congresses that sidestep their governments' ingenious diplomatic tactics. I didn't mean to draw this parallel, but the more I become acquainted with the international women's movement, the more I find a similarity between, say, French and Russian women, even though French women nowadays are the least advanced. Even so, these two groups share the same self-assuredness and the same almost contemptuous attitude toward others. Further analogy will reveal more positive similarities, and I will speak about these later.

Source: A. A. Kal'manovich, *Zhenskoe dvizhenie i ego zadachi. Kratkii istoricheskii ocherk (Doklad, chitannyi v Zheneve, Moskve i Peterburge)* [*The Women's Movement* and Its Mission: A Short Historical Sketch (A Speech Read in Geneva, Moscow, and St. Petersburg)] (St. Petersburg, 1908). Excerpted from pp. 1–4.

Translated by Karen L. Myers.

FIRST BALL

TATIANA SHCHEPKINA-KUPERNIK

Tatiana L'vovna Shchepkina-Kupernik (m. Polynova, 1874–1952) was an author of prose, a playwright, a translator, an actress, a journalist, and an author of memoirs. Over her sixty-year career, she accomplished much in each of these genres. She translated fifty-nine plays from six languages; these translations were acclaimed and include works by Hugo, Molière, and Shakespeare. One of her own plays, A Happy Woman (1911), won the Griboedov prize for best play of the season. Like this play, her poetry and prose fiction often focused on women: her first collection of poetry, for example, was entitled From Women's Letters (1898). Her prose fiction takes up three major themes: the theater, the underprivileged, and women's lives.

Published originally in a collection of Shchepkina-Kupernik's stories entitled It Happened Yesterday (1907), "First Ball" depicts a different kind of political activism than that seen with Elena Likhacheva and Anna Kalmanovich. Reflecting the split between "feminists" and "social revolutionaries" concerning both ends and means, the chief character in the story is motivated by an outrage over social injustice that is not focused specifically on the position and rights of women—and she accepts terror as a legitimate response and means of struggle. Although the heroine in the story is not portrayed as being part of a political organization, Russian women in the late imperial period played a prominent role in the political groups that employed terror as a tactic.

The dress came out delightfully: white tulle and innumerable flounces and gathers, so that it looked a bit like a cloud, a bit like sea spray, a bit like the first snowfall . . . in a word, it looked like something airy and innocent. The general's wife had overseen its making far more than had Olga Nikolaevna, for whom it had been made. The general's wife even had them bring it to her in her bedroom after she had retired for the evening. It would be shown off, dressed on a mannequin, and Maria Filipovna would turn it around, this way and that, and the general's wife, wallowing in her pillows, would inspect it through her lorgnette, and delight in it.

The spacious bedroom was warm and cozy. A little lamp burned in front of the icon case, and the little stove, guzzling, devoured fuel. The general's wife would not give away the huge double bed made of red wood, in spite of her almost decade-long widowhood. The bed was resplendent in elegant, snow-white sheets— a pride and weakness of the general's wife, immaculate, like her weaknesses.

The general's wife was a plump woman, not old quite yet. She lay in a fresh batiste blouse under the satin of the featherbed, and her face protected its expression of tranquil contentment. Next to her, on a narrow little stool, stood two cups of tea, a jar of jam, and a flask of rum; the general's wife liked to have her evening tea in bed when she didn't have guests. It was cozier than sitting as a pair in the big, solemn dining room, where, no matter what, Olga never came to tea. Either Olga wasn't home or she was in her room, serving tea to some sort of "shaggy, disheveled" people, as the general's wife called Olga's friends, with good-natured contempt.

Olga's closed nature frightened her somehow, [as did] her habit of leaving the city for two or three days, darkly explaining that she was going "to her girl-friend's." Her books, her horseback riding, her habit of shooting at empty bottles in the garden every morning, and the endless quantity of books that she subscribed to—all were decidedly frightening. But the general's wife had never argued with anyone her whole life: arguments and explanations gave her migraines. She couldn't even dismiss a servant; she had Maria Filipovna do it for her.

Everyone, herself included in this number, thought the general's wife an angel. She so slipped into the role that, if she didn't like something, she would simply raise her eyes toward heaven, saying: "Such is my life!" Then she tried to think no more of it.

But now the general's wife was in a simply rose-colored frame of mind: a week or so ago Olga had suddenly declared her desire to go to the ball. This was the first time she had done this her whole life, and the general's wife brightened up straightaway. She called all of the tailors to her without delay, and all week, forgetting even her usual soft idleness, she lived in an atmosphere of tulle and lace, silk and flowers—in a word, all that she had lacked all of these years. The general's wife was a deeply virtuous woman, and truly kept the memory of her husband. From the day of his death she ceased to dress up and go out, but on the other hand dreamed of how she would send out her beautiful little Olga. But little Olga grew up—and destroyed all of those dreams: she displayed completely different tastes, "she didn't dress, but simply covered herself," as the general's wife would say with a display of grief. Finishing secondary school, Olga had prepared to go to Petersburg to study, but somehow classes had never started, and she had lived at home for almost two years now, and instead of going out and receiving guests, she locked herself up with her books, or left to see unknown and unpleasant friends, in the general's wife's opinion.

Instead of proper society, she had over these "shaggy, disheveled" people, and still constantly took in all of these different, ragged people whom she fed and dressed and took to the train stations. Her means were her own, and the general's wife spared her no money, but she had already begun to fear that Olga would waste her life finally, and would never find a well-situated husband. She was already twenty years old! As she sat at home, locked up, finding a proper man was difficult. God forbid, she still imagined that she could go wherever, for whatever purpose . . . in a blouse! The general's wife turned cold all over at the thought.

And suddenly Olga cheered her up: she said herself that she wanted to go to the ball! True, it was a small disappointment that the question of the dress and the flowers and all the rest was left entirely in the hands of the mother, who took it up with painstaking energy, but, all the same, that lack of interest in Olga about such important things was slightly distressing. The general's wife time and again spoke out with regard to her astonishment in conversations with her confidante, Maria Filipovna,[19] or, as all of her friends called her—"Widow," although her husband was alive and only located in some obscure absence. Widow was a thin, dry, fifty-year-old woman. She lived on her own very small means, and rented a furnished room from the deacon's wife, but this room, for the most part, served as a shelter for her trunk, as she herself spent day and night at the home of the general's wife. To the general's wife she was irreplaceable: no one could pour tea so deliciously, massage in petroleum jelly with alcohol and make raspberry tea so well in case of a light cold, pick up something at the store that couldn't be entrusted to the servants, and so on, and so on. Besides that, the general's wife, occasionally suffering from nervous heart palpitations, was unable to sleep alone: then the dressing-room door was opened, and Widow slept in there on the big sofa. The dressing room was becoming her domain, piece by piece; she left her unimportant toilet necessities there, and her work, and even a portrait of her missing husband. But she would never agree to move in completely with the general's wife, and that is why, possibly, that between them, they governed a perfect world.

Widow, silently stepping shod in little cloth shoes, went over to the bell and rang twice for the young mistress's maid.

Dora appeared at the summons; she was a thin, little gypsy type with burning eyes in a black dress. She silently gathered up the mannequin.

"What is the young mistress doing?" asked the general's wife.

"Lying down, reading," quietly answered Dora. "Do you need anything else?"

"Nothing. Tell the young mistress not to read too much, or tomorrow her eyes will be red!"

Dora had a nervous twitch in the corner of her mouth. She lowered her head and left.

"And what kind of servant she is," sighed Widow. "That Dora is a surprisingly insolent girl!"

"What? Has she said something to you?" worried the general's wife, not liking it if her Widow had been offended.

"No, it would be a sin to raise false accusations. She knows, my golden ones, how angelically you treat me. Really, what would she say? But she is impertinently silent, somehow. She never says, 'She's lying down, madame, reading, madame,' but 'lying down, reading' . . . well, is that really proper?"

"Yes, it's true. But Olga loves her terribly, and she's so honest. . . . "

"The young mistress permits her too much. She goes everywhere with her, like a companion; they read, they chat as if they were equals. That's why she's grown proud."

"It is already Olga's affair. She found her herself, brought her from somewhere. I said, 'Does she have recommendations?' And she said to me, 'Don't worry, I know her.' So, let her do as she pleases."

"But she's such a little heathen! It's her second year with you, and not once has she fasted, not once has she kept Lent! On Good Friday she was drinking milk!"[20] said Widow with horror.

"She learned that from Olga too," sighed the general's wife.

"I was thinking, my precious ones, mightn't she be Jewish?"

"To think of that! Why, I have her passport myself: citizen of Pskov, Daria Telegina. . . . "

"Yes, of course, her face doesn't look Russian at all!"

"Well, devil take her! Call Duniasha, Widow, ask her to have your bed made, and go to bed. It's late."

"Why should I bother Duniasha? I can do it myself, I have everything I need . . . I'll just gather up the cups. . . . "

In a few minutes everything was quiet and dark, and only by the light of the little lamp did a long figure with a deacon's braid shine white, bowing to the ground.

The general's wife fell asleep peacefully and sweetly to the murmur of prayerful whispers.

The next evening the Zarubov house was unusually alive. Dressmakers and maids threw themselves from room to room; everything smelled of perfume, and powder, and irons. The French hairstylist heated the crimping tongs over the spirit lamp. The general's wife dressed in her room in front of a big pier glass in which candles burned; Widow helped her, and the dressmaker, and Duniasha, and among them flew incessant chatter and stories, groans and laughter.

All was quiet in Olga Nikolaevna's room. Her big room, with books standing on every dresser and shelf, was more reminiscent of a student's room than that of a young mistress.

The dress, all prepared, lay helplessly spread out on the narrow iron bed.

Olga Nikolaevna sat at the writing desk. It was her favorite, an old table with an oilcloth casing all spotted with ink, scratched and cut with a knife. A small bust of Tolstoi had been standing there since her childhood, and she could not bring herself to send it away, although she had long ago outgrown her period of its influence. It stared angrily at the gloves tossed on the table, the lace fan on its white ribbon, the bouquet of violets; at everything that the general's wife had chosen for her with such interest. The young girl already wore white stockings on her shapely legs, stretched thin, like cobwebs, so that her pink skin glistened through the semi-transparent material; little white shoes adorned her feet. They exhibited a strange contrast to her modest, virginal underclothes without any sort of adornment or ornamentation. Her heavy strawberry-blonde hair, which she usually wore plaited into two braids, lay in two luxuriant waves on her shoulders. She sat, stretching forth her uncovered hands, and embracing her knees with them, and stared steadily at one fixed point. Dora stood by the bed, equally silent and motionless. It was as if both, the young mistress and the maid, had forgotten that it was time to dress. There was a knock on the door. Both of them gave a start. Duniasha brought in a batiste peignoir.

"Your mother sent this to you. Might the Frenchman do your hair?"

Dora slipped the peignoir onto Olga, and behind Duniasha appeared the dark, smiling Frenchman with a large-toothed comb behind his ear.

Olga knitted her brows a little when his hands, which were not entirely clean and smelled of greasy pomade, grasped her head. Dora, following all of Olga's motions with her burning eyes, blushed all over, and quickly asked, "Might I comb your hair?"

"No matter what, Mama won't be still until he's disfigured me," answered Olga, and then casually resigned her head to the disposal of Monsieur Jules. She sat silently and mechanically glanced into the mirror placed before her. It reflected exactly the strangeness of her face, how changed it was by the fashionable hairstyle. Parted in two, her hair hid her forehead, so it became low, and her eyes, already wide and dark, became darker from the proximity of the golden curls. Up above, Monsieur Jules cut off its corners.

"A la grècque! [In the Greek style!]" he explained. "The mademoiselle has such a lot of hair, there would be nothing else to do with it. Oh, ce qu'une parisienne aurait donnée pour ces cheveux! [Oh, what a Parisian woman would do for this hair!] Our ladies have no hair, only false hair. Maybe a sprig of violets here? How mademoiselle is reminiscent of mademoiselle Mierise from Quo Vadis!"

He pronounced it "Quo vadi," and kept on chattering for quite some time, as is the way with hairstylists, paying no attention to the fact that they go unanswered. Finally he finished the hairstyle and withdrew.

Olga stood up and cast her eyes around the room. Her eyes stopped on one object, then another. She was delaying something . . . then her eyes fell on the dress, and on the motionless Dora.

"Well, it's time to get dressed," she suddenly said decidedly.

Dora handed her the dress. Both were silent. Dora's heartbeat was audible. Loudly, strongly, exactly, someone beat on Dora's chest with little hammers, until she fastened the dress up the back. Again, there was a knock at the door.

Widow came in and brought with her a lace shawl from the general's wife.

"Your mama forgot to give this to you . . . Oh my soul, Olga Nikolaevna! What a beauty you are! Simply a bride in white!"

Widow looked at her with feeling; her hands were even folded as if in prayer. Olga smiled at her with her mouth only, and reflecting, repeated, "A bride. . . . "

Widow shook her head again.

"You should always wear white, Olga Nikolaevna, and you are always in black, like some kind of nun. Your Mama is entirely ready, and she asks that you come to her when you are all dressed."

"I will be ready in a moment," said Olga in an apathetic voice. "I'll be right there."

Widow left. Dora continued to fasten the bodice. Her fingers were shaking so badly that the hooks would not fall into the loops. Olga Nikolaevna turned suddenly.

"Dora, do I look like a bride?" she asked.

Dora abruptly slid to the floor, and grasping Olga Nikolaevna's knees with both hands, pressed them to her and froze. Only her shoulders were shuddering.

Olga bent toward her and, trying to raise her up, stroked her head, like a child. "Dora, Dora! . . . Where is our strength of will?"

Her face would have been perfectly calm, albeit deathly pale, had her nostrils not quivered. Now her entire being, tall, shapely, beautiful, seemed stronger and older than Dora, although she was younger by some seven years.

"Why couldn't it be me? Why couldn't it be me!" groaned Dora, shaking all over with soundless weeping.

"Dora, Dora!" said Olga impatiently, seeing that the other would not be soothed. "You are making me hurt more. Is that your way of helping me? I am not crying."

"I am crazy, but I won't be any more!" whispered Dora. All the same, she would not rise from her knees. She bowed down still lower and stuck her lips to the little white shoes.

"Dora!" Olga blushed, and wanted to be angry. But the expression on Dora's face was such that she extended her hand, and clasped the rising Dora to herself.

They stood quietly for a minute, embracing. Olga closed her eyes. A deep horizontal wrinkle cut across her forehead. Her lips were pressed tight.

With a quick motion, she abruptly almost knocked Dora down. "Well, of course . . . enough. Let's go to mama now . . . there. Better now, so that there won't be any. . . . Tell everyone I said hello. Goodbye, Dora, goodbye!"

She clenched her hand tightly, tossed her head, and left.

"Take everything to Mama. Those . . . things."

The general's wife was already dressed in a lavender-velvet dress, radiant in diamonds and smiles.

Seeing her daughter she gasped, and without warning began to cry: the general's wife cried easily as a rule.

"What's wrong with you, Mama?" said Olga, kissing her mother's hand.

"I'm so sorry that you lost two entire years!" sobbed the general's wife, wiping her eyes with a wad of batiste handkerchief. "Everything under lock and key. Always in black, just like some sort of poor student. And white looks so good on you. Oh, what a beauty I have!" She embraced her daughter and kissed her, pressing her to her cheeks wet with tears.

Something flickered suddenly across Olga's face.

"Mama, maybe . . . you won't be going?" she asked perfectly unexpectedly.

The general's wife was dumbfounded, and even stopped crying. "What is the matter with you?"

Olga was abashed. "I just thought . . . well, that maybe, you . . . you aren't in the habit of . . . and you'll grow so tired, or in a mood. And Anna Viktorovna will be there. . . . " she explained with some confusion.

"Oh, you, my sweet, Heaven take you!" objected the general's wife, offended. "It seems I'm not a Queen of Spades[21] yet, I won't crumble from senility. As if I suddenly wouldn't go to your first ball!"

Olga lowered her head. Her mother looked her over from every angle, turned her about, looked again and again under the sighs of Widow and Duniasha, corrected this little fold, fixed that small lock. Then they began to look for her gloves. Then they lost the lorgnette. Then a piece of lace ripped off.

Finally, after a lot of bothering about, Duniasha announced that the horses had been brought around, and they all poured down the flight of stairs. The general's wife sailed into the carriage in her sable, then a ray of light from the street lamp lit up the golden head with a sprig of violets.

"Dora, don't catch cold!" cried Olga, her voice breaking, when she saw Dora standing on the stairs in only a dress and with her head uncovered.

"It's all the same, now!" answered Dora with a voice full of despair.

Widow's indignant call was heard, "Is that really how you answer your mistress?"

And the carriage moved away.

In the drawing room, in the corner under the palm trees, where the town's most respectable ladies sat (indeed, the governor's wife, the deputy's wife, and the chairman's wife were all there), there arose a sort of sanctum sanctorum. All of the arriving guests headed there first of all; they kissed hands, inquired after health, and headed off. The respectable ladies were in the big hall, the young people were in the far drawing room where there were open card tables; many of the ladies were in there as well, admiring their own creations in multicolored dresses.

The general's wife quickly found a place, and good friends, in the respectable corner. Compliments flew:

"*Votre fille est charmante!* [Your daughter is charming!]"

"Is this her first ball? How unfair you have been, my dear, not to have shown us this delight before now."

"You will see. She will be the belle of the ball. *Ravissante, ravissante!* [Ravishing, ravishing!]"

The ladies whispered quietly between themselves. They wondered how old Olga might be; they found that she held herself too haughtily for her first ball.

"*Elle manque de* [She lacks] femininity, my dear," said the thin attorney's wife, who looked like an old maid. "In a girl, *n'est-ce pas important* [it is so important]—femininity. Beauty alone *ne vaut rien!* [is worth nothing!]"

"But it looks good on her type of beauty!" answered the goodhearted chairman's wife.

"You shall see how quickly she is stolen away from you!" commented the attorney's wife to the general's wife aloud. "She won't be dancing for long!"

The ladies conversed in each other's ears, so it wouldn't be a surprise if Olga Zarubova happened to come and sit by her mother's hand. She had, at least, one hundred thousand in dowry!

"Oh, *ma chère*, more than that: two thousand acres of land in the city alone!"

"But they say that her character is very disagreeable. She's some kind of old blue stocking. Self-confident, bold, eccentric . . . she doesn't care a fig for her mother. Yes, it's obvious: *voyez les airs qu'elle se donne!* [look at the airs she puts on!]"

And they sang aloud: "*Délicieuse, délicieuse!* [Delicious, delicious!]"

The general's wife beamed.

Olga sat for a little while in the drawing room. The governor's wife's attaché from the Baltics hurried over and was presented to her. He was the best dancer in town, and he presented to her a few other cavaliers. She turned down the *pas d'espagne*, which was just beginning, as she had not learned it in school. She promised the waltz to the baron, the quadrille to someone else, and the mazurka to a third. The baron was joyfully excited, and handsome, resplendent in a dazzling chemisette and polished shoes, and stockings that shone like two little suns. He hurried off to the ballroom, while she remained in her place near the arch, from which spot the entire ballroom was visible.

The gold room was flooded with light, with its huge chandelier on whose pendants played rainbow-colored lights and its electrical sconce on the wall. The orchestra was lodged on a large platform beneath a portrait of the Tsar. The ladies sat along the walls, and the young mistresses would sit for a while, then flutter off, like butterflies from flowers.

Around the room, in a huge, free space, meandered a many-colored, elegant garland of dancing couples.

Olga watched them. From lack of habit, from the bright lights and the bright colors, from the sounds of the music or the low rumble of the crowd, a well-educated rumble in which could be heard the rustling of silk skirts, and fans, and French phrases; from all of this, Olga's head began to spin slightly. She suddenly remembered her friend Sonia Gregorovius. She was a pale, sickly little girl who had been forbidden to dance at the age of fourteen. She had told Olga, "Do you know what I do, so that I don't become envious? I sit here every night at Zhenia Kromskaia's, and I used to want to dance so badly that I would become jealous. I stopped up my ears really tightly, so that I couldn't hear the music. And suddenly I wasn't envious anymore; it was just funny. Everyone jumping about, making all sorts of strange gestures, red and straggling, completely crazy . . . I haven't become jealous once since then!"

The picture before her of the ball presented a similar sensation in Olga. After her normal life, which she led in a completely different setting, surrounded by people who lived in the middle of hard labor and war, people frighteningly devoted to one collective goal, people who were, for the most part comrades not only in labor but also in necessity—and harassment, deprivation, and self-renunciation . . . it seemed to her that creatures from another world had gathered here. It was as if these people were unaware of what occurred this very minute to their own people in their own country. They may as well have been Kaffirs or Zulus, judging by their relationship with their own people. It was as if they suspected nothing, knew nothing, and continued, undisturbed and with enthusiasm, depending on the character, to surrender to their happy dances, the caress of the music, the distraction of flirting and coquetry . . .

Olga watched them with eyes wide open, and suddenly she shuddered as if from electric shock.

A young officer approached the governor's wife, his spurs melodically ringing slightly. He was a very tall, well-built man of ideal beauty, with a head like Anthony, which was only a little spoiled by his not overlarge, gray, excessively cold eyes. The eyes watched everything brightly and coldly, but they were disguised by a bewitching smile, parted crimson lips, and an opening row of teeth that were white, like almonds. He respectfully kissed the hand of the governor's wife and told her in exquisite French that his Excellency was looking for her.

She stood, clasped his hand, and left with him.

The ladies became agitated in his wake.

"Well, how do you like our new lion, Prince Gordynsky?" the chairman's wife asked the general's wife.

"Remarkably attractive!" enthusiastically answered the general's wife, not removing the lorgnette from her eyes. "And, well . . . is he well-situated?"

"Not really, but *très bien né* [from a good family] and on a path to glory. So young, and already a colonel . . . He carried out his orders marvelously here, you know: everything was accomplished in two days. Really, he is a lion, and not a man at all; he simply doesn't understand what fear is. . . . "

Olga, frozen from head to toe, watched after Gordynsky. He led the governor's wife to her husband, and returned to the ballroom. He walked up to a stylish little brunette, who simply lit up. He bowed, and after a minute they already occupied a space among the dancers. He danced marvelously, with grace and strength together, and it wasn't funny, even for a minute. He somehow protected his light little damsel and dominated her at the same time. Many were admiring the attractive couple.

Olga watched most attentively and fixedly of all. She could not tear her eyes away. She somehow could not blend in her head that beauty, that enthusiasm for the dance, that face, with what she knew had brought her here. She shut her eyes for a minute. And there, not at all like Sonia, an entirely different sensation appeared.

The music continued to sound, now flowing, now passionate, a laughing and teasing, light, bright melody, joining the simplicity of a Spanish folksong and the gracious manner of modern dances. Silk rustled, spurs jangled, everything smelled of perfume and flowers . . . In front of her closed eyes, Olga saw a very different picture under that music; different motions, toward a bright horror.

There was a wretched, little room . . . A woman kneaded dough for bread, the children played on the floor, dressing a wood-chip doll in rags. A young worker prepared to rest . . . noise . . . the sound of spurs, those very same spurs! A loud voice:

"Are you Vasiliev?". . . . "I am.". . . . "Come here.". . . . "Good heavens, what for?" exclaims the woman. "You are looking for Iakov Vasiliev, aren't you, and this is Dmitri?". . . . "It's none of your business!" she is rudely cut short. The woman obediently becomes silent. She whispers, "Again a week or two in jail to satisfy them . . . I hope they don't want more!" At that moment there is shooting in the courtyard, an entire round . . . She is senseless from fear, she throws herself to the door, her children behind her, clutching at her skirt . . . The poor woman, the wall spattered with blood . . . There is no owner, they shot him without a trial, upon the order of the commander. *For a similar last name!* The woman told this to them, standing before them with those children clinging to her skirt, shuddering from sobs without tears . . . Olga was at the hovel herself, had seen the blood stains on the white walls . . . But was that woman really alone? Tens, hundreds, of women form a line in front of her. Such a long troop that it now winds around the ball-room underneath the music; slaughtered, harassed women, rags and tatters and earthy faces . . . Young women, little girls, scarcely more than children—a dis-graced, dishonored band of "punishers" . . . There is a senile old woman in front of whom they shot her only son because he had not gone to work . . . There is a woman with a baby nursing at her breast, which had lost its milk that day when they killed her husband because they discovered he had a revolver . . . Another mother, in front of whom they shot her eleven-year-old son because he had not moved off the road when ordered . . . All of the beggarly, orphaned, hungry chil-dren, dying from starvation . . . Oh, what a frightening procession! . . . They strive onward, they lament, they pull out their hair, scratch at their dry breasts with their nails . . . Their eyes are full of bloody tears, their gums are swollen and whitened from hunger . . . How many of them, how many of them . . .

Olga opened her eyes in terror. But in the place of these frightening visions, the pink, blue, multicolored garland of elegant, smiling women swam around the ball-room . . .

The orchestra fell silent, but not for long. After a moment, the sound rose, the scraping of feet, curtseying and bowing, the movement of chairs, conversations. Then the conductor cried out in an exaggeratedly meaningful tone of voice:

"*La valse, s'il vous plaît!* [The waltz, please!]"

The thin conductor flourished his baton. The orchestra was imitating a gypsy band. The sweet, pretty melody rose and sang—the melody of the "Blue [Danube] Waltz." The baron stood in front of Olga, bowing and smiling, glanced at her face; he just had time to appraise its novelty and beauty, and he waited for the waltz with impatience.

"*C'est la valse promise!* [It is the promised waltz!]"

Olga, still not really understanding what was wrong with her, or where she was, stood mechanically and went with him to the ballroom. She placed his hand on her shoulder, and succumbed to the slow tempo of the waltz. In her head flashed images, thoughts, pictures—but, little by little her nervous excitement calmed her, stole her away with the waltz, and hid those images so that they would give way to a new sensation, unexpected and unfamiliar.

Knowing these dances only from mandatory classes at secondary school, in which her whole circle of friends looked upon them as beating out an insufferable obligation, Olga had never imagined what it would be like to dance with a good dancer. The baron danced splendidly. He held his lady expertly, gently and strongly at the same time, almost lifting her from the floor for minutes at a time; the floor just swam under her. In time, she was enveloped in a full drowsiness and feeling of physical happiness, like in childhood when she swung on the swings. Her breath caught and tickled her throat, and finally her head was spinning so that she had to stop and whisper: "I cannot, my throat has become too dry!"

"Then you need some fresh air. Come on, I'll get you something to drink," anxiously offered the baron, and, expertly threading a path between the dancers, he led Olga to the buffet in the next room.

He handed her a goblet of something sparkling. She greedily drank it down. The icy stream gently pricked her throat; fresh, fragrant, feeling like cold fire, it spread to every nerve.

"What is this?"

"*Coupe glacée* [Iced champagne]," he answered. "But after that you absolutely must dance, or you will catch a cold. That was a bit of military cunning; *je ne vous ferai pas grâce de cette valse* [I won't let you decline this waltz]."

Smiling, he again drew her into the ballroom, and pressed her to him a little more strongly. They stood there like that, waiting for the moment to enter the waltz. And again she was taken up off of the ground . . . She was unused to champagne, and it made her head spin. The waltz itself seemed intoxicating. The violins shivered and sighed, as if from pleasure, and they gave themselves up to the hidden depth of her being. The violets faded on her breast, and the warm air blowing past her face was sweet smelling and caressing. It seemed to her that she felt as if she would overflow with the crimson blood that pulsed beneath her skin.

"*Vous dansez comme une fée!* [You dance like a fairy!]" the baron whispered to her.

He did not want to let her go, and she herself did not want him to. She did not want this waltz to end, and with every turn she was all the closer to something fated and inevitable. If only she could postpone its ending! It would be eternal, like the shades of Dante's hell, like a dry leaf in a tuft of wind, drifting along like that, not knowing, or feeling, or thinking . . .

She closed her eyes halfway. The waves of sweet, exasperating music wrapped her up in lassitude, then picked her up and hurried off to somewhere. The sea sounded all around her, and through that noise of the sea it seemed to her as if someone unseen, but powerful, whispered to her, "I will give you everything if, having fallen, you humble yourself to me!"

And all of that was possible for her! Was it worth it to turn down that to which she had condemned herself? Was it worth it to desire?

She was young and pretty, she could see that in the enthusiastic eyes of the men; hot blood played in her young, strong body. Her refined hands were created for caresses . . . Desire? And all of this—the splendor, the diamonds, the smell of flowers, that music . . . The visions, the torment, the shackles, the torture, for which she had been prepared, disappeared like a shadow, and there was only the light, and the joy, and that music . . . Sweet, sweet music . . .

But the music abruptly broke off. The charm and fascination disappeared; only reality was at hand.

"Permit me to take you to your *maman?*" asked the baron.

"No . . . I'll just rest a moment. I danced too much."

He fanned her with her lace fan for a few minutes. They were preparing for the quadrille in the ballroom. The orchestra played some type of introduction.

Olga suddenly got even paler.

"Are you going to faint?" asked the baron, frightened.

"No . . . it's stuffy! Get me some ice cream. . . . " Olga ordered quickly. The baron disappeared. Olga stood up to her full height, leaving her left hand on the back of the chair. They were leading Gordynsky to her. He walked with his conqueror's gait, proudly holding his perfect head. He had not reached Olga when he stopped. Olga stared at him, not looking away. It seemed to the officer that there was something painful in that look. The energy in that stare was unusual, with something that was not quite horror, not quite despair, looking out of those wide-open eyes, which were almost black from their dilated pupils. That strange, almost panicked horror was transmitted to him, and he suddenly went pale.

For a minute they stared into each other's eyes.

"There, there he is. . . . " flashed through Olga's head. A thought of her mother bore into her for only an instant. Everything around her suddenly reeled, and collapsed into an abyss. The lights dimmed; she clearly saw in front of her only the handsome, pale, cruel face from which the smile had vanished . . . She slipped her hand behind her corsage with one quick motion. Something glistened in her hand. It shot once, again, three times . . . The officer flung up his hands, and fell.

The music stopped. Women's wailing could be heard.

When the stunned crowd came to itself and rushed into the room, the policeman on duty was already running about.

Olga stood motionless, clutching the revolver in her hand.

Gordynsky lay dead on the spot.

Source: Tat'iana L'vovna Shchepkina-Kupernik, "Pervyi bal," *Tol'ko chas* [*Only an Hour*], ed. Viktoriia Vasil'evna Uchenova (Moscow, 1988), pp. 317–34. Originally published in 1907 in Shchepkina-Kupernik's collection of short stories *Eto bylo vchera* [*It Happened Yesterday*]. Excerpted.

Translated by Melissa Merrill Floyd.

WOMEN SUPPORTING WOMEN IN OPPOSITION: REMINISCENCES OF NATALIA ARMFELDT

EKATERINA BRESHKO-BRESHKOVSKAIA

Opposition to the imperial government and its policies could result in the extreme consequences of prison or death sentences. Cultural ideas about women offered some initial protection, holding them outside of suspicion and often allowing them to act in situations when men could not (for example, in peasant protests). Once women had committed crimes against the state or its servitors, however, their gender did not protect them from

punishment. Many women were sentenced to long prison terms, and some were exe-
cuted, for revolutionary activity. Female comrades in prison, as in the underground
movements, supported one another to survive difficult conditions. Ekaterina Breshko-
Breshkovskaia (1844–1934), long active in socialist revolutionary groups and known as
"the little grandmother of the revolution," describes life in prison by painting a portrait
of Natalia Armfeldt (1850?–1887), an imprisoned comrade. The commitment women
had both to the causes they served and to each other is apparent in this excerpt, and might
well be compared to that of the religious women seen in chapter 5.

Natalia Aleksandrovna Armfeldt was a Muscovite. Her father was an educated
man, a lover of foreign languages, which he knew very well. For many years he
served in Moscow as an inspecting officer of the Nikolaev Women's Institute,[22]
and his two daughters—the elder, subsequently the wife of the naturalist Fed-
chenko, and the second, Natalia Aleksandrovna—studied in this institute.

Her mother, a very educated woman, was widowed at a young age, but managed
to create for herself a position of such respect among the best of Moscow society
that the most highly educated people of the day took her opinion into account.
Count L. N. Tolstoi[23] treated her with particular respect. Anna Vasilevna Armfeldt wanted her daughters to gain practical knowledge of foreign languages, so
there were always English and French women in her home. Natalia Aleksandrovna sought to continue her education after finishing the Institute, and since
there were no institutions of higher education [for women] in Moscow, she was
allowed to go abroad.

At Heidelberg she attended courses in the mathematical sciences and did very
well in them, which did not prevent her also from studying music and painting.
It must be supposed that it was the *narodnik* (populist)[24] movement that, from the
very beginning of the [18]70s, compelled Natalia Aleksandrovna to return to Russia and take part in the work of the established movement. I do not know the
number and composition of the Moscow circles of the day, but as regards Natalia
Aleksandrovna, I know that her closest comrade in revolutionary work in
Moscow was Batiushkova;[25] their close friendship was interrupted only by Natalia
Aleksandrovna's death.

I know likewise from N. A. herself that, during the time of her [populist] activity in Moscow, she was arrested six times. She would be held at the police station, released, and then find herself there again. The last of her Moscow arrests
ended with her administrative exile to the town of Bui, in Kostroma province.[26]
She would often reminisce about her residence there, and in a light-hearted tone
would tell stories of her acquaintance with local inhabitants and how she took
part in agricultural labor and how she liked life among the simple, unsophisticated
people who were surrounded by equally artless nature.

When she had completed her administrative exile, she returned home to
Moscow, to her mother [and] her brothers, who were also subject to relentless persecution by the gendarmes. Soon she was convinced that, being so well-known to

the Moscow gendarmes, it was impossible for her to continue her revolutionary work, and in 1879 she moved to Kiev, joined a local organization of revolutionaries, and in the spring of that same year was arrested on Zhilianskii Street, together with many others (Debogorii-Mokrievich,[27] the brothers Ivechevich, and others), as a result of armed resistance during which the gendarme Kazankin was killed. Others on both sides were also killed and wounded. Natasha[28] was struck by a bullet that ricocheted off a wall. The bullet struck her on the right side of her breast and tore her dress, but did not wound her bodily. The black cashmere dress came to Kara,[29] where we examined this trophy with great curiosity. It was never clarified whose bullet killed Kazankin. The shot was attributed to Brandt, and, despite the fact that Natalia Aleksandrovna took responsibility for this shot, Brandt was still hanged.

The trial of the Zhilianskii Street Group occurred at the same time as the trial of Osinskii and S. Leshern.[30] This trial resulted in three death sentences. Of the Zhilianskii Group, the majority were sentenced to fourteen years' hard labor, including Natasha; at the time she was about thirty years old.

And thus Natalia Aleksandrovna Armfeldt had in front of her fourteen years of hard labor. She accepted her sentence with her innate courage and good spirits, prepared to share all of the hardship and privation that awaited her comrades on their voyage and at hard labor. No one ever saw N. A. melancholy or mournful as regards the loss of the lavish earthly and familial blessings which she enjoyed living under the roof of her adoring mother. But she was frequently and profoundly anxious about the state of mind of her mother, whose every thought was directed at her beloved daughter's difficult and bleak life.

Before my arrival in Kara I had never seen N. A. and had heard little of her, which strengthened the impression made by my acquaintance with this bright and beautiful spirit. It was extremely pleasant for me to observe her gentle and heartfelt treatment of me from the very first hours of our meeting. And our meeting occurred as follows: on the first day of Easter in 1882 I was brought to the gates of the Kara Women's Prison. I was admitted to the courtyard where, on the porch of a small building that served previously as a guardhouse, I was met by a group of [female] political convicts, hitherto unknown to me. Among them Armfeldt and Kutitonskaia somehow became especially interested in me, although I was equally glad to see them all, since for more than two years I had been deprived of female society and longed for it. My mood was very joyous; straightaway I began to make everyone's acquaintance and to inquire about who they were and where they were from. It turned out that M. A. Kolenkina was in this prison, but she lay ill in her small cell. I had long been friendly with her; in 1874 we went out to the people together. The remaining inhabitants of this prison were new and unknown activists to me: N. A. Armfeldt, Kutitonskaia, Bogomolets, Kovalskaia, Shekhter, Kriukovskaia, Leshern, Rossikova, and Levenson;[31] the last three at this time were in the hospital.

The prison was divided into four cells, the doors of which opened out onto a corridor where there was an oven with a tea-urn and a stove. The appearance of

the cells surprised me by its familial character—there were flowers in the windows, in one cell there was a sewing machine, and in the one where Armfeldt and
Kutitonskaia lived there was an easel and an enormous Italian accordion on the
table. My joyful state at the sight of this dear female society was infectious—we
chatted, joked, laughed, and within an hour Armfeldt was playing dance music
on her Italian accordion, and I was dancing furiously, moving from one woman to
another. I cannot say how long I was in this excited condition, but I remember
that after my last turn with the last of my women, I swayed and fell on the pile of
my traveling clothes, which lay in the corner on the floor. I also know that I was
unable to get up by myself, that Armfeldt's powerful arms lifted me and carried me
to someone's bed in the adjacent cell.

She was prepared to sacrifice herself for the sake of anyone needing her self-
sacrifice. It goes without saying that the ideal of the universal happiness of man-
kind was the base on which her social activism developed, and her loving heart
was not satisfied with mere abstractions, but demanded the expression of this ideal
in everyday life. Of course, Natasha also had her antipathies, but she was able to
force herself to make peace with them, once she saw that her harsh attitude could
destroy the general harmony of the prisoners' life.

II.

Having arrived at Kara, I managed to take advantage of the privileges enjoyed
by the Sredne-Kara women's prison. The escape of a comrade from the men's
prison led to significant repression, too, in the women's prison. The men responded
to the repression with a hunger strike, which we also joined. No one passed the five
days of our hunger strike with as much cheer and spirit as did Natasha. The cells
were still open, so we could communicate, but many of the women lay on their
beds in order to save their strength. But Natasha was on her feet the whole time,
going from one cell to another, joking, making humorous comments about our situation, and [she] even proposed that all gather around the weaker ones, organizing a game of cards, [a pack of] which by some miracle had remained in the prison.
Her spirited attitude toward the calamity that had befallen us greatly softened the
severity of our situation. All of our books had been confiscated. The easel, the accordion, and the sewing machine had disappeared somewhere. The flowers had
been thrown out of their pots. The prison detachment that had arrived finally
locked us up in separate cells, but not without violence. They let us out only for
cleaning the cell toilets and curtailed all of our household needs to a minimum.
They served us prison slop from a common caldron and a ration of black bread.
And even in these conditions Natasha was distinguished by her energetic character, always looking after the needs of her neighbors. She even contrived to dash
outside to water her garden where various vegetables were growing and which was
already covered with a luxuriant green growth. I should say that even in the early

spring, when the women were not yet deprived of their relative freedom, Natasha had planned a small but rational vegetable garden in the little courtyard of the prison guardhouse. The beds were luxuriant, fertilized, and covered with good black earth. From Moscow "Mama" sent her gardening seeds suitable for a northern climate and by the end of May the beds were impressive with their green growth of radishes, cucumbers, turnips, carrots, and other vegetables. She [Natasha] tended her vegetable garden zealously and lovingly. It was in exemplary order. One can imagine her chagrin when soon after the hunger strike the cossack prison detachment announced to us the departure from the Sredne-Kara mine to the Ust-Kara lockup.

At Ust-Kara began a three-month period of cold, hungry lockup. [After] three months of the cruel regimen had passed, we were permitted to use our money and books, and were permitted to take orders for handwork. We were once again allowed to take charge of household affairs.

Source: Ekaterina Breshko-Breshkovskaia, "Vospominanie: [Chast'] II. N. A. Armfel'd," *Golos minuvshego* ("Reminiscences: [Part] II. N. A. Armfeldt," *Voice of the Past*), nos. 10/12 (1918), pp. 169–235. Excerpted.

Translated by Sally Kux.

PEASANT WOMEN PROTEST: POLICE REPORTS

Both before and after the Emancipation, Russian peasant women participated in acts of resistance against both landlords and the state. But the provisions of the Emancipation added another source of conflict by favoring former serf owners, who received the best lands at the expense of their peasants whose land allotments in turn also were frequently reduced in size. Saddled with poorer lands, inadequate access to forests and meadows, high taxes and land redemption payments to the state, and some continuing obligations to landowners, peasants often had to rent lands from neighboring landowners and other villages or supplement their agricultural pursuits with domestic industry, trade, laboring on nearby estates, and migratory work. The rapid growth of the population after the 1860s intensified the pressure on peasant households to increase their income. Despite such grievances and pressures, however, peasants engaged in risky, overt acts of resistance relatively rarely, preferring instead more passive forms of resistance that were unlikely to provoke a conflict with authorities. When more overt acts of resistance did occur, they generally involved an entire village, or at least the majority of its households, acting collectively. The incidence of such acts of resistance escalated at the beginning of the twentieth century, and then intensified greatly during the Revolution of 1905.

Women as well as men engaged in both passive and overt forms of resistance. The following documents present the actions of peasant women in overt protest, seen through the observations of the officials who worked to combat unrest. From this perspective readers can examine when and how women acted, under what circumstances, and how those in authority understood their actions. It is particularly noteworthy that in some cases, peasant men stood aside to let their wives engage in protest—even though they did not allow women a voice in village assemblies.

A. Village of Chernech, Baltskii District, Podolia Province

16 MAY 1885—"STATEMENT OF THE PROSECUTOR OF THE KAMENETS-PODOL'SKII CIRCUIT COURT,[32] V. V. BAZILEVSKII, TO THE PROSECUTOR OF THE ODESSA JUDICIAL CHAMBER, V. A. ARISTOV, CONCERNING THE RESISTANCE OF THE PEASANTS OF THE VILLAGE OF CHERNECH TO THE SURVEYING OF LAND."

The assistant prosecutor Garf informed me in a statement from 14 May of the following information concerning disturbances occurring in the village of Chernech, Baltskii district [Podolia province].

As a result of a persistent disagreement among the peasants of the village of Chernech over the demarcation of boundaries around the land they had bought, two companies of the Dneprovskii militia were dispatched by the governor of Podolia, with the agreement of the governor-general, to Chernech to render assistance in the demarcation of boundaries that had been begun on 5 May by the peace mediator Savitskii.[33] A crowd of peasants, trying to head out to the field where the work was going on, was detained in the village by the police chief with the aid of the invited troops, but at the same time a throng of women reached the field unnoticed, grabbed and led the local elder and an agricultural laborer who defined the boundaries away from there, cursed the peace mediator and the surveyor who was with him, threatened the witness present at the boundary markings, broke the land markers placed there, tore the shovels out of the hands of the laborers, and wanted to take away the chain, but the women were not allowed to do that, and both the peace mediator and all those persons accompanying him were forced to stop working and return to the village, where that same crowd of women, gathered at the economic office, shouted, making some kinds of demands that were impossible to understand.

In accordance with the governor's telegram, further work in demarcating boundaries was suspended until his arrival, while the records of the inquiry into the events of 5 and 6 May compiled by the police were given over to the judicial investigator[34] of the third sector of Baltskii district, who, beginning the investigation on 6 May, summoned six women in this regard, Maria Kushnirova, Natalia Lavrinova, Lukeria Babieva, Praskovia Garachkunova, Aleksandra Forostianova, and Praskovia Doskacheva, the accused in the case, and on 11 May completed the investigation.

Meanwhile, the peasants of the village of Chernech continued to be agitated by rumors coming from who knows where that the demarcation of boundaries around the land would be to their detriment, and crowds continued to form, ignoring the demands of the police to disperse. And only with the governor's arrival on the spot on 8 May was order restored after the governor's explanations, which the peasants finally believed; the work in demarcating the boundaries around the land was completed, and the troops were led out of the village of Chernech.

I have the honor of reporting the foregoing to your Excellency as a supplement to statement no. 10164 from 11 May and also to report that the matter of disorders in the village Chernech of 14 May is before the assistant prosecutor Garf.

Signed by the assistant prosecutor, prosecutor Bazilevskii.

B. Hamlet of Zubovskoe, Korotoiaskii District, Voronezh Province

4 AUGUST 1889—"REPORT OF THE VORONEZH VICE-GOVERNOR V. G. KARNOVICH TO THE MINISTER OF THE INTERIOR, I. N. DURNOVO, ABOUT THE ATTACK OF PEASANTS OF THE HAMLET OF ZUBOVSKOE, KOROTOIASKII DISTRICT [VORONEZH PROVINCE] AND THEIR SEIZURE OF LANDOWNERS' LANDS."

The Korotoiaskii district police chief reports that the carrying out by the bailiff of the decision of the Korotoiaskii Council of peace mediators regarding the restoration of the landowners Bondarevs' property, infringed upon by the peasants of the hamlet of Zubovskoe and local village leadership, was subject to resistance.

In regard to this the police chief's assistant was ordered to provide the bailiff assistance; having arrived on the spot on the 25th of this past July, he summoned the peasants of the hamlet of Zubovskoe. Upon reading the council's decision to the peasants, it was suggested that they take down the fencing around their gardens that should be returned to the Bondarevs, but the peasants refused to carry out that demand on that occasion as well.

Then the police chief's assistant and bailiff began to remove the fencing, but once again met resistance on the part of the women who expressed themselves as follows: at the sign of one of the women who was standing near, a whole crowd of them, armed with sticks, rakes, pokers, etc., flung themselves toward the fencing with shouts: "Don't approach—we won't give them over!"

Despite all exhortations [to the contrary], the women refused to hand over the fencing, while the bearers of responsibility—their husbands, stood off to the side, apparently, not taking any part, convinced that they [the authorities] would not touch their wives, and only rarely did a few run out of the crowd, inciting the leader of the police, summoned there to help the bailiff, to commit insubordination.

After this, almost all of the policemen, summoned from neighboring settlements, with few exceptions, flatly refused to tear down the fencing.

When the police official and three guards and a few policemen began to get close to the people, the women attacked them and knocked down one of the guards, as a result of which one woman was injured; seeing her with a bloody face, the men also began to beat the officials and police.

When the crowd quieted down, they began to exhort them again to let them carry out the judicial decision, but the peasants firmly refused to submit to this.

At the present time I think it helpful to billet a company of soldiers in the hamlet of Zubovskoe as a punitive measure for two to three weeks. The peasants must comprehend that governmental power exists not only in the guise of policemen upon whom they send armed *baby*. With the presence of military force the decision of the court would obviously be carried out.[35]

Vice-governor Karnovich

C. Village of Arkhangelskoe, Urzhumskii District, Viatka Province

1 DECEMBER 1890—"REPORT OF THE VIATKA GOVERNOR A. F. ANISIN TO THE DEPARTMENT OF POLICE CONCERNING THE RESISTANCE OF THE PEASANTS OF THE VILLAGE OF ARKHANGELSKOE, WHICH WAS CONNECTED TO THE REFUSAL TO PAY ARREARS AND THE DEMAND THAT THE CARVING UP OF THE LAND BE CARRIED OUT."

The peasants of the village of Arkhangelskoe, Urzhumskii district [Viatka province], owed arrears of 2,000 rubles on state and land taxes, which out of obstinacy they had not wanted to pay for the duration of four years.

On the 22nd of last November the police officer of the 1st section of Urzhumskii district, having a commission to declare to the above-mentioned peasants the provincial decree on peasant matters regarding the business of abandoning without benefit of a petition their postponement of payment of the aforesaid arrears, arrived in the village of Arkhangelskoe together with the Mazarskaia canton *starshina* [elder], two constables, and eighty policemen of lower ranks. Having gathered the peasants in the assembly hut, the police officer informed them about the provincial office's decision concerning their plea and suggested that they give him a signed statement to that effect, but all of the peasants in the hut (about 200 persons) announced that they would not give the requested statement until they received the additional allotment of land. Being in an agitated state, the peasants answered the officer's demand for payment of the arrears with an absolute refusal. Seeing this and the unsuccessful nature of persuasion, the officer, in the presence of the above-mentioned officials, read out to the peasants the appropriate articles of the Criminal Code, warning what punishment awaited those guilty of disobeying the authorities. After that, the officer intended to draw up a list of the property of the more obstinate tax delinquents and set off for the homes of the village elder Danil Rezvykh and peasant Aleksandr Rezvykh for that purpose, but there a crowd of almost all the residents of both sexes of the village of Arkhangelskoe met him with an expression of open resistance to his instruction to inventory the movable property of those tax delinquents. Moreover, several inhabitants took the liberty of taking insolent actions against both the officer and the officers with him. Thus, by the way, the peasant woman Varvara Stepanova threw a clump of mud at the officer's face, while she threatened a police officer with a stick, a second peasant woman—Stepanida Totmeninova—hit a police officer with a stick, the peasant woman Irina Kozhevnikova tore a scarf from the neck of one of the officials, the peasant women Evdokiia Rezvykh and Efrosiniia Evstigneeva shoved another official in the chest. Besides that, the entire crowd shouted, branding the district police chief, officials, and policemen as thieves, robbers, and brigands. Such unruly behavior of the peasants forced the officer to discontinue his attempts to recover the arrears and return to his apartment, where the peasants gathered, locked the gate, and yelled that they would not let either the officer or officials out; but after some time, learning about the officer's dispatching a courier to an Urzhumskii official with a report about what had happened, the peasants dispersed to their homes. Upon the arrival on the spot of the requested police chief's assistant, the peasants, persuaded after various explanations and reprimands of the correctness of the demands for their arrears, acknowledged their guilt and began unquestioningly to hand over money owed to the tax collector. From the evidence provided thereafter by the police chief, it is clear that the said peasants voluntarily paid 1,200 rubles on 22–24 November and that the payments are continuing.

I have the honor of informing the Department of Police about the incident; further developments on this subject will be reported by me in a timely fashion.

Governor Anisin

D. Village of Bunino, Bolkhovskii District, Orel Province

"THE SECRET REPORT OF 5 AUGUST 1906 OF THE OREL GOVERNOR TO THE DEPARTMENT OF POLICE"

As a supplement to the already reported information about peasant disorders in Bolkhovskii district [Orel province], I am informing the Department of Police that on the night of 5 July on the estate of the landowner Beer near the village of Bunino, in the canton of that same name, shocks of grain from two *desiatin* were carried off by some unknown person and on the 5th a rumor spread that on the following night a pogrom of the farmstead would take place. They sent for the district police officer, who arrived with guards that very day. On the night of the 6th and for the whole time until 8 o'clock, it was completely quiet; work was in full swing, and no signs of the impending plunder were evident, as a result of which the officer, having received a report about misunderstandings on the estate of the landowner Karpov, on the 8th at 4 o'clock in the afternoon rode out of Bunino, leaving two guardsmen there. At 10 o'clock in the evening the two guards, the local policeman and two estate laborers rode round [the estate] but did not see anything in the fields. Upon their return to the farmstead at 3 o'clock at night they heard the rumbling of carts and once again headed out to the field where they saw up to fifty carts; they were met by seven gunshots, but they did not respond, and from a distance began to track which of the peasants was in the field. Having noticed this, one of the peasants took aim with his rifle, while another began to shout: "Seize them, beat them." From that moment onward the open carting of grain right in front of the farmstead began: when the landowner Beer and the steward Kalugin's family got up, they [peasants] carted grain past them out in the open all day, during which the elders, walking past, turned away or hid their faces with their hands, while the youths insolently looked Beer in the eye. This continued until 2 o'clock on 9 July, and during that time the peasants managed to cart away all of Beer's rye and oats. After this an assembly was convened, after which they came to get the wheat, and by 7 o'clock in the evening had carted off all of it as well. In total, up to 1,700 shocks of grain had been plundered. By evening a rumor spread that during the night they would plunder and carry off the whole farmstead, Beer and Kalugin's entire family left the estate, and starting at 9 o'clock in the evening the district police officer returned with his guards, and the peasants from that time onward sat tight in their huts and did not show themselves anymore that evening.

On 10 July the local land captain[36] arrived in Bunino and summoned an assembly, but did not come up with any results since the peasants wouldn't agree to any concessions, and all of them maintained that they didn't have anything to eat (that does not correspond with reality since the harvest was decent) and that they took the grain out of necessity. It is characteristic that the peasants considered their action completely normal: "They will do what they want with us, if they have the right to do something," they said. At that time, an assistant to the provincial administration, Rutkevich, whom I summoned, arrived at the meeting [and . . .] also tried to reason the peasants into returning the pilfered grain, but without success. Having waited the appropriate time, he came to the meeting with newly arrived dragoons. The entire village, including women and even babes in arms, was at the meeting. The officer of the police guards, Fau, ordered the women to stand apart from the men, but without any provocation they began such a forced wailing that it was impossible to speak. When they quieted down a bit, the councilor asked the assembly what they had decided and received the answer that they would cart the grain back, but asked permission to begin at dawn, which was granted to them. With that the councilor explained to the assembly that all of their actions would be investigated thoroughly and that those guilty would have to bear a legal punishment and then ordered them to disperse. The men obeyed that demand, but the women unexpectedly started up their earlier howling, shoved their children forward, got down on their knees, beat themselves in the chest, and shouted: "There is nothing to eat, but he made a fortune; we didn't steal but as a whole community decided to take the grain so that we wouldn't die of hunger; take, take us all, beat us, kill us and kill our children." All of this occurred before the cantonal administration near Beer's farmstead and was conducted with a lot of fervor, but it was clear that all of this was learned, insincere. The councilor ordered the elder and several of the old men to take the *baby* away, but he did not succeed in this. Then he ordered the guards to leave, and they quickly rode away behind him and the dragoons. The women at this time stopped shouting and dispersed.

On the second day, i.e., 11 July, it poured, as a result of which no one carted the shocks of grain. On the morning of the 12th the assembly of peasants appeared on the estate and asked the councilor to negotiate with them. Seeing that the peasants had appeared once again with all the women and children, he announced that he could speak only with the assembly, but not with the women. Then the women left, and almost all the men followed them. There remained only twenty men who announced that they would return everything, and that everything would go well, only if they were relieved of responsibility and no one was seized. Rutkevich explained that it was not in his authority to forgive them, but that if they didn't cart back the plundered grain and did not hand over the culprits, then that would be carried out by force, and if it appeared that he didn't have enough soldiers, then he would bring in double, quadruple, ten times the number of troops, he would destroy the entire village, and what needed to be done would be done. This resulted in a dispirited mood among the peasants, and they announced that they would do everything they were ordered to. And indeed, as soon as the bad weather lifted, they quickly set about carting the shocks of grain and delivered almost all the grain. At the same time, under the guidance of the councilor Rutkevich an inquiry was carried out by the police officer, during which twenty individuals of the neighboring villages were arrested and handed over to the purview of the judicial investigator, while the main leaders—the village teacher Otdelnov and gentryman Derevitskii[37]—were taken into custody on the pretext of their protection, and as for them and also the peasant Shevyrev, identified by the judicial investigator, I will go with the recommendation of administrative exile.

After the arrests everything quieted down all around. The arrests of Otdelnov and Derevitskii affected the peasants especially hard. They are even afraid of talking loudly about their previous actions. Undoubtedly, the village of Bunino was the center from which the peasant movement spread all over Bolkhovskii district. Now the population is quiet, is not troubling itself with any hostile activities, as a result of which the dragoons stationed there by the civil authorities for [the purposes of providing] assistance have returned to the place of their permanent billet in the town of Orel.

For the governor, vice-governor Bel'gard

Source: Krest'ianskoe dvizhenie v Rossii v 1881–1889 gg.: Sbornik dokumentov [The Peasant Movement in Russia in 1881–1889: A Collection of Documents], ed. A. S. Nifontov and B. V. Zlatoustovskii (Moscow, 1960). Excerpted from pp. 434–45 and

679–81. *Krest'ianskoe dvizhenie v Rossii v 1890–1900 gg.: Sbornik dokumentov [The Peasant Movement in Russia in 1890–1900: A Collection of Documents]*, ed. A. V. Shapkarin (Moscow, 1959). Excerpted from pp. 33–34. *1905: Materialy i dokumenty: Agrarnoe dvizhenie v 1905–1907 gg. [1905: Materials and Documents: The Agrarian Movement in 1905–1907]*, vol. 1, ed. S. Dubrovskii and B. Grave (Moscow, 1925). Excerpted from pp. 216–18.

Translated and partially annotated by Christine Worobec

WORKING WOMEN IN THE GAPON ASSEMBLY: MEMOIRS

VERA KARELINA

The government of Nicholas II responded to a growing workers' strike movement at the turn of the century by creating government-sponsored unions. These unions were meant to keep workers from joining the various socialist revolutionary movements that were also active at the time. The founder of the thousands-strong St. Petersburg Assembly of Russian Factory and Mill Workers was Father Georgii Gapon, one of a group of socially activist clergy in the St. Petersburg diocese who were attempting to fend off challenges to Russian Orthodoxy by making it relevant to the lives of urban workers. While the Gapon Assembly, like others of its type, had rules against women holding administrative posts, Vera M. Karelina (b. 1870, m. 1890 to Aleksei Karelin) was an active participant and the first woman to rise into the Assembly's leadership. Karelina, herself a working woman, was reared by a foster mother in a village near St. Petersburg. She worked at the St. Petersburg Maternity Hospital after the death of her foster mother. In her free time, Karelina studied in a radical workers' circle based in a neighboring cotton-spinning factory. Although composed of workers, such circles generally were conducted by radical students or members of underground revolutionary organizations. In this circle Karelina read the classics of Russian radicalism (Chernyshevskii and Pisarev,[38] for example) and took part in the formation of a separate women's circle. When the police broke the circle in 1892, Karelina was sentenced to prison and exile for three years. Her activities in the Gapon Assembly were similar. She again founded separate women's sections and recruited female members. By the end of 1904 about a thousand women belonged to the women's sections in St. Petersburg. All of this work ended when police and military detachments crushed the Gapon Assembly on January 9 [January 22, New Style], 1905, the day known as Bloody Sunday and the event that triggered the Revolution of 1905.

The working class [members] struggled in various ways to better their lives. Over the decades there were many strikes, many victims, and many deaths in prisons and prison camps. The government, seeing that the workers' consciousness was growing, tried its best to halt its development. Severe treatment and prisons did not help. Then, hypocritically wishing to show its goodwill toward workers, the government began to organize special societies for factory workers in Moscow and Petersburg. In Petersburg the famous priest Gapon was the leader of these societies. The government hoped that with their aid it could distance the working masses from revolution and win them over to the tsar and the government. Until the January 9th massacre, workers trusted the societies and joined them.

After the January 9th massacre, the vast masses of workers understood that revolution was the only way to win themselves a better life. Toward the end of summer 1904 the Petersburg factory workers' society began an intense expansion in all working-class areas, not just in the city but also in Kolpino and Sestroretsk.[39] Masses of working women poured into the organization, but initially were not very active. The reason for this was that most of them were semiliterate; in addition, men's attitudes toward women were different than they are now [1926]. Most workers then thought that organizational concerns were not a woman's affair. A woman had her own concerns: her machine at the factory, and her family, diapers, and pots at home.

I remember what a battle I had to endure when the issue of whether a woman could be a Society member was debated. Working women were not even mentioned, as if they did not even exist, as if they were some kind of afterthought in the industrial world, even though all the while there were factories where the workers were almost exclusively women.

It was no wonder that with attitudes like these, women themselves felt uncomfortable in the Society and were reluctant to participate actively and speak their minds. We used to gather after assemblies to talk over tea, and the women would immediately feel completely different, more relaxed, since conversations over tea were more family-like. They would state their opinions about almost anything they had heard at the meetings, and were almost always right.

I would often try to convince and entreat them to speak up at the general assemblies. But I would get this answer: "Well, sometimes I want to say what's on my mind, but then I think: how can I talk? There's so many people, they'll all be looking at me. . . . and then someone'll laugh at me: look, there she goes with her babble—and your heart goes cold from thoughts like those, you get scared and you sit and shut up, but your heart's on fire."

When quite a large number of working women started to attend Society meetings, I began to wonder if it would be possible to channel women into separate groups or assemblies. I knew well that they would be less embarrassed among other women.

In one of my frequent encounters with Gapon I expressed my thoughts about a women's organization within the Society. Gapon willingly agreed to it, and said that it had to be done for women so that they would become more active, or else they would keep coming to the meetings in silence and leaving them in silence.

"But you have to handle organizing the women's assemblies."

Frankly speaking, I felt with my whole heart that an organization like this was needed, but it had never occurred to me to take it upon myself, in spite of my

burning desire to draw the broad masses of working women into active participation in the Society. Additionally, I knew from my experience working in underground political groups that women, drawn into active participation, would
put their lively minds and sensitive emotions into it, and the organization would
flourish.

But all the same it wasn't an easy task for me. I didn't feel adequately prepared
for this endeavor; it was serious and required experience and a skillful approach.
But there was nothing else I could do; I had to take the initiative, since there were
hardly any educated men, let alone women, in the Society.

I didn't consent immediately. I discussed the matter beforehand with my comrades at my apartment. They advised that I had to take on this task, and promised
their help.

At the next board meeting I gave a report about organizing separate women's assemblies. The board heard my report, responded very sympathetically to its contents, and also entrusted me with the organization. During the same meeting it was
decided to begin this task immediately, without any delay. They designated one
day per week—Thursday—as the day for women's assemblies. The board didn't
write up any instructions, relying instead on me, and confined itself to informing
all the chapters and concerned groups in the chapters about the women's assemblies. Gapon took the responsibility of arranging things at city hall, since the Society's bylaws did not provide for a separate women's organization. There was
even a stipulation in one paragraph of the bylaws where it said that women were
restricted to being members of the Society and could not hold any responsible positions.

Before me was the question of where to start and how to approach the women.
I knew well what kind of life these women had led: most were illiterate, worn
down by the burden of factory work. Women worked alongside men, but were
paid much less. They spent the same long, dreary hours at their machines that the
men did, but after work they would run home to their children, pots, and diapers.
Sometimes children would get sick, and during work hours women would have to
leave them in the care of their landladies. While at work their hearts ached for
their children, but they couldn't stay with them. Their pay would be reduced, or
they would be fired altogether. Often a woman would stay up all night with her
sick children, never closing an eye, and head back to her machine early in the
morning. And that was the way a working woman's life went, day in, day out, year
in, year out. She experienced neither light nor joy.

It was no better when she was younger; she had few joys. She began going to
the factory at the age of ten to twelve years old. If she was not put on a machine,
then she got work that was just as hard. She worked the same hours as the adults,
but got paid pennies. She grew up almost illiterate, never seeing anything good,
just a bleak marriage and her machine at the factory, until her dying day.

Besides difficult conditions at work and horrible exploitation, working women
were forced to suffer a great deal morally. Sometimes they were harassed, not only
by scoundrels, such as the foremen, but also by those in positions of power at the

factory. How were they supposed to learn and become politically conscious? The church and its teachings oppressed them still further. I took all this into account, and was well aware that I needed to find some way to reach the average woman that would appeal to her. I had to find a cautious approach. First I would have to touch upon those painful issues that were part of women's lives, the lives of working women. To find a starting point I began looking in various books for something suitable. Initially I wanted to read something to them, to awaken their interest in one issue or another. I looked mostly in literature. At that time, short but very descriptive articles and stories from workers' lives were beginning to slip into print. I found just the thing, a short story entitled "At the Entry," written by V. Temnykh. It vividly described how a woman worker was frisked upon leaving the factory at the end of the day.

It must be noted that these searches were often quite disgraceful. They were often conducted in the presence of foremen or other administrators. Of course, it was obvious why they gathered at the women's exit. During the searches, particularly those of the young women, they let loose with wisecracks you would not care to repeat. There was no reason for the men to be polite to the women; they took it all, no matter what was said. The middle-aged women cursed back, and the young women hurried to leave. There was no mercy, even on the ten- to thirteen-year-old girls; everyone had their turn.

When I myself worked at the factory, after a fourteen-hour day[40] working at our machines, unable, as the saying goes, to relax from exhaustion, we would leave work only to be further and more vulgarly insulted.

This particular simple story which, unnoticed, found its way into literature, played a major part in organizing women in the Society. It touched upon the most painful issue of women's lives. It so appealed to the hearts of working women that I read it at all the chapters where women's assemblies were held. It used to be that you would go to women's assemblies in some regional chapter, and they would already know that in some other chapter a very interesting story had been read, and would ask if it could be read to them. Or else the day before a planned chapter assembly, a woman from that chapter would come to me and ask me to bring a story that had been read somewhere else.

Honestly speaking, I got sick and tired of this story, since I had to read it many times over. But I was always willing to read it. This particular simple story played a major role in organizing women in the Factory Workers' Society. It allowed them to approach these painful issues that weighed upon their hearts. This pain, known only to female factory workers, accumulated throughout their lives but was never expressed. The working women bore it as they did all the other burdens of the working class.

This story also allowed me to address more easily the overall situation of workers, particularly women, in Russia. That's the way I began the mass organization of women in the Factory Workers' Society in 1904.

The women's assemblies were quite well attended, particularly those of the Narva, Vasilevskii Island, Rozhdestvenskoe-na-Peskakh, Vyborg, and Kolomenskoe chapters.[41] Two hundred to five hundred women used to meet in the Narva chapter, and no less than that in the others. The connection with factories and plants was almost universal, since workers, Society members, were more often registered by place of residence than by factories or plants. Many workers lived in one place and worked in another, so it was always possible to find out what was going on where, and what was being done and discussed in what chapter. My personal ties to the working women were very close even though I no longer worked at a factory, having become a housewife. I did not lose my ties with the working women. How could I lose them when I was proletarian to the bone? My husband was a worker, as was I, so naturally I was not a stranger to them, nor they to me. So our relationship quickly and easily got off on a firm footing, and they felt that I was one of them.

Many of them also knew me from my earlier work in the Society. Some girls and women entered the Society from our underground organization. They worked together with me in the Society, too. They were all underground workers from Social Democrat groups.[42] There were also some young women from the Kirchner factory. Some of them worked in workers' political groups and also conducted propaganda campaigns directed at women.

At first I had to direct all the women's assemblies and organization, but as soon as things settled down somewhat, each chapter elected its own chairwoman and secretary, who had the right to vote and go to the executive levels of their chapters. From these chairwomen and secretaries we formed something resembling an organizational committee, where we formulated concise instructions governing the conduct of women's assemblies. The meeting agenda was delineated by individual chapters.

It seems strange that there were two organizations within one Society, but that's the way it was. But we weren't coequal members; according to regulations, it was illegal to elect women to responsible positions within the Society, which meant: come and listen, but don't make your presence known; be ballast within the Society. That's why we used to discuss how to win civil rights within the Society during our women's assemblies.

All the instructions would be carried out at the women's general assemblies, and gradually women began to establish a position within the Society. At first they were elected to host concerts and dances. Then they were elected to library and lecture-budget committees. And as women entered unnoticed into the life of each chapter, they became practically indispensable to the Society. They began to make their presence known and to speak out at the combined meetings.

Women were irreplaceable on some commissions. In addition, they had higher moral standards. If one of the men cursed, he would then look around, or others would remind him that a girl or woman was present, and the next time he was more careful. Gradually many workers who had earlier opposed the idea of women joining the Society began to change their minds. Relationships improved, and more mutual interests appeared. We became simply comrades. Women, particularly young women, often told me that men had changed their attitudes toward them. "Now when we leave the factory, we talk completely differently than we used to, and they've even started to help us at work." It used to be that women couldn't do one thing or another because they weren't strong enough, and they would have to call an apprentice over. Now a comrade would help and there were no stoppages, which used to significantly affect pay.

All this was truly new and unusual for its time. There were underground organizations, but they were persecuted and punished by the government. Participants were arrested and sent to prison. The most politically conscious men and women workers joined the underground Party organizations, while the broad masses joined the Gapon societies.

Thus, when things settled down somewhat in the women's assemblies, elections for chairwomen and secretaries of the women's assemblies were held. Elena Petrovna Inozemtseva, the wife of a worker at the Putilov factory,[43] was elected chairwoman of the first, or so-called Narva, chapter. The secretary, a seamstress in a workshop, was the wife of another Putilov employee whose name I don't remember. Khaiko, a cigarette maker from the Laferme factory, was elected chairwoman of the Vasilevskii Island chapter. Her husband used to work at the Nakhimson (formerly Trubochnyi) plant. He was a member of our SD/Bolshevik group, and was killed in Tula while escaping from prison in 1906. Pania Usanova was the secretary. The chairwoman of the women's assemblies at Kolomenskoe chapter was Maria Vasilevna Soldatova, who worked at a cigarette factory, though I don't remember which one. She was the wife of M. P. Soldatov, a worker at the Baltic Factory. She was a middle-aged woman, forty years old and illiterate. But she possessed inexhaustible energy and natural organizational ability, and could understand and think quickly. She was witty and resourceful. Everyone in her chapter liked her for her friendliness and kindness. She knew everything and was always informed about what was happening in the chapter.

And so in spite of her illiteracy, M. V. was unanimously elected chairwoman of the women's assemblies. She often lamented and complained about her illiteracy, and would always say, "If only I could read and write, I could do so much more for the factory and the Society." When someone offered to teach her to read and write, she began to study zealously. But I don't know if she ever learned to read or write, since I lost track of her shortly after January 9th. She left for the country with her husband, who had fallen ill. I heard that she, too, died soon thereafter. Her secretary was a young seamstress, V. A. Andrigina. She was called Ekaterina Vasilevna. Her husband worked at the Baltic plant too.

More or less politically conscious women were elected as chairwomen and secretaries of the other chapters. The wife of Ivan Vasilevich Vasilev worked hard for the Vyborg chapter. He was the chairman of the board of the Industrial Workers' Society, and was killed during the January 9th demonstration at the Narva Gates.[44]

In each chapter there were men and women workers who wielded influence over the masses. Of course there were initially some amusing incidents during the women's assemblies. The men were extremely interested in hearing what the women said and how their assemblies went. And of course the curious among them tried by hook and by crook to sneak into the women's assemblies. But the women themselves had resolved that while they were still getting accustomed to speaking, no man would be allowed to attend their assemblies. The women used to say: "If they come and listen, then we'll say something stupid, and they'll blab it all over the factory and at meetings. So it's better if nobody's there. That way they can't bother us. Our sister workers won't badmouth us since they aren't big talkers either."

It should be noted that women of all ages, even the elderly ones, would come to the assemblies. I attribute this to Father Gapon's cassock and to the recitation of prayers before the meetings were opened. Of course, that meant nothing to the young people. But the prayers were recited somewhat mechanically, and immediately afterward discussions would begin that were far from religious in nature. When it was necessary to discuss religion and the church with the women, extreme caution was required. No ridicule was permitted. If religious issues arose, both my comrades and I would try to point out the most obvious facts. But we never had specific discussions. If religious issues came up, it was only in passing. More attention was devoted to mass organization. No member of the Society could help but notice that when women began to actively participate in its work, the scope of the organization's activity expanded, because women gave so much of themselves to it. Large numbers of women poured into the Gapon societies. On January 9th working women, along with men, went to the tsar to seek the truth. Then the women played an enormous part; otherwise the January 9, 1905, movement would never have been so majestic. They did not dissuade their husbands and brothers from participating in the demonstration; on the contrary, many of them called upon others to participate in it.

Women did not march behind men in the procession. Weren't they in the first ranks, side by side with the men? Didn't many women and children fall from tsarist bullets that day?

And when on the morning of January 9th I appealed to working women with a summons to join the men in seeking truth for the people from the tsar, I explained then and there to those who had gathered that the unknown awaited us that day. Armed soldiers were everywhere. Perhaps we, too, would have to die. And then the entire hall answered as one, simply and calmly: "Well, then, we'll all die for our truth." I will never, until the day I die, forget those words, pronounced with such simplicity and calm. On the night of January 9th, when I passed out scarves with red crosses that I had sewn to those who wished to be volunteer nurses, a sea of women's hands stretched toward me. Every girl and woman wanted to contribute something to the cause.

Separate women's assemblies didn't last long—from October 1904 until the end of December. In January 1905 new events began, sweeping working women into their maelstrom and drawing them into the October 1905 strike, forcing them to fight along with the entire working class for their liberation.

Source: Vera M. Karelina, "Rabotnitsa v gaponskikh obshchestvakh," *Rabotnitsa v 1905 g. v S.-Peterburge* ["The Woman Worker in the Gapon Societies," in *The*

Woman Worker in 1905 in St. Petersburg], ed. P. Kudelli (Leningrad, 1926). Excerpted from pp. 14–26.

Translated by Lisa Renée Taylor.

CIVIC ACTIVISM

A. Charitable Work

1. A Personal Act of Charity

NATALIA ZAGRAZHSKAIA

Although the nature of private charity evolved in the eighteenth and nineteenth centuries, the charitable ideal continued to be informed by the teachings of the Orthodox Church. Orthodox believers were encouraged to follow the examples of especially holy people and devote themselves to service to the poor and needy. While women and men both participated in charity work, even as Russians moved from a charitable culture based in personal donations to one of active participation in voluntary societies, the belief intensified that women were especially well suited for it. The following selections illustrate two types of charitable work possible in the nineteenth century.

Charity was considered part of an eighteenth- or nineteenth-century noblewoman's household responsibilities. Women could fulfill this responsibility by feeding poor relations and acquaintances or by dispensing alms. In the first selection, we see that Natalia Kirilovna Zagrazhskaia took seriously the obligation to aid the truly needy. She exercised judgment and care in the transfer of a sum of money to a needy family (for a similar example of personal charity, see the Labzina selection in chapter 3).

Particularly after the latter part of the eighteenth century and through the remainder of the imperial period, however, charity work constituted the most accessible form of public activity for Russian women. Empresses and Grand Duchesses gave their financial and ceremonial support to educational and social welfare institutions. They also encouraged the foundation of nursing societies and the Russian Red Cross; during wars, women of the imperial family often devoted their efforts to caring for wounded soldiers. Women of the nobility and the middling social estates organized charitable societies and played important roles in the many voluntary organizations that were founded after the Great Reforms. After the 1860s they also campaigned for reform in such areas as public health, protective labor legislation, and education, and they coordinated battles against poverty, alcoholism, and prostitution. In the second selection, Evgenia Berkut offers an example of this form of charitable activity. Working with the Municipal District Trusteeships in Moscow provided women, such as Berkut, not only with an opportunity for civic activism but also with a kind of training in governmental service; such opportunities were still rare for women in this period. Berkut discusses different kinds of aid and remarks upon the social estate of both providers and recipients of aid.

Your Gracious Majesty Konstantin Markovich,[45]

I received a letter dated 8 December from the town of Myshkin, Yaroslavl province, from the retired Lieutenant Peter Gerasimov Tolbuzin who is living there in the house of the bourgeois Nastasia Burinina. He wrote that during a fire in his apartment on 19–20 November, he and his wife and five children barely escaped with their lives; all their belongings were destroyed in the fire; and now they are in the most dire of straits; this is why he is asking for assistance, citing Your Excellence as able to verify the veracity of the events he described.

In view of his misfortune, I have collected on his behalf 130 rubles in credit notes, which I have affixed to this letter, and humbly ask Your Excellency to inform me whether Tolbuzin's request is fair, and if it is fair, to order that he be sent the money so as not to leave such a large, impoverished family in your care. I myself would be honored to receive word of what you can discover of this matter.

I ask that You kindly forgive me for burdening you with such a commission. I'm doing this, confident that compassion for the poor is not alien to you.

You may be confident of my utmost respect.

Your Excellency's humble servant
N. Z.

26 December 1838
St. Petersburg
To His Excellency K. M. Poltoratsky
Her Excellency Natalia Kirilovna Zagrazhskaia

Source: Shchukin, vol. X, pp. 481–82.

Translated by Valentina Baslyk.

2. Publicly Organized Charity: Memoirs of a District Trustee

EVGENIA BERKUT

Often when speaking with people engaged in philanthropic activity and interested in issues of charity for the poor, I have mentioned the activity of the *Moscow Municipal Trusteeships* and have always been surprised by the complete ignorance of this large and beneficial activity, in which so many people work and which has produced such real and tangible results.

Even though while working in the *Trusteeships* I had to become familiar with the darkest aspects of life, the memories left by this activity are the brightest and most gratifying, which is a result of the realization that it is possible to achieve much even with few resources and a small expenditure of effort.

The *Moscow Municipal District Trusteeships* were established in December 1894 on the basis of the plan and project of *Vladimir Ivanovich Gere*, a member of the Municipal Duma[46] and a distinguished professor at Moscow University. The *Provisional Statute of Municipal District Trusteeships for the Poor in Moscow* was approved on March 15, 1894, by the Ministry of Internal Affairs and contained the following main provisions:

1) The *Municipal Board*[47] shall establish, so far as possible and within the means available, *municipal district trusteeships for the poor* composed of people of both sexes who have taken upon themselves the obligation of aiding the cause of charity for the poor through monetary contributions defined by themselves or through personal work.

2) The chairman of the trusteeship and the members of the council are elected for four years and are approved in their position by the Municipal Board. People wishing to serve the trusteeship through their personal labor declare this to the trusteeship, defining at the same time the obligations that they will assume—visiting the poor, caring for the sick, or [providing] medical treatment for the latter. Associates are invited by the trusteeship to sessions of the council with a right to vote on those matters that involve their personal participation. All members of the trusteeship participate in the general meetings convened by the trusteeship.

3) With the agreement of the Municipal Board, each newly opened trusteeship is assigned a particular territorial district for its activity.

Aid can be of two kinds: temporary and permanent. Permanent aid can consist of concern for the placement of young children, enfeebled elderly people, or people unable to work due to infirmity or chronic illness in appropriate charitable institutions or the assignment to them of a permanent monetary or other allowance and in general of firmly securing their fate. With the agreement of the Municipal Duma, the trusteeships are permitted to establish charitable institutions.

These, in brief, are the rights and obligations that were conferred on the municipal district trusteeships. Their activity began in 1894 with the organization of work in each district, in which the place of residence played the main part. The activity of associates was based on the principle of help by a *good neighbor*. All members of the trusteeship had to live in their district, as did associates, and although it was possible to work in another district, that happened only rarely, in view of the inconvenience that was caused by long distances and transportation time.

The activity of the trusteeship's associates, who were accepted only upon the recommendation of two people and after exacting inquiries about their character, consisted of visits to the poor, the collection of money, sewing clothes for the poor, and management of the children's shelter, the crèche, the almshouse, the dormitory apartment, and so on.

Each *municipal district trusteeship* had an office, which was managed by a salaried person. The poor who wished to receive help would inform the office, where their address would be recorded. The chairman of the trusteeship then would send the nearest associate with a list of questions regarding the status, age, health, and marital status of a given person. After visiting the petitioner, the associate recorded his testimony on the questionnaire and gave his own conclusion, which was based on his impression of the personality and the situation of the petitioner. At the end of the questionnaire he wrote his opinion on whether and what particular kind of help was needed, and then reported personally on this at a meeting of the trusteeship, where he had the right to vote on the case. Sometimes a second visit was necessary in order to verify the first impression. Of course, there were mistakes committed on one side and deception on the other, but in the end, after several visits and questions, it was possible to form a clear understanding of the situation of a given person, of his ability to work, and of his actual or invented need.

Aid was given in the form of money, payment for an apartment, clothing, medicine, milk, bread, tea, and even payment to educational institutions and placement into various establishments for sick children and the elderly.

An associate had to deliver the assistance rendered himself. It was not permitted to *send it through a servant,* and only in the case of illness was it possible to transfer the case to a fellow associate.

As I mentioned already, assistance could be temporary or permanent. Temporary assistance usually was necessary in cases of impoverishment due to illness, unemployment, the death of the breadwinner in the family, and so on. Permanent assistance had to be given either to elderly people who had spent their entire life in hard labor [and] now were deprived of the possibility of work due to old age, a lack of strength, or chronic illness, or to children, who in the poor families of charwomen often are left untended for entire days and who equally need both daily bread and moral guidance and instruction. For such children the trusteeship established daily shelters or crèches.

Medical help was given by the doctor-associates of the trusteeships, and many pharmacies dispensed medicine with a large discount.

The almshouses were established for elderly people who were unable to earn their sustenance through personal labor, and I personally had to establish the first almshouse for elderly women in the Arbat[48] trusteeship and to manage it for several years. Even with the still-limited resources of the trusteeships, it was very easy to establish almshouses, and while doing so we sought only to make sure that the poor whom we admitted had warm accommodation, a clean bed, and simple but nourishing and healthful food. Initially twenty-two elderly women were admitted into the first almshouse of the Arbat trusteeship, among whom was a cook who was also old but relatively energetic and still able to work. She received a small wage and was obliged to cook dinner and supper and to keep the kitchen and the dining room tidy; two of the residents helped her, taking turns. The residents had to make their beds and tidy their rooms themselves, taking turns, with those who were so feeble that they could not do anything for themselves enjoying the services of the others. The majority of the elderly women were either disabled or chronically ill, but, being placed in good conditions, they still could perform light work in their almshouse, with the exception of a few very old or very sick.

Every summer, the crèche of the Arbat trusteeship is transferred to the countryside, from where the children reappear ruddy, healthy, and cheerful. Needless to say, the amount spent on the stay in the country was insignificant compared with the benefit which this stay brought to the poor children, who had never seen the fields and the forest and who were brought up in the back courtyard of some large building, where instead of air they breathed various miasmas, and instead of nature they saw pieces of the sky blackened with smoke.

For example, the report of the Arbat trusteeship for 1900 relates: "The stay in the country: transportation there and back—136 rubles, 48 kopecks; during the winter there were 30 children in the shelter, 15 who lived there and 15 who came each day, and all 30 were taken to the country." And this insignificant sum saved these young people from the perilous influence of destitution, from unavoidable filth, and from the ignorance, drunkenness, and harmful examples that surround them. Filth, disorderliness, and drunkenness are unavoidably linked to destitution, and despair [is] inseparable from a hopeless mood that sometimes forces a good worker to give up everything and start drinking. Of course, quarrels and discord arise in such a family, and the children become the involuntary witnesses of coarse and difficult scenes. The issue here is not money, but the work invested in this cause by the people involved with the children's shelters, organized by the trusteeships, and the love with which they related to these children.

The almshouse accepted people of all faiths and social estates. Incidentally, during my management of the almshouse there died an eighty-year-old woman, the daughter of a marshal of the nobility,[49] who had finished a course of studies in an institute[50] and who was a former governess, because her entire fortune had been spent on the financial speculations of her close relative. When she was finally unable to work and all her relatives had died, she had no option other than to rent a corner in a basement, and finally she could not afford even to pay for that. When she was placed in the almshouse, and I learned her history, I tried as much as I could to alleviate her life among the coarse and ignorant old women. But she endured her situation humbly and was so kind and gentle that her small privileges did not evoke jealousy, and she exerted a beneficial influence on her co-residents, weaning them from swearing.

Soon after the establishment of the almshouse, some members of the Arbat trusteeship's council noted that the trusteeship was assisting only the most helpless people who were unable to work, leaving without support those who needed limited help, such as with the payment for an apartment. The idea arose at that point to establish a so-called dormitory apartment for single individuals, where the lodging would be given free and everything else would have to be earned on one's own. The dormitory apartment was organized in a basement, which the trusteeship cleaned up and renovated, making it comfortable, clean, and bright. It was managed by an associate who looked after its cleanliness, order, and calm and visited it daily. Later the need emerged for a second dormitory apartment. Finally, having become convinced that a good clean lodging, the obligatory order in it, and its more hygienic living conditions facilitated not only the physical but also the moral health of the poor, the trusteeship planned to take upon itself the organization of apartments for the poor, renting beds to them for a small fee and thereby not giving the landlord the possibility of exploiting needy people.

It is, of course, not the place here to expand upon the enormous significance that the improvement of hygienic conditions in the apartments of the poor had for the general health of the city. Everyone knows how often floor-polishers, laundresses, and upholsterers act as sources of infection, bringing from their dirty, damp, and dark lodgings every possible germ into the bright and wealthy apartment where they happen to work. To what extent the trusteeship was able to realize its intentions I do not know, since I left Moscow.

I spoke of temporary aid, and this activity of the trusteeship was the most gratifying because its results were tangible and visible. It was worth supporting a person or a family during a difficult moment or during an illness, and little by little the individual began himself to get out of difficulty and manage independently. Among these, I cannot fail to mention here one vivid example, which in its time aroused the attention of many of the trusteeships in Moscow. I had received from the chairman of the Arbat trusteeship, Mr. S., an address and a questionnaire, and, as was the custom, the chairman had written requesting me to pay particular attention to this case. I arrived: the apartment was in the yard of a wooden house, but not in the basement. I rang the bell, and the door was opened by a university student, who, having learned that I was from the trusteeship (to which, as it turns out, he had turned with a request for wages, since the trusteeship provided even this form of aid), departed with embarrassment, leaving me alone with a young woman. In her hands she was holding a young child, and another one was holding the hem of her skirt. The children were wearing only shirts and were barefooted, despite the fact that it was chilly in the apartment. This was the student's wife. Seeing before me a face from the milieu of the intelligentsia, I carefully and even fearfully began to pose the usual questions, trying to spare her self-esteem and not touch upon a sore topic. At first Mrs. V. kept silent, and then, placing her head on the table, she began to cry and whispered *"We have not eaten for two days."*

There is no need even to mention that as soon as I reported this fact to the chairman and his deputy, immediately, within an hour, the V. family was provided with everything necessary.

At the present time, the student V. already has finished his course of studies, received a position, and, perhaps, in his turn is working in some trusteeship to help those as poor as he once was.

The Arbat trusteeship organized two more shelters, then a second almshouse appeared, and at present forty-nine people and a cook are supported in the united almshouses, thirty people in the dormitory apartment, and fifty people in the two shelters.

In addition to this help, the Arbat trusteeship has placed many people in municipal almshouses, shelters, and hospitals (for instance, the Bakhrushin Hospital for the incurably ill), and has continually distributed linen, clothes, and warm clothing from its material storehouse. The storehouse was formed from donations and is managed by an associate.

People often turned to the trusteeship for legal advice, which was given free by the jurist-associates.

In the Presnenskii trusteeship, neighboring that of the Arbat, and where I also happened to work, one more form of help has been organized for some time. This was a workshop for those who were seeking work. It had sewing machines and also handed out work to be done at home. The Presnenskii trusteeship entered into an agreement with various institutions, for example hospitals, educational establishments, and so on, and would take orders for the sewing of simple clothing, which would then be shared out among poor women to perform at home.

This form of help proved to be expedient to the highest degree: by giving a constant and certain wage, and by bringing poor women into contact with the people from the intelligentsia who managed the workshop, it not only secured them materially, but also provided moral support.

Source: Evgenia Berkut, "O gorodskikh uchastkovykh popechitel'stvakh v Moskve (Vospominaniia sotrudnitsy)," *Trudovaia pomoshch'* ["About the Municipal District Trusteeships in Moscow (Memoirs of an Associate[51])," *Labor Aid*], no. 3 (1903), pp. 352–62. Excerpted.

Translated by William G. Wagner and Igor Timofeyev.

B. Prostitution and Alcoholism

1. Prostitution and Alcoholism

MARIA POKROVSKAIA

In chapter 3 we met Maria Pokrovskaia, whose work on prostitution was well known in Russia at the turn of the century. In the following excerpt we see how she considered prostitution as connected with other social ills, and linked it with the problem of alcoholism. Pokrovskaia's views on prostitution, however, were somewhat idiosyncratic, and should be contrasted with those of Ekaterina Gardner in the following selection. Like the movement against prostitution, the temperance movement attracted numerous women activists. Religious rejoinders against overindulgence in alcohol appeared in Russia as early as the thirteenth century, but secular temperance efforts began only in the 1830s. In the 1860s doctors, journalists, and intellectuals took up the question of alcohol abuse as part of the general concern about social welfare during the reform period. The state also became concerned with the problem about this time, most often viewing it as an issue for police resolution. Only in the 1880s and 1890s, however, did an organized temperance movement appear in Russia. For the most part, these efforts concentrated on educating people about the dangers of alcoholism and providing entertainment that did not involve drinking. Because alcoholism was considered to be primarily a working-class problem, moreover, efforts by civic groups, religious organizations, and the state were directed principally at that group of people.

In modern society prostitution and alcoholism are inextricably bound, as D. N. Borodin's report has illustrated. For my part I want to supplement and confirm the connection between prostitution and alcoholism.

I happened to hear about a young woman who had a nervous breakdown in a brothel and was placed in an insane asylum, where she got better. They wanted to find a respectable job for her, but she refused, saying that she knew how to get her customers to drink a lot of liquor and for this the madam rewarded her. Upon her return from the hospital she was to receive a special dress from the madam, a Polish-made one, I think.

One prostitute who works in a bordello of the lowest sort told me that on major holidays like Christmas and Easter, each woman has a truly incredible number of customers—between sixty and eighty. To enable them to endure this work the madam bolsters the women with glasses of vodka so that, when all is said and done, a woman "performs her obligation in a state of complete disregard for her actions." She also told me that when they have to go to their medical examinations, the madam gives them each a glass of vodka for courage.

According to information gathered at my request by Mrs. Baar, it is evident that all the prostitutes at Kalinkin Hospital use alcohol, and more than half of those asked use it in significant quantities.[52] More than half of the women asked said that without alcohol they would not be able to practice their trade.

Alcohol and obligation are the means by which brothel keepers control the women. As soon as a young girl falls into a madam's clutches, she is inured to drink. The madam gets her drunk, as do the patrons. With her senses constantly dulled by alcohol, the girl is in no condition to comprehend her position and make an attempt to get out of it at the very beginning of her career as a prostitute, when she is still capable of returning to honest work.

Very often a young girl will give herself the first time under the influence of al-cohol, but in fact, alcoholism begins for her when she becomes a professional prostitute, that is, one who is under surveillance.[53] Landing up in a state-licensed brothel, she finds herself in real servitude. Although there is an administrative order which states that not even her debts can keep her there, she is in no con-dition to leave without outside assistance. At this point her ignorance plays an enormous role; she doesn't know whether or not she can leave without paying off the debts, of which the madam keeps tab. Fairly often the madam treats the girl violently. She is not allowed to go out at all and is kept under lock and key. Dur-ing this time the process of turning her into a professional prostitute takes place. She is made drunk, inured to debauchery and wild partying. When she develops a taste for this life, then she is given her freedom. The madam knows that now she will not leave.

Mandatory checkups are undoubtedly offensive to a woman. Besides this, the examinations of those "under surveillance" are often conducted in the most dis-graceful conditions. According to Dr. Stürmer, in Baku checkups of independent prostitutes (odinochki) are held in the police station. The women must wait their turn along with a motley crowd, enduring all kinds of harassment. Prostitutes have repeatedly requested permission to rent a room at their own expense for these examinations. "We're too ashamed to go to the checkups sober," they have said. In Tula[54] the examinations of independent prostitutes are held in a close, dark cell at the police station, with no privacy from other people or policemen. Younger women are afraid to go there for their checkups.

Dr. Stürmer also noted that many Petersburg prostitutes, especially those from the brothels, come drunk to their mandatory examinations. This is because the examination is hard to bear.

The existence of the "yellow ticket" makes drinking inevitable for both prostitutes from brothels and independents under surveillance.[55] Medical-police surveillance places a heavy burden on the women. The "yellow ticket" places her outside the law and makes her prey to the whim of even the lowest-ranked police officer. She becomes a plaything of the police, and her civilian rights disappear. Laws that protect the rights of citizens from arbitrariness cease to exist for her. Thus the existing system of medical-police regulation of prostitution creates alcoholics not only among brothel prostitutes but also among independents. It also contributes significantly to alcoholism among men.

The medical-police regulatory system places women in the position of having to live exclusively by their own and their customers' depravity. It's not at all surprising that they resort to getting men drunk, wishing to get the most money they can out of them. Male depravity is a matter of life and death for the supervised prostitutes. Alcohol serves them as a good ally. Prostitutes corrupt young men and accustom them to drinking. One may conclude, then, that many men become alcoholics thanks to supervised prostitution.

In modern society prostitution and alcoholism are closely interconnected. One of them usually gives rise to the other. Thus, to successfully fight alcoholism it's important to combat prostitution, and vice versa. Without question, regulated prostitution in large cities is an important cause of alcoholism in men and women. The abolition of the regulation of prostitution, thus, is crucial in the fight against alcoholism.

The medical-police regulatory system of prostitution is defended in the name of public health. Its advocates rally around the issue of hygiene. But can a system that creates outcasts in modern society, that reduces a woman to total degradation and drives her to alcoholism, that compels her to become debauched and get men drunk, really be protecting the nation's health? This patronizing system of trade in ignorant and defenseless young girls turns a blind eye to the cruder instincts of the population, encourages the spread of alcoholism, provides young people with corrupt models, and is ruining the future of the country. It's impossible to protect public health in this way. Therefore I propose that the Commission petition the government to repeal the medical-police regulation of prostitution and to take energetic steps in the struggle against prostitution.

Source: Maria I. Pokrovskaia, "Prostitutsiia i alkogolizm," *Zhurnal russkago obshchestva okhraneniia narodnago zdraviia* ["Prostitution and Alcoholism," *Journal of the Russian Society for the Protection of Public Health*], nos. 5–6 (1905), pp. 216–23. Excerpted.

Translated and partially annotated by Teresa L. Polowy.

2. On Abolishing Brothels: Speech, 1910

EKATERINA GARDNER

In 1910 Ekaterina Gardner joined Aleksandra Dementeva and other activists in pre-senting an address to the Congress on the Abolition of State-Licensed Brothels (see chapter 4). An active feminist and member of both the Women's Mutual Philanthropic Society and the League of Equal Rights for Women,[56] *Gardner began her speech by placing her opposition to brothels in an international context, again indicating the high degree of international awareness and involvement of many women activists by the end of the imperial period. Like the other participants at the Congress, Gardner viewed prostitution from the perspective of an elite woman (see chapter 3 for the views of sixty-three prostitutes on their exclusion from the Congress). In her address, she enumerated the reasons why, contrary to the claims of bawdy-house supporters, state-licensed brothels in no way protected public health. Although most of her arguments purport to be scientifically and statistically based, they also incorporate elements of Russian nationalism, anti-Semitism, and an equation of (male) sexual desire with depravity, as well as an unwillingness to see prostitutes as anything other than victims.*

We hope that the minutes from this congress will soon help Russia throw off from itself the hypocritical cloak of protection of public health that covers the infamous, immoral business enslaving the body and soul of a human being for the sake of indulging depravity.

Illusions about protecting public health by regulating prostitution in brothels become clear to all who familiarize themselves with this matter. There is sufficient scholarly research on this issue in both foreign and Russian literature. We shall argue mainly on the basis of data we received while working from 1900 to 1903 on the "Commission for the Discussion of the Issue of Medical-Police Surveillance over Prostitution as It Is Connected with the General Issue of the Struggle against It [Prostitution]," which was convened by the Second Section of the Society for the Protection of Public Health. These data, signed by the fourteen members of the commission, were presented by a representative of the Second Section to the general assembly.

I shall not stand solely on the grounds of a moral point of view; rather, I shall criticize the position of brothels' defenders from a sanitary point of view. I shall enumerate here the more serious arguments that are often cited in defense of preserving brothels, as well as the objections to them, citing sometimes from official sources.

1. Defenders of state-licensed brothels argue that brothels are preferable to street prostitution, that it is easier [in them] to establish good sanitary surveillance over women by the aid of frequent examinations and, in such a manner, to prevent the spread of syphilitic infections by dispatching those who fall ill to the hospital.

I can cite a great deal of evidence from Russian and foreign specialists and syphilologists who maintain that, in its dormant period, syphilis is difficult to detect, that its initial symptoms are easily overlooked, and that a healthy woman, after sexual relations with an infected man, can pass on the disease to others with whom she has relations in the capacity of a simple go-between. And if cases exist where a doctor poorly diagnoses the disease and warns against passing it on, then it makes no difference whether prostitutes are examined frequently or seldom.

Doctors know quite well, and this was also known to the Commission, that a serious cure of syphilis requires from three to five years, and that, moreover, in its second phase, which is characterized by an absence of external symptoms, the disease is impossible to diagnose but can be passed on.[57] Judging by this it is obvious that the removal of sick prostitutes from state-licensed brothels to hospitals does not cure them, but only subjects them to a so-called *blanchissage*[58] and lets them out with evidence of their "health."

2. Defenders of state-licensed brothels also argue that by removing a syphilitic from a state-licensed brothel to the hospital they have reduced the spread of this disease. To this it is possible to answer that to replace those who were removed, traders in female bodies seek and seduce new prostitutes and, of course, cultivate new syphilitics in place of the others.

3. The beneficial significance of frequent medical examinations of women in state-licensed brothels—twice a week according to the rules—is negated both by the previously mentioned impossibility of diagnosing syphilis in its dormant form and by the possibility of passing on the disease after receiving the syphilitic poison from a sick client. This capability remains with both frequent and infrequent examinations.

4. The possibility of contracting an infection from medical instruments also counteracts the favorable significance of the examinations of prostitutes in state-licensed brothels: speculums, tongue depressors, and so forth are used for both sick and healthy prostitutes. Dr. Stürmer deals with this in his paper to the 1897 congress of Russian physicians and syphilologists.[59] Professor Fournier[60] also reports about this in the 1895 *Bulletin Médical*, providing many examples of syphilitic infections contracted through poor cleansing of medical instruments.

5. Defenders of state-licensed brothels maintain that the latter are preferable to street prostitution because the sanitary condition of prostitutes in brothels can be supervised more easily than that of streetwalkers. One can respond to this with the following: if it is acknowledged that a sick prostitute must infect all the men who have relations with her, then in a state-licensed brothel she will infect a greater number of guests than a streetwalker in the same amount of time because, for the sake of the madam's profit, in a brothel the prostitute must take a greater number of men each night.

6. As for the opinion that in state-licensed brothels the madams themselves, interested in the health of the prostitutes, promote sanitary surveillance over them—this, too, has no basis. Such care may be taken in unique cases in the more expensive dens, but the average landladies and the cheap brothels continually employ all means possible to hide sick women during examinations because not only are they deprived of the income from women who have been put in the hospital but the madams also must pay for their treatment. Moreover, it is well known that at night in state-licensed brothels, in addition to the prostitutes registered in them, outsiders also practice their trade, living there in the capacity of hired laborers. There can of course be many syphilitics among these unregistered women.

The unsanitary significance of state-licensed brothels increases still more because of the close cohabitation of healthy and infected women. It is well known that in our countryside, and with all probability in our cities, syphilis is predominantly spread through nonsexual means,[61] as a consequence of contact among members of families, relatives, and acquaintances. It would be odd to assume that the close relations between sick and healthy women would not have similar results.

It is also well known that owners of state-licensed brothels, who comprise a close-knit group of people interested in the trade in women,[62] use all their power to evade all the restrictive rules and laws. By exchanging women not only within the same city but also with other cities and states, owners of brothels can also easily sell an infected woman to another city where she can pass as healthy for a time and spread infection.

[7.]

8. With such a high level of infection distinguishing the contingent of prostitutes in state-licensed brothels, the existence of these houses cannot be justified. State-licensed brothels can only be allowed if examinations of the visitors will be obligatory and if there will be no syphilitics in the condyloma phase[63] among the number of prostitutes living in these houses. In other words, syphilitics in the condyloma phase must be forbidden from entering state-licensed brothels, and those sick with syphilis must quickly be excluded from state-licensed brothels.

Terrible facts about a shocking carelessness toward the protection of public health reveal themselves in the last lines of Dr. Stürmer's paper—that syphilitics in the condyloma phase are allowed in state-licensed brothels and that there is an indirect means for spreading disease. Professor V. M. Tarnovskii[64] has also spoken out about the inadvisability of licensing brothels so long as there are no obligatory medical examinations of the guests. He argues, "The examination of men must be introduced because otherwise, in the form they now exist and as the present commission (of the Medical Department) projects, state-licensed brothels provide the most glaring and graphic proof of the futility of existing surveillance over prostitution."

9. The statistics cited in regard to how men supposedly contract fewer infections in state-licensed brothels than from street prostitutes are contradictory, and

the means of collecting them also does not stand up to criticism, as they rely on a sample of infected men who tend to go to the doctor long after having been infected.

Several proponents of state-licensed brothels from among the members of the commission of the Second Section of the Society for the Protection of Public Health also acknowledged the necessity of examining male guests, but, together with this, they pointed out the supposedly insurmountable obstacle of putting this into practice; they said that not one doctor would agree to sit in a state-licensed brothel and examine drunken visitors. We suggest that it is also not becoming to examine drunken and diseased prostitutes.

10. Though I do not wish to defend street prostitution, which is a product of many evils of life—the gloom of ignorance, poverty, hereditary illness, etc.—I nevertheless must say that the streetwalker never sinks to the abysmal depths that are the lot of the victims of state-licensed brothels. First, to a certain extent, she is her own boss, and the customers brought to her cannot venture to exert such disgraceful humiliation of her as that which befalls women in state-licensed brothels. In the latter, good money can buy any outrage. The facts of male licentiousness are encountered by everyone whose fate it is to enter into humane, sincere relations with the victims of social temperament.

State-licensed brothels are humiliating to a woman, and they also corrupt men, arousing abnormal instincts in them in relation to women—with which their wives then have to reckon. Their offspring also have to reckon with this, because the perverted instincts of the fathers are passed on to the children and disrupt the improvement of society.

Only the concerted strength of all society can help reduce the spread of syphilis. But this reduction will not occur through state-licensed brothels but by evolutionary means, through the development of enlightenment and in connection with the habits of order, cleanliness, and sanitary self-care.

I am suggesting that the moral grounds for abolishing state-licensed brothels, where both women and men are deeply corrupted, are evident to all. On the basis of everything already said, I am turning to the congress with a request that it petition for the immediate closing of state-licensed brothels, and I hope that the decisions of the congress will be made with consciousness of the necessity for the state to stop administratively legalizing the indulgence of vice, which is leading Russia toward degeneration, and also in the spirit of Christian morality. The congress has gathered during the great holy days [Easter], when cries resound: "Christ has risen!" that is, "Love has risen!" Yes, love is rising in the hearts of all those present at the congress, and they will kindle the hearts of the rulers and all their fellow citizens with the flame of love and truth!

Source: Ekaterina I. Gardner, "Ob unichtozhenii domov terpimosti," *Trudy pervago vserossiiskago s"ezda po bor'be s torgom zhenshchinami i ego prichinami proiskhodivshchago v S.-Peterburge s 21 do 25 aprelia 1910 goda* ["On Abolishing State-Licensed Brothels," in *Works of the First All-Russian Congress on the Struggle against* the *Trade in Women and Its Causes, Which Took Place in St. Petersburg 21–25 April 1910*], vol. 2 (St. Petersburg, 1911–1912). Excerpted from pp. 356–62.

Translated and partially annotated by Laurie Bernstein.

C. On the Outskirts of St. Petersburg: Memoirs

SOFIA PANINA

Countess Sofia Vladimirovna Panina (1871–1956), a member of the Kadet party and Deputy Minister of Welfare and Education in the Provisional Government,[65] *developed her political skills by engaging in charitable work. Among her many activities, Panina founded, funded, and administered the Ligovo People's House in St. Petersburg. The programs of this pioneering community center in an industrial slum reflected Panina's dedication to education and cultural enlightenment as the means to political and social progress. The center served working-class adults and children, providing a subsidized cafeteria, day care, adult education classes, vocational training, a library, art exhibitions, a theater, and other activities. It is still in operation today, serving some of the same purposes.*

In the following excerpt from her memoirs (written in exile), Panina recounts her confrontation with the Bolshevik government. In it we see the clash of diametrically opposed views of class relations and the beginnings of the process that led eventually to the suppression of all autonomous social and political organizations, including feminist ones, under the Soviet regime.

When the Provisional Government changed the voting laws for municipal self-government and granted the same rights to women that were given to men, I was elected in 1917 as a deputy of the Petrograd City Duma and I fell into the thick of political events.

Until then I had never belonged to any political party, and my interests were concentrated on questions of education and general culture, which alone, I was deeply convinced, could provide a solid basis for a free political order. But since many of those around me considered me a socialist, by reason of the nature of my activity and because of the fact that the latter [her activity] proceeded among workers and the most deprived strata of the urban population, I considered it necessary, at the moment when the political struggle intensified, to establish my position with complete precision and dissociate myself from the socialist madness that had seized the country; I joined the Party of Popular Freedom (K.-D.), which alone at that time, out of all the nonsocialist parties, openly battled with advancing Bolshevism. My entire future fate was determined by this moment.

In May of 1917 I became Deputy Minister of State Welfare in the Provisional Government, under Minister Prince D. I. Shakhovskoi, and in August I was appointed Deputy Minister of Popular Education, the head of which at that time was S. F. Ol'denburg.[66] I was put in charge of administering the Department of Adult Education. The Bolshevik October Revolution found me at this post.

The Ministers of the Provisional Government were arrested and imprisoned in the Peter and Paul Fortress. Elections to the Constituent Assembly, called for [at] the end of November, were going on throughout Russia.[67] Legal authority no longer existed in the country, and therefore on the first morning after the Revolution,[68] with the complete agreement of all the Ministry's senior employees, I signed an order to take out of the Ministry those monies that were kept as cash reserves and to deposit them into a bank in the name of the Constituent Assembly, which alone could be a competent manager of government funds. I should add to this that the greater part of the 93,000 [rubles] that were in the Ministry's cash reserves consisted of Ministry employees' salaries, not taken out at the proper time. Several hours later the Ministry was seized by the Bolsheviks, and in a month, the night before the proposed opening of the Constituent Assembly, I was arrested and taken away to Smolnyi.[69] There, at the interrogation, they presented me with the order I had signed about removing Ministry funds and demanded the return of this money to the Bolshevik government. Upon my refusal to do this, it was announced to me that I would be placed in prison and brought to trial on a charge of plundering and embezzling the people's property. That same day, at the same time as I sat in Smolnyi, the Constituent Assembly was dispersed by the Bolsheviks.

They brought me to prison about midnight.[70] An old clerk was dozing in the overheated, barely lit, and smoke-filled prison office. Cigarette butts, scattered across the entire floor, gathered like living things and lay thick around the burning-hot small iron stove; empty and half-drunk glasses of tea were piled up on the tables and window sills. My military guard left me, having handed me over to the old clerk, truly right out of Gogol's[71] time. Having barely wakened from a sweet slumber, steamed into a sweat and bored, he, without raising his eyes, pulled over to himself a thick register book, took pen in hand, and set about fulfilling his responsibilities.

"Your name?"

"Panina, Sofia Vladimirovna."

"Rank?"

"Countess."

Eyes tear themselves from the paper and look at me for the first time with surprise over the iron rims of eyeglasses. Big, kind, blue eyes.

"Your occupation?"

"Deputy Minister of Popular Education."

A pause.

"Please be seated."

He himself stands up, long and skinny, and transfers me to the jurisdiction of the entering prison matron, who is to take me to my cell.

"My God, My God, and what will happen next!" the matron clutches at her head.

"What is so surprising?" I ask.

"As if we had not heard about the People's House!"

The door of the solitary cell closes after me with a bang.

"Sofia Vladimirovna, is that you?" Through the little window of my solitary cell, the very first morning of my incarceration, a young female face is staring. It is one of the criminals, who take turns cleaning the cells, corridors and staircases of the prison, bringing us food and carrying out various jobs around the prison.

"It is. And who are you?"

"Why, Niusha, Niusha Evseeva, don't you remember? I was often at your People's House, I looked at the pictures, listened to the music. But how could you remember all of us! But I remember you well. Good Lord, my God, whatever for did they put you in here, the monsters?"

"And you, Niusha, why are you here?"

A muddled and very incomprehensible story follows about some theft, immediately establishing in both of us a belief in our common innocence and our solidarity against the common enemy.

And every day at the little window of my cell there began to appear ever new Niushas, Ksiutas, Grushas, and Manias, who knew me from the People's House and now tried their hardest to brighten my life. They washed my cell with special effort and polished the state-issued copper basin and pitcher that served me for washing. When, once a week, I was taken to the bath, one of them without fail ran ahead and scrubbed and cleaned the bath. They brought me extra pieces of bread, since the portion fixed for us was very small, and were terribly upset if I refused them. No sisters or friends could have been more attentive and solicitous than those dear young women, who had somehow gotten tangled up in the snares of life.

The "most revolutionary" and "freest" power of that time, of course, had abolished the obligatory work in laundries, kitchens, and various prison workshops that was imposed as a duty on prisoners under the tsarist regime and was literally their salvation. The majority of these women did not know how to read. As a result, except for those few women on duty around the prison whose work I mentioned above, all of them were literally dying of boredom and idleness in their cells. I constantly observed one of them, whose cell was just opposite mine. She had remarkable red curly hair, which she constantly combed and arranged. This was her only entertainment and comfort. The quiet of the prison was broken only by the completely wild-animal-like yawning of the prisoners—the boredom and idleness were that unbearable.

Having looked closely at this situation and having talked with some of the women, I proposed to the prison administration—that is, to the Bolshevik commissar running the prison—teaching the prisoners to read. Permission was not granted.

At the same time the People's House, or rather that outlying district of Petersburg with which I was so closely connected, took on a new, unforgettable role for me, compelling me now to recall that time as the most significant and happiest of my life.

By a strange and inexplicable chance, overcoming all the havoc and losses I have lived through, a packet of letters written to me then in prison and after prison is preserved to this day in my hands. Among those who wrote were very many well-known names, still more were not only names completely unknown but also individuals who were unknown to me. Of course, the larger part of the sentiments expressed to me then related less to me personally than to the symbol that I represented at that moment, but it is exactly this that is dear to me, that is, those "good feelings" that "I awakened with a lyre" are dear.

The first session of the Military Revolutionary Tribunal opened on December 10 in the former palace of Grand Duke Nikolai Nikolaevich, on the Petersburg Side.[72] The public, among whom were many of my friends, so filled up the hall that people were turned away, and when I, under security guard, approached the building, we had to fight our way through a thick crowd of people who already could not enter the hall. When I entered the courtroom, the entire public rose and gave me a loud ovation. At the judge's bench, which stood on a platform, presided the worker Zhukov, who was a student at the Smolensk Evening Courses, an organization related to our People's House.

There were no "sworn" defenders[73] or prosecutors at this improvised court, and professional Petersburg lawyers refused on principle to appear at these new courts, which were considered by them to be a parody of a real court. Therefore, on the eve of this day when they told me in prison about the impending trial on the morrow and suggested that I invite a defender of my own choice for myself, I telephoned not a lawyer, but my long-time acquaintance and co-worker, Ia. Ia. Gurevich, asking him to take on my defense. Gurevich was director of the gymnasium founded in Petersburg by his father, and was a close collaborator in the [work of the] theater section of the People's House.

The ritual of the new legal procedures required that the chairman of the court, after finishing the formal questioning of the defendant, invite anyone from the public who wished to make a speech for the prosecution. No one responded to this offer. Then the offer was extended to those wishing to speak for the defense. Gurevich rose and spoke his calm, friendly words. The atmosphere in the hall, although it was tense, nevertheless still stayed within the bounds of "moderation and scrupulousness." Then, however, something unforeseen happened. "Someone in gray" from the public asked to speak.

"Your name?"

"Ivanov."

"Occupation?"

"Worker."

Ivanov . . . —one of those countless Russian Ivanovs—made a speech in my defense . . . Even now I remember its content and, more important, I remember its simplicity of form and sincerity. He was completely unknown to me personally, but he turned out to be a resident of our outlying district and a visitor to the People's House.[74]

His speech produced the effect of a bomb exploding in the hall, and provoked unusual agitation among the judges. Stuchka,[75] the People's Commissar of Justice, who was also present here and led the entire production, began to fuss. One of the

Bolshevik orators was immediately produced with a speech for the prosecution; his right hand, by adopted tradition, began to spin around like a windmill, barely keeping pace with the machine-gun speed of the words that flew from his lips. He talked incredible nonsense. Cries began to be heard from the public: "You're lying!" and "Lies!" and so on. I was then given a final word, in which I said that I had carried out only what I considered to be my duty of service to the country, and I tried to express to all those present the gratitude that filled my heart to over-flowing after Ivanov's speech. After this a recess was announced and the court withdrew to confer, Stuchka immediately darting away behind the scenes into the judges' conference room, a fact completely impermissible in the legal traditions of former times.

How many dear and friendly faces did I discern then in the hall! And how many of them did I see then without myself suspecting that it was for the last time!

I do not remember whether the judges conferred for a long time, but when they finally took their places again on the platform, at the bench, the sentence that they passed on me was surprisingly mild: "in light of my former service" only a "public reprimand" to me was declared, and freedom was offered under the condition, however, of paying the sum of money taken out of the Ministry to the judicial tribunal.

"Do you agree to pay in that money, citizeness Panina?"

"On the grounds of everything already said by me earlier—no."

"Then you will be returned to prison."

"You have the power."

When the guard again led me through the hall by a narrow passage through the crowded spectators, the public gave me a stormy ovation. People applauded, shouted things, hands reached out to me—my trial turned into my triumph.

But the prison doors once again slammed shut after me—and this time, it seemed, soundly. There was no way out of the situation: in no way could I hand over state funds, whose safekeeping was my responsibility, to a power that I did not consider legitimate; this same power could not renounce its demand. I began mentally preparing for a long stay in prison. The only improvement in my situation as "one who had been sentenced" compared to the situation of "one under investigation" lay in the fact that meetings with visitors were now permitted in the normal way, in the prison reception room, and did not take place across a distance of two sets of bars, between which walked a guard.

Christmas was approaching, and bearing in mind the fact that during holidays all kinds of indulgences to the prisoners were permitted, in the form of extra visits and parcels, I proposed to the prison administration to organize a reading for the prisoners with a magic lantern, obtaining all the necessary materials for this from the People's House.[76] This permission was granted, and several days before Christmas both the lantern of the People's House and the pictures I had indicated arrived at the prison office.

This second term of mine lasted, however, only ten days. One splendid evening the wardress entered my cell at an unusual hour and said that I was called to the office "with my things." I quickly descended with my little suitcase in hand. In the office stood Professor I. M. Grevs, O. K. Nechaeva, and my friend Aleksandra Mikhailovna Petrunkevich.[77] The Bolshevik commissar of the prison announced to me that I was free.

It turned out that while I sat in ignorance behind bars, my friends continued their energetic efforts to get me freed. The All-Russian Union of Teachers opened a subscription to collect the 93,000 [rubles] that were necessary to ransom me out of prison. The first ruble on the list was contributed by a worker.

My dealings with the prison did not end with this episode, however.

As dearest O. K. Nechaeva, with face beaming, took me into her broad embrace and all of us, conversing animatedly, began to say goodbye to the blue-eyed clerk and the Bolshevik commissar of the prison, the latter suddenly turned to me with the question:

"Well, but what about the Christmas reading that was promised to the prisoners?"

"Yes, the reading. . . . " the clerk and wardress repeated with bewilderment and disappointment in their voices.

"If you permit it, I will come to you with pleasure on Christmas Day and hold the promised reading," I said.

The little commissar, in leather jacket and with a revolver at his belt, went up to me, took my hand, and kissed it.

On Christmas Day my cousin and I tramped through the deep snowdrifts with which the uncleared streets of Petrograd were blocked that winter. The snowdrifts on the Vyborg Side, near the prison, had turned into real mountain ranges.

The big hall of one of the prison buildings was jammed with prisoners. In the first row, under special guard, sat women murderers, in manacles, as far as I recall; further off huddled the criminal small-fry, all my Niushas and Ksiutas. I chose as my theme "The Nativity of Christ." I showed them scenes of Palestine, read the Gospel text describing the event, showed reproductions of paintings depicting the Nativity by great artists of various nationalities, and read one of the legends of Selma Lagerlöf, from her *Legends about Christ*.[78] When I finished, the prison commissar asked me to repeat the reading the next day for prisoners of another prison building, whom the hall could not accommodate, and I, of course, gladly fulfilled his request.

So, for a brief moment, a link between two outlying districts of the city was established and a bridge of mutual understanding was thrown across the gulf between all of us, people of such different "classes," education, political views, and spiritual and intellectual cultures.

For me those days remained forever the emblem of open opportunities.

Source: S. V. Panina, "Na peterburgskoi okraine," *Novyi zhurnal* ["On the Outskirts of St. Petersburg," *New Journal*] 49 (1957), pp. 189–203. Excerpted from pp. 191–99.

Translated and partially annotated by Adele Lindenmeyr.

Notes

1. Since a substantial body of primary sources by, and relating to, women who were involved in the revolutionary movement already is available in English, we have included little such material in this volume. For such works, see the list of suggested English-language readings.

2. Located in Vladimir province, which borders Moscow province on the east.

3. Located in Moscow province.

4. Russian Orthodox believers observed four periods of fasting during the year.

5. Women's institutes were state-run boarding schools that generally combined upper primary and secondary levels of education. Although their forerunner was the Smolnyi Institute, established by Catherine II, most institutes were founded in the first half of the nineteenth century. Intended to produce enlightened wives and mothers faithful to the ideals of the autocracy, the Orthodox Church, and the established social order, they offered a fairly narrow curriculum until after the 1850s. See chapter 4 for more information on both the Smolnyi Institute and women's institutes in general.

6. On peasant women's braids, see the selection under "Arranging Marriages" in chapter 3 on peasant marriage practices.

7. On Tolstoi, see chapter 4, note 34.

8. Konstantin Nikolaevich Bestuzhev-Riumin (1829–1897), an academician and professor of history at St. Petersburg University, was the first director of the St. Petersburg Higher Women's Courses; hence the courses generally were known as the Bestuzhev Women's Courses.

9. The courses therefore paralleled somewhat the structure of existing university departments, which at this time consisted of history and philology, natural science, mathematics, medicine, and law. A department of law was added to the Courses in 1906.

10. On the State Council, see chapter 4, note 35.

11. Considered an extreme reactionary, Prince M. S. Volkonskii had earlier chaired another commission that limited women's medical training to midwifery courses. The Volkonskii commission on women's education worked from 1884 to 1888, but its proposals were not submitted to the State Council for consideration until 1893, thus ensuring that all Higher Women's Courses except those in St. Petersburg would have ceased to exist as a result of the "temporary" ban on admissions instituted in 1886.

12. The third position in the Table of Ranks established by Peter the Great in 1722; it conferred hereditary noble status on non-nobles. Likhacheva's husband, however, was an editor of the moderate newspaper *New Times* [*Novoe vremia*].

13. Founded during the Revolution of 1905, the All-Russian Union for Women's Equality was the largest and most influential feminist organization active in imperial Russia between 1905 and 1907. It advocated specific rights for women (e.g., equality of the sexes before the law, coeducation at all levels, equal land rights for peasant women), protective legislation for female workers, and radical-liberal reforms in general. The union foundered after 1907 due both to repressive governmental policies and to divisions within its ranks. Many of its members, including Kalmanovich, then turned to the League of Equal Rights for Women, which after 1909 became the chief feminist organization in imperial Russia until it was suppressed after the October Revolution in 1917. Both organizations combined political activism with charitable activities and other forms of advocacy.

14. Emmeline Pankhurst and her daughters were leaders in the British women's suf-frage campaign, and usually are credited with developing the direct, violent action of the "suffragettes."

15. A commercial and industrial center on the middle course of the Volga River that served as a place of exile for those convicted of political crimes.

16. As political unrest mounted over the summer and fall of 1905, various political groups began to hold gatherings to facilitate political discussion that was banned in a more public setting.

17. That is, "It suited their plans."

18. Kalmanovich refers here to the Russo-Japanese War (1904–1905).

19. Maria Filipovna is a typical *"prizhival'ka,"* or hanger-on, figure. Women who lacked adequate independent means and did not marry or were widowed had a difficult time earn-ing a living and so often lived with families in a kind of companion role.

20. That is, she was not observing fasting practice.

21. A reference to the elderly Countess in Pushkin's novelette "The Queen of Spades" (1833), on which Tchaikovsky based his opera of the same name (1890).

22. One of the women's institutes in Moscow. See note 5 in this chapter, and also chapter 4.

23. The author Leo Tolstoi.

24. The term "populism" embraces a diverse array of radical and revolutionary groups that first appeared in the late 1860s and that, despite their differences, emphasized the revo-lutionary potential of the peasantry and the possibility of a non-capitalist path of economic development incorporating transformed peasant institutions.

25. Varvara Nikolaevna Batiushkova-Tsvileneva (1852?–1894), the daughter of a high government official, became involved in revolutionary groups while studying in Zurich, Switzerland, in the early 1870s. Returning to Russia, she became active in the revolu-tionary underground while also working as a teacher in a rural school. She was arrested in 1875 and sentenced to hard labor for nine years, but the sentence was commuted to exile to the Siberian city of Irkutsk.

26. Located north and east of Moscow, in the central industrial region, but also in the southern taiga zone.

27. Vladimir Karpovich Debogorii-Mokrievich (1848–1926), populist revolutionary, author, and civil engineer.

28. Natasha is a nickname formed from the formal name Natalia.

29. The Kara prison complex was located on the Kara River in a valley of the Iablonskii Mountains, a gold-mining region privately owned by the emperor. The complex was made up of the following prisons: Ust-Kara [Kara Mouth], the Lower Prison, the Political Prison, the Lower Diggings, Sredne-Kara [Middle Kara], Upper Kara, and the Upper (Amurskii) Prison.

30. Sofia Aleksandrovna Leshern (1842?–1898), a revolutionary populist and the first woman in the Russian empire to receive a death sentence, which was commuted to life imprisonment.

31. Of these, the following have been identified: Maria Kutitonskaia, a revolutionary assassin who also received a death sentence, later commuted to penal servitude for life; Elizaveta Kovalskaia (1849, 1850, or 1852–1933), one of the few women revolutionaries to have been born a serf.

32. On the circuit courts, see chapter 5, note 42.

33. Chosen from among the landowning nobility, peace mediators were local administrative officials introduced at the time of the Emancipation to help with the implementation of the reform.

34. In the system created by the 1864 judicial reform, the official charged with conducting criminal investigations. Also translated as "examining magistrate."

35. The vice-governor decided first to warn the peasants of Zubovskoe that if they did not obey the law he would bring in the military. He also ordered that the ringleaders be imprisoned.

36. Established in 1889, a local official in rural areas who combined administrative and judicial functions and who was appointed by the Minister of Internal Affairs from among the local landowning nobility.

37. The tsarist authorities believed that it was impossible for the peasants to disturb the peace on their own and always looked for ringleaders among other classes in society. Teachers were particular targets during the 1905 Revolution.

38. Nikolai Gavrilovich Chernyshevskii (1828–1889) and Dmitrii Ivanovich Pisarev (1840–1868) were radical journalists and literary critics influential in the 1850s and 1860s. Chernyshevskii's novel *What Is to Be Done?* (1863), which proposed a radical solution to the "woman question" and other social problems, was regarded as akin to a new gospel by radical youth.

39. Small cities near St. Petersburg.

40. At that time, there was no fixed working day specified by law. In some industries, such as bast [fiber] processing and others, the workday was eighteen hours. It was only after a major strike by textile workers and others broke out in May of 1896 that a shorter workday and its legal regulation were proposed. After the strike, an eleven-and-a-half-hour workday was introduced and, at some factories, a ten-and-a-half-hour one.

41. These are all districts of St. Petersburg.

42. Social Democrats (SD): the Russian Social Democratic Labor Party was founded as a clandestine Marxist organization in 1898. In 1903 disagreements over ideology and tactics caused the organization to split into two factions: the Mensheviks (the minority) and the Bolsheviks (the majority).

43. A well-known, privately owned metalworking plant; a large part of its production was in armaments.

44. A triumphal arch in St. Petersburg.

45. The use of this honorific to address Poltoratsky and its later use in Zagrazhskaia's closing suggest that the two were nobles and social equals; however, nothing more is known about them.

46. The elected councils established by the reform of municipal government in 1870 to manage important aspects of city government. Election to the councils was based on property and educational qualifications that narrowly limited the electorate.

47. The executive boards created by the reform of municipal government in 1870 that served as the basis of municipal administration. The executive board in each city was elected by the municipal duma and chaired by the mayor.

48. An area in Moscow west of the Kremlin that, in addition to containing fashionable sections, was inhabited by numerous small shopkeepers, artisans, and other poorer urban groups.

49. Established in 1775, marshals of the nobility were elected by the provincial and district noble assemblies and played an important role in provincial and district administration.

50. See note 5 above.

51. The Russian term here is *"sotrudnitsa/sotrudnik,"* which in this context denoted a particular association with the trusteeships that is defined in the text.

52. Kalinkin Hospital was the best facility in Russia for prostitutes with venereal disease, yet it was understaffed and overcrowded, as were all Russian hospitals at the turn of the century.

53. *Podnadzornaia prostitutka* referred to a registered prostitute, one who was under the surveillance (*nadzor*) of the medical-police regulatory system. Registered prostitutes could work in brothels or be independent streetwalkers (*odinochki*).

54. Famed for its metallurgical industry, Tula is the administrative center of Tula province, which is located immediately south of Moscow province in the central industrial region.

55. On the "yellow ticket" (*zheltii billet*), see chapter 4, notes 47 and 50.

56. On these organizations, see the selection by Kalmanovich above.

57. In fact, after 1906 syphilis could be detected in its dormant state through the Wasserman test. Of course, in the Russian empire, few medical-police committee physicians had access to modern equipment, nor would they necessarily have been trained in the latest medical findings.

58. French for whitewashing.

59. In 1897 Konstantin Stürmer presented an overview of the Russian empire's regulatory system to a huge gathering of syphilologists, state bureaucrats, and physicians in an officially sponsored congress. Though Stürmer supported government regulation of prostitution, his report made the dismal state of Russia's system obvious to everyone.

60. Dr. Alfred Fournier was one of the first scientists to establish a link between syphilis and long-term chronic illness.

61. Although largely unfounded, belief in the nonsexual transmission of syphilis, especially among the peasant population, was common. *Inter alia,* it enabled members of the educated strata of society to preserve their idealized image of the peasantry and rural life, which was contrasted to the depravity of urban life.

62. This would appear to be a veiled reference to a common anti-Semitic perception at this time that Jews were at the forefront of brothel prostitution and the so-called "white slave trade."

63. The condyloma, or condylomatous, phase of syphilis is characterized by the presence of tumors.

64. Veniamin M. Tarnovskii (1837–1906), the first president of the Russian Syphilological and Dermatological Society and a professor at the Imperial Academy of Military Medicine, was the tsarist state's chief expert on prostitution. He nonetheless came to advocate closing down state-licensed brothels if the health of the male visitors was not monitored.

65. On the Kadet Party and the Provisional Government, see chapter 1, notes 37 and 38.

66. In 1917 the leading liberal politicians Prince Dmitrii Ivanovich Shakhovskoi (1862–1939) and his friend Sergei Fedorovich Ol'denburg (1863–1934) were members of the Constitutional Democratic Party's Central Committee along with Panina, as well as ministers in the Provisional Government.

67. The Bolsheviks arrested many of the ministers of the Provisional Government on October 26, 1917, when they seized power. A month later, early on the morning of November 28, they also arrested Panina, two more ministers of the now toppled Provisional Government, and another leader of the Constitutional Democratic Party. The date November 28 was significant: it was the date originally designated for the opening of the

Constituent Assembly, a popularly elected body that was supposed to draft a new constitution for Russia and decide on its future political order.

68. That is, after the Bolsheviks seized power on October 25–26, 1917. Since the Provisional Government's Minister of Education had been arrested that day along with other ministers, and the other Deputy Ministers were not in Petrograd, Panina became *de facto* head of the Ministry.

69. On Panina's arrest, see note 67 above. The Smolnyi Institute became the headquarters of the Petrograd Soviet of Soldiers' and Workers' Deputies during the Revolution.

70. Panina was incarcerated in the Vyborg Women's Solitary Prison, located in the working-class district of the city known as the Vyborg Side.

71. Nikolai Vasilevich Gogol (1809–1852), novelist, playwright, and short story writer, known especially as a humorist.

72. The Bolshevik government had just created the Military Revolutionary Tribunal for the purpose of exposing and prosecuting counterrevolution; Panina's trial was its first. The Tribunal appropriated the palace of Grand Duke Nikolai Nikolaevich (a cousin of Alexander III and commander-in-chief of the imperial Russian army at the outset of World War I).

73. A trained attorney and member of the bar established by the 1864 Judicial Reform.

74. Ivanov is an extremely common Russian last name, like "Smith" in English. In his speech, Ivanov declared that he had learned to read thanks to the People's House, and he praised Panina for her educational and cultural work, calling her "the best friend of the people."

75. Petr Ivanovich Stuchka (1865–1932), a lawyer and Bolshevik activist who helped to organize the Latvian Communist Party and, after the October Revolution, became one of the principal early theorists of Soviet law.

76. A magic lantern was an early type of slide projector; it used lenses and a light to project onto a screen a magnified image of a picture from a slide or card.

77. Ivan Mikhailovich Grevs (1865–1932), an eminent historian and pedagogue who participated actively in efforts to expand educational opportunities for women and who taught in the St. Petersburg Higher Women's Courses from 1892 to 1918. Active prior to 1917 in organizations that both provided aid to women in need and struggled against prostitution, Olga Konstantinovna Nechaeva (1860–1926) after the February Revolution was a member of the Petrograd committee of the Kadet Party. From a prominent family of liberal noble landowners, and Panina's stepcousin, Aleksandra Mikhailovna Petrunkevich (?–1960) graduated from the Bestuzhev Courses in 1896 and became a literary scholar and historian.

78. Selma Lagerlöf (1858–1940) was a Swedish novelist who won the Nobel Prize for Literature in 1909, the first woman and first Swedish writer to do so. She was especially known for her historical novels.

Glossary

The terms that occur in only one document are explained either in the text or in a note accompanying the document. All the terms defined here are used in more than one document.

archimandrite	The head of one or more monasteries; title given to distinguished celibate priests.
baba (plural, *baby*)	A married peasant woman or a peasant woman in general; also a wet nurse or midwife.
bania	A bathhouse or public bath; in the countryside, a popular meeting place for women and men, together or separately.
cossack	A member of a separate estate of settler-soldiers who formed regiments of irregular cavalry in the Russian army and, in the nineteenth century, were settled primarily in the southern and eastern borderlands of the empire.
desiatina (plural, *desiatiny, desiatin*)	A unit of area equivalent to 2.7 acres.
fel'dsher (m.), *fel'desheritsa* (f.; plural, *fel'dsheritsy*)	A person with a minimal level of medical training, often employed by the *zemstvo* to provide medical services to the rural population.
gendarme	A member of the political police established by Nicholas I in 1827.
gymnasium	A secondary school; although the curriculum of gymnasiums varied during the imperial period, it consistently included classical languages.
Holy Synod	Established by Peter the Great in 1721, the governing body of the Russian Orthodox Church until the restoration of the patriarchate in 1917.
institutka	A student at or graduate of a women's institute (boarding school).
intelligentsia	A term loosely applied to intellectuals, or more generally to people possessing a secondary or higher education; commonly used to describe such people who were critical of the imperial regime.

intelligentka	A female member of the Russian intelligentsia.
kasha (plural, *kashi*)	Cooked grain or groats.
kibitka	Covered wagon; also used specifically to refer to the wagon or carriage transporting the bride and groom in peasant weddings.
kisel'	Depending on the ingredients, a thick juice, sauce, or purée of fruit.
kulak	Literally, "fist," but used to mean a rich peasant; usually used pejoratively.
kulich	A rich, light cake (sometimes including raisins) baked in a cylindrical mold; commonly served for Easter.
lavra	The highest level of Orthodox monastic institution; there were four in prerevolutionary Russia.
metropolitan	The highest rank in the Russian Orthodox hierarchy from the church reforms of Peter the Great to the restoration of the patriarchate in 1917.
paskha	A type of cheesecake, in a cone-shaped mold, made specially for Easter.
pel'meni	Meat dumplings.
progymnasium	A secondary school having fewer classes (grades) than a gymnasium.
raznochinets (plural, *raznochintsy*)	A term appearing in the eighteenth century to denote people of various social estates or, more often, people who had left the estate of their parents but had not formally entered another one.
rusalka	A female water spirit, or water sprite, believed by the peasantry to be associated with the unclean dead and the cause of misfortune.
skit	Monastic hermitage or a separate monk's cell, usually located in a remote area.
soldatka	A soldier's wife.
soslovie	Formal rank or social estate.
Spiritual Consistory	An administrative board composed of clergy that assisted the bishop of an Orthodox diocese with the administration of the diocese.
Synod	See Holy Synod.
terem	During the Muscovite period, the women's quarters within the houses of the elite.

versta (plural, *versty*, *verst*)   One *versta* equals .66 miles or 1.067 kilometers.

zemstvo (plural, *zemstva*)   An elected organ of regional and local self-government charged with promoting public health, education, and general welfare. Established in 1864, it ceased to exist after the October Revolution in 1917.

Suggested English-Language Readings

Alexander, John T. *Catherine the Great: Life and Legend*. New York: Oxford University Press, 1989.

Alphin, Hugh Anthony. "M. S. Zhukova and E. A. Gan: Women Writers and Female Protagonists, 1837–1843." Ph.D. diss., University of East Anglia, 1988.

Andrew, Joe. "A Futile Gift: Elena Andreevna Gan and Writing." In *Gender Restructuring in Russian Studies: Conference Papers, Helsinki, August 1992*, edited by Marianne Liljeström, Eila Mätysaari, and Arja Rosenholm. Tampere: University of Tampere, 1993.

———. "Mothers and Daughters in Russian Literature of the First Half of the Nineteenth Century." *Slavonic and East European Review* 73, no. 1 (1995): 37–60.

———. *Narrative and Desire in Russian Literature, 1822–49: The Feminine and the Masculine*. New York: St. Martin's Press, 1993.

———. *Women in Russian Literature: 1780–1863*. New York: St. Martin's Press, 1988.

———. "Radical Sentimentalism or Sentimental Radicalism: A Feminist Approach to Eighteenth-Century Russian Literature." In *Discontinuous Discourses in Modern Russian Literature*, edited by Catriona Kelly, Michael Makin, and David Sheperd. Houndmills, England: Macmillan, 1989.

Anisimov, Evgenii V. "Anna Ivanovna." *Russian Studies in History* 32, no. 4 (1994): 8–36.

———. *Empress Elizabeth: Her Reign and Her Russia, 1741–1761*, translation and preface by John T. Alexander. Gulf Breeze, Fla.: Academic International Press, 1995.

Arora, Mandakini. "Boundaries, Transgressions, Limits: Peasant Women and Gender Roles in Tver' Province, 1861–1914." Ph.D. diss., Duke University, 1995.

Atkinson, Dorothy, Alexander Dallin, and Gail Warshofsky Lapidus, eds. *Women in Russia*. Stanford: Stanford University Press, 1977.

Awsienko, Nina. "Zinaida Hippius's Literary Salon in St. Petersburg." *Russian Language Journal* 26 (1978): 83–89.

Ayers, Carolyn. "Discourse in the Society Tale." Ph.D. diss., University of Chicago, 1994.

Barker, Adele Marie. *The Mother Syndrome in the Russian Folk Imagination*. Columbus, Ohio: Slavica, 1986.

Barker, Adele and Jehanne M Gheith, eds. *A History of Russian Women's Writing*. Cambridge: Cambridge University Press, 2001.

Bartlett, R. P., A. G. Cross, and Karen Rasmussen, eds. *Russia and the World of the Eighteenth Century*. Columbus, Ohio: Slavica, 1988.

Bergman, Jay. *Vera Zasulich: A Biography*. Stanford: Stanford University Press, 1983.

Bernstein, Laurie. *Sonia's Daughters: Prostitutes and Their Regulation in Imperial Russia*. Berkeley: University of California Press, 1995.

———. "Yellow Tickets and State-Licensed Brothels. The Tsarist Government and the Regulation of Urban Prostitution." In *Health and Society in Revolutionary Russia*, edited by Susan Gross Solomon and John F. Hutchinson. Bloomington: Indiana University Press, 1990.

Bisha, Robin. "The Promise of Patriarchy: Women, Marriage, and Property in Imperial Russia." Ph.D. diss., Indiana University, 1994.

Black, J. L. *Citizens for the Fatherland: Education, Educators, and Pedagogical Ideals in Eighteenth Century Russia*. With a translation of *Book on the Duties of Man and Citizen* (St. Petersburg, 1783). Boulder, Colo.: East European Quarterly; distributed by Columbia University Press, 1979.

———. "Educating Women in Eighteenth-Century Russia: Myths and Realities." *Canadian Slavonic Papers* 20, no. 1 (March 1978): 23–43.

Bobroff, Anne. "The Bolsheviks and Working Women, 1905–1920." *Soviet Studies* 26, no. 4 (1974): 540–67.

———. "Russian Working Women: Sexuality in Bonding Patterns and Politics of Daily Life." In *Powers of Desire: The Politics of Sexuality*, edited by Ann Snitow, Christine Stansell, and Sharon Thompson. New York: Monthly Review, 1983.

———. "Working Women, Bonding Patterns, and the Politics of Daily Life: Russia at the End of the Old Regime." 2 vols. Ph.D. diss., University of Michigan, 1982.

Bonnell, Victoria. *The Russian Worker: Life and Labor under the Tsarist Regime*. Berkeley: University of California Press, 1983.

Botchkareva, Maria. *Yashka: My Life as Peasant, Officer and Exile, as Set Down by Isaac Don Levine*. New York: Frederick A. Stokes, 1919.

Bowman, Rebecca Linton. "Russian Society Tales: A Gendered Genre." Ph.D. diss., University of Virginia, 1997.

Brennan, James F. *Enlightened Despotism in Russia: The Reign of Elizabeth, 1741–1762*. New York: Peter Lang, 1987.

Breshko-Breshkovskaia, Ekaterina. *The Little Grandmother of the Russian Revolution: Reminiscences and Letters of Catherine Breshkovsky*. Edited by Alice Stone Blackwell. Boston: Little, Brown & Co., 1930.

Breshkovskaia, Catherine. *Hidden Springs of the Russian Revolution*. Edited by Lincoln Hutchinson. Stanford: Stanford University Press, 1931.

Briker, Olga Lee. "The Poetic Personae of Karolina Pavlova (1807–1893)." Ph.D. diss., Columbia University, 1996.

Broido, Vera. *Apostles into Terrorists: Women and the Revolutionary Movement in the Russia of Alexander II*. New York: Viking Press, 1977.

Burgin, Diana Lewis. "After the Ball Is Over: Sophia Parnok's Creative Relationship with Marina Tsvetaeva." *Russian Review* 47, no. 4 (1988): 425–44.

———. "Signs of a Response: Two Possible Parnok Replies to Her 'Podruga'." *Slavic and East European Journal* 35, no. 2 (1991): 214–27.

———. *Sophia Parnok: The Life and Work of Russia's Sappho*. New York: New York University Press, 1994.

———. "Sophia Parnok and the Writing of a Lesbian Poet's Life." *Slavic Review* 51, no. 2 (1992): 214–31.

Bushnell, John. "Did Serf Owners Control Serf Marriage? Orlov Serfs and Their Neighbors, 1773–1861." *Slavic Review* 52, no. 3 (1993): 419–45.

Catherine II, Empress of Russia. *Memoirs of Catherine the Great*. Translated by Katharine Anthony. New York: Knopf, 1927.

————. *Two Comedies by Catherine the Great, Empress of Russia: "Oh, These Times!" and "The Siberian Shaman."* Edited and translated by Lurana D. O'Malley. *Russian Theatre Archive,* vol. 15. Amsterdam: Harwood Academic Publishers, 1997.

Chester, Pamela. "Engaging Sexual Demons in Marina Tsvetaeva's 'Devil': The Body and the Genesis of the Woman Poet." *Slavic Review* 53, no. 4 (1994): 1025–45.

Clark, Rhonda Lebedev. "Forgotten Voices: Women in Periodical Publishing of Late Imperial Russia, 1860–1905." Ph.D. diss., University of Minnesota, 1996.

Clements, Barbara Evans. *Bolshevik Feminist: The Life of Aleksandra Kollontai.* Bloomington: Indiana University Press, 1979.

————. *Bolshevik Women.* Cambridge: Cambridge University Press, 1997.

————. "Working Class and Peasant Women in the Russian Revolution, 1919–1923." *Signs* 8, no. 2 (1982): 215–35.

Clements, Barbara Evans, Barbara Alpern Engel, and Christine D. Worobec, eds. *Russia's Women: Accommodation, Resistance, Transformation.* Berkeley: University of California Press, 1991.

Clyman, Toby W., and Diana Greene, eds. *Women Writers in Russian Literature.* Westport, Conn.: Greenwood Press, 1994.

Confino, Michael, ed. *Daughter of a Revolutionary: Natalie Herzen and the Bakunin-Nechaev Circle.* Translated by Hilary Steinberg and Lydia Bott. La Salle, Ill.: Library Press, 1973.

Conroy, Mary Schaeffer. "Women Pharmacists in Nineteenth- and Early Twentieth-Century Russia." *Pharmacy in History* 29, no. 4 (1987): 155–64.

Coole, Diana. "Social Democrats and Bolsheviks: Socialism and the Woman Question." In *Women in Political Theory: From Ancient Misogyny to Contemporary Feminism,* edited by Diana Coole. 2nd ed. Boulder, Colo.: L. Rienner, 1993.

Cooper, Nancy L. "Secret Truths and Unheard-of Women: Poliksena Solov'eva's Fiction as Commentary on Vladimir Solov'ev's Theory of Love." *Russian Review* 56, no. 2 (1997): 178–91.

Cornwell, Neil, ed. *Reference Guide to Russian Literature.* London: Fitzroy Dearborn Publishers, 1998.

Corten, Irina H. "Feminism in Russian Literature." In *Modern Encyclopedia of Russian and Soviet Literature.* Vol. 7. Edited by Harry B. Weber. Gulf Breeze, Fla.: Academic International Press, 1984.

Costlow, Jane T. "The Gallop, The Wolf, The Caress: Eros and Nature in *The Tragic Menagerie.*" *Russian Review* 56, no. 2 (1997): 192–208.

————. "Speaking the Sorrow of Women: Turgenev's *Neschastnaia* and Evgeniia Tur's *Antonina.*" *Slavic Review* 50, no. 2 (1991): 328–35.

Costlow, Jane T., Stephanie Sandler, and Judith Vowles, eds. *Sexuality and the Body in Russian Culture.* Stanford: Stanford University Press, 1993.

Cunningham, Rebecca. "The Russian Women Artists-Designers of the Avant Garde." *T D & T* 34, no. 2 (1998): 38–51.

Curtiss, John Shelton. "Russian Sisters of Mercy in the Crimea, 1854–1855." *Slavic Review* 25, no. 1 (1966): 84–100.

Curtiss, Mina. *A Forgotten Empress: Anna Ivanovna and Her Era, 1730–40.* New York: Ungar, 1974.

Dashkova, Ekaterina. *Memoirs of the Princess Dashkova*. Edited and translated by Kyril Fitzlyon. London: J. Calder, 1958. Reprint; intro., Jehanne M Gheith and afterword, Alexander Woronzoff-Dashkoff. Durham, N.C.: Duke University Press, 1995.

Dolgorukaia, Natalia. *Memoirs of Princess Natalija Borisovna Dolgorukaja*. Edited and translated by Charles Townsend. Columbus, Ohio: Slavica, 1977.

Donald, Moira. "Bolshevik Activity Amongst the Working Women of Petrograd in 1917." *International Review of Social History* 27, no. 2 (1982): 131–60.

Dorfman, Leslie Jane. "Serapion Sister: The Poetry of Elizaveta Polonskaja." Ph.D. diss., University of Michigan, 1996.

Drumm, Robert Elmer. "The Bolshevik Party and the Organization and Emancipation of Working Women, 1914 to 1921; Or, A History of the Petrograd Experiment." Ph.D. diss., Columbia University, 1977.

Dudgeon, Ruth Arlene Fluck. "The Forgotten Minority: Women Students in Imperial Russia, 1872–1917." *Russian History* 9, no. 1 (1982): 1–26.

———. "Women and Higher Education in Russia, 1855–1905." Ph.D. diss., George Washington University, 1975.

Dukes, Paul. *Russia under Catherine the Great*. 2 vols. Newtonville, Mass.: Oriental Research Partners, 1977.

Durova, Nadezhda. *The Cavalry Maiden: Journals of a Russian Officer in the Napoleonic Wars*. Edited and translated by Mary Fleming Zirin. Bloomington: Indiana University Press, 1988.

Edmondson, Linda H. "Equality and Difference in Women's History: Where Does Russia Fit In?" In *Women in Russia and Ukraine*, edited and translated by Rosalind Marsh. Cambridge: Cambridge University Press, 1996.

———. *The Feminist Movement in Russia, 1900–1917*. Stanford: Stanford University Press, 1984.

———. "Russian Feminists and the First All-Russian Congress of Women." *Russian History* 3, no. 2 (1976): 123–49.

———. "Women's Emancipation and Theories of Sexual Difference in Russia, 1850–1917." In *Gender Restructuring in Russian Studies: Conference Papers, Helsinki, August 1992*, edited by Marianne Liljeström, Eila Mätysaari, and Arja Rosenholm. Tampere: University of Tampere, 1993.

———, ed. *Women and Society in Russia and the Soviet Union*. Cambridge: Cambridge University Press, 1992.

Eidelman, Dawn Diane. "George Sandism and the Woman Question in Nineteenth Century Russia: Desire and Culpability in the Love Triangle in Ten Russian Selections." Ph.D. diss., Emory University, 1990.

Engel, Barbara Alpern. *Between the Fields and the City: Women, Work, and Family in Russia, 1861–1914*. New York: Cambridge University Press, 1994.

———. "Engendering Russia's History: Women in Post-Emancipation Russia and the Soviet Union." *Slavic Review* 51, no. 2 (1992): 309–21.

———. *Mothers and Daughters: Women of the Intelligentsia in Nineteenth-Century Russia*. New York: Cambridge University Press, 1983. Reprint, Evanston, Ill.: Northwestern University Press, 2000.

———. "Peasant Morality and Pre-Marital Relations in Late Nineteenth Century Russia." *Journal of Social History* 23, no. 4 (1990): 695–714.

———. "Socially Deviant Women and the Russian Peasant Community, 1861–1914." In *Gender Restructuring in Russian Studies: Conference Papers, Helsinki, August 1992,* edited by Marianne Liljeström, Eila Mätysaari, and Arja Rosenholm. Tampere: University of Tampere, 1993.

———. "St. Petersburg Prostitutes in the Late Nineteenth Century: A Personal and Social Profile." *Russian Review* 48, no. 1 (1989): 21–44.

———. "The Woman's Side: Male Out-Migration and the Family Economy in Kostroma Province." *Slavic Review* 45, no. 2 (1986): 257–71.

———. "Women Medical Students in Russia, 1872–1882: Reformers or Rebels?" *Journal of Social History* 12, no. 3 (1979): 394–415.

———. "Women, Men, and the Languages of Peasant Resistance, 1870–1907." In *Cultures in Flux: Lower-Class Values, Practices, and Resistance in Late Imperial Russia,* edited by Stephen P. Frank and Mark D. Steinberg. Princeton: Princeton University Press, 1994.

———. "Women, Work and Family in the Factories of Rural Russia. " *Russian History,* 16, nos. 2–4 (1989): 223–37.

———. "Women's Rights à la Russe." *Russian Review* 58, no. 3 (July 1999): 355–60.

Engel, Barbara, and Clifford Rosenthal, eds. and trans. *Five Sisters: Women against the Tsar.* New York: Knopf, 1975. Reprint, New York: Routledge, 1987.

Engelgardt, Aleksandr Nikolaevich. *Letters from the Country, 1872–1877.* Edited and translated by Cathy A. Frierson. New York: Oxford University Press, 1993.

Engelstein, Laura. "Gender and the Juridical Subject: Prostitution and Rape in Nineteenth-Century Russian Criminal Codes." *Journal of Modern History* 60, no. 3 (1988): 458–95.

———. *The Keys to Happiness: Sex and the Search for Modernity in Fin-de-Siècle Russia.* Ithaca: Cornell University Press, 1992.

———. "Lesbian Vignettes: A Russian Triptych from the 1890s." *Signs* 15, no. 4 (1990): 813–31.

———. "Morality and the Wooden Spoon: Russian Doctors View Syphilis, Social Class, and Sexual Behavior, 1890–1905." *Representations* 14 (Spring 1986): 169–208.

Farnsworth, Beatrice. *Aleksandra Kollontai: Socialism, Feminism, and the Bolshevik Revolution.* Stanford: Stanford University Press, 1980.

———. "The Soldatka: Folklore and the Court Record." *Slavic Review* 49, no. 1 (1990): 58–73.

Farnsworth, Beatrice, and Lynne Viola, eds. *Russian Peasant Women.* New York: Oxford University Press, 1992.

Farrow, Lee A. "Peter the Great's Law of Single Inheritance: State Imperatives and Noble Resistance." *Russian Review* 55, no. 3 (1996): 430–47.

Feiler, Lily. *Marina Tsvetaeva: The Double Beat of Heaven and Hell.* Durham: Duke University Press, 1994.

Feinstein, Elaine. *A Captive Lion: The Life of Marina Tsvetayeva.* New York: Dutton, 1987.

Fieseler, Beate. "The Making of Russian Female Social Democrats, 1890–1917." *International Review of Social History* 34, no. 2 (1989): 1–17.

Figner, Vera Nikolaevna. *Memoirs of a Revolutionist.* 2 vols. Translated by Camilla Chapin Daniels et al. New York: International, 1927. Reprint, Westport, Conn.: Greenwood Press, 1968.

Forrester, Sibelan. "Bells and Cupolas: The Formative Role of the Female Body in Marina Tsvetaeva's Poetry." *Slavic Review* 51, no. 2 (1992): 232–47.

Frank, Stephen P. "Narratives within Numbers: Women, Crime, and Judicial Statistics in Imperial Russia, 1834–1913." *Russian Review* 55, no. 4 (October 1996): 541–66.

Fraser, Eugenie. *The House by the Dvina: A Russian-Scottish Childhood.* New York: Walker, 1987.

Frierson, Cathy. *Peasant Icons: Representations of Rural People in Late Nineteenth-Century Russia.* New York: Oxford University Press, 1993.

Gheith, Jehanne M. "In Her Own Voice: Evgeniia Tur, Author, Critic, Journalist." Ph.D. diss., Stanford University, 1992.

———. "The Superfluous Man and the Necessary Woman: A 'Re-vision'." *Russian Review* 55, no. 2 (1996): 226–44.

Giffin, Frederick C. "The Prohibition of Night Work for Women and Young Persons: The Russian Factory Law of June 3, 1885." *Canadian Slavic Studies* 2, no. 2 (1968): 208–18.

Glants, Musya and Joyce Toomre, eds. *Food in Russian History and Culture.* Bloomington: Indiana University Press, 1997.

Glickman, Rose L. *Russian Factory Women: Workplace and Society, 1880–1914.* Berkeley: University of California Press, 1984.

Goldberg, Rochelle. "The Russian Women's Movement." Ph.D. diss., University of Rochester, 1976.

Good, Jane E., and David R. Jones. *Babushka: The Life of the Russian Revolutionary Ekaterina Breshko-Breshkovskaia (1844–1934).* Newtonville, Mass.: Oriental Research Partners, 1991.

Goscilo, Helena, and Beth Holmgren, eds. *Russia, Women, Culture.* Bloomington: Indiana University Press, 1996.

Greene, Diana. "Karolina Pavlova's 'At the Tea Table' and the Politics of Class and Gender." *Russian Review* 53, no. 2 (1994): 271–84.

Griffiths, David. "Catherine II: The Republican Empress." *Jahrbücher für Geschichte Osteuropas* 21, no. 3 (1973): 323–44.

Haight, Amanda. *Anna Akhmatova: A Poetic Pilgrimage.* New York: Oxford University Press, 1976. Reprint: 1990.

Harussi, Yael. "Women's Social Roles as Depicted by Women Writers in Early Nineteenth-Century Russian Fiction." In *Issues in Russian Literature before 1917: Selected Papers from the Third World Congress for Soviet and East European Studies*, edited by Douglas Clayton. Columbus, Ohio: Slavica, 1989.

Heldt, Barbara. "Feminism and the Slavic Field." *The Harriman Review*, November 1994, 11–18.

———. "Men Who Give Birth: A Feminist Perspective on Russian Literature." In *Discontinuous Discourses in Modern Russian Literature*, edited by Catriona Kelly, Michael Makin, and David Shepherd. Houndmills, England: Macmillan, 1989.

———. *Terrible Perfection: Women and Russian Literature.* Bloomington: Indiana University Press, 1987.

Herold, Kelly. "Russian Autobiographical Literature in French: Recovering a Memoiristic Tradition (1770–1830)." Ph.D. diss., University of California at Los Angeles, 1998.

Holmgren, Beth. "Why Russian Girls Loved Charskaia." *Russian Review* 54, no. 1 (1995): 91–106.

Hoogenboom, Hilde Maria. "A Two-Part Invention: The Russian Woman Writer and Her Heroines from 1860–1917." Ph.D. diss., Columbia University, 1996.

———. "Vera Figner and Revolutionary Autobiographies: The Influence of Gender on Genre." In *Women in Russia and Ukraine*, edited and translated by Rosalind Marsh. Cambridge: Cambridge University Press, 1996.

Hubbs, Joanna. *Mother Russia: The Feminine Myth in Russian Culture*. Bloomington: Indiana University Press, 1988.

Hughes, Lindsey. "Peter the Great's Two Weddings: Changing Images of Women in a Transitional Age." In *Women in Russia and Ukraine*, edited and translated by Rosalind Marsh. Cambridge: Cambridge University Press, 1996.

———. *Russia in the Age of Peter the Great*. New Haven: Yale University Press, 1998.

Hutton, Marcelline. *Russian and West European Women, 1860–1939: Dreams, Struggles, and Nightmares*. Lanham, Md.,: Rowman & Littlefield, 2001.

Hyde, H. Montgomery. *The Empress Catherine and Princess Dashkov*. London: Chapman & Hall, 1935.

Joffe, Muriel and Adele Lindenmeyr. "Daughters, Wives, and Partners: Women of the Moscow Merchant Elite." In *Merchant Moscow: Images of Russia's Vanished Bourgeoisie*, edited by James L. West and Iurii A. Petrov. Princeton: Princeton University Press, 1998.

Johanson, Christine. "Autocratic Politics, Public Opinion, and Women's Medical Education During the Reign of Alexander II, 1855–1881." *Slavic Review* 38, no. 3 (1979): 426–43.

———. *Women's Struggle for Higher Education in Russia, 1855–1900*. Montréal, Québec: McGill-Queen's University Press, 1987.

Karlinsky, Simon. *Marina Tsvetaeva: The Woman, Her World and Her Poetry*. Cambridge: Cambridge University Press, 1986.

Kelly, Catriona. *An Anthology of Russian Women's Writing, 1777–1992*. New York: Oxford University Press, 1994.

———. *A History of Russian Women's Writing, 1820–1992*. New York: Oxford University Press, 1994.

———. "Life at the Margins: Women, Culture and Narodnost' 1880–1920." In *Gender Restructuring in Russian Studies: Conference Papers, Helsinki, August 1992*, edited by Marianne Liljeström, Eila Mätysaari, and Arja Rosenholm. Tampere: University of Tampere, 1993.

———. "Teacups and Coffins: The Culture of Russian Merchant Women, 1850–1917." In *Women in Russia and Ukraine*, edited and translated by Rosalind Marsh. Cambridge: Cambridge University Press, 1996.

Kelly, Catriona, Michael Makin, and David Sheperd, eds. *Discontinuous Discourses in Modern Russian Literature*. Houndmills, England: Macmillan, 1989.

Kelly, Rita Mae Cawley. "The Role of Vera Ivanovna Zasulich in the Development of the Russian Revolutionary Movement." Ph.D. diss., Indiana University, 1967.

Khvoshchinskaya, Nadezhda. *The Boarding School Girl*. Translated and annotated by Karen Rosneck. Evanston, Ill.: Northwestern University Press, 2000.

Knight, Amy. "Female Terrorists in the Russian Socialist Revolutionary Party." *Russian Review* 38, no. 2 (1979): 139–59.

———. "The *Fritschi*: A Study of Female Radicals in the Russian Populist Movement." *Canadian-American Slavic Studies* 9, no. 1 (1975): 1–17.

Koblitz, Ann Hibner. "Career and Home Life in the 1880s: The Choices of Sofia Kovalevskaia." In *Uneasy Careers and Intimate Lives: Women in Science*, edited by Pnina G. Abir-Am and Dorinda Outram. New Brunswick, N. J.: Rutgers University Press, 1987.

———. *A Convergence of Lives: Sofia Kovalevskaia: Scientist, Writer, Revolutionary*. Boston: Birkhauser, 1983.

———. "Science, Women, and the Russian Intelligentsia: The Generation of the 1860s." *Isis*, 79, no. 297 (1988): 208–26.

Kollontai, Aleksandra. *Diaries*. New York: Random House, 1985.

———. *A Great Love*. Translation and introduction by Cathy Porter. New York: W. W. Norton, 1982.

Konz, Louly Peacock. "Marie Bashkirtseff (1858–1884): The Self-Portraits, Journals, and Photographs of a Young Artist." Ph.D. diss., University of North Carolina at Chapel Hill, 1998.

Korovushkina, Irina. "Marriage, Gender, Family, and the Old Believer Community, 1760–1850." Ph.D. diss., University of Essex, 1998.

Labzina, Anna. *Days of a Russian Noblewoman: The Memories of Anna Labzina, 1758–1821*. Edited and translated by Gary Marker and Rachel May. DeKalb: Northern Illinois University Press, 2001.

Ledkovsky, Marina, Charlotte Rosenthal, and Mary Zirin, eds. *Dictionary of Russian Women Writers*. Westport, Conn.: Greenwood Press, 1994.

Lenin, Vladimir. *On the Emancipation of Women*. Moscow: International Publishers, 1965.

Lewin, Moshe. "Customary Law and Russian Rural Society in the Post-Reform Era." *Russian Review* 44, no. 1 (1985): 1–19.

Liljeström, Marianne, Eila Mätysaari, and Arja Rosenholm, eds. *Gender Restructuring in Russian Studies: Conference Papers, Helsinki, August 1992*. Tampere: University of Tampere, 1993.

Lindenmeyr, Adele. "Maternalism and Child Welfare in Late Imperial Russia." *Journal of Women's History* 5, no. 2 (1993): 114–25.

———. *Poverty Is Not a Vice: Charity, Society, and the State in Imperial Russia*. Princeton: Princeton University Press, 1996.

———. "Public Life, Private Virtues: Women in Russian Charity, 1762–1914." *Signs* 18, no. 3 (1993): 562–91.

———. "The Rise of Voluntary Associations during the Great Reforms: The Case of Charity." In *Russia's Great Reforms, 1855–1881: New Perspectives*, edited by Ben Eklof, John Bushnell, and Larissa G. Zakharova. Bloomington: Indiana University Press, 1994.

Listova, T. A. "Russian Rituals, Customs, and Beliefs Associated with the Midwife (1850–1930)." In *Russian Traditional Culture: Religion, Gender, and Customary Law*, edited by Marjorie Mandelstam Balzer. Armonk, N.Y.: M. E. Sharpe, 1992.

Madariaga, Isabel de. *Catherine the Great: A Short History*. New Haven: Yale University Press, 1990.

———. "The Foundation of the Russian Educational System by Catherine II." *Slavonic and East European Review* 57, no. 3 (1979): 369–95.

———. *Russia in the Age of Catherine the Great*. New Haven: Yale University Press, 1981.

Makowiecka, Maria Hanna. "Women's Departures: Rewriting Voyage/Rethinking Female Travel 'Recits'." Ph.D. diss., City University of New York, 1996.

Marker, Gary. "The Enlightenment of Anna Labzina: Gender, Faith, and Public Life in Catherinian and Alexandrian Russia." *Slavic Review* 59, no. 3 (2000): 369–90.

Marrese, Michelle Lamarche. "The Enigma of Married Women's Control of Property in Eighteenth-Century Russia." *Russian Review* 58, no. 3 (1999): 380–95.

———. "Women and Westernization in Petrine Russia." In *Russia in the Age of Peter the Great: Old and New Perspectives*, edited by Anthony Cross. Vol I. Cambridge: Cambridge University Press, 1998.

Marsh, Rosalind. *Gender and Russian Literature: New Perspectives*. Cambridge: Cambridge University Press, 1996.

———, ed. and trans. *Women in Russia and Ukraine*. Cambridge: Cambridge University Press, 1996.

Marshall, Bonnie. "The Radical Voices of Russian Romanticism: Women Prose Writers, 1800–1840." *Woman and Earth [Zhenshchina i zemlia]* 3, no. 1 (1994–1995): 24–27.

Maxwell, Margaret. *Narodniki Women: Russian Women Who Sacrificed Themselves for the Dream of Freedom*. New York: Pergamon Press, 1990.

Mazour, Anatole G. *Women in Exile: Wives of the Decembrists*. Tallahassee, Fla.: Diplomatic Press, 1975.

McCormack, Kathryn Louise. "Images of Women in the Poetry of Zinaida Gippius." Ph.D. diss., Vanderbilt University, 1982.

McNeal, Robert H. *Bride of the Revolution: Krupskaya and Lenin*. Ann Arbor: University of Michigan Press, 1972.

———. "Women in the Russian Radical Movement." *Journal of Social History* 5, no. 2 (1971–1972): 143–63.

McReynolds, Louise. "Journalists in Prerevolutionary Russia." *Journalism History* 14, no. 4 (1987): 104–110.

Meehan, Brenda. *Holy Women of Russia: The Lives of Five Orthodox Women Offer Spiritual Guidance for Today*. San Francisco: Harper San Francisco, 1993.

———. "Popular Piety, Local Initiative, and the Founding of Women's Religious Communities in Russia, 1764–1807." In *Seeking God: The Recovery of Religious Identity in Orthodox Russia, Ukraine, and Georgia*, edited by Stephen K. Batalden. DeKalb: Northern Illinois University Press, 1993.

———. "Wisdom/Sophia, Russian Identity, and Western Feminist Theology." *Cross Currents* 46, no. 2 (1996): 149–68.

Meehan-Waters, Brenda. "The Authority of Holiness: Women Ascetics and Spiritual Elders in Nineteenth-Century Russia." In *God's Servants: Church, Nation, and State in Russia and Ukraine*, edited by Geoffrey A. Hosking. London: Macmillan, 1991.

————. "Catherine the Great and the Problem of Female Rule." *Russian Review* 34, no. 3 (1975): 293–307.

————. "From Contemplative Practice to Charitable Activity: Russian Women's Religious Communities and the Development of Charitable Work." In *Lady Bountiful Revisited: Women, Philanthropy, and Power,* edited by Kathleen McCarthy. New Brunswick, N.J.: Rutgers University Press, 1990.

————. "Metropolitan Filaret (Drozdov) and the Reform of Russian Women's Monastic Communities." *Russian Review* 50, no. 3 (July 1991): 310–23.

————. "Russian Convents and the Secularization of Monastic Property." In *Russia and the World of the Eighteenth Century,* edited by R. P. Bartlett, A. G. Cross, and Karen Rasmussen. Columbus, Ohio: Slavica, 1988.

Meincke, Evelyn. "Vera Ivanovna Zasulich: A Political Life." Ph.D. diss., State University of New York at Binghamton, 1984.

Monter, Barbara Heldt. "*Rassvet* (1859–1862) and the Woman Question." *Slavic Review* 36, no. 1 (1977): 76–85.

Morsberger, Grace Anne. "The Russian Woman Writer in the Salon: Issues of Gender and Literary Space." Ph.D. diss., University of California at Berkeley, 1997.

Mullaney, Marie Marmo. "Gender and the Socialist Revolutionary Role, 1871–1921: A General Theory of the Female Revolutionary Personality." *Historical Reflections* 11, no. 2 (1984): 99–152.

————. "The Female Revolutionary, the Woman Question and European Socialism, 1871–1921." Ph.D. diss., Rutgers University, 1980.

Nagrodskaia, Evdokia. *The Wrath of Dionysus: A Novel.* Edited and translated by Louise McReynolds. Bloomington: Indiana University Press, 1997.

Nash, Carol S. "Educating New Mothers: Women and the Enlightenment in Russia." *History of Education Quarterly* 21, no. 3 (1981): 301–16.

————. "The Education of Women in Russia, 1762–1796." Ph.D. diss., New York University, 1978.

————. "Students and Rubles: The Society for the Education of Noble Girls as a Charitable Institution." In *Russia and the World of the Eighteenth Century,* edited by R. P. Bartlett, A. G. Cross, and Karen Rasmussen. Columbus, Ohio: Slavica, 1988.

Naumov, V. P. "Elizaveta Petrovna." *Russian Studies in History* 32, no. 4 (1994): 37–72.

Nemec Ignashev, Diane M., and Sarah Krive, eds. *Women and Writing in Russia and the USSR: A Bibliography of English-Language Sources.* New York: Garland, 1992.

Norton, Barbara T. "E. D. Kuskova: A Political Biography of a Russian Democrat, Part 1 (1869–1905)." Ph.D. diss., Pennsylvania State University, 1981.

————. "The Making of a Female Marxist: E. D. Kuskova's Conversion to Russian Social Democracy." *International Review of Social History* 34, no. 2 (1989): 227–47.

Norton, Barbara T. and Jehanne M Gheith, eds. *Women Journalists.* Durham, N.C.: Duke University Press, 2001.

Oldenbourg, Zoë. *Catherine the Great.* New York: Pantheon Books, 1965.

O'Malley, Lurana Donnels. "Masks of the Empress: Polyphony of Personae in Catherine the Great's *Oh, These Times!*" *Comparative Drama* 31, no. 1 (1997): 65–85.

————. "The Monarch and the Mystic: Catherine the Great's Strategy of Audience Enlightenment in *The Siberian Shaman*." *Slavic and East European Journal*, no. 2 (1997): 224–42.

Pachmuss, Temira. *Zinaida Hippius: An Intellectual Profile*. Carbondale: Southern Illinois University Press, 1971.

————, ed. and trans. *Women Writers in Russian Modernism: An Anthology*. Urbana: University of Illinois Press, 1978.

Pavlova, Karolina. *A Double Life*. Translation and introduction by Barbara Heldt Monter. Ann Arbor, Mich.: Ardis, 1978. Reprint, Oakland, Calif.: Barbary Coast Books, 1987.

Pavlovskaya, Marianna E. "Everyday Life and Social Transition: Gender, Class, and Change in the City of Moscow." Ph.D. diss., Clark University, 1998.

Pedrotti, Louis. "The Scandal of Countess Rostopčina's Polish-Russian Allegory." *Slavic and East European Journal* 30, no. 2 (1986): 196–214.

Pennar, Karen. "Daily Life among the Morozovs." In *Merchant Moscow: Images of Russia's Vanished Bourgeoisie*, edited by James L. West and Iurii A. Petrov. Princeton: Princeton University Press, 1998.

Porter, Cathy. *Alexandra Kollontai: A Biography*. London: Virago, 1980.

————. *Fathers and Daughters: Russian Women in Revolution*. London: Virago, 1976.

Pozefsky, Peter C. "Love, Science, and Politics in the Fiction of *Shestidesiatnitsy* N. P. Suslova and S. V. Kovalevskaia." *Russian Review* 58, no. 3 (1999): 361–79.

Proffer, Carl B., and Ellendea Proffer. "Women in Russian Literature." *Russian Literature Triquarterly* 9 (1974).

Pushkareva, Natalia. *Women in Russian History: From the Tenth to the Twentieth Century*. Edited and translated by Eve Levin. Armonk, N.Y.: M. E. Sharpe, 1997.

Raeff, Marc. *Catherine the Great: A Profile*. New York: Oxford University Press, 1972.

Raleigh, Donald J., ed. *The Emperors and Empresses of Russia: Rediscovering the Romanovs*. Compiled by Akhmed A. Iskenderov. Armonk, N.Y.: M. E. Sharpe, 1996.

Ramdas, Mallika Urvashi. "Through Other 'I's: Self and Other in Russian Women's Autobiographical Texts." Ph.D. diss., Columbia University, 1996.

Ramer, Samuel C. "The Transformation of the Russian Feldsher, 1864–1914." In *Imperial Russia, 1700–1917: State, Society, Opposition. Essays in Honor of Marc Raeff*, edited by Ezra Mendelsohn and Marshall S. Shatz. DeKalb: Northern Illinois University Press, 1988.

————. "Traditional Healers and Peasant Culture in Russia, 1861–1917." In *Peasant Economy, Culture, and Politics of European Russia, 1800–1921*. Edited by Esther Kingston-Mann and Timothy Mixter. Princeton: Princeton University Press, 1991.

Ransel, David L. *Mothers of Misery: Child Abandonment in Russia*. Princeton: Princeton University Press, 1988.

————. "Problems in Measuring Illegitimacy in Prerevolutionary Russia." *Journal of Social History* 16, no. 2 (1982): 111–27.

————. "Undervaluation of Females: Evidence from the Foundling Homes." In *Russia and the World of the Eighteenth Century*, edited by R. P. Bartlett, A. G. Cross, and Karen Rasmussen. Columbus, Ohio: Slavica, 1988.

————. *Village Mothers: Three Generations of Change in Russia and Tataria.* Bloomington: Indiana University Press, 2000.

————, ed. *The Family in Imperial Russia: New Lines of Historical Research.* Urbana: University of Illinois Press, 1978.

Rappoport, Philippa Ellen. "Doll Folktales of the East Slavs: Invocations of Women from the Boundary of Space and Time." Ph.D. diss., University of Virginia, 1998.

Rasmussen, Karen. "Catherine II and the Image of Peter I." *Slavic Review* 37, no. 1 (1978): 51–69.

Resing, Mary Catherine. "Vera Fedorovna Kommissarzhevskaia: A Life in Performance." Ph.D. diss., University of Michigan, 1997.

Rice, Tamara Talbot. *Elizabeth, Empress of Russia.* New York: Praeger, 1970.

Roosevelt, Priscilla R. *Life on the Russian Country Estate.* New Haven: Yale University Press, 1995.

Rosenholm, Arja. *Gender Awakening: Femininity and the Russian Woman Question of the 1860s.* Helsinki: Kikimora Publications, 1999.

Rosenthal, Charlotte. "Zinaida Vengerova: Modernism and Women's Liberation." *Irish Slavonic Studies* 8 (1987): 97–105.

Ross, Dale. "The Role of the Women of Petrograd in War, Revolution and Counter-Revolution, 1914–1921." Ph.D. diss., Rutgers University, 1973.

Rosslyn, Wendy. *Anna Bunina (1774–1829) and the Origins of Women's Poetry in Russia.* Lewiston, N.Y.: Mellen Press, 1997.

————. "Making Their Way into Print: Poems by Eighteenth-Century Women." *Slavonic and East European Review* 78, no. 3 (2000): 407–38.

————. ed. *Women and Gender in Eighteenth-Century Russia.* Aldershot, England: Ashgate Publishing, forthcoming 2002.

Ruane, Christine. "Divergent Discourses: The Image of the Russian Woman Schoolteacher in Post-Reform Russia." *Russian History* 20, nos. 1–4 (1993): 109–23.

————. "Caftan to Business Suit: The Semiotics of Russian Merchant Dress." In *Merchant Moscow: Images of Russia's Vanished Bourgeoisie,* edited by James L. West and Iurii A. Petrov. Princeton: Princeton University Press, 1998.

————. *Gender, Class, and the Professionalization of Russian City Teachers, 1860–1914.* Pittsburgh: University of Pittsburgh Press, 1994.

————. "The Vestal Virgins of St. Petersburg: School Teachers and the 1897 Marriage Ban." *Russian Review* 50, no. 2 (1991): 163–82.

Ruthchild, Rochelle Goldberg, ed. *Women in Russia and the Soviet Union: An Annotated Bibliography.* New York: G. K. Hall & Co., 1994.

Salmond, Wendy. "The Solomenko Embroidery Workshops." *Journal of Decorative and Propaganda Arts* 5 (Summer 1987): 126–43.

Satina, Sophie. *Education of Women in Pre-Revolutionary Russia.* Translated by Alexandra F. Poustchine. Foreword by Myra Sampson. New York: Sophie Satina, 1966.

Scepansky, Anne Johnson. "Vera Ivanovna Zasulich: From Revolutionary Terror to Scientific Marxism." Ph.D. diss., George Washington University, 1974.

Schlosberg, Laura Elyse. "Converging Realms, Exclusive Consumption: The Salons of the Nineteenth-Century Russian Nobility," Ph.D. diss., Duke University, 2000.

Schuler, Catherine. "Female Theatrical Entrepreneurs in the Silver Age: A Prerevolutionary Revolution." *Theatre History Studies* 13 (Spring 1993): 79–94.

———. "The Silver Age Actress as Unruly Woman Starring Lidia Lavorskaia as Madonna." *Theatre Survey* 34, no. 2 (1993): 55–76.

———. *Women in Russian Theatre: The Actress in the Silver Age*. New York: Routledge, 1996.

———. "Zinaida Gippius: An Unwitting and Unwilling Feminist." In *Theatre and Feminist Aesthetics*, edited by Kathleen Laughlin and Catherine Schuler. Madison, N.J.: Fairleigh Dickinson University Press, 1995.

Scott, Mark Chapin. "Her Brother's Keeper: The Evolution of Women Bolsheviks." Ph.D. diss., University of Kansas, 1980.

Sendich, Munir. "Moscow Literary Salons: Thursdays at Karolina Pavlova's." *Die Welt der Slaven* 17, no. 2 (1973): 341–57.

Siegel, George. "The Fallen Woman in Nineteenth Century Russian Literature." *Harvard Slavic Studies* 5 (1970): 81–107.

Stites, Richard. "M. L. Mikhailov and the Emergence of the Woman Question in Russia." *Canadian Slavic Studies* 3, no. 2 (1969): 178–99.

———. "Prostitute and Society in Pre-Revolutionary Russia." *Jahrbücher für Geschichte Osteuropas* n.s. 31, no. 3 (1983): 348–64.

———. "Women and the Revolutionary Process in Russia." In *Becoming Visible: Women in European History*, edited by Renate Bridenthal, Claudia Koonz, and Susan Stuard. 2nd ed. Boston: Houghton Mifflin, 1987.

———. *The Women's Liberation Movement in Russia: Feminism, Nihilism, and Bolshevism, 1860–1930*. Princeton: Princeton University Press, 1978; new edition with afterword, 1990.

Taubman, Jane. *A Life Through Poetry: Marina Tsvetaeva's Lyric Diary*. Columbus, Ohio: Slavica Press, 1989.

Tian-Shanskaia, Olga Semyonova. *Village Life in Late Tsarist Russia*. Edited by David L. Ransel. Translated by David L. Ransel and Michael Levine. Bloomington: Indiana University Press, 1993.

Tolstaia, S. A. *The Diaries of Sophia Tolstoy*. Translated by Cathy Porter. New York: Random House, 1985.

Tomei, Christine D., ed. *Russian Women Writers*. 2 vols. New York: Garland Publishing, 1999.

Toomre, Joyce, trans. and intro. *Classic Russian Cooking: Elena Molokhovets' A Gift to Young Housewives*. Bloomington: Indiana University Press, 1992.

Tovrov, Jessica. "Action and Affect in the Russian Noble Family from the Late Eighteenth Century through the Reform Period." Ph.D. diss., University of Chicago, 1980.

Trotsky, Leon. *Women and the Family*. 2nd ed. New York: International Publishers, 1973.

Troyat, Henri. *Catherine the Great*. Translated by Joan Pinkham. New York: Dutton, 1980.

Tuve, Jeanette E. *The First Russian Women Physicians*. Newtonville, Mass.: Oriental Research Partners, 1984.

Wagner, William G. *Marriage, Property, and Law in Late Imperial Russia*. New York: Oxford University Press, 1994.

———. "The Trojan Mare: Women's Rights and Civil Rights in Late Imperial Russia." In *Civil Rights in Imperial Russia*, edited by Olga Crisp and Linda Edmondson. Oxford: Oxford University Press, 1989.

Weickhardt, George. "Legal Rights of Women in Russia, 1100–1750." *Slavic Review* 55, no. 1 (1996): 1–23.

Whittaker, Cynthia. "The Women's Movement during the Reign of Alexander II: A Case Study in Russian Liberalism." *Journal of Modern History* 48, no. 2 (1976): iii [abstract].

Wilmot, Martha and Catherine. *The Russian Journals of Martha and Catherine Wilmot*. Edited by The Marchioness of Londonderry and H. M. Hyde. London: Macmillan and Co., Ltd, 1935.

Worobec, Christine D. "Customary Law and Property Devolution among Russian Peasants in the 1870s." *Canadian Slavonic Papers* 26, nos. 2–3 (1984): 220–34.

———. "Death Ritual among Russian and Ukrainian Peasants: Linkages between the Living and the Dead." In *Cultures in Flux: Lower-Class Values, Practices, and Resistance in Late Imperial Russia*, edited by Stephen P. Frank and Mark D. Steinberg. Princeton: Princeton University Press, 1994.

———. *Peasant Russia: Family and Community in the Post-Emancipation Period*. Princeton: Princeton University Press, 1991.

———. *Possessed. Women, Witches, and Demons in Imperial Russia*. DeKalb: Northern Illinois Press, 2001.

———. "Reflections on Customary Law and Post-Reform Peasant Russia." *Russian Review* 44, no. 1 (1985): 21–25.

———. "Victims or Actors? Russian Peasant Women and Patriarchy." In *Peasant Economy, Culture, and Politics of European Russia, 1800–1921*, edited by Esther Kingston-Mann and Timothy Mixter. Princeton: Princeton University Press, 1991.

———. "Witchcraft Beliefs and Practices in Prerevolutionary Russian and Ukrainian Villages." *Russian Review* 54, no. 2 (1995): 165–87.

Woronzoff-Dashkoff, A. "Princess E. R. Dashkova's Moscow Library." *Slavonic and East European Review* 72, no. 1 (1994): 60–71.

Wortman, Richard. "Images of Rule and Problems of Gender in the Upbringing of Paul I and Alexander I." In *Imperial Russia 1700–1917: State, Society, Opposition. Essays in Honor of Marc Raeff*, edited by Ezra Mendelsohn and Marshall S. Shatz. DeKalb: Northern Illinois University Press, 1988.

Yablonskaya, M. N. *Women Artists of Russia's New Age, 1900–1935*. Translated by Anthony Parton and Felicity O'Dell Vnukova. New York: Rizzoli, 1990.

Yedlin, Tova, ed. *Women in Eastern Europe and the Soviet Union*. New York: Praeger, 1980.

Zguta, Russell. "The Ordeal by Water (Swimming of Witches) in the East Slavic World." *Slavic Review* 36, no. 2 (1977): 220–30.

Zirin, Mary F. "Butterflies with Broken Wings? Early Autobiographical Depictions of Girlhood in Russia." In *Gender Restructuring in Russian Studies: Conference Papers, Helsinki, August 1992*, edited by Marianne Liljeström, Eila Mätysaari, and Arja Rosenholm. Tampere: University of Tampere, 1993.

Index